E.C. ANTITRUST PROCEDURE

THIRD EDITION

AUSTRALIA

The Law Book Company
Brisbane · Sydney · Melbourne · Perth

CANADA

Carswell
Ottawa · Toronto · Calgary · Montreal · Vancouver

AGENTS

Steimatzky's Agency Ltd., Tel Aviv
N.M. Tripathi (Private) Ltd., Bombay
Eastern Law House (Private) Ltd., Calcutta
M.P.P. House, Bangalore
Universal Book Traders, Delhi
Aditya Books, Delhi
MacMillan Shuppan KK, Tokyo
Pakistan Law House, Karachi, Lahore

E.C. ANTITRUST PROCEDURE

THIRD EDITION

by

C.S. KERSE
LL.B., Solicitor

LONDON
SWEET & MAXWELL
1994

Published in 1994 by
Sweet & Maxwell Limited of
South Quay Plaza, 183 Marsh Wall, London E14 9FT.
Computerset by Tradespools Ltd., Frome, Somerset.
Printed and bound in Great Britain by
Hartnolls Ltd., Bodmin.

No natural forests were destroyed to make this product;
only farmed timber was used and re-planted.

A CIP catalogue record for this book is available from the British Library

ISBN 0 421 50310 6

Preface

My task in preparing this third edition has been to describe and explain in detail the procedure of the Commission of the European Community in antitrust cases under Articles 85 and 86 of the E.C. Treaty. The roles of the Community courts and national courts in the enforcement of the competition rules are also considered. The book is intended to complement the established texts on the substantive law and to provide a practical procedural handbook for lawyers. But others, businessmen, students, etc. will, I hope, find it helpful and instructive.

There have been many developments and changes since the second edition was published in 1987. The impact of the Court of First Instance has been substantial, both as regards the procedural rules in Regulation 17 as well as those being developed under general principles of Community law. More cases have come forward in the transport sector and I have taken the opportunity in this edition to explain points of similarity and difference under the relevant implementing regulations for inland, maritime and air transport.

I have endeavoured to state the law as at March 1, 1994. The original intention was to finish at an earlier date but I was persuaded to take a little extra time in order to add a commentary, at appropriate points in the text, on the implications of and practice under the EEA. This extra time has also provided the opportunity to note other recent developments. Moreover the title of the book has been changed, to reflect the new order of things after Maastricht.

All opinions expressed are personal and do not necessarily reflect those of Her Majesty's Government.

Finally, I would like to acknowledge my debt and express my thanks to those friends and colleagues, especially John Cook and Henry Emden, who not only encouraged me to prepare this third edition but also gave comments and suggestions which have, I am sure, improved it. Special thanks must also go to Norman Hasker, law librarian, who for many years now has greatly helped me to keep up to date. I remain personally responsible for all errors and omissions.

C.S. Kerse
March 28, 1994

Contents

1. INTRODUCTORY

2. STARTING THE MACHINERY

3. FACT-FINDING

4. RIGHTS OF THE DEFENCE

5. INVOLVEMENT OF NATIONAL AUTHORITIES

6. COMMISSION DECISIONS

7. FINES AND PENALTIES

8. GENERAL LEGAL RULES

9. JUDICIAL REVIEW BY THE EUROPEAN COURT OF JUSTICE

10. NATIONAL COURTS AND NATIONAL LAW

Table of Cases

---

* For full citation please cross-refer to numerical lists.

1. ALPHABETICAL LIST OF CASES BEFORE THE EUROPEAN COURTS*

* Cases before the European Court of First Instance can be identified by the "T"
prefix in the case number.

xix

Table of Cases

Table of Cases

Table of Cases

Table of Cases

2. EUROPEAN COURT OF JUSTICE

Table of Cases

Table of Cases

Table of Cases

Table of Cases

3. EUROPEAN COURT OF FIRST INSTANCE

4. COMMISSION DECISIONS

Table of Cases

Table of Cases

Table of Cases

Table of Cases

5. NATIONAL CASES

Belgium

Canada

Germany

Ireland

Netherlands

United Kingdom

United States

6. INTERNATIONAL TRIBUNAL CASES

Table of Legislation

7. EUROPEAN UNION TREATIES AND CONVENTIONS

8. REGULATIONS

9. DIRECTIVES

10. COUNCIL DECISIONS

11. NOTICES

12. RULES OF PROCEDURE

13. NATIONAL LEGISLATION

Table of Legislation

14. INTERNATIONAL TREATIES AND CONVENTIONS

1

Introductory

1.01 Articles 85 and 86 of the Treaty of Rome constitute an essential part of the Community's competition policy. Restrictive agreements and cartels are prohibited. Undertakings with a dominant position may not abusively exploit that position. Both the Member States and the Community institutions have responsibilities in connection with the competition rules. The Commission, in particular, has the day to day job of applying and enforcing them and is empowered to investigate and, where necessary, bring to an end violations of Articles 85 and 86. In performing this duty, the Commission is subject to the supervision of the Court of Justice.[1] This book is primarily concerned with the procedure of the Commission but also looks at appeals to the Court in antitrust cases and other enforcement issues under the E.C. Treaty. It does not deal with the special rules and procedures relating to mergers.[2] This chapter sets the scene. It contains a brief introduction to the substantive rules in Article 85 and 86[3] and a description of the Commission and the Court. It also describes briefly the competition regime under the Agreement for the European Economic Area (EEA). Finally, as a framework for the chapters which follow, it outlines the Commission's procedure.

I. THE COMPETITION RULES

The Treaty context

1.02 Articles 85 and 86 must be seen in the context of the objectives and purposes of the Treaty. The Common Market is not simply a customs union. In addition to the elimination of customs duties, tariffs, quotas, etc. The Treaty provides, *inter alia*, for

---

[1] The Single European Act amended the Treaty to provide for the establishment, at the request of the Court, of the Court of First Instance to be attached to the Court. Its jurisdiction includes competition cases.

[2] See Cook and Kerse, *EEC Merger Control* (1991). New edition in preparation.

[3] On the substantive law relating to the EEC competition rules and to Arts. 85 and 86 in particular, see, generally, *Bellamy and Child Common Market Law of Competition* (ed. by V. Rose) (4th ed., 1993); Deringer, *The Competition Law of the European Economic Community* (1968); Goldman, *European Commercial Law* (1973); Goyder, *EEC Competition Law* (2nd ed., 1993); Hawk, *United States, Common Market and International Anti-trust*; Korah, *An Introductory Guide to EEC Competition Law and Practice* (4th ed., 1990); Ritter, Braun and Rawlinson, *EEC Competition Law: A Practitioner's Guide* (1991); Whish, *Competition Law* (3rd ed., 1993); Wyatt and Dashwood, *European Community Law* (3rd ed., 1993). On the economics of competition policy see, generally, Hay and Morris, *Industrial Economics* (1979); Rowley, *Anti-Trust and Economic Efficiency* (1973); Scherer, *Industrial Market Structure and Economic Performance* (2nd ed., 1980).

the free movement of goods, services, labour and capital between Member States and, not least, "a system ensuring that competition in the internal market is not distorted" (Article 3(g)). Articles 85 and 86 are matched by rules for Member States directed to the same objective, in particular Articles 90, 92 and 93. National protection measures having been abolished, firms are not permitted to erect private barriers to trade. The advent of the Internal Market (and then the EEA) and the consequent disappearance of national economic boundaries may further discourage attempts at compartmentalisation by firms but the temptation may well remain so long as geographic, cultural and political differences persist. Community competition policy is aimed at the stimulation and maintenance of competition in an integrated common market. Articles 85 and 86, the Court of Justice has said, must be interpreted and applied in the light of the general principles contained in Articles 2 and 3 of the Treaty.[4] This is an important practical rule of construction which the Court has applied in a number of cases.[5] For example, in relation to Article 86, the Court of Justice has on several occasions[6] referred to Article 3 when determining what may amount to an abuse of a dominant position. It is now well established that the rules are equally applicable to services, including transport, as to goods.[7]

Article 85

1.03 The wording of Article 85 is characterised by the formulation of a rule of prohibition (Article 85(1)) and of its effects (Article 85(2)), tempered by the exercise of a power to grant exemptions from the rule (Article 85(3))[8] An academic analysis of the Article is, however, simpler than its practical application. Whether or not a particular agreement[9] falls within the prohibition contained in Article 85(1) involves an evaluation, sometimes complex, of both economic and legal elements[10] and it is trite but true to say that each case must be carefully considered on the basis of its own facts and circumstances. Some assistance may be given by the examples listed in Article 85(1),

---

[4] Cases 6 & 7/73, *Instituto Chemioterapico Italiano SpA and Commercial Solvents Corporation* v. *Commission*: [1974] E.C.R. 223, [1974] 1 C.M.L.R. 309, at para. 25. The establishing of a system of undistorted competition is not the only objective mentioned in Article 3 and other objectives (*e.g.* the CAP) may take priority. See Case 139/79, *Maizena GmbH* v. *Council*: [1980] E.C.R. 3393, at para. 25.

[5] For example, Case 32/65, *Italy* v. *Council and Commission*: [1966] E.C.R. 389, [1969] C.M.L.R. 39, at para. 7.

[6] Case 6/72, *Europemballage Corp. and Continental Can Co. Inc.* v. *Commission*: [1973] E.C.R. 215, [1973] C.M.L.R. 199, at paras. 23–26. The court refers in particular to Art. 3(f), now renumbered 3(g) after Maastricht. See also *Commercial Solvents*, above, and Case 85/76, *Hoffmann-La Roche* v. *Commission*: [1979] E.C.R. 461, [1979] 3 C.M.L.R. 211.

[7] Case 172/80, *Züchner* v. *Bayerische Vereinsbank*: [1981] E.C.R. 2021, [1982] 1 C.M.L.R. 313 (banking); Case 45/85 *Verband der Sachversicherer* v. *Commission*: [1987] E.C.R. 405 (insurance), and Cases 209–213/84, *Ministère Public* v. *Lucas Asjes and others*: [1986] E.C.R. 1425, [1986] 3 C.M.L.R. 173 (air transport).

[8] Case 10/69, *Portelange SA* v. *Smith Corona Marchant International SA*: [1969] E.C.R. 309, [1974] 1 C.M.L.R. 397, at para. 9.

[9] Article 85(1) also refers to "decision" and "concerted practices". For the sake of brevity the term "agreement" will be used throughout this book to include such decisions and concerted practices unless the context clearly indicates the contrary.

[10] Case 56/65, *La Technique Minière* v. *Maschinenbau Ulm GmbH*: [1966] E.C.R. 235, [1966] C.M.L.R. 357 and Case 31/80, *L'Oréal NV and L'Oréal SA* v. *De Nieuwe A.M.C.K. Pvba*: [1980] E.C.R. 3775, [1981] 2 C.M.L.R. 235.

by the cases decided by the Court of Justice and the Court of First Instance[11] and the decisions of the Commission in application of the competition rules.[12] The Commission also from time to time issues Notices giving guidance as to its views of the application of Article 85 in particular areas. Notices currently apply in relation to exclusive commercial agents,[13] co-operation agreements,[14] minor agreements,[15] Japanese imports,[16] sub-contracting,[17] the block exemptions for exclusive distribution and exclusive purchasing agreements[18] and for motor vehicle distribution,[19] activities of motor vehicle distribution intermediaries,[20] co-operation with national courts[21] and joint ventures.[22] Whilst any measure on the part of the Commission bringing transparency to the operation of the competition rules is to be welcomed, such notices should not be relied upon too heavily. They do not have any legal force in relation to particular cases.[23] They may be overtaken by subsequent changes in Commission policy and practice. They are general in nature and are often difficult to apply in a particular case.[24]

Prohibition in Article 85(1)

1.04 Article 85(1) prohibits:

> "as incompatible with the common market: all agreements between undertakings, decisions by associations of undertakings and concerted practices which

---

[11] Judgments are reported in the (official) *European Court Reports* (E.C.R.) and the (unofficial) *Common Market Law Reports* (C.M.L.R.). Where possible, both references are given in this book.

[12] Commission decisions are published in the *Official Journal of the European Communities* (O.J.), Legislation (L) series. There is also a "C" series. This contains information, preparatory acts (draft legislation), Notices, written questions to the European Parliament, etc.

[13] Notice on Exclusive Agency Contracts made with Commercial Agents: J.O. 2921/62. Applied, for example, in *ARG/Unipart*: [1988] O.J. L45/34. The position of the exclusive agent should not be confused with that of the exclusive distributor. See Regs. 1983/83 and 1984/83 and note the attitude taken by the Commission in *Pittsburgh Corning Europe*: [1972] J.O. L272/35, [1973] C.M.L.R. D2 and the Court in the *Sugar* case (see n. 62, below), and in Case 311/85, *Vereniging van Vlaamse Reisbureaus* v. *Sociale Dienst van de Plaatselijke en Gewestelijke Overheidsdiensten*: [1987] E.C.R. 3801, [1989] 4 C.M.L.R. 213, at paras. 19 and 20. The Commission has announced that it is revising the Notice on contracts with commercial agents to bring it up to date with the caselaw and developments in distribution systems since 1962: Twenty-first Report on Competition Policy, point 133.

[14] Notice concerning agreements, decisions and concerted practices in the field of co-operation between enterprises: [1968] J.O. C75/3 and C84/14, [1968] C.M.L.R. D5. Applied, for example, in *Eurotunnel*: [1988] O.J. L311/36.

[15] Notice of 3 September 1986 concerning agreements of minor importance which do not fall under Article 85(1) of the Treaty establishing the European Economic Community: [1986] O.J. C231/2. Applied, for example, in *Quantel International-Continuum/Quantel SA*: [1992] O.J. L235/9.

[16] Notice on imports of Japanese products: [1972] J.O. C111/13.

[17] Notice of 18 December 1978 concerning its assessment of certain sub-contracting agreements in relation to Article 85(1) of the EEC Treaty: [1979] O.J. C1/2, [1979] 1 C.M.L.R. 264.

[18] Notice concerning Commission Regulations 1983/83 and 1984/83: [1984] O.J. C101/2.

[19] Notice concerning Regulation 123/85: [1985] O.J. C17/4.

[20] Notice on the clarification of the activities of motor vehicle intermediaries: [1991] O.J. C329/20.

[21] Notice on co-operation between national courts and the Commission in applying Articles 85 and 86 of the EEC Treaty: [1993] O.J. C39/6.

[22] Notice concerning the assessment of co-operative joint ventures pursuant to Article 85 of the EEC Treaty: [1993] O.J. C43/2.

[23] Reliance on a Notice may be a mitigating factor in relation to fining. See para. 7.35.

[24] The former minor agreements Notice was, for example, extremely difficult to apply. See, for example, the Commission's decision in *Kawasaki*: [1979] O.J. L16/9, [1979] 1 C.M.L.R. 448.

may affect trade between Member States and which have as their object or effect the prevention, restriction, or distortion of competition within the common market."

There are thus three essential requirements which must be satisfied for Article 85(1) to apply:

(a) Some form of agreement, decision or concerted practice between undertakings, which
(b) may affect trade between Member States, and
(c) has the object or effect of restricting or distorting competition within the Common Market.

Undertakings

1.05   It is significant that Articles 85 and 86 do not refer to "persons" but to "undertakings", a much looser and wider concept.[25] The Treaty does not define "undertakings" for these purposes[26] but, broadly speaking, "undertaking" encompasses any body, whether company, partnership, sole trader, etc. carrying on economic activities. An economic rather than a legal approach is necessary. So the Court of Justice has said that the term "undertaking" embraces any entity carrying on an economic activity regardless of its legal status or the way it is financed.[27] Further, autonomous commercial activity is more relevant than legal personality in this context. The approach is thus a functional one and no useful distinction can be drawn from the different legal forms which a business may take, or its precise status under domestic law.[28] Individuals may be "undertakings"; for example, a self-employed inventor commercially exploiting his patents by licensing, a commercial adviser and even artistes when they commercially exploit their artistic performances.[29] The term may include non profit-making

---

[25] Per A.G. Warner in *Commercial Solvents*, above, n. 3.

[26] "Undertaking" is defined in the Treaty for other purposes, see Arts. 52 and 80 EEC. See also Art. 80 ECSC and Art. 196 Euratom. Under the EEA, for the purposes of the division of enforcement responsibility under the competition regime, Art. of Protocol 22 defines "undertakings" as "any entity carrying out activities of a commercial or economic nature."

[27] Case C–41/90, *Höfner and Elser* v. *Macrotron*: [1991] I E.C.R. 1979, [1993] 4 C.M.L.R. 306. In its Notice regarding concentrative and co-operative operations under Reg. 4064/89 (Merger Control Regulation) "undertaking" is defined as "an organised assembly of human and natural resources intended to pursue a defined economic purpose on a long term basis": [1990] O.J. C203/10, para. 8.

[28] See *Aluminium*: [1985] O.J. L92/1, [1987] 3 C.M.L.R. 813, where East European trade organisations were held to be undertakings. They engaged in trading activities and could not claim sovereign immunity. *Cf. Amersham/Buchler*: [1982] O.J. L314/34, [1983] 1 C.M.L.R. 619, where the Commission described Amersham before the time of the agreements as "essentially a government agency rather than a commercial enterprise." But a public body acting as a public authority in granting a concession to an undertaking is not itself an undertaking. See Case 30/87, *Bodson* v. *Pompes Funèbres des Régions Libérées SA*: [1988] E.C.R. 2479, [1989] 4 C.M.L.R. 984, at para. 18, and Cases C 159 & 160/91, *Christian Poucet* v. *AGF and Camulrac* and *Daniel Pistre* v. *CancaVa*: [1993] O.J. C70/7 ("undertaking" does not include certain bodies entrusted with the management of social security schemes). See also Case C–69/91, *Ministère Public* v. *Decoster and others*: judgment of October 27, 1993, not yet reported, and Case C–364/92, *SAT Fluggesellschaft mbH* v. *Organisation européenne pour la sécurité de la navigation aérienne (Eurocontrol)*: judgment of January 19, 1994, not yet reported.

[29] *A.O.I.P./Beyrard*: [1976] O.J. L6/8, [1976] 1 C.M.L.R. D14; *Vaessen/Moris*: [1979] O.J. L19/32, [1979] 1 C.M.L.R. 511; *Reuter/BASF*: [1976] O.J. L254/40, [1976] 2 C.M.L.R. D44 and *RAI/UNITEL* [1978] O.J. L157/39, [1978] 32 C.M.L.R. 306. And note the position of Mr. De Rooij in Case 42/84, *Remia and Nutricia* v. *Commission*: [1985] E.C.R. 2545, [1987] 1 C.M.L.R. 1, at paras. 49–51.

bodies.[30] An undertaking is an "undertaking" for the purposes of Articles 85 and 86 even if it has its seat outside the Community.[31]

Agreements, decisions, etc.

1.06 Some element of collusion[32] is necessary for the purposes of Article 85 and this finds legislative expression in the three terms, "agreements between undertakings", "decisions by associations" and "concerted practices". The notion of what amounts to an "agreement" is not too formalised or precise[33] and there is no requirement that there be a legally enforceable contract. The so-called "gentleman's agreement" will be caught.[34] It is sufficient if the undertakings in question have expressed their joint intention to conduct themselves on the market in a specific way. There are no rules as to the form of the agreement. So the rules and regulations of a commodity market may comprise an agreement.[35] In one case[36] the Commission considered that it did not matter that the formal agreement was not signed or dated as the parties had acted in compliance with its terms. Notification to the parties and tacit accession has been considered enough to evidence an agreement.[37] Pressure by a supplier on a dealer, wholesale or retail, to accept an export ban does not negate the finding of an agreement between them for these purposes.[38] Article 85 is also applicable to agreements which are no longer formally in force but which continue to produce their effects.[39] Various activities of trade associations (and associations of associations)[40]

---

[30] See, *e.g. GVL*: [1981] O.J. L370/49, [1982] 1 C.M.L.R. 221, and *P & I Clubs*: [1985] O.J. L376/2, [1989] 4 C.M.L.R. 178. In Case 41/83, *Italy* v. *Commission*: [1985] E.C.R. 873, [1985] 2 C.M.L.R. 368, the Court of Justice defined economic activity as activity, whether or not profit making, that involves economic trade.

[31] *Continental Can*, above, n. 6, at para. 16.

[32] National rules (legislative or administrative) freezing prices do not as such involve any "agreement": Case 5/79, *Procurer General* v. *Hans Buys and others*: [1979] E.C.R. 3203, [1980] 2 C.M.L.R. 493, at paras. 29–31. Nor rules imposing RPM: Case 231/83, *Cullet* v. *Leclerq*: [1985] E.C.R. 305, [1985] 2 C.M.L.R. 524. But an agreement remains an "agreement" even if it is endorsed and extended by government regulation: Case 123/83, *BNIC* v. *Guy Clair*: [1985] E.C.R. 392, [1985] 2 C.M.L.R. 43.

[33] See, for example, *Italian Cast Glass*: [1980] O.J. L383/19, [1982] 2 C.M.L.R. 61 or, more recently, *Moosehead/Whitbread*: [1990] O.J. L100/32, [1991] 4 C.M.L.R. 391 where the Commission treated a number of agreements as a "single agreement". *Cf. Olivetti/Canon*: [1988] O.J. L52/51, [1989] 4 C.M.L.R. 940 where there were separate agreements in a formal legal sense which were for the purposes of Article 85(1) recognised as such but then considered as a whole and not as one agreement.

[34] *Quinine*: Cases 41, 44 & 45/69, *ACF Chemiefarma* v. *Commission*; *Buchler* v. *Commission*; *Boehringer Mannheim* v. *Commission*: [1970] E.C.R. 661, 769. For a recent example, see *Flat Glass*: [1989] O.J. L33/44, [1990] 4 C.M.L.R. 535.

[35] See *The GAFTA Soya Bean Meal Futures Association Ltd.*: [1987] O.J. L19/18, [1989] 4 C.M.L.R. 287.

[36] *BP Kemi–DDSF*: [1979] O.J. L286/32, [1979] 3 C.M.L.R. 684. And see the arguments of the Belgian undertakings in *Welded Steel Mesh*: [1989] O.J. L260/1, [1991] 4 C.M.L.R. 13.

[37] See *BVB/ABB*: [1987] O.J. L7/27. In *Viho/Toshiba*: [1991] O.J. L287/39, [1992] 5 C.M.L.R. 180 an understanding between parties that an export ban should apply was treated as being within their supply agreement.

[38] Cases 32 & 36–82/78, *BMW Belgium SA and Others* v. *Commission*: [1979] E.C.R. 2435, [1980] 1 C.M.L.R. 370. See, *e.g. Fisher-Price/Quaker Oats Ltd.–Toyco*: [1988] O.J. L49/19, [1989] 4 C.M.L.R. 553. Cheating does not negate the existence of an agreement, *Flat Glass*, above.

[39] Case 243/83, *Binon & Cie SA* v. *Agence et Messagerie de la Presse SA*: [1985] E.C.R. 2015, [1985] 3 C.M.L.R. 800, at para. 17.

[40] See, for example, *Hudson's Bay-Dansk Pelsdyravlerforening*: [1988] O.J. L316/43, [1989] 4 C.M.L.R. 340 and *Scottish Salmon Board*: [1992] O.J. L246/37. In Case T–61/89, *Dansk Pelsdyravlerforening* v. *Commission*: [1992] II E.C.R. 1931, the Court of First Instance held that the particular obligations of the association (a co-operative) did not preclude the application of Art. 85(1).

5

may fall within Article 85 and the term "decision by associations" is not construed narrowly. The Court of Justice has held that it will include recommendations made by an association to its members in circumstances where the members are not required to comply with them.[41] Finally, it should be noted that parties cannot contract out of the prohibition in Article 85(1) or exclude it by suitable words in the contract or agreement.[42]

Economic entity

1.07   The Court of Justice has developed the concept of enterprise or economic entity in its treatment of related companies.[43] This has two main practical applications. First, the fact that a subsidiary company has its own legal personality cannot exclude the possibility that its conduct may be imputed to its parent company in circumstances such that the latter may be considered to be responsible for the conduct of the subsidiary.[44] So a parent may be the appropriate addressee of a decision and fined for the activities of its subsidiaries.[45] A parent company may be a party to the infringement even though it may be established outside the Community.[46] Second, the fact that a number of undertakings having separate legal personalities may be part of the same economic entity may rule out the question of there being an "agreement" between them for the purposes of Article 85(1). The Court of Justice has held that the prohibition in Article 85(1) does not apply to the relationship between a subsidiary and a parent company in circumstances where the subsidiary does not enjoy real autonomy of action on the market.[47] The Commission has taken the view that there is no agreement caught by Article 85(1) between a parent and a subsidiary where the agreement is in effect related to a distribution of tasks within a single economic entity,[48] or, for example, between a parent and subsidiary or between the subsidiaries *inter se* where the parent in

---

[41] Case 8/72, *Vereeniging van Cementhandelaren* v. *Commission*: [1972] E.C.R. 977, [1973] C.M.L.R. 7; Cases 96–102, 104, 105, 108 & 110/82, *NV IAZ International Belgium SA* v. *Commission*: [1983] E.C.R. 3369, [1984] 3 C.M.L.R. 276. See, *e.g. Publishers Association–Net Book Agreements*: [1989] O.J. L22/12, [1989] 4 C.M.L.R. 825 and *Concordato Incendio:* [1990] O.J. L15/25, [1991] 1 C.M.L.R. 199.

[42] *Aluminium*, above, n. 28, and *John Deere*: [1985] O.J. L35/58, [1985] 2 C.M.L.R. 554.

[43] The concept was first mentioned by the Court in the *Dyestuffs* case: Cases 48, 49 & 51–57/69, *ICI and others* v. *Commission*: [1972] E.C.R. 619, [1972] C.M.L.R. 557.

[44] Case 107/82, *AEG-Telefunken* v. *Commission*: [1983] E.C.R. 3151, [1984] 3 C.M.L.R. 325, at paras. 47–53. For examples of cases where parents and subsidiaries have been treated as one undertaking, see *Eurofix-Bauco* v. *Hilti*: [1988] O.J. L65/19, [1989] 4 C.M.L.R. 677; *Decca Navigator Systems*: [1989] O.J. L43/27, [1990] 4 C.M.L.R. 627; *Soda ash-Solvay CFK*: [1991] O.J. L152/16 and *Viho/Parker Pen*: [1992] O.J. L233/27.

[45] See, *e.g. Moët et Chandon (London) Ltd.*: [1982] O.J. L94/7, [1982] 2 C.M.L.R. 166; *Benelux Flat Glass*: [1984] O.J. L212/13, [1985] 2 C.M.L.R. 350; *Fatty Acids*: [1987] O.J. L3/17, [1989] 4 C.M.L.R. 445. On the implications for imposition and collection of fines, see paras. 7.11 and 7.50.

[46] See, *e.g. Aluminium*: [1985] O.J. L92/1, [1987] 3 C.M.L.R. 813 and *Wood Pulp*: [1985] O.J. L85/1. [1985] 3 C.M.L.R. 474. This aspect of the economic entity concept is discussed further in Chap. 8 under the heading "Jurisdiction" where the problems of the possible extraterritorial application of the competition rules is discussed in more detail.

[47] See Case 22/71, *Béguelin Import Co* v. *GL Import-Export SA*: [1971] E.C.R. 949, [1972] C.M.L.R. 81, at para. 8 and Case 16/74, *Centrafarm BV and De Peijper* v. *Winthrop BV*: [1974] E.C.R. 1183, [1974] 2 C.M.L.R. 480. The point is before the Court of First Instance in Case T–102/92, *Viho Europe BV* v. *Commission*: [1993] O.J. C1/10.

[48] *Christiani & Nielsen*: [1969] J.O. L165/12, [1969] C.M.L.R. D36; Contrast *Langenscheidt/Hachette*: [1982] O.J. L39/25, [1982] 1 C.M.L.R. 181 and *Gosme/Martell-DMP*: [1991] O.J. L185/23, [1991] 5 C.M.L.R. 586, where the Commission held that an agreement between a company and its 50 per cent. owned joint venture company was an agreement within the meaning of Art. 85(1).

fact exercises control by issuing precise instructions to the subsidiaries and it is impossible for the subsidiaries to act independently of the parent or *inter se* in the areas governed by the parent company.[49] Importantly, the Court of Justice has held that a parent and subsidiary may be one party for the purposes of qualifying for a block exemption.[50]

The Commission has said that in the case of a large industrial group it may be appropriate (according to the circumstances) to apply the term "undertaking" to a parent or to a subsidiary company or to the economic unit formed by the parent and subsidiaries together.[51] Ownership (50+ per cent.) may in some cases imply a single undertaking of the parent and subsidiary. But the real test is whether the subsidiary operates as a separate commercial entity so that it cannot be considered as forming the same economic unit.[52] Indeed, there is no authority for the proposition that if one member of a corporate group enters into an agreement or concerted practice infringing Article 85(1) then all, some or even one other member of the group is automatically considered as party to the agreement or practice or as participating in or as responsible for the infringement. In *BMW Belgium* v. *Commission*,[53] the Court of Justice pointed out that "the bond of economic dependence existing between a parent company and the subsidiary does not preclude a divergence in conduct or even a divergence in interests between the two companies." And in *AEG-Telefunken* v. *Commission*[54] the Court required some evidence that the parent actually influenced the subsidiary's behaviour. In relation to Article 86, in *Metro II*[55] the Court held that parent and subsidiaries were independent in the absence of evidence that the undertakings were "not only linked at the level of capital but also pursue a co-ordinated marketing strategy in accordance with the directions of their parent company or with a plan agreed between themselves." Where, however, members of the same group are to be treated as the economic unit Article 86 may apply to the group's behaviour.[56]

Agreement, decision or concerted practice?

1.08 Although Article 85(1) uses three terms, "agreement between undertakings", "decision by associations of undertakings" and "concerted practices", not a great deal is to be achieved by trying to differentiate rigidly between them. The precise meanings of the first two may be relatively unimportant if, as would appear to be the case, "concerted practices" will sweep up lesser degrees of collusion.[57] The object of the

---

[49] *Kodak*: [1970] J.O. L147/24 and [1970] J.O. L159/22, [1970] C.M.L.R. D19.

[50] For the former exclusive purchasing exemption in Reg. 67/67. Case 170/83, *Hydrotherm* v. *Andreoli*: [1984] E.C.R. 2999, [1985] 3 C.M.L.R. 244.

[51] *Welded Steel Mesh*: [1989] O.J. L260/1, [1991] 4 C.M.L.R. 13.

[52] *Polypropylene*: [1986] O.J. L230/1, [1988] 4 C.M.L.R. 347. For a more recent example, see the treatment of BBC and BBC Enterprises in *Magill TV Guide/ITP BBC and RTE:* [1989] O.J. L78/43, [1989] 4 C.M.L.R. 749.

[53] Above, n. 38 at para. 24.

[54] Above, n. 44.

[55] See Case 75/84, *Metro-SB-Grossmarkte GmbH & Co. KG* v. *Commission*: [1986] E.C.R. 3021, [1987] 1 C.M.L.R. 118, at para. 84.

[56] Case 30/87, *Bodson* v. *Pompes Funèbres de Régions Libérées SA*: [1988] E.C.R. 2479, [1989] 4 C.M.L.R. 984, at para. 21.

[57] See Hawk, *op. cit.* Indeed there may be situations where some parties are linked to a collusive arrangement by "agreement" and others, with lesser involvement, by concerted practice. See, *e.g.* *PVC*: [1989] O.J. L74/1, [1990] 4 C.M.L.R. 345.

Treaty in creating a separate concept of concerted practice is to forestall the possibility of undertakings evading the application of Article 85 by colluding in an anticompetitive manner falling short of a definite agreement. Moreover, the Commission has on occasion deliberately neglected to reach a conclusion on the existence of an "agreement" if there is a concerted practice. Indeed in a particular case nothing may turn on the precise form of the collusion,[58] provided that always the Commission can adduce evidence to the requisite standard of proof.[59] When holding that Article 85 is applicable to parallel conduct continued after the discontinuance of the old agreement without a new agreement being made, the Court of Justice has said that the competition rules "are concerned with the economic results of agreements or any comparable form of concerted action or co-ordination rather than their legal form."[60] What is important therefore is the difference between collusion, in whatever shape and form, which falls within Article 85(1) and mere parallel behaviour with no element of concentration.

Concerted practices

1.09 Article 85(1) prohibits "concerted practices". Undertakings cannot escape the competition rules by colluding in an anti-competitive manner short of an agreement. In the *Dyestuffs* case,[61] the Court of Justice defined a concerted practice as "a form of co-ordination between undertakings which, without going so far as to amount to an agreement properly so called, knowingly substitutes a practical co-operation between them for the rules of competition." The Court took the view that although parallel conduct did not by itself constitute a concerted practice it might give a strong indication of such a practice. In the *Sugar* case,[62] the Court substantially repeated the definition of "concerted practice" given in Dyestuffs and touched further on the problem of "conscious parallelism":

---

[58] See *Dyestuffs*: [1969] J.O. L195/11, [1969] C.M.L.R. D23; *G.I.S.A.*: [1972] J.O. L303/45, [1973] C.M.L.R. D125 and *Hasselblad*: [1982] O.J. L161/18, [1982] 2 C.M.L.R. 233. The "concerted practice" may also be used as a long stop. See *Floral*: [1980] O.J. L39/51, 55, [1980] 2 C.M.L.R. 285, 293: "The co-operation between the relevant companies … is based on an agreement or at least a concerted practice." In Case T–7/89, *Polypropylene, Hercules SA* v. *Commission*: [1991] II E.C.R. 1711, [1992] 4 C.M.L.R. 84, at para. 264, the Court of First Instance upheld the Commission's characterisation of the infringement in question as "an agreement and a concerted practice". The Court said that such dual characterisation "must be understood, not as requiring, simultaneously and cumulatively, proof that each of those factual elements presents the constituent elements both of an agreement and of a concerted practice, but rather as referring to a complex whole comprising a number of factual elements some of which were characterised as agreements and others as concerted practices for the purposes of Article 85(1) EEC, which lays down no specific category for a complex infringement of this type."

[59] See Antunes, "Agreements and Concerted Practices under EEC Competition Law: Is the Distinction Relevant?" (1991) 11 Y.E.L. 57.

[60] Case 243/83, *Binon et Cie* v. *SA Agence et Messageries de la Presse*: [1985] E.C.R. 2015, [1985] 3 C.M.L.R.. 800, at para. 17.

[61] *ICI and others* v. *Commission*, above, n. 43, at para. 64, followed in *Züchner* v. *Bayerische Vereinsbank*, above, n. 7.

[62] Cases 40–48, 50, 54–56, 111, 113 & 114/73, *Sugar: Cooperative Vereniging 'Suiker Unie' UA and others* v. *Commission*: [1975] E.C.R. 1663, [1976] 1 C.M.L.R. 295, at paras. 173 and 174. Relied upon by the Commission in *Polypropylene*, above, n. 52 and upheld by the Court of First Instance in that case, *Hercules*, above, at para. 258.

"... each economic operator must determine independently the policy which he intends to adopt on the common market including the choice of persons and undertakings to which he makes offers or sells. Although it is correct to say that this requirement of independence does not deprive economic operators of the right to adapt themselves intelligently to the existing and anticipated conduct of their competitors, it does however strictly preclude any direct or indirect contact between such operators, the object or effect whereof is either to influence the conduct on the market of an actual or potential competitor or to disclose to such a competitor the course of conduct which they themselves have decided to adopt or contemplate adopting on the market."

The Court's approach to "conscious parallelism" has been the subject of critical analysis and discussion.[63] There is no short answer to the question of what conduct is acceptable and the problems of definition may be acute particularly in the area of oligopoly pricing. In *Rolled Zinc*, the Court recognised that evidence of parallel synchronous behaviour by competitors may not be sufficient to establish a concerted practice where evidence of other circumstances allows another explanation indicative of independent action by the parties.[64] More recently in *Wood Pulp II*, the Court of Justice placed a heavy burden of proof on the Commission. In determining the probative value of factors, such as a system of regular price announcements and the simultaneity and parallelism of price announcements it must be noted, the Court said, that "parallel conduct cannot be regarded as furnishing proof of concentration unless concertation constitutes the only plausible explanation for such conduct".[65] It is outwith the scope of this book to enter into the necessarily complex and detailed discussion as to the point when parallel conduct may fall foul of Article 85. Undertakings should eschew any form of collusive conduct or behaviour which may have the effects described in Article 85(1). Note particularly that the Commission may be entitled, once a concerted practice has been established, to rely on a presumption of continuance until the concerted practice is shown to have been terminated.[66]

Anti-competitive object or effect

1.10   The agreement must have as its object or effect the prevention, restriction or distortion of competition within the Common Market. The reference to object or effect has the consequence that there is no requirement to show the actual effects of an agreement provided it appears that it has clearly the object of restricting, preventing or distorting competition.[67] In order to determine whether an agreement has as its object

[63] See, for example, Korah, *Competition Law of Britain and the Common Market* (1975), p. 177 and Hawk, *op. cit.*

[64] Cases 29–30/83, *Compagnie Royale Asturienne des Mines SA and Rheinzink GmbH* v. *Commission*: [1984] E.C.R. 1679, [1985] 1 C.M.L.R. 688, at paras. 16–18.

[65] Cases C 89, 104, 114, 116, 117 & 125–129/85, *A Åhlström Osakeyhtio and Others* v. *Commission*: [1993] 4 C.M.L.R. 407, at para. 71.

[66] Per A.G. Slynn in Case 86/82, *Hasselblad* v. *Commission*: [1984] E.C.R. 883, [1984] 1 C.M.L.R. 559.

[67] Cases 56 and 58/64, *Consten Sarl and Grundig-Verkaufs GmbH* v. *Commission*: [1966] E.C.R. 299, [1966] C.M.L.R. 418, and, *e.g.* more recently in *Building and Construction in the Netherlands*: [1992] O.J. L92/1. Indeed lack of success in achieving the desired effect, *e.g.* a ban on exports, will not matter. See Case 19/77, *Miller International Schallplatten GmbH* v. *Commission*: [1978] E.C.R. 131, [1978] 2 C.M.L.R. 334. On the other hand, Art. 85 may apply to agreements which are no longer in force where such agreements continue to produce their effects after they have formally ceased to be in force. See Case

the restriction of competition it is not necessary to determine which party took the initiative in inserting a particular clause or to verify that the parties had a common interest at the time of making the agreement.[68] The Court of Justice has stressed that when considering the object or effect of an agreement what is necessary is to consider the agreement in its economic and legal context.[69] This requires an examination of the relevant market and an analysis and appraisal of all the circumstances bearing upon the case. As the Court indicated in the *Perfumes* cases, it may be necessary to look at what the competitive situation would have been in the absence of the agreement in question.[70] Further, particular consideration should be given to the nature and quantities, limited or otherwise, of the products to which the agreement relates, and the position and importance of the parties on the market for the relevant products. It may also be important to consider the significance of the agreement not in isolation[71] but in the context of any other similar agreements.[72] This may be especially so in the case of distributorship agreements where the whole of the distribution system should be examined and the contracts assessed in the context within which they are operated.

The Commission has been criticised[73] for not attempting a realistic economic analysis and for considering almost any restrictive provision[74] in an agreement as contrary to Article 85(1), with the result that, the only escape route being Article 85(3), there has built up a substantial backlog of cases.[75] The Court of Justice has however given several indications that an economic analysis is necessary for Article 85(1).[76] So

---

51/75, *EMI Records Ltd.* v. *CBS United Kingdom Ltd.*: [1976] E.C.R. 811, [1976] 2 C.M.L.R. 235, at para. 30, and the *Binon* case, above, n. 60, at para. 17.

[68] See the *Rolled Zinc* case, above, n. 64, at para. 26. As the Commission indicated in *Bayo-n-ox*: [1990] O.J. L21/71, [1990] 4 C.M.L.R. 930, the term "object" has an objective meaning in this context. It does not matter what the intention subjectively pursued by the parties is.

[69] Case 56/65, *La Technique Minière* v. *Maschinenbau Ulm*: [1966] E.C.R. 235, [1966] C.M.L.R. 357 and Case 5/69, *Völk* v. *Vervaecke*: [1969] E.C.R. 295, [1969] C.M.L.R. 273.

[70] Case 99/79, *Lancôme* v. *Etos and Albert Heijn Supermart*: [1980] E.C.R. 2511, [1981] 2 C.M.L.R. 164, at para. 24, and see the Court's first ruling in Case 31/80, *L'Oréal NV and L'Oréal SA* v. *De Nieuwe A.M.C.K. Pvba*: [1980] E.C.R. 3775, [1981] 2 C.M.L.R. 235.

[71] It is well established that Art. 85 applies to both vertical and horizontal agreements. It can apply to agreements between undertakings competing at the same level (*e.g.* between two retailers) or situated at different levels (*e.g.* between a manufacturer and a distributor). See *Consten and Grundig*, above, and Case 32/65, *Italy* v. *Council and Commission*: [1966] E.C.R. 389, [1969] C.M.L.R. 39.

[72] The Court has adopted this approach in the context of certain tied house agreements in the Belgian beer trade. See Case 23/67, *Brasserie de Haecht* v. *Wilkin (No. 1)*: [1967] E.C.R. 407, [1968] C.M.L.R. 26, and Case 47/76, *De Norre and de Clerq* v. *NV Brouwerij Concordia*: [1977] E.C.R. 65, [1977] 1 C.M.L.R. 378. But the approach is not restricted to tied house arrangements. See, *e.g. Distribution of package tours during the 1990 World Cup*: [1992] O.J. L326/31.

[73] See, *e.g.* Korah, "EEC Competition Policy—Legal Form or Economic Efficiency" [1986] *Current Legal Problems* 85.

[74] For an example of the Commission disregarding a restriction because it was not an applicable restriction, see *Villeroy & Boch*: [1985] O.J. L376/15, [1988] 4 C.M.L.R. 461, at para. 30. Where no clauses contain appreciable restrictions on competition, then negative clearance is appropriate; see, *e.g. Petroleum Exchange of London Ltd.*: [1987] O.J. L3/27, [1989] 4 C.M.L.R. 280.

[75] Various methods have been employed to reduce the backlog, principally the use of block exemptions, comfort letters, and other forms of settlement.

[76] Most notably in the *Maize Seed* case Case 258/78, *Nungesser and Eisele* v. *Commission*: [1982] E.C.R. 2015, [1983] 1 C.M.L.R. 278, and Case 262/81, *Coditel (No. 2)*: [1982] E.C.R. 3381, [1983] 1 C.M.L.R. 49, where the Court found that exclusive licences did not in themselves infringe Art. 85(1). And see the recitals to Reg. 2349/84, the block exemption for patent licences.

the Court has recognised that in certain contexts (e.g. franchising) there may be agreements which restrict the freedom of undertakings without there being any restriction on competition within the meaning of Article 85(1).[77] Some have talked of applying a "rule of reason" to Article 85(1),[78] although recent cases do not suggest that the Court will embrace that concept, at least as it is understood in U.S. anti-trust law. It is true however that the Commission has in some areas taken a less legally formalistic approach to Article 85(1); for example, it has accepted a doctrine of ancillary restraints.[79]

Article 85(1) contains a non-exhaustive list of types of agreement that may prevent, restrict or distort competition. It includes agreements involving price fixing, market sharing, the restriction of production, terms of supply or other unreasonable conditions. Although the emphasis on the necessity of some form of market analysis tends against the creation of *per se* infringements, the Court of Justice has said that:

> "by its very nature, a clause prohibiting exports constitutes a restriction on competition, whether it is adopted at the instigation of the supplier or of the customer since the agreed purpose of the contracting parties is the endeavour to isolate a part of the market."[80]

The restriction on competition need not be the only or sole objective and the presence of a further quite legitimate objective (*e.g.* protecting public health) will not exclude Article 85(1).[81] It must nevertheless be shown that competition within the Common Market is actually or potentially prevented, restricted or distorted to an appreciable or significant extent.[82] In this respect the size of the parties may be important. The Court of Justice has said that a large undertaking which is responsible for the entire production of a product whose market share may be minimal in relation to competing products may not be able to rely on 'insignificance'.[83]

---

[77] See the approach taken by the Court in Case 161/84, *Pronuptia de Paris* v. *Schillgalis*: [1986] E.C.R. 353 [1986] 1 C.M.L.R. 414.

[78] See, *e.g.* Scheckter, "The Rule of Reason in European Competition Law" [1982] 2 L.I.E.I. 1. and Whish and Sufrin, "Article 85 and the Rule of Reason" (1987) 7 Y.E.L. 1

[79] See the Commission decisions in *Reuter/BASF*, above, n. 29; *Nutricia*: [1983] O.J. L376/22, [1984] 2 C.M.L.R. 165; *Mecaniver–PPG*: [1985] O.J. L35/54, [1985] 3 C.M.L.R. 359, and *ARG/Unipart*, above, n. 13.

[80] *Miller International Schallplatten*, above, n. 67, at para. 7.

[81] See the *NAVEWA/ANSEAU* case, Cases 96–102, 104, 105, 108 & 110/82, *NV IAZ International Belgium SA* v. *Commission*: [1983] E.C.R. 3369, [1984] 3 C.M.L.R. 276, at para. 25.

[82] Case 5/69, *Völk* v. *Vervaecke*: [1969] E.C.R. 295, [1969] C.M.L.R. 273; Case 19/77, *Miller International Schallplatten* v. *Commission*: [1978] E.C.R. 131, [1978] 2 C.M.L.R. 334. Hawk, *op. cit.*, commenting on the notion of "appreciable effect" as it finds expression in the *Völk* case and the Notice on Minor Agreements notes that the Commission and the Court have been reluctant to find a lack of "appreciable" effect where the agreement is either a hardcore restraint like price fixing or is one which is detrimental to single market integration such as export bans.

[83] Case 30/78, *Distillers* v. *Commission:* [1980] E.C.R. 2229, [1980] 3 C.M.L.R. 121, at para. 20.

Effect on inter-State trade

1.11   The agreement must be one "which may affect trade between Member States." This criterion is common to both Articles 85 and 86 and determines the scope of application of Community law and also its objective of one single market.[84] As will be explained below, it is also important in the division of responsibilities in the enforcement of the competition regime under the EEA. In the context of Articles 85 and 86 the Court of Justice has explained it as follows:[85]

> "The interpretation and application of the condition relating to effects on trade between Member States contained in Articles 85 and 86 of the Treaty must be based on the purpose of that condition which is to define, in the context of the laws governing competition, the boundary between the areas respectively covered by Community law and the law of the Member States. Thus Community law covers any agreement or any practice which is capable of constituting a threat to freedom of trade between Member States, in particular by partitioning the national markets or by affecting the structure of competition within the common market. On the other hand, conduct, the effects of which are confined to the territory of a single Member State, is governed by the national legal order."

The requirement that there be some effect on inter-State trade does not confer exclusivity on the Commission to deal with all problems having this effect.[86] Moreover the reader should not be misled by the apparent simplicity of the statements made by the Court. In practice, if it is likely that the structure of competition within the Community may be affected, agreements or practices which might at first glance be thought to be purely domestic or national agreements may be subject to Article 85(1).[87] Anti-competitive conduct confined to the territory of a single Member State is capable of having repercussions on patterns of trade and competition in the Common Market.[88] The Commission does not have to show that trade between Member States has been affected but merely that it may be affected. In this context, the Court on a number of occasions has said:[89]

---

[84] It is clear from, *e.g.* the Merger Control Regulation, Reg. 4064/89, that the concept of an effect on inter-state trade can change its complexion depending on the circumstances. *Quare* whether it will do so in the light of the development of the principle of subsidiary and the decentralisation of Community competition law. See generally para. 8.27A–B.

[85] Case 22/78, *Hugin Kassaregister A/B and Hugin Cash Registers Ltd.* v. *Commission*: [1979] E.C.R. 1869, [1979] 2 C.M.L.R. 345, at para. 17. Adopted by the Court of First Instance in Case T–70/89, *BBC* v. *Commission*: [1991] II E.C.R. 535, [1991] 4 C.M.L.R. 669, at para. 64. But see also the cases cited at n. 92 below, which show that the Court of Justice has also taken a more extensive view of the phrase "affect trade between Member States".

[86] There is still room for conflict in the relationship between Community and national competition laws. See, generally, Chap. 10.

[87] *Brasserie de Haecht* v. *Wilkin (No. 1)*, above, n. 72. The Court has applied a similar test to national legislation. Does it have the effect of preventing access to the market for new national and foreign competitors? Case 234/89, *Delimitis* v. *Henninger Bräu*: [1991] E.C.R. 935, [1992] 5 C.M.L.R. 210. For a case where national legislation failed this test and therefore there was no effect on inter-state trade, see Case C–60/91, *The State (Portugal)* v. *Morais*: [1992] 2 C.M.L.R. 533 (restriction on driving lessons outside district of establishment of driving school).

[88] Case T–66/89, *Publishers Association* v. *Commission*: [1992] II E.C.R. 1995, [1992] 5 C.M.L.R. 120, at para. 55.

[89] Cases 56 and 58/64, *Consten Sarl and Grundig-Verkaufs GmbH* v. *Commission*: [1966] E.C.R. 299, [1966] C.M.L.R. 418. A formula repeated in later judgments of the Court of Justice and followed recently

"it must be possible to foresee with a sufficient degree of probability on the basis of a set of objective factors of law or of fact that the agreement may have an influence, direct or indirect, actual or potential, on the pattern of trade between Member States."

In the case of express export bans from one Member State to another there is virtually an automatic presumption that the criterion is satisfied.[90] In other cases it may be necessary to enter into a detailed analysis of the relevant products and of the likely effects of the agreement in question. So, for example, an export ban to a non-Member State may nevertheless be contrary to Article 85 if there is a reasonable possibility that without such a ban the goods having been exported would be re-imported into the Community.[91] However, judgments of the Court have in the past shown a noticeable trend to find an effect on inter-State trade where there is almost any material degree of contact, actual or theoretical, with another Member State.[92] But in theory the effect on inter-State trade must be an appreciable one.[93] A *de minimis* rule should apply here.[94]

Article 85(2)—automatic nullity

1.12 Article 85(2) provides that agreements and decisions subject to the prohibition in Article 85(1) are automatically void. Nullity under Article 85(2) is, as it says, automatic and is not therefore contingent on any act or finding of the Commission or any other Community or national authority. And as Articles 85 and 86 are directly applicable provisions of Community law,[95] Article 85(2) renders unenforceable any agreement caught by Article 85(1) before a national court, whether between the parties to the agreement or as against a third party.[96] The Court of Justice has however, qualified the apparent rigour of Article 85(2) in two important respects.

by the Court of First Instance in *Publishers Association* v. *Commission*, above, at para. 55.

[90] *Miller International Schallplatten*, above, n. 82. Arguments that a party has no interest in preventing trade because prices are almost the same throughout Europe are not compelling: Case 107/82, *AEG Telefunken* v. *Commission*: [1983] E.C.R. 3151, [1984] 3 C.M.L.R. 325. There remains the possibility that restrictions may affect inter-state trade because market and price conditions may change at any time. See *Bayer Dental*: [1990] O.J. L351/46, [1992] 4 C.M.L.R. 61.

[91] This may be particularly important in cases where the ban operates in relation to countries where the Community has a free trade agreement. See the Commission's decision in *SABA*: [1976] O.J. L28/19, [1976] 1 C.M.L.R. D6; *Junghans*: [1977] O.J. L30/10, [1977] 1 C.M.L.R. D82, and *Campari*: [1978] O.J. L70/69, [1978] 2 C.M.L.R. 397. See, generally, Bellis, "International Trade and the Competition Law of the European Economic Community" (1979) 16 C.M.L.Rev. 647.

[92] See Case 243/83, *Binon & Cie SA* v. *Agence et Messagerie de la Presse SA*: [1985] E.C.R. 2015, [1985] 3 C.M.L.R. 800, at para. 9; *Pronuptia de Paris* v. *Schillgalis*, above, n. 78, at para. 26; Case 193/83, *Windsurfing International Inc.* v. *Commission*: [1986] E.C.R. 611, [1986] 3 C.M.L.R. 489, at paras. 96–97; Cases 240–242, 261, 262, 268 & 269/82, *Stichting Sigarettenindustrie* v. *Commission*: [1985] E.C.R. 3831, [1987] 3 C.M.L.R. 661, at paras. 48–50; Case 45/85, *Verband der Sachversicherer* v. *Commission*: [1987] E.C.R. 405, at paras. 48–51, and Case 247/86, *Alsatel* v. *Novosam*: [1988] E.C.R. 5987, [1990] 4 C.M.L.R. 434, at para. 11.

[93] *Völk* v. *Vervaecke*, above, n. 82. See also comment at n. 84 above.

[94] Per A.G. Warner in *Miller International Schallplatten*, above, n. 82. And see question 5.3 in Part IX of the Complementary Note to Form A/B.

[95] Consten and Grundig, above, n. 89.

[96] Case 22/71, *Béguelin Import Co* v. *GL Import-Export SA*: [1971] E.C.R. 949, [1972] C.M.L.R. 81.

First, the Court has held that it is not necessarily the entire agreement that is void but only those parts which fall within the prohibition of Article 85(1), provided they are severable from the agreement. In *La Technique Minière* v. *Maschinenbau Ulm GmbH*[97] the Court said:

> "Article 85(2), which is aimed at ensuring respect of the Treaty, may only be interpreted in the light of its finality within the Community and should be limited to that context. The automatic nullity in question applies only to those elements of the agreement which are subject to the prohibition or to the agreement as a whole if those elements do not appear severable from the agreement itself. Consequently, all other contractual provisions which are not affected by the prohibition, since they do not involve the application of the Treaty, fall outside the Community law."

The question whether a particular element of an agreement is severable is a question of national law. So, too, the consequences of nullity for other aspects of the agreement and, for example, for any orders and deliveries made on the basis of the agreement and the resulting financial obligations are not a matter of Community law.[98] It is for the national court to determine in accordance with the applicable national law (which need not necessarily be that of a Member State) the consequences in the event that certain provisions are void.[99] In *Chemidus Wavin Ltd.* v. *Société pour la Transformation et l'Exploitation des Résines Industrielles SA*,[1] Buckley L.J. Said:

> "It seems to me that in applying Article 85 to an English contract one may well have to consider whether, after the excisions required by the Article of the Treaty have been made from the contract, the contract could be said to fail for lack of consideration or any other ground, or whether the contract could be so changed in its character as not to be the sort of contract that the parties intended to enter into at all."

In practice parties frequently include quite detailed provisions so that their wishes can, in so far as the law permits, govern the consequences of Article 85(2) being found applicable.

Second, the Court of Justice has held[2] that a national court cannot apply Article 85(2) to 'old agreements'[3] duly notified or exempt from notification[4] until after the Commission has taken a decision granting or refusing exemption under Article 85(3). Legal certainty requires such agreements to be treated as being valid and enforceable pending the Commission's pronouncement on Article 85(3). A Commission decision

---

[97] Above, n. 10, at p. 250.
[98] Case 319/82, *Société de Vente de Ciments et Bétons de l'Est SA* v. *Kerpen & Kerpen GmbH & Co. KG*: [1983] E.C.R. 4173 [1985] 1 C.M.L.R. 511.
[99] Case 10/86, *V.A.G. France SA* v. *Etablissements Magne SA*: [1986] E.C.R. 4071, [1988] 4 C.M.L.R. 98.
[1] [1978] 3 C.M.L.R. 514, at 519. Applied in *Inntrepreneur Estates Ltd.* v. *Mason*: [1993] 2 C.M.L.R. 293.
[2] Case 48/72, *Brasserie de Haecht* v. *Wilkin (No. 2)*: [1973] E.C.R. 77, [1973] C.M.L.R. 287.
[3] "Old agreements" are agreements in existence on March 13, 1962 when Reg. 17 came into force and which were notified in due time or fall within Art. 4(2) of Reg. 17. "Accession agreements", *i.e.* those in existence on January 1, 1973, January 1, 1981 or January 1, 1986 as the case may be, and which came within Art. 85(1) solely as a result of accession, may be treated in the same way as "old agreements". See paras. 10.04–07. Note the potential application for agreements under the EEA.
[4] By virtue of Art. 4(2) of Reg. 17. See paras. 2.09–15.

finding infringement and refusing exemption under Article 85(3) will trigger off nullity under Article 85(2) which has not only prospective but also retrospective effect.[5] Moreover, the Court has held that a comfort letter sent by the Commission may in certain circumstances also withdraw such "provisional validity".[6] Provisional validity has taken on renewed significance in the context of the EEA.

Article 85(3)—exemption

1.13 Article 85(3) sets out the conditions which must be satisfied for an agreement to be exempted from the prohibition in Article 85(1). The agreement must satisfy four conditions, two positive and two negative. It must:

(a) contribute to improving the production or distribution of goods or to promoting technical or economic progress; and
(b) allow consumers a fair share of the resulting benefit.

It must not:

(c) impose restrictions which are not indispensable; and
(d) afford the possibility of eliminating competition in respect of a substantial part of the products in question.

The improvement in the production or distribution of the goods in question must show appreciable objective advantages which outweigh the disadvantages they may cause to competition.[7] As the Court of Justice has pointed out, the powers conferred upon the Commission under Article 85(3) show that the requirements for the maintenance of workable competition may be reconciled with the safeguarding of objectives of a different nature and that to this end certain restrictions on competition are permissible, provided that they are essential to the attainment of those objectives and that they do not result in the elimination of competition for a substantial part of the Common Market.[8] The Commission is entitled to consider all the circumstances surrounding the application of the agreement. How it has been worked in practice may be very material. The Commission will take account of the nature of the market in question and the effect on competition in the Community. The Commission is not obliged however to undertake a detailed examination of all the advantages and disadvantages likely to flow from the agreement where it believes the agreement has been used to partition the

---

[5] *Brasserie de Haecht (No. 2)*, above, at para. 27. But note the approach of the Commission in *Velcro/Aplix*: [1985] O.J. L233/22, [1989] 4 C.M.L.R. 157. See further para. 10.11.
[6] Case 99/79, *Lancôme* v. *Etos and Albert Heijn Supermart*: [1980] E.C.R. 2511, [1981] 2 C.M.L.R. 164, at para. 17.
[7] Cases 56 and 58/64, *Consten Sarl and Grundig-Verkaufs GmbH* v. *Commission*: [1966] E.C.R. 299, at p. 348. This requirement to balance the interests involved arguably creates a fifth condition to be satisfied before exemption can be granted. For recognition of the existence and importance of the "fifth condition", see *Ford Werke AG (Distribution System)*: [1984] O.J. L327/31, [1984] 1 C.M.L.R. 596, and *Fire Insurance (D)*: [1985] O.J. L35/20, [1985] 3 C.M.L.R. 246.
[8] Case 75/84, *Metro-SB-Grossmarkte GmbH & Co. KG* v. *Commission*: [1986] E.C.R. 3021, [1987] 1 C.M.L.R. 118, at para. 65.

Common Market.[9] The burden is however on the applicants to prove that the agreement in question satisfies each of the conditions laid down in Article 85(3).[10]

1.14 By virtue of Article 9(1) of Regulation 17 the Commission has the sole power to grant exemptions under Article 85(3).[11] An agreement may have the benefit of an exemption either because it is the subject of an individual decision taken by the Commission or because it falls within a category of agreements for which a group or block exemption applies. Acting under the powers in Article 87 the Council has in Regulation 19/65 given power to the Commission to make block exemptions for certain categories of exclusive dealing agreements and for certain agreements relating to industrial property rights. Regulations 1983/83 and 1984/83 contain block exemptions for exclusive distribution agreements and exclusive purchasing agreements. Regulation 2349/84 exempts certain patent licensing agreements. Regulation 123/85 gives a block exemption for certain motor vehicle distribution and servicing agreements. Regulation 4087/88 exempts categories of franchise agreements. Regulation 556/89 exempts certain know-how licensing agreements. By Regulation 2821/71 the Council empowered the Commission to make block exemptions for certain agreements concerning the application of standards or types, research and development and specialisation. In Regulation 417/85, the Commission has exercised the power in relation to certain types of specialisation agreement, and in Regulation 418/85 for research and development co-operation agreements. By Regulation 1534/91 the Council empowered the Commission to make block exemptions for certain activities, including common risk premiums, tariffs and common standard policy conditions, in the insurance sector. This the Commission has done in Regulation 3932/92. The scope of the block exemptions relating to specialisation, R&D, patent licensing and know-how licensing was recently extended by Regulation 151/93.[12]

1.15 Individual exemptions can, as a general rule,[13] only be granted if the agreement is notified to the Commission. A block exemption, on the other hand, automatically exempts an agreement without any need for notification[14] or a formal decision by the Commission provided, of course, the conditions specified in the terms of the block exemption are satisfied in relation to the agreement. But there is also the possibility under certain block exemptions to notify under the so-called "opposition procedure" where the agreement in question has "grey" features.[15] There is clearly a very strong incentive to bring an agreement within the strict terms of a block exemption where

---

[9] Cases 25–26/84, *Ford Werke AG and Ford of Europe Inc.* v. *Commission*: [1985] E.C.R. 2725, [1985] 3 C.M.L.R. 528, at paras. 33 and 36. Unilateral behaviour outside the agreement may prejudice exemption. See also Case 107/82, *AEG-Telefunken* v. *Commission*: [1983] E.C.R. 3151, [1984] 3 C.M.L.R. 325.

[10] And to set out in Form A/B its position on each of those conditions. Case T–66/89, *Publishers Association* v. *Commission*: [1992] II E.C.R. 1995, [1992] 5 C.M.L.R. 120, at para. 69.

[11] See the Court's ruling in Case 31/80, *L'Oréal NV and L'Oréal SA* v. *De Nieuwe A.M.C.K. Pvba*: [1980] E.C.R. 3775, [1981] 2 C.M.L.R. 235. The jurisdictional implications of Art. 9 and the equivalent provisions in the transport implementing regulations in relation to national competition authorities are dealt with at para. 1.26 and in relation to the principle of subsidiarity at para. 8.27A.

[12] [1993] O.J. L21/10. The four block exemptions as amended are reproduced at [1993] 3 C.M.L.R. 151.

[13] By Art. 4(2) of Reg. 17, certain agreements are exempt from notification. This does not mean that they are exempt from the prohibition in Art. 85(1) but merely that any application for and granting of exemption will not be prejudiced by the absence of notification. See, generally, paras. 2.09–15.

[14] Case 1/71, *SA Cadillon* v. *Firma Hoss, Maschinenbau KG*: [1971] E.C.R. 351, [1971] C.M.L.R. 420.

[15] The procedure which is provided for in Regs. 2349/84, 417/85, 418/85, 4087/88 and 556/89 is discussed at paras. 2.40–52.

available.[16] But if an agreement contains restrictions which go beyond those permitted by the block exemption, then the block exemption will not apply at all and if the agreement needs[17] to be exempted it will have to be notified[18] and an application made for the Commission, by individual decision, to exempt it. The Commission has acknowledged that, as the concept of a restrictive agreement depends on changing economic conditions, it has considerable discretion when considering agreements for exemption in the light of the conditions ((a)-(d) above) laid down in Article 85(3).[19] Exempted agreements are valid and enforceable in national courts. Only an exemption, by individual decision or block exemption, made in accordance with Article 85(3) has the effect of precluding *erga omnes* the nullity resulting from Article 85(2).[20]

Article 86

1.16 Article 86 prohibits, as incompatible with the Common Market, any abuse by one or more undertakings of a dominant position within the Common Market or a substantial part of it in so far as it may affect trade between Member States. Size or, more accurately, dominance itself is not prohibited. The acquisition or increase of dominance by takeover or other merger is controlled under Regulation 4064/89, the Merger Control Regulation.[21] Article 86 is concerned with behaviour. It lists a number of activities which may constitute abuse: directly or indirectly imposing unfair trading conditions; limiting production, markets or technical development to the prejudice of consumers; applying dissimilar conditions to equivalent transactions with other trading parties; and making the conclusion of contracts subject to acceptance by the other parties of supplementary obligations having no connection with the subject of such contracts. Like the list of prohibited agreements contained in Article 85(1), the list of examples in Article 86 is not exhaustive.[22] It should be noted that unlike Article 85, Article 86 does not contain any provisions for an exemption or other approval to the granted.

---

[16] But block exemptions do not themselves specify mandatory rules for the contents of agreements or oblige the contracting parties to amend the contents of their contract to accord with the regulations. See *VAG France SA* v. *Etablissements Magne SA*, above, n. 99.

[17] A block exemption cannot however prejudice the applicability of Art. 85(1). In Case 32/65, *Italy* v. *Council and Commission*: [1966] E.C.R. 389, [1969] C.M.L.R. 39, at para. 9, the Court said: "to define a category is only to make a classification and it does not mean that the agreements which come within it fall within the prohibition. Nor does it mean that an agreement within the exempted category, but not exhibiting all the features of the said definition, must necessarily fall within the prohibition. Therefore to grant exemptions by categories cannot amount, even by implication, to passing any preconceived judgment on any agreement unless considered individually." If Art. 85 (1) is not applicable then the block exemption and therefore any opposition procedure under it does not apply. Negative clearance is appropriate in such circumstances—see, *e.g. Elopak/Metal Box-Odin*: [1990] O.J. L209/15, [1991] 4 C.M.L.R. 832.

[18] Unless exempted from notification by virtue of Art. 4(2) of Reg. 17.

[19] The European Community's Competition Policy, European Documents 1976/4, at p. 6.

[20] *Prodifarma I*: Case T–116/89, *Vereniging Prodifarma and Others* v. *Commission*: [1990] II E.C.R. 843, at para. 65.

[21] The application of Arts. 85 and 86 to mergers after Reg. 4064/89 is considered by Cook and Kerse, *EEC Merger Control* (1991), Chap. 8.

[22] Case 6/72, *Europemballage Corp. and Continental Can Co. Inc.* v. *Commission*: [1973] E.C.R. 215, [1973] C.M.L.R. 199. For a critical (and comparative) article on the scope of Art. 86, see Joliet, "Le contrôle des monopoles dans la C.E.E." [1976] *Journal des Tribunaux* 217.

Dominant position

1.17 Perhaps the most difficult question in connection with the application of Article 86 is the determination of the existence of a dominant position.[23] Market share is not the sole criterion as the Court of Justice pointed out in the *United Brands* case:[24]

> "The dominant position referred to in this Article relates to a position of economic strength enjoyed by an undertaking which enables it to prevent effective competition being maintained on the relevant market by affording it the power to behave to an appreciable extent independently of its competitors, its customers and ultimately of consumers. In general a dominant position derives from a combination of several factors which, taken separately, are not necessarily determinative."

The existence of a dominant position does not require the undertaking enjoying it to have eliminated all possibility of competition. But as the Court said in *AKZO*:

> "very large market shares are in themselves, and save in exceptional circumstances, evidence of the existence of a dominant position . . . That is the situation where there is a market share of 50% such as that found to exist in this case."[25]

A lesser, though large, share may not be (although the ratio of market share held by the undertaking concerned to those held by its competitors is an important indicator) and it will be necessary to look closely at all the other relevant facts in order to determine the degree of market power enjoyed. This depends on the height of any barriers to entry or expansion and the ease with which buyers can switch to substitute products. In *United Brands*, the Court considered a number of facts important, including the degree of vertical integration of UBC, its transport facilities, its technical knowledge, its quality control supporting its premier brand name (Chiquita) as well as the size of its market share (45 per cent.) in relation to its nearest competitor. Temporary unprofitability, or even losses, is not inconsistent with the existence of a dominant position.[26]

Article 86 expressly contemplates the situation where the dominant position is held by more than one undertaking.[27] The nature of the relationship between undertakings alleged to be jointly or collectively dominant was recently considered by the Court of First Instance in *Italian Flat Glass*.[28] The Court held that two or more independent economic entities may on a specific market be united by[29] economic links and together hold a dominant position *vis-à-vis* the other operators on the same market. The Court of First Instance gave the example of where two or more independent undertakings

---

[23] This is not a question which can be answered solely by legal analysis. See, generally, Baden Fuller, "Article 86 EEC: Economic Analysis of the Existence of a Dominant Position" (1979) 4 E.L.Rev. 423.

[24] Case 27/76, *United Brands Co.* v. *Commission*: [1978] E.C.R. 207, [1978] 1 C.M.L.R. 429, at paras. 65 and 66.

[25] Case C–62/86, *AKZO* v. *Commission*: [1991] I E.C.R. 3359, [1993] 5 C.M.L.R. 215, at para. 60.

[26] Case 322/81, *Michelin* v. *Commission*: [1983] E.C.R. 3461, [1985] 1 C.M.L.R. 292, at para. 59.

[27] Art. 86 speaks of any abuse "by one or more undertakings of a dominant position."

[28] Cases T 68 & 77/89, *Società Italiano Vetro SpA and Others* v. *Commission*: [1992] II E.C.R. 1403, [1992] 5 C.M.L.R. 302.

[29] The Court of First Instance appear to have firmly rejected the argument that joint dominance can only exist in circumstances where, for the purposes of Art. 85(1), the undertakings will be regarded as being one economic entity—see para 1.07.

jointly have, through agreements or licences, a technological lead affording them the power to behave to an appreciable extent independently of their competitors, their customers and ultimately their consumers.[30] The notion of joint or collective dominance has particular significance for the transport sector.[31]

Relevant market

1.18 The Commission must define the relevant market.[32] Such definition will normally be determined by reference to both product sector and geographic area in which the economic power of the undertaking in question is to be judged. The Court of Justice has indicated that an examination limited to the objective characteristics only of the relevant products is not enough: the competitive conditions and the structure of supply and demand on the market must also be taken into account.[33] In practice the Commission will look at the extent of the possibility of demand substitution and supply substitution. The Commission has sometimes tended towards a narrow product market involving a correspondingly narrow view of which product is substitutable for another. Both Commission and Court have in the past been criticised for concentrating on differentiation by reference to product description rather than by reference to price relationships and cross-elasticity of demand.[34] On the question of the relevant geographic market, the Court of Justice has said[35]:

> "The condition for the application of Article 86 to an undertaking in a dominant position presupposes the clear delineation of the substantial part of the Common Market in which it may be able to engage in abuses which hinder effective competition and this is an area where the objective conditions of competition applying to the product in question must be the same for all traders."

Thus, in *United Brands*, where the relevant product market was bananas, the whole of the Common Market excluding France, Italy and the United Kingdom (being Member States which operated special preferential tariffs for certain producer countries) was held to constitute the relevant geographical market. One cannot lay down any hard and fast rules as to what amounts to a "substantial part" of the Common Market. It is a question of identifying an area where the conditions of competition are homogeneous and the adjective "substantial" may only serve to import a *de minimis* rule into the formulation.[36] The pattern and volume of production and consumption of the product and

---

[30] *Italian Flat Glass*, above, at para. 358.

[31] See the Commission's recent decisions relating to shipping conferences: *French-West African Shipowners Committees*: [1992] O.J. L134/1 and *Cewal, Cowac and Ukwal*: [1993] O.J. L34/20.

[32] *Continental Can*, above, n. 22. The significance in the case of Art. 86 is not the same as in the case of Art. 85, where the position and importance of the undertakings concerned in the relevant market comes in at the later stage when considering whether the effect on trade of the restrictions on competition is appreciable: A.G. Mischo in Case 246/86, *Société Co-opérative des Asphalteurs Belges (Belasco) and Others* v. *Commission*: [1989] E.C.R. 2181, [1991] 4 C.M.L.R. 96.

[33] *Michelin*, above.

[34] See Korah, "Concept of a Dominant Position within the Meaning of Article 86: Recent Case Law of the Court" (1980) 17 C.M.L. Rev. 395. Korah criticises in particular the approach taken by the Court in United Brands. See also Baden Fuller, *op. cit.*

[35] Case 27/76, *United Brands Co.* v. *Commission*: [1978] E.C.R. 207, [1978] 1 C.M.L.R. 429, at para. 44.

[36] Per A.G. Warner in Case 77/77, *B.P. and others* v. *Commission*: [1978] E.C.R. 1513, [1978] 3 C.M.L.R. 174. But see his opinion in Case 177/78, *Pigs and Bacon Commission* v. *McCarren*: [1979] E.C.R. 2161, [1979] 3 C.M.L.R. 389, where he took the view that a particular current of trade, *in casu*, the export of Ir-

the habits and economic opportunities of vendors and purchasers are all matters which may be considered in this context.[37] This said, both the Court of Justice and the Commission have expressly recognised that the territories of both large and medium-sized Member States constitute a substantial part of the Common Market.[38]

Abuse

1.19 Article 86 contains a list of activities which may constitute an abuse.[39] This list is non-exhaustive[40] and does not restrict the character of the activities which may constitute an abuse. The prohibition in Article 86 encompasses both "exploitative" and "exclusionary" or "anti-competitive" abuses.[41] That "exploitative" abuses are caught can be seen from the examples set out in Article 86 and is acknowledged most clearly in the following statement of the Court of Justice in the *United Brands* case:[42]

> "It is advisable therefore to ascertain whether the dominant undertaking has made use of the opportunities arising out of its dominant position in such a way as to reap trading benefits which it would not have reaped if there had been normal and sufficiently effective competition."

A dominant undertaking may exploit its position by excessive pricing (Article 86(a)), limiting production, markets or technical development (Article 86(b)), discriminatory practices (Article 86(c)) and using tie-in sales (Article 86(d)).[43] But such activities can also be "exclusionary" or "anti-competitive": for example, a tie-in sale not only enables a dominant undertaking to exploit its position by requiring purchasers to take another product they may not want, but may also be exclusionary to the extent that such purchasers no longer acquire some or all of the tied product from competing suppliers.[44] Article 86 is aimed not only at practices which may cause damage to consumers directly but also those which are detrimental to them through their impact on effective competition.[45] That Article 86 covers exclusionary practices is well established. The Court of Justice said in *Hoffmann-La Roche*:[46]

---

ish bacon to Great Britain, did not constitute a "part of" the Common Market within the meaning of Art. 86.
[37] *Sugar:* Cases 40–48, 50, 54–56, 111, 113 & 114/73, *Cooperative Vereniging 'Suiker Unie' UA and others* v. *Commission*: [1975] E.C.R. 1663, [1976] 1 C.M.L.R. 295, at para. 371.
[38] Case 127/73, *B.R.T.* v. *S.A.B.A.M.*: [1974] E.C.R. 313, [1974] 2 C.M.L.R. 238 (Belgium); *Soda ash–ICI*: [1991] O.J. L152/40 (U.K.).
[39] See, generally, *Bellamy and Child*, n. 3, at Chap. 8.
[40] Case 6/72, *Europemballage Corp. and Continental Can Co. Inc.* v. *Commission*: [1973] E.C.R. 215, [1973] C.M.L.R. 199.
[41] See Temple Lang, "Monopolisation and the Definition of 'Abuse' of a Dominant Position under Article 86 EEC Treaty" (1979) 16 C.M.L.Rev. 345.
[42] Above, n. 35, at para. 249.
[43] *London European Airways–Sabena*: [1988] O.J. L317/47 is an example of both 86 (c) and (d).
[44] The theory about extending market power has however been seriously criticised by the Chicago School. See, generally, Posner, *Anti-trust Law an Economic Perspective* (1976).
[45] Case 6/72, *Europemballage Corp. and Continental Can Co. Inc.* v. *Commission*: [1973] E.C.R. 215, [1973] C.M.L.R. 199, at para. 26.
[46] Case 85/76, *Hoffmann-La Roche* v. *Commission*: [1979] E.C.R. 461, [1979] 3 C.M.L.R. 211, at para. 91. These words were repeated by the Court in Case C–62/86, *AKZO* v. *Commission*: [1991] I E.C.R. 3359,

"The concept of abuse is an objective concept relating to the behaviour of an undertaking in a dominant position which is such as to influence the structure of a market where, as a result of the very presence of the undertaking in question, the degree of competition is weakened and which, through recourse to methods different from those which condition normal competition in products or services on the basis of the transactions of commercial operators, has the effect of hindering the maintenance of the degree of competition still existing in the market or the growth of that competition."

The Court held, *inter alia*, that fidelity rebates and exclusive supply agreements were such abuses. As the Court of Justice added in *AKZO*:

"It follows that Article 86 prohibits a dominant undertaking from eliminating a competitor and thereby strengthening its position by using methods other than those which come within the scope of competition on the basis of quality."[47]

In *Continental Can*, the Court considered a merger will be an abuse where the dominant undertaking strengthens its position in such a way that the degree of dominance reached substantially fetters competition.[48] This case, as well as indicating that "anti-competitive" abuses fall within Article 86, also demonstrates that behaviour of a dominant undertaking may constitute an abuse notwithstanding that the undertaking's dominance is not being employed in relation to it.[49] The behaviour will, *a fortiori*, be abusive if the dominance is used.[50]

The following have been found by the Court of Justice to constitute an abuse or to be capable of so doing: refusal to supply;[51] requirements contracts;[52] loyalty or fidelity rebates;[53] excessive prices; discriminatory pricing;[54] predatory pricing;[55] tying.[56] In relation to industrial and intellectual property rights, the Court has held that the mere

---

[1993] 5 C.M.L.R. 215, at para. 69.

[47] *AKZO*, at para. 70.

[48] Above. The adoption of the Merger Control Regulation, Reg. 4064/89, has largely rendered the application of Art. 86 to mergers redundant. But see *Warner-Lambert/Gillette and BIC/Gillette*: [1993] O.J. L116/21. The Commission has also applied the rationale of *Continental Can* to certain related but non-merger situations. See *Tetra Pak I (BTG licence)*: [1988] O.J. L272/27, [1990] 4 C.M.L.R. 47 (acquisition of an exclusive licence).

[49] On the relationship between the dominance and the abuse, see, generally, Vogelenzang, "Abuse of a Dominant Position in Article 86: the Problem of Causality and Some Applications" (1976) 13 C.M.L.Rev 61.

[50] Temple Lang, *op. cit.*, at p. 349.

[51] Cases 6 & 7/73, *Instituto Chemioterapico Italiano SpA and Commercial Solvents Corporation* v. *Commission*: [1974] E.C.R. 223, [1974] 1 C.M.L.R. 309; Case 27/76, *United Brands Co.* v. *Commission*: [1978] E.C.R. 207, [1978] 1 C.M.L.R. 429, and Case 77/77, *B.P. and others* v. *Commission*: [1978] E.C.R. 1513, [1978] 3 C.M.L.R. 174.

[52] *Hoffman-La Roche*, above.

[53] *Ibid.* and *Michelin*, above, n. 31.

[54] *United Brands*, above. Case 226/84, *British Leyland* v. *Commission*: [1986] E.C.R. 2263, [1987] 1 C.M.L.R. 185, and see Siragusa, "The Application of Article 86 to the Pricing Policy of Dominant Companies: Discriminatory and Unfair Prices" (1979) 16 C.M.L.Rev. 179.

[55] *AKZO*, above. See also Case 298/83, *C.I.C.C.E.* v. *Commission*: [1985] E.C.R. 1106, [1986] 1 C.M.L.R. 486.

[56] Case 311/84, *CBEM Télémarketing* v. *Compagnie Luxembourgeoise de Télédiffusion*: [1985] E.C.R. 3261, [1986] 2 C.M.L.R. 558.

ownership of such rights does not imply the existence of a dominant position,[57] and the exercise of the right (to prevent infringement) is not considered an abuse merely because the proprietor occupies a dominant position on the market.[58] But in some circumstances the exercise of industrial and intellectual property can amount to an abuse, although this does not destroy the specific subject matter of the right itself.[59]

1.20 An abuse is only prohibited by Article 86 "in so far as it may affect trade between Member States." As in the case of Article 85(1), this criterion defines the sphere of application of the Community rules in relation to national laws. The criterion has not been narrowly construed and the Court of Justice has said that it must consider the consequences of an alleged abuse "for the effective competition structure in the Common Market."[60] In this context there may be no reason to distinguish between production (whether of goods or services[61]) intended for supply within the Common Market and that intended for export. If the conduct in question has, or will have, repercussions on the effective competitive structure in the Common Market then the criterion will be satisfied.

As already mentioned Article 86, unlike Article 85, does not contain any provision for an exemption to be granted. Article 86 does not permit any exceptions to its prohibition.[62] But not every exploitation of a dominant position is necessarily abusive. The two Articles, 85 and 86, are not, however, mutually exclusive. The same conduct may fall foul of both prohibitions.[63] The application of Article 85(3), whether by block exemption or individual decision, does not preclude the application of Article 86.[64]

---

[57] Case 96/75, *EMI Records Ltd.* v. *CBS Schallplatten GmbH*: [1976] E.C.R. 913, [1976] 2 C.M.L.R. 235, at para. 36.

[58] Case 102/77, *Hoffmann-La Roche* v. *Centrafarm*: [1978] E.C.R. 1139, [1978] 3 C.M.L.R. 217, at para. 16.

[59] Case 38/87, *Volvo AB* v. *Erik Veng (UK) Ltd*: [1988] E.C.R. 6211, [1989] 4 C.M.L.R. 122; Case 53/87, *CICRA* v. *Renault*: [1988] E.C.R. 6039, [1990] 4 C.M.L.R. 265. Applied by the Court of First Instance in Case T–70/89, *BBC* v. *Commission*: [1991] II E.C.R. 535, [1991] 4 C.M.L.R. 669 upholding the Commission decision in the *Magill* case that there was an abuse by the BBC and others limiting the scope of their copyright licensing policies and products so as to prevent entry on the market of a comprehensive TV guide.

[60] *Commercial Solvents*, above, at para. 33.

[61] Case 22/79, *Greenwich Film Productions* v. *SACEM*: [1979] E.C.R. 3275, [1980] 1 C.M.L.R. 629, at para. 11.

[62] *Continental Can*, above, at para. 25.

[63] See, *e.g. Decca Navigator Systems*: [1989] O.J. L43/27, [1990] 4 C.M.L.R. 627. But as the Court of First Instance said in *Italian Flat Glass* (Cases T 68 & 77/89, *Società Italiano Vetro SpA and Others* v. *Commission*: [1992] II E.C.R. 1403, [1992] 5 C.M.L.R. 302) the Commission cannot simply "recycle" the Art. 85 facts and deduce a breach of Art. 86. There has to be a proper market analysis and definition, etc., to justify a finding of infringement of Art. 86 (para. 360).

[64] Case T–51/89, *Tetra Pak Rausing SA* v. *Commission*: [1990] II E.C.R. 309, [1991] 4 C.M.L.R. 334.

Article 90—public undertakings

1.21 Articles 85 and 86 simply refer to "undertakings". They apply to both private and public undertakings.[65] Article 90 contains certain special provisions which relate, *inter alia*, to public undertakings.[66] Article 90(1) provides that in the case of public undertakings and undertakings to which Member States grant special or exclusive rights, Member States must not enact or maintain in force any measure contrary to the rules of the Treaty, including the competition rules in Articles 85 and 86. Article 90(1) is addressed to Member States and is a specific application of the general rule in Article 5 of the Treaty.[67] It contains no relaxation of the competition rules.[68] On the other hand, Article 90(2) does provide a limited exception to Articles 85 and 86:

> "Undertakings entrusted with the operation of services of general economic interest or having the character of a revenue-producing monopoly shall be subject to the rules contained in this Treaty, in particular to the rules on competition, in so far as the application of such rules does not obstruct the performance, in law or in fact, of the particular tasks assigned to them. The development of trade must not be affected to such an extent as would be contrary to the interests of the Community."

This derogation from the competition rules is narrowly construed by both the Commission and the Court.[69] Articles 85 and 86 apply to public undertakings whether or

---

[65] See, generally, Wyatt and Dashwood, *European Community Law* (3rd ed., 1993), at Chap. 19; Page, "Member States, Public Undertakings and Article 90" (1982) 7 E.L.Rev. 19.

[66] Wyatt and Dashwood, *ibid.* at p. 551 consider that "public undertaking" would include the following: the State and its regional and local subdivisions when they participate in the production or distribution of goods or in the provision of services, but not when they act in the exercise of sovereignty or purely as consumers; corporations established under public law, as in the U.K. statutory bodies such as British Coal, etc.; public services or authorities, *e.g.* a health authority with regard to the provision of private hospital treatment; and State controlled undertakings operating under private law.

[67] Art. 5 provides that Member States "shall abstain from any measure which could jeopardise the attainment of the objectives of this Treaty." The Court has consistently held that Arts. 85 and 86, in conjunction with Art. 5 require the Member States not to introduce or maintain in force measures, even of a legislative nature, which may render ineffective the competition rules applicable to undertakings. Case 267/86, *Pascal Van Eycke* v. *Aspa NV*: [1988] E.C.R. 4769, [1990] 4, C.M.L.R. 330, at para. 16. The development of the Court's jurisprudence in the area is traced by Joliet, "National Anticompetitive legislation and Community law" [1989] 12 Fordham Int. L.J. 163. The Court has not moved any further forward in its recent judgments in Cases C–2/91, *Meng*, C–185/91, *Reiff* and C–245/91, *Ohra*: November 17, 1993, not yet reported.

[68] See the judgments of the Court of Justice in Case C–260/89, *Elliniki Radiofonia Tileorassi* [1991] I E.C.R. 2925 and Case C–179/90, *Merci Convenziondi Porto de Genova* v. *Siderurgica Gabrielli*: [1991] I E.C.R. 5889.

[69] See Case 127/73, *B.R.T.* v. *S.A.B.A.M.*: [1974] E.C.R. 313, [1974] 2 C.M.L.R. 238; Case 172/80, *Züchner* v. *Bayerische Vereinsbank*: [1981] E.C.R. 2021, [1982] 1 C.M.L.R. 313; Case 7/82, *GVL* v. *Commission*: [1983] E.C.R. 483, [1983] 3 C.M.L.R. 645; the *NAVEWA/ANSEAU* case, Cases 96–102, 104, 105, 108 & 110/82, *NV IAZ International Belgium SA* v. *Commission*: [1983] E.C.R. 3369, [1984] 3 C.M.L.R. 276; the *British Telecom* case, Case 41/83, *Italy* v. *Commission*: [1985] E.C.R. 873, [1985] 2 C.M.L.R. 368; *CBEM Telemarketing*, above, n. 55; Case C–41/90, *Höfner and Elser* v. *Macrotron*: [1991] I E.C.R. 1979, [1993] 4 C.M.L.R. 306 and Case C–18/88, *RTT* v. *GB Inno-BM*: [1991] I E.C.R. 5941. See also the Commission's decisions in *Pabst and Richarz/BNIA*: [1976] O.J. L231/24, [1976] 2 C.M.L.R. D63; *Maize Seed*: [1978] O.J. L286/23, [1978] 3 C.M.L.R. 434; *Uniform Eurocheques*: [1985] O.J. L35/43, [1985] 3 C.M.L.R. 434; *Decca Navigator System*, above; *Magill TV Guide/ITP, BBC and RTE*: [1989] O.J. L78/43, [1989] 4 C.M.L.R. 757; *Film purchases by German television stations*: [1989] O.J. L284/36, [1990] 4 C.M.L.R. 841; *Screensport/EBU Members*: [1991] O.J. L63/32, [1992] 5

not they come within Article 90. Where they do, the enforcement of the rules remains with the Commission and the normal procedures under Regulation 17, etc. apply. In addition, Article 90(3) enables the Commission, where necessary, to address appropriate directives or decisions to Member States to ensure the application of Article 90. Such directives or decisions can, but need not be, limited to a particular case.[70] They can be general in nature, such as the Directive on the transparency of financial relations between Member States and public undertakings.[71] They can also be directed at the opening up of a particular sector of market, such as telecommunications.[72]

Applicability of the competition rules to different economic sectors

1.22   The area of operation of Articles 85 and 86 is not expressly restricted to any particular economic sectors. Activities relating to the supply of goods or services, or involving industrial or other property rights,[73] may fall within their ambit. The competition rules (and the principal implementing provision, Regulation 17) apply generally. There are, however, four areas where special provisions apply and the above statement must be qualified:

(i) *Coal and steel*

Coal and steel are the subject of the Treaty of Paris which created the European Coal and Steel Community (the ECSC). The EEC Treaty expressly provides that its provisions do not affect the provisions of the ECSC Treaty[74] which contains special

---

C.M.L.R. 273; *IJsselcentrale and others*: [1991] O.J. L28/32, [1992] 5 C.M.L.R. 154 and *Jahrhundertvertrag*: [1993] O.J. L50/14.

[70] See *Insurance in Greece of Public Property and Loans Granted by Greek State and Banks*: [1985] O.J. L152/25; *Provision in the Netherlands of express delivery services*: [1990] O.J. L10/47, [1990] 4 C.M.L.R. 947 and *Provision in Spain of express courier services*: [1990] O.J. L233/19, [1991] 3 C.M.L.R. 560.

[71] Dir. 80/723: [1980] O.J. L195/35. The validity of this directive was challenged but upheld by the Court of Justice in Cases 188–190/80, *France, Italy and United Kingdom* v. *Commission*: [1982] E.C.R. 2545, [1982] 3 C.M.L.R. 144.

[72] See Dir. 88/301 on competition in the markets in telecommunications equipment: [1988] O.J. L131/73 and Dir. 90/388 on competition in the markets for telecommunications services: [1990] O.J. L192/10. Both directives have been partially annulled by the Court of Justice; 88/301 in Case 208/88, *France* v. *Commission*: [1991] I E.C.R. 1223, [1992] 5 C.M.L.R. 552; 90/388 in Case 271, 281 & 289/90, *Spain, Belgium and Italy* v. *Commission*: not yet reported. In both cases the measures were annulled in respect of their dealing with "special rights" on the grounds of lack of reasoning. The Court has distinguished between "special or exclusive rights" referred to in the first sentence of Art. 90. See also Criminal proceedings against Case C–320/91, *Paul Corbeau* v. *Belgian Post Office*: *The Times*, July 21, 1993.

[73] See, *e.g. Bloemenveilingen Aalsmeer*: [1988] O.J. L262/27, [1989] 4 C.M.L.R. 500 (use of premises for flower auctions); *B & I Line/Sealink*: [1992] 5 C.M.L.R. 255; and *Sea Containers* v. *Stena Sealink*: [1994] O.J. L15/8.

[74] Art. 232(1) EEC. And see Art. 232(2) which provides that the provisions of the EEC Treaty do not derogate from the provisions of the Treaty establishing the European Atomic Energy Community (the Euratom Treaty). Note the Commission decisions exempting two nuclear fuel reprocessing agreements, *United Reprocessors* and *KEWA*: [1976] O.J. L51/7–15, [1976] 2 C.M.L.R. D1–15, and see *Amersham/Buchler*: [1982] O.J. L314/34, [1983] 1 C.M.L.R. 619.

rules on competition for coal and steel products as defined by that Treaty.[75] Such products are therefore outside the rules on competition contained in the EEC Treaty. This book does not deal with the special rules and procedures which apply by virtue of the ECSC Treaty although on occasion reference may be made to provisions of that Treaty, and judgments of the Court and decisions of the Commission relating thereto.[76]

(ii) *Transport*

As mentioned above, the principal implementing provision, Regulation 17, is not limited in its applicability to particular economic sectors. Regulation 141, however, exempted transport from the ambit of Regulation 17. Only gradually have implementing regulations been put in place in the transport sector and even now their coverage is still not complete. Regulation 1017/68[77] implements Articles 85 and 86 for the purposes of rail, road and inland waterway transport. Regulation 4056/86 lays down detailed rules for the application of Articles 85 and 86 to maritime transport.[78] Regulation 3975/87 supplies the implementing rules for air transport.[79] Broadly these regulations follow the scheme of Regulation 17 although there are some notable differences. This book does not deal in detail with transport cases but the main points of similarity and difference will be identified and special rules explained. Notwithstanding the Council's recent legislative activity, particularly in the air transport sector,[80] there are, as mentioned, still gaps in the coverage of the implementing regulations. Regulation

---

[75] See Arts. 65 and 66 ECSC. Measures taken by the Commission under the ECSC may impact upon the assessment under Arts. 85 and 86, and the level of any fine: see *Welded Steel Mesh*: [1989] O.J. L260/1, [1991] 4 C.M.L.R. 13. Where agreements cover both ECSC and non-ECSC products it may be appropriate to deal with them in one decision. See *Jahrhundertvertrag*: [1993] O.J. L50/14 (exemption under Art. 85(3) EEC coupled with authorisation under Art. 65(2) ECSC), and *National Association of Licensed Opencast Operators* v. *British Coal Corporation*: [1993] 4 C.M.L.R. 615 (rejection of complaint).

[76] Although useful comparison can sometimes be made with cases under the ECSC Treaty (see, *e.g.* Case 136/79, *National Panasonic U.K. Ltd.* v. *Commission*: [1980] E.C.R. 2033, [1980] 3 C.M.L.R. 169), not every problem can be solved by such comparison (see, *e.g.* at Case 6/72, *Europemballage Corp. and Continental Can Co. Inc.* v. *Commission*: [1973] E.C.R. 215, [1973] C.M.L.R. 199, at para. 22).

[77] Despite the age of Reg. 1017/68, there has been very little activity in this sector. But see *Cerafel*: [1979] 12 E.C. Bull. 31; *French Inland Waterway Charter Traffic: EATE Levy*: [1985] O.J. L219/35, [1988] 4 C.M.L.R. 698, upheld on appeal in Case 272/85, *ANTIB* v. *Commission*: [1987] E.C.R. 2201, [1988] 4 C.M.L.R. 677, and *Tariff structures in the combined transport of goods*: [1993] O.J. L73/38, and L145/31. Reg. 1017/68 was held to be not applicable in *Distribution of railway tickets by travel agents*: [1992] O.J. L366/47. The activity in question was not directly related to the provision of the transport service.

[78] Reg. 4056/86 came into operation on July 1, 1987. Decisions are now coming forward: see *Secrètema*: [1991] O.J. L35/23, [1991] 5 C.M.L.R. 76; *French-West African Shipowners Committees*: [1992] O.J. L134/1; *B & I Line/Sealink*, above; *Ukwal*: [1992] O.J. L121/45; *Mewac*: [1993] O.J. L20/6 and *Cewal, Cowac and Ukwal*: [1993] O.J. L34/20.

[79] Reg. 3975/87 came into force on January 1, 1988 in relation to international air transport between Community airports. The jurisdiction was extended by Reg. 2410/92 to include domestic flights in Member States. For Commission regulatory activity before Reg. 3975/87, see *Sterling Airways/SAS*: [1980] 12 E.C. Bull. 34, and *Olympic Airways*: [1985] O.J. L46/51, [1985] 1 C.M.L.R. 730. And see n. 81, below. Decisions under Reg. 3975/87 are now coming forward: see *British Midland* v. *Aer Lingus*: [1992] O.J. L96/34, [1993] 4 C.M.L.R. 596

[80] In particular the Third Liberalisation Package (See [1992] O.J. L240) followed by a Commission Reg. 617/93 (block exemptions for joint planning and co-ordination of schedules, joint operations, consultations on passenger and cargo tariffs on scheduled air services and slot allocations at airports) and Reg. 3652/93 (block exemption for computerised reservation systems—the code of conduct for such systems, Reg. 2298/89 was amended by Reg. 3089/93). Both block exemptions run until June 30, 1998.

4056/86 does not cover tramp shipping and Regulation 3975/87 air services between a Member State and State outside the Community. How are Article 85 and 86 enforced in these cases? Briefly the position is the same as it once was for all (other) sectors within the ambit of Articles 85 and 86 before Regulation 17. The power of the Commission to deal with possible violations of the competition rules is limited to that set out in Article 89 of the Treaty, *i.e.* to investigate, propose appropriate measures to bring an infringement to an end and, if necessary, authorise Member States to take such measures.[81] The "authorities in Member States"[82] can rule on the applicability of Articles 85 and 86 in accordance with their own law under Article 88 of the Treaty. So far as the enforceability of agreements is concerned, it appears that if an agreement falls within the prohibition in Article 85(1) solely because of some restriction relating, for example, to air transport services outside Regulation 3975/87, then it would not automatically be void under Article 85(2).[83] And this would seem to be the position until either (a) the Commission, under Article 89(2), or an authority of a Member State, under Article 88, takes a decision against the agreement, or (b) a Regulation under Article 87 is made further extending the scope of application of Regulation 3975/87.[84]

(iii) *Agriculture*

Article 42 of the Treaty provides that the rules on competition shall apply to the production of and trade in agricultural products only in so far as the Council has determined, taking account of the objectives of the Common Agricultural Policy (CAP).[85] Council Regulation 26 applies the competition rules to production of and trade in agricultural products. Agricultural products here mean those products listed in Annex II to the Treaty.[86] So far as the prohibition in Article 85(1) is concerned, Article 2 of Regulation 26 expressly provides that Article 85(1) shall not apply to agreements that form part of a national market organisation[87] or are necessary for the attainment of the objectives of the CAP set out in Article 39 of the Treaty. Certain farmers' associations of

---

[81] Before the introduction of Reg. 3975/87 the Commission took action against 10 airlines under Art. 89. See Sixteenth Report on Competition Policy, at point 36 and Seventeenth Report, at point 46.

[82] This term is discussed at paras. 1.26, 5.02 and 10.02.

[83] Such agreements would be provisionally valid. See the *Air Tariffs* case, Cases 209–213/84, *Ministére Public* v. *Lucas Asjes and others*: [1986] E.C.R. 1425, [1986] 3 C.M.L.R. 173 at paras. 60–69, and the discussion of Provisional Validity at paras. 10.04–11.

[84] Even in this latter event, the agreement would, provided it was duly notified, still be provisionally valid until such time as the Commission has pronounced on the question of Art. 85(3). See Case 48/72, *Brasserie de Haecht* v. *Wilkin (No. 2)*: [1973] E.C.R. 77, [1973] C.M.L.R. 287. But note the effect of Case 99/79, *Lancôme* v. *Etos and Albert Heijn Supermart*: [1980] E.C.R. 2511, [1981] 2 C.M.L.R. 164.

[85] Art. 42 of the Treaty recognises at one and the same time the primacy of agricultural policy in relation to the objectives of the Treaty as regards competition and the power of the Council to decide to what extent the rules of competition have to be applied in the agricultural sector. In the exercise of this power, as in the whole putting into effect of the CAP, the Council possesses a considerable discretion. See Case 139/79, *Maizena GmbH* v. *Council*: [1980] E.C.R. 3393, at para. 23.

[86] See Case 161/80, *Coöperatieve Stremsel-en Kleurselfabriek* v. *Commission*: [1981] E.C.R. 851, [1982] 1 C.M.L.R. 240, at paras. 19–21. Note, it is not sufficient that the particular product is a substance ancillary to the production of another product which itself comes within the Annex.

[87] Whilst this limb is largely redundant following the common organisation of the market (see the rules laid down in Reg. 804/68 and *Sugar beet*: [1990] O.J. L31/32, [1991] 4 C.M.L.R. 629) in *New potatoes*:

a co-operative nature are specifically excluded. The Court of Justice has said that even if there is little freedom of competition left after the regimes imposed by the CAP or national market organisations such freedom should be allowed to develop without interruption or hindrance by private measures.[88] Both Article 85 and 86 have been applied in cases concerned with agricultural products.[89]

(iv) *Products for military purposes*

Article 223(1)(b) of the Treaty provides that a Member State may take such measures as it considers necessary for the protection of the essential interests of its security which are connected with the production of or trade in arms, munitions and war material. Such measures must not "adversely affect the conditions of competition in the Common Market regarding products which are not intended for specifically military purposes." The exception is likely to be narrowly construed.[90]

II. ENFORCEMENT AT COMMUNITY LEVEL

Historical perspective

1.23   Prior to the taking of the necessary measures[91] for implementation in pursuance of Article 87 of the Treaty, the power of the Commission to deal with infringements of Articles 85 and 86 was restricted and it was for the "authorities in Member States" to rule on Articles 85 and 86 in accordance with Article 88. Article 89 of the Treaty imposed a duty on the Commission to ensure the application of the principles laid down in Articles 85 and 86 and set out the framework of a procedure within which the Commission could carry it out:

> "On application by a Member State or on its own initiative, and in co-operation with the competent authorities in the Member States, who shall give it their assistance, the Commission shall investigate cases of suspected infringement of these principles. If it finds that there has been an infringement, it shall propose appropriate measures to bring it to an end."

[1988] O.J. L59/25, the Commission took a decision under Art. 2 of Reg. 26 in effect exempting a national scheme relating to the production and marketing of new potatoes in France.

[88] See *Sugar* (Cases 40–48, 50, 54–56, 111, 113 & 114/73, *Cooperative Vereniging "Suiker Unie" UA and others* v. *Commission*: [1975] E.C.R. 1663, [1976] 1 C.M.L.R. 295) and Case 83/78, *Pigs Marketing Board* v. *Redmond*: [1978] E.C.R. 2347, [1979] 1 C.M.L.R. 177.

[89] See *Sugar, ibid.*; Case 71/74, *Frubo* v. *Commission*: [1975] E.C.R. 563, [1975] 2 C.M.L.R. 123, and the Commission's decisions in *Preserved Mushrooms*: [1975] O.J. L29/26, [1975] 1 C.M.L.R. D83; *Cauliflowers*: [1978] O.J. L21/23, [1978] 1 C.M.L.R. D66; *Maize Seed*: [1978] O.J. L286/23, [1978] 3 C.M.L.R. 434; *Cane Sugar*: [1980] O.J. L39/64, [1980] 2 C.M.L.R. 559; Rennet; [1980] O.J. L51/19, [1980] 2 C.M.L.R. 402; *Milchförderungsfonds*: [1985] O.J. L35/35, [1985] 3 C.M.L.R. 101, and *MEL-DOC*: [1986] O.J. L348/50, [1989] 4 C.M.L.R. 853. In Case T–61/89, *Dansk Pelsdyravlerforening* v. *Commission*: [1992] II E.C.R. 1931, the Court of First Instance concluded that furs were not agricultural products falling within the scope of Reg. 26/62.

[90] See *France/Suralmo*: Ninth Report on Competition Policy, at point 72. The question was left open in the merger case, *GEC–Siemens/Plessey*: [1990] O.J. C239/2.

[91] "Necessary" does not mean "required" in this context. See Case 32/65, *Italy* v. *Council and Commission*: [1966] E.C.R. 389, [1969] C.M.L.R. 39.

But as Article 89(2) indicates, it is a procedure the effectiveness of which is, in practical terms, limited[92] from the Commission's standpoint:[93]

> "If the infringement is not brought to an end, the Commission shall record such infringement of the principles in a reasoned decision. The Commission may publish its decision and authorise Member States to take measures, the conditions and details of which it shall determine, needed to remedy the situation."

Until the Commission was given, in pursuance of Article 87 of the Treaty, the necessary powers in Regulation 17 and the implementing regulations for the transport sectors to investigate and prosecute infringements of Articles 85 and 86, the main burden of enforcing these provisions of the Treaty was placed on the Member States in accordance with Article 88.[94] But, as is indicated below, Articles 87, 88 and 89 are not merely of historical importance.

Article 87—implementing powers

1.24　Article 87 of the Treaty enables the Council to adopt appropriate regulations or directives to give effect to the principles set out in Articles 85 and 86. Such regulations or directives shall be designed in particular:

> "(a) to ensure compliance with the prohibitions laid down in Article 85(1) and in Article 86 by making provision for fines and periodic penalty payments;
> (b) to lay down detailed rules for the application of Article 85(3), taking into account the need to ensure effective supervision on the one hand, and to simplify administration to the greatest possible extent on the other;
> (c) to define, if need be, in the various branches of the economy, the scope of the provisions of Articles 85 and 86;
> (d) to define the respective functions of the Commission and of the Court of Justice in applying the provisions laid down in this paragraph;
> (e) to determine the relationship between national laws and the provisions contained in this Section or adopted pursuant to this Article."

Regulation 17 was the first Council regulation implementing Articles 85 and 86 and, although it has been amended in certain respects,[95] it remains the principal regulation dealing with the practical application and enforcement by the Commission of the

---

[92] But this has not prevented the Commission from acting. See the proceedings brought against 10 airlines, Sixteenth Report on Competition Policy, point 36 and Seventeenth Report, point 46.

[93] And, it seems, a complainant's. Art. 89 makes no mention of individual complainants. It requires the Commission to investigate cases "on the application by Member States" and "on its own initiative." Even if this means that under the Treaty the Commission is under a specific duty to investigate each case reported to it where suspected infringement is alleged (and perhaps (*sed quaere*) to give reasons for not doing so) it does not seem that this is a duty owed to the person bringing the Commission' attention and enforceable at his initiative. Per A.G. Slynn in Case 246/81, *Lord Bethell* v. *Commission*: [1982] E.C.R. 2277, [1982] 3 C.M.L.R. 300. But it appears that a Member State can compel the Commission to take action under Art. 89 where appropriate—see the judgment of the Court of First Instance in Case T–24/90, *Automec Srl* v. *Commission*: [1992] 5 C.M.L.R. 431, at para. 76.

[94] See, generally, Deringer, "The Distribution of Powers in the Enforcement of the Rules of Competition under the Rome Treaty" (1963) 1 C.M.L.Rev. 30; Sharpe, "The Commission's Proposals on Crisis Cartels" (1980) 17 C.M.L.Rev. 75, 81–85.

[95] By Reg. 59, Reg. 118/63 and Reg. 2822/71 and by the Acts of Accession of 1972, 1979 and 1985.

Community competition rules. Subsequent Council regulations made with regard to Article 87 include Regulation 19/65 and Regulation 2821/71. In order to ease the administrative load these regulations empower the Commission to give block or group exemptions under Article 85(3) to certain categories of agreements. As mentioned above,[96] these powers have been exercised in relation to a number of different categories of agreements.

Article 87 also provides the basis for the three implementing regulations for the transport sector. But in relation to Regulations 1017/68 and 4056/86, other Treaty powers are also cited; Article 75 in the case of Regulation 1017/68, and 84(2) in the case of Regulation 4056/86. The former is probably explicable by the uncertainty as to the relationship between the common transport policy at that time and the latter by the need to give effect to the UNCTAD liner code as part of the common transport policy. Finally it should be noted that only in the case of air transport has the Council (by Regulation 3976/87) given the Commission power to make block exemption regulations.[97] As regards maritime transport, there is however an import block exemption, for liner conferences, contained in Regulation 4056/86 itself.

Regulation 17

1.25 Regulation 17 is the principal regulation dealing with the practical application and enforcement of Articles 85 and 86. It provides the basis for the Commission's procedures in relation to the giving of negative clearance, the taking of decisions requiring the termination of infringements and the granting of exemptions under Article 85(3). It makes provisions for the notification of agreements, for the relationship between the Commission and the authorities of the Member States, for the obtaining of information and the investigation of cases by the Commission, for the hearing of parties, for the imposition of fines and periodic penalty payments, for the publication of decisions and for the maintenance of professional secrecy.

By Article 24 of Regulation 17, the Commission is given the power to adopt implementing provisions (a) concerning the form, content and other details of applications for negative clearance and notifications for the purposes of exemption, and (b) concerning hearings. The implementing provisions laid down by the Commission presently comprise Regulation 27 (recently amended by Regulation 3666/93 to take account of the EEA) which relates to the form, content, etc. concerning applications and notifications, and Regulation 99/63 which relates to the hearings provided for in Article 19 of Regulation 17. In *ACF Chemiefarma* v. *Commission*[98] the applicant challenged the legal basis of Regulation 99/63, maintaining that the delegation of powers in Article 24 of Regulation 17 as it related to hearings was incompatible with Articles 87, 155 and 4 of the Treaty. The Court of Justice rejected this argument. It did not think that Article 87 prohibited the Council from giving power to the Commission to make regulations which were necessary to implement the rules which the Council had adopted. In Article 19 of Regulation 17 the Council had provided that undertakings shall be given the opportunity to be heard by the Commission. It was therefore lawful for the Council to entrust the Commission with the task of laying down the detailed

---

[96] See para. 1.14.
[97] See Reg. 1617/93 and Reg. 83/91 as extended by Reg. 1618/97.
[98] Case 41/69: [1970] E.C.R. 661, at paras. 59–70.

rules of procedure in this context. Such rules, in the opinion of the Court, constituted implementing provisions within the meaning of Article 155 of the Treaty.

Using its delegated powers in the respective transport regulations to make implementing provisions the Commission has made Regulation 1629/69 (on the form, content and other details of complaints, applications and notifications under Regulation 1017/68), Regulation 1630/69 (on hearings under Regulation 1017/68), Regulation 4260/88 (on communications, complaints and applications and hearings under Regulation 4056/86), and Regulation 4261/88 (on complaints, applications and hearings under Regulation 3975/87).

The authorities in Member States

1.26   Article 88 of the Treaty provides as follows:

> "Until the entry into force of the provisions adopted in pursuance of Article 87, the authorities in Member States shall rule on the admissibility of agreements, decisions and concerted practices and on abuse of a dominant position in the common market in accordance with the law of their country and with the provisions of Article 85, in particular paragraph 3, and of Article 86."

Although this Article appears at first sight to contain essentially transitional provisions and might therefore be thought to have been rendered redundant following the adoption of provisions adopted in pursuance of Article 87 (and in particular Regulation 17), this is not in fact the case and Article 88 remains, at least potentially, important in practice. First, it has to be noted that Regulation 17 did not remove or totally replace the jurisdiction given to the authorities in Member States under Article 88. Article 9(3) of Regulation 17 provides that as long as the Commission has not initiated any procedure[99] "the authorities of the Member States *remain competent*[1] to apply Articles 85(1) and 86 in accordance with Article 88 of the Treaty."[2] There are equivalent provisions in the three implementing regulations in the transport sector (Regulation 1017/68, Article 15; Regulation 4056/86, Article 14; Regulation 3975/87, Article 7), although they make no express reference to Article 88. Second, it has to be remembered that Regulation 4056/86 and Regulation 3975/87 do not extend to all types of sea transport and air transport respectively. Certain transport services therefore remain within the jurisdiction of the authorities in Member States under Article 88.[3]

[99] Under Art. 2, 3 or 6 of Reg. 17.

[1] Emphasis added.

[2] The jurisdiction is limited both as to time (until the Commission indicates a procedure) and extent (the national authorities can only apply Art. 85(1), and cannot grant exemption under Art. 85(3)—see Art. 9(1) of Reg. 17). See Deringer, *op. cit.*, at pp. 37–39. But the jurisdiction may be restored to the Member States under Art. 9(3) where, for example, the Commission closes its file (without a decision finding infringement) in a case. Per A.G. Mancini in Cases 142 & 156/84, *BAT and Reynolds* v. *Commission*: [1987] E.C.R. 4487, [1988] 4 C.M.L.R. 24.

[3] See para 1.22 above. The services not yet covered by implementing regulations are tramp shipping and air transport services between a Member State and a third state.

The Commission

1.27   Article 155[4] of the Treaty provides that in order to ensure the proper functioning and development of the Common Market the Commission shall:

(a)   ensure that the provisions of the Treaty and the measures taken by the institutions pursuant thereto are applied;

(b)   formulate recommendations or deliver opinions on matters dealt with in the Treaty;

(c)   have its own power of decision and participate in the shaping of measures taken by the Council and by the Parliament;

(d)   exercise the powers conferred on it by the Council for the implementation of the rules laid down by the latter.

The Commission thus has a variety of duties in connection with the Treaty. It may be the guardian of the Treaty and, for example, may take infraction proceedings under Article 169 against a Member State before the Court.[5] It may be the initiator of Community policy.[6] In relation to competition policy, the Commission acts foremost as the executive arm of the Community, applying the rules laid down in Article 85 and 86 of the Treaty in individual cases.

1.28   The Commission consists of 17 members (including a President and six Vice-Presidents) who are appointed by common accord of the Governments of the Member States.[7] Members must be nationals of the Member States, and are bound during the period of their office[8] to act completely independently of the Member States, the Council or any other body. Although the Treaty generally speaks of the Commission (acting as a collegiate body) adopting the various acts[9] required under or in implementation of the Treaty, it is expressly provided that the Commission may act by a majority.[10] Each Commissioner has responsibility for a particular area of Commission

---

[4] It is by no means clear to what extent the general duties set out in Art. 155 empower the Commission to take action in areas where express powers may be absent. In particular, in the context of competition policy, it may be arguable that the Commission may address an opinion (followed, if necessary, by a decision) to an undertaking acting contrary to the provisions of Arts. 3 and 30–36 of the Treaty in connection with the exercise of industrial property rights in circumstances falling outside Arts. 85 and 86. On the other hand the duties imposed on the Commission by Art. 155 do not appear to be sufficiently specific to base an action for failure to act under Art. 175. See para. 9.27.

[5] The Commission has the right, not a duty, to bring proceedings before the Court under Art. 169. A private party is not entitled to object (under Art. 175) that the Commission has failed to commence proceedings against a Member State: Case 247/87, *Star Fruit Company SA* v. *Commission*: [1989] E.C.R. 291, [1990] 1 C.M.L.R. 733, and Case C–371/89, *Emrich* v. *Commission*: [1990] I E.C.R. 1555.

[6] See, generally, Noel, "The Commission's Power of Initiative" (1973) 10 C.M.L. Rev. 123.

[7] Arts. 10 and 11 of the Treaty Establishing a Single Council and a Single Commission of the European Community (the "Merger Treaty"): [1967] J.O. 152, p. 2, as amended by Council Decision of January 1, 1973: [1973] O.J. L2/28, and by Art. 15 of the Acts of Accession of May 28, 1979 and June 12, 1985.

[8] A term of four years, which is renewable. Art. 11 of the Merger Treaty, *ibid.*

[9] There are basically five kinds of "acts" which the Commission can take: regulations, directives, decisions, recommendations and opinions. See Art. 189 of the Treaty. On the nature of these acts see, generally, Kapteyn and VerLoren van Themaat, *Introduction to the Law of the European Communities* (2nd ed., 1987), Chap. V.

[10] Art. 17 of the Merger Treaty. Because of the size, variety and complexity of the Commission's business, it almost goes without saying that not every matter can be discussed and voted on at meetings of the Commissioners. Hence a variety of procedural devices have been invented to facilitate the day to day running

activity. One Commissioner has responsibility for competition[11] but formal decisions[12] of the Commission in competition cases are nevertheless decisions of the Commission and only a limited delegation of powers is made.[13]

The Commission has a large staff which is divided into departments. Some of these departments are given the title Directorate-General and there are 22[14] of these covering the wide range of the Commission's activities. For example, separate Directorates-General deal with Agriculture (DG VI), Transport (DG VII) and Internal Market (DG XV). Other departments simply have a title which reflects their general function, for example, the Secretariat-General and the Legal Service. The Directorate-General for competition (DG IV) is responsible for Community competition policy under both the EEC and ECSC Treaties.[15] DG IV will also discharge the Commission's responsibilities for enforcing the competition regime under the EEA.

DG IV

1.29   The Directorate-General for Competition (DG IV) has a total staff of approximately 400 persons. It is headed by a Director-General[16] and is comprised of the Merger Task Force and five other directorates.[17] The Hearing Officer[18] is also a member of DG IV. There are three operational directorates, B, C and D, who are responsible for cases, from start to finish. Each of these directorates is in turn divided into divisions, each responsible for particular economic sectors.

Directorate A—*general competition policy and co-ordination*
Division 1:   general policy and international aspects; relations with the European Parliament and the Economic and Social Committee.
Division 2:   legal and procedural problems, regulation (*e.g.* block exemptions), infringement proceedings and intra-Community dumping.
Division 3:   economic questions and studies.

---

of affairs. Fairly straightforward matters may be dealt with by the so-called "written procedure". The Commissioners are sent particulars and the text of a proposed decision and if within a given period (usually one week) they have not entered reservations or objections the proposal is taken as adopted.

[11] The present Commissioner for Competition is Mr. Karel Van Miert.

[12] A decision is a formal act which, unlike a regulation, does not have general application but is binding in its entirety on those to whom it is addressed. Art. 189 of the Treaty. The majority of formal acts taken in competition cases are decisions. See, generally, Chap. 6.

[13] Delegation in relation to decisions in competition cases is discussed at paras. 6.46–47.

[14] They in fact number to DG XXIII (Enterprise Policy) but DG XXII is now closed.

[15] The comment is occasionally made that there is insufficient communication, co-ordination and co-operation between the different Directorates-General. In particular, it is sometimes suggested that DG IV should have greater contact with the Directorates-General dealing generally with industrial and commercial matters, in particular with subjects such as dumping and industrial property rights. The Commission has replied that it always takes care to ensure that its competition policy, which it does not view as an end in itself, operates in harmony with other common policies. See Answer to Written Question 710/79: [1979] O.J. C316/45.

[16] The present Director-General is Dr. Claus Dieter Ehlermann.

[17] DG IV underwent a fundamental reorganisation in the autumn of 1984. Most significantly the old division between Directorates A (inspections) and B (examining) disappeared, and the administrative unit became a directorate (then E) and is now more prominent (A). There was a further reorganisation in 1987.

[18] Dr. Hartmut Johannes. See, generally, para. 4.25. There is a separate Hearing Officer for merger cases under Reg. 4064/89.

Division 4: co-ordination of competition decisions.
Division 5: public enterprises and State monopolies[19] and implementation of Articles 101 and 102.

Directorate B—*restrictive practices, abuses of dominant positions and other distortions of competition I.*
Division 1: electrical and electronic manufactured products, information industries and telecommunications.
Division 2: mechanical manufactured products and the textile, clothing, leather and other manufacturing industries.
Division 3: banking, insurance and other service industries.
Division 4: the media, consumer electronics, music publishing and the distributive trades.

Directorate C—*restrictive practices, abuses of dominant positions and other distortions of competition II.*
Division 1: non-ferrous metals, non-metallic mineral products, construction, timber, paper, glass and rubber industries.
Division 2: energy (except coal) and basic chemical products.
Division 3: processed chemical products and agricultural products and foodstuffs.

Directorate D—*restrictive practices, abuses of dominant positions and other distortions of competition III.*
Division 1: steel and coal.
Division 2: ECSC Inspection.
Division 3: transport and tourism.
Division 4: motor vehicles, other means of transport and related manufactured mechanical products.

Directorate E—*State aids.*
Division 1: general aid schemes.
Division 2: aids for research and development.
Division 3: regional aids.
Division 4: sectoral aids I.
Division 5: sectoral aids II.
Division 6: evaluation (inventaire) and analysis.

The offices of DG IV are situated at 150 Avenue de Cortenberg, Brussels a short distance from the main Commission building, presently the Breydel. Whilst informal meetings and interviews take place in the offices on Cortenberg, oral hearings and meetings of the Advisory Committee are usually held at the Centre de Conference Albert Borschette,[20] 3 Rue Froissart, Brussels.

[19] This division, dealing with Arts. 37 and 90 questions, was formerly part of the directorate (then D) dealing with state aids.
[20] Again, only a short distance from the Breydel and Cortenberg.

Legal Service

1.30 The Commission's Legal Service (*Service Juridique*) is staffed by lawyers from all the Member States and provides legal advice, assistance and representation over the complete range of the Commission's activities under the Treaties. Within the flexible structure of the Legal Service, there are teams of lawyers working in particular fields (such as transport, agriculture, competition) under the direction of an experienced senior colleague (*chef d'equipe*). There is constant liaison between the team dealing with competition matters[21] in the Legal Service and DG IV throughout almost the entire procedure in a case likely to result in a formal decision.

It is important to note that the Legal Service is independent of the Directorates-General and its opinion must be sought on any formal act to be taken by the Commission.[22] If the Legal Service does not give a favourable opinion (*avis favorable*) then the matter must go to the Commission[23] itself to be determined. In the context of competition cases, the Legal Service's opinion must be sought, for example, before a statement of objections is sent to an undertaking concerned, a complaint is formally rejected, a preliminary draft decision is submitted to the Advisory Committee or a draft decision placed before the Commission.[23] In practice, the Legal Service will also be represented at the formal stages in the procedure, in particular, the oral hearing and the meeting of the Advisory Committee. The Legal Service assists at all meetings where either the Commission responsible for Competition or the Commission itself decides formal acts.

The Legal Service also represents the Commission in proceedings before the Court of Justice and Court of First Instance. For each such case, the President of the Commission appoints one of the Service's legal advisers to act as agent for the Commission.[24] The agent is responsible to the Commission for the handling of the case, may prepare and sign the written pleadings and may act as advocate at the oral stage of the proceedings. Because the Legal Service is responsible for defending Commission decisions in competition cases before the Court, it may look at whatever is proposed by DG IV from a different perspective from that of the examiner (*rapporteur*) in the case. In particular, it will try to ensure that any such proposals would be upheld by the Court.[25]

---

[21] In this context, Arts. 37, 85, 86, 90, 92 and 93 EEC and Arts. 65 and 66 ECSC.

[22] By Commission decision of 1958, the opinion of the Legal Service must be sought on any document which is likely to become a proposal to the Council or to be adopted in one of the forms provided for in Art. 189 of the Treaty (see above, n. 9).

[23] This is very much the last resort as in practice the matter will be debated between DG IV and the legal service going as far up through the grades as necessary.

[24] The position of the agent has been described as follows: "The Commission's agent has extensive but not unlimited freedom of action. Firstly, he must respect the principles which prompted the Commission to adopt the decision which is being challenged. Secondly, he must stand by the Commission's interpretation of certain legal provisions. Thirdly, he must work hand in hand with the appropriate DG in elaborating the line he will take not only on points of fact but also on points of law." (Commission's Staff Courier 372, p. 11)

[25] Van der Esch, "Due process in the administrative application of the European Communities' Competition Rules", lecture at A.I.E.C. Conference in Luxembourg on March 20, 1980.

The Court of Justice

Introduction

1.31 Article 164 of the Treaty requires the Court of Justice[26] to "ensure that in the interpretation and application of the Treaty the law is observed."[27] Article 164 sets out, in a nutshell, the essential role of the Court but scarcely indicates the significance of the Court as a Community institution. Its value and effectiveness are based on the importance of law and legal order to the creation, functioning and development of the Community and also on the Court's total independence. The Court of Justice's jurisdiction is wide and varied and the different capacities in which the Court may act have been briefly described as follows:[28]

> "administrative court (legality of Community measures, compensation for damage caused by wrongful Community acts, unlimited jurisdiction in regard to penalties), penal court (dismissal of Commissioners), internal administrative tribunal (appeals by civil servants), international court (conflicts between Member States or between the Commission and Member States), constitutional court (conformity of international agreements with the Treaties) and civil jurisdiction (attribution of competence in contracts concluded by the Community)."[29]

In practice many of the functions are now exercised by the Court of First Instance subject to appeal to the Court of Justice. For present purposes, it should suffice to outline two principal areas of competence and indicate their applicability in relation to competition cases.

Power to review Commission decisions

1.32 The Court of Justice may review the legality of Community acts. In particular, under Article 173, the Court has power to review the legality of acts (for example, regulations and decisions) of the Council and the Commission. The grounds on which such legality may be questioned are:

(a) lack of competence
(b) infringement of an essential procedural requirement
(c) infringement of the Treaty or of any rule of law relating to its application, and
(d) misuse of powers.

Actions under Article 173 may be brought by a Member State, the Council or the Commission. Further, it is expressly provided that any natural or legal person may

---

[26] See, generally, Lasok, *The European Court of Justice Practice and Procedure* (1984); Usher, *European Court Practice* (1983) and Brown, *The Court of Justice of the European Communities* (3rd ed., 1989).

[27] The law, as referred to in Art. 164, has been shown not to be a fixed or static commodity and the Court has been able in the interpretation and development of Community law to import concepts and principles of wide and general application not necessarily expressly provided for or referred to in the Treaty. See Brown and Jacobs, *op. cit.*, Chap. 13, and Usher, "The Influence of National Concepts on Decisions of the European Court" (1976) 1 E.L.Rev. 359.

[28] Mathijsen, *A Guide to European Community Law* (2nd. ed., 1975), p. 196.

[29] To this list one might add the Court's work under the Convention on Jurisdiction and the Enforcement of Judgments in Civil and Commercial Matters and (in the future) under the Community Patent Convention.

institute proceedings against a decision addressed to that person or against a decision which, although addressed to another person, is of direct and individual concern to the former. Under Article 172, the Court has unlimited jurisdiction where penalties are imposed in pursuance of Council regulations.[30] Both Articles 172 and 173 are important in practice in relation to the enforcement of the Community competition rules by the Commission. For it is by a decision (an "act" within the meaning of Article 173) that the Commission will, in individual cases, apply the competition rules against parties and may exercise its powers of investigation into alleged infringements of those rules.[31] The law and practice in relation to applications under Articles 172 and 173 are discussed further in Chapter 9. Most cases under Articles 172 and 173 are brought in the Court of First Instance.

References from national courts

1.33   Brief mention must be made of the Court of Justice's powers under Article 177 of the Treaty relating to references from national courts for preliminary rulings on questions of Community law.[32] Under Article 177 the Court has jurisdiction to give preliminary rulings on questions concerning, *inter alia*, the interpretation of the Treaty and the validity and interpretation of the acts of the institutions of the Community. Requests for preliminary rulings can come only from a court or tribunal of a Member State where such a question is raised before it and it considers that a decision on the question is necessary to enable it to give judgment.[33] Such a request must, as a general rule, be made when the national court or tribunal asked to apply Community

---

[30] For a useful introductory account of the plenary or full jurisdiction of the Court, see Brown, *op. cit.*, Chap. 8.

[31] On "decisions" in competition cases, see Chap. 6.

[32] See, generally, Brown, *op. cit.*, Chap. 10, and Dashwood and Arnull, "English Courts and Art. 177 of the EEC Treaty" (1984) 4 *Yearbook of European Law* 79.

[33] The reference must come from a court or tribunal (see Case 138/90, *Re Jules Borker*: [1980] 3 C.M.L.R. 638 and, more recently, Case C–24/92, *Pierre Corbeau* v. *Administration des Contributions*: not yet reported). The court or tribunal may itself raise the question for decision by the Court. The fact that the parties to the main action fail to raise the point of Community law before the national court does not preclude the latter from bringing the matter before the Court (Case 128/80, *Salonia* v. *Poidomani*: [1981] E.C.R. 1563, [1982] 1 C.M.L.R. 64). A national court making an Art. 177 reference (a) should explain on what grounds it considers an answer to its questions is necessary for judgment in the proceedings before it, if those grounds are not unequivocally evident from the file on the case, (b) should define the legal context in which the interpretation requested should be placed, and (c) if circumstances permit, it might be convenient if the facts of the case were established and questions of national law settled at the time when the reference to the Court is made: Cases 141–143/81, *Holdijk, Mulder and Veevoederbedrijf Alpuro BV*: [1982] E.C.R. 1299, [1983] 2 C.M.L.R. 635, at para. 5. It is not for the Court to verify the accuracy of factual findings in the reference order: Case 243/83, *Binon & Cie SA* v. *Agence et Messagerie de la Presse SA*: [1985] E.C.R. 2015, [1985] 3 C.M.L.R. 800, at para. 24. Most important, the Court's interpretation of Community law must be necessary to settle a genuine dispute: Case 104/79, *Foglia* v. *Novello*: [1980] E.C.R. 745, [1981] 1 C.M.L.R. 45. Where the link between the questions referred and the domestic legislation cannot readily be discerned and the referring court does not explain its reasons, the Court may still accept the reference in the interests of procedural economy, provided always that there is nothing to suggest the main proceedings are not in reality a procedural contrivance: Cases 98, 162 & 258/85, *Bertini* v. *Regione Lazio*: [1986] E.C.R. 1885, [1987] 1 C.M.L.R. 774. Recent cases have again shown that the Court will not answer questions of a hypothetical nature. The national court is required to define the factual and legal framework in which the questions it puts arise or at least explain the factual assumptions on which those questions are based. See Case C–83/91, *Meilicke* v. *ADV/ORGA F.A. Meyer AG*: *The Times*, October 20, 1992 and Cases C 320–322/90, *Telemarsicabruzzo SpA* v. *Circostel and Others*: not yet reported.

law is a court or tribunal against whose decisions there is no judicial remedy under national law.[34] There have been many and various requests for preliminary rulings made by the courts and tribunals of the different Member States. A good number have involved questions relating to the competition rules[35] or related matters such as the provisions of the Treaty relating to the free movement of goods[36] and services.[37]

Court of First Instance

1.33A   One of the important institutional reforms of the Single European Act was the establishment, at the request of the Court of Justice, of the Court of First Instance. It is not a separate institution of the Community but is attached to the Court of Justice. Its jurisdiction is not as extensive as that of the Court of Justice. It has jurisdiction to hear and determine at first instance certain claims of action or proceedings brought by natural or legal persons. It does, however, not have jurisdiction in cases brought by, or against Member States or to rule on questions referred from national courts under Article 177.[38] The object was to improve the judicial protection of individual interests, particularly in cases requiring the examination of complex facts, whilst at the same time reducing the workload of the Court of Justice.

The initial jurisdiction of the Court of First Instance comprised four subject matters: staff cases; certain cases under its ECSC Treaty; actions against the Commission relating to the enforcement of the EEC competition rules; and, finally, damages claims (under Article 215 of the Treaty), arising from an act or failure to act which is the subject of an action under one of the first three matters. The Court's jurisdiction was recently extended to cover all direct actions brought by natural or legal persons.[39] There is the potential still for cases to arrive in the wrong Community court and also for there to be concurrent jurisdiction.[40] The rules, therefore, provide for the division of jurisdiction between the two Courts and for actions to be stayed in appropriate circumstances.[41] Appeals lie from the Court of First Instance to the Court of Justice on points of law only.[41a] As Advocate General Vesterdorf said in *Polypropylene*:

---

[34] Although Art. 177(3) provides that a national court of final appeal must refer questions of Community law to the Court, the national court may not be so obliged in certain circumstances, see Case 283/81, *CIL-FIT* v. *Minister of Health*: [1982] E.C.R. 3415, [1983] 1 C.M.L.R. 472. For the position in relation to interlocutory proceedings, see Case 107/76, *Hoffmann-La Roche* v. *Centrafarm (No. 1)*: [1977] E.C.R. 957, [1977] 2 C.M.L.R. 334.

[35] The first reference under Art. 177 involved the question of the application by national courts of the Community competition rules: see Case 13/61, *Bosch* v. *De Geus*: [1962] E.C.R. 45, [1962] C.M.L.R. 1.

[36] For example, the series of cases involving the relationship between the free movement rules in Arts. 30–36 of the Treaty and industrial and intellectual property rights. See, generally, Korah, *An Introductory Guide to EEC Competition Law and Practice* (4th ed., 1990), Chap. 9.

[37] For example, see Case 52/79, *Procureur du Roi* v. *Debauve*: [1980] E.C.R. 833, [1981] 2 C.M.L.R. 362, and Case 62/79, *Coditel* v. *Cinè Vog*: [1980] E.C.R. 881, [1981] 2 C.M.L.R. 362.

[38] Art. 168A of the Treaty.

[39] By decision of the Council of Ministers of June 8, 1993: [1993] O.J. L144/21. The transfer took effect on August 1, 1993, except for anti-dumping cases where the date of transfer which was finally agreed by the Council was March 15, 1994.

[40] *E.g.* a Member State may challenge a decision of the Commission under Art. 85 at the same time as a party to the agreement in question.

[41] See Art. 47 of the Protocol on the Court of Justice. For an application of the rules in a case of concurrent jurisdiction, see Case C–48/90, *Netherlands* v. *Commission*: [1992] E.C.R. 565, and Case T–42/91, *Koninklijke PTT Nederland NV and PTT Post BV* v. *Commission*: [1991] II E.C.R. 273.

[41a] The Court of First Instance's appraisal of the factual evidence cannot be challenged before the Court of Justice except where the clear sense of that evidence has been distorted: see Case C–53/92P, *Hilti AG* v.

> "the very creation of the Court of First Instance as a court of both first and last instance for the examination of facts in the cases brought before it is an invitation to undertake an intensive review in order to ascertain whether the evidence on which the Commission rules in adopting a contested decision is sound."[42]

Experience has shown that the Court has not been reluctant to enter into a detailed factual examination of cases brought before it. It has already handled a variety of procedural and substantive law questions relating to the application of Articles 85 and 86, taking an active inquisitorial attitude.[43]

The Courts' personnel

1.34 The Court of Justice[44] consists of 13 judges who are assisted by six Advocates General and a Registrar. The Treaty requires the judges and Advocates General to be chosen from persons whose independence is beyond doubt and who possess the qualifications required for appointment to the highest judicial office in their respective countries. Like the members of the Commission, they are appointed by common accord of the governments of the Member States. There is no requirement relating to the nationality of the judges although in practice each Member State is represented. The judges elect a President from among themselves.[45]

The six Advocates General assist the Court and it is their duty to prepare and deliver an opinion in open court in order to assist the Court to see that the law is observed in accordance with Article 164 of the Treaty. The Advocate General's opinion will generally contain an analysis of the facts and the legal issues involved, an examination of the relevant legislation, case law and opinions of learned writers and on occasion a comparative study of the (different) national laws. The Advocate General will also put forward a proposal for the solution of the problem of questions at issue for consideration by the Court.[46]

The Court of First Instance has 12 judges, in effect one from each Member State. They are chosen from persons whose independence is beyond doubt and who possess the qualifications required for appointment to judicial office in their respective countries. Like the judges of the Court of Justice, they are appointed by common accord of the governments of the Member States. The Court of First Instance does not have advocates general as such but the rules of procedure provide for a judge to act as advocate general in a particular case.[47] This may be particularly helpful in complex multi-party competition cases.[48]

Commission: judgment of March 2, 1994, not yet reported, at paras. 10 and 42.

[42] *Polypropylene:* Case T–7/89, *Hercules SA* v. *Commission*: [1991] II E.C.R. 1711, [1992] 4 C.M.L.R. 84.

[43] See van der Woude, "The Court of First Instance, The First Three Years" [1992–93] 16 Fordham Int. L.J. 412.

[44] See Arts. 165, 166, 167 and 168 of the Treaty.

[45] Art. 167 of the Treaty. He is chosen by secret ballot and by simple majority.

[46] Art. 166 of the Treaty.

[47] See Arts. 17 and 18 of the Rules of Procedure, *i.e.* where the Court sits in plenary or there is a particularly difficult or complex case.

[48] The Court appointed an advocate-general in, *e.g.* the *Polypropylene* case, *Hercules* v. *Commission*, above.

Both Courts may sit as a full court or in chambers. Most cases are in practice assigned to chambers. Each judge and Advocate General may appoint his own legal secretaries who carry out investigations and research into the questions of Community and comparative law that may be raised in a particular case. Both Courts have a registrar who is responsible for the acceptance, transmission and custody of all documents and for effecting service.[49] All pleadings are entered in his register and he is responsible for drawing up the minutes of each hearing. Both Courts sit and have their offices at Luxembourg.

European Economic Area

1.34A In May 1992, the Community, its Member States and seven Member States of EFTA signed the Agreement on the European Economic Area (EEA). In March 1993, all the parties except Switzerland agreed a Protocol adjusting the Agreement to take account of Swiss withdrawal following rejection of the Agreement in a referendum of the Swiss people. The aim of the Agreement, which finally entered into force on January 1, 1994, is to promote a strengthening of trade and economic relations between the Contracting Parties with a view to creating a homogeneous European Economic Area.[50] The practical effect will be to create a large market of nearly 400 million consumers by extending to the EFTA States the free-trade advantages of E.C. membership. The EEA therefore provides for the making applicable in the EFTA States and between them and the Community a large body of Community law including the four freedoms which lay at the core of the Community (i.e. the free movement of goods, persons, services and capital). It establishes a competition regime (including rules on public undertakings, State aids, state monopolies and public procurement) and provides for closer co-operation in other fields including research and development, the environment and social policy.[51] There will however be no common external tariff or fiscal harmonisation and borders between the Community and EFTA countries will remain. Nor is the Common Agricultural Policy applicable.[52]

It was realised early in the negotiations that the competition rules in the EEA would in the interests of uniformity have to mirror closely the existing provisions in and made under the E.C. Treaty. Article 53 EEA therefore contains a prohibition on restrictive agreements based on the wording of Article 85 of the E.C. Treaty. Similarly Article 54 EEA prohibits abuses of dominant positions following the model of Article 86. Article 57 EEA reflects the Community's merger control regime in Regulation 4064/89. The EEA's provisions substitute the condition of affecting trade between Contracting Parties for trade between Member States under the E.C. Treaty. Again in the interests of uniformity the subordinate rules of the Community, in particular the block exemptions under Article 85(3), are mirrored in the EEA competition regime.[53] Moreover the EFTA States have accepted existing Community jurisprudence (including the case law on Articles 85 and 86) although under the EEA they are not formally bound by future decisions of the Court of Justice or the Court of First Instance on the interpretation of Articles 85 and 86. Similarly, they are not automatically bound by

---

[49] Art. 168 of the Treaty.
[50] Art. 1(1).
[51] Art. 1(2).
[52] Agriculture and fish are dealt with in Arts. 17–20.
[53] Art. 60 and Annex XIV.

the Community's subordinate legislation on competition.[54] As regards enforcement of the EEA competition regime the EEA provides what is generally described as a two-pillar approach and, at the same time, a one-stop shop.[55] Both the Commission and the EFTA States, the latter via a new body called the EFTA Surveillance Authority, have responsibility for the enforcement of the rules in Articles 53 and 54 EEA.[56] The EEA provides for the allocation of cases between these two enforcement authorities. Neither the Community nor the EFTA States had transferred any existing competence to the other party. This has taken on particular significance for the Community and for its competition rules in this context. In two Opinions under Article 228 of the E.C. Treaty the Court of Justice has held that the Community cannot surrender any of its competence.[57] Accordingly when it came to dividing up jurisdictional responsibility between the two enforcement authorities, the Commission and the EFTA Surveillance Authority, for handling cases under the new regime the Commission, because of its existing Community rules and jurisprudence, has emerged likely in practice to take the larger share. The rules allocating jurisdiction are set out in Article 56 EEA which for a better understanding has to be read against the background of the two Opinions of the Court. The result is as follows:

1.34B (i) *Restrictive agreements*

(a) Where the agreement or practice only affects trade between Member States of the Community the Commission will maintain its competence and apply the E.C. competition rules.[58]

(b) Where the agreement or practice in question only affects trade between EFTA States then the EFTA Surveillance Authority will be the competent authority, applying the EEA competition rules in Article 53.

(c) Where the effect on trade is "mixed", *i.e.* affecting trade between the Community and the EFTA States the Commission will be the competent authority where:

(i) the agreement or practice has an appreciable effect on trade between Member States and on competition within the Community; or

(ii) the combined turnover of the undertakings concerned in the territory of the EFTA States is less than 33 per cent of their turnover in the European Economic Area.

The EFTA Surveillance Authority therefore only has competence where there is no effect on trade between Member States (*e.g.* the only effect is on trade between one or more Member States and one or more EFTA States) or the effect on trade between Member States or on competition within the Community is not appreciable (in practice to be determined by applying the Commission's Notice on minor agreements)[59]

---

[54] Art. 6.

[55] See generally Jacob, "EEA and Eastern European Agreements with the European Communities". 19th Annual Conference, Fordham University 1992, and Stragier, "The Competition Rules of the EEA Agreement and their implementation" [1993] 1 E.C.L.R. 30.

[56] Art. 55(1) and 109(1). Art. 108(1) provides for the establishing of the EFTA Surveillance Authority.

[57] Opinion 1/91: [1992] 1 C.M.L.R. 245 and Opinion 1/92: [1992] 2 C.M.L.R. 217.

[58] This is the effect of the Court of Justice's Opinion 1/91. See also the Joint Declaration concerning Rules on Competition (Cm. 2073, p. 253).

[59] Annex XIV, para. 20; Agreed Minute on Art. 56(3) (Cm. 2073, p. 267).

and the turnover of the undertakings concerned in the territory of EFTA States is 33 per cent or more of their turnover in the European Economic Area.

(ii) *Dominant positions*

The Commission again retains its competence to deal with cases under Article 86 where the effect on trade is limited to the Member States.[60] Cases falling under Article 54 EEA shall be decided upon by the surveillance authority in the territory of which a dominant position is found to exist. Where dominance exists within the territories of both surveillance authorities then the jurisdiction division is the same as that for restrictive practices and in practice the Commission will more frequently have competence. The EFTA Surveillance Authority will only have competence to deal with cases where there is no appreciable effect on trade between Member States or on competition within the Community *and* the turnover of the undertaking concerned in the territory of the EFTA States equals 33 per cent or more of their turnover in the European Economic Area. Protocol 22 EEA provides a definition of terms "undertaking" and "turnover" for these purposes.

Protocol 23 contains practical rules for co-operation between the surveillance authorities, including rules for the transfer of cases at an early stage to the authority competent pursuant to the application of Article 56 described above.

1.34C As the substantive rules in Articles 53 and 54 EEA mirror those in Articles 85 and 86 of the E.C. Treaty so the procedural rules mirror Regulation 17 and the other implementing regulations.[61] The EEA itself provides special rules providing transitional arrangements for the notification and handling of agreements in existence at the time of entry into effect of the EEA.[62] Again these reflect the provisions made for the commencement of Regulation 17 and, later, the accession of new Member States. The transitional arrangements are discussed in Chapters 2 and 6. Appeals from the Commission go to the Community's courts. Those from the EFTA Surveillance Authority will go to the newly created EFTA Court.[63] The Agreement provides for co-ordination and co-operation in enforcement of the EEA competition rules by the Commission and the EFTA Surveillance Authority.[64] This is further considered in Chapter 5. The Competition Directorate of the latter is based in Brussels close to DG IV. So far as new Community competition legislation (*e.g.* new block exemptions) is concerned, the EFTA States have rights to be consulted and to participate in the discussions although ultimately it is the Community's legislation and the EFTA States have no right of vote or veto.[65] The new legislation can, however, only be added to the Annexes or Protocols to the EEA with the consent of the EFTA states via the EEA Joint Committee.[66] It is expected that the EFTA States will accept such new rules but, if not, the EEA Joint Committee must work to maintain the good functioning of the

---

[60] This is the effect of the Court of Justice's Opinion 1/91. See also the Joint Declaration concerning Rules on Competition (Cm. 2073, p. 253).
[61] Protocol 22, Arts. 1 and 3(1)(3)–(14).
[62] Protocol 21, Arts. 5–9, 10–13.
[63] Art. 108(2)(b).
[64] Arts. 3, 55, 109(2) and Protocol 24.
[65] Arts. 99, 100 and 102. See generally Reymond, "Institutions, Decision—Making Procedure and Settlement of Disputes in the European Economic Area" (1993) 30 C.M.L.R. Rev. 449.
[66] Arts. 98 and 102.

EEA. The EEA provides procedures for the resolution of differences which may emerge between EEC and EEA competition rules and their application.[67]

III. OUTLINE OF THE COMMISSION'S PROCEDURE

Introduction

1.35   Whilst the Community rules may be enforced by national competition authorities[68] and applied by national courts,[69] the Commission is the principal enforcement agency.[70] Regulation 17 (and in transport cases, the other implementing Regulations 1017/68, 4056/86 and 3975/87) provides the basis[71] for the Commission's enforcement procedure and gives it the power to take decisions requiring the termination of infringements and also to grant negative clearance[72] or an exemption to a particular agreement or practice. The procedure is essentially an administrative one.[73] The Commission investigates the facts, makes known its objections to the undertakings concerned, and finally, takes any decision necessary in the circumstances of the case. The Commission is not, however, without check, nor the parties without safeguard. Decisions of the Commission may be the subject of appeals to the Court of First Instance and from there, on points of law, to the Court of Justice.[74] Moreover, during the Commission's procedures the interests of the undertakings concerned are protected not only by express provisions in the relevant regulations relating, for example, to the right to be heard but also by all general principles of Community law which may be relevant, such as the principle of proportionality[75] and the right of the defence.[76]

Notification and complaints

1.36   The Commission may commence proceedings following a notification or a complaint, or by simply acting on its own initiative. This reflects the different ways by which information relating to a suspected infringement of the Community competition rules may be brought to the attention of the Commission. First, a good number of agreements are voluntarily notified to the Commission. There are two basic reasons

---

[67] Art. 111.

[68] Art. 88 of the Treaty. See generally, Deringer, *op. cit.*

[69] Arts. 85 and 86 are directly applicable provisions of Community law: Cases 56 and 58/64, *Consten Sarl and Grundig-Verkaufs GmbH* v. *Commission*: [1966] E.C.R. 299.

[70] Art. 87 of the Treaty. See para. 1.24. It has a primary responsibility for ensuring the application of Arts. 85 and 86.

[71] See para. 1.25.

[72] *I.e.* a decision by the Commission that on the information available to it has no cause to intervene. See paras. 2.02–06.

[73] *Consten and Grundig*, above, at para. 5.

[74] Art. 173 of the Treaty. See paras. 9.04–22.

[75] Discussed at paras. 8.25–26.

[76] In Case 85/76, *Hoffmann-La Roche* v. *Commission*: [1979] E.C.R. 461, [1979] 3 C.M.L.R. 211, the Court said: "Respect of the rights of the defence in any proceedings that may lead to the imposition of sanctions, and in particular to fines and penalties, constitutes a fundamental principle of Community law, which should be observed in administrative proceedings."

for this. An exemption under Article 85(3) cannot, as a general rule,[77] be granted by the Commission unless the agreement has first been notified to it. Fines cannot generally be imposed for infringement of Article 85 or 86 in respect of behaviour within the terms of the notification during the period after notification and before the Commission's decision in application of Article 85(3).[78] Second, evidence of a possible violation of the competition rules may be made known to the Commission in a complaint made by a third party. There is a formal complaints procedure available although the Commission can and does receive informal complaints.[79] Finally, the Commission may receive information from a variety of other sources including the regular perusal of trade journals, questions in the European Parliament, discussions with other antitrust authorities, etc. The Commission also has power (in fact rarely used) to conduct sector investigations[80] which are not limited to the activities of any one or group of undertakings but extend to a market generally. Sector inquiries may disclose particular infringements of the Treaty just as an investigation into one infringement may show up another infringement.

Fact-finding

1.37   The consideration and investigation of cases (the fact-finding stage) may proceed formally or informally.[81] It may not be necessary to use formal investigatory powers where, for example, parties voluntarily discuss with the Commission the terms and effects of an agreement which has been notified with a view to negative clearance or exemption. The Commission has, however, two major investigatory powers which it can use when and where necessary. They are a right of request for information[82] and a right of inspection of business records, books, etc.[83] Both can be reinforced by the use of formal decisions, failure to comply with which may lead to a further decision imposing a fine and/or periodic penalty payment.

The Commission is entitled to obtain all necessary information from undertakings.[84] The procedure relating to requests for information is a two-stage one. Undertakings must be given the opportunity to supply the information voluntarily in response to a simple written request. Only if this fails can the Commission take a decision ordering the necessary information to be supplied to it. It should be noted that requests for information can be made to all relevant undertakings and the Commission is not restricted to obtaining information only from undertakings suspected of infringing the competition rules. Although there is no legal obligation to comply with the simple written request, undertakings should take care if they do so because fines can

---

[77] Certain agreements need not be notified (see Art. 4 of Reg. 17) and block or group exemptions do not, of course, require the notification of the agreements to which they apply.

[78] *I.e.* a decision finding an infringement under Art. 85(1) but rejecting the application for exemption. Note that the immunity from fine may be withdrawn by a preliminary decision under Art. 15(6) of Reg. 17. See paras. 6.12–15.

[79] The procedure relating to complaints is dealt with in detail at paras. 2.29–37.

[80] Art. 12 of Reg. 17. See para. 3.43.

[81] Although this book concentrates on the formal procedures, the ability and practice of the Commission to act informally must not be underestimated. See paras. 6.53–61.

[82] Art. 11 of Reg. 17. See Chap. 3.

[83] Art. 14 of Reg. 17. See Chap. 3.

[84] See n. 82.

be imposed for intentionally or negligently supplying false information.[85] The vast majority of simple written requests are in fact answered voluntarily and without too much difficulty, and formal decisions requiring information are therefore extremely rare.

The Commission has a power to enter an undertaking's premises and to inspect and take copies of its books and business records.[86] Inspections may be ordered by decision of the Commission or take place under a simple mandate or authorisation given to the inspectors. There is no compulsory two-stage procedure here and the inspection may be ordered by decision without the Commission first having to offer the undertaking the opportunity to submit voluntarily. Inspections may be announced in advance to the undertaking or may be by surprise. Where an inspection is not ordered by decision, there is no legal obligation to submit to it, but if an undertaking does so voluntarily it should nevertheless take care. Fines can be imposed for intentionally or negligently producing the required books or other business records in incomplete form.[87] Where the inspection is ordered by decision and there is a failure to submit to the inspection as ordered, then a further decision can be taken imposing a fine and/or periodic penalty payment to compel compliance.[88] Officials from the competent authority of the relevant Member State may assist the Commission at these inspections.[89] Moreover where an undertaking opposes an inspection ordered by decision, the Member State must give the necessary assistance to the Commission officials to enable them to make their investigation.[90] In the past, the majority of inspections were without a decision and announced in advance to the undertakings concerned. Only very rarely did the Commission make an unannounced or surprise inspection or an inspection, whether announced or unannounced, ordered by decision. Unannounced inspections ordered by decision have, however, become more frequent since 1979.

Statement of objections

1.38 Following the fact-finding stage, if the Commission considers that the evidence points to an infringement which should be the subject of a decision, a formal procedure is opened[91] and a statement of objections[92] served on the undertaking concerned. This does not happen in every case as there is sufficient flexibility in the Commission's procedures for informal settlements involving, for example, the amendment or abandonment of the agreement or practice involved. A good number of cases are for instance concluded on the basis of so-called comfort letters.[93] The statement of objections sets out in written form the Commission's case against the undertakings concerned. It contains the basic facts as understood by the Commission

---

[85] Art. 15(1)(b) of Reg. 17. A similar offence is committed where the request is contained in a formal decision. But, in this latter case, periodic penalty payments can also be imposed under Art. 16(1)(c).

[86] See n. 83.

[87] Art. 15(1)(c) of Reg. 17.

[88] Arts. 15(1)(c) and 16(1)(d) of Reg. 17.

[89] Art. 14(5) of Reg. 17.

[90] Art. 14(6) of Reg. 17. There is also the possibility of the national officials carrying out the inspection for the Commission. See paras. 5.17–18.

[91] As to the nature and effects of the initiation of proceedings, see paras. 2.38–39.

[92] As to the statement of objections, its form and contents, see paras. 4.02–04.

[93] See para. 6.54.

relating to the agreement or practice in question. The reasons for the applicability of Article 85 or 86 are explained and, in the case of a notified agreement, the grounds for the refusal of an exemption under Article 85(3) are also set out. Relevant documentary evidence is usually annexed.

Parties' right to be heard

1.39   The undertakings concerned have a right to be heard.[94] This basically means the right to reply to the arguments put by the Commission and to make their own views known to the Commission. The Commission will also give access to its file on the case.[95] The right to be heard is normally and primarily exercised in writing by way of a reply containing observations on the accuracy of the facts, validity of the arguments, etc. of the statement of objections. The undertaking may also put in evidence of its own in support of its defence. The statement of objections will specify a time-limit (not less than two weeks) within which any written reply must be made. The undertakings concerned will also be offered the opportunity to be heard orally.[96] The date for the oral hearing is usually fixed by the statement of objections a few weeks after the expiry of the time for the written reply. The oral hearing is a relatively informal affair. It is not a formal trial by any stretch of the imagination although when a third party, such as a complainant, is present at the hearing, the proceedings may take on an adversarial character. Representatives of the Member States may take part in the oral hearings.[97] Witnesses may be heard.[98]

Where the Commission concludes after investigation that the agreement does not infringe Article 85(1) and may be suitable for a negative clearance, or that it infringes Article 85(1) but is nevertheless beneficial and suitable for an exemption under Article 85(3), then it may not be necessary for a statement of objections to be served on the undertaking concerned. There may, however, be some discussion with the undertaking before the final decision is taken particularly if the agreement has to be modified before any negative clearance or exemption is granted. If an exemption is made subject to any conditions,[99] then the undertaking concerned must be given a right to be heard on the subject of these conditions.[1] Third parties, such as complainants, may also have to be heard before such a decision is to be taken if their interests are likely to be affected.[2] Summaries of decisions granting negative clearance or an exemption must be published in the *Official Journal* and a period of at least one month allowed for any interested third parties to submit observations to the Commission.[3]

---

[94] Art. 19(1) of Reg. 17. See, generally, paras. 4.13–24.

[95] See paras. 4.07–12.

[96] The procedure at the oral hearing is discussed at paras. 4.28–33.

[97] Art. 8(2) of Reg. 99/63.

[98] Art. 3(3) of Reg. 99/63.

[99] Conditions and obligations may be imposed under Art. 8 of Reg. 17.

[1] See Case 17/74, *Transocean Marine Paint Association* v. *Commission*: [1974] E.C.R. 1063, [1974] 2 C.M.L.R. 459.

[2] Art. 19(2) of Reg. 17.

[3] Art. 19(3) of Reg. 17. In transport cases there is also the possibility to use the "objections" procedure whereby if no adverse comments are raised within 90 days of application the agreement is deemed exempt for a period of three years. See para. 2.17.

Advisory Committee

1.40   Before the final decision is taken, whether it is a termination of an infringement or negative clearance or an exemption, the Commission must consult the Advisory Committee on Restrictive Practices and Monopolies.[4] This Committee, made up
of officials competent in competition matters from the Member States, considers and
discusses the draft decision and records its opinion which is annexed to the draft decision put before the Commissioners. The Advisory Committee's opinion is not made
public or made known to the parties. The final decision is taken by the Commissioners
and then notified to the undertakings concerned.[5] Decisions are published in the *Official Journal.*[6]

Interim measures

1.41   The Court of Justice has held that the Commission has powers to take interim
measures in suitable cases.[7] The Court said:

> "It is obvious that in certain circumstances there may be a need to adopt interim
> protective measures when the practice of certain undertakings in competition
> matters has the effect of injuring the interests of some Member States causing
> damage to other undertakings, or unacceptably jeopardising the Community's
> competition policy. In such circumstances it is important to ensure that whilst
> enquiries are being carried out no irreparable damage is caused such as could
> not be remedied by any decision which the Commission might take at the con-
> clusion of the administrative procedure."

When taking such measures the Commission must have regard to the interests of the
undertaking concerned and essential safeguards such as the right to be heard must be
respected. Interim me. sures must be of a temporary and conservatory nature. The procedures for granting interim relief have been specially streamlined in aviation cases.[8]
Like other decisior of the Commission, decisions ordering interim measures are subject to appeal before the Court.

---

[4] Art. 10(3) of Reg. 17. The role of the Advisory Committee is discussed at paras. 5.21–28. The implementing regulation for the transport sector provide for separate Advisory Committees with different representation. See para. 5.
[5] In practice, the operative part (*dispositif*) of the decision is telexed straight away to the undertakings concerned. The full text follows in due course.
[6] Art. 21 of Reg. 17.
[7] Case 792/79R, *Camera Care Ltd.* v. *Commission*: [1980] E.C.R. 119, [1980] 1 C.M.L.R. 334, at para. 14.
The procedure is discussed at paras. 6.02–11.
[8] By Reg. 1284/91 which adds an Art. 4a to Reg. 3975/87.

2

Starting the Machinery

I. NOTIFICATION

Generally

2.01 Community law does not require all cartels or dominant positions to be notified to the Commission. In this respect it differs quite fundamentally, for example, from the registration system for restrictive agreements provided by the United Kingdom Restrictive Trade Practices Acts or indeed the Community's own regime for mergers in Regulation 4064/89. As will be seen, the primary purpose for notifying an agreement to the Commission will be to seek a ruling either that the agreement does not come within the terms of Article 85(1) at all (this is called negative clearance) or that the agreement is subject to the prohibition in Article 85(1) but that the provisions of Article 85(1) should be declared inapplicable in relation to the agreement by virtue of Article 85(3) (this is commonly called exemption). Strictly speaking, one makes an "application" for negative clearance and a "notification" for exemption. But the same form, Form A/B[1] is used for both and in practice, as will be explained later, it is usually prudent to apply for both at the same time. The term "notification" is generally used loosely to mean the process whereby copies of the agreement under cover of Form A/B are supplied to the Commission for the purposes of obtaining negative clearance or exemption.

In practice, very few agreements receive individual decisions of negative clearance or exemption and the block exemption regulations have a far greater import in releasing agreements from the prohibition in Article 85(1). Indeed the system of notification has been criticised for producing a system which although aimed at providing legal certainty in effect produces uncertainty because of the fact of large numbers of agreements sitting in the files of DG IV without hope of an individual decision.[2] Informal arrangements (such as comfort letters) can give the parties some assurance, albeit without legal security, and in practice comfort letters are frequently acceptable,

---

[1] Form A/B is set out in an annex to Regulation 27 (as amended in particular by Reg. 2526/85 and, most recently to take account of the EEA, by Reg. 3666/93). Form A/B is reproduced in Appendix F hereto. Copies may be obtained free of charge from the Commission's Press and Information Office, 8 Storey's Gate, London SW1P 3AT (tel. 071-973 1992).

[2] Forrester and Norall, "The Laicization of Community law, Self-Help and the Rule of Reason: How Competition Law is and could be applied" (1984) 31 C.M.L.Rev. 11. See also Brown, "Notification of Agreements to EC Commission: Whether to Submit to a Flawed System" (1992) 17 E.L.Rev. 323.

particularly if the comfort given is that an agreement appears not to fall within Article 85(1) at all. The block exemptions have been the most effective means of clearing the backlog, giving certainty in a generally deregulatory manner. Some, such as that for exclusive distribution (Regulation 1983/83) are more useful than others because they are capable of operating normatively and tend to apply to self-standing agreements whereas many other arrangements such as licences are agreed in the context of joint ventures, etc., where block exemptions are ruled out automatically. A development intended further to extend the block exemption has been the incorporation of the so-called "opposition procedure" allowing agreements to be notified and cleared quickly although the evidence so far is that the procedure is little used in practice. From April 1, 1993 new arrangements have been put in place to enable notifications to be dealt with more quickly, by analogy with the timetable for mergers under Regulation 4064/89. As will be explained in more detail later, Form A/B (and the forms for use in transport cases) has recently been amended to take account of the EEA. The Commission has also embarked upon informal consultation which may lead to a major revision of Form A/B.

Negative clearance

2.02 Article 2 of Regulation 17 provides:

> "Upon application by the undertakings or associations of undertakings concerned, the Commission may certify that, on the basis of the facts in its possession, there are no grounds under Article 85(1) or Article 86 of the Treaty for action on its part in respect of an agreement, decision or practice."

In short, the agreement is not caught. This may be, for example, because it does not restrict or distort competition within the Common Market, or does not affect trade between Member States appreciably or, more rarely, because the agreement is not made between independent undertakings.

As regards the transport sector, Article 3(2) of Regulation 3975/87 provides for negative clearance in appropriate air transport cases. But neither Regulation 1017/68 nor Regulation 4056/86 provides a negative clearance for maritime and other transport cases.[3]

2.03 Negative clearance must be distinguished from exemption. Although Regulation 27 speaks of applications under Article 2 of Regulation 17 relating to the "applicability" of Articles 85(1) and 86 of the Treaty, there is a semantic difficulty in describing negative clearance as a decision relating to the non- or inapplicability of Article 85(1). This is because Article 85(3), dealing with exemption, refers to the provisions of Article 85(1) being declared "inapplicable". An agreement cannot be granted exemption from the prohibition contained in Article 85(1) unless it is an agreement caught by Article 85(1) and it also satisfies the criteria for exemption laid

---

[3] Would the Court of Justice imply such a power if needed? The Court has shown that it will construe implementing regulations to give them maximum effectiveness, see Case 792/79R, *Camera Care Ltd.* v. *Commission*: [1980] E.C.R. 119, [1980] 1 C.M.L.R. 334.

down in Article 85(3). This is reflected in the practice of the Commission when drafting its decisions. A decision granting exemption will always contain the Commission's reasons for holding that the agreement falls within the prohibition contained within Article 85(1) as well as why it satisfies the criteria required for exemption, and its operative part (the *dispositif*) will state that the provisions of Article 85(1) are declared inapplicable under Article 85(3).[4]

2.04 Negative clearance can be sought for Article 85(1) and/or Article 86.[5] Formal applications under Article 86 alone are rare in practice, particularly since no exemption is possible equivalent to that under Article 85(3). A decision granting negative clearance will declare that on the basis of the facts in its possession there are "no grounds for action to be taken" by the Commission under the competition rules.[6] The ∨ form of words might be thought suitable to cover the situation where the Commission having examined an agreement and found that it falls within the terms of Article 85(1) considers that although the agreement has an appreciable effect on competition and inter-State trade it is of relatively little significance or importance, and chooses to exercise its administrative discretion not to proceed against it in the absence of any complaint or evidence of serious detrimental effect. Negative clearance is not appropriate for this type of case but only for those cases where the Commission considers the agreement does not come within the terms of Article 85(1).

Application for negative clearance

2.05 As regards Article 85(1), the application must be made on Form A/B and all the information requested by the form and the Complementary Note must be included.[7] Form A/B can also be used for negative clearance under Article 53(1) EEA. No special form is required for an application for negative clearance relating to the application of Article 86 (and/or Article 54 EEA), although Form A/B may be used and is strongly recommended.[8] Such application must, however, contain a full statement

---

[4] For recent examples, see *Ford/Volkswagen*: [1993] O.J. L20/14 and *Jahrhundertvertrag*: [1993] O.J. L50/14. The latter decision also contains an authorisation under Art. 65(2) of the ECSC Treaty.

[5] See *GEMA Statutes*: [1982] O.J. L94/12, [1982] 2 C.M.L.R. 482, where the decision is limited to Art. 86. Also *Mentaleurop SA*: [1990] O.J. L179/41, [1991] 4 C.M.L.R. 222. Contrast *Schlegel/CPIO*: [1983] O.J. L351/20, [1984] 2 C.M.L.R. 179, where the negative clearance for a know-how agreement covers both Arts. 85 and 86. See also *Mecaniver-PPG*: [1985] O.J. L35/54, [1985] 3 C.M.L.R. 359.

[6] For examples, see *Dutch banks*: [1989] O.J. L253/1; *A.P.B.*: [1990] O.J. L18/35, [1990] 4 C.M.L.R. 619 and *Elopak/Metal Box–Odin*: [1990] O.J. L209/15, [1991] 4 C.M.L.R. 832. Contrast *D'Ieteren Motor Oils*: [1991] O.J. L20/42, [1992] 4 C.M.L.R. 399, where the formula "does not fulfil the conditions for application of Article 85(1)" is used.

[7] Arts. 4(1) and (2) of Reg. 27. Before Form A/B was introduced in 1968, there were separate forms for negative clearance and exemption. The use of Form B (exemption) did not, however, exclude the possibility of negative clearance provided the necessary information was included on the form used. See *Nicholas–Vitapro*: J.O. 2287/64, [1964] C.M.L.R. 505. Note also the cases where notification was made "at large". See, for example, *Reickermann*: [1968] O.J. L276/25, [1968] C.M.L.R. D78, and *Association pour la Promotion du Tube d'Acier Soude Electriquement*: [1970] J.O. L153/14. *Cf. Limeburners*: [1969] J.O. L122/8, [1969] C.M.L.R. D15. On Form A/B, its use and completion, see paras. 2.18–27. In the present context note *SABA's EEC Distribution System*: [1983] O.J. L37/41, [1984] 1 C.M.L.R. 676, where limited negative clearance was granted in the context of a renewal of an exemption where a fresh Form A/B is not required. The fact that SABA had only sought by letter a renewal did not inhibit the Commission from granting negative clearance.

[8] Art. 4(4) of Reg. 27. The practice for which clearance is sought may involve agreements within the meaning of Art. 85(1) (for example, the contracts which a supplier makes with a distributor or certain retail pur-

of the facts and set out, in particular, the practice concerned and the position of the undertaking within the Common Market[9] (and/or the territory of the EFTA States) in relation to the relevant products or services.[10] In all applications for negative clearance the fullest disclosure of the appropriate factual information is desirable. Negative clearance is given on the basis of the facts in the Commission's possession and the measure of its value is therefore dependent on the amount of information available to the Commission at the time it is given.[11] Nor should the accuracy of the information be neglected. The Commission may by decision fine undertakings where they intentionally or negligently supply incorrect or misleading information in an application for negative clearance.[12]

An application for negative clearance alone does not confer immunity from fine under Article 15(5) of Regulation 17.[13] Only notification for exemption can do this.

Procedure

2.06 Although negative clearance involves the Commission in the initiation of a procedure, there will often be no need for all the further procedural steps common to cases of infringement of Article 85(1) or 86 of the Treaty. It may not be necessary, for example, for the Commission to serve a statement of objections on the undertakings concerned in order to establish the status of the agreement or practice. But if it be necessary to do so, then the undertakings must be given the opportunity of being heard on the matters to which the Commission has taken objection. An agreement may be modified or amended in order to render it fit for negative clearance.[14] The Commission is, however, required, before taking any decision giving negative clearance, to publish a summary of the relevant application and invite all interested third parties to submit their observations within a specified time being not less than one month.[15] The publication must have regard to the legitimate interests of undertakings in the protection

---

chasers may be agreements between undertakings for the purposes of Art. 85(1)—see the Commission's decisions in *Kodak*: [1970] J.O. L147/24, [1970] C.M.L.R. D19; *Gerofabriek*: [1977] O.J. L16/8, [1977] 1 C.M.L.R. D35, and see *Zanussi*: [1978] O.J. L322/26, [1979] 1 C.M.L.R. 81. *Cf. Sandoz*: [1987] O.J. L222/28). Negative clearance or exemption might be sought for such agreements, although it should be noted that the fact that agreements might fall within Art. 85 (and, in particular, within Art. 85(3)) does not preclude the application of Art. 86. See case 85/76, *Hoffmann-La Roche* v. *Commission*: [1979] E.C.R. 461, [1979] 3 C.M.L.R. 211, at para. 116 and Case T–51/89, *Tetra Pak Rausing SA* v. *Commission*: [1990] II E.C.R. 309, [1991] 4 C.M.L.R. 334, at para. 25.

[9] Or a substantial part thereof, Art. 4(4) of Reg. 27.

[10] In *Hoffmann-La Roche*, above, at para. 134, the Court of Justice emphasised the importance of Art. 2 of Reg. 17 as a precautionary measure to be taken for a ruling on the application of Art. 86 to doubtful cases.

[11] In the Complementary Note to Form A/B, the Commission says that a decision based on incomplete information could be without effect.

[12] Art. 15(1)(a) of Reg. 17. and see para. 7.05.

[13] *John Deere*: [1985] O.J. L35/58, [1985] 2 C.M.L.R. 554.

[14] See, *e.g. A.P.B.*: [1990] O.J. L18/35, [1990] 4 C.M.L.R. 619, where the case started as infringement proceedings.

[15] Art. 19(3) of Reg. 17. For a recent example, see *Konsortium E.C.R. 900*: [1989] O.J. C308/5, [1990] 4 C.M.L.R. 256. The publication in the O.J. does occasionally trigger off objections from interested parties. See *GEMA Statues*: [1982] O.J. L94/12, [1982] 2 C.M.L.R. 482. It may however produce support for an exemption. See *X/Open Group*: [1987] O.J. L35/36, [1988] 4 C.M.L.R. 542. It may produce comments on other matters possibly involving Article 85(1), see *D'Ieteren Motor Oils*: [1991] O.J. L20/42, [1992] 4 C.M.L.R. 399.

of their business secrets and therefore should not disclose them.[16] The publication is made in the *Official Journal*.[17]

The Commission has limited resources and must establish priorities. It takes the view that it is under no legal obligation to give negative clearances and has said that it does not usually issue such decisions in cases which, in its opinion, so clearly do not fall within the scope of the prohibition in Article 85(1) that there is no reasonable doubt for it to resolve by such a decision.[18] Generally, in relation to its decision-making powers, the Commission has said that it will concentrate on cases having particular political, economic or legal significance for the Community.[19]

Exemption

Generally

2.07   Under Article 85(3) of the Treaty, the provisions of Article 85(1) may be declared inapplicable to any agreement between undertakings which satisfies the specified criteria described above.[20] Although it is possible to apply for negative clearance in relation to the applicability of Article 86,[21] it is not possible to apply for exemption from Article 86, because Article 86 does not permit any exceptions to its prohibition.[22] There is understandably no power to approve abuses of dominant positions. Furthermore, the fact that agreements or practices might fall within Article 85(3) does not preclude the application of Article 86 in relation to them.[23]

2.08   The basic rule is that in order for an agreement, decision or concerted practice to be exempted it must be notified to the Commission. Article 4(1) of Regulation 17 provides: "Until they have been notified, no decision in application of Article 85(3) may be taken." The Court of Justice has made this a strict rule.[24]

There are, however, exceptions to this basic rule. The rule applies only to individual exemptions (*i.e.* those which are the subject of specific decisions of the Commission

---

[16] Case 53/85, *AKZO Chemie BV and AKZO Chemie U.K.* v. *Commission*: [1986] E.C.R. 1965, [1987] 1 C.M.L.R. 231.

[17] In the C series. No indication may be given as to whether a negative clearance or exemption is to be granted. The publication may simply refer to the Commission taking a "favourable decision". See *Encompass Europe*: [1992] O.J. C233/2, [1992] 5 C.M.L.R. 537. Or it may indicate the intention to grant exemption. See *Fiat/Deere III*: [1992] O.J. C87/3, [1992] C.M.L.R. 501. It may indicate that the Commission intends to close the procedure by sending a comfort letter, see *Infonet*: [1992] O.J. C7/3, [1992] 4 C.M.L.R. 493, and, more generally, para. 6.26.

[18] Part III of Complementary Note to Form A/B. On the obligation to give negative clearance, etc. see para. 9.28.

[19] Notice on co-operation between national courts and the Commission in applying Articles 85 and 86 of the EEC Treaty, paras. 13 and 14: [1993] O.J. C39/6.

[20] See para. 1.13.

[21] Art. 2 of Reg. 17 and Art. 4(4) of Reg. 27, see paras. 2.02–06.

[22] Case 6/72, *Europemballage Corp. and Continental Can Co. Inc.* v. *Commission*: [1973] E.C.R. 215, [1973] C.M.L.R. 199, at para. 25.

[23] Case 85/76, *Hoffmann-La Roche* v. *Commission*: [1979] E.C.R. 461, [1979] 3 C.M.L.R. 211, at para. 116 and Case T–51/89, *Tetra Pak Rausing SA* v. *Commission*: [1990] II E.C.R. 309, [1991] 4 C.M.L.R. 334, at para. 25. But the fact that there has been a notification may reduce any fine: see Case 27/76, *United Brands Continental BV* v. *Commission*: [1978] E.C.R. 207, [1978] 2 C.M.L.R. 429, at paras. 291 and 292.

[24] See, *e.g.* Case 126/80, *Salonia* v. *Poidomani*: [1981] E.C.R. 1563, [1982] 1 C.M.L.R. 64, at paras. 28–31, and, more generally, para. 2.19 below.

addressed to the parties concerned) and does not apply in the case of so-called block or group exemptions.[25] It is acknowledged that one of the primary purposes of the block or group exemption is to avoid hundreds, if not thousands, of agreements having to be notified to the Commission.[26] Second, Article 4(2) of Regulation 17 exempts from notification certain types of agreement. Finally, in transport cases all three implementing regulations provide that the Commission may grant an individual exemption even though the parties have not notified the agreement in question.[27] As in the case of agreements within Article 4(2) of Regulation 17 the operative date of the exemption may be prior to that of the exemption decision itself. Where parties notify agreements under the transport regulations the Commission will first consider the applicability of the "objections" procedure.[28]

Agreements exempt from notification

2.09 Four types of agreement are exempt from notification by virtue of Article 4(2) of Regulation 17 (Article 4(2) of Protocol 21 is the mirror image for the EEA). Before considering each type separately, certain general points should be made. First, the agreements are exempt only from notification and not from the prohibition contained in Article 85(1). Unless they also fall within the terms of a block or group exemption, it will still be necessary to obtain a decision from the Commission if they are to have the status of agreements exempted under Article 85(3). But if such a decision is made, it has an advantage in that it can be retrospective to the date of making of the agreement.[29] Secondly, in the case of agreements covered by Article 4(2) of Regulation 17 the Commission must examine whether the conditions laid down in Article 85(3) are met even where it becomes aware of the agreements as a result of its own investigation.[30] Thirdly, although notification is not required, agreements within the categories listed in Article 4(2) may still be notified. The principal benefit which arises is the immunity from fine conferred by Article 15(5) of Regulation 17. This only applies to agreements which have in fact been notified.[31] In the case of old and accession agreements an additional benefit of actual notification may be the application of the special provisions of Article 7 of Regulation 17.[32] Finally, it is sufficient to satisfy the criteria of one of the categories listed in Article 4(2). Failure under one head does not exclude qualification under another.[33]

There is no need to notify agreements, decisions or concerted practices where:

---

[25] For details of the block exemptions, see para. 1.14. And see *Sole Distribution Agreements for Whisky and Gin*: [1985] O.J. L369/19, [1986] 2 C.M.L.R. 664, where in the context of an exemption decision for the Commission made a declaration on the applicability of Reg. 1983/83.

[26] For example, some 25,000 cases were dealt with on the basis of Reg. 67/67 the forerunner to Regs. 1983/83 and 1984/83. See Ninth Report on Competition Policy, at point 16.

[27] Reg. 1017/68, Art. 11(4); Reg. 4056/86, Art. 11(4); Reg. 3975/87, Art. 4(3).

[28] See para 2.

[29] Art. 6(2) of Reg. 17, and see para. 6.28. Decisions exempting agreements governed by Art. 4(1) cannot take effect from a date prior to the date of notification.

[30] Cases 240–242, 261, 262, 268 & 269/82, *SSI-Stichting Sigarettenindustrie and others* v. *Commission*: [1985] E.C.R. 3831, [1987] 3 C.M.L.R. 661, at para. 75.

[31] *Ibid.* at para. 77. The benefits of notification are discussed at para. 2.18.

[32] See paras. 6.29–31. This also has significance in the context of the EEA. Protocol 21, Art. 7 has a similar provision to Art. 9 of Reg. 17.

[33] See, for example, *Vaessen/Moris*: [1979] O.J. L19/32, [1979] 1 C.M.L.R. 511.

(i) *the only parties thereto are undertakings from one Member State and the agreements, decisions or practices do not relate either to imports or to exports between Member States.*

2.10   An agreement falls within the prohibition of Article 85(1) of the Treaty only if it may "affect trade between Member States" and the classic example of an agreement contrary to Article 85(1), and the *bête noire* of the Commission, is one which contains an export ban or disincentive. It is clear that Article 4(2)(1) of Regulation 17 will not apply to an agreement containing an export ban.[34] It is, however, difficult at first sight to reconcile the requirement that trade between Member States be affected before Article 85(1) applies with the criterion that the agreement must not "relate either to imports or to exports between Member States" in order to benefit from Article 4(2)(1).

In *Bilger* v. *Jehle*,[35] the Court of Justice had to consider this problem in the context of a tied cafe contract. The Court thought it possible for one and the same agreement not to "relate either to imports or to exports between Member States" but nevertheless to "affect trade between Member States." The phrase "relate either to imports or to exports" must be given a narrower meaning than the phrase "affect trade between Member States."[36] The Court held that an exclusive supply agreement, the performance of which does not involve the crossing of national frontiers by the goods in question, may not relate to imports or to exports. But such an agreement, taken together with a number of similar agreements binding a significant number of dealers in the same Member State to several national suppliers, could in appropriate circumstances be capable of affecting trade between Member States.[37] In *Delimitis* v. *Henninger Bräu,* the Court recently confirmed the approach taken in *Bilger* v. *Jehle.* A beer supply agreement may satisfy the conditions of Article 4(2) even if it forms an integral part of a series of similar contracts.[38]

The Court of Justice looked again at the ambit of the condition that the agreement must not "relate either to imports or to exports between Member States" in the case of *Fonderies Roubaix-Wattrelos* v. *Fonderies A. Roux*.[39] It concerned the validity of an unnotified exclusive distribution agreement between two French firms relating to the marketing in France of goods originally imported from Germany. The Court said:[40]

> "This . . . condition must be interpreted with reference to the structure of Article 4 and its aim of simplifying administrative procedure, which it pursues by not requiring undertakings to notify agreements which, whilst they may be covered by Article 85(1), appear in general, by reason of their particular characteristics,

---

[34] *Moët et Chandon (London) Ltd.*: [1982] O.J. L94/7, [1982] 2 C.M.L.R. 166; *National Panasonic*: [1982] O.J. L354/22, [1983] 1 C.M.L.R. 497, and *Windsurfing*: [1983] O.J. L229/1, [1984] 1 C.M.L.R. 1. For other types of restrictions relating to exports in this context, see *AROW/BNIC*: [1982] O.J. L379/1, [1983] 2 C.M.L.R. 240 and *Milchförderungsfonds*: [1985] O.J. L35/35, [1985] 3 C.M.L.R. 101, and "relating to imports", *Roofing Felt*: [1986] O.J. L232/15, [1991] 4 C.M.L.R. 130.

[35] Case 43/69: [1970] E.C.R. 127, [1974] 1 C.M.L.R. 382.

[36] *Ibid.* at para. 5.

[37] On "network" agreements, see Case 23/67, *Brasserie de Haecht* v. *Wilkin (No. 1)*: [1967] E.C.R. 407, [1968] C.M.L.R. 26; Case 47/76, *De Norre and de Clerq* v. *NV "Brouwerij Concordia"* : [1977] E.C.R. 65, [1977] 1 C.M.L.R. 378; the *Perfumes* cases (Cases 253/78, 3, 37, & 99/79) [1980] E.C.R. 2327, [1981] 2 C.M.L.R. 99, and Case C–234/89, *Delimitis* v. *Henninger Bräu*: [1991] I E.C.R. 935, [1992] 5 C.M.L.R. 210.

[38] *Delimitis*, above, at para. 51.

[39] Case 63/75: [1976] E.C.R. 111, [1976] 1 C.M.L.R. 538.

[40] *Ibid.* at paras. 6, 7 and 8.

to be less harmful from the point of view of the objectives of this provision and which are therefore very likely to be entitled to the benefit of Article 85(3). In the majority of cases, agreements between two undertakings from one Member State will be so entitled if they grant exclusive sales concessions in relation to the marketing of goods, where the marketing envisaged by the agreement takes place solely within the territory of the Member State to whose law the undertakings are subject, even if the goods in question have at a former stage been imported from another Member State. Therefore, the fact that the products involved in such agreements have previously been imported from another Member State does not by itself mean that these agreements must be regarded as relating to imports within the meaning of Article 4(2) of Regulation 17."

The upshot of these decisions is that some local exclusive supply agreements may fall within Article 4(2)(1) even if the goods the subject of the agreement have at some previous stage been imported into the Member State concerned. But it is important to note the Court's reference (in the first part of the quotation) to agreements which are "less harmful" from the point of view of Article 85(1). So in *NAVEWA/ANSEAU*,[41] the Court of Justice found that the effect of the relevant agreement was to restrict the right to obtain conformity labels to certain manufacturers and sole importers of washing machines in Belgium with the alleged object and result of discouraging parallel imports and held that it concerned imports to a degree which could not be regarded as harmless. It therefore could not be exempt from the notification required for exemption under Article 85(3). It seems that it is necessary therefore to assess the importance of the agreement in the Member State concerned, its extent and significance on the market. In *SSI*,[42] both the Commission and the Court (*per* Advocate General VerLoren van Themaat) referred to the market share of the relevant goods. The nature of the restriction on the imported goods (in *SSI*, the price) may also be relevant. All this, as the reader will appreciate, may make Article 4(2)(1) difficult to apply in practice.

2.11   The necessity for the agreement to be truly local and not to have any direct impact on imports or exports has been made clear by the Commission.[43] In *BP Kemi/ DDSF*,[44] the Commission took the view that an agreement relating to the exclusive purchase of ethanol by DDSF, a Danish company, from BP Kemi, the Danish trading subsidiary of BPCL, a U.K. company in the BP group, "related to" imports and exports within the meaning of Article 4(2)(1). The subject matter of the agreement was ethanol imported into Denmark from the United Kingdom and the effect, the Commission stated, was to prevent the most important distributor in Denmark from importing from other sources of supply in the Community. It is also a condition of

---

[41] Cases 96–102, 104, 105, 108 & 110/82, *NV IAZ International Belgium SA* v. *Commission*: [1983] E.C.R. 3369, [1984] 3 C.M.L.R. 276, at paras. 30–35.

[42] *SSI*: [1982] O.J. L232/1, [1982] 3 C.M.L.R. 702, and on appeal, above, n. 30. Contrast the approach of the Commission in *Sugarbeet*: [1990] O.J. L31/32, [1991] 4 C.M.L.R. 629, where it proceeded on the basis that certain agreements of Belgian sugar producers, to the effect that Belgian growers received priority and French growers were excluded, fell within Art. 4(2). The Commission did not concern itself with the question whether the agreements related to imports or exports (they almost certainly related to the former).

[43] See, *e.g. GISA*: [1972] O.J. L303/45, [1973] C.M.L.R. D125; *Stoves and Heaters*: [1975] O.J. L159/22, [1975] 2 C.M.L.R. D1, and *Arthur Bell and Sons Ltd.*: [1978] O.J. L235/15, [1978] 3 C.M.L.R. 298.

[44] [1979] O.J. L286, 32, [1979] 3 C.M.L.R. 684.

Article 4(2)(1) that all the undertakings party must be "from one Member State." In *BP Kemi/DDSF*, the Commission said that although the parties who signed the purchase agreement were both situated in Denmark, the arrangements did not involve parties in only one Member State:

> "because one of the parties is selling only goods which are imported from a company in another Member State and this other company and the party in question are both controlled by the same third company. In effect, therefore, the arrangements, as admitted by the parties ... should be considered as having been made between BPCL and DDSF."

The Commission also emphasised that the benefit of Article 4(2) could not be obtained merely by delegating the formal conclusion of agreements to local subsidiaries. In *Fire Insurance (D)*,[45] the Commission indicated that parties will not be considered to be from one Member State where the head offices of some are situated outside the Member State albeit that those undertakings conduct business in the first Member State through local branches. In practice, therefore, great caution is necessary before relying on Article 4(2)(1).

2.12 Finally, it should be mentioned that whilst the present discussion of Article 4(2)(1) has concentrated to a great extent on the position of exclusive supply or purchase agreements, other types of agreement can of course come within its terms. For example, in *Vaessen/Moris*,[46] the Commission found that a patent licence between two undertakings from the same Member State fell within Article 4(2)(1) and was thus exempted from notification although it did not come within the terms of Article 4(2)(2)(b) discussed below.

(ii) *not more than two undertakings are parties thereto, and the agreements only restrict the freedom of one party to the contract in determining the prices or conditions of business upon which the goods which he has obtained from the other party to the contract may be resold.*[47]

2.13 Unlike (i) above, it does not seem to matter in this case whether the two undertakings are from different Member States or whether the agreement relates to imports or exports between Member States. The agreement must not contain any restrictions which do not relate to "the prices or conditions of business upon which the goods ... may be resold." The restriction must be on only one party[48] and must adhere to the goods "which he has obtained from the other party to the contract." There is no requirement that the goods must necessarily have been supplied under or in pursuance of the contract although this may well be the situation in many cases. A restriction on "prices" would presumably include a restriction as to the minimum, maximum or other level of prices to be charged, *i.e.* various forms of resale price maintenance. A

---

[45] [1985] O.J. L35/20.

[46] [1979] O.J. L19/32, [1979] 1 C.M.L.R. 511.

[47] Art. 4(2)(2)(a) of Reg. 17.

[48] See the *FEDETAB* case, Cases 209–215 & 218/78, *Heintz van Landewyck* v. *Commission*: [1980] E.C.R. 3125, [1981] 3 C.M.L.R. 134, at paras. 48–56, where the agreement failed to come within the terms of Art. 4(2) because it involved parties from more than one Member State and at least two accepted restrictions.

restriction on discounts would also appear to be included. The meaning of "conditions of business" is uncertain although it will not apparently include an export ban[49] (and the presence of such a provision will exclude the applicability of Article 4(2)(2)(a) even if the ban is not in fact applied.[50]) But it should presumably cover the terms and conditions on which the goods are to be resold. The restriction, whether as to prices or conditions of business, must not extend to goods which have not been obtained from the other party to the contract.

(iii) *not more than two undertakings are party thereto, and the agreements only impose restrictions on the exercise of the rights of the assignee or user of industrial property rights—in particular patents, utility models, designs or trade marks—or of the person entitled under a contract to the assignment, or grant, or the right to use a method of manufacture or knowledge relating to the use and to the application of industrial processes.[51]*

2.14 There is some doubt as to the ambit of this provision and it has been suggested that few agreements are likely to benefit from it.[52] The basic difficulty lies in making sure that any restrictions fall within the "rights" of the patent, trade mark, etc., In *Windsurfing*,[53] the Court of Justice held that Article 4(2)(2)(b) did not apply because the restrictive provisions exceeded the scope of the rights conferred by the patent because they also encompassed goods not covered by the patent and because there was a no-challenge clause relating to the patent and trade marks. A trade mark delimitation agreement has also been found to fall outside Article 4(2)(2)(b).[54] It is clear that no restriction may be accepted by the assignor/licensor or a third party.[55] It is therefore extremely doubtful whether an exclusive (or even sole) licence of, for example, a patent, comes within the terms of Article 4(2)(2)(b).[56] Anyone seeking to rely on this provision would be well advised to consider the Court's rulings in patent and trade mark licence cases, and also the block exemption on patent licensing agreements.[57]

---

[49] *Moët et Chandon (London) Ltd.*: [1982] O.J. L94/7, [1982] 2 C.M.L.R. 166.
[50] *Polistil/Arbois*: [1984] O.J. L136/9, [1984] 2 C.M.L.R. 594.
[51] Art. 4(2)(2)(b) of Reg. 17.
[52] Ritter, Brown and Rawlinson, *EEC Competition Law: A Practitioner's Guide* (1991), at p. 614 (n. 110).
[53] Case 193/83, *Windsurfing International Inc.* v. *Commission*: [1986] E.C.R. 611, [1986] 3 C.M.L.R. 489, at para. 100. In *Vaessen/Moris*, above, n. 41, the Commission had found similar restrictions excluded Art. 4(2)(2)(b).
[54] *Toltecs/Dorcet*: [1982] O.J. L379/19, [1983] 1 C.M.L.R. 412. On appeal, Case 35/83, *BAT Cigaretten-Fabriken* v. *Commission*: [1985] E.C.R. 363, [1985] 2 C.M.L.R. 470, *per* A.G. Slynn.
[55] See, *e.g. Advocaat Zwarte Kip*: [1974] O.J. L237/12, [1974] 2 C.M.L.R. D79.
[56] That is, to the extent the exclusive licence falls within Art. 85(1). See Case 258/78, *Nungesser and Eisele* v. *Commission*: [1982] E.C.R. 2015, [1983] 1 C.M.L.R. 276.
[57] Reg. 2349/84.

(iv) *agreements which have as their sole object:*

(a) the development or uniform application of standards or types; or
(b) joint research and development; or
(c) specialisation in the manufacture of products, including agreements necessary for the achievement thereof:
   (i) where the products which are the object of specialisation do not, in a substantial part of the Common Market, represent more than 15 per cent. of the volume of business done in identical products or those considered by the consumers to be similar by reason of their characteristics, price and use, and
   (ii) where the total annual turnover of the participating undertakings does not exceed 200 million units of account.[58]

2.15   The first thing to note is that the agreement must have as its "sole object" one of the matters listed (a) to (c). In practice this may well be a serious limiting factor.[59] Parties involved in agreements concerning (b) joint research or (c) specialisation are advised to consider carefully the block exemption for research and development agreements[60] and for specialisation agreements,[61] wherein lies greater legal security. They may also have regard to the Notice on Co-operation Agreements.[62] Under (c), the specialisation must not exceed the manufacturing stage. As will readily be apparent, the criteria specified in (c) (in particular, "substantial part of the Common Market" and "identical products") may not be applied easily or with any great degree of certainty in a particular case. In practice not many specialisation agreements come within the terms of Article 4(2)(3)(c).[63]

Notification for exemption — procedure

2.16   Notification for the purposes of seeking an exemption under Article 85(3) must be made on Form A/B[64] and contain the information requested by the Form and the Complementary Note.[65] There are no time-limits specified for such notification by

---

[58] Art. 4(2)(3) of Reg. 17, as amended by Reg. 2822/71.
[59] See, *e.g. Siemens/Fanuc*: [1985] O.J. L376/29 [1988] 4 C.M.L.R. 945. *Cf.* the importance of "sole object" in relation to the Notice on Co-operation Agreements, see *Roofing Felt*: [1986] O.J. L232/15, [1991] 4 C.M.L.R. 130.
[60] Reg. 418/85.
[61] Reg. 417/85.
[62] [1968] J.O. C75/3. But now dated and probably not that useful in practice. And note *Beecham/Parke Davis*: [1979] O.J. L70/11, [1979] 2 C.M.L.R. 157.
[63] See, *e.g. Italian Cast Glass*: [1980] O.J. L383/19, [1982] 2 C.M.L.R. 61.
[64] Art. 4(1) of Reg. 27.
[65] Art. 4(2) of Reg. 27. For discussion on completion Form A/B, see paras. 2.21–27. Any notification should make clear that exemption is sought—so asking for a declaration that a particular block exemption applies may not suffice if an individual exemption proves to be necessary. *Ivoclar*: [1985] O.J. L369/1, [1988] 4 C.M.L.R. 781. The parties' request for termination of proceedings against their agreement may indicate that their request for an examination under Art. 85(3) has lapsed. See *Video-Cassettes*: [1978] O.J. L47/42, [1978] 2 C.M.L.R. 160.

Regulation 17 and generally speaking an agreement may be notified to the Commission at any time.[66] Where agreements are formally amended, renotification may be appropriate.[67] There are, as might be expected, separate forms for use in transport cases: Form II for notifications under Regulation 1017/68, Form MAR under Regulation 4056/86 and Form AER under Regulation 3975/87. The procedure is also different and is described below. All the forms have been modified by Regulation 3666/93 to take account of the EEA.

For cases under Regulation 17 the Commission will initiate a procedure but, as in the case of negative clearance, there may not be any need for all the further procedural steps common to cases of infringement where the Commission proposes to take a decision under Article 3 of Regulation 17. It may be, however, that there are matters on which the undertakings must be given the opportunity to be heard: for example, in relation to the imposition of conditions or obligations under Article 8. It is also possible for the procedure to begin as for an infringement and then because, for example, the agreement is amended, to continue as for an exemption.[68] Indeed it is by no means unusual for agreements to be amended at some stage in order to secure favourable treatment.[69] The Court of Justice has recognised that the Commission's procedure provides an opportunity for the undertakings concerned to bring their agreements into conformity with the competition rules and that any negotiations with the Commission in order to determine what changes may be necessary to the Commission's objections are entitled to confidentiality.[70] Discussions and negotiations may also precede the formal procedure. The Commission is required, before taking any decision granting exemption, to publish a summary of the relevant notification and invite all interested third parties to submit their observations within a specified time limit being not less than one month.[71] The reactions of third parties may be particularly important where the Commission is using a proposed decision as a precedent for an industry practice.[72] The publication must have regard to the legitimate interests of undertakings in the protection of their business secrets. The publication is made in the *Official Journal*.

---

[66] See, *e.g. Nuovo CEGAM*: [1984] O.J. L99/29, [1984] 2 C.M.L.R., 484, where the notification was after the statement of objections. Note that "old" and "accession" agreements have to be notified within a specified time in order to benefit from the provisions of Art. 7 of Reg. 17. See para. 6.30. Such agreements may also be provisionally valid. See paras. 10.04–07.

[67] *VIFKA*: [1986] O.J. L291/46.

[68] See, *e.g. Optical Fibres*: [1986] O.J. L236/30 and *U.I.P.*: [1989] O.J. L226/25, [1990] 4 C.M.L.R. 749. In the latter case the parties also gave certain undertakings. See para. 6.61.

[69] *E.g. Pronuptia*: [1987] O.J. L13/39, [1989] 4 C.M.L.R. 355; *Yves Rocher*: [1987] O.J. L8/49, [1988] 4 C.M.L.R. 592, and *Eirpage*: [1991] O.J. L306/22, [1993] 4 C.M.L.R. 64.

[70] Cases 142 and 156/84, *BAT and Reynolds* v. *Commission*: [1987] E.C.R. 4487, [1988] 4 C.M.L.R. 24, at para. 23.

[71] Art. 19(3) of Reg. 17. For a recent example, see *GVst/VIK*: [1992] O.J. C249/3. Such a notice may propose a comfort letter as an alternative to an exemption decision, *e.g. ICL/Fujitsu*: [1986] O.J. C210/3. It seems to be the exception rather than the rule that the Art. 19(3) notices excites comments from third parties, but see, *e.g. EBU/Eurovision System*: [1993] O.J. L179/23. See also *SABA's EEC Distribution System*: [1983] O.J. L37/41, [1984] 1 C.M.L.R. 676, where the notice even sparked off a question in the Parliament (Written Question No. 669/83, [1983] O.J. C335/3) and *KSB/Goulds/Lowara/ITT*: [1991] O.J. L19/25, [1992] 5 C.M.L.R. 55, where it sparked a request for interim protective measures. Third party comments may trigger off wider investigations (*e.g.* into motor vehicle manufacturers' policy of not tolerating any parts-suppliers marks in addition to their own trademarks — see *Iveco/Ford*: [1988] O.J. L230/39) but not necessarily prejudice the procedure of the case in hand. Third parties may even provide support for exemption, see *X/Open Group*: [1987] O.J. L35/36, [1988] 4 C.M.L.R. 542.

[72] See *Yves Saint Laurent Parfums*: [1992] O.J. L12/24, [1993] 4 C.M.L.R. 120 and *Parfums Givenchy system of selective distribution*: [1992] O.J. L236/11.

It is for the undertakings in the first place to submit convincing information to the Commission to substantiate the economic justification for the exemption.[73] The applicant should show that each of the conditions laid down in Article 85(3) is satisfied and therefore should set out in Form A/B its position on each of those conditions.[74] The Commission must, as a matter of good administration, play its part, using the means available to it, to ascertain the relevant facts and circumstances.[75] It must, for example, take account of the special nature of certain economic sectors and of the problems peculiar to those sectors.[76] Where the Commission raises objections it may be necessary for the undertaking to submit alterations to accommodate these. Although the Commission can and may provide undertakings with information on possible alternative solutions, it is not legally obliged to do so.[77]

Transport cases — "objections" procedure

2.17 A special procedure for exemption is applicable in transport cases. Each of the three implementing regulations provides a procedure entitled "Objections"[78] but which is probably better described as an opposition procedure (this should not however be confused with the opposition procedure provided by several of the block exemptions and which is described at the end of this chapter). The scheme of the implementing regulations concerning transport envisages undertakings themselves, in the first instance, judging whether the predominant effects of their agreements, etc., are restrictive of competition or the economic benefits acceptable as justification for such restrictions. They appear to contemplate notification for exemption being the exception and provide a special "simplified" procedure for the case where undertakings wish to ensure that their agreements are in conformity with the competition rules. Under the procedure the Commission on receipt of a notification judges first whether the application is admissible and whether it is in possession of all the necessary information. The case must also be one where the Commission is not acting on a complaint or otherwise taking infringement proceedings against the agreement in question. The Commission then publishes in the *Official Journal* a summary of the application and invites the Member States and all interested third parties to submit comments within 30 days.[79] The publication in the *Official Journal* must have regard to the protection of business secrets. In the absence of any complaint from Member States or interested third parties and provided the Commission does not notify the applicant undertakings within 90 days[80] from the date of the publication in the *Official Journal* that there are

---

[73] Case 42/84, *Remia and Nutricia* v. *Commission*: [1985] E.C.R. 2545, [1987] 1 C.M.L.R. 1, at para. 45.

[74] Case T–66/89, *Publishers Association* v. *Commission*: [1992] II E.C.R. 1995, [1992] 5 C.M.L.R. 120, at para. 69. In *Ansac*: [1991] O.J. L152/54, the Commission said that the burden is on the applicant to show that the restrictions in question should bring about an objective improvement over the situation which would have existed in their absence.

[75] Cases 56 & 58/64, *Consten and Grundig* v. *Commission*: [1966] E.C.R. 299, 347, [1966] C.M.L.R. 418.

[76] Insurance, for example, Case 45/85, *Verband der Sachversicherer eV* v. *Commission*: [1987] E.C.R. 405, [1988] 4 C.M.L.R. 264, at para. 15.

[77] *Dutch Books*: Cases 43 & 63/82, *VBVB and VBBB* v. *Commission*: [1984] E.C.R. 19, [1985] 1 C.M.L.R. 27, at para. 52.

[78] See Reg. 1017/88 (Art. 12), Reg. 4056/86 (Art. 12) and Reg. 3975/87 (Art. 5).

[79] See, *e.g.* [1989] O.J. C204/12, Joint venture agreements between London City Airways and SAbena relating to a service between London City Airport and Brussels, and [1993] O.J. C57/5, Agreements in the rail transport and goods via the Channel Tunnel.

[80] The time period has led to difficulties on some cases. See Soames in *Butterworths Competition Law* Encyclopedia, para. 32, dealing with the *Air France/Air Inter* case.

serious doubts as to the legality of the agreement in question, the agreement is deemed exempted from the prohibition for the time already elapsed[81] and for a further period of three years in cases under Regulation 1017/68 or six years in other cases from the date of publication in the *Official Journal*. If the Commission finds, after the expiry of the 90-day period, but before the expiry of the exemption period, that the conditions of Article 85(3) are not satisfied, it can issue a prohibition decision. That decision may be retroactive where the undertakings concerned have given inaccurate information or where they have abused the exemption or have contravened Article 86. In maritime and air transport cases, the Commission is obliged, at the request of a Member State, to raise "serious doubts" and thereby stop the automatic procedure running. But the Member State must make its request within 45 days of the Commission forwarding the application to it and must base its request on Community competition rules considerations. Where "serious doubts" have been expressed,[82] whether following the request of a Member State or otherwise (for example, in response to representations from third parties), the agreement can still be considered for an individual exemption decision under Article 85(3), the Commission being satisfied that no serious doubts remain.

Benefits of notification

2.18

(a) The prime stated purpose[83] of notification is to enable the granting of exemption under Article 85(3). An agreement which has an exemption may be enforced in a national court without fear of the application of Article 85(2). But only the Commission can grant an exemption. If the agreement has not been notified, then a national court may (in the absence of an applicable block exemption) have little choice but to apply Article 85(2).[84] The enforceability of an agreement may be very important (particularly, for example, if it relates to valuable property such as patents or know-how).

(b) In the case of both "old" agreements[85] and "accession" agreements[86] duly and timeously notified, the Commission may retrospectively validate an agreement under Article 7 of Regulation 17 where it is subsequently modified in such

---

[81] From the date of the notification or of entry into force of the agreement in question. It is unclear but the latter is more consistent with the scheme of the transport regulations procedures.

[82] See Soames, *op. cit.*, at para. 91(2).

[83] Art. 4(1) of Reg. 17 provides that the Commission shall be notified of any agreements "for which those concerned wish to invoke Art. 85 para. 3." Except for agreements which fall within the categories of agreements exempted from notification under Art. 4(2) or within a block or group exemption, notification is a prerequisite for exemption under Art. 85(3).

[84] It cannot apply Art. 85(3) and unless the agreement is exempt from notification under Art. 4(2) of Reg. 17 there would seem to be little point in staying the proceedings unless the agreement has been notified so that the Commission could apply Art. 85(3) if appropriate. See Case C–234/89, *Delimitis* v. *Henninger Bräu*: [1991] I E.C.R. 935, [1992] 5 C.M.L.R. 210, at para. 51. The implications of this judgment and the Commission's recent Notice on co-operation with national courts are discussed at para. 10.13.

[85] *I.e.* those agreements in existence on the introduction of Reg. 17.

[86] *I.e.* those agreements in existence at the date of accession (January 1, 1973, January 1, 1981 or January 1, 1986, as appropriate) and to which Art. 85 applies be virtue of accession.

manner as to remove it from the prohibition in Article 85(1) or to enable it to satisfy the criteria of Article 85(3).[87]

(c) "Old" agreements, and most probably also "accession" agreements, which have been duly and timeously notified have provisional validity.[88]

(d) Fines in respect of infringements of Article 85(1) or 86 of the Treaty cannot be imposed by the Commission in respect of acts taking place after notification and before its decision in application of Article 85(3), provided they fall within the limits of the activity described in the notification.[89] The phrase "before its decision in application of Article 85(3)" does not mean that the immunity from fines exists only if an exemption is granted. A decision finding an infringement of Article 85(1) and refusing an exemption under Article 85(3) is a decision "in application of Article 85(3)". The proviso relating to acts within the limit of the activity described in the notification is very important and is unlikely to be construed otherwise than strictly by the Commission. Immunity from fine presupposes full disclosure. The notification must be a valid one.[90] Note that a mere application for negative clearance does not confer immunity from fine.[91] For this reason, applications are almost invariably coupled with a notification for exemption. Form A/B provides for this.

(e) Finally, as an official of the Commission has stated, notification may establish a party's bona fides and get its version of the story on the Commission's files first.[92]

In practice, the desire to obtain immunity from fine ((d) above) is a major consideration for the notification of many agreements, although a fine is usually dependent on the unacceptable nature of the infringement rather than failure to notify and indeed the notification of a clear infringement may be treated as an abuse of the process and invalid.[93] Enforceability in national courts is also considered an important factor particularly where third parties may be concerned or the agreement may be publicly visible (*e.g.* a major joint venture). The legitimate desire to gain greater (if not perfect) legal certainty where the agreement is of major commercial significance and the parties wish to be sure that they can rely on the obligations inter se may be uppermost in some cases. Many agreements continue to be notified, sometimes unnecessarily, because a block exemption applies. The decision whether to notify can be a difficult one.[94] Parties who fail to notify are not necessarily to be taken to be hiding something

---

[87] Art. 7 of Reg. 17 is discussed at paras. 6.29–31 There is an EEA equivalent which could be especially helpful in its early days.

[88] Provisional validity is discussed in Chap. 10, at paras. 10.04–11. This will be important in EEA cases.

[89] Art. 15(5) of Reg. 17, discussed at para. 7.33. and note Art. 15(6).

[90] *I.e.* it must comply with Art. 4 of Reg. 27, see *Sperry New Holland*: [1985] O.J. L376/21, [1988] 4 C.M.L.R. 306.

[91] *John Deere*: [1985] O.J. L35/58, [1985] 2 C.M.L.R. 554.

[92] See Temple Lang, "EEC Competition Policies: A Status Report" in *Enterprise Law of the 80s* (1980), at p. 38.

[93] This is the position under several Member States domestic law but the Court has yet to rule on this. See Korah, *An Introductory Guide to EEC Competition Law and Practice* (4th ed., 1990) at p. 155.

[94] See Siragusa, "Notification of Agreements in the EEC — To Notify or Not to Notify" [1986] Fordham Corp. L. Inst. 243, and Holley, "EEC Competition Practice: A Thirty Year Retrospective" 16 Fordham Int. L.J. 342, at pp. 350–357.

exceptionally harmful or offensive. Parties may not unnaturally wish to avoid disclosure, the burden of completing Form A/B and the regulatory process including intervention and possible renegotiation, perhaps years later, by the Commission involving
amendment of the agreement. They may order their affairs and conclude, quite hon-
estly and fairly after a full review of its status, that their agreement or practice is consistent with Article 85.[95] Notification will be considered mainly where the position
under Article 85 or 86 is unclear and where, if Article 85(1) applies, it may be possible
to obtain an exemption.[96] But at the end of the day, the decision is essentially a commercial one for the parties concerned.[97]

Importance of Form A/B

2.19 The importance which is attached to the use of Form A/B has been a feature of
a number of decisions of the Court. In *FEDETAB*,[98] the Court of Justice held that the
submission of an agreement in response to a request for information made by the
Commission under Article 11 of Regulation 17 did not constitute notification for the
purposes of exemption under Article 85(3). The Court considered that use of Form
A/B as provided for by the regulations was obligatory and an indispensable condition
of a valid notification. Justification for this view, the Court said, lay in Article 87(2)(b)
of the Treaty which specifies "the need to ensure effective supervision on the one
hand, and to simplify administration to the greatest possible extent on the other." If in
any doubt as to how to notify the whole or any part of any agreement, or additions or
amendments to an already notified agreement, use Form A/B. As the Court stressed in
Pioneer,[99] notification is not a mere formality but an indispensable condition for
obtaining benefits. An undertaking which does not notify takes the risk[1] of being fined
if its agreement is found to infringe Article 85(1). An undertaking cannot claim,
on being fined, that there was a hypothetical possibility that notification might
have led to an exemption. As Advocate General Warner said in *Distillers* v.
Commission:[2]

---

[95] See, generally, Forrester and Norall, "The Laicization of Community law, Self-Help and the Rule of Reason: How Competition Law is and could be applied" (1984) 31 C.M.L.Rev. 11., where it is suggested that
consistency with Art. 85 may be for reasons which are in part dependent on Art. 85(3) rather than Art.
85(1). The authors acknowledge the commercial risks involved.
[96] Siragusa, *op. cit.*, at p. 283.
[97] See, generally, Brown, "Notification of Agreements to EC Commission: Whether to Submit to a Flawed
System" (1992) 17 E.L. Rev. 323. At one time there appeared to be "notifying" and "non-notifying" na-
tionalities; see Holley, *op. cit.*, at p. 353
[98] Cases 209–215 & 218/78, *Heintz van Landewyck* v. *Commission*: [1980] E.C.R. 3125, [1981] 3
C.M.L.R. 134, at paras. 57–63. For a recent example of the need for Form A/B, see *Eco System/Peugeot*:
[1992] O.J. L66/1, [1993] 4 C.M.L.R. 42, where the Commission held that a circular sent in draft could
not be considered a notification for exemption.
[99] Cases 100–103/80, *Musique Diffusion Francaise* v. *Commission*: [1983] E.C.R. 1813, [1983] 3
C.M.L.R. 221, at paras. 92–93. One appellant claimed that the substantive conditions for exemption were
satisfied and that therefore it could have obtained an exemption by notification. The infringement was
therefore merely one of a procedural rule, namely the failure to notify. The Court firmly rejected this.
[1] See text to n. 97. Note the nature of the offence in *Pioneer*.
[2] Case 30/78: [1980] E.C.R. 2229, [1980] 3 C.M.L.R. 121.

"It would hardly be consistent with the aims there expressed to hold that an undertaking that had not complied with the Regulation was entitled to the same treatment as one that had. Moreover, apart from disclosing the agreement in question to the Commission, formal notification does three things: it establishes that, in case the agreement should be caught by Article 85(1), exemption under Article 85(3) is sought; it identifies the grounds on which such exemption is sought, and it fixes, in accordance with Article 6(1) of Regulation 17, the earliest date from which the exemption may take effect."

The Court of Justice's decision in *Distillers* indicates how strictly the rules will be applied and the critical consequences of any failure to comply. Distillers introduced new terms and conditions of supply (substituting differential prices for the export ban in its standard contract which had been notified two years previously). Customers were circulated but not the Commission who wrote to Distillers, followed by a request under Article 11, for particulars of the new terms. The Commission condemned both the old and new agreements, refusing exemption on two grounds, no notification and no merits.³ The Court upheld the Commission's decision, rejecting the argument that to refuse exemption because of non-use of Form A/B would be too formal an application and interpretation of the notification rules. Moreover, it did not matter that in its dealings the Commission had not insisted on notification and had used the same reference numbers throughout. The Court also rejected *sub silentio* Distillers' argument that the notification of its conditions of sale covered the price terms because the objective of the latter was the same as the export prohibition although they were less strict.⁴

2.20 The Court of Justice clearly regards Form A/B as having a most necessary and important function in connection with the Commission's ability to grant an exemption and consequent need for the information it contains. Having said this, the Court has on a number of occasions shown a more pragmatic and less formalistic approach. In *Eldi Records*,⁵ it held that where a complete text of the agreement had been supplied with the form of notification it did not matter that only some of the clauses containing restrictions had been identified provided that the description given in the form consti-

---

³ It has been the practice of the Commission even where an exemption is refused on the grounds of lack of notification to proceed to consider whether, had notification been effected properly, the agreement justified exemption on its merits. This saves administrative time and resources. If the Commission decision only dealt with the non-notification, it would be open to a party to notify and then the administrative procedure, including the oral hearing and consultation with the Advisory Committee, might have to be gone through again. Nonetheless, the Commission cannot and will not exempt on an "as if" notified basis. See *Zinc Producer Group*: [1984] O.J. L220/27, [1985] 2 C.M.L.R. 108.
⁴ Contrast the position in Case 106/79, *VBBB* v. *Eldi Records*: [1980] E.C.R. 1137, [1980] 3 C.M.L.R. 719, where one category of goods ceased to be subject to a general restriction and then later returned to it. The Court considered that this was covered by the original notification. The field of application had not been extended but merely limited temporarily.
⁵ *Ibid.*

tuted a fair and accurate record of the provisions which at the time were considered the most important. The Court said:[6]

> "If the agreement has been reduced to writing, and if a copy of its entire text is attached to the form, the information given on that form is intended solely to facilitate verification. If that information is correct, and above all it relates fairly to the provisions which at the time were considered the most important, the objectives of the notification seem to be obtained."

This is both fair and realistic having regard to the continually evolving state of Community competition law and the fact that years may pass between notification and final decision. The Court also took the view that an agreement must be regarded as properly notified in its entirety unless the intention to notify only a part of the agreement emerges clearly from the information supplied.[7] In *Metro II*,[8] the Court of Justice held that a formal application is not necessary for a renewal of an exemption even where the agreement has been substantially amended since the original notification. Where the new version does not differ in principle then a mere application (*e.g.* by letter) plus a communication of amendments will be sufficient.

Form A/B is not, however, to be regarded as simply a certificate or covering letter. It requires certain information to be provided, restrictions identified and justification given. The Court considers the answers to the questions in Form A/B necessary to put the Commission in a position to take a decision.[9] And, as the Commission has indicated, notification only makes eligible for exemption conduct which is sufficiently clearly described in the notification.[10] More recently the Commission has said that where an undertaking chooses to notify an agreement it must collaborate fairly with the Commission and no important information must be withheld. The Commission has referred to a principle of fair and full notification.[11] The present Form A/B requires more information and greater specificity than its predecessor. It is unclear how far the Court's words in *Eldi* (quoted above) remain good. It is to be hoped that both the Court and the Commission will continue to accept a fair and reasonable standard. There is a great deal of scope so far as the fullness and length of the notification is concerned and in practice the Commission has shown itself to be flexible and pragmatic.

---

[6] *Ibid.* at para. 10. Emphasis added.

[7] *Ibid.*

[8] See Case 75/84, *Metro-SB-Grossmarkte GmbH & Co. K.G.* v. *Commission*: [1986] E.C.R. 3021, [1987] 1 C.M.L.R. 118, at paras. 31 and 37. See also para. 6.36.

[9] *Eldi*, above, at para. 10, and *Distillers*, above, at para. 22. But it must be doubtful if any exemptions have been granted simply on the basis of the information on Form A/B. and see para. 2.17.

[10] *Aluminium*: [1985] O.J. L92/1, [1987] 3 C.M.L.R. 813.

[11] *Eurocheque: Helsinki Agreement*: [1992] O.J. L95/50.

Completion of Form A/B

(i) *Generally*

2.21   The present Form A/B was introduced on January 1, 1986[12] and was recently (by Regulation 3666/93) revised to enable its use for notifications for exemption under Article 85(3) and/or Article 53(3) EEA. It comprises one (double-sided) sheet which the undertaking must complete and to which it must annex all the other information sought in the Complementary Note (in particular under the seven headings set out in Part X of the Note). In view of the sanctions for an incomplete or incorrect submission (refusal of exemption, no immunity from fine and, possibly, even a fine under Article 15(1)(a)) the greatest care should be taken in relation to each and every question. The form is designed to be user-friendly but it nonetheless requires a considerable amount of information, some of it detailed and technical. Legal advisers completing the form for their clients should, as always, obtain the fullest instructions. Remember that it will be the commercial and economic implications of the agreements (or "arrangements" as the form designates them) which will concern the Commission, not just the legal considerations. For this reason the company secretary may not be the only or best person able to give instructions. It will be useful to speak, for example, to the commercial and marketing personnel who put the agreement together and others concerned in its day-to-day operation. A company cannot do more than employ best endeavours. Often good market information is not available.

Before looking in more detail at the form itself and the headings in Part X of the Complementary Note, some general points should be made:

(a)   The present form can be used for exemption under Article 85(1) and/or Article 53(3) EEA.[13]

(b)   It is quite clear that it is not just the questions on the two sides of the form which must be answered. Applications and notifications must contain all the information asked for in the Complementary Note.[14] In effect the questions listed in particular in Part X become questions on the form.

(c)   A good number of the questions can only be answered by giving estimates and opinions. This is particularly so where accurate information is not readily available and is nowhere more true than in relation to questions 2 (Market) and 3.3 and 3.4 (turnover and market share). Estimates, the Note says, must be identified as such and must be best estimates.[15]

(d)   All matters in the Form and the Note must be addressed. If the applicant believes any detail asked for to be unavailable or irrelevant, then it should not be passed over. An explanation must be given.

---

[12] Introduced by Reg. 2526/85 amending Reg. 27. See, generally, Reynolds, "Practical Aspects of Notifying Agreements and the new Form A/B" in Fordham University's 1985 Corporate law Institute's Antitrust and Trade Policy in the U.S. and EEC.

[13] The second recital to Reg. 2526/85 states: "It is desirable to adapt the design of Form A/B in the light of experience and, in particular, of the fact that the form used hitherto does not require applicants to give all the information necessary for a decision."

[14] Art. 4(2) of Reg. 27, as amended.

[15] Indeed the form itself requires the applicant to make a declaration to this effect and that all opinions expressed are sincere.

(e) As the Note indicates, an undertaking uncertain how to complete a notification or wishing further explanation may contact DG IV. Commission officials are available to discuss any problems or difficulties (such as what detail is relevant). But caution is necessary. Where preliminary meetings have been held with Commission officials prior to notification they do not absolve the parties from the duty and need to make a full and proper notification.[16]

(f) Business secrets[17] should be put in a second annex and references to that annex inserted in the main annex under the relevant heading. The second annex (each page clearly marked "Business Secrets") must repeat the affected heading and reference and give the information for which secrecy is claimed together with the reasons for this.

(g) Finally, although the Commission will acknowledge receipt (provided always that one copy of the slip is completed), if the notification is in some way deficient or faulty the fact that the Commission accepts and registers the form and annex and does not query or raise any objection does not amount to acceptance of its validity. Nor does it raise any estoppel to prevent the Commission later denying the validity of the notification.[18]

2.22   The Form itself requires the identification of the applicant and other parties,[19] definition of the purpose of the submission, and a formal declaration as to the correctness of information, etc. The section "Purposes of this application/notification" is noteworthy. It requires the applicant to answer quite precisely, yes or no, a series of questions which can leave neither the applicant nor the Commission in any doubt as to exactly what is being sought. As already mentioned, Form A/B can be used for both negative clearance and exemption (and also for the opposition procedure where available) and both can be applied for at the same time. The fact that a party applies in the alternative for exemption should not, it is submitted, be treated as an admission that the agreement falls within the prohibition in Article 85(1). For example, analysis of the effects of the agreement on competition will be relevant both to its significance under Article 85(1) and to the question, arising under Article 85(3), as to whether the agreement eliminates competition in respect of a substantial part of the products in question. Finally, it should be noted that the applicant is asked whether it would be satisfied with a comfort letter.[20] This question may not be the easiest to answer, the

---

[16] *Aluminium*, above, and more recently *Eco System/Peugeot*: [1992] O.J. L66/1, [1993] 4 C.M.L.R. 42.

[17] See, generally, paras. 8.18–21.

[18] *Aluminium*, above. This is equally true of notifications under the opposition procedure—see para. 2.43. But it will have to be seen whether the new practice of the Commission setting time-limits (see para. 2.28) affects the position.

[19] Negative clearances and exemptions can be sought without the consent, but not without the knowledge, of other parties to the agreement.

[20] See paras. 6.53–59.

theoretical limitations having to be balanced against the practical and procedural advantages in the particular case.[21] Most companies are satisfied with comfort letters as there may be timing and publicity benefits.

Heading 1 requires a brief description of the arrangements or behaviour in question. It should not present much difficulty. Full details of the arrangements are supplied under Heading 4. A brief description of the purpose of the arrangements must be given and three copies of the text attached (technical descriptions contained in know-how agreements may be omitted, but the omission must be indicated). Be sure to attach copies of the definitive texts of agreements if or as soon as available, else there is a risk that the notification may not be considered complete and an exemption granted only from receipt of the definitive text.[22] If the parties understand the agreement or any term of it in a way which is not the normal or natural interpretation of it, that should also be stated. Parties cannot rely on any ambiguity in the notification. It may be necessary to look carefully at and explain the application of an agreement. In *AEG-Telefunken*,[23] the Commission took the view that as AEG had not disclosed how its whole distribution system had worked in practice the notification was insufficient. Parties should not rely on the fact that something may have been publicly reported or is generally known.[24] Where the contents of agreements are not, or are only partially, reduced to writing then the fullest description must be given. The Commission considers that where no text is notified the parties have a special duty to state fully, exactly and fairly everything that is relevant.[24a] Where a framework or master agreement is notified care should be taken to disclose agreements operating below it.[25] 4.2 requires the parties to give details of any provisions which may restrict their freedom to take independent commercial decisions in relation to a variety of matters, such as prices, choice of markets and sources of supply. The list is long and not exhaustive. In *Eldi*,[26] the Court of Justice considered it sufficient to identify the restrictions which at the time were considered the most important. That case was under the old regime and the present Form A/B may require a greater effort here.

Heading 2 deals with the market. The nature of the goods or services affected and a brief description of the structure of the market must be given. The applicant does not have to provide a definition of the market as such but still has to assess and describe how competitive it is, its geographical extent, entry barriers and substitute products. Clearly there is room for differences of opinion and applicants may do no better than express bona fide opinion and supply best estimates. If there are any studies of the market of which the applicant knows, these should be pointed out.

---

[21] Brown, *op. cit.*, robustly advises that the answer should normally be "yes". The Commission is unlikely to take further action unless the circumstances change and national courts will take the Commission's stance into consideration.

[22] *BVB/ABB*: [1987] O.J. L7/27, [1989] 4 C.M.L.R. 141. Reynolds, *op. cit.*, discusses the question of notifying heads of agreement or a memorandum in advance of definitive texts in joint venture cases. He points to the Commission's notice in *PRB/Shell*: [1984] O.J. C189/2 as an example of the Commission's preparedness to clear heads of agreement. But Reynolds doubts whether this absolves the parties from the need to furnish final definitive texts.

[23] [1982] O.J. L117/15, [1982] 2 C.M.L.R. 386. See also *Hasselblad*: [1982] O.J. L161/18, [1982] 2 C.M.L.R. 233.

[24] *Aluminium*: [1985] O.J. L92/1, [1987] 3 C.M.L.R. 813.

[24a] *Ibid.*

[25] *SSI*: [1982] O.J. L232/1, [1982] 3 C.M.L.R. 702, where the framework agreement covered unnotified price agreements.

[26] Case 106/79, *VBBB* v. *Eldi Records*: [1980] E.C.R. 1137, [1980] 3 C.M.L.R. 719, discussed at para. 2.20. Remember that the old Form A/B required less information.

Heading 3 requires fuller details of the parties. In particular it is necessary to explain any group relationship (as defined in the Complementary Note) giving details of related companies and last sets of individual and group accounts. It is also necessary to give sales and turnover figures for each party, and estimates of market. It is necessary to give each party's total EEA-wide turnover, and the figures and percentage of that turnover achieved within the Community and within the EFTA States. Other detailed geographical breakdowns of turnover are also required. One should not underestimate this task.[27] Information is often not recorded or retained in a manner which enables it to be readily drawn on for the purposes of completing Form A/B. The Complementary Note acknowledges that best estimates may be all that can be supplied.

Heading 5 requires an applicant for negative clearance to explain why this is thought necessary (what provisions or effects raise questions of compatibility with the competition rules?), why the arrangements do not have an anti-competitive object or effect, and why inter-state trade is not appreciably affected. "Inter-State" trade here has a threefold dimension; between E.C. Member States, between the Community and one or more EFTA States, or between EFTA States. The intention is to encourage applications for negative clearance only where there is some genuine doubt to be resolved.

Heading 6, "Reasons for exemption", requires the applicant to explain how the arrangements satisfy all the criteria in Article 85(3) and/or Article 53(3) EEA. As the Court of Justice reaffirmed in *Nutricia*,[28] it is primarily the responsibility of the undertakings seeking exemption to provide the material, facts and reasons to justify exemption. The Note acknowledges that parties may wish to notify if only as a precaution but at the same time draws attention to the block exemptions, noting that if they apply the parties avoid the considerable bother and expense of submitting a notification where there is clearly no doubt.[29] One can write informally for confirmation that an agreement comes within a particular block exemption.

Heading 7, "Other information", is something of a catch-all, requiring, *inter alia*, parties to inform the Commission of any earlier proceedings or informal contacts with the Commission (there are obvious advantages for both the Commission and the parties), allowing applicants to indicate if it is intended to produce further supporting facts and arguments not yet available, and asking the applicant to state the urgency of the application or notification. In giving additional information under this heading the parties should maintain the same standard of care as regards accuracy and completeness as in the remainder of the submission.

---

[27] Reynolds, *op. cit.*, comments: "On any view the information required is complex and extensive quite apart from the problems which will arise if the notifier is uncertain as to what is the relevant market."

[28] Case 42/84, *Remia and Nutricia* v. *Commission*: [1985] E.C.R. 2545, [1987] 1 C.M.L.R. 1, at para. 45. Cited by the Commission recently in *Building and construction industry in the Netherlands*: [1992] O.J. L92/1.

[29] Part V of the Complementary Note. The recitals to the block exemptions point in the other direction, drawing attention to the ability to seek a declaration from the Commission on an individual exemption in a particular case. See Reg. 1983/83, rec. 14; Reg. 1984/83, rec. 22; Reg. 2349/84, rec. 27; Reg. 417/85, rec. 9; Reg. 418/85, rec. 18; and Reg. 4087/88, rec. 16.

(ii) *Particular points*

2.23 (i) *Persons entitled to submit.* An application (for negative clearance) or notification (for exemption) can only be made by an undertaking which is party to the agreement in question.[30] The application or notification does not have to be made by all the parties to the agreement in question. It is sufficient if only one makes the application or notification but if all the undertakings party to the agreement do not submit it, the party or parties making the application or notification must inform the others that it has been made.[31] There is no requirement that all the undertakings must consent to the application or notification.[32] Several participating undertakings can submit an application or notification on a single form.[33]

2.24 (ii) *Representatives.* Applications and notifications may be signed by representatives on behalf of the undertakings concerned. In this event, written proof of the representative's authority to act must be supplied.[34] Where a joint application or notification is submitted a joint representative should be appointed.[35]

2.25 (iii) *Copies, supporting documents and format.* It is necessary to supply 13 copies of each application and notification (*i.e.* the Form and Annex), three copies of any relevant agreement and one of other supporting documents.[36] It is not necessary to supply the originals of any supporting documents but copies must be certified as true copies of the original.[37] Applications and notifications must be made in one of the official languages of the Community or of an EFTA State. The working language of the EFTA Surveillance Authority (English) may also be used. Supporting documents must be submitted in their original language. Where this is not an official language, a translation in one of the official languages must also be supplied.[38]

The form is a single sheet and the party or parties notifying supplement this with an annex. The paper used should be A4 and must not be larger. A margin of at least 25mm or one inch must be left on the left hand side of the page and, if both sides are used, on the right hand side of the reverse.[39]

---

[30] Art. 1(1) of Reg. 27.

[31] *Ibid.*

[32] This is implied. See Art. 1(1) of Reg. 27.

[33] Art. 4(3) of Reg. 27.

[34] Art. 1(2) of Reg. 27. For example, a power of attorney or a certified copy of an extract from a board minute authorising the representative to act. Community law may be strict in relation to authorization rules. See Case 289/83, *G.A.A.R.M* v. *Commission*: [1984] E.C.R. 4295, [1986] 3 C.M.L.R. 15 (action before the Court dismissed because applicant failed to produce evidence of advocate's authorisation to act).

[35] Art. 1(3) of Reg. 27.

[36] Art. 2(1) of Reg. 27, as amended. 15 copies are required in order that the Commission may retain two and send one to each of the competent authorities in the Member States in pursuance of Art. 10(1) of Reg. 17, and one to the EFTA Surveillance Authority.

[37] Art. 2(2) of Reg. 27. A simple certification appears to be sufficient and it is not necessary to have the documents notarised.

[38] Art. 2(3) of Reg. 27. The use of the official languages is discussed generally at para. 8.31.

[39] Complementary Note, Part VI. Clearly the official Form A/B should be used but it is hoped that accidental failure to follow exactly the other formal requirements (*e.g.* as to size of margin) will not invalidate the notification.

2.26   (iv) *Effective date.* The application or notification is registered in the Registry of DG IV. The date of submission of an application or notification is the date on which it is received by the Commission.[40] Where the application or notification is sent by registered post, it is deemed to have been received on the date shown on the postmark of the place of posting.[40a] A form of acknowledgment of receipt is attached to Form A/B. The Commission will return this if completed.

2.27   (v) *Standard form contracts.* Form A/B provides that in the case of a standard contract[41] the normal information relating to the names and addresses of all the undertakings which are parties to the agreement, etc., need not be supplied.[42] Form A/B gives as an example of a standard contract "a contract appointing dealers". Terms of business are commonly notified in this manner.

Such notification is considered adequate for the effective supervision and control of such agreements which may come within the terms of Article 85. In *Parfums Marcel Rochas* v. *Bitsch*,[43] the Court of Justice said: "Because of its very nature, a standard contract, on being notified, draws the Commission's attention to the economic and legal context in which an agreement of this kind subsists." This statement probably requires some qualification given the changes in the amount of information required by Form A/B. Heading 2 (Market), for example, specifically requires the party notifying a standard contract to specify how many it expects to conclude. The administrative convenience to both parties and Commission alike can hardly be denied. If it is necessary for the Commission to obtain the information "omitted" from the Form A/B on account of the agreement being a standard contract, Article 11 of Regulation 17 may be used to acquire this as well as any other necessary information.

Agreements in the form of the standard contract duly notified enjoy the benefits of notification described above.[44] In particular, all contracts concluded after the entry into force of Regulation 17 which are exact copies of a standard contract concluded before that date and duly notified will be provisionally valid.[45] Further, retrospective

---

[40] Art. 3 of Reg. 27.

[40a] *Ibid.*

[41] In *European Glass Container Manufacturers*: [1974] O.J. L160/1, [1974] 2 C.M.L.R. D50, the Commission said that the erroneous description of the agreement as a "standard contract" did not affect the validity of the notification. The agreement had been notified as a "standard contract" when it was actually a collective agreement between the undertakings concerned. It is not, however, apparent how complete the notification was and the point does not appear to have been significant because no exemption was granted or fine imposed.

[42] Para. 2, Identity of other parties.

[43] Case 1/70: [1970] E.C.R. 515, [1971] C.M.L.R. 104, at para. 5.

[44] See para. 2.18.

[45] *Parfums Marcel Rochas* v. *Bitsch*, above, at para. 6. Some doubt was cast on the proposition laid down in *Rochas* following the Court's decision in Case 48/72, *Brasserie de Haecht (No. 2)*: [1973] E.C.R. 77, [1973] C.M.L.R. 287, but see the A.G. in the *Perfumes* case: [1980] E.C.R. 2327, [1981] 2 C.M.L.R. 90, [1980] E.C.R. 2481, [1981] 2 C.M.L.R. 143. Any doubt seems to have been removed by the Court of Justice in C–234/89, *Delimitis* v. *Henninger Bräu:* [1991] I E.C.R. 935, [1992] 5 C.M.L.R. 210, at para. 49. Art. 5 of Reg. 17, as amended by Reg. 59, specifies the dates by which agreements in existence when Reg. 17 came into force had to be notified. Such agreements had to be notified before November 1, 1962 with the exception of those to which not more than two undertakings are parties, in which case the date was February 1, 1963. A standard contract can be regarded as a contract to which not more than two undertakings are party (*Rochas*, at para. 11) but, presumably, only if the standard contract has in its model form two parties. On counting heads, see Case 170/83, *Hydrotherm* v. *Andreoli*: [1984] E.C.R. 2999, [1985] 3 C.M.L.R. 224.

validation under Article 7(1) of Regulation 17 is also possible where the standard contract is amended to the satisfaction of the Commission.[46] Similar benefits will accrue to EEA agreements.

(vi) *Amendments.* Paragraph VII of the Complementary Note states that it is important to inform the Commission of any material changes to agreements, etc., made after the application or notification. The safest course is undoubtedly to notify amendments,[47] including withdrawals of restrictions. If a restriction is expressly set out in the agreement including that term even though the parties may maintain that the restriction has not been applied for a long time and therefore should be considered as no longer valid, the parties should make a formal amendment of their agreement and notify it to the Commission.[48]

(vii) *Restrictive Trade Practices Act 1976.* Finally, the attention of the reader is drawn to the Registration of Restrictive Trading Agreements (EEC Documents) Regulations 1973.[49] These Regulations require parties to an agreement registrable in the United Kingdom under the Restrictive Trade Practices Act 1976 to inform the Director-General of Fair Trading of certain steps including any application or notification made to the Commission in relation to the agreement and the final decision of the Commission and any decision by the Court relating to the Commission's decision.[50] The register of restrictive agreements maintained by the Director-General under the 1976 Act should include a copy of any such decision by the Commission or the Court relating to an agreement on the register.

Setting time-limits—Commission's new procedure—revision of Form A/B

2.28 The Merger Control Regulation, Regulation 4064/89, has demonstrated that the Commission is capable of operating within strict and fairly tight time-limits. The Commission must carry out an initial examination within one month of notification to ascertain whether the merger falls within the scope of the Regulation and if so, whether serious doubts are raised as to its compatibility with the Common Market. If such doubt exists a further examination (up to four months in length) is set in motion.

---

[46] Art. 7(1) is discussed at paras. 6.29–31. For an example of its application to a standard contract, see Zanussi: [1978] O.J. L322/26, [1979] 1 C.M.L.R. 81.

[47] Case 30/78, *Distillers* v. *Commission*: [1980] E.C.R. 2229, [1980] 3 C.M.L.R. 121. But the position of the Commission appears ambivalent. See *London Sugar Futures Market Ltd.*: [1985] O.J. L369/25, [1988] 4 C.M.L.R. 138, where the amended agreements were notified and the negative clearance given to the agreement "as last notified." *Cf.* the *GAFTA Soya Bean Meal Futures Association*: [1987] O.J. L19/18, [1989] 4 C.M.L.R. 287, where again the agreement was amended to obtain negative clearance, but here the Commission did not require the amendment agreement to be notified and gave negative clearance to the agreement as notified on April 11, 1975!

[48] *Dutch Books*: Cases 43 & 63/82, *VBVB and VBBB* v. *Commission*: [1984] E.C.R. 19, [1985] 1 C.M.L.R. 27, at paras. 7 and 8. Contrast the position relating to the notification of state aids. Here it appears that amendments may be given to the Commission informally in the context of the consultations which ensue from the notification. See Cases 91 & 137/83, *Heineken Brouwerijen* v. *Inspecteur der Venootschapsbelasting*: [1984] E.C.R. 3425, [1985] 1 C.M.L.R. 389.

[49] S.I. 1973 No. 950.

[50] The parties should also inform the Director-General of the Commission's notification to them of the opportunity to be heard in relation to the objections raised against them.

At the end of 1992, the Commission announced[51] certain procedural changes aimed at speeding up the handling of notifications under Regulation 17 and thereby giving firms greater certainty in their dealings with each other and with the Commission. The changes, which are purely administrative and therefore not laid down in any regulation or even notice, make a distinction between "structural cases" and others and like the Merger Control Regulation introduce the notion of a two stage procedure.

In so-called "structural cases", in particular co-operative joint ventures[52] (if concentrative, the joint venture would fall within the scope of the Merger Control Regulation), the Commission will, within two months of receiving a complete notification on Form A/B, send the undertaking concerned either a comfort letter or a warning letter. The former will in effect give the parties the green light to go ahead. A warning letter, a new concept whose nature and legal effects are still uncertain, will on the other hand indicate serious competition problems but will also at the same time fix a second deadline whose duration will depend on the circumstances of the particular case, by which the Commission should reach its final decision. The first (two month) stage would not run until the Commission has the full information and the Commission has encouraged undertakings and their advisers to make contact with DG IV officials prior to notification to discuss the information that they should provide (this is in effect standard practice in cases under the Merger Control Regulation). A similar system is also proposed for all other notifications and complaints. But in this instance there is to be no standard deadline for the first stage. Each case will receive its own deadline for the first stage, which the Commission has said will be no more than a few months. As for structural cases, the second stage will be fixed having regard to the circumstances of the particular case. The Commission has indicated that if exceptional circumstances arise, in particular if an undertaking challenges before the Court an intermediate step in the decision making process, the clock will stop running. It is proposed to include in the Annual Report on Competition Policy a section giving details of the time taken for decisions along with a detailed analysis of how the new procedure is working.

To meet these timetables the Commission has taken the view that it may be necessary to change some of the rules in Regulation 27 and, in particular, the requirements of Form A/B. One of the reasons why the Commission is able to take speedy decisions under the Merger Control Regulation is the amount of information which must be provided (in Form CO) at the outset. The Commission is therefore considering amending Regulation 27 and Form A/B to require a similar level of information to be provided. Although the proposal seems directed primarily at the so-called structural joint venture, changes would not necessarily be restricted to such cases. Other provisions of the Merger Control regime which are also under consideration for Regulation 17 cases are the rules that the language of the notification becomes the language of the proceeding and that the Commission can waive the detailed requirements of notification in appropriate cases.

---

[51] Commission Press Release IP(92)1111, December 23, 1992.

[52] It seems that for a co-operative joint venture to be "structural" the joint venture must have some identity of its own after the regrouping and a significant number of assets transferred to it by its parents. Examples are likely to be found in production joint ventures, or joint ventures engaged in the production and marketing of certain products. See generally the Commission Notice concerning the assessment of co-operative joint ventures pursuant to Article 85 of the EEC Treaty: [1993] O.J. C43/2.

EEA–Notification

2.28A   As mentioned in Chapter 1 the procedural rules relating to the day-to-day enforcement of the EEA competition rules mirror those of Regulation 17 and the other implementing rules under the EEC Treaty. Thus, as Article 4(1) of Protocol 21 to the EEA lays down, notification is a prerequisite for exemption under Article 53(3) EEA. Notification gives immunity from fines.[53] There are special rules for transport (including the "objections" procedure) and as is the case under Regulation 17, notification is not required for certain types of agreement. Article 4(2) of Protocol 21 mirrors Article 4(2) of Regulation 17. The detailed rules for notification (numbers of copies, etc.) are set out, in the case of EFTA Surveillance Authority, in Protocol 4 to the EFTA Surveillance Agreement. In practice for notifications of agreements, whether to the EFTA Surveillance Authority or the Commission, the modified form A/B will be used which takes into account the need for extra information to cover the EFTA elements.

The EEA makes special transitional arrangements for agreements in existence at the time of entry into force of the EEA. Where parties seek exemption under Article 53(3) EEA, they must notify within six months.[54] This does not apply however to agreements excepted from the general notification obligation, *i.e.* those described in Article 4(2) of Protocol 21. The parties may however choose to amend their agreement either to bring it within the terms of a block exemption[55] or so as not to fall under the prohibition in Article 53(1) EEA anymore.[56] They have six months from the date of entry into force of the EEA in which to do this. The prohibition in Article 53(1) is treated as not applying to those agreements provided appropriate amendments are made within that time. Agreements which have prior to the date of entry into force of the EEA already been notified to the E.C. Commission are deemed to comply with the provisions of notification under the EEA.[57] So far as the application of the EEA competition rules are concerned, the competent surveillance authority may however require a form (prescribed for EEA purposes) to be completed and submitted within a prescribed period. Agreements which have the benefit of an individual exemption granted under Article 85(3) E.C. before the date of entry into force of the EEA continue to be exempted until the date of expiry specified in the exemption decision or until the Commission otherwise decides.[58] Other transitional relief, in particular as it relates to exemption decisions, is described in Chapter 6.[59]

The division of responsibility between the two surveillance authorities, the Commission and the EFTA Surveillance Authority, is described in Chapter 1. Undertakings must address notifications to the authority having competence in accordance with the jurisdictional rules in Article 56 EEA.[60] The EEA does, however, address the

---

[53] Protocol 21, Art. 9.
[54] Protocol 21, Art. 5(1)
[55] Protocol 21, Art. 11.
[56] Protocol 21, Art. 12. If the agreement cannot be so amended and is unsuitable for exemption under Art. 53(3) EEA, the parties may have no choice but to abandon it.
[57] Protocol 21, Art. 8.
[58] Protocol 21, Art. 13.
[59] See para. 6.31A
[60] Protocol 23, Art. 10(1). Complaints, however, can be sent to either surveillance authority.

question of what happens if a party notifies the wrong surveillance authority and provides a simple and pragmatic solution. The surveillance authority which is not competent must transfer it without delay to the competent surveillance authority.[61] However where certain procedural steps have already been taken in a particular case, it cannot be transferred. A case cannot be transferred after the publishing of the intention to give a negative clearance or an exemption, the issuance of a statement of objections to the undertakings concerned or, in the case of a complaint, the sending of a letter informing the applicant that there are insufficient grounds for pursuing the complaint.[62] The EEA also has a simple rule to exclude the possibility of a case being passed to and fro between surveillance authorities. Once a case is transferred it cannot be sent back.[63] Finally, there is a further rule which assists parties faced with the jurisdictional test in Article 56 EEA. The date of submission of an application or notification is the date on which it is received by the Commission or the EFTA Surveillance Authority, regardless of which of them is competent to decide on the case under Article 56.[64] When sent by registered post, the date shown on the postmark of the place of posting is treated as the date of receipt.

II. COMPLAINTS

2.29   Article 3 of Regulation 17 provides that the Commission may "upon application or upon its own initiative" find that there is an infringement and require its termination.[65] The transport regulations say more clearly that the Commission may act "on receipt of a complaint".[66] Application under Article 3 can be made by Member States[67] or by "natural or legal persons who claim a legitimate interest."[68] Regulation 17 does not define what is a "legitimate interest" and so far the Court has not been called upon to adjudicate on this question.[69] The category of persons who have a legitimate interest for the purposes of Article 3 is not limited to third parties but includes

---

[61] Protocol 23, Art. 10(2). Cases must also be transferred where, in the preparation or initiation of *ex officio* proceedings, it becomes apparent that the other surveillance authority is competent to decide on the case (Art. 10(3)).

[62] Protocol 23, Art. 70(4).

[63] *Ibid.*

[64] Protocol 23, Art. 11.

[65] Emphasis added.

[66] Reg. 1017/68, Art. 10; Reg. 4056/86, Art. 10; Reg. 3975, Art. 3.

[67] Member States do not have to show that they have a "legitimate interest." As in the case of interventions before the Court under Art. 37 of the Statute of the Court, they are presumed to have a sufficient interest. For an example of a complaint made by the Member States, see *Union Interprofessionnelle des Semences Fourragères*: [1976] 1 C.M.L.R. D95 or, more recently, *Cewal, Cowac and Ukwal*: [1993] O.J. L34/20.

[68] Art. 3(2)(b) of Reg. 17. See, generally, Temple Lang, "The Position of Third Parties in EEC Competition Cases" (1978) 3 E.L.Rev. 177, and "EEC Competition Actions in Member States' Courts—Claims for Damages, Declarations and Injunctions for Breach of Community Antitrust Law" (1984) Annual Proceedings of Fordham Corporate Law Institute; J. Shaw, "Competition Complainants: a comprehensive system of remedies?" (1993) 18 E.L. Rev. 427 and Vesterdorf, "Complaints concerning infringements of Competition Law within the context of European Community Law" [1994] 31 C.M.L.R.Rev. 77.

[69] But see *Metro I*: Case 26/76, *Metro-SB-Grossmarkte* v. *Commission*: [1977] E.C.R. 1875, [1978] 2 C.M.L.R. 1, where the Court indicated the relationship between Art. 3(2)(b) of Reg. 17 and Art. 173 of the Treaty.

persons party to the agreement or practice in question.[70] But something more than a sharing in the general interest that the law should be upheld is required. The interest of parties to an agreement would seem to be clearly affected if the agreement is found to be contrary to Article 85.[71] In the case of third parties, broadly speaking, any person who can show that it is suffering, or is likely to suffer, injury or loss directly from the alleged infringement should be regarded as having a "legitimate interest".[72] Examples of complainants accepted by the Commission include: a distributor or wholesaler who is unable to export goods because of an export ban or disincentive;[73] a member of a trade association who is being fined for breach of the rules;[74] a competitor who is being restricted in the supply of non-patented goods to licensees because of tie-in clauses in the patent licence[75] or a licensee against restrictive provisions in a plant breeding licence;[76] a wholesaler,[77] retailer,[78] or even competitor[79] who is the subject of a refusal to supply or of price restrictions;[80] a consumer who is unable to purchase goods for export on the grounds that export sales by dealers are prohibited;[81] the target

---

[70] See A.G. Mancini in Cases 142 and 156/84, *BAT and Reynolds* v. *Commission*: [1987] E.C.R. 4487, [1988] 4 C.M.L.R. 24; Deringer, *The Competition Law of the European Economic Community* (1968), at para. 2033, and Temple Lang, *op. cit.*

[71] For an example of a complaint made by a party to an agreement in question, see *Quantel International-Continuum/Quantel SA*: [1992] O.J. L235/9.

[72] Deringer, *ibid.* considers that "third parties may be considered to be affected where their economic interests could be injured in some way by the violation." Temple Lang, *ibid.* makes the point that any undertaking which has a right to compensation in a national court arising from the violation of the Community competition rules would have a right to intervene in a procedure before the Commission in respect of the same violation. In the cases which have come before the Court of Justice, the *Metro* cases (Case 26/76, *Metro-SB-Grossmarkte* v. *Commission*: [1977] E.C.R. 1875, [1978] 2 C.M.L.R. 1 and 75/84, *Metro-SB-Grossmarkte GmbH & Co. K.G.* v. *Commission*: [1986] E.C.R. 3021, [1987] 1 C.M.L.R. 118); Case 210/81, *Demo-Studio Schmidt* v. *Commission*: [1983] E.C.R. 3045, [1984] 1 C.M.L.R. 63; Case 298/83, *C.I.C.C.E.* v. *Commission*: [1985] E.C.R. 1105, [1986] 1 C.M.L.R. 486 and Case 43/85, *ANCIDES* v. *Commission*: [1987] E.C.R. 3131, [1988] 4 C.M.L.R. 821, a restriction or loss of business has been apparent. The question whether there is a "legitimate interest" may become more important in future. See n. 89, below.

[73] *Distillers*: [1978] O.J. L50/16, [1978] 1 C.M.L.R. 400; *Moët et Chandon (London) Ltd.*: [1982] O.J. L94/7, [1982] 2 C.M.L.R. 166; *Viho/Toshiba*: [1991] O.J. L287/39, [1992] 5 C.M.L.R. 180; *Newitt/ Dunlop Slazenger International and Others*: [1992] O.J. L131/32 and *Viho/Parker Pen*: [1992] O.J. L233/27. Or, for example, an importer suffering the effects of an export ban as in *Johnson & Johnson*: [1980] O.J. L377/16, [1981] 2 C.M.L.R. 287 or *Sperry New Holland*: [1985] O.J. L376/21, [1988] 4 C.M.L.R. 306.

[74] *Dutch Bicycles*: [1978] O.J. L20/18, [1978] 2 C.M.L.R. 194.

[75] *Vaessen/Moris*: [1979] O.J. L19/32, [1979] 1 C.M.L.R. 511.

[76] *Breeders' rights: Roses:* [1985] O.J. L369/9. Or a broadcaster denied a sublicence from a group of broadcasters who had acquired exclusive rights to a sporting event, *Screensport/EBU Members*: [1991] O.J. L63/32, [1992] 5 C.M.L.R. 273.

[77] The *Metro* cases, above, n. 72; *Gosme/Martell–DMP*: [1991] O.J. L185/23, [1992] 5 C.M.L.R. 586; or an association or self-service suppliers excluded from a selective distribution system: *Ideal Standard's Distribution System*; [1985] O.J. L20/38, [1988] 4 C.M.L.R. 627.

[78] Case 792/79R, *Camera Care Ltd.* v. *Commission*: [1980] E.C.R. 119, [1980] 1 C.M.L.R. 334, and see, more recently, *Fisher-Price/Quaker Oats Ltd.–Toyco*: [1988] O.J. L49/19, [1989] 4 C.M.L.R. 553.

[79] *Zoja-CSC-ICI*: [1972] O.J. L299/51, [1973] C.M.L.R. D50, and *Hudson's Bay–Dansk Pelsdyravlerforening*: [1988] O.J. L316/43, [1989] 4 C.M.L.R. 340.

[80] *VBBB/VBVB*: [1982] O.J. L54/36, [1982] 2 C.M.L.R. 344; *AROW/BNIC*: [1982] O.J. L379/1, [1983] 2 C.M.L.R. 240; *Napier Brown–British Sugar*: [1988] O.J. L284/41, [1990] 4 C.M.L.R. 196 and *Eco System/Peugeot*: [1992] O.J. L66/1, [1993] 4 C.M.L.R. 42.

[81] *Kawasaki*: [1979] O.J. L16/9, [1979] 1 C.M.L.R. 448, or a customers' trade association, *e.g.* the NFU in *John Deere*: [1985] O.J. L35/58, [1985] 2 C.M.L.R. 554.

company in a takeover subject to Article 86;[82] a local authority as major purchaser of services subject to alleged collusive tendering;[83] and a ferry operator seeking access to port facilities.[84]

Form of the complaint

2.30 There is no requirement in Regulation 17 that a complaint should be communicated to the Commission in any particular or special way or that the complainant should have exhausted national remedies.[85] But the Commission will almost certainly ask whether national remedies exist and could be tried.[86] A written application is expressly required in transport cases.[87] A complaint under Regulation 17 may be made orally or in writing although the latter is preferred and is necessary to evidence a formal complaint creating rights and duties on the complainant and the Commission respectively. There is a prepared form, Form C[88] (see Appendix G), which complainants may use. It was recently reviewed[89] to enable its use also in EEA cases. A simple letter will be sufficient provided it discloses the complainant's name and address and is signed. The only formal requirement is that where a complaint is signed by a representative, proof of the representative's authority to act must be produced.[90] The Commission receives so-called informal or unofficial complaints and even anonymous complaints. The Commission does not consider itself bound to pursue these although like any other source of information they may spark off an investigation by the Commission of its own motion. It is not the Commission's practice to disclose the identity of "unofficial" complainants or even whether a tip-off has been received.[91] Indeed, in *Stanley Adams*, the Court of Justice held that where information is supplied on a voluntary basis and accompanied by a request for confidentiality in order to protect the informant's anonymity the Commission is legally bound to comply with that condition.[92]

It is not unnatural for the complainant to fear retaliatory action from the undertaking complained of. English law has recognised the public interest in ensuring that the Commission can receive voluntary complaints and enforce the competition rules, and has, for the purposes of the law of defamation, accorded absolute privilege to the complaint.[93]

---

[82] *Continental Can*: [1972] O.J. L7/25, [1972] C.M.L.R. D11, and see Cases 160–161/73R, *Miles Druce* v. *Commission*: [1973] E.C.R. 1049, [1974] 1 C.M.L.R. 224.

[83] *Building and construction industry in the Netherlands*: [1992] O.J. L92/1.

[84] *B & I Line/Sealink Harbour*: [1992] 5 C.M.L.R. 255 and *Sea Containers* v. *Stena Sealink*: [1994] O.J. L15/8. These have also been cases in the air transport sector, see, *e.g. Air Europe/Lufthansa*: Press Notice IP(90)384, and *British Midland* v. *Air Lingus*: [1992] O.J. L96/34, [1993] 4 C.M.L.R. 596.

[85] Case 43/72, *Merkur* v. *Commission*: [1973] E.C.R. 1055, at para. 6. For an example of a complaint being made simultaneously with proceedings in a national court, see *Sugarbeet*: [1990] O.J. L31/32, [1991] 4 C.M.L.R. 629.

[86] See the discussion of the Commission's recent Notice at para 2.32.

[87] See Reg. 1629/69, Art. 1(1) (Form I); Reg. 4056/86, Art. 2; Reg. 4261/88, Art. 1.

[88] Form I may be used for cases under Reg. 1017/68.

[89] By Reg. 3666/93.

[90] Art. 1(2) of Reg. 27, which expressly refers to applications under Arts. 3(1) and 3(2)(b) of Reg. 17. And see n. 34 above.

[91] Joshua, "Information in EEC Competition Law Procedures" (1986) 11 Eur.L.R. 409.

[92] And may be liable in damages under Art. 214 if the duty is breached. Case 145/83, *Stanley Adams* v. *Commission*: [1985] E.C.R. 3539, [1986] 1 C.M.L.R. 506.

[93] *Hasselblad (GB) Ltd.* v. *Orbinson*: [1985] 1 All E.R. 173, [1984] 3 C.M.L.R. 679.

Contents of complaint

2.31 Although the contents of a complaint will largely depend on the circumstances of the particular case, what materials are available and who prepares and submits it, the following may serve as a general guide to what matters might be included in a formal complaint.

The complaint should give the names and addresses of the complainant, the undertaking or undertakings the subject of the complaint and any other relevant persons (*e.g.* persons who may be able to corroborate any statements made by the complainant or who can provide other information or assistance in the matter). The complainant should adduce evidence to show that he has a "legitimate interest" within the meaning of Article 3(2)(b) of Regulation 17. The substance of the complaint should be set out as clearly as possible: copies of all relevant correspondence and other documents, if any, should be attached. If a similar complaint has been made to any other authority (*e.g.* the competition authority in the relevant E.C. Member or EFTA State) or is the subject of proceedings in a national court, then the present position of such complaint or action should be made known to the Commission — again copies of correspondence, documents, etc., should be supplied. A description of the relevant products or services should be given, particularly if of a specialised or technical nature: where appropriate, photographs, diagrams, catalogues, price lists, etc., might be supplied. Some indication should be given of the nature and structure of the relevant market and position of the undertakings concerned in relation to it: any available statistical information and other published reports and materials might be referred to or copies or extracts supplied. Although the Commission will not necessarily adopt the complainant's legal analysis and arguments, the complainant should nevertheless indicate how Article 85 or 86 and/or Article 53 or 54 EEA is thought applicable in the circumstances:[94] in particular the complainant should show how trade between Member States, between the Community and one or more EFTA States, or between EFTA States is likely to be affected to an appreciable extent.

Where specific relief is sought the complainant should be careful to identify the type of relief which the Commission can and should in the circumstances grant. In *Automec II*, the complainant unsuccessfully sought injunctive relief requiring supply of vehicles to it for resale. The Court of First Instance held that although the Commission could have granted alternative forms of relief which might in fact have had the same result of resuming supply to the complainant it was not the Commission's duty to redefine the complainant's application.[95] A complaint should indicate clearly where it expects the Commission to take a decision ordering interim measures (see Chapter 6) in its favour. Where the complaint is signed by a representative, proof of authority to act should be produced. Finally, any material which is confidential and contains business secrets should be clearly marked and the Commission's attention drawn to any restrictions on its use. It is convenient to annex it separately so that the rest of the complaint can more easily be shown to the undertaking the subject of it.[96]

---

[94] Any other relevant provisions of the Treaty should be mentioned: *e.g.* Arts. 30–36 in industrial property cases.

[95] Case T–24/90, *Automec Srl* v. *Commission*: [1992] 5 C.M.L.R. 431, at paras. 52–54.

[96] Subject to the exclusion of business secrets the full complaint must be shown to the undertaking complained of—see A.G. Warner in *Distillers:* [1978] O.J. L50/16, [1978] 1 C.M.L.R. 400.

Commission's reaction to the complaint

2.32 Whether and how quickly the Commission will respond to an application under Article 3 of Regulation 17 will depend on a number of factors. As the Court of First Instance acknowledged in *Automec II*, the Commission, like many other public bodies with limited resources, has to set priorities compatible also with its legal obligations.[97] As an administrative body it must act in the public interest and consequently, the Court of First Instance has held, it is legitimate for the Commission to refer to the Community interest in order to determine the relevant degree of priority to accord to a particular matter.[98] This does not mean however that the Commission can simply claim lack of priority in the public interest as an excuse for not proceeding with a complaint. Although the Commission cannot generally be compelled to conduct an investigation into an alleged infringement of competition rules,[99] its decisions are susceptible to judicial review and therefore in accordance with Article 190 of the Treaty it must, in a particular case, set out the legal and factual considerations which leads it to conclude that there is not sufficient Community interest to pursue a complaint.[1] The Commission has for some time given importance to the seriousness of the alleged infringement, the urgency of obtaining a quick decision and the relationship with national proceedings as well as whether the case has broad significance for the Community's competition policy.[2] The Court of First Instance had indicated that in the circumstances of the particular case it is for the Commission to weigh up the importance of the alleged infringement for the functioning of the Common Market, the probability of being able to establish the existence of the infringement and the extent of the investigation measures necessary in order to fulfil successfully its task of securing compliance with Articles 85 and 86.[3] In its recent Notice on co-operation with national courts, the Commission has signified its intention, in exercising its decision-making powers, to concentrate on cases "having particular political, economic or legal significance for the Community".[4] In the absence of one of these features complaints, the Commission says, "should, as a rule, be handled by national courts or authorities." The Notice goes on to say:

> "there is not normally a sufficient Community interest in examining a case where the plaintiff is able to secure adequate protection of his rights before the national courts. In these circumstances the complaint will normally be filed."

Whether a national court can provide adequate protection may not always be easy to determine. Many complaints involve refusals to supply under Article 86 and national courts may be ill-suited to determine the economic issues involved. There may also be evidential and procedural hurdles to overcome,[5] as well as the risk of legal

---

[97] Above, at para. 77.

[98] *Ibid.* at para. 85.

[99] *Ibid.* at para. 87.

[1] *Ibid.* at para. 85.

[2] Seventeenth Report on Competition Policy, at point 7.

[3] *Automec II*, above, at para. 87.

[4] Notice on co-operation between national courts and the Commission in applying Articles 85 and 86 of the EEC Treaty: [1993] O.J. C39/6, at paras. 14 and 15. Discussed further at para. 10.13.

[5] Especially in the U.K. where cross-undertakings in damage are invariably sought by defendants and in many cases will rule out action by the complainant.

costs. But following the Notice, it is now clearly a matter which should be considered in more detail by a complainant and its advisers and addressed in any complaint made to the Commission. But as the Court of First Instance made clear in *Automec II*, the fact that a national court has jurisdiction to deal with the question is not *per se* sufficient reason for the Commission not pursuing the complaint.[6]

2.33 The Commission has "a duty of vigilance,"[7] on receipt of a complaint, to examine the facts and legal arguments put forward to see whether they disclose behaviour indicating that the competition rules are likely to have been infringed. Where the Commission has a power of appraisal it has, the Court of First Instance said recently in *Asia Motor France*,[8] to be exercised with the greatest respect for procedural guarantees, in particular the obligation to examine with care and impartiality the particular elements of the relevant case. At this stage in the proceedings there may be an informal exchange of opinions and information between the Commission and the complainant during which the latter will have the opportunity to substantiate its allegations in the light of the initial reactions of the Commission staff.[9] The complainant must co-operate and may be expected to supply information and assistance to the Commission if the Commission is to be able to proceed.[10] But as regards the undertaking accused the Commission is under no obligation immediately to inform it of the complaint.[11] Subject to the rights of defence the Commission has a discretion when to do this,[12] although it is the Commission's procedure to send the complaint to the undertaking concerned at an early opportunity to get its reaction. The right of a complainant to participate in the Commission's administrative procedure is discussed in Chapter 4.[13]

Rejection of complaint

2.34 Article 6 of Regulation 99/63 provides as follows:

> "Where the Commission, having received an application pursuant to Article 3(2) of Regulation 17, considers that on the basis of the information in its possession

---

[6] Above, at para. 88.

[7] Case 210/81, *Demo-Studio Schmidt* v. *Commission*: [1983] E.C.R. 3045, [1984] 1 C.M.L.R. 63, at paras. 19 and 22; Case 298/83, *C.I.C.C.E.* v. *Commission*: [1985] E.C.R. 1105, [1986] 1 C.M.L.R. 486, at para. 18, and *Automec II*, at para. 79.

[8] Case T–7/92, *SA Asia Motor France* v. *Commission*: judgment of June 29, 1993, not yet reported. And see earlier statement of the principle in Case T–44/90, *La Cinq* v. *Commission*: [1992] II E.C.R. 1, [1992] 4 C.M.L.R. 449, at para. 86.

[9] The preliminary observations given by Commission staff at this stage, whether in correspondence or otherwise, cannot be classified as acts which can be challenged in the Court. *Automec I*, at para. 45.

[10] *C.I.C.C.E.*, above, at para. 25, where the Court considered it reasonable for the Commission to require the complainant to provide details of pricing in particular cases, *i.e.* to provide specific evidence (within its control) rather than to make generalisations. The requirement of the complainant to collaborate is explored by Mancini in "Access to Justice: Individual Undertakings and EEC Antitrust Law — Problems and Pitfalls" (1989) 12 Fordham Int. L.J. 189.

[11] Joshua, *op. cit.*

[12] In *ECS/AKZO*: [1985] O.J. L374/1, [1986] 3 C.M.L.R. 273, for example, the complaint was communicated at the same time as the statement of objections.

[13] See paras. 4.18–20.

there are insufficient grounds for granting the application, it shall inform the applicants of its reasons and fix a time limit for them to submit any further comments in writing."

This provision (and the equivalent provisions in the transport regulations)[14] requires the Commission to give a preliminary or provisional view to the complainant prior to any rejection of the complaint by the Commission. If not forthcoming the complainant can use the procedure under Article 175 to compel the Commission to respond under Article 6. In *Asia Motor France*,[15] the Court of First Instance held that the Article 6 communication is an act other than a recommendation or opinion for the purposes of Article 175(3). In *GEMA*,[16] the Court of Justice explained the purpose and effect of Article 6 as follows:

> "As is shown by the phrase '... shall inform the applicants of its reasons', it follows that the communication referred to in Article 6 of Regulation 99/63 only seeks to ensure that an applicant within the meaning of Article 3(2)(b) of Regulation 17 be informed of the reasons which have led the Commission to conclude that on the basis of the information obtained in the course of the inquiry there are insufficient grounds for granting the application. Such a communication implies the discontinuance of the proceedings without, however, preventing the Commission from reopening the file if it considers it advisable, in particular where, within the period allowed by the Commission for that purpose in accordance with the provisions of Article 6, the applicant puts forward fresh elements of law or of fact."[17]

The Court held that such a communication from the Commission was an act constituting the "definition of its position" within the meaning of Article 175 and therefore rendered inadmissible an action for failure to act under that Article. It also made clear that a complainant under Article 3(2)(b) of Regulation 17 is not entitled to obtain a decision from the Commission on the existence of the alleged infringement. The Court did not, however, determine whether the Article 6 communication constituted a decision which might be challenged before the Court in an action for annulment under Article 173 of the Treaty.[18] The Court of First Instance addressed this question in *Automec II*.[19] The Court compared the Article 6 communication with the statement of objections. Both are the result of a preliminary examination of the facts, on the basis of which the Commission gives the recipient a time-limit in which to state its point of

---

[14] Reg. 1630/69, Art. 6; Reg. 4260/88, Art. 10; Reg. 4261/88, Art. 9.
[15] Case T–28/90, *Asia Motor France* v. *Commission*: [1992] 5 C.M.L.R. 431, at para. 29.
[16] Case 125/78: [1979] E.C.R. 3173, [1980] 2 C.M.L.R. 177.
[17] *Ibid.* at para. 17. But see A.G. Mancini in Cases 142 and 156/84, *BAT and Reynolds* v. *Commission*: [1987] E.C.R. 4487, [1988] 4 C.M.L.R. 24. He had difficulty with the last sentence of this statement from *GEMA*. He thought the purpose of Art. 6 was to give the complainant an opportunity to express its view before the Commission closed the investigation. He saw the obligation to give notice under Art. 6 as satisfying two interests: it enabled the complainant to check whether the matters of which it had complained had been properly assessed and the Commission to establish whether, on the basis of the comments submitted to it, the information in its possession was sufficient to justify the discontinuance of the proceedings.
[18] The Art. 6 letter was, in *GEMA*, the subject of annulment proceedings in the alternative, but the Court ruled that the Art. 173 application was inadmissible as it was made out of time.
[19] Case T–64/89, *Automec Srl* v. *Commission*: [1990] II E.C.R. 367, [1991] 4 C.M.L.R. 177.

view. Both are aimed at safeguarding procedural rights, albeit that the complainant's rights are not as extensive as the right to be heard of undertakings against which the Commission is conducting an investigation.[20] The Court of Justice has held that the statement of objections is not a decision but only a procedural act paving the way to a decision.[21] The Court of First Instance therefore concluded that the Article 6 communication was not a decision.[22]

2.35 A complainant may nevertheless be entitled to, or in fact may receive,[23] a decision from the Commission on the matter of its complaint. The position is clear in transport cases. There the implementing regulations provide that:

> "if the Commission, acting on a complaint received, concludes that on the evidence before it there are no grounds for intervention . . . in respect of any agreement, decision or concerted practice, it shall issue a decision rejecting the complaint as unfounded."[24]

Regulation 17 is, in contrast, silent. In *Automec II*, the Court of First Instance said: "The Court of Justice has held on several occasions that the Commission *may* adopt a final decision to reject the complaint and close the file."[25] Where the Commission, having heard the comments of the complainant in pursuance of Article 6 of Regulation 99/63, reaches a final view resolving to reject the complaint either wholly or in part and discontinuing the application, the complainant, it is submitted, should be entitled to a definitive measure rejecting the complaint. It is in the interests of legal protection and of good administration that the complainant should be able to learn of the Commission's position in a manner whereby the Court is able to review comprehensively and effectively the legality of the measure which the Commission has adopted with respect to the complainant.[26] The Court of Justice has yet to rule on the complainant's entitlement to a decision on the rejection of its complaint. It has recognised, in *Metro* and again in *Demo-Studio Schmidt*,[27] that it is in the interests of a satisfactory administration of justice and of a proper application of the competition rules that a person who is entitled under Article 3(2)(b) of Regulation 17 to request the Commission to find an infringement should be able, if the request is dismissed, to institute proceedings in order to protect his legitimate interests.[28] That protection, it is submitted,

---

[20] *BAT and Reynolds*, above, para. 20.

[21] Case 60/81, *IBM* v. *Commission*: [1981] E.C.R. 2639, [1981] 3 C.M.L.R. 635.

[22] Above, n. 19, at para. 46.

[23] See A.G. Warner's appraisal of the Commission's letter in Case 792/79R, *Camera Care Ltd.* v. *Commission*: [1980] E.C.R. 119, [1980] 1 C.M.L.R. 334.

[24] Reg. 1017/68, Art. 11(3); Reg. 4056/86, Art 11(3); Reg. 3975/87, Art. 4(2). No reference is made to cases under Art. 86, but there is no justification for treating these cases differently.

[25] Above, n. 19, at para. 47, emphasis added. The Court of First Instance cited *Demo Studio* (Case 210/81, *Demo-Studio Schmidt* v. *Commission*: [1983] E.C.R. 3045, [1984] 1 C.M.L.R. 63); Case 298/83, *C.I.C.C.E.* v. *Commission*: [1985] E.C.R. 1105, [1986] 1 C.M.L.R. 486C and Cases 142 and 156/84, *BAT and Reynolds* v. *Commission*: [1987] E.C.R. 4487, [1988] 4 C.M.L.R. 24. See also Case T–16/91, *Rendo NV and Others* v. *Commission*: [1992] II E.C.R. 2417.

[26] See A.G. Mancini in *BAT and Reynolds*.

[27] Above. The Court appeared to duck the question. But see para. 14.

[28] The particular interests must be sufficient to demand this degree of protection. Thus, A.G. Mancini in *BAT and Reynolds*, above, appeared to contemplate a right to bring an action against the measure rejecting the complaint only where, so far as may be reasonably foreseen, the measure will cause him to incur a loss.

if it is to be respected and effective, requires the Commission to reject the complaint by a definitive act reviewable by the Court.

The Commission has adopted the practice under which, if the complainant requests a definitive ruling, it will normally receive one where this is needed to enable the complainant to raise the matter before the Court. Such a statement will contain either a rejection or acceptance of the complaint depending on the Commission's reaction to the further arguments supplied in response to the Article 6 communication. Where a complaint is rejected, the letter rejecting the complaint will list all the documents in the file and indicate those to which the complainant may have access. But the letter need not (although it may) contain a ruling on the existence of the alleged infringement. As mentioned above, the Court held in *GEMA* that a complainant is not entitled to a decision on this.[29] Where the statement definitively rejects the complaint this has been held by the Court of Justice and the Court of First Instance to be a decision which could be challenged by the complainant under Article 173.[30] The essence of such a decision is the ruling by the Commission that on the basis of the facts and information in its possession the complaint is unjustified. This does not necessarily imply that there has been no infringement[31] of Article 85 or 86 and in this respect it does not constitute a decision on that question for the undertaking complained of or estop the Commission from investigating the alleged infringement at a later date. The ambit of any appeal under Article 173 may thus be limited.[31a] It is not, however, limited to the submissions and points made by the complainant in answer to the Article 6 communication. The Court will look at all the arguments and evidence before the Commission at the time of the definitive decision to close the file.[32]

2.36   The position therefore appears to be as follows. The complainant is entitled first to a statement from the Commission under Article 6 of Regulation 99/63 provisionally rejecting the complaint and giving the complainant the opportunity to submit comments. This may, if necessary, be obtained by way of the procedure under Article 175. In its reply to the Article 6 communication the complainant may always request the Commission to give a definitive ruling on the complaint and if he has a serious case to bring before the Court he can expect to obtain one. The Court of Justice has yet to rule on whether he is entitled to a decision rejecting the complaint. The fact that the Commission has closed the file does not stop it from reopening it,[33] although it has been noted that experience suggests that the re-opening of a file recently closed rarely

[29] Above, n. 16 at p. 3189 (E.C.R.) and p. 195 (C.M.L.R.). Followed by the Court of First Instance in *Automec II*, at para. 75. Nor is a complainant entitled to have the Commission take a decision under Art. 15(6) of Reg. 17 (the so called "provisional decision") by which the Community from fine of a notified agreement is lost. See *Prodifarma II*: Case T–3/90, *Vereniging Prodifarma* v. *Commission*: [1991] II E.C.R. 1.
[30] See text to and cases cited above at n. 25.
[31] But where it does give reasons why there is no breach of the competition rules that will suffice. The Commission is not required to explain any difference from any statement of objections directed at the undertakings the subject of the investigation. *BAT and Reynolds*, above, at para. 70.
[31a] But see Vesterdorf, *op.cit.*, commenting on *Rendo*, above, n. 25.
[32] *C.I.C.C.E.*, above, at para. 20.
[33] *Ibid.* at para. 27.

is a matter of urgency.[34] Where the complainant's arguments are expressly or impliedly rejected in a formal decision addressed to the undertaking complained of (for example, as in *Metro I*,[35] the Commission gives exemption under Article 85(3) to the agreement at the root of the complaint) the complainant may also be able to challenge the decision under Article 173. In *Metro I*, the Court held that a complainant with a legitimate interest under Article 3(2)(b) of Regulation 17 should be able, if its request is not complied with wholly or in part, to institute proceedings to protect that interest and therefore, for the purposes of Article 173, must be considered to be a person directly and individually concerned by the decision in question.

EEA—Complaints

2.37   The EEA expressly provides that complaints may be addressed to either surveillance authority.[36] Complaints sent to a surveillance authority which, pursuant to the rules in Article 56 EEA dealing with the division of responsibility for enforcement,[37] is not competent to decide on a given case must be transferred without delay to the competent surveillance authority.[38]

III. INITIATION OF A PROCEDURE

Generally

2.38   It does not seem to matter that the formal act on the part of the Commission commencing the proceedings is not communicated straight away to the undertakings concerned.[39] Nor, for example, is the initiation of a procedure necessary before the Commission can exercise its powers of investigation.[40] The communication of the commencement of proceedings to an undertaking may have legal significance in relation to the interruption of time running against the Commission under the limitation regulation, Regulation 2988/74.[41] It may be important in cartel cases where the Commission may have to show it acted in time or risk being time-barred. The primary legal significance, however, of the formal commencement or initiation of proceedings by the Commission relates to the jurisdiction of the authorities in the Member States[42] to apply Articles 85(1) and 86 of the Treaty. Article 9(3) of Regulation 17 provides:

---

[34] Mancini, *op. cit.*
[35] Case 26/76, *Metro-SB-Grossmarkte* v. *Commission*: [1977] E.C.R. 1875, [1978] 2 C.M.L.R. 1, at para. 13.
[36] Protocol 23, Art. 10(1).
[37] See para 1.34B.
[38] Protocol 23, Art. 10(2).
[39] Cases 48, 49, 51–57/69, *Dyestuffs, ICI and others* v. *Commission* [1972] E.C.R. 619, [1972] C.M.L.R. 557.
[40] Indeed, such powers are commonly exercised in advance of the formal commencement of proceedings against an undertaking. See, *e.g. National Panasonic*: [1982] O.J. L354/22, [1983] 1 C.M.L.R. 497.
[41] See, generally, paras. 7.46–49.
[42] The meaning of the term "the authorities in the Member States" is discussed at para. 5.02. But **note** the initiation of a procedure under Art. 2, 3 or 6 of Reg. 17 cannot exempt a national court (*soit a son titre* incident) before which the direct effect of Art. 85(1) is pleaded from giving judgment. See *Perfumes* (Cases 253/78, 3, 37 & 99/79: [1980] E.C.R. 2327, [1981] 2 C.M.L.R. 99), at para. 13.

"As long as the Commission has not initiated any procedure under Article 2, 3 or 6, the authorities of the Member States shall remain competent to apply Article 85(1) and Article 86 in accordance with Article 88 of the Treaty."

It has been in the context of Article 9(3) that much of the Court's consideration of what amounts to the initiation of proceedings has taken place.

In *Brasserie de Haecht* v. *Wilkin (No. 2)*,[43] the Court of Justice took the view that Article 9(3) clearly contemplated an official act on the part of the Commission indicative of its intention to proceed to a decision under the Articles cited. The Court drew a distinction between an official act (*acte d'authorité*) and an administrative formality (*acte de correction administrative*). The simple acknowledgement of an application for negative clearance or notification for exemption could not, in the opinion of the Court, be taken as an initiation of a procedure for these purposes. In *B.R.T.* v. *S.A.B.A.M.*,[44] Advocate General Mayras considered that the Court in *Brasserie de Haecht (No. 2)* had laid down two conditions:

(a) the necessity for an authoritative act of the Commission; and
(b) the necessity for such act to evidence its intention to take one of the decisions referred to in Article 2, 3 or 6 of Regulation 17.

He did not think that this required the Commission to make a formal record of the initiation of the procedure although this is in fact the Commission's practice. In the *Perfumes* cases, the Court held that an administrative letter (*lettre administrative*) informing the undertaking concerned that the file on its case had been closed did not amount to the initiation of a procedure pursuant to Article 2, 3 or 6 of Regulation 17.[45]

The initiation of a procedure is not a decision and a challengeable act within the meaning of Article 173 of the Treaty, notwithstanding its legal character and consequences (in particular as regards Regulation 2988/74 and Article 9(3) of Regulation 17) described above. In *IBM*,[46] the Court of Justice held that it was merely a procedural measure adopted preparatory to the decision which represent its culmination.

---

[43] Case 48/72, *Brasserie de Haecht (No. 2)*: [1973] E.C.R. 77, [1973] C.M.L.R. 287, at para. 16.
[44] Case 127/73: [1974] E.C.R. 51, [1974] C.M.L.R. 238,.
[45] Case 37/79, *Anne Marty SA* v. *Estée Lauder SA*: [1980] E.C.R. 2481, [1981] 2 C.M.L.R. 143, at para. 16. But where a procedure has been initiated the closing of the file may cause the reversion of jurisdiction to the authorities in the Member States under Art. 9(3)—see A.G. Mancini in Cases 142 and 156/84, *BAT and Reynolds* v. *Commission*: [1987] E.C.R. 4487, [1988] 4 C.M.L.R. 24. This may become more important in practice if the Commission relies more on national authorities to pursue cases—see generally the Commission's Notice on co-operation with national courts discussed at para 10.13.
[46] Case 60/81, *IBM* v. *Commission*: [1981] E.C.R. 2639, [1981] 3 C.M.L.R. 635, at para. 21.

Practice

2.39 In practice what is likely to happen is that the Commissioner responsible for competition matters will, in the name of the Commission, sign a form declaring the proceedings open.[47] The competent authorities in the Member States and the undertakings concerned will be informed in due course.[48]

There does not appear to be any requirement on the Commission immediately to notify the undertakings concerned that proceedings have been initiated. So far as the rights of the defence are concerned the statement of objections is the crucial document. In the *Dyestuffs* case,[49] it was argued that the Commission had violated the procedural rules contained in Regulation 17 by communicating to the parties its statement of objections at the same time as it announced the commencement of proceedings to determine whether any infringements had taken place. The complaint was also made that the communication relating to the commencement of proceedings contained no reference to the possible imposition of a fine under Article 15(2) of Regulation 17 and that this violated the essential formal provisions relating to the right to be heard. The Court of Justice rejected both these arguments, stressing that the statement of objections is the important document. The fact that the Commission had not separated chronologically or in substance the communication of the initiation of proceedings from the statement of objections could not in the Court's view injure the rights of the defence.[50] On the second point, the Court said that the communication referred to Regulation 17 as a whole, and thus to Article 15.[51]

IV. OPPOSITION PROCEDURE

Introduction

2.40 Individual exemptions under Article 85(3) can, as a general rule, only be granted if the agreement is notified to the Commission.[52] A block exemption on the other hand, typically exempts an agreement without any need for notification or a formal decision by the Commission provided always that the conditions specified in the terms of the block exemption are satisfied. Whether or not an agreement falls within a block exemption can, if required, be determined by national courts.[53] If an agreement

---

[47] Formerly the nature of the act taken by the Commission to commence proceedings differed depending on whether the case was based on a notification or complaint, or whether the Commission was acting of its own motion. In the last case the Commissioners acting collegiately took a decision to this effect. Now, following a habilitation, the Commission responsible for competition can now act in all three cases. On delegation of powers by the Commission, see paras. 6.46–47.

[48] The fact that a procedure has been initiated is not normally made public, but see [1993] O.J. C107/4 concerning Case IV/34.631 —Agreements relating to the combination of the Galileo and Covia CRSs, where the Commission declared the publication of the notice under Art. 19(3) of Reg. 17 as the initiation of procedure for the purposes of Art. 9(3).

[49] Above, n. 39.

[50] *Ibid.* (Case 57/69), at para. 14.

[51] *Ibid.* (Case 52 & 53/69), at para. 8.

[52] See para. 2.08.

[53] See Case 63/75, *Fonderies Roubaix-Wattrelos*: [1976] E.C.R. 111, [1976] 1 C.M.L.R. 538. Case 59/77, *De Bloos* v. *Bouyer*: [1977] E.C.R. 2359, [1978] 1 C.M.L.R. 511 and Case 170/83, *Hydrotherm* v. *Andreoli*: [1984] E.C.R. 2999, [1985] 3 C.M.L.R. 224. *Sed quaere* where the Commission has made a declaratory decision on the applicability of a block exemption, as in *Sole Distribution Agreements for Whisky*

contains restrictions other than those permitted by the block exemption, the general rule is that the block exemption will not be applicable and if the agreement is to be exempted it will have to be notified and an application made for the Commission, by individual decision, to exempt it.[54] But in the case of five types of agreement, patent licences, research and development, specialisation, franchising and know-how licences, their block exemptions offer another possibility.[55] This is provided by the so-called opposition procedure.[56] The procedure is not applicable where an agreement, although having some features of a type of agreement falling within a relevant block exemption, does not meet the tests of the block exemption in question.[57] But as will be seen, the opposition procedure enables a wider band of agreements to benefit from the block exemption though they cannot do so without notification to the Commission. Before the introduction of the opposition procedure, block exemption would typically specify a particular category of agreements to be exempted. An agreement fell within the terms of the block exemption, or it did not. There were no grey areas, no safety net.

Outline of the procedure

2.41   Where the agreement contains restrictions which are not expressly permitted ("white")[58] or expressly condemned ("black")[59] then the agreement ("grey" in character) may be notified to the Commission and provided the Commission does not oppose exemption within a period of six months, the exemption provided by the block exemption applies to the agreement.[60] The Commission may raise an opposition at any time within the six months. It must do so if requested by a Member State within three months of the transmission to the Member State of the notification.

The Commission may withdraw its opposition at any time, not necessarily within the six-month period. Where this is because the undertakings concerned have shown that the conditions of Article 85(3) are met, the exemption applies as from the date of notification. But where it is because the agreement has been amended in order to satisfy Article 85(3), the exemption applies from the date on which the amendments take

---

and Gin: [1985] O.J. L369/19, [1986] 2 C.M.L.R. 664.

[54] See, *e.g. Alcatel Espace/ANT Nachrichtentechnik:* [1990] O.J. L32/19, [1991] 4 C.M.L.R. 208, where the agreement went beyond R&D and extended to the marketing of products. Being outside the scope of the block exemption (Reg. 418/85) the opposition procedure was also not available to the parties.

[55] The block exemptions for patent licences (Reg. 2349/84), specialisation agreements (Reg. 417/85) research and development agreements (Reg. 418/85), franchising agreements (Reg. 4087/88) and know-how licensing agreements (Reg. 556/89). The procedure can be found in Arts. 4, 4, 7, 6 and 4 of those Regs. respectively. For convenience and economy, references hereafter are restricted to the relevant provisions in Reg. 2349/84 these provisions are reproduced in Appendix J.

[56] See, generally, Venit, "The Commission's Opposition Procedure—Between the Scylla of Ultra Vires and the Charybdis of Perfume: Legal Consequences and Tactical Considerations" (1985) 22 C.M.L.Rev. 167; Korah, *R & D and the EEC Competition Rules: Regulation 418/85* (1986), Chap. 7; and Cook, "Procedural Implications of the New Patent Regulation", paper for ESC Conference, October 30, 1984.

[57] See *Alcatel Escpace/ANT Nachrichtentechnik,* above, and *Quantel International-Continuum/Quantel SA:* [1992] O.J. L235/9 (subject to appeal on this point, Cases T 29 and 36/90). Application of the opposition procedure also presupposes the application of Art. 85(1) and it will therefore not apply if the agreement must be given negative clearance—see *Elopak/Metal Box-Odin:* [1990] O.J. L209/15, [1991] 4 C.M.L.R. 832.

[58] Arts. 1 and 2.

[59] Art. 3.

[60] Art. 4.

effect. Where the opposition has been raised following a request from a Member State and that request is maintained, the opposition can only be withdrawn after consultation with the Advisory Committee. Where the opposition is maintained the consequences of notifying are governed by Regulation 17.

Vires

2.42 The vires of the opposition procedure have not escaped comment.[61] Regulations 2349/84, 4087/88 and 556/89 are made under Regulation 19/65, Regulations 417/85 and 418/85 under Regulation 2821/71. Both enabling provisions require two matters to be specified in the block exemption:[62] first, the restrictions and provisions which must not be contained in the agreements[63] and second, the clauses which must be contained "or the other conditions which must be satisfied." Can a block exemption apply to agreements where the restrictive provisions are not identified and prohibited or permitted? Does the power to specify "other conditions" include procedural conditions rather than conditions which go to the definition of the agreements covered or other objective criteria such as market share or behaviour, in particular where those procedural conditions require notification whereby the benefit of exemption in a particular case will depend on a determination and the exercise of discretion by the Commission? Can a block exemption in effect bypass Regulation 17, with its safeguards for third parties and involvement of the Member States, and provide a procedure whereby agreements may have exemption, perhaps often individual consideration but without an individual exemption? It can, however, be argued that the enabling provisions do not limit what "conditions" can be imposed and necessarily exclude procedural provisions. The effect of the new procedure is not to allow another distinct category of agreements to be exempted but merely to permit some relief at the edges where a strict definitional control might work arbitrarily. Merely because something is novel or different does not mean that it is *ultra vires*. Less automaticity of application may not be desirable in a perfect world, but the Court of Justice will almost certainly be sympathetic to the Commission's position in view of the history of backlogs, the limited resources of the Commission and hence the small number of individual exemptions which can be granted. The Court may not wish to turn the clock back. Moreover, the Commission's discretion may still not go unchecked[64] and the position of third parties is no worse than under other block exemptions.

Notification

2.43 (i) *Regulation 27 and Form A/B*

The five block exemption regulations all provide that agreements must be notified

---

[61] Venit, *op. cit.*, and Korah, *op. cit.*

[62] Art. 1(2) of Reg. 19/65, Art. 1(2) of Reg. 2821/71.

[63] Typically, the "black" list.

[64] See para. 2.52.

"in accordance with Commission Regulation 27,"[65] that is in accordance with the detailed procedural rules governing notification under Regulation 17. The principal consequence is that Form A/B[66] must be used. But the other rules of Regulation 27 (*e.g.* as to notice, proof of authority, certification, etc.) must not be neglected. Since notification in accordance with Regulation 27 is a condition precedent to obtaining the benefit of the procedure it may be that these other[67] requirements become mandatory even if in other circumstances the Court of Justice and the Commission might be prepared to treat them as directory only.

(ii) *Need to invoke opposition procedure*

Express reference must be made in the notification to the relevant article of the block exemption regulation in question.[68] There is a special question and space in Form A/B to enable parties to do this.[69]

(iii) *Complete and accurate information*

Regulation 27 requires notifications to contain all the information asked for in Form A/B and the Complementary Note.[70] The block exemption regulations require the information to be "complete and in accordance with the facts."[71] It is uncertain whether this requires the parties to provide more information than is required for a "normal" notification using Form A/B.[72] It is thought probably not, except possibly where, as the Complementary Note indicates, more specificity or detail is required for the opposition procedure.[73] Particular care should be taken, especially in those cases where the Note requests certain information "if possible".[74] The Commission expects parties to provide all the facts that can and should be in the notification.[75] But the obligation to supply "complete" information cannot be at large. There must be objective limits, both as regards materiality and what the parties knew or ought reasonably to have known in the circumstances and at the relevant time.

---

[65] Art. 4(1)

[66] Art. 4(1) of Reg. 27, as amended by Reg. 2526/85. As the Complementary Note indicates, Form A/B has been constructed to accommodate, *inter alia*, the opposition procedure. And see Recital 3 to Reg. 2526/85.

[67] Other, that is, than the requirement to use Form A/B.

[68] Art. 4(3)(a).

[69] The fourth question in the box "Purpose of this application/notification" on the second side of the form.

[70] Art. 4(2) of Reg. 27.

[71] Art. 4(3)(b).

[72] On completing Form A/B, see, generally, paras. 2.21–27.

[73] See, *e.g.* Headings 4.2 and 6.3 in Part X of the Complementary Note. Moreover the introduction of the new procedures described in para. 2.28 above may lead to more information having to be supplied generally with Form A/B.

[74] *E.g.* Heading 3.1 of Part X.

[75] See the second para. of Part VII of the Complementary Note.

(iv) *The six month period*

The six month period runs from the date on which the notification is received by the Commission.[76] Where registered post is used the period runs from the date shown on the postmark of the place of posting.[77]

(v) *Failure to satisfy a condition precedent*

If a condition has not been met, and that condition (such as notification on Form A/B) is mandatory for the application of the opposition procedure, the exemption will not apply and it is not necessary for the Commission to object by raising opposition or otherwise. The Commission is not obliged to correct the parties' misapprehension that they have satisfied the conditions. There could be circumstances where it might be unfair to the parties if the Commission took the view that a notification was incomplete or defective in some way and yet did not draw this to their attention. The Complementary Note to Form A/B suggests that the Commission may notify the parties.[78] But it is for the parties and their legal advisers to ensure that they have satisfied all preconditions and receipt by the Commission does not stop the Commission from later asserting the inadequacy of the notification.[79] Nor does it prevent a national court from ascertaining whether all conditions precedent have been satisfied. If an agreement is challenged by a third party before the Commission or a national court,[80] the party seeking to rely on exemption under the opposition procedure will, if put to proof, have to show that the conditions have been met.

Confidentiality

2.44 The block exemption regulations contain their own rules on confidentiality and use of information.[81] They follow Article 20 of Regulation 17. There are differences, but it is doubtful if they will be important in practice. So they provide that any information acquired pursuant to the opposition procedure (including the notification) shall only be used for the purposes of the block exemption regulation.[82] The prohibition on disclosure[83] makes no reference to hearings or publication in the *Official Journal* for the opposition procedure does not contemplate these steps. Like Regulation 17 the restriction on confidentiality is limited to information of the kind covered by the obligation of professional secrecy.[84]

---

[76] Art. 4(2).
[77] *Ibid.*
[78] Part VII. The Note contemplates the Commission raising an opposition in these circumstances. This, it is submitted, is the wrong procedure; see para. 2.45.
[79] *Aluminium*: [1985] O.J. L92/1, [1987] 3 C.M.L.R. 813.
[80] As *Fonderies Roubaix-Wattrelos* and the other cases cited in n. 53 indicate, the Commission does not have exclusive jurisdiction here.
[81] This may be because of the uncertainty of the relationship with Reg. 17 and whether Art. 20 would apply. See Korah, *op. cit.* Indeed the block exemptions appear to treat notifications under the opposition procedure as being separate from Reg. 17.
[82] This could theoretically involve a greater restriction on Member States than is found in Art. 20(1) of Reg. 17. See para. 3.45.
[83] Which also purports to bind the "authorities of the Member States." Korah, *op. cit.*, questions the vires to do this.
[84] See, generally, paras. 8.18–21.

Opposition

2.45   The block exemption regulations lay down no rules as to when and how the opposition is to be made and communicated to the parties. It is implicit, however, that the Commission can exercise the power at any time up to the end of the six-month period. It is reasonable to suppose that the opposition will be evidenced in writing even if initially made orally. It is submitted that the opposition can have effect only when notified to the parties. Opposition demands a manifest act which in the absence of any provision in the regulations for publication must be made known to the parties. Furthermore, the communication must be made within the six months.[85]

No grounds for opposition are set out in the regulations. It is submitted that the opposition is confined to the merits of the agreement for inclusion in the relevant block exemption. The Commission would not therefore need to raise an opposition if the block exemption cannot apply because the agreement, for example, is not grey but black or otherwise outside the terms of the block exemption,[86] or because there has been a failure to fulfil the conditions specified for activating the procedure.[87] It is important to make this distinction since in principle a national court is entitled, and may be called upon, to decide whether an agreement fits the negatively defined category of agreements which fall within the block exemption and whether conditions for proper notification have been fulfilled,[88] whereas it is the exclusive preserve of the Commission to deny the benefit of exemption by raising and maintaining an opposition on the basis that the conditions of Article 85(3) are not, in the context of the block exemption, satisfied.

The burden

2.46   The burden is on the Commission to raise an opposition, but once raised it seems that the burden shifts to the applicant to justify exemption. Under the block exemption the applicant is then in a position somewhat similar to the applicant for an individual exemption, *e.g.* it is for the undertaking to submit convincing material to the Commission which allows economic justification for an exemption to be established.[89] Whether the applicant will have to show as much in order to cause an opposition to be withdrawn as may an applicant for individual exemption will in large part depend on the circumstances of the particular case. In some instances it may well be more burdensome because under the opposition procedure the Commission cannot impose a time-limit on the exemption.[90] Nor can it impose conditions or obligations.[91]

---

[85] Although the regs. are silent on this, legal certainty requires that the parties should be able to rely without more on the lapse of time and then be able to enforce the agreement among themselves and, if necessary, rely on it against third parties.

[86] See the decision mentioned, above, n. 57.

[87] But the Complementary Note to Form A/B (Part VII) contemplates raising an opposition in order to allow time for information to be supplied so that the information in the notification is "complete".

[88] See *Fonderies Roubaix-Wattrelos*, and the other cases cited at n. 53.

[89] *VBVB and VBBB*: [1982] O.J. L54/36, [1982] 2 C.M.L.R. 344, at para. 52. If the Commission puts forward objections it is for the undertakings to put forward amendments. Although the Commission may provide undertakings with information on possible alternative solutions, it is not legally obliged to do this.

[90] As the Commission can in the case of individual exemptions. See Art. 8 of Reg. 17.

[91] *Ibid.*

Therefore the Commission may be more cautious and may suggest that the undertakings put forward amendments to the agreements.[92]

Legal effect of notification

2.47 It is important to establish the precise legal effect of notification under the opposition procedure. As long as an agreement within Article 85(1) does not have the benefit of exemption, it is subject to the sanction in Article 85(2), unenforceable (at least as regards its restrictions) and liable to be attacked. It is necessary therefore to ascertain whether an agreement notified under the opposition procedure has the benefit of exemption immediately but subject to the possibility of opposition, or at the end of the six-month period and then with or without retrospective effect. The block exemption regulations are silent on this except for the provision which says that where the opposition is withdrawn because the undertakings have shown that the conditions of Article 85(3) are met, the exemption applies from the date of notification.[93] This suggests that in other cases exemption runs automatically from the date of notification. Indeed it would be odd if an agreement which is unopposed were in a worse position than an agreement opposed and then released. There are two possibilities. The exemption applies immediately on notification, the absence of opposition being a condition subsequent.[94] This avoids a hiatus in the legal status of the agreement and is not inconsistent with the avowed aim of the procedure to extend legal certainty. Alternatively it is arguable that the exemption attaches at the end of the six months, and, subject to the condition precedent that no opposition has been raised, relates back to the date of notification. The position, although not unreasonable in principle, demands a lot from the silence of the regulations, and does not avoid a legal hiatus, at least temporarily. It will be appreciated that the question of the legal effect of notification may be significant for the status of the acts of raising, maintaining and withdrawing opposition described below.

Relationship with Regulation 17

2.48 From a practical standpoint it is sensible that an agreement which has been notified for the purposes of the opposition procedure using Form A/B should also be treated as a notification for the purposes of Regulation 17 with the benefits of such, namely immunity from fine and eligibility for individual exemption.[95] But in order to achieve this at the point of notification it seems that the parties must apply additionally for individual exemption when completing Form A/B.[96] The regulation governing the opposition procedure merely provides that where the Commission raises an opposition and does not withdraw it "the effect shall be governed by the provisions of Regulation 17."[97] This suggests that Regulation 17 may not be applicable to the notification

---

[92] If it is commercially feasible, the easier course for the applicant faced with an opposition may be to remove the provisions whose effect is to colour the agreement grey, leaving the remainder white and therefore exempt. The Commission cannot deny the benefit of the block exemption to such a remnant without a formal decision withdrawing the benefit of the block exemption (*e.g.* under Art. 9).

[93] Art. 4(7).

[94] Korah, *op. cit.*, takes this view.

[95] See para. 2.18.

[96] The applicant must supply all the information necessary for the opposition procedure and an individual exemption.

[97] Art. 4(9).

until some point when the Commission has decided not to withdraw the opposition,[98] which need not be within the six-month period. In theory therefore, if an agreement is not at the same time notified for the purposes of individual exemption, there is no immediate immunity from fine. But it is most unlikely that the Commission would fine where the parties have notified under the opposition procedure. On the other hand, if the parties have notified under the opposition procedure there seems no reason why the Commission could not issue an Article 15(6) decision suspending immunity from fine immediately on opposition.[99] The opposition is not by itself a decision under Article 15(6). Whilst the relationship between Regulation 17 and the opposition procedure is uncertain it does not appear to have given rise to problems in practice.

Role of the Member States

2.49   The only aspect of the opposition procedure which is elaborated to any extent is the involvement of the Member States. Opposition may be triggered by a Member State.[1] There is an implied obligation on the Commission to send copies of the agreement and notification to the Member States and one would expect them to be sent to the designated competent authorities for the purposes of Article 10(1) of Regulation 17.[2] There is also an implied obligation to send the documents in good time in order to enable the Member States to exercise their rights under the regulations.[3] Any request made by a Member State for the Commission to raise an opposition must be justified on Community competition law grounds. It is not certain what a Member State must show but presumably the arguments and any other material must be directed towards showing that the agreement does not fulfil the conditions of Article 85(3) in the context of the block exemption, or at least should be put to further proof and examination. The Commission might reasonably expect the Member State to give it sufficient material so that the Commission can on that basis legitimately move an opposition against the agreement.[4] Where the opposition is raised at the request of a Member State and the request is maintained, it may be withdrawn only after consultation of the Advisory Committee.[5]

---

[98] And it is difficult to see how there are the vires in Reg. 19/65 or 2821/71 to apply Reg. 17 where the parties do not notify formally under the Reg. Contrast the approach taken in relation to mergers. See Arts. of Reg. 2367/90 and note the recitals in that regulation relating to vires, and in particular the second to fifth "having regard to" clauses.

[99] See, generally, paras. 6.12–15.

[1] Art. 4(5). The request to raise an opposition must be made within three months of the transmission of the notification of the agreement to the Member State.

[2] Although the regs. refer simply to the Member States, the competent authority is the obvious channel of communication. It is apparently open to the Member States to designate a different body for the purposes of the block exemptions. Moreover, even if the documents are sent to the Reg. 17 competent authority it is possible for the documents to be passed on to other authorities within the Member State.

[3] That is not later than three months from the date of notification. There seems no good reason why the documents should not be sent "forthwith" as is required under Reg. 17 (Art. 10(1)).

[4] At first sight this might appear an unreasonable burden to place on the Member States, but it should be remembered that the Commission is obliged to raise an opposition at the Member State's request and therefore may, given the time factors involved, have little opportunity in which to verify or amplify the grounds for opposition. Of course, if the Commission itself can raise an opposition with little justification or explanation the burden on the Member State will correspondingly be less.

[5] Art. 4(6).

Third parties

2.50   The opposition procedure makes no express provision for third parties,[6] and in particular complaints. Nor are there any rules for publication. Contrast the position under Regulations 17[7] and 99/63.[8] The absence of any express recognition or protection for third parties does not mean that the interests of third parties can be totally disregarded by the Commission and that third parties go unprotected.[9] The express rules in Regulations 17 and 99/63 concerning third parties are merely specific applications of a general principle of Community law. But the absence of publicity in the opposition procedure (as compared to the objections procedure in transport cases) may defeat third party interests at the critical time. Complainants can always complain, and in view of the time factors relating to the opposition procedure, should never delay. The ability of third parties to challenge the key steps in the procedure being at best uncertain,[10] a complainant who comes late may only hope to persuade the Commission to withdraw the exemption.[11]

Review by the Court

2.51   Which steps, if any, in the opposition procedure may be challenged before the Court? Generally, any measure the legal effects of which are binding on, and capable of affecting the interests of, the applicant by bringing about a distinct change in his legal position is an act or decision challengeable under Article 173.[12] But, as the Court of Justice has indicated, where a procedure involves several stages, it is necessary to distinguish between the final decision and the provisional measures which pave the way for the decision. Provisional measures are not challengeable acts unless they have the effects described above and they are themselves the culmination of a special procedure distinct from the final decision.[13] Whilst the efficacy of the opposition procedure would be considerably jeopardised if the possibility of legal challenge existed at every (or even several) stages,[14] the procedure does involve an exercise of discretion on the part of the Commission and the interests of parties may be adversely affected. The key steps will be considered separately.

(i) *Opposition*

It is extremely doubtful whether the act of opposition can itself be challenged. It is essentially a preliminary step, not involving any definitive act by the Commission. It is a holding measure, maintaining the status quo ante (*i.e.* that the agreement because of

---

[6] That is apart from Member States.

[7] See paras. 2.29–37.

[8] Especially Art. 6, discussed at para. 2.34.

[9] The absence of protection has been criticised. Indeed it has been suggested that it impinges upon the vires of the block exemption regs. See Venit, *op. cit.*, and Korah, *op. cit.*

[10] See para. 2.52.

[11] Under Art. 9, an uphill task for complainant and Commission.

[12] Case 60/81, *IBM* v. *Commission*: [1981] E.C.R. 2639, [1981] 3 C.M.L.R. 635, at para. 9. See, generally, paras. 9.06–09.

[13] *Ibid.* at para. 10.

[14] If only for this reason, the Commission is likely to argue strenuously against steps being challengeable acts.

its greyness is not within the block exemption). A party who notifies under the opposition procedure has no legal guarantee or expectation that its agreement will retain or be given the benefit of exemption since the possibility of opposition is a clear feature of the regime. Most important, whether the opposition will be withdrawn or an individual exemption under Regulation 17 granted is still open.[15]

(ii) *Non-opposition*

If the Commission does not raise an opposition and the six months pass, then by force of the terms of the block exemption the agreement is exempt. Whilst it is clear that complainants may be able to challenge individual exemptions,[16] it does not seem that non-opposition gives rise to a challengeable act. The complainant cannot call upon the Commission to act under Article 175, the opposition not being a measure addressed to him,[17] and therefore it seems that the complainant must be content with a decision on his complaint.[18]

(iii) *Maintaining opposition*

The block exemptions do not require the Commission to inform the parties that the opposition is to be maintained and it is doubtful whether maintaining opposition is itself challengeable. As in the case of the opposition described above the status quo ante remains. There is the possibility of a withdrawal (with retrospective effect) or even an individual exemption under Regulation 17. But the position may be different where, perhaps pursuant to a request from the parties, the Commission gives a definitive statement refusing withdrawal of the opposition. This, it could be argued, is the culmination of a special procedure within the meaning of *IBM*[19]—the Commission has determined to close the gate on the opposition procedure's route to exemption.[20]

(iv) *Withdrawal of opposition*

It is unlikely, but not inconceivable,[21] that a party to the agreement would wish to challenge the withdrawal of opposition, having as it does the consequence of exemption under the regulation. The legal effect on the parties is immediately discernible — the agreement can be enforced by the parties inter se and can be relied upon against third parties without fear of Article 85(2). The determination and exercise of discretion by the Commission in the circumstances is tantamount to granting an individual exemption and a party to the agreement or a third party with sufficient interest[22] may be able

---

[15] See Venit, *op. cit.*, and Korah, *op. cit.*

[16] See the *Metro* cases (Case 26/76, *Metro-SB-Grossmarkte* v. *Commission*: [1977] E.C.R. 1875, [1978] 2 C.M.L.R. 1 and 75/84, *Metro-SB-Grossmarkte GmbH & Co. K.G.* v. *Commission*: [1986] E.C.R. 3021, [1987] 1 C.M.L.R. 118).

[17] Case 246/81, *Lord Bethell.* v. *Commission*: [1982] E.C.R. 2277, [1982] 3 C.M.L.R. 300, and more recently, Case T–3/90, *Vereniging Prodifarma* v. *Commission*: [1991] II E.C.R. 1.

[18] As to the complainant's entitlement to such a decision, see para. 2.35.

[19] Above, at para. 10.

[20] Venit, *op. cit.*, also contemplates the possibility of challenge in these circumstances.

[21] See, *e.g.* the example given by Korah, *op. cit.*

[22] As in the *Metro* cases, above.

to challenge this.[23] An appeal might also be brought by a Member State, particularly one which had triggered the opposition.[24]

Practice

2.52   It appears that few agreements are notified under the opposition procedure. The annual Competition Policy Reports briefly describe how they have been dealt with.[25] In practice as long as black-listed clauses are avoided, companies appear more prepared to rely on their own determination that remaining clauses do not constitute restrictions on competition contrary to Article 85(1) than to notify a grey agreement.

---

[23] See Venit, *op. cit.*, contra.
[24] See Venit, *op. cit.*
[25] Twenty-first Report on Competition Policy, points 112–130.

3

Fact-Finding

3.01 This chapter deals with the Commission's formal investigatory powers. The Commission can, of course, obtain information from the parties, complainants, national authorities, etc., informally, and often does so. Newspapers and trade journals also provide a source of information. The formal powers are, however, frequently used in practice and must be taken seriously. Regulation 17 and, similarly, the implementating regulations in the transport sector give the Commission two important powers relating to the obtaining and verification of factual information.[1] Article 11 of Regulation 17 enables the Commission to obtain "all necessary information from the Governments and competent authorities of the Member States and from undertakings and associations of undertakings." Article 14 enables the Commission to undertake "all necessary investigations into undertakings and associations of undertakings" and contains a list of powers which shows straightaway just how wide the scope of investigations may be.[2] The Commission's inspectors are empowered:

> "(a) to examine the books and other business records;
> (b) to take copies of or extracts from the books and business records;
> (c) to ask for oral explanations on the spot;
> (d) to enter any premises, land and means of transport of undertakings."[3]

---

[1] See, generally, Deringer, *The Competition Law of the European Economic Community* (1968); Ehlermann and Oldekop, "Due Process in Administrative Procedure" Vol. 3 of the papers of the FIDE Conference in Copenhagen 1978; Thiesing-Schroter-Hochbaum, *Les Ententes et les Positions Dominantes dans le Droit de la CEE* (1977); Joshua, "The Element of Surprise: EEC Competition Investigations under Article 14(3) of Regulation 17" (1983) 8 E.L.Rev. 3; Kreis, "EEC Commission Investigation Procedures in Competition Cases" (1983) 17 Int. Lawyer 19; House of Lords Select Committee on the European Communities, Session 1983–1984, 18th Report, Commission's Powers of Investigation and Inspection. And note the Commission's general power to collect information, etc., set out in Article 213 of the Treaty.

[2] Cases 46/87 & 227/88 *Hoechst AG* v. *Commission*: [1989] E.C.R. 2859, [1991] 4 C.M.L.R. 410, at para. 26.

[3] *Cf.* s. 46 of the German Act against Restraints of Competition (Gesetz gegen Wettbewerbsbeschrankungen–GWB, the English text of which can be found at [1982] 1 *Commercial Laws of Europe* 1) which gives the Bundeskartellamt similar powers in the case of administrative proceedings: "(1) To the extent necessary for the performance of its duties under this Act, the cartel authority may 1. require information from enterprises and associations of enterprises concerning their economic circumstances; 2. inspect and examine business documents at the premises of enterprises and associations of enterprises during normal hours of business; 3. require information from trade, industrial or professional organisations concerning their rules, resolutions and the number and names of members to whom the resolutions are directed." For the investigation powers of U.K. competition authorities, see Fair Trading Act 1973, ss. 44–46 and 85; Restrictive Trade Practices Act 1976, ss. 36 and 37, and Competition Act 1980, ss. 2(5), 3(7) and (8).

Both powers are prefaced by the words "In carrying out the duties assigned to it by Article 89 and by provisions adopted under Article 87 of the Treaty."[4] Articles 87 and 89 are discussed above.[5] The duties are those concerning the enforcement of the Community competition rules.

As will be seen, Regulation 17 accords certain guarantees to the undertaking under investigation and the Court of Justice has held that the Commission's powers cannot be interpreted in such a way as to give rise to results which are incompatible with the general principles of Community law and in particular with fundamental rights.[6] This said, as the Court indicated in *Orkem*:

> "Regulation 17 does not give an undertaking under investigation any right to evade the investigation on the ground that the results thereof might provide evidence of an infringement by it of competition rules. On the contrary, it imposes on the undertaking an obligation to co-operate actively, which implies that it must make available to the Commission all information relating to the subject matter of the investigation."[7]

This duty on undertakings to co-operate should not be overlooked in practice, although its main relevance is in relation to Article 14. The Court has however recognised the need to respect and protect the confidentiality of lawyer/client communications (this is discussed in Chapter 8) and the need not to undermine the rights of defence of the undertaking concerned (the issue of protection against self-incrimination is dealt with later in this chapter[8]).

I. REQUESTS FOR INFORMATION

Undertakings

3.02   Article 11(1) gives the Commission the power to obtain all necessary information "from undertakings."[9] The meaning of undertaking in the context of Articles 85 and 86 is discussed in Chapter 1[10] and it is reasonable to suppose that the same meaning should be given to the term in Article 11 although it does not necessarily follow.[11] The undertakings from whom information can be sought under Article 11 are not described by reference to their participation or involvement in any breach of the Community competition rules and the Commission takes the view that it is entitled to

---

[4] The powers in the transport regulations are however prefaced by the words "In carrying out the duties assigned to it by this Regulation."

[5] See paras. 1.23–24.

[6] *Hoechst*, above, at para. 12.

[7] Case 374/87, *Orkem* v. *Commission*: [1989] E.C.R. 3283, [1991] 4 C.M.L.R. 502, at para. 27.

[8] See para. 3.44.

[9] And from Governments and competent authorities of the Member States, see para. 5.14.

[10] See para. 1.05

[11] *Quaere* the Commission's powers to obtain information from a body (not being an undertaking) to ascertain its status as an undertaking. It is arguable that the Commission's powers should be sufficient to cover this. The body may of course have an interest in giving the information voluntarily.

request information under Article 11 from undertakings against which there is no suspicion of infringement of Article 85 or 86 of the Treaty.[12] So, for example, it is not uncommon for the Commission to request a complainant formally under Article 11 to supply further and better particulars of, or supplementary information relating to, his complaint.[13] The Commission may make inquiries of competitors of parties to an agreement or concerted practice in order to obtain a better picture of the relevant market for the goods or services the subject of the agreement or practice, and will often use Article 11 to obtain such information. In the same way, the Commission may obtain information from the customers of a dominant firm about that firm's conduct or behaviour. Third parties are an important source of information for the Commission and it is the better view that the Commission is entitled to obtain information from such parties where the information is necessary for the enforcement of the competition rules.[14]

Necessary information

3.03 Article 11 contains few express restrictions on the Commission's power to request information from undertakings. The principal limitation is that indicated by the prefatory words "in carrying out the duties assigned to it by Article 89 of the Treaty and by the provisions adopted under Article 87." It is a limitation of purpose and therefore there must be a relationship between the information requested and the infringement being investigated. The Commission almost certainly has a substantial discretion in this context. The Court of Justice has held that it is for the Commission to decide whether particular information is necessary to define the scope of the infringement, its duration, the identity of the parties, etc., subject always to the supervision of the Court.[15] Necessary information is that which is requisite for the Commission to establish the applicability of Articles 85 and 86 in pursuance of its obligations and duties

---

[12] *Cf.* the position of the Director-General of Fair Trading under the Restrictive Trade Practices Act 1976. Under s. 36(1) he can only address a notice to a person believed to be a party to a registrable agreement, and under s. 36(3), to a person who has furnished particulars of an agreement or who is party to an agreement. The Director-General has wider powers under ss. 44–46 of the Fair Trading Act in connection with the obtaining of statistical information prior to monopoly references and under s. 2(5) of the Competition Act 1980. The Monopolies and Mergers Commission had wide powers under s. 85 of the Fair Trading Act, and similarly the Director-General under s. 3(7) and (8) of the Competition Act. The powers of the Bundeskartellamt under s. 46 of the GWB do not appear to be restricted only to enterprises which are suspected of engaging in anti-competitive practices. In the United States, the powers of the Justice Department in civil proceedings under the Sherman Act to issue a civil investigative demand (a CID) to obtain information are not limited to prospective defendants but, by virtue of the Hart-Scott-Rodino Antitrust Improvements Act of 1976, may also be used in the case of any party believed to have information which will aid the investigation.

[13] See, *e.g.* Case 298/83, *C.I.C.C.E.* v. *Commission*: [1985] E.C.R. 1106, [1986] 1 C.M.L.R. 486, at para. 5. The formal use by the Commission of its powers under Article 11 may protect a complainant. In any event the complainant will want to respond positively. The Commission has indicated that it will only take up a complaint where there is a particular Community interest in doing so. See the Notice on co-operation between national courts and the Commission in applying Articles 85 and 86 of the EEC Treaty: [1993] O.J. C39/6. Discussed at para. 10.13.

[14] The question has never been considered by the Court but, bearing in mind the Court's readiness to construe the provisions of Reg. 17 so as to give them maximum practical effectiveness, it is most likely that the Court would uphold the Commission's viewpoint. And see Kreis, *op. cit.*, at p. 26.

[15] *Orkem*, above, at paras. 15 and 16. The Court will look to see whether the information requested exceeded what might be rejected as necessary in the light of the investigation. See also paras. 3.30 and 3.32.

under the Treaty and where appropriate to take a decision in relation to such applicability under Regulation 17.[16] So requests for information that are purely precautionary or solely for documentary purposes would be improper.[17] The Court of First Instance has said that "the Commission may require the production only of information likely to enable it to verify the presumptions of an infringement which justify the conduct of the investigation and which are stated in the request for information."[18] The risk is that in practice there may be little real control on the Commission except where information is patently irrelevant. It is a separate question whether the power to request information should be exercised in a reasonable manner,[19] or in a manner consistent with the principle of proportionality and with a limited measure of intervention.[20]

Primary and secondary sources

3.04   Article 11 does not contain any express restrictions on the number or type of undertakings from which it can request information nor on the number of requests that can be made to any undertaking. The Commission is therefore not limited to asking for information from only one party to an agreement and, as already mentioned, information can be sought from third parties.[21] In *SEP*, the Court of First Instance stated clearly that in addition to the requirement that there be a connection between the information sought and the infringement "the obligation on an enterprise to furnish information shall not represent a burden for the enterprise which is disproportionate to the needs of the investigation."[22] It is a nice question whether and, if so, to what extent the Commission is entitled to request information under Article 11 from "secondary" sources such as lawyers, accountants, bankers, etc., acting for an undertaking. A firm of solicitors or accountants or a bank may constitute an undertaking for the purposes of Articles 85 and 86 and of Regulation 17. And in so far as the information does not touch upon the relationship between the lawyer, accountant, banker, etc., and a client undertaking, then providing it is "necessary" in performance of the Commission's duties, any refusal to supply the information might be unjustifiable.[23] Where the information sought relates to the client relationship then the position is less clear. The confidential nature of the information would not itself seem to be a good reason for refusing to supply information under Regulation 17, because the Commission is bound by Article 20(2) of Regulation 17 and Article 214 of the Treaty to keep secret

---

[16] See, for example, the recitals in *RAI/UNITEL*: [1978] O.J. L157/39, [1978] 3 C.M.L.R. 306.

[17] See Kreis, *op. cit.*, at p. 27.

[18] Case T–39/90 *SEP* v. *Commission*: [1991] II E.C.R. 1497, [1992] 5 C.M.L.R. 33, at para. 25.

[19] See Deringer, *op. cit.*, para. 2211.

[20] *Per* A.G. Roemer in Case 31/59, *Acciaieria e Tubificio di Brescia* v. *High Authority*: [1960] E.C.R. 71, 88, 89. And *Deutsche Castrol*: [1983] O.J. L114/26, [1983] 3 C.M.L.R. 165, at para. 7, the Commission stated that the questions posed did not go beyond what was relevant to the case and what Castrol might reasonably be expected to reply. The principle of proportionality is discussed generally at paras. 8.25–26.

[21] For an example of inquiries of customers, see *Bayo-n-ox*: [1990] O.J. L21/71, [1990] 4 C.M.L.R. 930, at para. 32.

[22] Above, n. 18, at para. 51. The issue in that case was not the burden or cost of ascertaining and providing the information but its particular confidentiality. The plea of lack of proportionality was rejected on the grounds that sufficient protection of confidentiality existed by virtue of Art. 214 of the Treaty and Art. 20 of Reg. 17.

[23] Disclosure under compulsion of law would not constitute a breach of the banker's duty of secrecy (*Tournier* v. *N.P. Bank*: [1924] 1 K.B. 461) or the solicitor's duty of confidentiality (*Parry-Jones* v. *Law Society*: [1968] 1 All E.R. 17).

information governed by the obligation of professional secrecy.[24] Whilst legal professional privilege/legal confidence may justify a refusal by a lawyer it is very doubtful whether similar protection is given to others who might be bound by the *secret professionel*.[25]

Who supplies the information

3.05 Article 11(4) provides as follows:

> "The owners of the undertakings or their representatives and, in the case of legal persons, companies or firms, or of associations having no legal personality, the persons authorised to represent them by law or by their constitution shall supply the information requested."[26]

Although it appears to place the responsibility to supply the information firmly on the shoulders of the officials specified, Article 11(4) is not supported by sanctions which can be imposed on such officials. If incorrect information is supplied in response to a request under Article 11(3) or a decision under Article 11(5), or if information is not supplied within the time limit fixed by a decision under Article 11(5), then it is the undertaking which may be fined and not the officials concerned.[27] Where the information is correct, complete and in time but is given by a person who is "incompetent" or unauthorised as regards Article 11(4) then provided the information has been supplied by or on behalf of the undertaking there should be no liability to penalty under Article 15. In any event it would be a simple matter for an official who is competent for the purposes of Article 11(4) to ratify the acts of the person who in fact supplied the information. The purpose of Article 11(4) appears to be to enable the Commission to rely on the person supplying the information to bind the undertaking. The undertaking will also wish to make this clear. Replies to Article 11 requests are therefore best given by properly authorised officials of the undertaking. Indeed the Commission may insist that they are so given, so that it can rely on them.

---

[24] See paras. 8.18–21.

[25] See Deringer, *op. cit.*, paras. 2211, 2212. In Continental systems the obligation of professional secrecy may extend beyond the lawyer-client relationships. *Cf.* the position of patent agents and registered trade mark agents who have professional privilege under U.K. law (see Copyright; Designs and Patents Act 1988, ss. 280 and 284). On the lawyer-client relationship, see, generally, paras. 8.13–17.

[26] *Cf.* s. 46(2) of the GWB (above, n. 3) which provides that "the proprietors of enterprises or their representatives or, in the case of legal persons or companies and societies without legal capacity, the persons appointed to represent them by statute or articles of association, and the agents appointed under section 36(2), shall have a duty to give the information required, to produce the business documents and to suffer examination thereof and permit entry to business offices and premises." The GWB therefore covers both authority to supply information and to permit investigations in administrative proceedings. Art. 14 of Reg. 17 contains no equivalent to Art. 11(4).

[27] And the Commission may not be impressed by any argument that the person giving the information lacked authority to do so. *Cf. Viho/Parker Pen*: [1992] O.J. L233/27 where the plea that the official of the company concerned did not have relevant authority to put an export ban into the contract failed. The company remained liable *culpa in eligendo* or *culpa in vigilando*.

Two-stage procedure

3.06 Article 11 contemplates a two-stage procedure[28] for obtaining information from undertakings: a simple request for information under Article 11(3) followed, if necessary, by a decision under Article 11(5) requiring information to be supplied. The Commission has acknowledged that undertakings are under no legal obligation to supply information unless it has taken a formal decision to that effect.[29] It is, however, clear from the wording of Article 11 that before taking such a decision under Article 11(5) there must be a default on the part of the undertaking in supplying the information voluntarily in response to a simple request under Article 11(3). As to the purpose of this two-stage procedure, in *Transocean Marine Paint Association* v. *Commission*,[30] Advocate General Warner said:

> "Whatever purpose can this two-stage procedure serve, unless it be to afford the opportunity for any observations of the 'undertakings or associations of undertakings' concerned, as well as of the competent authorities of the relevant Member State or Member States, to be made and considered before the Commission reaches a final decision."

Two Commission officials have indicated that the two-stage procedure also enables an undertaking to put arguments to the Commission before a decision is taken under Article 11(5). In this way, they say, due process is assured.[31] The Commission's intentions are made known through the simple request under Article 11(3) and the Commission must consider any opposing arguments made by the undertaking before taking a decision. It also provides the opportunity in practice to have the ambit of the request and its underlying purpose clarified and therefore to avoid the Commission having to proceed to a decision under Article 11(5). There is, however, no right to a formal hearing in these circumstances. The Court of Justice has held that there is a substantive difference between decisions taken in exercise of investigatory powers and those taken to terminate an infringement or to declare that an agreement or practice is incompatible with Article 85.[32] This substantive difference explains the wording of Article 19(1) which provides for the right to be heard and makes no reference to Article 11 or 14 but only to those Articles of Regulation 17 under which the Commission may take decisions in exercise of its judicial powers. In relation to these more important decisions the rights of defence require the undertakings concerned to be given greater protection.[33]

---

[28] Case 136/79, *National Panasonic (UK) Ltd.* v. *Commission*: [1980] E.C.R. 2033, [1980] 3 C.M.L.R. 169, at para. 10. For an example of the use of both stages, see *Baccarat*: [1991] O.J. L97/16, [1992] 5 C.M.L.R. 189.

[29] Answer to Written Question No. 677/79: [1979] O.J. C310/30.

[30] Case 17/74: [1974] E.C.R. 1063, 1089, 1090, [1974] 2 C.M.L.R. 459, at 471–472.

[31] Ehlermann and Oldekop, *op. cit.*, at p. 6.

[32] *National Panasonic (UK) Ltd.* v. *Commission*, above, at para. 21.

[33] Art. 19 of Reg. 17 and the right to be heard are discussed in Chap. 4.

Requests for information

3.07 It is normally assumed that requests under Article 11(3) must be in writing. The request must be made in a form which can be copied to the relevant competent authority in accordance with Article 11(2). In practice requests are usually made in writing and are set out in the text of a letter. The request must state the legal basis and the purpose of the request and also the penalties provided for in Article 15(1)(b) of Regulation 17 for supplying incorrect information in response to the request.[34] The information sought should be identified precisely. Not only will this assist the undertaking to comply, but because of the two-stage procedure only information requested under Article 11(3) can, if not supplied pursuant to that request, be the subject of a decision under Article 11(5). The request will usually specify a time-limit within which the information should be supplied to the Commission. There is no legal requirement for this in Article 11(3), but it is one of the conditions to be satisfied before the Commission can take a decision under Article 11(5) that the undertaking has not supplied the information requested "within the time limit fixed by the Commission." Any decision under Article 11(5) must fix an appropriate time-limit within which the information must be supplied. It is submitted that any time-limit fixed by the Commission in respect of information under Article 11(3) must similarly be "appropriate", *i.e.* it must be reasonable in view of the circumstances of the undertaking and the nature and amount of information sought. If the time is not enough in order to provide a proper answer, this should be explained to the Commission and extra time requested. Reasonable requests are usually granted.

There is no legal obligation on an undertaking to comply with a request under Article 11(3).[35] But this does not mean that an undertaking which complies can do so without risk. The Commission may impose a fine (from 100 to 5,000 ECUs) on an undertaking which intentionally or negligently supplies incorrect information in response to a request under Article 11(3).[36] In this context the Commission does not accept that there is any distinction between information supplied in response to an Article 11(3) request and that to a decision under Article 11(5). In *Telos*,[37] the Commission defined what it considers to be "incorrect" information:

> "Any statement is incorrect which gives a distorted picture of the true facts asked for, and which departs significantly from reality on major points. Where a statement is thus false or so incomplete that the reply taken in its entirety is likely to mislead the Commission about the true facts, it constitutes incorrect information within the meaning of Article 15(1)(b)."

Moreover for the purposes of Article 15(1)(b) a request for information means the complete document containing all the elements listed in Article 11. It is not, the Commission says, limited to the particular questions seeking information. The request

---

[34] Art. 11(3) of Reg. 17.

[35] See above, n. 29 and the text relating thereto.

[36] Art. 15(1)(b) of Reg. 17. Discussed at para. 7.06. See *Telos*: [1982] O.J. L58/19, [1982] 1 C.M.L.R. 267; *National Panasonic (Belgium) NV*: [1982] O.J. L113/18, [1982] 2 C.M.L.R. 410; *National Panasonic (France) SA*: [1982] O.J. L211/32, [1982] 3 C.M.L.R. 623; *Comptoir Commercial d'Importation*: [1982] O.J. L27/31, [1982] 1 C.M.L.R. 440, and *Peugeot*: [1986] O.J. L295/19. See also *Secrétama*: [1991] O.J. L35/23, a decision under the equivalent provisions in Reg. 4056/86 (maritime transport).

[37] *Ibid.*

must be viewed not only in the light of the questions asked but also of the objective being pursued. An undertaking may not therefore rely simply on the listed questions but should have regard to the spirit and purpose of the request.[38] The Commission will look at the undertaking's reply in its entirety and will not limit its consideration to the specific answers to the individual questions set out in the request. The Commission takes the view that for the purposes of Article 15(1)(b) a reply must be taken to include not only the answers to the actual questions asked, but also information supplied which goes beyond the particular scope of the questions, as well as information supplied by the undertaking on its own initiative which does not directly relate to the questions.[39] But presumably any "extra" information supplied must be relevant and material to the request if its incorrectness is to attract a fine under Article 15.

The request for information should therefore be scrutinised carefully. Even if the questions are uncertain or even ambiguous, the answers should not be. And as indicated there is a danger if an undertaking gives too little or too much![40] An undertaking should not hesitate to seek legal advice. It is important that the undertaking is aware of the Commission's current interpretation and practice as regards Articles 85 and 86. Much may be at stake, not just for Article 15 purposes, but perhaps more importantly for the future of the proceedings. Care should be taken lest any statement be construed, perhaps wrongly, as an admission, for example, as to the existence of an agreement or understanding between undertakings.[41] It should also be borne in mind that any reply may ultimately be disclosed to other parties under the "access to the file" procedure.[42] Having said all this, it is a fact that the vast majority of requests for information are complied with voluntarily and effectually and it is only rarely that recourse has to be made to the second stage in the procedure, the formal decision under Article 11(5).

Although Article 11(2) requires the Commission, when sending a request for information under Article 11(3) to an undertaking, to forward at the same time a copy to the competent authority of the Member State in whose territory the seat of the undertaking is situated, there is no express requirement in Article 11 for the competent authority to be supplied with a copy of any reply given by the undertaking and in practice copies are not routinely sent to it. If the reply is a relevant document in a later procedure the Commission may have to do so by virtue of its general obligation in Article 10(1) of Regulation 17.[43]

---

[38] The Commission seems to expect firms to reveal all relevant information which although it is not specifically requested the Commission would need if it knew the whole story! It is debatable whether the duty to co-operate (see *Orkem*, above, n. 7) extends this far.

[39] On this point there is an interesting difference between the German text of Art. 15(1)(b) and the other languages. In the German, the phrase "in response to a request" is adjectival and qualifies "information" whilst in the other texts it is capable of being treated as adverbial, qualifying "supply". Consider also the implications of this approach for Art. 15(1)(a) and "extra" information provided under Heading 7 of Part X of the Complementary Note to Form A/B.

[40] It has been suggested that firms will be less keen to respond voluntarily to Art. 11(3) requests and may well wait for an Art. 11(5) decision where they are not so likely to supply incorrect information by mistake or omission. See Korah, "Narrow or Misleading Replies to Requests for Information" (1982) 3 Bus. Law Review 69.

[41] See *Peroxygen Products*: [1985] O.J. L35/1, [1985] 1 C.M.L.R. 481.

[42] See generally para. 4.08. However, in *Plasterboard*, the Court of First Instance did not criticise the Commission for failing to disclose the answer to a request for information: Case T–65/89, *BPB Industries plc and British Gypsum* v. *Commission*: [1993] 4 C.M.L.R. 143, at paras. 31–33.

[43] If the reply is not a relevant document or if there is no subsequent procedure, it will probably not make much difference if the national authority never gets it. So the absence of any express legal duty to supply

Decisions requiring information

3.08 Before the Commission can take a decision under Article 11(5) it must first have requested the information from the undertaking under Article 11(3) and thereby have given the undertaking the opportunity to supply the information voluntarily. Therefore, unlike inspection decisions, there can be no "surprise" decisions requiring information. Where an undertaking does not supply the information requested under Article 11(3) within the time-limit fixed by the Commission, or supplies incomplete information,[44] the Commission may by decision require the information to be supplied.[45] Article 11(5) requires the decision to:

(a) specify what information is required,
(b) fix an appropriate time-limit[46] within which the information is to be supplied to the Commission, and
(c) indicate:
    (i) the penalties provided for in Articles 15(1)(b) and 16(1)(c) of Regulation 17, and
    (ii) the right to have the decision reviewed by the Court.[47]

Decisions must be notified to those to whom they are addressed and take effect upon such notification.[48] The Commission must send a copy of the decision to the competent authority of the Member State in whose territory the seat of the undertaking is situated.[49] But the Commission is not required to consult with the relevant competent authority before taking a decision under Article 11(5) as it is under Article 14 in connection with decisions ordering investigations.

---

copies of replies in all cases may not be important. Art. 10(1) is discussed further at para. 5.05.
[44] *Quaere* when information is incorrect. It would appear that incorrect information may not be "complete". See Art. 16(1)(b) of Reg. 17 which enables the Commission to impose periodical penalty payments in order to compel an undertaking "to supply *complete and correct* information which it has requested by decision taken pursuant to Art. 11(5)." Emphasis added.
[45] Decisions have been taken in a number of cases. See, for example, *C.I.C.G.–ZVEI/ZPU*: [1971] J.O. L34/13; *Asphaltoid-Keller*: [1971] J.O. L161/32; *S.I.A.E.*: [1971] J.O. L254/15; *Rodenstock*: [1972] J.O. L267/17, [1973] C.M.L.R. D40; *Misal*: [1972] J.O. L267/20, [1973] C.M.L.R. D37; *CSV*: [1976] O.J. L192/27; *RAI/UNITEL*: [1978] O.J. L157/39, [1978] 3 C.M.L.R. 306; *Fire Insurance (D)*: [1982] O.J. L80/36, [1982] 2 C.M.L.R. 159; *Deutsche Castrol*: [1983] O.J. L114/26, [1983] 3 C.M.L.R. 165; *Olympic Airways*: [1985] O.J. L46/51, [1985] 1 C.M.L.R. 730; *Baccarat*: [1991] O.J. L97/16, [1992] 5 C.M.L.R. 189. These decisions have been published although Art. 21 of Reg. 17 does not oblige the Commission to do so. The use of decisions is sometimes revealed in final decisions—see, for example, *PVC*: [1989] O.J. L74/1, [1990] 4 C.M.L.R. 345, at para. 6, and *LdPE*: [1989] O.J. L74/21, [1990] 4 C.M.L.R. 382, at para. 8. A number of decisions have also been taken in the context of sector enquiries under Art. 12. See para. 3.43.
[46] In *Baccarat*, above, two weeks was given.
[47] See below, n. 19 to para. 3.24.
[48] Art. 191 of the Treaty.
[49] Art. 11(6) of Reg. 17.

3.09   The decision must state the reasons on which it is based.[50] It appears that this requirement will be satisfied if the Commission sets out the purposes for which the information is required. In *Brescia*,[51] the Court of Justice said:

> "Contrary to the complaint made by the applicant and although the decision is imperfectly formulated as regards the need for the request for information, sufficient reasons are given for the decision, since the mere reference to the performance of its tasks by the High Authority is supplemented by the statement of the purposes for which the information was intended."

In *National Panasonic*,[52] the Court indicated that it is sufficient for the purpose of Article 14(3) decisions to set out the information specifically required by the Article and the Commission need go no further. If the same applied to Article 11(5) decisions then it could be sufficient for the Commission to set out the matters (a) to (c) listed in the previous paragraph above. But considering the essential constituents listed in Article 14(3) in comparison with those in Article 11(5) and having regard to what the Court said in *Brescia* (quoted above), the Commission should also include a statement of the purpose for which the information is required. Some statement of the factual background may also need to be given. This will not necessarily require the Commission to recite at length the facts and grounds for suspecting an infringement. It is not required for decisions under Article 14 (3)[53] and Articles 11 and 14 being, in the words of the Court of Justice, analogous provisions[54] a more stringent test should not apply to Article 11. Indeed one would hardly expect the Commission to have to set out such detailed factual statements and legal arguments as may be required in a final decision. A decision under Article 11(5) may be at an early stage in the investigation, and may be adopted either to get background information or on reasonable suspicion only, which would not of course be enough for a final decision. But as the Court of First Instance made clear in *SEP*, the Commission must demonstrate a connection between the information sought and the alleged infringement under investigation.[55] On the other hand, provided the Commission complies with the obligations in Article 11 a party cannot complain if the decision sets out in detail the Commission's suspicions and arguments.[56]

Documents—information

3.10   What is information? Article 11 is entitled "Requests for information" and the question has been raised whether the Commission is entitled to obtain copies of documents under Article 11 as opposed to being informed merely as to the contents. It seems to be a distinction without a difference, at least in practice. In a number of decisions under Article 11(5),[57] the Commission has ordered the furnishing, *inter alia*,

---

[50] Art. 190 of the Treaty.
[51] Above, n. 20 at p. 82.
[52] Above, n. 28, at paras. 25–27.
[53] Case 85/87, *Dow Benelux NV* v. *Commission*: [1989] E.C.R. 3137, [1991] 4 C.M.L.R. 410, at para. 10.
[54] Case 374/87, *Orkem* v. *Commission*: [1989] E.C.R. 3283, [1991] 4 C.M.L.R. 502, at para. 10.
[55] Case T–39/90, *SEP* v. *Commission*: [1991] II E.C.R. 1497, [1992] 5 C.M.L.R. 33 at para. 25. The detailed analysis in the judgment is noteworthy.
[56] *Orkem*, above, at para. 11.
[57] See, *e.g. C.I.C.G.–ZVEI/ZPU, S.I.A.E., CSV, RAI/UNITEL*, above, n. 45, and *National Panasonic (Belgium) NV* and *Comptoir Commercial d'Importation*, above, n. 36. But note the Commission's Rejoinder

of the complete texts of certain documents or, simply, the documents identified in the decision. In *Orkem*, the Court of Justice made it clear that Article 11 entitles the Commission to require the disclosure of documents.[58] The fact that there has been or could be an inspection under Article 14 enabling the Commission to see and copy the document does not restrict or lessen the investigatory powers given by Article 11. Article 11 and 14 are quite independent procedures.

Confidentiality or secrecy of the information

3.11 It appears to be no justification for refusing to supply information to say that the information requested contains business secrets, is confidential or is subject to the obligation of professional secrecy. In *Brescia*,[59] in the context of an investigation under the ECSC rules, the Court of Justice said:

> "It is not necessary to restrict the power of the High Authority to examine all the accounts of an undertaking whose production is mixed on the ground that it may divulge information which is harmful to such undertakings since, in the light of the duty of professional secrecy imposed on the inspectors of the High Authority, no vital interest of the undertakings is likely to be adversely affected by such a general examination."

In its decision in *CSV*,[60] the Commission expressly stated that neither the Commission nor its staff were released from their obligation of professional secrecy[61] simply because the information sought had been supplied to an organisation outside the Community. Where secret or confidential information is supplied to the Commission then it is advisable that the document in which the information is contained should be clearly marked so as to indicate its character and, unless it is obvious from the very nature of the material that it is deserving of protection as being secret or confidential, the reasons why the information should be so treated should be made known to the Commission. If practicable, confidential material should be put in a completely separate document in order to avoid any possible confusion. Where it is likely that the reply to the Article 11 request might be shown to a third party (*e.g.* a complainant) for comment, it may also be useful to submit an edited or "watered down" version which could be shown by the Commission.

in *National Panasonic*, quoted at n. 83 to para. 3.34, below.

[58] Above, at para. 14, making clear what the Court said in Case 155/79, *A.M. & S.* v. *Commission*: [1982] E.C.R. 1575, [1982] 2 C.M.L.R. 264, at para. 16.

[59] Case 31/59, *Brescia* v. *High Authority*: [1960] E.C.R. 71, at p. 82. Confidentiality is no excuse or defence for failure to disclose documents under Art. 14: *FNICF*: [1982] O.J. L319/12, [1983] 1 C.M.L.R. 575. Nor breach of a fidiciary duty: *Fides, Milan*: [1979] O.J. L57/33, [1979] 1 C.M.L.R. 650.

[60] Above, n. 45.

[61] See generally paras. 8.18–21.

Service under Article 11—Extraterritoriality

3.12   It is a vexed question to what extent, if any, the Commission can use its Article 11 powers to obtain information from undertakings situated outside the Common Market.[62] There have been cases in practice where the jurisdictional point has been taken and others where full replies have been volunteered. The nature of the response has been a matter of the corporate policy of the undertakings concerned. Powers under Article 11 can only be used by the Commission "in carrying out the duties assigned to it by Article 89 and by the provisions adopted under Article 87 of the Treaty," *i.e.* in the enforcement of the Community competition rules. But substantive jurisdiction over undertakings outside the Community does not necessarily imply "investigatory jurisdiction" and jurisdiction clashes may be avoided by co-operation agreements. Under the EEA the EFTA States have expressly agreed that the Commission can send requests to firms within their territory, provided copies are sent to the EFTA Surveillance Authority.[63] The extent generally to which the Community can exercise its legislative and investigatory powers extraterritorially is dealt with later.[64] There remains the practical problem of whether or not the undertakings concerned can be properly served with a request or decision under Article 11.[65] If the undertaking has itself some presence within the Community such as a branch or sales office then that is sufficient and the request or decision can be served at that address.[66] If the undertaking itself does not have any commercial presence within the Community but has a wholly-owned subsidiary within the Community then it seems that service on the parent undertaking can be effected through the subsidiary.[67] In the absence of a subsidiary

---

[62] Deringer (*op. cit.*, at para. 2207) has taken the view that undertakings from non-Member States are in principle obliged to supply information in so far as their activities produce effects within the Community. Although as a general rule information may only be obtained from persons domiciled or with their usual place of residence in the Community, this does not in his view prevent the Commission from addressing requests for information to undertakings outside the Community or from penalising such undertakings by attaching their assets within the Community. Goldman (*European Commercial Law* (1973), at para. 947) considers the Commission is not entitled to subject undertakings from non-Member States to inquiries and investigations under Arts. 11 and 14 of Reg. 17. But although he considers that the Commission cannot obtain information by decision and carry out investigations on the premises of such undertakings, he says: "it may be doubted whether the Commission would be exceeding its powers in sending any 'simple' request for information to enterprises from third party States." And note the 8th preamble to Reg. 17 which provides that the Commission must be "empowered, *throughout the common market*, to require such information to be supplied . . ." Emphasis added. The question is discussed further at para. 8.07.

[63] Protocol 23, Art. 8(1).

[64] Jurisdiction is discussed generally at paras. 8.01–08A. The E.C.–U.S. Co-operation Agreement is discussed there.

[65] See also paras. 4.05 and 6.44.

[66] In Case 8/56 *ALMA* v. *High Authority*: [1957] E.C.R. 95, 99, the Court said: "application may be made of a principle of law recognised in all countries of the Community, namely that a written declaration of intention becomes effective as soon as it arrives in due course within the control of the addressee." In U.S. law, the basic test is that laid down in *International Shoe Co.* v. *Washington*, 326 U.S. 310 (1945), namely, that there must be such business contacts with the forum as make it reasonable to require the undertaking to defend the particular action brought there. The leading case on what constitutes "transacting business" for the purposes of the Clayton Act is *United States* v. *Scophony Corp.*, 333 U.S. 795 (1948).

[67] Cases 48, 49 & 51–57/69, *Dyestuffs, ICI and Others* v. *Commission*: [1972] E.C.R. 619, [1972] C.M.L.R. 557. ICI, a British firm, was served with a decision through its German subsidiary. The Court said (Case 48/69, at paras. 42 and 43): "It is apparent that the applicant had complete knowledge of the text of the decision and made use, within the time limits, of its right to bring an action. In these circumstances, the question of any irregularities of notification becomes immaterial."

within the Community, then if there is no applicable agreement between the Community and the State within which the undertaking is situate, service may be made direct on the undertaking. In *Dyestuffs*, the statement of objections was sent direct by post to the undertaking's address in Switzerland.[68] This was described by the Court of Justice as "service in accordance with the provisions of Community law." In *Continental Can*,[69] the Court of Justice said: "A decision is properly notified within the meaning of the Treaty if it reaches the addressee and puts the letter in a position to take cognizance of it." The Court appears to adopt a pragmatic approach. If in fact an instrument is served on an undertaking, it cannot invoke its own refusal to take notice of the decision to render such service invalid.[70]

Location of information

3.13 If the information is subject to the ownership or control of an undertaking situate within the Community then in principle the Commission's powers should not be frustrated merely by the fact that the information required by the Commission is situate outside but is available in the Community.[71] An undertaking which has its domicile, resides or carries on business within the Community must accept the responsibilities as well as the benefits from so doing and should not be able to avoid those responsibilities, for example, by transferring or storing information outside the Community even if this is legitimate and practicable in the day to day conduct of its business. Practical problems may increase as information comes to be stored in a central computer, with local networks and terminals hundreds or thousands of miles apart.

Foreign law defences

3.14 An undertaking may try to refuse to make available information on the grounds that its production is prohibited by the laws of a non-Member State or is objected to by the Government of such a state. The United States experience has shown that such objections to the production of information may be based on a variety of reasons including the confidential nature of the information, the fact that the information is concerned with matters of state, or that the foreign state objects to the application of U.S. anti-trust laws extraterritorially or in matters concerning them.[72] As mentioned above, confidentiality will not be a defence. The obligation on the Commission not to

---

[68] *Ibid.* Cases 52 & 53/69, *Geigy AG and Sandoz AG* v. *Commission*. It is understood that there have been other instances in practice.

[69] Case 6/72, *Europemballage Corp. and Continental Can Co. Inc.* v. *Commission*: [1973] E.C.R. 241, [1973] C.M.L.R. 199, at para. 10.

[70] *Ibid.*

[71] The test of control rather than location of the documents has been adopted by U.S. courts in antitrust proceedings. See *Re Grand Jury Subpoena Duces Tecum Addressed to Canadian Int'l Paper Co.*, 72 F.Supp. 1013 (S.D.N.Y. 1947). The same rule applies to both U.S. and foreign enterprises.

[72] See, generally, Griffin, "United States Antitrust Laws and Transnational Business Transactions: An Introduction" (1987) 2 Int. Lawyer 307. Considerable interest has arisen in this subject as a result of the *Westinghouse Uranium Contracts* litigation. See *Rio Tinto Zinc Corp, and others* v. *Westinghouse Electric Corp.*: [1978] 1 All E.R. 434, [1978] 1 C.M.L.R. 100 (H.L.). And note the Protection of Trading Interests Act 1980. On "blocking" legislation generally, see Lowe, *Extraterritorial Jurisdiction* (1983).

disclose information of the kind covered by the obligation of professional secrecy applies to all such information supplied under Regulation 17 and, it is submitted, no distinction should be made as to whether the information originates inside or outside the Community.

In *CSV*,[73] the Commission made a decision requiring CSV, the joint selling agency for nitrate fertilisers manufactured by two Dutch undertakings, to supply information concerning its exports outside the EEC. The information sought by the Commission involved CSV's relationship with Nitrex AG, an international combine established in Switzerland, which was responsible for the operation of an agreement bringing together all European manufacturers' sales of nitrate fertilisers outside the EEC. CSV argued that disclosure of the information would involve an offence under the Swiss Criminal Code and therefore requested the Commission to take the decision in order that, if prosecutions were subsequently brought in Switzerland, it would be possible to plead, by way of defence, compulsion.[74] The Commission rejected CSV's reasons for refusing to supply the information without a decision. The fact that information was available within the Community and that part of it had also been supplied to a body established in Switzerland did not affect the Commission's rights to call for it. The Commission went further:

"Even if Swiss law could be interpreted to mean that the supply of information amounted to unlawful disclosure, this would still not warrant delaying the performance of obligations imposed by the Commission in order to enforce the competition rules."[75]

In United States law, a foreign prohibition against producing information will not necessarily deprive the court of the power to order a party subject to the jurisdiction to submit evidence although it may provide a sufficient defence to a charge of contempt in a U.S. investigation, at least where a party has made an effort in good faith to comply.[76] The position so far as Community law is concerned is uncertain. The decisions of the Commission in *CSV* would indicate the likelihood of the Commission taking a firm line in such circumstances.[77]

Relationship with Article 14

3.15 The Commission's powers under Article 11 can be used at virtually any stage in the Commission's procedure.[78] And in particular the powers of investigation under Article 14 are in no way dependent or conditional on the exercise of its powers under

---

[73] Above, n. 36.

[74] The defence of 'ètat de contreinte' under s. 34 of the Swiss Criminal Code.

[75] Above, n. 45, at p. 28.

[76] See *Societe Internationale pour Participations Industrielles et Commerciales* v. *Rogers*, 357 U.S. 197, and *Re Westinghouse Electric Corporation Uranium Contracts Litigation*, 563 F. 2d 992 (10th Cir. 1977). And note the reaction to blocking statutes in the recent ruling of the Supreme Court in *Société Nationale Industrielle Aerospatiale* v. *U.S. District Court*, referring to the Restatement s. 437.

[77] *Quaere* whether the Commission is entitled to draw negative inferences on questions of fact where information is not forthcoming because of a prohibition or objection by a non-Member State. See, generally, Case 18/62, *Barge* v. *High Authority*: [1963] E.C.R. 259.

[78] *E.g.* at a very early stage to follow up a complaint, as described in Case 298/83, *C.I.C.C.E.* v. *Commission*: [1985] E.C.R. 1106, [1986] 1 C.M.L.R. 486, or at a later stage, to verify a defence, as in *Wood Pulp*: [1985] O.J. L85/1, [1985] 3 C.M.L.R. 474.

Article 11. In the *National Panasonic* case the Court of Justice drew attention to the distinction made by Regulation 17 between "information" in Article 11 and "investigations" in Article 14.[79] The eighth recital of the preamble to Regulation 17 provides that the Commission "must . . . be empowered, throughout the common market, to require such information to be supplied and to undertake such investigations as are necessary to bring to light" infringements of Article 85 or 86. Regulation 17 thus provides for separate procedures, subject to different rules and conditions, in order to satisfy the diversity of needs likely to be met in the accomplishment of this task.[80] The two procedures, Article 11 and Article 14, are entirely independent — the powers given to the Commission by one do not limit the powers given by the other.[81] Article 11 can be used before[82] or after inspections.[83] Indeed use of Article 11 often follows inspections. The Commission may ask for information to strengthen the evidence it already has; for example, it may request documents from undertaking X to see if that undertaking has copies of documents which the Commission has already found at the premises of undertaking Y.

II. INSPECTIONS

Preliminary points

3.16   Article 14(1) of Regulation 17 provides that "the Commission may undertake all necessary investigations into undertakings." Several points arise from this apparently simple statement.

First, although it is provided that the Commission may undertake investigations into undertakings, it is not clear at first sight what obligation, if any, this places on the undertaking the subject of the investigation. Article 14 contemplates two basic types of investigation: an investigation ordered by decision under Article 14(3) and investigations not so ordered but where the Commission's officials may nevertheless exercise the specific investigatory powers conferred by Article 14(1) upon production of a written authorisation specifying certain matters in accordance with Article 14(2). As mentioned at the beginning of this chapter the Court of Justice has held that the undertaking is under an obligation to co-operate actively with the Commission.[84] However the Court has also said that in interpreting Article 14 regard must be had to particular rights of defence. It is necessary to prevent those rights from being irremediably impaired during the Commission's fact-finding, whether under powers in Article 11 or 14.[85]

---

[79] Case 136/79, *National Panasonic (UK) Ltd.* v. *Commission*: [1980] E.C.R. 2033, [1980] 3 C.M.L.R. 169, at para. 15.
[80] *Ibid.* at para. 9 and para. 13.
[81] Case 374/87, *Orkem* v. *Commission*: [1989] E.C.R. 3283, [1991] 4 C.M.L.R. 502, at para. 14.
[82] See, e.g. *Ford Agricultural*: [1993] O.J. L20/1, at para. 5.
[83] See, *e.g. Peroxygen Productions*: [1985] O.J. L35/1, [1985] 1 C.M.L.R. 481, at para. 9 and *Welded Steel Mesh*: [1989] O.J. L260/1, [1991] 4 C.M.L.R. 13, at para. 20.
[84] Orkem, above, at para. 27.
[85] Cases 46/87 & 227/88, *Hoechst AG* v. *Commission*: [1989] E.C.R. 2859, [1991] 4 C.M.L.R. 410, at paras. 14 and 15.

Where the investigation is ordered by decision then there is clearly a legal obligation to comply with the terms of the decision[86] and failure to do so may result in the Commission taking a further decision imposing a fine and/or periodical penalty payment[87] and in national courts' orders. If the undertaking is subject to a duty and this seems clear from the words "undertakings shall submit" in Article 14(3), then the Commission has a right to investigate and for its authorised officials to exercise the specified investigatory powers to this end. It is submitted that this right is enforceable in the English courts and a remedy given by way of injunction in suitable circumstances.[88]

Where the investigation is not ordered by decision and the Commission officials merely proceed to exercise their powers on production of the authorisation specified in Article 14(2), then there is no duty on the undertaking to comply with the Commission's investigatory requests. The Commission has said that undertakings are under no legal obligation to supply information or to submit to investigations unless it has taken a formal decision to that effect.[89] But if the undertaking submits to the investigation and proceeds to produce the required books or other business records in an incomplete form the undertaking may be liable to be fined in respect of such incomplete production.[90] Two examples can be seen in the Commission's decisions in *Fabbrica Pisana*[91] and *Fabbrica Sciarra*,[92] cases arising out of the Commission's investigation of the manufacture and marketing of glass in the Community. In both cases, the Commission's inspectors were acting simply under authorisation in accordance with Article 14(2) and without decisions. The fining decisions[93] record that the attention of the undertakings was drawn to the provisions of Articles 14 and 15 of Regulation 17 and that "when they were duly called upon, the undertakings' representatives expressed willingness to submit to the investigations."

---

[86] If an undertaking doubts its legality, the decision may be appealed to the Court under Art. 173 of the Treaty. The decision is, and should be treated as, valid until declared otherwise by the Court. See Case 101/78, *Granaria BV* v. *Hoofdproduktschap voor Akkerbouwprodukten*: [1979] E.C.R. 623, [1979] 3 C.M.L.R. 124, referred to in *Hoechst*, above, at para. 64.

[87] The decision ordering the investigation must indicate the penalties provided for in Arts. 15(1)(c) and 16(1)(d) of Reg. 17 but cannot itself impose them. Daily penalties are not suspended during an appeal unless the Court so orders under Art. 185 of the Treaty.

[88] See the later discussion of assistance by Member States under Art. 14(6) of Reg. 17, paras. 5.17–18. It is a separate yet unanswered question whether the Commission can ex parte seek a protective order in advance of opposition. In *Hoechst*, above, at para. 32, the Court of Justice indicated that the Commission had the *power* but Member States (and their Courts) were not obliged to make an order assisting the Commission in such circumstances.

[89] Answer to Written Question No. 677/79: [1979] O.J. C310/30. *Cf.* the position taken by the Court in Case 31/59, *Brescia* v. *High Authority*: [1960] E.C.R. 71. Dealing with an appeal against a decision ordering an investigation under Art. 47 of the ECSC Treaty the Court said (at p. 79): "By providing in a single section the two propositions that 'The High Authority may obtain the information it requires to carry out its tasks. It may have any necessary checks made,' the first para. of Art. 47 establishes, first the *duties* of undertakings to provide information and, secondly, the extent of the inquiries, which may be made at the same time. Nothing in the wording of this provision allows one to infer from it the implied provision that a preliminary decision is to be adopted before any check is made." Emphasis added. The Court appears to consider that the undertaking here is under a duty whether or not the investigation is ordered by decision.

[90] Under Art. 15(1)(c) of Reg. 17.

[91] [1980] O.J. L75/30, [1980] 2 C.M.L.R. 354.

[92] [1980] O.J. L75/35, [1980] 2 C.M.L.R. 362.

[93] Both decisions are discussed further in this chapter and also in Chap. 7 dealing with fining. See para. 7.07.

It would be wrong to imagine that an undertaking can, by refusing to submit voluntarily, buy much time.[94] As the *AKZO* case[95] shows, the Commission can take an Article 14(3) decision very quickly if necessary, the power to do so having been vested in the Commissioner for competition matters.

3.17 Second, the investigation must be "necessary". As in the case of Article 11 discussed above, it is important to note the prefatory words: "In carrying out the duties assigned to it by Article 89 and by provisions adopted under Article 87 of the Treaty." The restriction relates to the purpose of the investigation and not its reasonableness in the circumstances. In *FNICF*,[96] the Commission asserted:

> "Undertakings . . . which are the subject of an investigation are not entitled to assess whether a request for documents to be produced is justified or whether the period in respect of which they are required is appropriate."

Such a bald assertion has yet to receive the approval of the Court of Justice. An investigation must be "necessary", *i.e.* requisite to establish the applicability of Articles 85 and 86. This gives the Commission a very substantial measure of discretion.[97] It is certainly arguable that the power to carry out investigations should be exercised in a reasonable manner,[98] and in a manner consistent with the principle of proportionality and with a limited measure of intervention.[99]

3.18 Third, investigations under Article 14 can only be made in respect of "undertakings and associations of undertakings."[1] Article 14 contains no reference to Governments and competent authorities of Member States as does Article 11 dealing with requests for information. They cannot be made the subject of investigations by the Commission under Article 14. But Government owned or controlled bodies are not immune from investigation as such and, provided they are "undertakings", may be investigated.[2] Finally, as in the case of Article 11, there does not seem to be any restriction as to which undertakings can be investigated. The Commission's powers of investigation are not limited to those undertakings believed to be infringing Articles 85 and 86. Third party undertakings may therefore be investigated under Article 14. The principles of proportionality and of limited measure of intervention may, however, be applicable and act as a restraint on the Commission's exercising its powers of inspection of the books and other business records, etc., of third parties.[3]

---

[94] Although Hoechst bought time before the German courts, the result of the litigation both in the national and European Court may not give such opportunity again.
[95] Case 5/85, *AKZO Chemie BV (Netherlands) and AKZO Chemie UK Ltd. (UK)* v. *Commission*: [1986] E.C.R. 2585 [1987] 3 C.M.L.R. 716.
[96] *FNICF*: [1982] O.J. L319/12, [1983] 1 C.M.L.R. 575.
[97] *Cf.* the position under Art. 11, described in para. 3.03.
[98] See Deringer, *op. cit.*, para. 2211.
[99] See above, n. 20. In practice it is very difficult to assert these seemingly reasonable limits.
[1] It most probably does not matter if the undertaking has ceased to carry on business completely in the relevant goods or services. See Case 108/63, *Merlini* v. *High Authority*: [1963] E.C.R. 1, [1965] C.M.L.R. 109. There is no power to investigate the premises, etc., of individuals as such. Whilst the Merger Control Regulation, Reg. 4064/89, permits the use of Art. 11 type powers in relation to individuals, it rightly draws the line at Art. 14 investigations.
[2] See para. 1.21 and generally Wyatt and Dashwood, *European Community Law* (3rd ed., 1993) Chap. 19.
[3] See, generally, paras. 8.25–27.

Two basic types of inspection

3.19   Article 14 contemplates two basic types of investigation,[4] one ordered by decision of the Commission under Article 14(3), the other pursuant to Article 14(1) without decision but with a simple mandate or authorisation in the form contemplated by Article 14(2). In both types, the Commission officials are empowered to examine books, take copies, enter premises, etc., in accordance with Article 14(1). The powers are no greater or more extensive where the inspectors are acting under a decision. Although there are two basic types of investigation this does not mean that there is intended to be, or necessarily is, a two-stage procedure as in Article 11 (requests for information).[5] The Commission's first investigation of an undertaking can be ordered by decision. There is no express requirement that an undertaking be investigated without decision in pursuance of Article 14(1) before it can be investigated by decision under Article 14(3).[6] As the Court of Justice explained in the *National Panasonic* case, the "two procedures do not necessarily overlap but constitute two alternative checks the choice of which depends upon the special features of each case."[7]

Decisions made under Article 14(3) were relatively rare before 1979, most investigations being with a simple mandate or authorisation.[8] In recent years, the Commission has made more frequent use of decisions under Article 14(3). Simultaneous unannounced investigations,[9] the so called "dawn raids", are now more common (and can attract much publicity). Undertakings should be ready to deal with publicity attendant on leaks that investigations have taken place. Recent experience in the United Kingdom suggests that voluntary investigations are being much less used and "dawn raids" are becoming more frequent. In part this may be explicable on the grounds that the Commission is targeting its resources on suspected larger cartels, that competent authorities in other Member States may insist on Article 14(3) being used rather than Article 14(2) and the demise of the professional investigator in DG IV.

3.20   There is no obligation on the Commission to publish details of decisions under Article 14(3) ordering investigations.[10] The Commission may publish such details and, although it is not its practice to publish such decisions in the *Official Journal*, has done so in certain cases.[11] In the *Quinine* case,[12] the Court of Justice pointed out that

---

[4] Art. 13(1) of Reg. 17 speaks of "investigations which the Commission considers to be necessary under Art. 14(1), or which it has ordered by decision pursuant to Art. 14(3)." And note the different acts which may be penalised under Art. 15(1)(c).

[5] The Court has rejected the notion that Art. 14 involved a two-stage procedure. See *National Panasonic (UK)*, above, n. 79, at paras. 8–16.

[6] Compare the wording of Art. 14 with that of Art. 11 which not only contemplates two types of request for information but expressly requires the first type to be tried and have been unsuccessful before the second type can be employed.

[7] Above, n. 79, at para. 12. Followed in *Hoechst*, below, n. 14, at para. 22.

[8] See Answer to Written Question No. 677/69: [1979] O.J. C310/30 for a detailed breakdown. Only 31 investigations were ordered by decision in the period between January 1, 1973 and November 6, 1979.

[9] See, *e.g. Polypropylene*: [1986] O.J. L230/1, [1988] 4 C.M.L.R. 347; *Welded steel mesh*: above n. 67, at para. 18 and in the transport sector *Mewac*: [1993] O.J. L20/6, at paras. 5 and 9.

[10] For the decisions which the Commission is required to publish, see Art. 21 of Reg. 17.

[11] *Vereinigung Deutscher Freiformschmieden, Dusseldorf*: [1978] O.J. L10/32, [1978] 1 C.M.L.R. D63; *Fides, Milan*: [1979] O.J. L57/33, [1979] 1 C.M.L.R. 650 and *A.M. & S. Europe Ltd., Bristol*: [1979] O.J. L199/31, [1979] 3 C.M.L.R. 376.

[12] Case 41/69 *ACF Chemiefarma v. Commission*: [1970] E.C.R. 661, at para. 104.

the publication by the Commission of its decisions may contribute to ensuring the observance of the competition rules of the Treaty. It has increasingly become the practice of the Commission, in final decisions, to describe the procedural steps, and in particular the use of its powers of inspection.[13] In this way the fact that the Commission has carried out investigations (even unannounced) and the evidence they revealed may be disclosed.

3.21   The undertaking may be informed in advance, usually by telephone, of the proposed investigation. There is an obvious advantage for the Commission: the undertaking can prepare itself and have appropriate representatives ready to meet the inspectors. Where by surprise, the inspectors will ask at the door to speak to a particular director or senior employee by name or rank to whom they will identify themselves and their business. The undertaking can decide then and there to refuse admission. Once in the premises the inspectors will present their authorisations, staff cards and any decision. The undertaking can take immediate legal advice[14] but cannot delay unduly and must quickly decide whether to submit. Where it submits, the inspectors will explain and discuss with the undertaking how they wish to proceed. There is no set pattern. But the inspectors normally ask to see the offices and files *in situ* before examining particular files and papers.

Authorisations

3.22   Article 14(2) provides that Commission officials authorised for the purpose of investigations under Article 14 shall exercise their powers:

> "upon production of an authorisation in writing specifying the subject-matter and purpose of the investigation and the penalties provided for in Article 15(1) (c) in cases where production of the required books or other business records is incomplete."

The Commission officials receive a general authority to undertake investigations and a specific written authorisation for each investigation. The authorisation does two jobs. It defines in broad terms the scope of the enquiry and it evidences the authority of the particular inspectors.[15] A copy of the form of authorisation normally used is reproduced in Appendix H. The Commission inspectors will have such authorisations whether or not the investigation is ordered by decision. They will be produced at the beginning of the inspection. The identity of the "authorised" official is usually established by his Commission staff card bearing his photograph. If the inspection is not ordered by decision then the authorisation is the key document and it should be examined carefully to discover the subject matter of the investigation. Where there is

---

[13] See, *e.g. Zinc Producer Group*: [1984] O.J. L220/27, [1985] 2 C.M.L.R. 108, at para. 64, referring to some 19 inspection visits during the case. More recent examples can be found in *Newitt/Dunlop Slazenger International and Others*: [1992] O.J. L131/32 and *Viho/Parker Pen*: [1992] O.J. L233/27.

[14] The Court of Justice has recognised that the right to legal representation is one of the rights of defence which must be respected at both the investigation and contentious proceedings stage. Cases 46/87 & 227/88, *Hoechst AG* v. *Commission*: [1989] E.C.R. 2859, [1991] 4 C.M.L.R. 410, at para. 16. See para 3.40

[15] Joshua, *op. cit.*

a decision, this will define the scope and although the authorisation should still be checked and copies taken, it is less important.

Explanatory notes

3.23   The Commission has prepared two Explanatory Notes to the authorisations to investigate. One note is applicable in the case of inspections under Article 14(2) (*i.e.* without decision), the other in the case of inspections under Article 14(3) (*i.e.* with decision). Copies of the Notes are reproduced in Appendix H. As the Notes say, they are for information only and therefore without prejudice to any formal interpretation of the Commission's powers of enquiry. A glance at Appendix H will show that the two Notes are in broad terms similar. They explain how the inspectors prove their identity and set out the inspectors' powers. The position of the officials of the competent authority of the Member State concerned is described. The undertaking is advised of its rights to have a lawyer present[16] and its entitlement to a copy of the inspectors' minutes recording oral explanations[17] and a signed inventory of the copies and exhibits taken by the inspectors.[18] There are some important differences between the two Notes, reflecting the different legal bases of investigation. Where the investigation is backed simply by authorisation the Note says that before starting the investigation the inspectors shall at the undertaking's request provide explanations of the subject matter and purpose of the proposed investigation and on procedural matters. Where, on the other hand, the inspection is backed by a decision, the Note states that the inspectors cannot be required to enlarge upon the subject matter as set out in the decision or to justify in any way the taking of the decision. But explanations can be given on procedural matters and the possible consequences of a refusal to submit to the inspection.

Decisions under Article 14(3)

3.24   Article 14(3) provides that the decision must:

    (a) specify the subject matter and purpose of the investigation,
    (b) appoint the date on which it is to begin, and
    (c) indicate:
        (i) the penalties provided for in Articles 15(1)(c) and 16(1)(d) of Regulation 17, and
       (ii) the right to have the decision reviewed by the Court.[19]

---

[16] See para. 3.40. There can be no undue delay.
[17] See paras. 3.34–36.
[18] See para. 3.33.
[19] Ehlermann and Oldekop, *op. cit.*, suggest that the obligation to state that the decision may be challenged before the Court may be explained by the fact that decisions under Arts. 11 and 14 are situated in the initial stages of the Commission's procedure and that therefore, at that moment, the undertakings concerned may not yet have had the occasion to consult a lawyer with regard to their rights of defence. They acknowledge that it is uncertain what the consequences are of the Commission's failure to fulfil its obligation to inform the undertakings of their rights (illegality of the decision or merely non-applicability of the two months' time limit for lodging an appeal as, *e.g.* under German law).

The Court of Justice has held that the obligation to state the subject matter and purpose comprises a fundamental requirement, safeguarding the rights of defence, whose object not only shows that the investigation is justified but also enables the undertaking to assess the scope of its duty to co-operate.[20] The decision will of course name the firm or firms concerned. Where a number of firms are suspected and there are to be simultaneous visits it is the Commission's practice to take one decision naming all the firms. But where there is no apparent complicity a separate decision will be made for each firm.[21]

3.25 The decision must state the reasons on which it is based.[22] In *Brescia*,[23] the Court of Justice indicated that this requirement would be satisfied by reference to the performance of its tasks by the Commission supplemented by a statement of the purposes for which the investigation is made. In *National Panasonic*,[24] the Court referred to Article 14(3) which, it said, "lays down the essential constituents of the statement of reasons upon which a decision ordering an investigation is based." Provided that the decision contains the matters, listed (a) to (c) above, the Court was satisfied that the requirements of Article 190 of the Treaty, that a decision must state the reasons on which it is based, were met. In *Hoechst*,[25] the Court said that the decision need not indicate all the information known to the Commission concerning the alleged infringement. The decision must however indicate the presumed facts which it is intended to investigate. Stating in concise terms the type of infringement suspected and how the undertaking in question is involved[26] would appear to suffice. Provided the essential information is given there is no need to specify precisely the relevant market, the exact legal nature of the presumed infringements, nor the period during which the infringements were committed.[27] Nor is it necessary for the Commission to give reasons why it considers it appropriate to proceed with a decision under Article 14(3) rather than with a simple authorisation under Article 14(2). It does not have to set out, for example, its reasons for fearing that an undertaking might conceal or destroy evidence.[28] On the other hand the reasons for adopting a decision under Article 14(3) may well appear from the recitals and statement of the subject matter and purpose of the investigation: for example, that there has been a refusal to make books available during an investigation under a straightforward authorisation under Article 14(2),[29] or there is evidence of serious breach of the competition rules.[30] Nor where an undertaking has indicated its unwillingness to submit under Article 14(2) is the Commission required in its decision under Article 14(3) to reply to the arguments of the undertakings concerned. Article 14(3) enables the Commission to carry out investigations without the undertaking's agreement and without prior warning. The Commission is not therefore

---

[20] *Hoechst*, above, n. 14, at paras. 29 and 41.

[21] Joshua, *op. cit.*

[22] Art. 190 of the Treaty.

[23] Case 31/59, *Brescia* v. *High Authority*: [1960] E.C.R. 71, at p. 82.

[24] Case 136/79, *National Panasonic (UK) Ltd.* v. *Commission*: [1980] E.C.R. 2033, [1980] 3 C.M.L.R. 169, at para. 25.

[25] Above, n. 14, at para. 41.

[26] Joshua, *op. cit.*

[27] Case 85/87, *Dow Benelux NV* v. *Commission*: [1989] E.C.R. 3137, [1991] 4 C.M.L.R. 410, at para. 10.

[28] *National Panasonic*, above, *per* A.G. Warner.

[29] As, for example, in *A.M. & S. Europe Ltd.*, above, n. 11.

[30] *National Panasonic (UK)*, above.

obliged to give more extensive reasons for its decision than it would have had to give if it had proceeded immediately under Article 14(3).[31]

3.26 The decision must specify the subject matter and purpose of the investigation.[32] It does not seem that the Commission need be very specific. In *Brescia*,[33] the Court of Justice said:

> "The High Authority must of course give reasons for its decision and in the absence of any legal grounds for it, the terms of the Treaty are infringed. However, as the Court has just held, checks carried out by the High Authority when obtaining the information may guide its inquiries and the subject–matter of such inquiries could not be defined in detail in the statement of reasons.
>
> Furthermore, the need for information required by the High Authority must emerge from the decision with certainty. In view of this it is only the object in view which must serve as the criterion and not an a priori statement of the results expected which, drawn up unilaterally and without knowledge of the facts, may change by reason of the checks when they are carried out."

In its decision *Fides*,[34] the Commission required Fides to submit to investigations at its premises and

> "in particular, to allow the Commission officials responsible for the investigation to enter its premises during normal office hours and produce for examination the books and papers required by those officials and pertaining to the object of the enquiry."[35]

In other cases the Commission has been more precise as to what books, records, etc., are to be produced for examination. The need for particularity is best met by a concise description of the nature of the suspected violation.[36] The undertaking concerned should have particular regard to the terms of the decision. If in doubt as to what it covers, the undertaking should ask the Commission inspectors for any necessary explanation. The inspectors should know what it is they are investigating and the undertaking's informed reaction may facilitate the identification and production of the materials required for examination.

---

[31] *AKZO*, above, n. 95, at para. 19.
[32] Art. 14(3) of Reg. 17.
[33] Above, n. 23, at pp. 80, 81.
[34] *Fides, Milan*: [1979] O.J. L57/33, [1979] 1 C.M.L.R. 650.
[35] *Cf.* A.G. Roemer in *Brescia* v. *High Authority*, above, n. 23, at p. 97: "It is not enough to order the person to whom the decision is addressed to comply with the instructions of the inspectors, which amounts in fact to leaving the task of putting the decision in concrete form to the officials carrying out the inspection. Since the subject-matter of the check varies according to its purpose, the statement of its purpose may, in a specific case, be sufficient to show which documents are involved in the inspection. However, this is not so in every case. Where it is not clear that certain documents are necessary for a particular check, the documents to be examined must be indicated exactly."
[36] Joshua, *op. cit.*

Liaison with relevant competent authority

3.27 Before it undertakes any investigation pursuant to Article 14(1) the Commission must inform the competent authority of the Member State in whose territory it is to be made of the investigation and of the identity of the authorised Commission inspectors.[37] Although this need not be done in writing,[38] it must be done "in good time." Officials of the competent authority may at the request of such authority or the Commission assist the Commission's inspectors in carrying out the investigation.[39] Where the Commission takes a decision ordering an investigation pursuant to Article 14(3), it must first consult with the competent authority in the relevant Member State.[40]

Notification of decisions under Article 14(3)

3.28 Decisions must be notified to those to whom they are addressed and take effect upon such notification.[41] In the case of decisions under Article 14(3) it appears to be the Commission's practice to specify in the decision that it shall be notified to the undertaking concerned by being served immediately before the investigation is to commence by the Commission's officials authorised for the purposes of the investigation.[42] Notification is usually effected by the delivery of a certified copy of the decision. The copy does not have to be signed by the Commissioner. It is sufficient if it is duly certified as authentic by signature of the Secretary General of the Commission.[43] The undertaking is requested to acknowledge receipt by signing a minute of notification. This minute merely serves as proof of notification of the decision. It has no prejudicial effect, and would not prevent a later challenge to the validity of the decision or the way in which it had been implemented. Signature by the recipient does not imply submission by the undertaking to the investigation.[44] A copy of the form normally used is reproduced in Appendix H.

---

[37] Art. 14(2) of Reg. 17.

[38] *Cf.* Art. 11(6) in connection with decisions under Art. 11(5) requesting information.

[39] Art. 14(5) of Reg. 17. In practice, investigations in the U.K. are attended by officials from the Office of Fair Trading.

[40] Art. 14(4) of Reg. 17. Again there is no need for writing—see *AKZO*, above, n. 95—although in practice the competent authority may insist on seeing a draft of the decision. The OFT nowadays always does this and agrees minutes of consultation with DG IV. In relation to the subject matter of this para., see, generally, paras. 5.10–11 and 5.15–18.

[41] Art. 190 of the Treaty.

[42] For example, see Art. 3 of the Commission's decision in *A.M. & S. Europe Ltd.*, above, n. 11. Unless the investigation is by surprise/ unannounced, the undertaking will be informed a few days in advance of the intended investigation and of the decision ordering it. The undertaking will not however, have sight of the decision until it is notified in accordance with its terms. In the *National Panasonic* case, above, n. 24, although no point was taken as to the manner in which the decision had been notified, A.G. Warner noted that the method of service described in the text above is entirely consistent with a surprise investigation.

[43] Cases 97, 98 & 99/87, *Dow Chemical Iberica S.A. and others* v. *Commission*: [1989] E.C.R. 3165, [1991] 4 C.M.L.R. 410, at para. 59.

[44] Explanatory Note, para. 3.

Review by the Court

3.29   Article 14(3) provides that the decision must specify the right to have the decision reviewed by the Court. As the Commission said in *CSM-NV*,[45] it is up to the company itself in the first instance to assess its rights in relation to the inspection. But if it wishes to take issue over its rights with the Commission it cannot take things into its own hands. An appeal to the Court is the proper course. This may in theory be made under Article 173 within two months.[46] It will not have any suspensory effect but a separate application for a stay of execution of the Commission's decision may be made under Article 185.[47] It is, however, doubtful whether in the circumstances of a surprise investigation an appeal and application for a stay could, as a practical matter, be made immediately following notification of the decision in time to prevent its being carried out. Nor is it clear to what extent the Court would be flexible as regards the procedural requirements and would, for example, accept applications by telex. Even if the practical and procedural hurdles can be quickly overcome, it is unlikely that the Court would grant a stay in the absence of proof of serious and irreparable damage to the undertaking if the inspection were to continue.[48] An undertaking may be faced, as in the *Hoechst* case, with little choice but to refuse to submit to the investigation and appeal to the Court whilst under the shadow of a further decision imposing periodical penalty payments. But whilst an appeal may not prevent the inspection taking place, if ultimately successful the Court may prohibit the Commission from using any evidence obtained by means of an unlawful investigation or outside the scope of the investigation decision.[49] Further, misconduct of or at the inspection may give rise to an action for damages against the Commission for breach of the "general principles common to the laws of the Member States" under Article 215 of the Treaty.[50]

Proportionality and use of Article 14(3)

3.30   In *National Panasonic*, it was argued that an investigation ordered by decision under Article 14(3) where there had not been a previous investigation with simple authorisation under Article 14(2), is only justified if the situation is very grave and there is the greatest urgency and the need for complete secrecy prior to the investigation. The Court of Justice refused to accept the necessity of such conditions:[51]

> "The Commission's choice between an investigation by straightforward authorisation and an investigation ordered by a decision does not depend on the facts relied upon by the applicant but on the need for an appropriate inquiry, having regard to the special features of the case."

---

[45] [1992] O.J. L305/16.

[46] See generally, Chap. 9.

[47] *Ibid.*

[48] See Case 31/59R *Acciaieria e Tubificio di Brescia* v. *High Authority*: [1960] E.C.R. 98.

[49] See the Orders of the President in Case 46/87R, *Hoechst* v. *Commission*: [1987] E.C.R. 1549, at para. 34, and Case 85/87R, *Dow Chemical Nederland BV* v. *Commission*: [1987] E.C.R. 4367, at para. 17.

[50] Such an action may not be dependent on the invalidity of the Commission's decision. See Temple Lang, *The Common Market and the Common Law* (1966), p. 459. The Court appears prepared, in an appropriate case, to attribute improper behaviour to the Commission when done by a responsible official in the performance of his duties. See Case 5/85, *AKZO* v. *Commission*: [1986] E.C.R. 2585, [1987] 3 C.M.L.R. 716, at para. 15.

[51] Above, n. 24, at para. 29.

The Court considered that there had been no violation of the principle of proportionality.[52] The Commission's decision under Article 14(3) had not been disproportionate to the objective pursued, the collection of necessary information to determine whether or not there had been an infringement of Article 85.

The Court therefore imposed no limitation on the Commission's use of Article 14(3) other than "the special features of the case." What sort of circumstances may lead the Commission to take a decision under Article 14(3) and to carry out the investigation without prior notice? The following may be important:

(a) the serious nature of the infringement; for example, export bans, naked market-sharing, collective boycotts and collusive tendering or price fixing;
(b) the likelihood that evidence may be concealed or destroyed if not examined *in situ*;
(c) evidence that information or materials have been concealed.

The undertaking's conduct in the past may also be relevant: for example, where there has been a lack of voluntary co-operation; where the Commission suspects the undertaking of having deceived or misled it in correspondence or a notification; or where it has been fined for similar violations.[53] There is however a case for saying that, given the need for the Commission to concentrate its enforcement efforts on cases of significance and importance to the Community interest,[54] if in fact an investigation is warranted at all, there is probably also justification for a surprise visit supported by a decision under Article 14(3) where the undertaking is a suspected infringer. Announced visits are more likely to be made to complainants and other third parties where information is being verified or use of the Commission's formal powers may help protect the position of the complainant.

The inspector's powers

(i) *To examine the books and other business records*

3.31   "Books and other business records" is a wide term and includes all papers, official and unofficial, relating to the undertaking's business.[55] It would include, for example, photographic materials, magnetic tape and other more sophisticated means of information storage.[56] It is extremely doubtful whether an undertaking is entitled to resist the retrieval and inspection of information contained in sophisticated storage systems (*i.e.* to deny the inspectors access to and use of the undertaking's machines

---

[52] *Ibid.* at para. 30.

[53] Joshua, *op. cit.*

[54] See Notice on co-operation with national courts, above n. 13.

[55] *E.g.* a trade association's correspondence, internal memoranda and records of meetings with other trade organisations, as well as minutes and records of the management organs of the association, will constitute "business records": *FNICF*: [1982] O.J. L319/12, [1983] 1 C.M.L.R. 575.

[56] Decision 279/84, defining inspection powers under Art. 47 ECSC, provides expressly that books and business records includes "records held in automated systems of any kind". As regards the discovery and production of documents before the English Court, tape recordings have been held to be "documents," *Grant* v. *Southwestern and Country Properties Ltd.*: [1974] 2 All E.R. 465, and also a computer database which formed part of the business records of a company, *Derby & Co Ltd. and Others* v. *Weldon and Others (No. 9)*: [1991] 2 All E.R. 901.

necessary to check the contents of the tape, microfilm, fiche, disc, back-up tape, etc.). It is thought likely that the Commission (and the Court) would construe the words "to examine", so as to include the right of reasonable access and use of necessary facilities for the examination and copying (in whatever manner was appropriate, *e.g.* by obtaining a printout) of such records. This would be particularly justified where copies could not be obtained without such access and use. In practice inspectors ask for computer material and have their own software to interrogate databases and electronic mail.

There is, of course, no obligation to maintain books and business records for competition law purposes (as there may be for certain purposes of company and tax laws).[57] Indeed the paperless office is a reality in some companies. Some firms have a document retention policy (which is, of course, a systematic destruction policy although in practice is often not complete). However, unusually premature destruction may give rise to suspicion unless a reasonable explanation can be produced.[58] Destruction after the Commission's procedure has begun would be foolhardy and risks the imposition of sanctions. In its decision in *Stahlwerke Rochling Burbach GmbH*[59] under the ECSC Treaty, the Commission ordered the production and inspection of certain books and papers which the undertaking's management had stated had been destroyed on its instructions. The books and papers had been withheld from officials of the German Bundeskartellamt during an investigation carried out nine months previously on the grounds that the Cartel Office had no authority in relation to the relevant products.[60] The Commission inspectors had discovered during their investigation that the files described by the Cartel Office were no longer kept at the premises visited. The undertaking had provided no written explanation of the destruction despite the Commission's request and the undertaking's promise to do so. The Commission suspected that the relevant books and papers were being kept elsewhere and therefore ordered the undertaking to submit them for inspection. An undertaking is clearly in a dilemma in such circumstances. The late production of the books may cast doubt on its honesty. Failure to produce the books without satisfactory explanation exposes it to risk of fine and/or daily penalty until the books are produced.[61] It is clear, moreover, that the Commission's power of inspection is not limited to books, etc., located on the business premises. Article 14(1)(d) does not restrict Article 14(1)(a).

3.32 The Commission takes the view that it is not sufficient for an undertaking merely to make all books, etc., and files available to the Commission's inspectors. It is sometimes said that there is a duty to find. In *Fabbrica Pisana*,[62] the undertaking contended that it had fulfilled its obligation to submit the required documents to the inspectors by stating that all its records were at their disposal. The inspectors, not

---

[57] But see *Raffinerie Tirlemontoise*: [1971] 11 Bull. E.C. 55. See also Companies Act 1985, s. 450, relating to the destruction of documents, etc., to "defeat the law."

[58] It will be for the Commission to consider whether the non-production is justified having regard to the provisions of any relevant legislation and drawing the appropriate conclusions from them. See Cases 5–11 & 13–15/62, *San Michele and Others* v. *High Authority*: [1962] E.C.R. 449, [1963] C.M.L.R. 13.

[59] [1977] O.J. L243/20, [1977] 2 C.M.L.R. D25.

[60] S. 101 of the German Act against Restraints of Competition (GWB) provides: "This Act shall not apply ... 3. To the extent that the Treaty establishing the European Coal and Steel Community, dated 18 April 1951, contains special provisions."

[61] And note the comments made in *Pioneer Hi-fi*: [1980] O.J. L60/21, [1980] 1 C.M.L.R. 457 in relation to the absence of minutes of a critical meeting.

[62] [1980] O.J. L75/30, [1980] 2 C.M.L.R. 354.

knowing where the documents in question were kept, duly examined records kept in various of the undertaking's departments and offices but not those in the "administrative department", where the relevant documents were kept. The Commission's decision states:[63]

> "The argument that Fabbrica Pisana had satisfactorily fulfilled its obligations by generally putting all its files at the investigator's disposal must be rejected, since the obligation on undertakings to supply all documents required by Commission inspectors must be understood to mean *not merely giving access to all files but actually producing the specific documents required.*
>
> Nor can the argument that the Commission's inspectors did not examine the business records of the administration department be accepted, as none of the undertaking's representatives had told them that the documents requested were, or might be, kept in that department and where there was otherwise no reason to suppose that documents of that nature might be found there."

In *Orkem*, the Court of Justice stated that the undertaking concerned has an obligation to co-operate actively.[64] This means that it must provide the documents required by the inspectors.[65] It is right, as the Commission indicates in the Explanatory Notes, that undertakings should be advised to draw the inspectors' attention to any "favourable" factors (for one thing the time available for inspections is short) but the Commission cannot, of course, simply pass over the principal burden of investigation to the undertaking being investigated. Indeed it has not conceded that the undertaking can determine which documents (or parts of documents) are relevant[66] and as the Court has acknowledged on several occasions it is in principle for the Commission, and not the undertaking or a third party, to decide whether or not a document must be produced to it.[67] In *CSM–NV*,[68] the company refused to make available 12 documents claiming that they were not relevant (it could not be argued, they said, that the documents could prove any fact specified in the written authorisation presented by the Commission officials). After some reflection the company handed over four of the documents sought, but the remaining eight were not produced until the Commission had taken a decision under Article 16(1) of Regulation 17 imposing a periodic penalty payment. The Commission held to its view that it is for it to determine what is relevant but in its decision

---

[63] *Ibid.* at p. 33. Emphasis added.

[64] Case 374/87, *Orkem* v. *Commission*: [1989] E.C.R. 3283, [1991] 4 C.M.L.R. 502, at para. 27. The obligation can only be derogated from by providing proof of the existence of an overriding principle of Community law (including fundamental rights), para. 28. *Cf.* the duty to co-operate in investigations under ECSC Art. 47. In Case 18/62, *Barge* v. *High Authority*: [1963] E.C.R. 259, at p. 278, the Court said: "It is for the business concerned to enable the High Authority to carry out its duties by voluntarily furnishing it with the information it needs."

[65] *Orkem*, above, at para. 27.

[66] There seems little doubt that the Commission can examine books, etc., to confirm that they do not relate to the subject matter of the investigation. See *Brescia*, above, n. 23.

[67] Case 155/79, *A.M. & S.* v. *Commission*: [1982] E.C.R. 1575, [1982] 2 C.M.L.R. 264, at para. 17. See also Cases 46/87 & 227/88, *Hoechst AG* v. *Commission*: [1989] E.C.R. 2859, [1991] 4 C.M.L.R. 410, at para. 31 and Case 374,87 374/87, *Orkem* v. *Commission*: [1989] E.C.R. 3283, [1991] 4 C.M.L.R. 502, at para. 15. For an example of the Commission's reliance on this statement of principle, see *FNICF*, above, n. 55. But the principle may be subject to exceptions, one being documents subject to the legal protection for lawyer/client communications recognised by the Court in *A.M. & S.* See paras. 8.13–17.

[68] Above, n. 45.

conceded that there may be circumstances where production can be refused. The decision stated that inspectors "are under an obligation not to examine business records, or to stop examining such records, if they are obviously or in the Commission official's opinion, not related to the subject matter of the investigation."

How does all this work in practice? The selection of books, etc., for inspection is made by the Commission. If the request is for "the letter from A to B dated 1 April 1987," there can be little room for uncertainty or arguments on the part of the undertaking. But less specific requests, "all papers, etc., relating to the sale of widgets in the U.K. and France between 1983 and 1986," may give rise to problems especially if the undertaking is not aware of the particular suspected infringement with which the Commission is concerned. In such circumstances, in the absence of any further explanation or more specific request by the inspectors, it may be legitimate for the undertaking to explain its difficulty to the inspectors, actually produce (take the inspectors to the files, etc., and point them out to them — as already mentioned, the inspectors expect to see the files *in situ*) all its relevant books and records and indicate that some or all of them might possibly relate to the subject matter of the investigations. The undertaking could hardly be said to be "intentionally or negligently" producing the required books or other business records in incomplete form. By producing too much the undertaking can hardly be penalised for producing nothing or too little! Finally, it should be noted that it will be no defence for the undertaking's representative to refuse production of documents on grounds that they cannot be disclosed to the Commission without the agreement or authority of a higher officer or organ of the undertaking.[69]

It is commonly said that the inspectors cannot "fish" for information.[70] And whilst the powers listed in Article 14(1) are undoubtedly extensive there is no right of search as such.[71] The extent of the Commission's powers have, however, been controversial and the question of the power to search is discussed further later in this chapter.[72] In practice the exercise of the power to examine books and business records provides much valuable evidence of infringements. For an example of the sort of matters revealed, see the extensive list set out in the *Polypropylene* case.[73] The Commission commonly asks for records of telephone and fax numbers used over a particular period and may interrogate fax machine for numbers made documents. This is of value where the infringement is current or recent. An itemised bill from a telephone company is a business record of the subscriber. The question has been raised whether documents written independently by one party to an agreement or practice (*e.g.* internal memoranda) can be used as evidence against the other parties. The Commission accepts the need to treat such documents with caution. But where, for example, the documents contain a sufficiently large number of clear and consistent statements, they may be used as factual evidence against parties, including those who did not have any part in writing them.[74]

---

[69] *FNICF*, above, n. 55.

[70] On fishing expeditions, see Joshua, *op. cit.*, at p. 11.

[71] This, the Court of Justice made clear in *Hoechst*, above; *Dow Chemical Iberia*, above, n. 43 and Case 85/87, *Dow Benelux* v. *Commission*: [1989] E.C.R. 3137, [1991] 4 C.M.L.R. 410.

[72] See para. 3.37.

[73] Above, n. 9. And see the discovery of the "pirate" file in *British Leyland*: [1984] O.J. L207/11, [1984] 3 C.M.L.R. 92, and the "red notes" in *Peroxygen Products*: [1985] O.J. L35/1, [1985] 1 C.M.L.R. 481.

[74] See *Zinc Producer Group*, above, n. 13, and *Roofing Felt*: [1986] O.J. L232/15, [1991] 4 C.M.L.R. 130.

(ii) *To take copies of or extracts from the books and business records*

3.33   It is not necessary for the undertaking to supply copies[75] nor, it is submitted, to make available secretarial or photocopying facilities for this purpose. It is, however, normal practice for undertakings to make their photocopying facilities available at the request of the inspectors. Where this is done the inspectors are authorised at the request of the undertaking to pay for the copies made.[76] If an undertaking does not make its copying facilities available then the inspectors may have to take a longhand note of all the relevant documents and the investigation will be consequently protracted and the normal work, etc., of the officers representing the undertaking further disrupted. An undertaking may make the copies for the Commission. This can be useful because the undertaking can (i) check and record what is being copied, and (ii) take an extra copy at the same time for his own purposes (*e.g.* to be shown to the undertaking's lawyers if not present). The inspectors will keep an inventory of copies taken. The undertaking is entitled to a signed copy.[77] The undertaking or its legal advisers might be wise to make its own inventory and send it in the Commission, particularly where there may be four or five inspectors all making separate lists. The Commission has acknowledged that where inspectors take copies of records which, in the opinion of the undertaking concerned, are not related to the subject matter of the investigation, the undertaking can ask the Commission to return the copies taken.[78] But the Commission is unlikely to return them if their relevance is still an issue.

(iii) *To ask for oral explanations on the spot*

3.34   It is not clear how far the power to ask for oral explanations under Article 14(1) (c) extends.[79] Does it permit the inspectors to ask whatever questions they choose in connection with the investigation in progress and its subject matter?[80] Or are the inspectors restricted to requesting explanations of the books and other business records they are examining in exercise of their power in Article 14(1)(a)? Some commentators have taken the view that requests for explanations must relate to the documents which are being examined.[81] Any other questions are therefore informal or, if formal, must be put in a written request for information under Article 11. In practice much may depend on the experience of the Commission officials as to the extent to which

---

[75] *Cf.* Art. 13.1(b) of the Merger Control Regulation, Reg. 4064/89. Authorised officials are empowered to "take copies or *demand* copies of or extracts from the books and business records." Emphasis added.

[76] See Explanatory Notes, Appendix H.

[77] *Ibid.*

[78] *C.S.M.–N.V.*: [1992] O.J. L305/16.

[79] *Cf.* Art. 14 of Council Reg. 11 of 1960 which gives a power "to require explanations on all points relating to the books and records of undertakings."

[80] Ferry appears to construe the power widely. He paraphrases it by the words "take oral statements"—see "Procedure and Powers of the EEC Commission in Anti-trust Cases" [1979] E.I.P.R. 126, 127.

[81] Deringer, *op. cit.*, para. 2255. Van Bael, "EEC Antitrust Enforcement and Adjudication as seen by Defence Counsel" (1979) 7 *Revue Suisse du Droit International de la Concurrence* 1, 15. Note that the House of Lords Select Committee (*op. cit.*) took a narrow view of the scope of the power to require oral explanations: "it appears probably to be limited to requiring explanations of specific questions arising out of the books and business records which the Commission officials examine."

the inspection is a paper exercise. If the power contained in Article 14(1)(c) is very extensive then it does raise serious doubts as to the purpose and value of the protection and rights given to an undertaking in the procedures set out in Article 11. If the exercise of the power to ask for oral explanations on the spot during an investigation enabled the Commission to obtain any necessary information then an undertaking's right to supply information (i) on the basis of a written request (ii) voluntarily and (iii) within an appropriate period of time would be seriously undermined.

The matter was raised before the Court of Justice in the *National Panasonic* case[82] and in the context of the discussion of the relationship between Articles 11 and 14. In the report of the written procedure, the following is attributed to the Commission:

> "It is not true to say that the Commission may obtain information by requiring explanations on the spot at the time of an investigation by means of a decision under Article 14 and thus avoid the safeguards of the procedure under Article 11. In fact officials of the Commission undertaking an investigation are empowered to require explanations of specific concrete questions arising out of the books and business records which they examine, which has nothing to do with the power to ask general questions requiring careful consideration and perhaps gathering of information by the firm."[83]

Advocate General Warner opined that the only explanations that can be sought under Article 14(1)(c) are explanations relating to the books and records under examination or their contents.[84] The Court's judgment did not deal with the matter directly and is not decisive on the point. But in relation to the distinction between the procedures in Article 11 and those in Article 14, the Court said:[85]

> "The fact that the officials authorised by the Commission, in carrying out an investigation, have *the power to request during that investigation information on specific questions arising from the books and business records which they examine* is not sufficient to conclude that an investigation is identical to a procedure intended only to obtain information within the meaning of Article 11 of the regulation."

It would be dangerous to conclude that the words emphasised contain an exhaustive definition of the Commission's powers under Article 14(1)(c). It is significant, however, that the Court adopts words similar to those of the Commission and arguably appears to go beyond the Advocate General.

---

[82] Above, n. 24.

[83] The Commission's Rejoinder said: "The power to ask for oral explanations on the spot (Art. 14(1)(i)) relates to explanations of specific concrete questions rising out of books and business records. It is not a power to ask general questions requiring careful consideration and perhaps gathering of information by the firm: Thiesing-Schroter-Hochbaum, pp. 528, 529. The Commission could not use the narrow power under Art. 14 for the wider purpose, even if it wanted to, and therefore could not avoid the safeguards of Art. 11 as Panasonic suggests. In any case, there would be no object in adopting a decision ordering an investigation to get information which could more easily be got by using Art. 11. There is nothing to be gained by surprise when all that is required is information, not copies of documents."

[84] A.G. Warner also indicated that the Commission had conceded this. Having regard to the statements quoted in the text to n. 83 and in n. 83 itself, this is, with the greatest respect to the A.G., by no means so clear.

[85] Case 136/79 *National Panasonic (UK) Ltd.* v. *Commission*: [1980] E.C.R. 2033, [1980] 3 C.M.L.R. 169, at para. 15.

3.35 There is a distinction between "information" and investigations, and the procedures in Articles 11 and 14 are both separate and different.[86] It is submitted that the Commission's powers in Article 11 and 14(1)(c) are complementary but not co-extensive. Article 11 clearly contemplates and requires that undertakings be allowed a reasonable time in which to respond to the Commission's request for information. In contrast, the period of an investigation may be short (often one day, rarely longer than two or three) and explanations may not be requested until near the end. In these circumstances practicality and common sense require that any questions should be specific and capable of being answered if not spontaneously and immediately then within a short time allowed for consideration and any necessary research or consultation. Explaining the meanings of initials, abbreviations, group names, etc., is a good example. Used properly the power is to be encouraged as it may prevent misunderstandings arising and thus help clarify issues at an early stage in the proceedings. As a matter of law, the exercise of the powers given in Article 14(1)(c) should not be permitted to undermine the safeguards given in Article 11. Questions must therefore be specific and capable of being answered in the circumstances of an investigation.

Assuming that the narrower interpretation is preferred the Commission should nonetheless be entitled to require the following kinds of explanation:

(a) explanations relating to the whereabouts, organisation and maintenance[87] of the undertaking's books and business records, including explanations of the "absence" of such books, etc., where relevant;

(b) explanations of the books and records under examination or their contents; and

(c) explanations of matters arising from the books and business records under examination and relating to the subject matter of the investigation as defined by the terms of the Commission's decision.

It will be appreciated that (c) will in most cases include (b) but that whilst (c) goes wider than (b) it is limited by the terms of the decision. It does not therefore give the Commission a power to ask questions about all and anything but restricts it to the subject matter of the inquiry. It does, however, enable the Commission to ask questions about the conduct under investigation as opposed to simply the books or their contents, provided such questions arise from the examination of such books.[88]

3.36 Who is required to give the explanations requested? The simple answer to this is the undertaking, and in practice undertakings designate senior, often managerial, staff to do so. Under Regulation 17 responsibility always rests with the undertaking and only undertakings may be liable to fines or periodical penalty payments under Articles 15 and 16. It would therefore seem to be for the undertaking to determine in what manner it should fulfil any obligations it may have under Regulation 17 and thus to select which officer, employee or other person should represent it and supply any necessary explanation. The position is, however, by no means certain. As has been pointed out, it is logical that oral explanations of any document should be given by the person who wrote it, received it, performed the activity ordered or described in it, or

---

[86] *Ibid.* at paras. 12, 13 and 15 and *Orkem*, above, n. 67, at para. 14.

[87] It is arguable that the power to ask questions directed to the whereabouts of the books, etc., is necessary to, and therefore implicit in, the power to examine in Art. 14(1)(a).

[88] The classification in this para. acknowledges the Court's tacit recognition (by the choice of similar words) of the explanation given by the Commission in the pleadings.

engaged in discussions about its formation, execution or purpose.[89] The undertaking probably cannot prevent the inspectors putting any question (which is within the terms of the decision, etc., as mentioned above) to an employee about matters which may be within his knowledge and the undertaking may not be able to prevent the employee from answering.[90] Indeed this may rarely be practicable when inspectors are operating in several different offices. But as it is clear that directors or other officials of the undertaking cannot be made personally to supply information or give evidence, so it is for the undertaking to nominate and authorise the persons to supply any explanation under Article 14.[91] Support for this view can also be found in the Commission's decision in *Fabbrica Pisana*[92] where it is stated:

"It is not for the Commission's inspectors to assess or dispute the competence or extent of knowledge of the representatives of the undertaking they are investigating. The undertakings named in investigation authorisations are alone responsible for designating their representatives."

If the undertaking is "alone responsible" then the Commission cannot therefore choose or nominate any particular person to reply to its inquiries or requests for explanations, but this does not necessarily excuse the undertaking from putting forward whatever employee can best respond to the inspector's question. The duty to cooperate must not be neglected. In practice the Commission name individuals to whom they wish to talk, as having been in a meeting or the writer or recipient of a letter, and will ask for people to be made available. It is in this and for other matters during the investigation in the undertaking's interest to try to agree with the inspector, at an early stage, which senior managers need to remain accessible.

Care should be taken in the selection of persons to represent the undertaking at an investigation. The absence of appropriate officers on the premises is not however a good reason to refuse to submit to the investigation.[93] It may be desirable that all questions should be put to competent representatives who, if and where necessary, can check or consult before any reply is made. Trying to channel all replies, although sometimes advised out of caution, may not be productive. It may even be construed as being obstructive! It is in the interests of both the undertaking and the Commission that the most correct and complete answers be given. Questions must, however, be answered "on the spot" and the taking of advice, etc., must not delay the giving of the reply unreasonably. In practice there are few problems. There is no interrogation or cross-examination of employees. Undertakings explain, for example, handwriting,

---

[89] See Davidow, "EEC Fact-Finding Procedures in Competition Cases: An American Critique" (1977) 14 C.M.L.Rev. 175, 181.

[90] Co-operation is to be advised here. For it has been suggested that refusal to let the inspectors see the persons who can most easily provide explanations could in an extreme case so obstruct an investigation as to amount to a refusal to submit. Joshua, *op. cit.*, at p. 12. Kreis, *op. cit.*, also contemplates this amounting to obstruction and refusal to submit to the investigation.

[91] Van Bael, *op. cit.*, at p. 15. Where someone does speak for the company it may be difficult later to deny his authority and therefore responsibility for what is said: see Case T–7/89, *Hercules NV* v. *Commission*: [1992] 4 C.M.L.R. 84, at paras. 102–105, and *Viho/Parker Pen*: [1992] O.J. L233/27.

[92] Above, n. 62, at pp. 32 and 33. The undertaking in its defence to an infringement of Art. 15(1)(c) (production of documents in incomplete forms) argued inter alia that its representative had only recently taken up the post of sales manager and could not supply any information relating to the agreement in question because he was unaware of its existence and had played no part in it.

[93] *Mewac*: [1993] O.J. L20/6.

obscure references in documents, figures, technical terms, abbreviations. This avoids confusion and false conclusions being drawn, and can speed things up considerably.[94] The undertaking is entitled to a copy of the inspectors' minutes recording oral explanations. The undertaking can always correct anything said by an employee on the spot although it probably cannot repudiate what the employee said simply on the grounds that he was not authorised to say it. It is advisable to supply any corrections and additional information in writing as soon as possible after the investigation. The Commission cannot compel answers. The consequences of refusing to supply oral explanations or of giving a false or incorrect explanation are discussed in Chapter 7.[95]

(iv) *To enter any premises, land and means of transport of undertakings*

3.37 As the Court of Justice said in *Hoechst*, the powers listed in Article 141 are intended to permit the Commission to obtain evidence of infringements in places in which such evidence is normally to be found, *i.e.* on the business premises of undertakings.[96] Article 14(1)(d) refers to any premises, etc., of the undertaking and it is reasonable to infer that the inspectors have a right of access to all the premises specified in the relevant decision or authorisation and to all parts of those premises. It would render the power totally ineffectual if the undertaking could dictate where the inspectors could go and what they could see once over the threshold. The Court, again in *Hoechst*,[97] stated:

> "The right of access would serve no useful purpose if the Commission officials could do no more than ask for documents or files which they could identify precisely in advance. On the contrary, such a right implies the power to search for various items of information which are not already known or fully identified. Without such power it would be impossible for the Commission to obtain the information necessary to carry out the investigation if the undertakings refused to co-operate or adopted an obstructive attitude."

It is clear, however, that Article 14(1)(d) gives no right to the Commission's inspectors to make a forcible entry, to oblige the staff of the undertaking to give them such access, or to carry out searches without the party's agreement.[98] Article 14(1)(d) merely gives a power to enter premises, etc., in order to exercise the other powers contained in Article 14(1)(a), (b) and (c), so that the Commission can exercise the power to have shown to them the documents they request and to have shown to them the contents of a piece of furniture they indicate. But as will be explained below that position becomes entirely different if the undertaking opposes the investigation. It is the Commission's practice to ask to see the books, etc., *in situ* and therefore to be taken to the rooms where they are kept. The absence of a forcible power to search does not mean that the inspectors can be closeted in an empty room and periodically fed files! However, only the undertaking's premises, etc., may be entered.[99] The inspectors have no

---

[94] Joshua, *op. cit.*
[95] See para. 7.08
[96] Above, n. 67 at para. 26.
[97] *Ibid.* at para. 27.
[98] *Ibid.* at para. 31.
[99] Thiesing-Schroter-Hochbaum, *op. cit.*, p. 529.

power to visit, for example, the private home of a director of the undertaking concerned even if they suspect that some of the undertaking's files or papers are kept there, but they could go with him to collect papers if they were not, for some reason, at the office.[1] The power to enter the undertaking's premises does not as such imply a power to enter the premises of the solicitors, accountants or bank used by the undertaking although such persons may well hold "books or other business records" belonging to the undertaking being investigated.[2] If the inspectors wish to see them the correct procedure is for the Commission to require the undertaking being investigated to produce the relevant books, etc., and not to seek to enter the premises of other undertakings in order to examine them.

Assistance from competent authority

3.38   At the request of the competent authority or of the Commission, officials of the competent authority of the Member State in whose territory the investigation is to be made may assist the Commission inspectors in carrying out the investigation.[3] In the United Kingdom officials from the Office of Fair Trading normally accompany the inspectors. On an unannounced visit with decision the official is usually a lawyer. There are no formal guidelines governing the behaviour of such officials. Their job is to facilitate co-operation in the carrying out of the investigation.[4] They are not present to act as any form of umpire or referee between the Commission and the undertaking.[5] They are there to "assist" the inspectors. This means to help the Commission and may involve active participation in the investigation, for example, by scrutinising files of documents and putting questions relating to the papers to the representatives of the undertaking. Where an undertaking opposes an investigation ordered by a decision, the Member State concerned shall afford the necessary assistance to the authorised Commission officials to enable them to make their investigation.[6] This compensates for the Commission's lack of coercive powers. Such assistance may, but need not necessarily, be given by the competent authority. The procedure is a matter for national law.[7]

Refusals/opposition

3.39   The Commission may face refusal to submit not just at the doorstep or the outset of the inspection but at any time before completion. The duty to submit is a continuing one and therefore any obstruction of the inspection is potentially liable to amount to a refusal.[8] An undertaking may agree to the inspection and then, when it is

---

[1] *Quaere* the position of a self-employed person who works from his home.
[2] Rights of entry should be narrowly construed having regard to the need to protect fundamental rights. Contract Decision 379/84, defining inspection powers under Art. 47 ECSC, which enables inspectors to enter the premises "of any third party with whom books or business records have been deposited."
[3] Art. 14(5) of Reg. 17.
[4] Parliamentary Question of November 8, 1979, House of Lords Hansard, col. 1084.
[5] Kreis, *op. cit.*, at one point (p. 41) describes the representative of the competent authority as being a neutral third party. This is not so.
[6] Art. 14(6) of Reg. 17. The equivalent provision in Reg. 4056/86 (Art. 18(6)) was invoked in *Ukwal*: [1992] O.J. L121/45.
[7] See paras. 5.17–18.
[8] It must, however, be a question of degree. See Joshua, *op. cit.*, and Kreis, *op. cit.*, who both deal quite fully with various types of refusal to submit.

made, try to stop it or to impose restrictions on what the inspectors can see or where they can go. A temporary refusal to supply documents may be treated as a refusal to submit to the investigation and lead to a fine.[9] Such acts may be construed as refusal by the Commission. Where the Commission inspectors encounter opposition from the undertaking being investigated by decision, they have no additional powers to meet that opposition. Article 14 does not enable them to force entry or break into cupboards. It is for the Member State concerned in accordance with Article 14(6) to "afford the necessary assistance to the officials authorised by the Commission to enable them to make their investigation."[10] Acting on the basis of the national measures taken under Article 14(6) the inspectors may without the co-operation of the undertakings search for any information necessary for the investigation with the assistance of the national authorities. National law and assistance from the national authorities must enable the Commission officials to perform their duties and complete the investigation.[11] Moreover the Commission may by further decision impose a fine[12] of from 100 to 5,000 ECUs where, intentionally or negligently, it refuses to submit to an investigation ordered by decision and may impose periodical penalty payments[13] of from 50 to 1,000 ECUs per day in order to compel the undertaking to submit to the investigation.

Presence of legal advisers

3.40 Whilst the Commission cannot object to the undertaking concerned having its legal advisers present at the investigation to advise, assist and represent it where necessary, and the Court of Justice has recognised the right to legal representation as one of the rights of defence,[14] it does not seem that the undertaking is entitled to delay unduly the commencement of the investigation until the arrival of its legal advisers. This was made clear in *National Panasonic*.[15] The Commission inspectors arrived unannounced at about 10.00 a.m. at the undertaking's premises at Slough. The decision was served on the undertaking's sales director. The undertaking's solicitor (in Norwich) was contacted by telephone and arrangements made for him to be brought by air and road to Slough. The inspectors refused a request that the investigation be postponed until the solicitor's arrival and commenced the investigation a 10.45 a.m. National Panasonic argued before the Court of Justice that a fundamental right had been infringed, "the right" to prepare for their investigation by taking legal advice, marshalling the documents considered by the undertaking to be relevant and not privileged from disclosure and ensuring that "suitable senior executives and lawyers" can be present. Advocate General Warner rejected this plea: "I think it is enough to say that no authority whatsoever was cited on behalf of the Applicant for the existence of any such right." The Court, in its judgment, did not deal expressly with the point. It

---

[9] As in *C.S.M.–N.V.*: [1992] O.J. L305/16.

[10] See paras. 5.17–18.

[11] Cases 46/87 & 227/88, *Hoechst AG* v. *Commission*: [1989] E.C.R. 2859, [1991] 4 C.M.L.R. 410, at para. 32.

[12] Art. 15(1)(c) of Reg. 17.

[13] Art. 16(1)(d) of Reg. 17. As happened in the *Hoechst AG* case. For a recent example see the penalty payment imposed on AKZO Chemicals BV, European Commission Press Release: IP(23)893 of October 19, 1993.

[14] *Hoechst*, above, at para. 16.

[15] Above, n. 85.

did, however, consider whether the Commission's decision involved any infringement of fundamental rights and concluded that it did not.[16]

The Commission has however said that the inspectors must allow the company a reasonable time to secure, during the period of the investigation, the resources of an in-house legal adviser or a lawyer of its choice.[17] In practice, there should be a problem only where the investigation is unannounced for where the investigation is announced in advance there should be little difficulty in making suitable arrangements for attendance, etc. When unannounced (and this is becoming the norm), the Commission will in practice allow a solicitor to be contacted so that immediate advice on the decision and its implications can be taken. Such consultation must not, however, unduly delay the investigation. The Commission's Explanatory Note[18] indicates that the inspectors will only accept a minimal delay, and that subject to two conditions. First, the management of the undertaking must undertake that the business records will remain in the place and state they were in when the officials arrived. Secondly the inspectors must not be hindered from entering and remaining in occupation of offices of their choice. The Commission's recent decision in *Mewac*[19] suggests that the Commission may be prepared to wait longer than the 45 minutes in *National Panasonic*, where they can see a commencement time. In that case the inspectors appeared ready to await the arrival in Marseilles of the Secretary General of the organisation in question and his lawyer both coming from Paris. But the Commission will not await the arrival of an external lawyer when the undertaking has an in-house legal service available. Where the in-house lawyer is not on the premises or nearby the Commission may expect another (more local) legal adviser to be contacted.

Record and results of inspection

3.41   It is advisable to make a detailed note of the investigation for future reference. It may be useful to set down: which rooms and files were viewed and which investigated in detail; which documents were requested, produced and examined by the inspectors; which documents were requested but were not or could not be produced and any reasons given; any replies given to inquiries or requests for explanation; and which documents or parts of documents were copied. Such a record can best be made contemporaneously if suitable staff are available to do so. The Commission inspectors will keep their own record which may not be made available to the undertaking.[20] In particular where, for example, books or records cannot be produced or are withheld by the undertaking or the undertaking refuses to supply an explanation when requested, the inspectors will prepare a formal minute setting out the position. The undertaking will be invited to record its viewpoint in the minute. The minute will be signed by all parties and a copy left with the undertaking. But the undertaking cannot be compelled to sign or receive a copy. If it refuses, that fact is also recorded.

---

[16] *Ibid.* para. 20.

[17] Answer to written question No. 284/92: [1992] O.J. C168/45.

[18] Set out in Appendix H. In *Mewac*, above, n. 9 the Commission said "Naturally the Commission representatives are prepared to wait for a lawyer to be present before commencing an inspection, provided that the delay is reasonable and that no documents are removed from the premises or destroyed in the meantime." And see para. 3.23 above.

[19] *Mewac*, above, n. 9.

[20] Because it may be treated as an internal document for the purposes of access to the file (see para. 4.08). For examples, see the Commission's decisions in *Fabbrica Pisana* and *Fabbrica Sciarra*, above, nn. 91 and 92. A copy of the form of minute normally used is reproduced in Appendix H.

Regulation 17 lays down no rules for informing undertakings of the results of investigations. The complaint is sometimes made[21] that it may be years before the results are notified and investigations may be shelved or discontinued by the Commission without the undertakings being told. At least in part the remedy is in the hands of the undertaking. Its lawyer or other representatives may write, telephone or call on the Commission and in practice this is often done. The Commission will give such information as it can at that stage of the procedure, although confidentiality and secrets have to be respected.

Supplementary inquiries

3.42   Although the discussion of the investigatory powers of the Commission (Articles 11–14) has, for convenience' sake, been dealt with between the initiation of proceedings and the preparation of the statement of objections and reply, one should not assume from this that the powers given to the Commission in Articles 11 and 14 can be used only at this stage in the procedure and not earlier or later. Not only is the Commission allowed to take into account events occurring after the initiation of proceedings and before the statement of objections is delivered to the parties,[22] but the Commission is entitled and in certain cases may be under a duty to make fresh inquiries during the course of the administrative proceedings if the course of the proceedings brings out the need for supplementary investigations.[23] The powers contained in Articles 11 and 14 may be used in such supplementary investigations. It is not unknown for the Commission to use an Article 11 request to verify the factual arguments put by a particular undertaking during its hearing in order to top up its information on a particular undertaking (turnover figures, etc.) prior to the taking of the final decision in the procedure.[24] The Commission has also used Article 11 to obtain information from undertakings after a decision has been made and when it is before the Court in the context of an action for annulment under Article 173.

Sector inquiries

3.43   Article 12(1) of Regulation 17 provides:

"If in any sector of the economy the trend of trade between Member States, price movements, inflexibility of prices or other circumstances suggest that in the economic sector concerned competition is restricted or distorted within the

---

[21] See the House of Lords Select Committee Report, *op. cit.*, at pp. xviii, 83 and 116.
[22] Cases 48, 49 & 51–57/69, *Dyestuffs, ICI and Others* v. *Commission*: [1972] E.C.R. 619, [1972] C.M.L.R. 557.
[23] *Dyestuffs: Francolor* v. *Commission* (Case 54/69), at paras. 16–18. The Court held that the Commission was entitled and may even be under a duty in some cases to make fresh enquiries during the course of the administrative procedure, if the course of the proceedings brings out the need for supplementary investigations. If as a result of such enquiries the Commission raises new charges against the undertakings concerned or there is an appreciable alteration in the evidence proving the disputed infringements, it must serve a further statement of objections on the parties (see para. 4.06).
[24] In *Wood Pulp*: [1985] O.J. L85/1, [1985] 3 C.M.L.R. 474, Art. 11 was used to check certain unsubstantiated allegations made in the parties' replies to the statement of objections, that transaction prices differed widely from announced prices. More than 100,000 invoices and credit notes were then submitted by the

common market, the Commission may decide to conduct a general enquiry into that economic sector and in the course thereof may request undertakings in the sector concerned to supply the information necessary for giving effect to the principles formulated in Articles 85 and 86 of the Treaty and for carrying out the duties entrusted to the Commission."

This rather complex provision (which is not present in all the transport implementing regulations[25]) enables the Commission to conduct a general inquiry into a particular economic sector. It will be noted that it is not necessary for the Commission to have evidence of or suspect any particular infringement of Article 85 or 86, but merely that circumstances such as the trend of trade, price movements, etc.,[26] suggest that competition within the Common Market is being restricted or distorted. Such an inquiry may reveal specific infringements of Articles 85 and 86, but there are no sanctions applicable without a full Article 85 or 86 procedure. But there is no restriction on the Commission's using information gleaned in a sector inquiry in order to initiate a procedure against a particular undertaking leading to a decision under Article 3 of Regulation 17.

Article 12(1) empowers the Commission to obtain "necessary" information from undertakings in the economic sector being examined. "Necessary" means necessary for the purpose of "giving effect to the principles in Articles 85 and 86" and of "carrying out the duties entrusted to the Commission." The duties are almost certainly those assigned to the Commission by Article 89 and by the provisions adopted under Article 87 of the Treaty, *i.e.* the enforcement of the competition rules. It is clear that the Commission can, if appropriate, seek information from every undertaking in the relevant economic sector. Article 12(2) provides that the Commission "may *in particular* request every undertaking or association of undertakings in the economic sector" for details of agreements, etc., which are exempt from notification under Article 4(2) and 5(2) of Regulation 17.[27] As is clear from the words emphasised, Article 12(2) is an example of and does not limit the general power given in Article 12(1). Similarly the power given by Article 12(3) to make inquiries of dominant firms as to their structure and behaviour in order to appraise their positions under Article 86 is expressed to be exercisable by the Commission when making inquiries under Article 12(2) calling up non-notifiable agreements. It is submitted that this is also merely an example of a particular application of the general power in Article 12(1) and cannot restrict the extent or exercise of that power.

Article 12(4) provides that "Article 10(3) to (6) and Articles 11, 13 and 14" apply in the context of a sector inquiry. The Advisory Commission on Restrictive Practices and Monopolies[28] should therefore be consulted prior to the taking of the decision to commence the inquiry and any decision in relation to its closure or termination. The Commission can use its normal investigative procedures as and when appropriate.

firms concerned.
[25] It is only mirrored in Reg. 1017/68 (rail, road and inland waterways).
[26] "Or other circumstances" indicates that the category of factors which may suggest competition is being restricted or distorted is not closed.
[27] The agreements, decisions and practices listed in Art. 4(2) of Reg. 17 are exempted from notification because they are considered to be "less prejudicial to the development of the common market"—see 4th preamble to Reg. 17. See, generally, paras. 2.09–15.
[28] See, generally, paras. 5.21–28.

There are three reported examples of decisions taken under Article 11 in the context of a sector inquiry: *Brasserie Esperance-Alba*,[29] *Union des Brasseries*[30] and *Brasserie Maes*.[31]

In practice, the Commission has made little use of Article 12. There have been two reported examples of sector inquiries.[32] The first lasted three years and related to margarine.[33] During the inquiry, certain restrictions (bonuses for exclusive purchases) being practised by a dominant supplier were suppressed. The second related to the brewery sector,[34] and had the principal purpose of assessing the extent of the "brewery contracts" or "tied house" system. There have been other general inquiries without resort to Article 12,[35] for example, into the behaviour of the oil companies, commissions charged by credit institutions, and more recently the beer market.

Self-incrimination

3.44 The nature and extent under Community law of any privilege against self-incrimination for undertakings subject to the Commission's investigatory powers is related to the rights of defence of the undertakings concerned. In *A.M. & S.*, Advocate General Warner took the view that if a party could not be required to answer incriminatory questions under Article 11 of Regulation 17 that might defeat the very purpose of the Article or at least render it largely ineffective.[36] In the past, the Commission appeared not to recognise any such protection, having on occasion fined firms for failure to produce incriminatory documents.[37] Regulation 17 itself is silent on the existence of such a privilege and in *Orkem*, the Court of Justice found that a comparative analysis of the laws of the Member States did not indicate the existence of such a principle in relation to enforcement of competition laws.[38] Similarly the Court concluded that no support for the existence of such a principle in Community law could be found in the European Convention on Human Rights or the International Covenant on Civil and Political Rights.[39] But in *Hoechst*, the Court said that it is necessary to prevent the

---

[29] [1971] J.O. L161/2.

[30] [1971] J.O. L161/6.

[31] [1971] J.O. 1161/11.

[32] The Commission has stated that general and frequent recourse to sector enquiries is not possible, partly because of the basic conditions to be fulfilled and partly because of the heavy administrative work involved—First Report on Competition Policy, point 124.

[33] [1965] 8 E.C. Bull. 35, and [1970] 8 E.C.Bull. 69.

[34] [1969] J.O. C148/3.

[35] See Fifth Report on Competition Policy, point 9 and *Irish Banks' Standing Committee*: [1986] O.J. L295/28, at para. 8, and the Twentieth Report on Competition Policy, point 84.

[36] Case 155/79, *A.M. & S.* v. *Commission*: [1982] E.C.R. 1575, [1982] 2 C.M.L.R. 264.

[37] *Fabbrica Pisana* [1980] O.J. L75/30, [1980] 2 C.M.L.R. 354, and *Fabbrica Sciarra* [1980] O.J. L75/35, [1980] 2 C.M.L.R. 362. And see the views of Joshua, *op. cit.*, and Kreis, *op. cit.*

[38] Case 374/87, *Orkem* v. *Commission*: [1989] E.C.R. 3283, [1991] 4 C.M.L.R. 502, at para. 29. The Court found that the privilege is restricted to individual persons charged with a criminal offence. The privilege against self incrimination is restricted in English civil proceedings: see *A.T. & T. and Others*: [1992] 3 All E.R. 523. Generally it does not apply to investigations under statutory powers, see, *e.g. Bishopsgate Investment* v. *Maxwell*: [1992] 2 All E.R. 856 (Insolvency Act 1986), *In re London United Investments plc*: January 17, 1992 (Companies Act 1985) and *Bank of England* v. *Riley and Another*: [1992] 1 All E.R. 769 (Banking Act 1987).

[39] *Ibid.* at paras. 30 and 31.

rights of defence "from being irredeemably impaired during preliminary inquiry procedures which may be decisive in providing evidence of the unlawful nature of conduct engaged in by undertakings and for which they may be liable."[40] Applying this in *Orkem*, the Court held that whilst the Commission, in order to give effect to the powers in Article 11, is entitled to compel an undertaking to provide all necessary information and documents in its possession, even if this can be used to establish against it or another undertaking, the existence of an infringement of Article 85 or 86, it cannot compel an undertaking "to provide it with answers which might involve an admission on its part of the existence of an infringement which it is incumbent upon the Commission to prove."[41] Consequently the Court struck down three of the questions in the Commission's decision. These questions went beyond seeking factual clarification of the subject matter and the implementation of certain measures taken to determine prices. They related to the purpose or objective of the measures or tried to obtain from the undertaking an acknowledgment of its involvement in what was referred to as a market-sharing arrangement.[42] As has been pointed out,[43] this rules out questions of the "have you stopped beating your wife?" type. It does not stop the Commission asking simple factual questions (*e.g.* was there a meeting? who was present? what was discussed?). But the undertaking cannot be compelled to reply to questions which require it to assess its position as regards the application of the competition rules in any response (*e.g.* how did you check that everyone complied with the method of pricing discussed?). The extent of the privilege is thus narrow and in practice is no inhibition on the Commission provided that leading incriminatory questions are avoided.[44] The privilege, such as it is, should also be available in responding to questions asked during an Article 14 investigation.[45]

It is also necessary to consider the existence of any such privilege not just in relation to the protection of an undertaking against a finding of infringement and a fine under Regulation 17 but also in relation to criminal sanctions before another instance. Even in this case it is thought unlikely that the Court would go further in allowing the interest of the firm (to avoid prosecution and possible punishment in another forum) to outweigh the Community's (own public) interest in the effective investigation and curtailment of anti-competitive practices affecting the common market.[46] The undertaking already has the protection described above and also under Article 20(1) and (2) of Regulation 17.[47] The Court, it is submitted, should consider these safeguards sufficient.[48]

---

[40] Above, n. 11, at para. 15, quoted in *Orkem*, above, n. 38, at para. 33.

[41] *Orkem*, at paras. 34 and 35.

[42] *Ibid.* at paras. 38 and 39. The detail of the questions can be found in the Report to the hearing set out in the law reports.

[43] Lasok, "The Privilege Against Self-incrimination in Competition Cases" (1990) II E.C.L.R. 90.

[44] The scope of any privilege after *Orkem* might usefully be reviewed in the light of the judgment of the European Court of Human Rights in *Funke* v. *France*: [1993] 1 C.M.L.R. 897.

[45] An undertaking should not, during an inspection, be faced with the alternative either to have to incriminate itself by recognising its participation in a prohibited agreement etc, or to run the risk of being fined for inaccurate information: Guerrin and Kyriazis, "Cartels: Proof and Procedural Issues" 16 Fordham Int. L.J. 266, at p. 334.

[46] The considerations may be different where the proceedings are between two private parties. See para. 10.24.

[47] The House of Lords Select Committee (*op. cit.*, at para. 39) recognised that the essential safeguard, especially of self-incriminating evidence, is the duty of confidentiality imposed on the Commission.

[48] As regards the application of the *Orkem* principle in private proceedings before a national court, see para. 10.24, discussing the Court of Justice's recent judgment in Case C–60/92, *Otto* v. *Postbank NV*: not yet

Use of information

3.45   Article 20 of Regulation 17 is headed "Professional secrecy". It in fact deals with two separate matters which may be, but are not necessarily, related. Article 20(1) provides that "information acquired as a result of the application of Articles 11, 12, 13 and 14 of Regulation No. 17 shall be used only for the purpose of the relevant request or investigation." Article 20(2) prohibits the disclosure of information acquired as a result of the application of Regulation 17 and of the kind covered by the obligation of professional secrecy. Ostensibly Article 20(1) is a restriction on *use* of information obtained by the use of the Commission's investigatory powers,[49] whilst Article 20(2) is a restriction on *disclosure* of a certain class of information whatever its source under Regulation 17. Article 20(3) contains a limited exception to the prohibitions in Article 20(1) and (2). It permits the use and disclosure of information to enable the publication of general information surveys which do not contain information relating to particular undertakings.

3.46   Article 20(1) appears quite explicit. The information cannot be used except for the purposes of the relevant request or investigation. Such a restriction should assist the Commission's inquiries if the undertakings knows the information cannot be used elsewhere it is more likely to co-operate and supply it. The Court of Justice has however identified the purpose of Article 20(1) as being one to protect the rights of defence:

> "These rights could be seriously endangered if the Commission could rely on evidence against undertakings which was obtained during an investigation but was not related to the subject matter or purpose thereof."[50]

But this, the Court said, does not mean that the Commission is barred from initiating an inquiry in order to verify or supplement information which it happened to obtain during the previous investigation if that information demonstrates conduct contrary to the competition rules. Such a bar would go beyond the needs of professional secrecy and the rights of the defence and would be an unjustified hindrance to the Commission performing its task of enforcing the competition rules.[51] So notwithstanding the express wording or Article 20(1) the Commission has used information for an investigation into one thermoplastic product to launch investigations in relation to another such

---

reported.

[49] In *Hasselblad (GB) Ltd.* v. *Orbinson*: [1985] 1 All E.R. 173, [1984] 3 C.M.L.R. 679, the Court of Appeal took the view that Art. 20(1) did not apply to information acquired otherwise than by the application or threat of compulsion contained in Arts. 11 and 14. Art. 20(1) did not therefore protect a complainant's letter from use in a libel action. But the Court of Justice has extended the principle of Article 20(1) to information acquired under Articles 2, 4 and 5 of Reg. 17 (notifications and applications for exemption). In Case C–67/91, *Dirección General de Defensa de la Competencia* v. *Asociación Española de Banca Privada and Others*: The Times, November 26, 1992, the Court did not regard the omission of references to those Articles as meaning that the same principle did not prevent Member States' competent authorities from using the information so obtained. The principle would, it is stated, apply equally to the Commission.

[50] *Dow Benelux*, above, n. 71, at para. 18.

[51] *Ibid.* at para. 19.

product.[52] But the information cannot be given to other authorities (for example, customs or revenue authorities) which might be interested in having the information. National competition authorities assisting the Commission need not, however, suffer "acute amnesia" but cannot use the information as evidence in domestic proceedings.[53]

Although Article 20(2) prohibits the disclosure of certain information, it will be appreciated that in practice it may impose a serious restraint on the use of information by the Commission where such use would involve the information being made available to a party not entitled to see it. The scope of the obligation of professional secrecy and its implications for the Commission's procedures are discussed in more detail in Chapter 8.[54]

---

[52] See *PVC*: [1989] O.J. L74/1, [1990] 4 C.M.L.R. 345, at para. 6, and *LdPE*: [1989] O.J. L74/21, [1990] 4 C.M.L.R. 382, at para 8. See also *UK Agricultural Tractor Registration Exchange*: [1992] O.J. L68/19, [1993] 4 C.M.L.R. 358 where the existence of an information exchange agreement covering sales figures and market shares was discovered by the Commission when investigating complaints of interference with parallel trade.

[53] The position regarding the use of information by national authorities is discussed in Chapter 5. See para. 5.15 dealing with the *Spanish Banks* case, above, n. 49.

[54] See paras. 8.18–21. See also Lavoie, "The Investigation Powers of the Commission with respect to Business Secrets under Community Competition Rules" (1992) E.L. Rev. 20.

4

Rights of the Defence

4.01 The rights of the defence in competition cases[1] before the Commission connote two basic things: an obligation on the Commission to make its case known to the undertakings concerned and the right of the undertaking to reply. This was most clearly stated by the Court of Justice in *Consten & Grundig* v. *Commission*:[2]

> "The proceedings before the Commission concerning the application of Article 85 of the Treaty are administrative proceedings which implies that the parties concerned should be put in a position to present their observations on the complaints which the Commission considers must be upheld against them. For that purpose, they must be informed of the facts upon which these complaints are based."

These two essential features find legislative expression in Regulations 17 and 99/63. In particular, Article 19(1) of Regulation 17 requires the Commission, before taking certain decisions, to give the undertakings concerned the opportunity of being heard on the matters to which the Commission has taken objection. It is clear that the undertakings are to see all the evidence on which the Commission bases its case. In *Polypropylene*,[3] the Court of First Instance said:

> "regard for the rights of the defence requires that an applicant must have been put in a position to express, as it sees fit, its views on all the objections raised against it by the Commission in the statement of objections addressed to it and on the evidence which is to be used to support those objections and is mentioned by the Commission in the statement of objections or annexed to it."

Article 4 of Regulation 99/63 provides that the Commission in its decision may deal only with those objections raised against undertakings in respect of which they have been afforded the opportunity of making known their views.

---

[1] See generally, Ehlermann and Oldekop, "Due Process in Administrative Procedure", Vol. 3 of the papers of FIDE conference in Copenhagen, 1978; Korah, "The Rights of the Defence in Administrative Proceedings under Community Law" [1980] *Current Legal Problems* 73; Sedemund, "Due Process in Competition Procedures," paper given on September 11, 1979 to the IBA in Zürich; Joshua, "The Right to be Heard in EEC Competition Procedures" (15) Fordham Int. L.J. 16. Guerrin, *L'accès au dossier*. Paper given at Commission seminar on competition procedures, Brussels September 27–28, 1993.
[2] Cases 56 & 58/64: [1966] E.C.R. 299, [1966] C.M.L.R. 418, at para. 5.
[3] Case T–7/89, *S.A. Hercules NV* v. *Commission*: [1992] 4 C.M.L.R. 84, at para. 51.

138

The right to be heard is not, however, limited by or to such legislative provisions. As Advocate General Warner said in the *Japanese Ballbearings* case:[4]

> "It is a fundamental principle of Community law that, before any individual measure or decision is taken, of such a nature as directly to affect the interests of a particular person, that person has a right to be heard by the responsible authority; and it is part and parcel of that principle that, in order to enable him effectively to exercise that right, the person concerned is entitled to be informed of the facts and considerations on the basis of which the authority is minded to act. That principle ... is enshrined in many a judgment of this Court, and ... applies regardless of whether there is a specific legislative text requiring its application ..."

More recently, in *Al-Jubail*, the Court of Justice annulled an anti-dumping regulation for infringement of the right to a fair hearing. The Community institutions responsible had not discharged "their duty to place at the applicants' disposal all the information which would have enabled them effectively to defend their interests."[5] The importance of this general principle will be shown when dealing with matters such as a party's right of access to information on the Commission's file, on which the regulations are silent.

Finally, the Commission must conduct its procedure fairly. It is not required to act as a judicial tribunal but in its administrative proceedings must respect the basic procedural guarantees provided by Community law.[6] It must address itself to the particular case with a mind open to all the evidence and all the arguments that may be put to it. The right to be heard, which is guaranteed by Article 19 of Regulation 17 and the general principles of Community law, would not in any real sense be observed if the Commission's mind were closed to all persuasion.[7]

I. THE COMMISSION'S CASE

Statement of objections

4.02 Article 2 of Regulation 99/63 provides that the Commission must inform undertakings in writing of the objections raised against them. This is done in the so-called statement of objections. It must clearly set out the facts and legal arguments on the basis of which the Commission contends that there is or has been infringement of Article 85 or 86 and should make clear what substantive conclusions the Commission

---

[4] Cases 113 & 118–121/77, *NTN Toyo Bearing Co. Ltd. and Others* v. *Council*: [1979] E.C.R. 1185, [1979] 2 C.M.L.R. 257. See also Case 34/77, *Oslizlok* v. *Commission*: [1978] E.C.R. 1099 and the other staff cases discussed by Korah, *op. cit.*, at pp. 74–76, and, in relation to state aids, Case 40/85, *Belgium* v. *Commission*: [1966] E.C.R. 2321, at para. 28 and Case C–292/90, *British Aerospace plc and Rover Group Holdings plc* v. *Commission*: [1992] 1 C.M.L.R. 852, at paras. 12–14.

[5] Case C–49/88, *Al-Jubail Fertilizer Co* v. *Council*: [1991] 3 C.M.L.R. 377, at para. 18.

[6] Cases 209–215 & 218/78, *Heintz Van Landewyck Sarl & Others (FEDETAB)* v. *Commission*: [1980] E.C.R. 3125, [1981] 3 C.M.L.R. 134, at para. 87.

[7] Per A.G. Slynn in Case 86/82, *Hasselblad (GB) Ltd.* v. *Commission*: [1984] E.C.R. 883, [1984] 1 C.M.L.R. 559, at p. 567. If there is evidence that the Commission's mind was made up from the outset, so that the procedure was followed for the sake of form only, there may be grounds for annulling the decision.

intends to draw from the facts and legal considerations of the case.[8] The statement of objections is, in the Court of Justice's words:

> "a procedural and preparatory document, intended solely for the undertakings against which the procedure is initiated with a view to enabling them to exercise effectively their right to a fair hearing."[9]

It is a most important document because in its final decision the Commission can deal only with the objections in respect of which the undertakings have been afforded the opportunity of making known their views.[10]

In practice, the statement of objections is sent under cover of a letter usually signed by the Director-General of DG IV. The letter states briefly what the Commission proposes to do in the case: for example, to find that certain acts constitute infringements of Article 85(1), to refuse the application for negative clearance or exemption, and to impose a fine. It will point out that the undertaking has the opportunity to make known its views in writing within a given period[11] and offer an oral hearing. The main body of the statement of objections is normally divided into two parts. First there is a statement of facts as understood by the Commission. This will describe the industry/economic sector concerned, the undertakings involved and their position in the relevant market, the details of any notified agreement and/or the facts which establish the infringement. Secondly, there is the legal assessment. This sets out the Commission's reasoning relating to the applicability of Article 85(1), the non-applicability of Article 85(3), and the basis for any fine which is proposed. At this stage the assessments, both legal and factual, are purely provisional in character. The length of the statement of objections will of course depend on the nature and the type of case involved. It can be a very substantial document, running to well over a hundred pages, in a complex multiparty case. The Commission commonly annexes the documentary evidence.[12] As a result the body of the statement of objections may be shorter and the undertakings have the immediate opportunity to see the evidence against them.[13] Otherwise it may have to visit the Commission in Brussels to inspect the documentary evidence.

It is well established, however, that the Commission is not required to set out or recite in detail and at great length in the statement of objections every fact or matter on

---

[8] Case C–62/86, *AKZO* v. *Commission*: [1991] I E.C.R. 3359, at para. 29, followed by the Court of First Instance in the *Cement* cases, Cases T 10, 11, 12 & 15/92R, *S.A. Cimenteries CBR and Others* v. *Commission*: [1993] 4 C.M.L.R. 243, at para. 33. And see *Wood Pulp II*: Cases C 89, 104, 114, 116, 177 & 125 to 129/85, *Åhlström and Others* v. *Commission*: [1993] 4 C.M.L.R. 407, at paras. 40–54 and 152–154.

[9] Cases 142 & 156/84, *BAT and Reynolds Industries* v. *Commission*: (Order of the Court on application for discovery) [1987] 2 C.M.L.R. 551, at para. 14.

[10] Art. 4 of Reg. 99/63. And see the third recital to Reg. 99/63 making express reference to the "rights of defence" in this context.

[11] See para. 4.24.

[12] In the *AKZO* case there were some 127 such annexes. See Case 53/85, *AKZO Chemie* v. *Commission*: [1986] E.C.R. 1965, [1987] 1 C.M.L.R. 231, at para. 5. In Case T–65/89, *BPB Industries plc and British Gypsum Ltd.* v. *Commission*: [1993] 4 C.M.L.R. 143, there was an annex containing a list summarising the 2095 documents which made up the Commissions file. See para. 31 of the judgment.

[13] Separately the undertakings will have access to the Commission's file, see paras. 4.07–12 below.

which it may rely. In the *Quinine* case,[14] the Court of Justice said: "The notice of complaints fulfils this requirement since it sets forth clearly, albeit succinctly, the essential facts on which the Commission relies." Again in the *Dyestuffs* case,[15] the Court said:

> "To safeguard the rights of the defence in administrative proceedings it suffices that undertakings be informed of the essential factual elements on which the objections are based."

The fact that the statement of objections may be brief and need contain only the essential facts should not deny the undertakings concerned knowledge of and access to other facts and documents on which the Commission may rely to establish the alleged infringement.[16] The general principle of fairness requires the Commission not to conceal exculpatory evidence.[17]

4.03 When the Commission proposes to impose a fine, the statement of objections must state, as an essential factor, the duration of the infringement established by the Commission on the information it has at that time. The Commission may extend the period thus stated if further information obtained during the administrative proceedings so justifies, provided the undertaking has had the opportunity to make its views known in that respect.[18] But whilst the statement of objections must state the duration of the infringement, it is not necessary for the Commission to set out the criteria on which it proposes to calculate the fine, the amount or even the approximate size of the fine or the possibility of a change in fining policy. It is sufficient if the Commission indicates that it is considering imposing a fine and gives the main factual and legal criteria capable of attracting a fine, such as the gravity and duration of the alleged infringement and whether committed intentionally or negligently. To go further and to give indications as to the level of the fine envisaged before the undertaking has been heard would be to anticipate the decision and would therefore be inappropriate.[19] But it has been argued that the undertakings should in fairness be given an idea of the sort of size of fine in the mind of the Commission so that they can address argument on the point.[20]

The statement of objections may deal with more than one infringement and it may be addressed to more than one undertaking. For example, in the *Sugar* case, the Commission's statement of objections was sent in identical form to some 48 undertakings

---

[14] Cases 41, 44 & 45/69, *ACF Chemiefarma and Others* v. *Commission*: [1970] E.C.R. 661, Case 41/69, at para. 26. Followed by the Court of Justice in many cases including, recently, *Wood Pulp II*, at para. 42.

[15] Cases 48, 49, 51–57/69, *ICI and others* v. *Commission*: [1972] E.C.R. 619, [1972] C.M.L.R. 557, Case 48/69, at para. 22. See also the *FEDETAB* case: Cases 209–215 & 218/78, *Heintz van Landewyck Sarl and others* v. *Commission*: [1980] E.C.R. 3125, [1981] 3 C.M.L.R. 134, at para. 39 and Case 7/82, *GVL* v. *Commission*: [1983] E.C.R. 483, [1983] 3 C.M.L.R. 645.

[16] See the discussion relating to access to the Commission's file at paras. 4.07–12 below.

[17] Joshua, *op. cit.*, p. 51 introduces this point with the word "obviously".

[18] *Pioneer*: Cases 100–103/80, *Musique Diffusion Francaise and others* v. *Commission*: [1983] E.C.R. 1823, [1983] 3 C.M.L.R. 221, at para. 15. In *Pioneer*, the Commission's statement of objections alleged that the infringements subsisted during the period "late January/early February 1976". The decision referred to a longer period and the undertakings argued on appeal that they had not had the opportunity to make known their views as regards that period. The Court accepted this submission and held that in assessing the duration of the infringements regard must be had to the shorter period.

[19] *Ibid.* at paras. 20–22. See also Case 322/81, *Michelin* v. *Commission*: [1983] E.C.R. 3461, [1985] 1 C.M.L.R. 282, at paras. 17–21.

[20] Joshua, "The Right to the Heard in EEC Competition Procedures" (15) Fordham Int. L.J. 16, at p. 34.

concerned although not every alleged infringement involved each of them. The Court of Justice rejected the argument that the statement of objections did not set out with sufficient accuracy the complaints and evidence against a particular undertaking.[21] Further, where several complaints relate to the same infringement(s), it may be sufficient to deal with them all in one statement of objections without any need to join together formally the complaints by reasoned decision.[22] Practice in multiparty proceedings may permit a statement of objections comprised of a section common and relevant to all parties followed by sections dealing with particular undertakings, infringements or geographical markets.[23] As explained below particular care and attention needs to taken by the Commission in relation to the disclosure of documentary evidence in such cases.

4.04   The statement of objections is essentially a procedural matter preparatory to the decision which is the culmination of the Commission's administrative procedure. It is not therefore a decision or other act which may be challenged before the Court under Article 173.[24] So even where as in the *Cement* case the Commission in one statement of objections addresses several alleged infringements in different Member States but chooses not to disclose the whole of the statement to all the undertakings, but only those parts dealing with the national markets in which they participated, the Court of First Instance held that it is not possible for this alleged procedural defect to be challenged before the Commission's final decision.[25] The failure of existing rules and practice to provide a definitive ruling at an early stage in the procedure has been criticised.[26]

The Commission is not prevented from withdrawing its objection in whole or in part, or from modifying or amending them. Indeed it may, following the undertakings' response, be obliged to do so. As the Court of Justice has said,[27] the Commission is under a duty to revise its factual and legal assessments in the light of the explanations provided by the undertakings and of any amendments made to the agreements or practices in question. It must take into account the factors emerging in order either to abandon any objections discovered to be unfounded or to amend and supplement its arguments, both in fact and in law, in support of the objections it maintains. It is not unknown for allegations to be dropped[28] or the character of the proceedings to change.[29]

---

[21] [1973] O.J. L140/17, [1973] C.M.L.R. D65, and on appeal to the Court, Cases 40–48, 50, 54–56, 111, 113 & 114/73, *Cooperative Vereniging "Suiker Unie" UA and others* v. *Commission*: [1975] E.C.R. 1663, [1976] 1 C.M.L.R. 295, at paras. 423–428. But as the recent *Cement* cases show there may be difficulties where different material markets are involved and not all the information is given to all the undertakings concerned. Above, n. 8 and see para. 4.04.

[22] *FEDETAB*, at paras. 29 and 32.

[23] Joshua, *op. cit.*, at p. 32. But the practice is not without its problems as the *Cement* case, Cases T 10, 11, 12 & 15/92R, *S.A. Cimenteries CBR and Others* v. *Commission*: [1993] 4 C.M.L.R. 243 shows.

[24] Case 60/81, *IBM* v. *Commission*: [1981] E.C.R. 2639, [1981] 3 C.M.L.R. 635, at para. 21. See generally, paras. 9.06–09.

[25] Above n. 8, at para. 47.

[26] See the evidence of the Joint Working Party on Competition Law to the House of Lords Select Committee on the European Communities' 1993 Report, Enforcement of Community Competition Rules.

[27] *BAT and Reynolds Industries* v. *Commission*, above, n. 9, at paras. 13 and 14.

[28] See Thompson, "EEC: Commission Hearings in Competition Cases" J. World Trade Law 448, at p. 449.

[29] *E.g.* from infringement to exemption, as in *Optical Fibres*: [1986] O.J. L236/30.

Service of statement of objections

4.05 Article 2 of Regulation 99/63 simply provides that the statement of objections must be addressed to each of the undertakings concerned or to a joint agent appointed by them.[30] It is also possible for the Commission to inform undertakings of the objections raised against them by giving notice in the *Official Journal*. This may be done "if from the circumstances of the case this seems appropriate": for example, where there are a number of undertakings and no joint agent has been appointed. The Commission cannot, however, impose a fine or periodic penalty payment on an undertaking where it has been constructively notified in such manner.[31]

Where an undertaking concerned is situated outside the Common Market, then in the absence of an appropriate agreement between the Community and the state within which the undertaking is situated, the statement of objections may be sent direct to the undertaking. In the *Dyestuffs* case,[32] it was sent direct by post to the undertaking's address in Switzerland. The Court of Justice described this as "service in accordance with the provisions of Community law." If the undertaking has some presence, such as a sales or branch office or a subsidiary, within the Community, then it is probably sufficient if the statement of objections be sent to that address.[33]

Supplementary statement of objections

4.06 Whilst the statement of objections is a key document, it is not, as already shown, final. It is clear that it can be amended or added to by the Commission in the light of new evidence or information which comes to hand, whether from its own investigations, from the reply of the undertaking concerned, or in the light of legal or other argumentation contained in the reply. In the *Dyestuffs* case,[34] the Court of Justice clearly indicated that if, as a result of fresh inquiries conducted by the Commission after the issuance of the statement of objections, new facts are to be used against the undertakings or there is a material alteration in the evidence of the contested infringements, the Commission must send an additional statement of objections to the undertakings concerned. In another case, a supplementary statement of objections

---

[30] See Case 71/74, *Frubo* v. *Commission*: [1975] E.C.R. 563, [1975] 2 C.M.L.R. 123, where applicant associations complained that the Commission had addressed the statement of objections not to them but to their members. The Court said (at para. 13): "The applicant cannot complain that they were not informed by the undertakings which they organise, because the subject of the statement of objections was, of course, the agreement concluded between the two associations."

[31] Art. 2(3) of Reg. 99/63 provides that fines can only be imposed when the statement of objections has been notified in accordance with Art. 2(1), *i.e.* addressed to each undertaking or to a joint agent appointed by them.

[32] Cases 52 & 55/69, *Geigy AG and Sandoz AG* v. *Commission*, above, n. 15, at para. 10 and 11.

[33] See Case 8/56, *ALMA* v. *High Authority*: [1957] E.C.R. 95; Cases 48, 49 & 51–57/69, *ICI and others* v. *Commission*: [1972] E.C.R. 619, [1972] C.M.L.R. 557, and Case 6/72, *Europemballage Corp. and Continental Can Co. Inc.* v. *Commission*: [1973] E.C.R. 215, [1973] C.M.L.R. 199.

[34] *Francolor* v. *Commission* (Case 54/69), above, at paras. 15–18. But see *Frubo* v. *Commission*, above, where there had been an amendment to the agreement in question, but the Court held that the second statement of objections served by the Commission was not in fact necessary (paras. 12–14), and Cases 209–215 & 218/78, *Heintz van Landewyck Sarl and others* v. *Commission*: [1980] E.C.R. 3125, [1981] 3 C.M.L.R. 134, where the Court held that where later complaints substantially duplicated earlier complaints which had been dealt with in the statement of objections it was not necessary to have a supplementary statement of objections but was sufficient that copies of the complaints had been sent to the parties for their observations.

was issued which clarified the Commission's position in relation to material and argument contained in the undertaking's reply to the original statement of objections.[35] Where the Commission, for whatever reasons, has left out of the statement of objections an objection which it may later wish to include in its decision, it must send a supplementary statement to the undertakings concerned so as to "guarantee the full exercise of their right to be heard."[36] Usually this is done by letter: there is no requirement for a formal document entitled "supplementary statement of objections."[37]

Access to the Commission's file

4.07   In *Consten & Grundig*,[38] the Court of Justice acknowledged that the undertakings concerned must be put in a position to reply to the complaints made against them by the Commission. The Court said:

> "For that purpose, they must be informed of the facts upon which these complaints are based. It is not necessary, however, that the entire contents of the file should be communicated to them."

In *Hoffmann-La Roche & Co. AG* v. *Commission*,[39] the Court said:

> "the undertakings concerned must have been afforded the opportunity during the administrative procedure to make known their views on the truth and relevance of the facts and circumstances alleged and *on the documents used by the Commission to support its claim that there has been an infringement of Article 86 of the Treaty.*"[40]

Whilst, perhaps surprisingly, Regulation 99/63 is silent on the question of disclosure of documentary evidence it is clear that the Commission is required to make available

---

[35] Van Bael, "EEC Antitrust Enforcement and Adjudication as seen by Defence Counsel" (1979) 7 *Revue Suisse de Droit International de la Concurrence* 1, 16.

[36] Ehlermann and Oldekop, "Due Process in Administrative Procedure", Vol. 3 of the papers of FIDE conference in Copenhagen. See, *e.g. Eurocheque: Helsinki Agreement*: [1992] O.J. L95/50 where the Commission delivered a supplementary statement of objections relating to Art. 85(3) where notwithstanding the agreement had been in operation nearly 7 years the parties had formally notified the agreement just a fortnight before the Commission issued the statement of objections. See also *Screensport/EBU Members*: [1991] O.J. L63/32, where application for exemption was received three weeks after statement of objections. But as the Court of First Instance pointed out in the *Eurocheque* case, it is the Commission's duty to address such supplementary statements of objection to all interested parties if it wishes to rely on these objections against them all. The Court partially annulled the Commission's decision and cancelled Eurocheque International's fine where it had only been set a copy for information of the supplementary statement of objections sent to the French financial institutions without proper opportunity to answer. Cases T39 & 40/92, *Groupement des cartes bancaires "CB" and Europay International SA* v. *Commission*: judgment of February 23, 1994, not yet reported, at paras. 46-62.

[37] Joshua, *op. cit.*, at p. 35. It is the substance rather than the form which is important.

[38] Cases 56 & 58/64: [1966] E.C.R. 299, [1966] C.M.L.R. 418, at para. 5. See generally Vaughan, "Access to the File and Confidentiality" in P.J. Slot & A. McDonnell (eds.), *Procedure and Enforcement of E.C. and U.S. Competition Law: Proceedings of the Leiden Europa Instituut Seminar on User-Friendly Competition Law* (1993), and Doherty, "Playing Poker with the Commission: Rights of Access to the Commission's Files in Competition Cases" (1994) 15 E.C.L.R. 8.

[39] Case 85/76: [1979] E.C.R. 461, [1979] 3 C.M.L.R. 211, at para. 11. Cited by A.G. Darmon in Case 226/84, *British Leyland plc* v. *Commission*: [1986] E.C.R. 3263, [1987] 1 C.M.L.R. 184, at p. 215.

[40] Emphasis added.

sufficient material to establish the infringement. It should be noted, however, that the Court does not refer to the making available of the entire file or the documents and other evidence which the Commission may have but on which it does not rely or does not need to. However, not only may that evidence itself be of value and assistance to the undertaking concerned in its defence, it may also be useful to indicate the selective process of the Commission and thereby to make clearer the basis of the Commission's reasoning and argumentation. Moreover where a document is disclosable it should, subject to the possible deletion of business secrets, be the whole document which the undertaking sees. The Commission has on occasion taken the view that it need only disclose sufficient material to support its allegations. If facts A and B each prove the case to the Commission's satisfaction, it may not disclose B if it discloses A. Concealment should not be allowed to deny an undertaking the opportunity, for example, to refute facts erroneously stated by a complainant or to use facts in support of the undertaking's case.[41] If the views of third parties are relevant to the Commission's decision making process then the undertaking concerned should also be informed of them.[42]

There is, however, no general or absolute principle of Community law which requires information to be disclosed by the institutions of the Community to persons affected by Community acts in the absence of express provision and in the absence of litigation.[43] As regards the competition rules, the Court of Justice stated in the *Dutch Books* case,[44] and reiterated more recently in *AKZO*,[45] that there is no rule which lays down that the Commission is obliged to divulge the contents of its files to the undertakings concerned. Internal documents will rarely, if ever, be disclosable.[46] But the Commission must nevertheless respect the rights of the defence. So when the Commission has based its decision on documents not shown to the undertakings, the Court has disregarded the contents of those documents when considering the substantive validity of the decision.[47] The document will be admissible in its entirety. As Advocate General Vesterdorf said in *Polypropylene*: "It is thus established that it is not the Commission's task to assess what the undertaking can use for its defence."[48]

---

[41] Per A.G. Warner in Case 30/78, *Distillers* v. *Commission*: [1980] E.C.R. 2229, [1980] 3 C.M.L.R. 121.

[42] See Case 259/85, *France* v. *Commission*: [1987] E.C.R. 4393, [1989] 2 C.M.L.R. 30.

[43] Per A.G. Slynn in Case 64/82, *Tradax* v. *Commission*: [1984] E.C.R. 1359.

[44] Cases 43 & 63/82, *VBVB and VBBB* v. *Commission*: [1984] E.C.R. 19, [1985] 1 C.M.L.R. 27.

[45] Case C–62/86, *AKZO* v. *Commission*: [1991] I E.C.R. 3359, [1993] 5 C.M.L.R. 215, at para. 16. See Vaughan, *op. cit.*, on the need now for the Court of Justice to reconcile the various decisions of the Court and the Court of First Instance in this context.

[46] Cases 142 & 156/84, *BAT and Reynolds Industries* v. *Commission*: (Order of the Court on application for discovery) [1987] 2 C.M.L.R. 551 and Case 212/86, *ICI plc* v. *Commission*: [1987] 2 C.M.L.R. 500. As A.G. Vesterdorf said in *Polypropylene* (above, n. 3, at p. 107), the only reasonable ground which might exist for producing such a document was mentioned by the Court of Justice in *BAT and Reynolds*, namely if such a document might be capable of throwing light on the question whether there had been any misuse of powers.

[47] See *Pioneer*: Cases 100–103/80, *Musique Diffusion Francaise and others* v. *Commission*: [1983] E.C.R. 1823, [1983] 3 C.M.L.R. 221, at paras. 24–30; Case 107/82, *AEG-Telefunken* v. *Commission*: [1983] E.C.R. 3151, [1984] 3 C.M.L.R. 325, at para. 30, and AKZO above, at paras. 18–24.

[48] Case T–7/89, *S.A. Hercules NV* v. *Commission*: [1992] 4 C.M.L.R. 84, at p. 115.

4.08 Much of the controversy over disclosure was removed when in 1982 the Commission announced its intention of allowing firms to have access to the file in a particular case.[49] The Commission's practice is described in the Twelfth Report on Competition Policy:[50]

> "Undertakings are informed of the contents of the Commission's file by means of an annex to the statement of objections or to the letter rejecting a complaint, listing all the documents in the file and indicating documents or parts thereof to which they may have access.
>
> They are invited to come and consult these documents on the Commission's premises. If an undertaking wishes to examine only a few of them the Commission may forward copies.
>
> However, the Commission regards the documents listed below as confidential and accordingly inaccessible to the undertaking concerned:
>
> > (i) documents or parts thereof containing other undertakings' business secrets;
> >
> > (ii) internal Commission documents, such as notes, drafts or other working papers;
> >
> > (iii) any other confidential information, such as documents enabling complainants to be identified where they wish to remain anonymous, and information disclosed to the Commission subject to an obligation of confidentiality.
>
> Where an undertaking makes a justified request to consult a document which is not accessible, the Commission may make a non-confidential summary available.
>
> In order to facilitate the determination of the accessibility of documents, undertakings are henceforth requested, when supplying information, to state whether and to what extent it should be regarded as confidential.
>
> It should be possible to apply the procedures relating to access to the file as described without any problem, except for files assembled before they were introduced, for which these new arrangements could not be taken into account; they will have to be dealt with on a case-by-case basis."

Access to the file implies access to material additional to the documentary evidence which it is now the Commission's practice to annex to the statement of objections. In the course of an inquiry the Commission will have collected and filed many documents (thousands in some cases) not all of which will be used as documentary evidence. If the case involves only a few documents the Commission may along with the list of all the documents which comprise the file send a copy of the accessible documents to the parties. Recent practice, however, has been to send copies even where quite large numbers of documents are involved. Otherwise the parties will be invited

---

[49] At para. 35.

[50] The question has been raised, what is the file? A notification and a complaint may enter DG IV separately and create in fact two files. When requested by the Head of Unit or Director, the registry may consolidate the two under one common file number. Johannes (Festschrift fur A. Deringer, 1993) queries whether this request, or the decision of the registrar to proceed as described, is sufficient to give access to the entire (new) file. Other potential problems arise where a case has been earlier dealt with by means of a comfort letter and then a cause arises which may make the earlier file's contents relevant.

to Brussels to inspect the file at the Commission's offices. The undertakings can examine and take copies of all the documents on the Commission's file[51] except "internal" documents, business secrets and other confidential information. In some cases this can exclude the major portion of the file. As mentioned the list will be supplied at the same time as the statement of objections and the right to inspect the file has to be exercised within the time specified for the delivery of the written reply. So the undertakings cannot delay here.

To the extent that the Commission's practice of giving access exceeds the legal obligations described by the Court of Justice in such cases as *Hoffmann-La Roche* and *Dutch Books*, it is an important and valuable concession. Indeed "concession" may no longer be the appropriate word. In *Polypropylene*, the Court of First Instance has inferred from the Twelfth Report that the Commission has an obligation to make available all documents, whether in their favour or not, which it has obtained in the course of the investigations, save where the business secrets of other undertakings, the internal documents of the Commission and other confidential information are involved.[52] In *Cement*, the Court of First Instance said that access to the file is:

> "one of the procedural guarantees intended to protect the rights of the defence and to ensure, in particular, that the right to be heard provided for in Article 19(1) of Regulation No 17 and Article 2 of Regulation No 99/63 can be exercised effectively."[53]

The debate has yet to be settled as to whether, and to what extent, access to the file is a fundamental right or legitimate expedition dependent on the Commission's procedure.

It seems clear, however, that to the extent that access to the file is a fundamental right,[54] or the means of exercising one (the right to be heard), it does not allow access to the entire file. In *Plasterboard*, the Court of First Instance examined what documents could be refused disclosure on the grounds that they were purely internal documents or other confidential information. The Court held that the parties could not complain because they had not been able to see, in addition to internal Commission documents, certain correspondence with Member States, published documents and studies, reports of inspections, the answer to a request for information made by the Commission and certain correspondence with third party undertakings. The Court observed:

---

[51] See n. 50 above.
[52] *Hercules*, above, at para. 54, followed in Cases T 10, 11, 12 & 15/92R, *S.A. Cimenteries CBR and Others v. Commission*: [1993] 4 C.M.L.R. 243, at para. 4.
[53] *Cement*, at para. 38.
[54] As to the requirements under the European Convention on Human Rights see *Edwards* v. *United Kingdom*: (1992) 15 E.H.R.R. 417, at para. 36.

> "An undertaking to which a Statement of Objections has been addressed, and which occupies a dominant position in the market, may, for that very reason, adopt retaliatory measures against a competing undertaking, or supplier, or a customer, who has collaborated in the investigation carried out by the Commission."[55]

4.09   In addition to the disclosure of facts, documents, etc., which it may be required to make to the undertaking concerned, the Commission is also required to tell the undertaking how and to what extent such facts may have been used by the Commission, for example, in calculating an undertaking's market share. In *Japanese Ballbearings*,[56] (a dumping case) Advocate General Warner rejected the Commission's contention that the presentation and disclosure of information required by the anti-dumping regulation referred only to the factual material itself and not the way in which the material is used (in calculations or otherwise). He went further and said:

> "It was not enough for the Commission to put those persons in a position to indulge in conjecture. The Commission's duty was to tell them as clearly and as fully as the circumstances permitted, what its case against them was."

The need for the Commission to act with due diligence in such circumstances has been underlined by the Court of Justice in *Timex* and, more recently, *Al-Jubail*.[57] The Court of Justice pointed out in *AEG-Telefunken*,[58] that it is not the documents in themselves which are important but the conclusions drawn from them by the Commission. The Court held that if documents were not mentioned in the statement of objections, AEG could reasonably conclude that they were not important for the case. If a party is to be able effectively to exercise its rights of defence, the Commission must, it is submitted, not only disclose the materials it has used to build its case but also the manner of their employment, where not self-evident.

4.10   The Commission cannot use the obligation to maintain professional secrecy or confidentiality under Article 20(2)[59] of Regulation 17 to frustrate the rights of defence.[60] Nor should it be tempted to do so.[61] The Court of Justice in *Hoffmann-La Roche* was particularly concerned to reconcile the provisions of Article 20(2) with the

---

[55] Case T–65/84, *BPB Industries plc and British Gypsum Ltd.* v. *Commission*: [1993] 4 C.M.L.R. 143, above n. 12, at paras. 31–33.

[56] Cases 113 & 118–121/77, *NTN Toyo Bearing Co. Ltd. and Others* v. *Council*: [1979] E.C.R. 1185, [1979] 2 C.M.L.R. 257. The A.G. gave several examples of matters on which the parties had been afforded no opportunity to make known their views. In particular, that actual margins of dumping were never revealed to the parties or the Court, nor how the margins were calculated. The Commission had not revealed until the proceedings before the Court that the domestic prices had been "constructed" by the addition of a notional profit nor that such prices, but not export prices, had been updated. See also Korah, *op. cit.*

[57] Case 264/82, *Timex* v. *Council and Commission*: [1985] E.C.R. 849, [1985] 3 C.M.L.R. 550, cited in Case C–49/88, *Al-Jubail Fertilizer Co* v. *Council*: [1991] 3 C.M.L.R. 377, at para. 17.

[58] Case 107/82, *AEG-Telefunken* v. *Commission*: [1983] E.C.R. 3151, [1984] 3 C.M.L.R. 325, at paras. 24–28.

[59] Professional secrecy is discussed at paras. 8.18–21.

[60] The position as regards disclosure of confidential information to third parties may be different. See para. 4.20.

[61] The Commission sought to explain the tampering with the documentary evidence in *Italian Flat Glass* on the need to protect confidentiality. This was criticised by the Court: Cases T 68 & 77–78/89, *Societá Ital-*

undertaking's fundamental right to be heard. The Court noted that Article 20(2) was expressly provided to be "without prejudice to Article 19" which gives the undertaking the right of reply to the Commission's statement of objections.[62] The Court, however, went on to say that Article 20(2) does not allow the Commission:

> "to use to the detriment of the undertakings involved in a proceeding referred to in Regulation 17, facts, circumstances or documents which it cannot in its view disclose if such a refusal of disclosure adversely affects the undertaking's opportunity to make known effectively its views on the truth or implications of those circumstances on those documents or again on the conclusions drawn by the Commission from them."[63]

In *AEG-Telefunken*,[64] the Court said that the Commission should not have used as evidence a document which it had not, on the grounds of professional secrecy, shown to AEG and held that it should not be considered as proper evidence in the case before the Court. The upshot seems to be, therefore, that the Commission should try to find a way of communicating the substance of the secret or confidential material without breach of the obligation of Article 20(2),[65] or not use or rely on the material in its case unless disclosed to the undertakings concerned. Business secrets have special protection under Regulation 17[66] and as a general principle should not be disclosed during the Commission's procedure without the consent of the relevant party. Other material covered simply by the obligation of professional secrecy may, it seems, more readily be disclosed but as has been pointed out,[67] confidentiality should be respected by the Commission because of the fundamental obligation in Article 214 of the Treaty and in Article 20(2) of Regulation 17 and also because, as a practical matter, the Commission might not otherwise be supplied (at least, voluntarily) with such information. As

---

iano Vetro v. *Commission*: [1992] II E.C.R. 1403, [1992] 5 C.M.L.R. 302.

[62] *Above*, n. 39, at para. 13.

[63] *Ibid.* at para. 14. See also *Pioneer*: Cases 100–103/80, *Musique Diffusion Francaise and others* v. *Commission*: [1983] E.C.R. 1823, [1983] 3 C.M.L.R. 221, at paras. 5–10.

[64] *Above*, n. 47, at paras. 22–25 (M. Iffli's letter). See also Case C–62/86, *AKZO* v. *Commission*: [1991] I E.C.R. 3359, [1993] 5 C.M.L.R. 215, at paras. 18–24.

[65] Cases 41, 44 & 45/69, *ACF Chemiefarma and Others* v. *Commission*: [1970] E.C.R. 661, Case 41/69, at paras. 31–43. The Court referred to the possibility of the Commission requesting the opinion of the undertakings with regard to the applicant's request for sight of the documents relating to them. In its defence in *Hoffmann-La Roche*, the Commission took the position that it had been unable to produce the data relating to the market shares of other undertakings without having obtained their consent. After the adoption of the contested decision, the Commission agreed in principle to Roche inspecting the whole file, but made the authorisation to inspect the documents containing business secrets subject to the consent of the relevant undertakings. That consent was not given by the competing undertakings and only in some cases by Roche's customers who were involved in the investigations. Roche and the Commission managed to agree on an estimate of the market shares for the majority (but not all) of the vitamins concerned. Other documents were produced by the Commission at the request of the Court.

[66] See Case 53/85, *AKZO Chemie* v. *Commission*: [1986] E.C.R. 1965, [1987] 1 C.M.L.R. 231, at para. 28 and Case 142 & 156/84, *BAT and Reynolds* v. *Commission*: [1987] E.C.R. 4487, [1988] 4 C.M.L.R. 24. Although AKZO was concerned with the disclosure of business secrets to third parties, the Court does not appear to contemplate any relaxation of the principle of non-disclosure of business secrets. *Cf.* the opinion of A.G. Lenz. See paras. 8.20–21.

[67] Korah, "The Rights of the Defence in Administrative Proceedings under Community Law" [1980] *Current Legal Problems* 73, at p. 89. Note the consideration for the position of third parties expressed by the Court of First Instance in *Plasterboard*, above n. 55.

the dumping cases show clearly, the Commission must act with due diligence to provide the undertakings concerned, so for as compatible with the obligation not to disclose business secrets, with information relevant to the defence of their interests, choosing, if necessary on their initiative, the appropriate means of providing such information.[68] But in the end the Commission may have to disclose confidential material, including business secrets, needed to support its case or where its nondisclosure would otherwise materially jeopardise the rights of defence. There is a difficult balancing exercise here, with competing public interests. The Commission has said that the recognition of extensive protection for confidential information is subject to an important exception justified by the public nature of documents does not preclude their disclosure where the Commission relies upon the information as necessary evidence of an alleged infringement of Articles 85 and 86.[69]

Multiparty cases may raise special problems. Whilst it is well established that evidence in documents obtained from one undertaking which incriminates others can be used in pleadings against all the undertakings concerned,[70] problems can arise where documents contain sensitive commercial information relating to a particular undertaking. The Commission may edit the document and, where it can, rely on the edited document which can be disclosed to all undertakings concerned to justify its case. Disputes can still arise as to how much an undertaking is entitled to see. This was, for example, a major issue in the recent *Cement* case where parties were only allowed to see documents pertaining to the geographical market to which the Commission alleged their infringement related. The governing principle seems reasonably clear. Advocate General Vesterdorf said in *Polypropylene*:

> "It must be warrantable to conclude that the case law of the Court of Justice is at all events not inconsistent with the view that the applicants ought also to have access to the document used against other undertakings."[71]

Undertakings may otherwise be tempted to forms of self-help. In both *PVC* and *LdPE*,[72] the parties made a joint approach to the Commission and, on the basis of reciprocal assurances of confidentiality, made arrangements for the exchange of documents among themselves. But in its decisions in these cases, the Commission drew attention to the overriding public interest in ensuring that competitors are not informed of each others commercial activities and intentions. Perhaps the time has come to explore the possibility of there being some express provision in Community law enabling the disclosure of sensitive material to counsel for the interested parties who might be allowed to have sight of confidential documents subject to the proviso that he must respect their confidentiality even in dealings with his own client.[73]

---

[68] Case C–49/88, *Al-Jubail Fertilizer Co* v. *Council*: [1991] 3 C.M.L.R. 377, at para. 17.

[69] See Eighteenth Report on Competition, at point 43.

[70] A recent example can be seen in *Soda-ash Solvay, CFK*: [1991] O.J. L152/16.

[71] Above n. 3.

[72] [1989] O.J. L74/1 and L74/21 respectively.

[73] See the discussion of this by A.G. Darmon in *Al-Jubail* above, referring in particular to the practice and experience under U.S. law. Self-help is clearly unsatisfactory for the reasons given by Vaughan, *op. cit.* The possibility of mutual exchange between co-defendants, who in cartel cases will almost always be competitors, is not a substitute for proper access to the file. Co-operation will not always be forthcoming and a party's defence should not be dependant on the discretion of its competitors any more than that of the Commission. Not even the fullest of mutual exchanges will enable the parties to see the documents obtained by the Commission from third parties.

4.10A More generally as regards questions affecting access to the file, it has been proposed, and it seems likely that the Commission will accept, that the terms of reference of the Hearing Officer be extended to enable him to have a role in deciding on any complaints or requests for further documentation. Undertakings would receive, as is presently becoming the practice, together with the statement of objections all the documents to be disclosed and a list of all the documents on file. If an undertaking then believes it has reasonable grounds to see additional documents, a reasoned and specific request should be to the Hearing Officer who will examine it and decide on its merits.[74]

4.11 The documents, etc., on which the Commission relies should be disclosed at the time of or shortly after the statement of objections is served and certainly in good time to enable the undertaking to exercise its rights of defence and reply fully and effectively. This appears to be the practice of the Commission.

In this context it is important to note that the Court of Justice in *Hoffmann-La Roche* appeared to contemplate a default by the Commission being rectified during the appeal proceedings before the Court:

> "However, if such irregularities have in fact been put right during the proceedings before the Court they do not necessarily lead to the annulment of the contested decision in so far as remedying them at a later stage has not affected the right to be heard."[75]

This should not be taken as a licence for the Commission to refuse to produce its documents, etc., until the proceedings before the Court with the consequence that an undertaking might have to appeal to the Court to discover those documents on which it might have grounds for appeal. It is significant that the Court specified that the opportunity to make known its views on, *inter alia*, the documents used by the Commission must be given "during the administrative procedure." Indeed, more recently in *Wood Pulp II*,[76] the Court of Justice partially annulled the Commission's decision on the grounds that there had been a disregard of the rights of defence where the Commission relied, in establishing the infringement relating to transaction prices allegedly established within KEA, on documents gathered after the statement of objections had been drawn up and consequently the undertakings concerned had no opportunities to make known their views on those documents. Other cases,[77] where the Court has disregarded documentary evidence not divulged to the undertakings at the earlier correct

---

[74] Ehlermann, "A View from the Commission", Nabarro-Nathan-CBI Conference, London, February 1, 1994.

[75] Case 85/76: [1979] E.C.R. 461, [1979] 3 C.M.L.R. 211, at para. 15. This statement has been strongly criticised: see Herrmann, *European Law Letter*, June 1979, p. 68: Maitland-Walker, "Hoffmann-La Roche—the Judgment of the European Court Appraised" (1979) 1 E.I.P.Rev. 357; Sedemund, above n. 1, at p. 16. See generally, Sen, "Can Defects in Natural Justice be cured on Appeal?" (1993) 42 I.C.L.Q. 369.

[76] *Wood Pulp II*: Cases C 89, 104, 114, 116, 177 & 125–129/85, *Åhlström and Others* v. *Commission*: [1993] 4 C.M.L.R. 407, at paras. 133–138.

[77] In particular Cases 100–103/80, *Musique Diffusion Francaise and others* v. *Commission ("Pioneer")*: [1983] E.C.R. 1823, [1983] 3 C.M.L.R. 221, and *AEG-Telefunken*, above, n. 47 and *AKZO*, above n. 45. Commenting on the approach of the Court in cases such as *AEG-Telefunken*, Joshua, *op. cit.*, has submitted that it may not always be appropriate for the Court simply to ignore the contents of a document not put to the defendant. There may, he says, be cases where the "undisclosed" document is material to the decision but the omission to put it formally to the firm has caused no substantial prejudice to the defence.

time,[78] are inconsistent with the above-quoted statement in *Hoffmann-La Roche* but, perhaps unfortunately, the Court has not yet expressly overruled it.

4.12 It is imperative that an undertaking which, notwithstanding the Commission's procedure (described above), finds it necessary to ask the Commission to make documents available to it should do so at the earliest opportunity. And any such request should be quite specific, particularising the document or documents sought.[79] The fact that the Commission has refused to make available some or all of its file cannot be invoked to challenge the validity of the decision where, for example, the request is made after the decision.[80] The refusal must be shown to be capable of having and to have had an effect on the administrative procedure.[81] The relevant time would thus appear to be before the undertaking has delivered its written reply to the statement of objections and any further observations at the oral hearing. Even though refusal of access, in whole or part, to the file may constitute an infringement of the rights of the defence, the refusal may only be challenged in the context of the final decision.[82]

II. THE REPLY

4.13 When looking at the detailed rules relating to the hearing of parties (Article 19 of Regulation 17 and the hearings regulation, Regulation 99/63) it is important to bear in mind that the "hearing" may be both written and oral. The clearest indication of this appears in the preamble to Regulation 99/63 which provides:

[78] In Case 30/78, *Distillers* v. *Commission*: [1980] E.C.R. 2229, [1980] 3 C.M.L.R. 121, A.G. Warner pointed out: "To hold that ... the Commission's infringement of an undertaking's right to be heard does not vitiate the Commission's decision if the undertaking is subsequently given a fair hearing in this Court, would, it seems to me, amount to saying that the Commission may neglect essential procedural requirements with impunity because either the undertaking concerned will not appeal to this Court or, if it does, the irregularity can be put right in the course of the appeal". A.G. Warner considered that the Court's jurisdiction under Art. 173 to review the legality of acts of the Commission was concerned with their legality at the time when they were adopted. He referred to the Court's judgment in Cases 15 & 16/76, *France* v. *Commission*: [1979] E.C.R. 321, delivered shortly before its judgment in *Hoffmann-La Roche*, where the Court had said (paras. 7 and 8): "in the context of an application for annulment under Article 173 of the Treaty, the legality of the contested measure must be assessed upon the basis of the elements of fact and of law existing at the time when the measure was adopted. Rectification subsequent to that date cannot therefore be taken into account for the purposes of such assessment." See also the observations of A.G. Jacobs in Case 301/87, *France* v. *Commission*: [1990] I E.C.R. 307, on the failure of the Commission, in a state aids case, to produce the observations of third parties until requested by the Court.
[79] FEDETAB: Cases 209–215 & 218/78, *Heintz van Landewyck Sarl and others* v. *Commission*: [1980] E.C.R. 3125, [1981] 3 C.M.L.R. 134, at paras. 36–39.
[80] *Ibid.* at para. 40.
[81] *Quaere* whether the Commission's refusal to make documents available amounts to a decision which could be challenged under Art. 173. See generally, paras. 9.06–09.
[82] So in *Cement*: Cases T 10, 11, 12 & 15/92R, *S.A. Cimenteries CBR and Others* v. *Commission*: [1993] 4 C.M.L.R. 243, the Court of First Instance held that refusing access to the file produced in principle only limited effects, characteristic of a preparatory measure forming part of a preliminary administrative procedure. Following *IBM*, it held that only measures immediately and irreversibility affecting the legal situation of the undertakings concerned will be of a nature as to justify, before the completion of the administrative procedure, the admissibility of an action for annulment (para. 42). See the evidence at n. 26 above and, more generally, para. 9.08. The House of Lords Report (para. 112) recommends procedures designed to enable decisions on matters such as access to the file to be speedily adjudicated by a judge of the Court of First Instance.

"Whereas the various persons entitled to submit comments must do so in writing, both in their own interest and in the interests of good administration, without prejudice to oral procedures where appropriate to supplement the written evidence."

As this statement indicates and as will be clear form the account which follows, in practice the right to be heard is exercised primarily in writing,[83] the Commission's procedure being essentially a written one.

The right to be heard

4.14 Article 19 of Regulation 17 expressly provides that an undertaking must be given the opportunity to be heard before any of the following decisions are taken:

(a) negative clearance,
(b) termination of infringement,
(c) exemption,
(d) revocation of exemption,
(e) the imposition of a fine,
(f) the imposition of a periodic penalty payment.

Before taking interim measures under Article 3 of Regulation 17 the Commission should also hear the undertakings concerned under Article 19.[84] Decisions made pursuant to Article 15(6) (so-called preliminary decisions)[85] are not contained in the list set out in Article 19, but the right of a party to be heard (but not necessarily orally) before such a decision is taken has been acknowledged by the Court of Justice[86] and by the Commission.[87] Formal rejection of complaints should, only be made after the complainant has had the opportunity of being heard.[88]

4.15 There remain several decisions which the Commission can take without apparently having to afford the party the subject of the decision the opportunity to be heard. These include decisions under Article 11 of Regulation 17[89] requiring information to be supplied and decisions under Article 14[90] ordering investigations. In *National Panasonic (U.K.) Ltd.* v. *Commission*,[91] the Court of Justice explained the absence of any reference to the investigatory decisions (*i.e.* under Articles 11(5) and 14(3)) in Article 19(1). There is, the Court said, a "substantive difference" between

---

[83] Where interim measures are sought, the oral aspect may become more important in view of the time factors involved and the likely adversarial nature of the proceedings in such cases if there is a complainant.
[84] Case 792/79R, *Camera Care Ltd.* v. *Commission*: [1980] E.C.R. 119, [1980] 1 C.M.L.R. 334, at para. 19.
[85] See generally, para. 6.12–15.
[86] Cases 8–11/66, *Cimenteries* v. *Commission*: [1967] E.C.R. 75, [1967] C.M.L.R. 77.
[87] See the decisions discussed at para. 6.13.
[88] Principally by the complainant's response to the Commission's communication under Art. 6 of Reg. 99/63: Case T–64/89, *Automec* v. *Commission*: [1991] 4 C.M.L.R. 177, at para. 46. See generally, paras. 2.34–37.
[89] See generally, paras. 3.08–09. Art. 11 of Reg. 17 involves a two-stage procedure, and the undertaking has the opportunity to comply voluntarily before a decision can be taken.
[90] See generally, paras. 3.24–26.
[91] Case 136/79: [1980] E.C.R. 2033, [1980] 3 C.M.L.R. 169.

decisions taken in exercise of investigatory powers and those taken to terminate an infringement or to declare that an agreement or practice is incompatible with Article 85. In the latter case the rights of defence require the undertakings concerned to be given the opportunity to be heard. The Court implies that in the case of investigatory decisions the rights of defence are not affected in the same way because at that stage the Commission is solely concerned with the collection of the necessary information. It is submitted that this does not necessarily mean that principles of due process are not relevant or in fact cannot be recognised in the procedures in Articles 11 and 14.[92]

Who must be heard

4.16 Article 19 of Regulation 17 draws a distinction between parties who must be given the opportunity of being heard and those who may be given such an opportunity. Article 19(1) provides that before certain decisions[93] are taken:

> "the Commission shall give the undertakings or associations concerned the opportunity of being heard on the matters to which the Commission has taken objection."

Article 19(2) provides that the Commission "may also hear other natural or legal persons" if the Commission or the competent authorities of the Member States[94] consider it necessary. Such "other" persons must be heard "where they show a sufficient interest."

4.17 "Concerned" in Article 19(1) appears to have the same meaning that it has in Article 3 of Regulation 17, *i.e.* those persons whose conduct is the subject of the proposed decision and to whom the decision may be addressed. The Court of Justice has held that Article 19(1) is clearly directed to the hearing of the undertakings whose agreements or behaviour are the subject of the proceedings, and not third parties.[95] "Concerned" is not to be given any wider meaning as might be suggested by such words as "of direct and individual concern" contained in Article 173 of the Treaty (dealing with the rights of persons to challenge the validity of certain acts of the Council or Commission).[96] This narrow interpretation of "concerned" in Article 19(1) does not, however, prejudice the rights of any person who might be entitled to bring proceedings under Article 173. If he is entitled to bring such proceedings he will *a fortiori* have a "sufficient interest" for the purposes of Article 19(2) of Regulation 17 and therefore must be heard by the Commission if he wishes to be heard.[97]

---

[92] See Ehlermann and Oldekop, *op. cit.*, at p. 6 and Case C–49/88, *Al-Jubail Fertilizer Co* v. *Council*: [1991] 3 C.M.L.R. 377, at para. 15, referring in turn to Case 85/87, *Dow Benelux* v. *Commission*: [1989] E.C.R. 3137, [1991] 4 C.M.L.R. 410.

[93] *I.e.* decisions under Arts. 2, 3, 6, 7, 8, 15 and 16 of Reg. 17.

[94] *Quaere* whether all the Member States must consider it necessary and, if so, how they are to agree on such necessity and communicate it to the Commission. It is submitted that all the Member States need not have to agree to such action and it is consistent with the letter and intention of Art. 19(2) that one Member State should be able to request the Commission to hear the person concerned.

[95] Case 43/85, *ANCIDES* v. *Commission*: [1987] E.C.R. 3131, [1988] 4 C.M.L.R. 821, at para. 7.

[96] Art. 173(2) states: "Any natural or legal person may . . . institute proceedings against a decision addressed to that person or against a decision which, although in the form of a regulation or decision addressed to another person, is of direct and individual concern to the former." See para. 9.05.

[97] See generally, Temple Lang, "The Position of Third Parties in EEC Competition Cases" (1978) 3 E.L.Rev. 177, and the discussion of "sufficient interest" at para. 4.19.

Article 7 of Regulation 99/63 appears, at first sight, to qualify the right of an undertaking "concerned" to be heard. Article 7(1) provides:

> "The Commission shall afford to persons who have so requested in their written comments the opportunity to put forward their arguments orally, if those persons show a sufficient interest or if the Commission proposes to impose on them a fine or periodic penalty payment."

Whereas Article 19(1) is concerned with the right to be heard generally, Article 7(1) is concerned specifically with the right to be heard orally and makes it a condition precedent that a party must make a request to do so in its written observations. In practice the Commission will draw a party's attention to this in its statement of objections and ask the undertaking to let it know as soon as possible if it wishes to be heard orally. It is difficult to conceive of a situation where a person who is to be the addressee of a decision does not have a "sufficient interest" to be heard orally. It must, however, be noted that Article 7(1) is not simply dealing with undertakings "concerned" within the meaning of Article 19(1) of Regulation 17. But the alternative, "if the Commission proposes to impose on them a fine", etc., does seem to suggest that an addressee of a decision does not have an automatic right to be heard orally where he is not to be fined. The author knows of no case where the Commission has refused to allow an addressee of a final decision (not involving a fine) the right to be heard orally. Article 7(1) of Regulation 99/63 cannot restrict in any way the right to be heard contained in Article 19(1) of Regulation 17. Regulation 99/63 is a Commission regulation made pursuant to Article 24 of Regulation 17 to implement the provisions in Regulation 17 concerning hearings. The Commission is thus enabled to lay down the detailed rules[98] of procedure but cannot thereby limit, qualify or amend the substantive provisions contained in Regulation 17. Nor, it is submitted, can a fundamental principle of Community law be prejudiced by such rule-making. In practice the Hearing Officer decides whether parties should be heard orally.[99]

Third parties

4.18 The Commission may always hear third parties[1] (*i.e.*, persons not the addressees of the proposed decision), if the Commission or the competent authorities of the Member States consider it necessary.[2] Such third parties would include a complainant who might be competent to give evidence not only as to the fact of infringement (for example, that he was the victim of a boycott) but also as to the facts about the relevant market for the purposes of Article 85 or 86.[3] Witnesses brought by the undertakings alleged to be in breach of Articles 85 or 86 are not, it is submitted, third parties

---

[98] And see Cases 41, 44 & 45/69, *ACF Chemiefarma and Others* v. *Commission*: [1970] E.C.R. 661, at paras. 59–70.

[99] See Art. 4(3) of the terms of reference (Appendix L). The office and role of the Hearing Officer is discussed at para. 4.25.

[1] *I.e.* "other natural or legal persons" in the terms of Art. 19(2) of Reg. 17.

[2] Art. 19(2) of Reg. 17.

[3] See, *e.g. Ford Werke AG (Distribution System)*: [1983] O.J. L327/31, [1984] 1 C.M.L.R. 596, where the Commission heard "interested parties"; several Ford dealers in the U.K. arguing for the maintenance of the Ford distribution system, and also BEUC the European consortium of consumer organisations. In its hearing relating to *ECO System/Peugeot*: [1992] O.J. L66/1, the Commission received statements from two trade associations and from BEUC which spoke in favour of ECO System.

for these purposes. Although Article 3(3) of Regulation 99/63 is permissive in character (it provides that undertakings "may also propose that the Commission hear persons who may corroborate" the facts relied on by the undertakings) and therefore an undertaking cannot be required to produce witnesses, it is undoubtedly the undertaking's right to be heard and the hearing of witnesses for the undertaking, being a part of the exercise of that right, is as much the duty of the Commission as is the receipt and consideration of the written observations, relevant documents and oral presentations made by or on behalf of the undertaking concerned in the course of its defence. An undertaking should make it clear to the Commission whether it intends to call witnesses under Article 3(3) and who they are so that there can be no misunderstanding as to either the nature of the request or the capacity of the parties under Article 3(3). This is probably best done in writing at the same time as the written reply to the statement of objections or as soon as possible thereafter.[4]

4.19   Where a third party has a "sufficient interest" the Commission must hear such party.[5] An application has to be made.[6] The Court has recognised that a person who has a "legitimate interest" for the purposes of Article 3(2)(b) of Regulation 17 (*i.e.*, to make an application to request the Commission to find an infringement of Article 85 or 86) may be entitled as a person "directly and individually concerned" to challenge the validity of the Commission's decision under Article 173 of the Treaty.[7] For if the request is dismissed either wholly or in part, such a person must be able to commence proceedings to protect its "legitimate interest". There seems little doubt that such a person has a "sufficient interest" to be heard for the purposes of Article 19(2) of Regulation 17. But it appears that a lesser interest may be sufficient.[8] In *Deutscher Komponistenverband* v. *Commission*,[9] Advocate General Roemer said:

> "It is clear that these two proceedings are governed by different criteria: with regard to the hearing it is sufficient to establish an interest, whereas with regard to bringing an action [under Article 173] it is necessary that the contested decision should be of direct and individual concern to the applicant."

The Court of Justice has not, however, been called upon to define what amounts to a "sufficient interest". It is probably necessary to show an economic or legal interest

---

[4] *FEDETAB*, above, at para. 24.

[5] Art. 19(2) of Reg. 17 provides: "Applications to be heard on the part of such persons shall, where they show a sufficient interest, be granted". Contrast the position under the Community's Merger Control regime, whereby "members of the administrative or management organs of the undertakings concerned or recognised workers' representatives" are treated as having a sufficient interest ex officio. See Reg. 2367/90, Art. 15. This specific reference to management and unions puts beyond doubt their status in merger cases. It does not cut down the width of the rights of others who claim to have a "sufficient interest" either under the Merger Control Regulation or more generally under Reg. 17 and the other implementing regulations.

[6] In this respect there is no automatic right to be heard, per A.G. Lenz in Case 53/85, *AKZO Chemie* v. *Commission*: [1986] E.C.R. 1965, [1987] 1 C.M.L.R. 231. There is no special form. If a third party does not ask to be heard, he cannot complain that Art. 19(2) has been ignored. See Case 43/85, *ANCIDES* v. *Commission*: [1987] E.C.R. 3131, [1988] 4 C.M.L.R. 821, at para. 8.

[7] Case 26/76, *Metro-SB-Grossmarkte* v. *Commission*: [1977] E.C.R. 1875, [1978] 2 C.M.L.R. 1. And see, generally, para. 9.05.

[8] See Temple Lang, *op. cit.*, at p. 181.

[9] Case 8/71: [1971] E.C.R. 705, 717, 718, [1973] C.M.L.R. 902, 911.

which is or may be detrimentally affected by the infringement or the Commission's decision.[10] A general interest in the clarification of the law will not be enough.[11]

In practice the question of what is a "sufficient interest" may become academic as the Commission may hear third parties if it considers it necessary to do so and it is unlikely that the Commission will deliberately refuse to hear any person who wished responsibly to give relevant information or assistance to it. Whether the Commission would acknowledge that the person has a right to be heard is another matter and in one case the Commission, whilst declining to acknowledge the right of a representative group of lawyers to put forward argument on a particular point of procedure, was nevertheless prepared to listen informally to them.

Provided a third party is heard or is given an opportunity to be heard under Article 5 of Regulation 99/63 he cannot challenge the validity of any subsequent decision on the ground of procedural irregularity or take proceedings against the Commission for failure to act merely because the Commission does not take a position on whether or not he has a sufficient interest to be heard.[12]

4.20   As in the case of the undertakings concerned, third parties must exercise their right to be heard primarily in writing. But Article 7(2) of Regulation 99/63 provides: "The Commission may likewise afford to any other person the opportunity of orally expressing his views." In *Dutch Books*,[13] the Court of Justice recognised that under that provision the Commission has a reasonable margin of discretion to decide how expedient it may be to hear persons whose evidence may be relevant to the inquiry. Where they have been given an opportunity to make their point of view known in writing and they have effectively made use of this possibility, a subsequent decision of the Commission may not be overturned on the ground that the third party was not invited to be present at the oral hearing.[14]

---

[10] In *AKZO*, above, A.G. Lenz said: "He will generally be able to do so if he has been affected by the conduct of the undertaking against which the competition proceedings have been initiated." Ehlermann and Oldekop, *op. cit.*, refer to "an appreciable actual or potential economic or legal interest."

[11] See Deringer, *The Competition Law of the European Economic Community* (1978), para. 2359. And see the position of the CCBE in Case 155/79, *A.M. & S. Europe Ltd.* v. *Commission*: [1982] E.C.R. 1575, [1982] 2 C.M.L.R. 264.

[12] *Deutscher Komponistenverband* v. *Commission*, above, n. 9. The German Composers' Association requested that it be heard in the various proceedings initiated by the Commission against GEMA, as a "legal person" with a "sufficient interest" under Art. 19(2) of Reg. 17 and Art. 5 of Reg. 99/63. When the Association insisted on being heard orally, the Commission replied that it had no legal interest in obtaining a decision on its admission to the oral procedure, because it had already been granted the opportunity to make known its views in writing. The Association commenced proceedings against the Commission under Art. 175 for failure to act. The Court of Justice held the application inadmissible. It referred to a letter from the Commission which stated that without prejudice to the question whether the Association was a person having a "sufficient interest", the Commission was giving it the opportunity to submit its written observations within a month. This period was extended on two occasions. The Court held that the Commission had acted under Art. 5 of Reg. 99/63 and therefore could not be said to have refrained from acting when called upon to do so.

[13] Cases 43 & 63/82, *VBVB and VBBB* v. *Commission*: [1984] E.C.R. 19, [1985] 1 C.M.L.R. 27, at paras. 17 and 18, regarding the complaint that the Commission had refused to hear orally a person in his capacity as an author.

[14] *FEDETAB*: Cases 209–215 & 218/78, *Heintz van Landewyck Sarl and others* v. *Commission*: [1980] E.C.R. 3125, [1981] 3 C.M.L.R. 134, at para. 18.

Most importantly, the right of a third party to be heard under Article 19(2) of Regulation 17 does not give it the right to receive confidential information.[15] If he is to participate effectively the complainant may need to be shown evidence and other matter but the Commission must take care, for example, before transmitting to a complainant the written reply to the statement of objections for comment. Any confidential information belonging to the undertaking (*e.g.* investment plans, financial arrangements) concerned should be edited out. In practice, the Commission should be careful and separate genuine business secrets from the evidence and argumentation. As already indicated, business secrets are in a special category and must never be shown to a third party.[16]

4.21 Article 19(3) of Regulation 17 provides a further opportunity for third parties to make their views known. Where the Commission intends to give a negative clearance or an exemption, it must publish a summary of the relevant application or notification and invite all interested third parties to submit their observations within a time-limit being not less than one month. A person need not delay putting forward his views until such notice is published if he learns previously of the proposed favourable decision of the Commission. Provided he has the necessary interest he could make an application under Article 3 and/or require to be heard under Article 19(2).[17]

The reply to the statement of objections

4.22 The undertaking's reply to the Commission's statement of objections is first written and second, if necessary, oral. The undertaking has the right to be heard on "the matters to which the Commission has taken objection."[18] These "matters" are in effect the arguments with supporting reasons contained in the statement of objections. It is clear that the right to be heard on such "matters" includes the right to comment on the accuracy of the facts relied on by the Commission and to present new factual material. Article 3(3) of Regulation 99/63 provides that the undertaking may attach relevant documents in proof of the facts set out in its reply and this is usual in practice. The undertaking may also propose that the Commission hear persons who can corroborate those facts. It is equally clear that the undertaking can put forward legal and economic arguments in its defence and can challenge not only the factual but the legal and economic bases of the Commission's case. Undertakings are entitled in their written comments to set out "all matters relevant to their defence,"[19] and this, it is submitted, must allow the undertaking to include in its defence such factual, legal and economic arguments and material as it considers necessary to rebut the arguments put by the Commission relating to the applicability of Article 85 or 86. Where an undertaking puts forward a document by way of defence of one allegation, it cannot later complain

---

[15] *Ibid.* at para. 46. Moreover information which is afforded confidential treatment in the administrative proceedings before the Commission may be afforded, upon application by the parties concerned, confidential treatment *vis-à-vis* third parties/interveners in proceedings before the Court. See Case T–30/89A, *Hilti* v. *Commission*: [1990] 4 C.M.L.R. 602.

[16] Case 53/85, *AKZO Chemie* v. *Commission*: [1986] E.C.R. 1965, [1987] 1 C.M.L.R. 231. See para. 4.10 above.

[17] If he does not, but relies on Art. 19(3), he cannot complain that the rights of defence have been violated. See Case 43/85, *ANCIDES* v. *Commission*: [1987] E.C.R. 3131, [1988] 4 C.M.L.R. 821, at paras. 7–10.

[18] Art. 19(1) of Reg. 17.

[19] Art. 3(2) of Reg. 99/63.

if the Commission uses that document to support a different allegation against the undertaking.[20] Factual arguments may require corroboration from, for example, independent third parties and can be tested at the oral hearing.[21] Where use is made of experts, such as economists, it is important that they can see and speak on the basis of the relevant evidence, not just on theory.[22] Economic evidence may need to be handled and presented carefully, bearing in mind that although they can have recourse to economic advice DG IV staff may not always be trained or best equipped to handle detailed economic evaluations and argumentation.[23]

4.23   The question has arisen as to whether it is open to a party to contest a point before the Court which it has accepted in the administrative proceedings. In *Distillers* v. *Commission*,[24] DCL sought to annul, on the grounds of certain irregularities in the Commission's procedure, parts of the decision relating to the question of infringement of Article 85(1), in particular as regards its price terms. DCL had not contested this in the administrative proceedings. Advocate General Warner said:

> "It would indeed be very odd if, for instance, the Court were now to hold that the decision was void in so far as it declared that the price terms were caught by Article 85(1), when, in the administrative proceedings, DCL (quite rightly in my opinion) accepted that they were."

But with respect to the learned Advocate General the better view is found in *Hilti*[25] where the Court of First Instance held that an undertaking is not bound by admissions made by it during the Commission's administrative proceedings. Hilti had admitted contravening Article 86 on the assumption that it held a dominant position in the market without stating its view on the problems of defining the relevant geographic market and the effects on inter-state trade.[26] The Court noted the Community law does not compel an undertaking to reply to the statement of objections and that co-operation is desirable but not mandatory.[27] The Court of First Instance held that the admission would not be construed as an implicit acknowledgement on its part of the truth of the Commission's claims. Hilti was not therefore constrained in the exercise of its rights as a litigant to take issue on the points on appeal to the Court.[28]

---

[20] *Polypropylene*: Case T–11/89, *Shell* v. *Commission*: [1992] II E.C.R. 757.
[21] See *Soda-ash Solvay, CFK*: [1991] O.J. L152/16, at para. 8.
[22] See *Soda-ash Solvay, ICI*: [1991] O.J. L152/1, at para. 44
[23] See Holley, "EEC Competition Practice: A Thirty Year Retrospective" 16 Fordham Int. L.J. 343 at pp. 396–400. See also the reactions of A.G. Darmon in *Wood Pulp II*: Cases C 89, 104, 114, 116, 177 & 125–129/85, *Åhlström and Others* v. *Commission*: [1993] 4 C.M.L.R. 407, when confronted with "a substantial body of economic argument, referring at times to theoretical models which, whilst doubtless familiar to an economist, are nevertheless, in my view at any rate, of manifest complexity."
[24] Case 30/78, *Distillers* v. *Commission*: [1980] E.C.R. 2229, [1980] 3 C.M.L.R. 121.
[25] Case T–30/89, *Hilti AG* v. *Commission*: [1991] II E.C.R. 1439, [1992] 4 C.M.L.R. 16.
[26] See *Eurofix Bauco* v. *Hilti*: [1988] O.J. L65/19, [1989] 4 C.M.L.R. 677. Hilti had admitted the practices and sought to justify its behaviour, *inter alia*, on safety grounds.
[27] For similar reasons companies may decide not to accept the invitation an oral hearing.
[28] Above n. 25, at para. 35.

Time-limit for reply

4.24   The statement of objections will fix a time-limit within which the undertaking must deliver its written defence.[29] It will also offer the undertaking the opportunity to be heard orally and propose a date for such hearing. In fixing a time-limit for the written reply to the statement of objections the Commission must have regard both to the time required for the preparation of comments and to the urgency of the case.[30] The minimum time-limit allowed is two weeks.[31] In practice, except in interim measures cases a longer period is usually specified. The time-limit can be extended, but this is at the discretion of the Commission.

In *Ist. CI and Commercial Solvents* v. *Commission*,[32] Advocate General Warner said that it was:

> "plainly implicit in Article 2(4) that the Commission must fix a reasonable time limit enabling the respondent undertakings fully and effectively to exercise their rights under Article 3."

In that case a year had elapsed between the Commission receiving the complaint and its sending the statement of objections to the undertakings which were then given only 15 days in which to answer. The Advocate General thought that a fortnight was "patently unreasonable" given the complexity of the case and said that the matter was made worse by the Commission's holding the oral hearing three weeks after the service of the statement of objections. Nevertheless, this was not considered sufficient to invalidate the final decision of the Commission although the Court of Justice did reduce the fine as a result.

It is submitted that the length of time taken by the Commission in its investigation and preparation of the case is not necessarily a major factor to be taken into account when fixing the time-limit for the reply, although it may suggest the case involves a heavy burden of documents and is wide ranging. The complexity of the case when measured, for example, by reference to the number of parties, the facts and economic and legal issues involved is more relevant.[33] The undertaking's ability to respond should also be considered—for example, its geographical situation if outside the Community, or its access to facts, statistics and professional advice which may reasonably be required in order to exercise fully its rights of defence. Article 11(1) expressly refers to "the urgency of the case." This is clearly most relevant where there is a complainant who may be suffering immediate loss as a result of the alleged violation of Articles 85 and 86.[34]

---

[29] Art. 2(4) of Reg. 99/63. This will in fact be set by the Director of the relevant division of DG IV.

[30] Art. 11(1) of Reg. 99/63. The Court has held that where the legislation does not fix a minimum period, the Commission must give a sufficient time for the exercise of the right to be heard. See Case 19/70, *Almini* v. *Commission*: [1971] E.C.R. 623.

[31] See n. 30 above.

[32] Cases 6 & 7/73: [1974] E.C.R. 223, [1974] 1 C.M.L.R. 309, 334, 335.

[33] In the *Sugar* case: Cases 40–48, 50, 54–56, 111, 113 & 114/73, *Cooperative Vereniging "Suiker Unie" UA and others* v. *Commission*: [1975] E.C.R. 1663, [1976] 1 C.M.L.R. 295, a case of some considerable complexity, a time-limit of two months was considered sufficient.

[34] Usually Art. 86 in practice. Relief by way of interim measures may be appropriate in such a case. See paras. 6.02–11. Where such relief is given by the Commission, the "urgency" factor under Art. 11(1) may be lessened in importance in final decision cases.

Whilst the Commission has in the past attempted to set "more reasonable" periods for reply,[35] it has not, however, been unusual for parties to complain at the oral hearing that they have not had sufficient time to give their written reply. The Commission has recently announced its intention to standardise the time given to undertakings to respond to the statement of objections. In normal cases two months will be allowed and in complex cases three months. An additional two weeks will be added automatically if the period includes Christmas or Easter. A month will be added if the period falls in August. As a maximum therefore the undertakings concerned will have four months in a complex case. Recognising that much shorter periods may be needed where interim measures are being proposed, the undertaking concerned will only be given two weeks in which to reply in such cases.[36] The setting of such standard time-limits cannot absolve the Commission from its responsibilities under general principles of administrative law which require individual cases to be examined on their merits and prohibit bodies such as the Commission from fettering their discretion. Nonetheless it is expected that the Commission will follow the above guidelines in most cases. In the past the Commission has considered extensions of time. Are these now ruled out? Strictly speaking they cannot be. If an undertaking has genuine difficulty in replying within the period specified it should communicate this as soon as possible to the Commission. The application for an extension should state the reasons why it is considered necessary and indicate the length of time required.

When fixing a date for the oral hearing enough time must be given for the Commission to consider the parties' response and for all parties to assemble and prepare. In practice, the availability of rooms and translation services will also be an important factor. If the undertaking wishes to be heard orally,[37] but the proposed date[38] for the oral hearing is not convenient (for example, its representative, witness or lawyer may not be available), it should inform the Commission as soon as possible explaining the reasons why the date is not suitable and putting forward some alternative dates.

The oral hearing

Hearing Officer

4.25 Article 9(1) of Regulation 99/63 provides that hearings shall be conducted by the persons appointed by the Commission for the purpose. Formerly, the procedure was to appoint the Director responsible for the Directorate dealing with the case. In 1982, the Commission, in response to various criticisms,[39] created the special post of

---

[35] See Ferry, "Procedure and Powers of the EEC Commission in Anti-Trust Cases" (1979) E.I.P.R. 126, 129.

[36] Normally without the possibility of extension. See generally para. 6.09.

[37] A party may always waive its right to an oral hearing. See, *e.g. Johnson & Johnson*: [1981] O.J. L377/16, [1981] 2 C.M.L.R. 287, where the undertakings did so because their case was so "fully and clearly set out in the reply" and see also *Benelux Flat Glass*: [1984] O.J. L212/13, [1985] 2 C.M.L.R. 350, and *Decca Navigator System*: [1989] O.J. L43/27, [1990] 4 C.M.L.R. 627 and *Ford Agricultural*: [1993] O.J. L20/1.

[38] The Hearing Officer may already have been in touch with the parties and their representatives. The limited availability of rooms with full translation facilities often requires the Commission to fix well in advance the date for the oral hearing.

[39] There were various calls for an "independent person" whose function would include the conduct of the oral hearing. See, *e.g.* The House of Lords Select Committee on the European Communities (Session 1981–82, Eighth Report on Competition Procedure). In its recent (1993) report: Enforcement of Community Rules, the Committee points to the success of the role of Hearing Officer and makes a number of recommendations for extending his powers and responsibilities (paras. 111, 112).

Hearing Officer.[40] He is attached directly to the Director-General, and is not part of the operational Directorates. The Hearing Officer's duties include ensuring that the rights of the defence are respected and draft decisions take due account of the relevant facts. The terms of reference of the Hearing Officer are set out in Appendix L. The independent character of the office is referred in Article 1(3), according the Hearing Officer direct access to the Commissioner with responsibility for competition matters.[41] The Twelfth Report on Competition Policy describes his work as follows:[42]

"(a) The Hearing Officer organises preparations for the hearing, fixing the date, duration and place; he may also let the undertakings concerned know in advance the matters on which he would particularly like them to set forth their points of view. To this end he may organise a meeting with the parties concerned and, if necessary, with the relevant Commission departments to prepare for the hearing. He may also ask for prior submission in writing of the main content of statements by persons who are to speak on behalf of the undertakings concerned.

(b) The Hearing Officer is fully responsible for the actual hearing and decides whether to admit new documents in the course of the hearing, to hear persons who may corroborate the facts relied upon and also whether to hear the persons concerned separately or in the presence of other persons admitted to the hearing. On completion of the oral stage of the hearing, he ensures that the essential content of the statements made by each person heard are recorded in the minutes, which the person concerned must read and approve.

(c) As regards the role of the Hearing Officer in the steps to be taken after the hearing, he reports to the Director-General for Competition on developments at the hearing and on his conclusions. He submits comments on the continuation of the procedure. These comments may concern, *inter alia*, the need for additional information, withdrawal of certain objections or an additional statement of objections."

His responsibility is essentially for the chairing and conduct of the oral hearing. He does not have the power therefore to control the written procedure: he does not, *e.g.*, set the time-limits for delivery of the written reply to the statement of objections or deal with access to the file. But if lack of access to the file is pleaded at the oral hearing as a violation of the rights of the defence the Hearing Officer is duty-bound to address this plea, if sustained, in his report to the Director-General.[43]

It has recently been proposed that the powers of the Hearing Officer be increased to enable him to deal with problems concerning the time-limits for the reply to the statement of objection and access to the file, and thus encourage resolution of such problems at an early stage. The fact that the Commissioners themselves are not present and

---

[40] M. Roland Mussard was appointed with effect from September 1, 1982. He was succeeded by Dr. Hartmut Johannes. When Dr. Johannes has not been available, another official from DG IV has taken his place. As the Law Society/Bar's evidence to the House of Lords Select Committee, above, indicates, much may turn on who actually exercises the functions of the office in a particular case.

[41] Johannes, *op. cit.*, points out that as a civil servant in the Commission the Hearing Officer is special, if not unique, in being an A3 enjoying irremovability and non-transferability.

[42] At point 36.

[43] Johannes, *op. cit.*, referring to Art. 2 of the terms of reference.

do not personally take part in the hearing does not constitute grounds for invalidating the decision. This argument was rejected by the Court in the *Quinine* case.[44] Further, providing the Hearing Officer is present throughout the oral proceedings it does not matter that other Commission officials who may be involved with the case come and go from time to time.[45] Where several persons have been appointed to hear a given case, Article 9 of Regulation 99/63 does not require the simultaneous presence at hearings of all the persons appointed or certain of them.[46]

The Hearing Officer does not act as a judge in the proceedings. He does not have to consider or balance the weight of the evidence and arguments put by the Commission and the parties although his report may touch upon the adequacy of the Commission's reasoning and the existence of the alleged infringement. He is appointed by the Commission to conduct the hearing in the manner described above. It is therefore his job to ensure that the parties can present their case freely and fairly, to ensure that the Commission properly receives that case and that it is duly recorded, and, if necessary, to keep order. In this respect the powers of decision given to the Hearing Officer by Article 4(3) of the terms of reference are particularly noteworthy. He can decide whether fresh documents should be admitted during the hearing, whether persons should be heard pursuant to Articles 3(3) and 7(2) of Regulation 99/63, and whether the undertaking concerned should be heard separately or with others.

Representation at oral hearing

4.26 Article 9(2) of Regulation 99/63 provides that persons summoned to attend shall either appear in person or be represented by legal representatives or by representatives authorised by their constitution. Undertakings and associations of undertakings may also be represented by a duly authorised agent appointed from among their permanent staff. Persons heard may be assisted by lawyers, or by other qualified persons. Outside lawyers are not, as a general rule, admitted without their client. In practice few difficulties have arisen. Undertakings and their legal representatives are generally co-operative, particularly in large multiparty cases where numbers may have to be restricted if only because of the size of rooms available.

While it is therefore clear that an independent lawyer may always assist an undertaking in the presentation of its case (thus safeguarding the rights of the defence),[47] the lawyer is not a representative, "legal" or "authorised", and cannot, it would appear, act as such.[48] Representation by a lawyer appears possible only if he is permanently employed by the undertaking. In the words of the Court of Justice in the Dyestuffs

---

[44] Case 44/69, *Buchler* v. *Commission*, at para. 20. See also Case 45/69, at para. 20. (Cases 41, 44 & 45/69, *ACF Chemiefarma and Others* v. *Commission*: [1970] E.C.R. 661).

[45] *FEDETAB*: Cases 209–215 & 218/78, *Heintz van Landewyck Sarl and others* v. *Commission*: [1980] E.C.R. 3125, [1981] 3 C.M.L.R. 134, at para. 27.

[46] *Dutch Books*: Cases 43 & 63/82, *VBVB and VBBB* v. *Commission*: [1984] E.C.R. 19, [1985] 1 C.M.L.R. 27, at para. 16.

[47] "It must be considered a general principle of due process, valid also in the area of Community law, that a person whose rights or legitimate expectations could be affected by administrative action may seek the assistance of a qualified lawyer for the exercise of his right to be heard"—Ehlermann and Oldekop, *op. cit.* The Court of Justice recognised the right to be assisted by Counsel as being included in the rights of defence in Case 115/80, *Demont* v. *Commission*: [1981] E.C.R. 3147 (a staff case).

[48] The position relating to legal representation in the submission of written observations is less certain. There are no express rules on the matter. According to Ehlermann and Oldekop, *op. cit.*: "In practice, the Commission does not refuse to accept briefs signed by duly authorised independent lawyers which are written on behalf of the persons or enterprises concerned."

case: "Undertakings may only be represented by a duly authorised agent in their regular employment, and by a statutory or otherwise properly admitted representative."[49] The justification for this is, in the opinion of the Court, that:

> "such persons are usually the most instructed as regards the facts and as regards those technical or economic aspects of the activities of their undertakings which are relevant as regards the applicability of the rules of competition."[50]

The Court thought that without the participation of such persons the hearing of the parties would serve no real purpose. This argument would, it is submitted, ring more true if there was some requirement that the representative had such experience and first hand knowledge of the subject of the alleged infringement. But the Commission has no right to demand the presence of such a person as a representative nor that its questions be put to such a person.

Minutes of hearing

4.27   A record must be made of the oral hearing. Article 9(4) of Regulation 99/63 provides that the essential content of the statements made by each person heard shall be recorded in minutes which shall be read and approved by him. The provision is designed to assure the persons heard that the minutes contain a true record of the substance of what they have said.[51] It is also intended to supply to the Commission (*i.e.*, the Commissioners) and the Advisory Committee complete information on the essential content of the statements made at the hearing of the parties.

In the *Quinine* case,[52] Buchler complained that only a preliminary version of the minutes had been available to the Commission and the Advisory Committee. The Court of Justice said:

> "The preliminary nature of the minutes of the hearing submitted to these bodies could only amount to a defect in the administrative procedure capable of vitiating the decision which results therefrom on the grounds of illegality if the document in question was drawn up in such a way as to be misleading in a material respect."

In the *Dyestuffs* case,[53] there was a delay of some six months before the minutes were sent to the parties pursuant to Article 9(4) of Regulation 99/63 and the Commission made its decision before the parties were able to make their observations. The minutes had only been sent to the parties about four weeks before the decision was taken. The Court thought that the delay complained about could only affect the legality of the decision where there was doubt about the accuracy of the reproduction of the parties'

---

[49] *Dyestuffs*: Case 49/69, *BASF* v. *Commission*, above, n. 15. Concerning the lawyer's position, A.G. Mayras said: "while not being permitted to be *represented* by a representative *ad litem* nothing prevented BASF asking its counsel to assist its legal representatives" (emphasis added).
[50] *Ibid.*
[51] *Dyestuffs*: Case 48/69, *ICI* v. *Commission*, above, n. 15, at para. 29.
[52] *Buchler* v. *Commission* (Case 44/69), above.
[53] Above, n. 11 (Case 48/69), at para. 32.

statements. It therefore seems that there will be a breach of an essential procedural requirement if the Commission and the Advisory Committee are presented with draft minutes that are so incomplete or inaccurate as to be liable to be misleading.

In *RTE* the Court of First Instance addressed the case where no minutes, draft or final, were presented to the Advisory Committee.[54] The Court held that the minutes were in principle one of the "most important documents" to which the Advisory Committee should have access, the purpose of Article 10(5) being to enable to Committee to carry out its advisory task in full knowledge of the facts. The Court said that the Committee must have "entirely objective information on the views and essential arguments of those undertakings expressed in their comments on all the objections raised against them by the Commission". Whether the minutes of the oral hearing must be supplied to the Advisory Committee is a question to be determined in relation to the circumstances of each case. The Court of First Instance said:

> "it is not an essential procedural requirement that the minutes of the hearing be sent to the Advisory Committee unless, in a specific case, it proves necessary in order to enable the committee to deliver its opinion in full knowledge of the facts, that is to say without being misled in a material respect by inaccuracies or omissions. That is not the case when the minutes of the hearing do not contain any important new information not contained in the written comments, accompanying the notice convening the Advisory Committee, made by the undertaking concerned in reply to the statement of objections."

The burden is therefore on the applicant to show that there is a difference between the written comments in reply to the statement of objections and the observations it made at the oral hearing and that the Committee is likely to be misled in a material respect if it does not have the minutes identifying this.

In practice nowadays, the Commission prepares the minutes which are taken verbatim from the tape recordings of the oral hearing. Two copies are sent to each party, one for its retention and the other to be signed and returned to the Commission. Any change proposed must be agreed by the Hearing Officer.

Procedure at the oral hearing

4.28 Although there is no set form of procedure laid down in the Regulations, the procedure at the oral hearing is broadly as follows:

(a) the Hearing Officer[55] opens the hearing and invites the *rapporteur* (case officer) in the case to summarise briefly the facts and principal arguments of the Commission;

(b) the party (or parties) being heard is then given an opportunity to speak on the subject-matter of the case;

(c) questions may be put by the Hearing Officer and other members of the Commission's staff present,[56] and the party may reply;

---

[54] Case T–69/89, *Radio Telefis Eireann* v. *Commission*: [1991] 4 C.M.L.R. 586, at paras. 21–23.
[55] See para. 4.25.
[56] For example, the *chef de file*, the *rapporteur*, and the representative of the Legal Service.

(d) the representatives of the competent authorities of the Member States are invited by the Hearing Officer to put to the party any questions they may have and the party may reply;

(e) before closing the oral hearing, the Hearing Officer may invite the party to make any final or concluding remarks or observations.

This said it is the practice of the Hearing Officer to try to agree the agenda with the parties and their lawyers.[57] This is especially important in cases involving a number of undertakings. In practice the agenda tends to follow the order of the statement of objections. There is therefore scope for the lawyers to take the opportunity to organise matters and use to the best the co-ordination of representations. This avoids unnecessary repetition without prejudice to the rights of defence. If no agreement and co-ordination can be obtained the Hearing Officer will have to allocate and police time-limits for speaking. The oral hearing is not normally a lengthy affair, usually no longer than a day, but there have been a number of cases where the hearing has gone on for three weeks.[58] The basic order of procedure is not fixed and may be varied in whole or in part as the circumstances of the case demand. This might be, for example, where there is a multiplicity of parties involved, or where a third party such as a complainant[59] may be present. The Hearing Officer will rule on whether a party should be heard separately in order, for example, to protect confidential information. Where a complainant is present the procedure may take on an adversarial character,[60] the complainant being given an opportunity to put forward his argument before stage (b) above and to reply to the points made by the party at the appropriate time. Article 9(3) Regulation 99/63 lays down that hearing shall not be public.

It is of course important that the hearing is properly prepared and in particular that questions of fact are clarified as far as possible. The Commission should have considered the parties' responses to the statement of objection prior to the hearing. The Hearing Officer independently examines the statement of objections and the reply. He may, prior to the hearing, put a list of questions to the firms and their lawyers in order to clarify the issues. Occasionally this may involve preliminary discussions with the parties. He may also request that the essential contents of statements of parties being called by the undertakings are notified in writing before the hearing. All these measures help to focus the hearing on the key issues.[61] It may be useful to comment in more detail on the various stages (a) to (e) mentioned above.

---

[57] For an example of the Hearing Officer meeting with legal advisers in advance of the hearing to discuss and agree the procedural arrangements, see Case T–7/89, *S.A. Hercules NV* v. *Commission*: [1992] 4 C.M.L.R. 84, at para. 7.

[58] Big cases may take longer. In the recent *Cement* case, for example, there were some 75 parties and the oral hearing took up the best part of a month.

[59] The position of the complainant is discussed generally at paras. 4.18–20.

[60] However, in Case 53/85, *AKZO Chemie* v. *Commission*: [1986] E.C.R. 1965, [1987] 1 C.M.L.R. 231, A.G. Lenz was keen to point out that the presence of a complainant did not make the proceedings adversarial in character: "The complainant is limited to a role which corresponds to the position, under criminal proceedings, of a person who reports the matter to the authorities."

[61] Eighteenth Report on Competition, at point 44.

4.29 (a) *The introduction.* The undertaking being heard will have received the written statement of objections (or in "procedural cases",[62] a statement of the facts and legal arguments which form the basis of the proposed decision) and will have had the opportunity to put in a written reply by way of defence. The summary given by the *rapporteur* at the beginning of the oral hearing is merely an outline of the case from the Commission's point of view. In theory a party may take the opportunity at the stage of his own oral presentation to put forward corrections of any inaccuracies of fact he considers it may contain or to counter any arguments put forward. In practice the summary is frequently short and a formal step, and may not contain sufficient detail for the parties to do this. The oral hearing is not, however, an opportunity for a party to cross examine or question the Commission on the factual, legal or other bases of the statement of objections or the rapporteur's/case officer's summary. The summary should be regarded simply as a useful opening statement for the purposes of the oral hearing—by no stretch of the imagination can it be construed as the reading of an indictment or as a full statement of the Commission's case. This said, it is particularly useful for the representatives of the Member States to have the Commission's up to date view of the case. The Hearing Officer may introduce the summary in this way as for the benefit of the Member States.

4.30 (b) *The party's oral presentation.* As the undertaking's written defence may be wide-ranging and deal with any or all of the factual, legal and economic points raised by the statement of objections, so the oral presentation may be similarly wide-ranging. It is not restricted to points which have been made previously in the reply to the statement of objections, but an oral presentation which merely reproduces the reply may have little purpose or effect and is discouraged. The Commission has pointed out that the oral hearing is the place to clarify certain matters which have not been settled during the written procedure and to emphasise the main lines of the case.[63] The Court of Justice has indicated that parties should not neglect the opportunity to make known their views on any differences of opinion between themselves and the Commission which the written procedure may have revealed.[64]

The opportunity may be taken to produce or corroborate factual evidence. The Hearing Officer will not generally rule on evidence, although he may comment on it. He can, however, rule on the admission of documents. Parties do not speak on oath, nor is there any requirement that parties can only speak as to facts of which they have first-hand knowledge although it is useful to have representatives there who can do so because they tend to be listened to more closely. Third parties may be called to corroborate what is said. Even this evidence is not given on oath. Where third parties or expert witnesses are produced it is advisable that the Commission be supplied with a statement of what they will say and details of their qualifications.[65] If this has not already been supplied with the reply, it should be done in reasonable time before the

---

[62] Cases where the Commission proposes to fine for failure to comply with a decision under Art. 11 or 14 of Reg. 17.

[63] Eleventh Report on Competition Policy, point 27.

[64] Case C–62/86, *AKZO* v. *Commission*: [1991] I E.C.R. 3359, at para. 33. AKZO could not complain because it had had the opportunity at the oral hearing to clarify the position on cost arguments in response to the Commission's questions.

[65] Again this need not be under oath although such evidence has been given in the form of a statutory declaration. For an example of the types of technical and expert evidence which may be given, see *ANSAC*: [1991] O.J. L152/54.

hearing, in order that it can be examined in advance by the Commission.[66] In practice, the Hearing Officer will ensure that the essential contents of such statements are supplied before the hearing. The real value of an expert witness may be in his ability to respond to any questions put by the Commission after they have had the time to consider his evidence. If a party has any special requirements for its presentation, *e.g.* the use of an overhead projector, the Hearing Officer should be told beforehand.

As a general rule, copies of any documents to be referred to at the oral hearing should be supplied in advance. Most will have been supplied with the reply, but any others should be supplied as early as possible before the oral hearing. There is little to be gained from surprise but much from the Commission having had the chance to consider the documents before the hearing. Remember that it is the Hearing Officer who decides whether fresh documents can be admitted during the hearing. Where documents are produced at the hearing, sufficient copies should be available—allow at least six for the Commission representatives and remember that the Member States may each be separately represented. Confidential information and business secrets should be clearly identified. If any such material is to be used or mentioned at the hearing, the Hearing Officer should be advised at the outset in order that the hearing room can be cleared of all other parties (such as competitors and complainant) as may be present and to whom disclosure should not be made. A party may find it convenient to introduce such material either at the very beginning or end of his oral presentation in order that the clearing of the hearing room causes the minimum disturbance to the presentation.

Where a matter is not set out in the statement of objections, but is discussed at the oral hearing and the undertaking concerned is thereby given the opportunity to make its views known and adduce evidence in that regard, there can be no complaint that the decision does not coincide with the statement of objections in this respect.[67]

Persons addressing the Commission should speak slowly and avoid long or over-complicated sentences. Not all the other persons present will necessarily be able to listen and comprehend in the language of the speaker. Although the speech will normally be simultaneously translated into the other Community languages there can be great difficulty if a person speaks too fast. The greatest care should be taken when reading extracts from a document: there is a natural tendency to speed up. If it is intended to quote at length from a document (not generally a practice to be encouraged) or if, for example, unusual technical terms may be used in the speech, then it may be useful to give a copy of the quotation, the speaker's text or notes and a list of the terms and explanations to the interpreters before the hearing commences.

There is no time-limit fixed for the length of the oral presentation, but because the procedure is essentially a written one and the written reply will have preceded the oral hearing, a party is expected to keep his individual presentation to three hours or less.[68]

4.31 (c) *Questions from the Commission*. It is the Commission's practice to put questions to the parties. These are usually related to the information or points made in the oral presentation and may invite the party to explain a point or to expand or develop an argument. Occasionally the Commission may put questions to a party before

---

[66] The Commission may also be able to agree the evidence and the necessity of the witness attending may thus be avoided.

[67] *Pioneer*: Cases 100–103/80, *Musique Diffusion Francaise and others* v. *Commission*: [1983] E.C.R. 1823, [1983] 3 C.M.L.R. 221, at paras. 18 and 19.

[68] Ferry, *op. cit.*, at p. 130.

he makes his oral presentation: for example, the reply to the statement of objections may have raised something which it is better to clear up at the beginning to avoid any further confusion or disagreement.

It is by no means clear whether, as a matter of law, a party is obliged to reply to these questions . There appears to be no express obligation to do so and no penalty is incurred for failure to do so. To the extent that such questions may amount to the cross-examination of a party or witness then it is arguable that it does not necessarily follow that a party's right to be heard gives the Commission a right to cross-examine. But in practice this may not be avoided and the Commission regard it as a particularly useful feature of the oral hearing. A party may assist its case by replying to such questions and they may be extremely useful to both sides in making their respective positions and arguments clearer. There are, nevertheless, potential pitfalls. The best person to reply may not be present[69] and an undertaking may consider that an answer requires time for consideration or consultation of the business records, etc., or other factual sources. It is often most effective for a Company's director or manager to give the oral presentation or explanation himself rather than an outside lawyer. If a question cannot be properly answered straightaway the undertaking should give a qualified reply and ask the Commission if it can supply a fuller answer in writing within a reasonable period of time.

The greatest care should always be taken in reply to such questions. But it should be remembered that the immediate reply may not only underline the honesty and candour of the respondent but may even take the Commission by as much surprise as the question did the respondent! It does not seem that a party can usefully complain if the Commission does not ask any questions during the oral hearing.[70]

Although it was not formerly the case, with the advent of the Hearing Officer questions may now, subject to his direction, be put by the parties to the Commission. But it is not a question of "cross-examining" Commission officials who are not of course witnesses to the facts.[71] A party should not rely on the possibility of putting options to the Commission. In practice the Hearing Officer usually will not allow them.

4.32   (d) *Questions from the competent authorities of the Member States.* Representatives of competent authorities of the Member States are entitled to participate in the hearing and may take the opportunity to ask questions. As the Hearing Officer is not the judge, neither are the representatives of the Member States the jury. Remember that they may not have had the opportunity to see all the documents in their language and may be listening to the party's oral presentation in translation over the headphones. The Hearing Officer will invite the representatives of the Member States to put any questions they may have. Although any such questions are put direct to the party concerned, the answer is of course made not simply to the representative but also to the Commission staff and others present. The general points made in (c) above are

---

[69] The undertaking determines who shall represent it and speak on its behalf at the oral hearing. Although Art. 9(2) of Reg. 99/63 refers to the summoning of "persons" to attend, the summons is essentially an invitation to the undertaking to the oral hearing. The Commission has no power to require the attendance of any undertaking or any person on its behalf. Nor is there any sanction or penalty for non-attendance or failure to respond to the "summons".

[70] See the opinion of A.G. Roemer in Case 6/72, *Europemballage Corp. and Continental Can Co. Inc.* v. *Commission*: [1973] E.C.R. 215, [1973] C.M.L.R. 199.

[71] Joshua, *op. cit.*, at p. 65.

equally applicable here. It does not seem that a party can usefully complain if the representatives of the Member States do not ask any questions during the oral hearing.[72]

4.33 (e) *Concluding remarks.* These should be kept short. If it is necessary to make any fresh points or to qualify anything previously said in the light of something said by the Commission or other parties, then the opportunity should be taken to do so. If a question put by the Commission or a representative of a Member State has not been answered and the party intends to do so in writing following the hearing, or if a party realises that more information or documentation should be supplied to the Commission to make clear its case, then the party should mention this and agree with the Commission the time within which the material, etc., will be supplied.

4.34 Finally, the oral hearing does not necessarily conclude the procedure between the Commission and the undertakings concerned. As indicated above, the Hearing Officer will report to the Director-General for competition. The Commissioner with responsibility for competition will regularly be informed of the results. In practice a copy of the Hearing Officer's report to the Director General will be sent to the Commissioner's *cabinet.* Only rarely has it been necessary for the Hearing Officer to exercise his formal right to refer his observations direct to the Commissioner.[73] The Hearing Officer's report is not available to the parties, even in later proceedings before the Court. It is not a decisive factor[74] or a formal opinion for the purposes of Article 190 of the Treaty.[75] Further exchanges may take place, as necessary, between the Commission and the parties.[76] Communications may also continue with a view to settlement, for example by way of amendment of the agreement or practice and/or an undertaking.[77]

---

[72] *Ibid.*

[73] See Eighteenth Report on Competition, at point 44. Johannes, *op. cit.*, has said that in about 60 per cent. of cases the report is essentially formal (recording that the oral hearing has taken place, that in his opinion there has been no infringement of the rights of defence and that he agrees with the relevant Directorate of DG IV on the application of Article 85 or 86). In 25 per cent. of cases he may propose changes in the reasoning and in 10 per cent. he may recommend a reduction or withdrawal of the fine. Only in 5 per cent. of cases has he found no infringement of the competition rules or some other defect, such as incomplete access to the file having been given.

[74] *ICI* v. *Commission*, above.

[75] Case T–7/89, *S.A. Hercules NV* v. *Commission*: [1992] 4 C.M.L.R. 84, at para. 33.

[76] See, *e.g. Sperry New Holland*: [1985] O.J. L372/21, [1988] 4 C.M.L.R. 306, where additional documents relevant to the objections were produced after the oral hearing and sent to the undertaking for comment.

[77] On undertakings generally, see para. 6.61.

5

Involvement of National Authorities

I. THE COMPETENT AUTHORITIES

Introduction and definition

5.01 Regulation 17 and the other implementing regulations require the Commission to act "in close and constant liaison with the competent authorities of the Member States."[1] The preamble to Regulation 17 sets out the purpose as follows:

> "Whereas, in order to secure uniform application of Articles 85 and 86 in the common market, rules must be made under which the Commission, acting in close and constant liaison with the competent authorities of the Member States, may take the requisite measures for applying those Articles."

Regulation 17 does not define "competent authorities". This is because the term is derived from the Treaty itself. The reference in the preamble[2] to Regulation 17 to securing the uniform application of Articles 85 and 86 relates to the scheme of enforcement of the Community competition rules laid down by Articles 87, 88 and 89 of the Treaty and it is there that one finds the key to the nature and function of the "competent authorities" referred to in Regulation 17.[3]

5.02 The provisions of Articles 88 and 89 of the Treaty contemplate that, until the Council has adopted under Article 87 what that Article calls "appropriate regulations and directives to give effect to the principles set out in Articles 85 and 86", the authorities in Member States shall have the main responsibility for giving effect to those principles. Under Article 88 the "authorities in Member States" can "rule on the admissibility of agreements, decisions and concerned practices and on abuse of a dominant position in the common market." Under Article 89, the Commission has the duty

---

[1] Reg. 17, Art. 10(2); Reg. 1017/68; Art. 16(1); Reg. 4056/86, Art. 15(1); Reg. 3975/87, Art. 8(1). This requirement must not however prejudice the supremacy of Community law. Thus an infringement of the Community competition rules is not vindicated simply because national authorities under domestic competition or other economic laws have sanctioned or approved the agreement or conduct. See, *e.g. Fire Insurance (D)*: [1985] O.J. L32/20, [1985] 3 C.M.L.R. 246, at para. 28 and generally, Chap. 10.
[2] The recital is also to be found in Reg. 1017/68, but not in the other transport regulations.
[3] See generally, Deringer, "The Distribution of Powers in the Enforcement of the Rules of Competition under the Rome Treaty" (1963) 1 C.M.L.Rev. 30.

to ensure that the principles laid down in Articles 85 and 86 are applied but, in the express terms of Article 89, has limited powers of enforcement. If, following an investigation, an infringement continues the Commission can record the fact of infringement in a reasoned decision and authorise the Member State to take the necessary measures to remedy the situation. The investigation is carried out by the Commission "in cooperation with the competent authorities in the Member States, who shall give it their assistance." Although Articles 88 and 89 are primarily transitional provisions (Article 88 begins with the words: "Until the entry into force of the provisions adopted in pursuance of Article 87"), their force is not yet spent. In particular Regulation 17, the first "appropriate regulation" made under Article 87, does not remove from the authorities in Member States the powers derived from Article 88 to enforce Articles 85 and 86. Article 9(3) of Regulation 17 provides that as long as the Commission has not initiated any procedure[4] "the authorities of the Member State shall *remain competent* to apply Articles 85(1) and 86 in accordance with Article 88 of the Treaty."[5] In *B.R.T.* v *S.A.B.A.M.*,[6] the Court of Justice made it clear that the "authorities" referred to in Article 88 of the Treaty and Article 9(3) of Regulation 17 are the national competition authorities and that such authorities derive their "competence" direct from Article 88. In the *Air Tariffs* case,[7] the Court identified which national authorities were concerned:

> "The term 'authorities in Member States' in Article 88 refers to either the administrative authorities entrusted, in most Member States, with the task of applying domestic legislation on competition subject to the review of legality carried out by the competent courts, or else the courts to which, in other Member States, that task has been especially entrusted."

In order to give effect to the scheme of enforcement envisaged by the Treaty and therefore to secure the uniform application of Articles 85 and 86, references to "competent authorities" in Regulation 17 must mean the same authorities referred to in Articles 88 and 89 of the Treaty, that is the national competition authorities as explained by the Court of Justice.[8]

---

[4] The initiation of a procedure is discussed at paras. 2.38–39. Prior to Reg. 17 an informal arrangement had been developed by which the Commission was consulted by the Member States about proceedings of theirs that came under Art. 85 or 86. See Edwards, *Control of Cartels and Monopolies. An International Comparison* (1967).

[5] Emphasis added. There are similar provisions in the transport regulations. Where the Commission later closes the file the Member States' authorities' jurisdiction may return. See A.G. Mancini in Cases 142 & 156/84, *BAT and Reynolds Industries* v. *Commission*: [1987] E.C.R. 4487, [1987] 2 C.M.L.R. 551.

[6] Case 127/73: [1974] E.C.R. 51, [1974] 2 C.M.L.R. 238, at para. 18.

[7] Cases 209–213/84, *Ministère Public* v. *Asjes and others*: [1986] E.C.R. 1425, [1986] 3 C.M.L.R. 173, at para. 55. The term "authorities in Member States" does not on this basis include the criminal courts whose task is to punish breaches of the law (para. 56). A.G. Lenz did not limit the definition of authorities to competent authorities. He thought that Article 88 gave Member States freedom, *e.g.* in the aviation field, to entrust enforcement of the competition rules to the air transport authorities.

[8] It is unclear how this jurisprudence will translate in relation to the EEA. Under the Agreement on the European Economic Area Art. 55 mirrors Art. 89 EEC — see n. 93 below. But there is no equivalent to Art. 88 EEC, at least in the sense of putting an enforcement responsibility on national authorities in the interim period. Particularly, Art. 9(3) of Reg. 17 is repeated *mutatis mutandis* in Chapter 11 of Protocol 4 to the EFTA Surveillance Agreement but without an Art. 88 EEC it is difficult in theory to see if and how an EFTA national authority will have "competence" to apply Arts. 53 and 54. Presumably the national laws of EFTA states will fill any gaps in practice.

5.03 The question of what body (or bodies) within a Member State is a competent authority is therefore a matter of both Community and national law. National law will determine which body is a national competition authority.[9] Such authorities derive their competence to enforce the Community rules by virtue of Article 88 of the Treaty.[10] But this does not mean that where there are in a particular Member State more than one such authority competent by Article 88, they all act as "competent authorities" for all purposes in this context. It would be impractical for the Commission to have to communicate with, send documents to, consult with, etc., a number of such authorities in any Member State. Accordingly it is the practice for Member States to specify the national authority which will exercise the functions of the "competent authority" where that term is used (for example in Regulation 17, Articles 10, 11, 13, 14 and 19). The designation itself is a matter of national law and appears to be consistent with Community law[11] and the Commission's practice since 1962. Such designation will not oust the competence of other national authorities in the same State to enforce the Community competition rules in pursuance of Article 88 of the Treaty and in accordance with Article 9(3) of Regulation 17 or the equivalent provisions of the transport regulations.

5.04 In the United Kingdom, the Secretary of State for Trade and Industry and the Director General of Fair Trading act as "competent authority" for the purposes of Regulation 17.[12] The day to day casework is dealt with by the Director-General, whilst the Secretary of State has responsibility for policy matters.[13] There has been no formal legislative act appointing the Director-General to act as "competent authority", an administrative designation on behalf of the Crown being sufficient in the circumstances.[14] The Office of Fair Trading has a good working relationship with the Commission. Officials are in frequent touch on the telephone or face to face, discussing cases, their background and evidence on them.[15]

5.04A The enforcement regime of the EEA contemplates co-operation between the

---

[9] The question whether national courts applying Arts. 85 and 86 are "authorities" within the meaning of Art. 9(3) of Reg. 17 and the equivalent provisions of the transport regulations is discussed at para. 10.02.

[10] The procedure relating to such enforcement is, however, a matter for national law. Art. 88 provides that the national authorities shall rule on the admissibility of agreements, etc., "in accordance with the laws of their country." The Treaty does not lay down any rules of procedure in such circumstances and thus national law applies. See Deringer, *op. cit.*, at p. 37. In the *Air Tariffs* case (above, n. 7) the Court spoke of action being taken "within the framework of the laws relating to competition in their countries" (para. 62).

[11] At least in the sense that it enables the provisions of Reg. 17 to be construed in an effective way. See Case 792/79R, *Camera Care Ltd.* v. *Commission*: [1980] E.C.R. 119, [1980] 1 C.M.L.R. 334.

[12] House of Lords Select Committee on the European Communities, Session 1983–84, 18th Report, Commission Powers of Investigation and Inspection, at pp. 41 and 49. The same applies for Reg. 1017/68, 4056/86 and 3975/87.

[13] This is not true for Merger Regulation cases (*i.e.* Reg. 4064/89) where the Secretary of State is concerned with casework which may spill over into Reg. 17 in joint venture cases.

[14] In so far as it is necessary that any powers derived as a matter of Community law from the Treaty be conferred on the Director-General under domestic law, this, it is submitted, is achieved by s. 2(1) of the European Communities Act 1972. The designations are now in the form of declarations made by the Secretary of State. A formal declaration is not strictly necessary but is clearly helpful in demonstrating, to all who need to know, who the competent authorities are. Until 1980 reliance was simply placed on a letter sent to the Commission in 1973. Inglese, "E.C. Competition Law Procedure: Role of the Competent Authority" (1993) 14 E.C.L.R. 197.

[15] Inglese, *op. cit.*

Commission, the E.C. Member States, the EFTA Surveillance Authority and the EFTA States to ensure the functioning of the EEA's competition rules. The rules governing the relationship between the two surveillance authorities are discussed at the end of this chapter.

Obligations of the Commission as regards the competent authorities

(i) *To supply information*

5.05   Article 10(1) of Regulation 17 and equivalent provisions in the transport regulations require the Commission to send copies of certain documents to the competent authorities of the Member States. The purpose, as the Court of Justice indicated in the *Spanish Banks* case, is twofold; first, to inform Member States of the Community procedures concerning undertakings situated on their territory (in theory and in practice the competent authority's interest will be much wider); and second, to allow the competent authority to give its views to the Commission and to enable the Commission better to evaluate and use the information.[16] The competent authority should receive a copy of the applications and notifications together with copies of the most important documents lodged with the Commission for the purposes of establishing the existence of infringements of Article 85 or 86 of the Treaty or of obtaining negative clearance or a decision in application of Article 85(3). The Commission has claimed a wide margin of discretion in deciding whether a document is "most important" and therefore to be sent to the national authorities. The Commission often waits until the formal initiation of proceedings under Article 9(3) of Regulation 17 before deciding whether to transmit a document or not.[17] The precise timing of the transmission of documents to Member States has a particular significance in certain transport cases. Under the objections procedure[18] as it applies to maritime and air transport[19] a Member States can, within 45 days of the forwarding of the relevant documents to it, request the Commission to notify the parties to the agreement in question that there are serious doubts as to its compatibility with Article 85(3). The request from the Member State must be justified on the basis of consideration relating to the competition rules of the E.C. Treaty.

In practice the competent authority will receive numerous documents from the Commission, including:

    (a) Applications by parties:
        (i)   applications for negative clearance,[20]
       (ii) notifications for purposes of exemption,[21]
      (iii) applications for extension of exemption,[22]
      (iv) other applications for exemption (for example, in connection with Article 2 of Regulation 26, applying the rules of competition to production of and trade in agricultural products).[23]

---

[16] Case C–67/90, *Dirrección General de Defensa de la Competencia* v. *Associatión Española de Banca Privada and Others*: The Times, November 26, 1992.
[17] Case T–39/90, *S.E.P.* v. *Commission*: [1992] 5 C.M.L.R. 33, at para. 45.
[18] See para. 2.
[19] See Reg. 4056/86, Art. 12(4) and Reg. 3975/87, Art. 9(4).
[20] See, generally, paras. 2.02–06.
[21] See, generally, paras. 2.07–17.
[22] See, generally, para. 6.36.
[23] The applicability of Arts. 85 and 86 to the agricultural sector is discussed at para. 1.22.

(b) Reports of infringements and complaints.
(c) Commission decisions to initiate proceedings.[24]
(d) Written notifications in which the Commission makes a statement of its legal position:
   (i) statements of objections
  (ii) notification of reasons why the Commission does not intend to follow up a complaint,
 (iii) notification that the Commission after preliminary examination is of the opinion that exemption from the prohibition in Article 85(1) is not justified.[25]
 (iv) publication of a summary of an agreement which the Commission proposes to clear or exempt.[26]
(e) Written comments by undertakings concerned and by third parties on the notifications mentioned above.
(f) Minutes of hearings of parties involved or of third parties.
(g) Decisions concluding proceedings.
(h) Withdrawal of proceedings.

A considerable amount of information may thus be supplied by the Commission to the competent authority. The competent authority may, if it asks for them, see the replies of undertakings to requests for information under Article 11. It may also see the books and business records, etc. of undertakings when it assists the Commission at investigations. Under the so-called opposition procedure provided in the block exemptions for patent licensing agreements, specialisation agreements, research and development agreements, franchising agreements and know-how licensing agreements, there is an implicit obligation on the Commission to send copies of the agreements and notifications to the Member States.[27] One would expect them to be sent to the designated competent authority for the purposes of Article 10(1) of Regulation 17.[28] In the case of the United Kingdom, copies go to the Office of Fair Trading.

5.06   To what extent is this information available for use by the national authority in satisfaction of its own domestic functions and duties? The argument can be made that as a general rule the national authority should be free to use the information. Otherwise the situation could arise where the competent authority in Member State might learn through information supplied by the Commission of a patent infringement of the Member State's own competition laws and would not be able to carry out its duty to enforce those laws or perform the functions specifically given to it. As explained in Chapter 10, Community competition law does not prevent the application of national law in appropriate circumstances and indeed in some cases the latter may provide a

---

[24] See paras. 2.8–39.
[25] The so-called "preliminary decision" under Art. 15(6) of Reg. 17 is discussed at paras 6.12–15.
[26] In pursuance of Art. 19(3) of Reg. 17.
[27] Reg. 2349/84, Reg. 417/85, Reg. 418/85, Reg. 4087/88 and Reg. 556/89 respectively. The opposition procedure is discussed at paras. 2.40–52. The Committee is also consulted in relation to the quasi-opposition "objections" procedures in Regs. 1017/68 and 4056/86.
[28] This is the obvious avenue of communication, but the regs. appear to leave it open to a Member State to designate a different authority for the purpose of the block exemptions. The regs. refer simply to the "authorities" of the Member States. On the other hand, the new Form A/B appears to treat the notification as one under Reg. 17.

more speedy and effective remedy, albeit limited by national procedures and boundaries. It is, however, necessary to see to what extent, if any, the competent authority is restricted in the use of the information. Article 20 of Regulation 17 is relevant here.[29] Additional restrictions may apply in the case of notifications under the opposition procedure.

5.07   Although entitled "Professional Secrecy"[30] Article 20 deals with two separate matters: the use of certain specified information, and the non-disclosure of information "covered by the obligation of professional secrecy." Article 20(1) broadly states:

> "Information acquired as a result of the application of Articles 11, 12, 13 and 14 shall be used only for the purpose of the relevant request or investigation."

Article 20(2) provides:

> "The Commission and the competent authorities of the Member States, their officials and other servants shall not disclose information acquired by them as a result of the application of this Regulation and of the kind covered by the obligation of professional secrecy."

There are similar rules in the transport regulations.

In the *Spanish Banks* case, the Court of Justice made it clear that the restraints (such as they may be) contained in Article 20(1) and (2) apply both to the Commission and to the competent authorities of the Member States.[31] Indeed the reference to Article 13 in Article 20(1) clearly brings the competent authorities within the ambit of that paragraph to some extent and in principle there seems little reason why the competent authorities should be more free than the Commission to use the information outside the enforcement of the Community competition rules. Article 20(2) expressly refers to the competent authorities.

A distinction, however, appears to be drawn in Article 20 as to the information the subject of the prohibition on use or disclosure. Article 20(1) refers specifically to "information acquired as a result of the application of Articles 11, 12, 13 and 14" whilst Article 20(2) refers to "information acquired … as a result of the application of this Regulation." But in the *Spanish Banks* case, the Court of Justice was not persuaded that the absence, from Article 20(1), of any reference to Articles 2, 4 and 5 of Regulation 17 necessarily meant that the information in notifications and applications for exemption could be freely used by national authorities. In the Court's view regard had to be had to the legal context of the procedure in which the information was acquired. Firms notify agreements in order to obtain certain advantages, especially immunity from fine under Article 15(5)(a). A firm would weigh such advantages in the balance when deciding on disclosure to the Commission with its consequent risk of a finding of infringement and fining for any activity prior to notification. There are benefits to the Commission, reducing its investigative tasks, but there also has to be benefits in the undertakings. The Court of Justice therefore concluded that national competent

---

[29] There are equivalent provisions in the transport regulations.
[30] See, generally, paras. 8.18–21.
[31] Above n. 16.

authorities are not entitled to use information in requests and notifications provided by Articles 2, 4 and 5 as evidence in order to support national procedures and penalties.[32]

5.08 It would appear from the wording of Article 20(1) that information obtained pursuant to Articles 11 to 14 is not available for any use by the competent authorities under their own competition laws. The restriction of use contained in Article 20(1) is necessary to offset or balance the broad power of enquiry in Articles 11 to 14. But as the Court of Justice indicated in the *Spanish Banks* case, Article 20(1) does not require the competent authorities in the Member States to suffer "acute amnesia". They are not bound to ignore the information but can take it into consideration in deciding whether to initiate national proceedings. But the documents, etc., supplied via Article 10 cannot be used as evidence by the national competent authority. Facts underpinning proceedings to enforce the Member State's competition law must be proved otherwise in accordance with national rules of evidence and in accordance with the guarantees for the rights of the undertakings provided by national law.[33] The information cannot however be used for other purposes. In *S.E.P.* v. *Commission*,[34] there was concern that a confidential document affecting the supply of natural gas would if sent to a Member State pursuant to Article 10 be used by it for the purpose of determining the sales policy of certain public enterprises in that Member State. Article 20, the Court of First Instance said, would not permit any such leakage of information by the competent authority (which *in casu* was part of the same Government body) responsible for energy matters.

By contrast, Article 20(2) is a more general provision reflecting the fundamental rule contained in Article 214 of the Treaty. Information covered by professional secrecy should not be disclosed, whether to other national authorities or third parties There cannot, however, be any unlawful disclosure to the undertaking whose secret it is and, therefore, a national authority may, subject to Article 20(1), use such information in its investigation, etc., relating to that undertaking provided, of course, it is not disclosed to a third party. This proviso may operate, in practice, as a serious restraint on the use of the information. Moreover the Court of First Instance has pointed out that Article 5 of the Treaty requires Member States to fulfil their obligations arising from Article 20 of Regulation 17. They must ensure that the provisions of that Article are fully effective by taking care that they are not disregarded for the benefit or detriment of any enterprise especially enterprises which they themselves control.[35]

As indicated already notification under the so-called opposition procedure appears to contain further restrictions. The five block exemptions in question all contain a proviso to the effect that information acquired pursuant to the opposition procedure (*i.e.* contained in the agreement or in the accompanying Form A/B and correspondence, or otherwise volunteered to the Commission during the procedure) shall only be used for

---

[32] *Ibid.*

[33] *Ibid.* Similarly, the Commission may not be able to use information obtained as a result of proceedings in a national court where the proceedings do not have the same safeguards as the Commission's: see Case C–60/92, *Otto BV* v. *Postbank NV*: judgment of November 1993, not yet reported.

[34] Case T–39/90: [1992] 5 C.M.L.R. 33, at para. 56. But, on appeal in Case C–36/92P, A.G. Jacobs has taken the contrary view. It is not sufficient simply to rely on Art. 20 the Commission need to balance the issues of confidentiality in appropriate cases (Opinion of December 15, 1993).

[35] *Ibid.* at para. 57.

the purposes of the relevant block exemption regulation.[36] The block exemption regulations also contain restrictions on the disclosure of information similar to Article 20(2) and (3) of Regulation 17.[37]

(ii) *To notify procedural steps*

5.09 In addition to the requirement to supply copies of documents, etc., under Article 10(1), the Commission is required to notify the competent authorities of certain steps in the procedures under Regulation 17. Similar rules apply in transport cases.

(a) *Requests for information under Article 11*

When sending a request for information to an undertaking, the Commission at the same time forwards a copy of the request to the competent authority of the Member State in whose territory the (seat of the) undertaking is situated.[38] Further, where an undertaking does not supply the information in response to the simple written request and the Commission takes a decision requiring the information to be supplied, the Commission must at the same time forward a copy of its decision to the relevant competent authority.[39] There are similar requirements in relation to sector enquiries under Regulation 17 and Regulation 1017/68.[40]

5.10 (b) *Investigations under Article 14*. In connection with all investigations (*i.e.* whether with simple mandate or by decision, announced or surprise) the Commission is required "in good time before the investigation" to "inform the competent authority of the Member State in whose territory the same is to be made of the investigation and of the identity of the authorised officials."[41] The competent authority has a right, or may be requested by the Commission, to send officials to participate and assist in the investigation.[42]

5.11 Before taking a decision under Article 14(3) ordering an investigation the Commission must first consult with the competent authority of the Member State in whose territory the investigation is to be made.[43] There is no such consultation before taking a decision under Article 11(4) requiring information and the consultation requirement of Article 14(4) may be explained by the fact that, as already mentioned,

---

[36] Reg. 2349/84, Art. 13(1); Reg. 417/85, Art. 5(1); Reg. 418/85, Art. 8(1); Reg. 4087/88, Art. 7(1); and Reg. 556/89, Art. 11(1). If not also notified under Reg. 17 such information could not be used by the Commission under that Regulation. If on the other hand Reg. 17 applies (because the parties have applied for negative clearance or notified for individual exemption) then it is arguable whether the competent authorities under Reg. 17 are restricted in the use of information contained in the notification. The power to make block exemptions, Reg. 19/65 and Reg. 2821/71 cannot, it is submitted, be used to amend Reg. 17 except so far as those Regulations expressly provide.

[37] Reg. 2349/84, Art. 13(2) & (3); Reg. 417/85, Art. 5(2) & (3); Reg. 418/85, Art. 8(2) & (3); Reg. 4087/88, Art 7(2) & (3); and Reg. 556/89, Art. 11(2) & (3). Again, it must be questioned how far such rules are necessary if the notification is governed by Reg. 17, and Art. 20(2) & (3) therefore applies.

[38] Art. 11(2) of Reg. 17. See para. 3.07.

[39] Art. 11(6) of Reg. 17. See paras. 3.08–09. Note there is no requirement to consult the competent authority prior to the taking of such decision. *Cf.* Art. 14(4), discussed below.

[40] Art. 12(4) of Reg. 17 and Art. 18(3) of Reg. 1017/68. See para. 3.43.

[41] Art. 14(2) of Reg. 17.

[42] Art. 14(5) of Reg. 17.

[43] Art. 14(4) of Reg. 17.

the competent authority has the right, as well as an obligation if requested by the Commission, to participate and assist in the investigation.[44] Regulation 17 does not specify any particular form the consultation should take. The Commission considers that "consultation" means:

(a) the competent authority is notified that the Commission is planning to order an investigation and is informed of the content of the proposed decision;
(b) it is given the opportunity to submit its comments;
(c) the Commission takes note of its comments.[45]

There is no legal obligation on the Commission to adopt the comments or advice of the competent authority. The obligation is only to consult and the competent authority has no power of veto.

In practice the "consultation" involves the Commission officials responsible for the investigation meeting officials of the relevant competent authority, handing over the full text of the draft decision and supplying any further explanations requested. In the case of the United Kingdom this normally takes the form of a meeting (usually in Brussels) between the Commission officials and the OFT at which the draft is produced and the Commission explains the reasons for the investigation and is expected to make its case.[46] The competent authority can put forward any observations or comments it may have. The OFT in practice always puts its views in writing. A memorandum is signed by both the DG IV official and the representative of the competent authority recording the view of the latter. The Commission has said that this written note is made merely as a matter of record and good administrative practice, for the exclusive use of the services of the Commission and of the competent authority concerned.[47] The written record is confidential and not made available to the undertaking concerned. But any reservations of the competent authority will be recorded in the note and should go forward when the decision is taken. The record might also be produced to the Court as evidence to show that consultation has taken place. Circumstances may demand a less formal consultation, perhaps without an agreed written record. In the *AKZO* case, where the Commission's decision was taken within a matter of hours of the parties notifying the Commission of the intention to refuse to submit to inspection under Article 14(2), the Court held that an informal consultation over the telephone (*in casu*, with the OFT) and without a written note or record being prepared, was sufficient consultation.[48] The Court opined that the Commission must be in a position to take its decision without being subject to formal requirements which would cause delay. Consulting the relevant competent authority is, it is submitted, nonetheless an essential procedural requirement and the validity of the Commission's decision may be challenged under Article 173 of the Treaty in the (unlikely) event of the Commission failing to do so. There are similar requirements in relation to sector inquiries under Article 12(4) of Regulation 17 and Article 18(3) of Regulation 1017/68.

---

[44] Art 14(5) of Reg. 17. See para. 3.27.
[45] Answer to Written Question No. 677/79: [1979] O.J. C310/30 at 37.
[46] The draft decision will have been scrutinised by the OFT's own lawyers. The Commission has not infrequently been persuaded against having a dawn raid. Inglese, *op. cit.*, above n. 14.
[47] Answer to Written Question No. 1474/79: [1980] O.J. C99/31.
[48] Case 5/85, *AKZO Chemie BV (Netherlands) and AKZO Chemie UK Ltd. v. Commission*: [1986] E.C.R. 2585, [1987] 3 C.M.L.R. 716, at paras. 20–23.

5.12   (c) *Hearings*. Article 8(2) of Regulation 99/63 requires the Commission to send a copy of the summons (to the parties to attend the hearing) to the competent authorities of the Member States who may appoint an official to take part in the hearing.[49] Involvement in the oral hearing is described in Chapter 4. The U.K. experience is that parties frequently seek to get in touch with the OFT as competent authority. The OFT is receptive to approaches which might enable it to have a better understanding of the case.[50] The OFT cannot of course act as advocate for the parties.

5.13   (d) *Initiation of proceedings*. Although Regulation 17 and the other implementing regulations do not expressly impose any obligation on the Commission to inform the competent authorities of the initiation of proceedings, the Commission should in fact do so promptly in view of the legal consequences which follow from such event.[51] The national authorities cease to be competent to apply Article 85(1) and Article 86 in accordance with Article 88 of the Treaty.[52]

Assistance, etc., from the competent authorities

(i) *Information*

5.14   Article 11(1) of Regulation 17 provides that the Commission may obtain all necessary information from, *inter alia*, competent authorities of the Member States.[53] These are similar provisions in the transport implementing regulations. For an example of the use of this power see *Cast Iron and Steel Rolls*,[54] where the Commission obtained information from the Cartel Office of the Federal Republic of Germany.

(ii) *Investigations*

5.15   Article 14(5) of Regulation 17 provides that:

> "officials of the competent authority of the Member State in whose territory the investigation is to be made may, at the request of such authority or of the Commission, assist the officials of the Commission in carrying out their duties."

This provision and the similar provisions in the transport implementing regulations give the competent authority the right ("at the request of such authority") or the duty ("at the request . . . of the Commission") to assist at the investigation. The competent authority has to be informed "in good time" of any investigations in the territory of the Member State in order, *inter alia*, that it can arrange for its officials to be available to assist the Commission inspectors.[55] In practice, OFT officials assist at all inspections

---

[49] There are similar provisions in the transport regulations.
[50] Inglese, *op. cit.*, above n. 14.
[51] They do so in practice. See para. 2.38.
[52] See Art. 9(3) of Reg. 17 an the equivalent provisions for transport cases.
[53] See, generally, Fair Trading Act 1973, s. 133; Restrictive Trade Practices Act 1976, s. 41(1); and Competition Act 1980, s. 19. The Commission may also obtain information from Member States and, of course, undertakings (see paras. 3.02 and 3.04). And note that Art. 223(1)(a) of the Treaty provides that no Member State is obliged to supply information the disclosure of which it considers contrary to the essential interests of its security.
[54] [1983] O.J. L317/1, [1984] 1 C.M.L.R. 694.
[55] Art. 14(2) of Reg. 17.

in the United Kingdom. In the case of dawn raids the DTI, the fellow competent authority, will have been informed in advance by the OFT that an investigation is going to take place.[56]

5.16 Article 13 of Regulation 17 deals with the situation where the competent authority does not simply assist the Commission inspectors, but itself undertakes the investigation on behalf of the Commission. Article 13(1) provides that "at the request of the Commission, the competent authorities of the Member States shall undertake the investigations which the Commission considers to be necessary" under Article 14. There are similar provisions in the transport implementing regulations. The officials of the competent authority conducting the investigation are required to exercise their powers upon production of written authorisation issued by the competent authority, which shall specify the subject-matter and purpose of the investigation. Commission officials may assist the officials of the competent authority conducting the investigation. Such assistance can be requested by the Commission or by the relevant competent authority. Article 13 was used in the United Kingdom in 1992 for the first time. This was only the second time in the history of the Community that a competent authority has been asked to conduct an investigation for the Commission.[57] Concern has been expressed that too frequent use of Article 13 could lead to uneven enforcement as between different Member States.[58]

5.17 Under Article 14(6) of Regulation 17 and the equivalent provisions in the transport implementing regulations, Member States are required to "afford the necessary assistance" to the Commission inspectors in circumstances where an undertaking opposes an investigation ordered by decision under Article 14. It will be remembered that the Commission inspectors are not entitled to use force and have no additional powers to deal with the situation where an undertaking opposes the investigation. The Commission can, of course, take a further decision imposing a fine and/or periodic penalty payment on the undertaking concerned. Article 14(6), however, contemplates stronger medicine. The "necessary assistance" given by the Member State must be sufficient to "enable" the inspectors "to make their investigation." Such assistance may be given by the competent authority, but not necessarily. Precisely what form the assistance takes is a matter for the Member State and national law. It must, however, be consistent with the Community legal order and the uniform application of Community law. As the Court of Justice pointed out in *Hoechst*,[59] it is for each Member State to establish appropriate procedural rules which can provide guarantees for the undertakings concerned. Where the Commission requests assistance under Article 14(6) it must ensure that the national court or other body authorised has all the information necessary to exercise its supervisory powers. Whilst the national court or authority cannot question the need for the investigation (this is a matter for the Court

---

[56] Inglese, *op. cit.*, above n. 14.

[57] *Ibid.* There were five simultaneous raids in the U.K. investigating a cartel in PVC. Three were led by OFT officials and two by the Commission with support from the OFT. The documents obtained went straight to Brussels, no copies being retained by the OFT.

[58] In its 1993 Report, Enforcement of Community Competition Rules, the House of Lords Select Committee recommended that procedural guidance to national inspectors be identical with that issued to Commission inspectors and that national inspectors be assisted by at least one Commission inspector (para. 115).

[59] Cases 46/87 & 227/88, *Hoechst AG* v. *Commission*: [1989] E.C.R. 2859, [1991] 4 C.M.L.R. 410, at para. 33.

of Justice under Article 173 in any appeal against the Commission's decision) it is entitled:

> "to consider whether the measures of constraint envisaged are arbitrary or excessive having regard to the subject matter of the investigation and to ensure that the rules of national law are complied with in the application of these measures."[60]

The assistance must be speedy and ultimately effective — it must be sufficient to enable the Commission officials to perform their duties. Although Article 14(6) only requires Member States to give assistance where there has been actual opposition to the investigation, the Commission may request it in advance,[61] but presumably only in extreme circumstances where there is a serious risk of the destruction of evidence.

5.18   In the case of the United Kingdom, no specific measures have been taken.[62] The provisions of Regulation 17 and the other implementing regulations create rights, duties and obligations which are directly applicable in the United Kingdom without further enactment.[63] The rights of the Commission to carry out its investigation using the powers contained in Article 14(1) and the equivalent provisions relating to transport may therefore be enforced by an English court. The procedure is for an ex parte application[64] to be made in the name of the Attorney General to a judge of the High Court in chambers to obtain the order necessary to compel the undertaking concerned to submit to the investigation as ordered by the Commission's decision.[65] It is not the Court's function to question the merits of the decision but, as described above, there remains a discretion in the Court and a supervisory responsibility. The judge has to be satisfied that the decision is formally valid and that the undertaking has opposed the investigation. Evidence of the latter will normally be shown by the affidavit of the OFT lawyer assistant at the investigation. Although ex parte, the undertaking may be informed of the application and be able to attend. In practice the application can be

---

[60] *Ibid.* at para. 35.

[61] *Ibid.* at para. 32. The Commission has not done so in the U.K.

[62] For the position in other Member States in relation to Arts. 13 and 14 of Reg. 17, see Belgium, Royal Decree of January 18, 1966; Denmark, Act. No. 505 of November 29, 1972; France, Decree No. 72–151 of February 18, 1972; Germany, Act of August 17, 1967 implementing Reg. No. 17 of the Council of the European Economic Community; Italy, Decree of the President of the Republic September 22, 1963 No. 1884; Luxembourg, Grand Ducal Regulation of May 26, 1965; Netherlands, Act of July 10, 1966 implementing Reg. 17 of the Council of the European Economic Community; Spain, Royal Decree No. 1882/1986 of August 29, 1986. Some of these laws contemplate the use of force to overcome the undertaking's opposition and may involve police intervention. At the request of the Commission, the OFT has arranged for police support to be available in the vicinity at the time of seeking entry to the undertaking's premises, in order to guard against the possibility of a breach of the peace. This should not be confused with the assistance under Art. 14(6) described in this para.

[63] European Communities Act 1972, s. 2(1).

[64] In the run-up to the investigations the OFT will have liaised with the Treasury Solicitor's Department and counsel will have been briefed to be standing by. Inglese, *op. cit.*, above n. 14.

[65] The procedure has been used on at least two occasions in relation to Reg. 17 — see the House of Lords Select Committee Report (above n. 10) at pp. 46 and 78. On one occasion only a negative injunction was obtained.

heard within an hour or two of the refusal. The order may be both positive and negative. It would require the undertaking to permit the inspectors to carry out the investigation (*i.e.* to enter premises, examine books, etc.) and to prohibit the removal and destruction of the undertaking's books and business records. Breach of the Court's order would constitute contempt of court and would be punishable accordingly with imprisonment or a fine.

(iii) *Hearings*

5.19 So far as hearings are concerned, Article 19(2) of Regulation 17 provides that "if the Commission or the competent authorities of the Member States consider it necessary, they may hear other natural or legal persons", *i.e.* third parties, persons other than the undertakings concerned in the alleged infringement. Thus where the third party does not show a sufficient interest entitling him to be heard, the competent authorities have the right to require the Commission to hear a third party where they consider it necessary for such party to be heard. In practice this is most unlikely to cause any friction between the Commission and the competent authorities in view of the Commission's practice of hearing responsible third parties where they may have anything useful and relevant to contribute.

5.20 Article 8(2) of Regulation 99/63, dealing with the procedure and conduct of hearings in more detail, provides that the Commission must send a copy of the summons (to the parties to attend the hearing) to the competent authorities "who may appoint an official to take part in the hearing." The representatives of the competent authorities present at the oral hearings are therefore not merely observers but have the right "to take part". In practice, this right is exercised by the national representatives putting questions to the undertakings being heard. Similar rules apply in transport cases.

II. THE ADVISORY COMMITTEE ON RESTRICTIVE PRACTICES AND MONOPOLIES

Constitution and function

5.21 Particulars of the constitution and function of the Advisory Committee on Restrictive Practices an Monopolies (the Advisory Committee) are contained in Article 10(3)–(16) of Regulation 17. It is composed of "officials competent in the matter of restrictive practices and monopolies."[66] An official is appointed by each Member State.[67] Although there is no requirement that the official should come from the competent authority of the Member State, in practice it is often the case that he or she does. Separate committees exist for the transport sector: the Advisory Committee on Restrictive Practices and Monopolies in the Transport Industry, under Regulation 1917/68; the Advisory Committee on agreements and dominant positions in maritime transport, under Regulation 4056/86; and the Advisory Committee on Agreements and Dominant Positions in Air Transport, under Regulation 3975/87. For each of

[66] Art. 10(4) of Reg. 17.
[67] *Ibid.* If the appointed official is prevented from attending, another official may replace him.

these committees each Member State nominates two officials, competent in the relevant transport field (*i.e.* rail, road and inland waterway or maritime or air transport respectively) and in "agreements and dominant positions".

5.22   The Advisory Committee must be consulted prior to the taking of the following decisions:

(a) any decision establishing the existence of infringements of Article 85 or 86 of the Treaty, giving negative clearance or in application of Article 85(3);[68]

(b) any decision concerning the renewal, amendment or revocation of a decision pursuant to Article 85(3);[69]

(c) any decision imposing a fine or periodic penalty payment.[70]

The requirement of consultation applies similarly in the context of sector inquiries.[71] The Commission must also consult the Advisory Committee before publishing a draft regulation relating to a block or group exemption and again before adopting such a regulation.[72] It appears that there is no obligation to consult the Advisory Committee prior to a preliminary decision under Article 15(6).[73] There is no express obligation to do so in relation to interim measures,[74] but in practice the Commission does consult the Committee in such cases. The Commission has also developed the practice of consulting the Committee where it envisages sending out a comfort letter (administrative letter) to the undertakings concerned following publication of a notice under Article 19(3) of Regulation 17.[75]

Occasionally the Advisory Committee may meet to discuss general questions.[76] These may not necessarily be restricted to the organisation and functioning of the Committee and its work. They may range wider and deal with general matters of competition policy, *e.g.* recent developments both at Community and national level, the parallel application of national and Community competition laws and current problems such as merger control, know-how licensing and franchising. The Commission

---

[68] Art. 10(3) of Reg. 17. And note *NAVEWA/ANSEAU*: [1982] O.J. L325/20, [1983] 1 C.M.L.R. 470, where the Committee was consulted prior to the decision amending the earlier decision in the case ([1980] O.J. L167/39) by rectifying the position of one of the parties and withdrawing its fine.

[69] Art. 10(3) of Reg. 17. There are similar provisions in the transport regulations.

[70] Arts. 15(3) and 16(3) of Reg. 17. There are similar provisions in the transport regulations.

[71] Art 12(4) of Reg. 17 and Art. 18(3) of Reg. 1017/68.

[72] Art. 6 of Reg. 19/65, Art. 6 of Reg. 2821/71, Art. 6 of Reg. 3976/87, and Art. 6 of Reg. 1534/91.

[73] See A.G. Roemer in Cases 8–11/66, *Cimenteries* v. *Commission*: [1967] E.C.R. 75, 109, [1967] C.M.L.R. 77, and the Commission's practice in Art. 15(6) cases (see para. 6.14) upheld by the Court of First Instance in Case T–19/91, *Vichy* v. *Commission*: [1992] II E.C.R. 415.

[74] The question came before the Court of Justice in the *Ford* case (Cases 228 & 229/82: [1984] E.C.R. 1129, [1984] 1 C.M.L.R. 649), but the Court did not deal with it in its judgment quashing the decision. A.G. Slynn did say that the Committee must be consulted prior to a decision imposing interim measures, especially where, as in the *Ford* case the interim decision imposes a periodic penalty payment. He rejected the argument that the Committee need only be consulted prior to the second of the two stages. But in *Hoechst*, above, n. 58, the Court ruled that it was not necessary to consult the committee at the first stage, because this would occasion delay which might jeopardise the effectiveness of the decision in question (*in casu* — one ordering an investigation). It is nevertheless arguable that there is an implicit obligation to consult the Advisory Committee before taking a decision imposing interim measures. In Reg. 1284/91 (providing an expedited procedure for interim measures in air transport cases) special provision is made to excuse the Commission from consulting the Advisory Committee.

[75] Nineteenth Report on Competition Policy, at point 4, and Twentieth Report, at point 3.

[76] Thirteenth Report on Competition Policy, at point 79, and Sixteenth Report, at point 6.

also from time to time calls meetings of National Government Experts to discuss general issues of concern and promote co-operation between the Commission and national authorities.[77] For the United Kingdom, a representative from the Government department with the policy lead (*e.g.* DTI, DoT) will normally attend such meetings together with the OFT.

Procedure

5.23   The procedure for consultation of the Advisory Committee is as follows. The consultation takes place at a joint meeting of the Committee and the Commission.[78] This meeting is convened by the Commission and held in Brussels. The Commission sends a notice convening the meetings to the members of the Committee and the meeting must not be held earlier than 14 days after dispatch of the notice.[79] The notice must, in respect of each case to be examined, be accompanied by a summary of the case together with an indication of the most important documents,[80] and a copy of the preliminary draft decision.[81] The "most important documents" for this purpose would include any complaint, the letter initiating the procedure, the statement of objections, the undertakings' replies and the minutes of the oral hearing. The availability of an accurate version of the minutes of the oral hearing has been controversial. The Court of Justice has said that there will only be a defect in the administrative procedure capable of vitiating the Commission's decision if the minutes are drawn up in such a way as to be misleading in a material respect.[82] The Court of First Instance has adopted a similar test in the case where the Committee has not been presented with minutes, final or draft.[83] The 14-day rule has also come under scrutiny. In *RTE*, the Court of First Instance said that the 14-day notice period imposed under Article 10(5) is a purely internal procedural rule.[84] Failure to comply with it does not, by itself, render defective a subsequent decision by the Commission. The Advisory Committee must be given sufficient time to acquaint itself with the important aspects of the case and to formulate its opinion in full knowledge of the facts.

In practice, the meeting is chaired by the Director of the relevant Directorate of DG IV, Directorate A–General Policy. The Commission will also be represented by the case chairman (*chef de file*) and case officer (*rapporteur*) concerned. Other Commission officials, and in particular a member of the Legal Service, may be present. Following the opening of the meeting by the chairman and a short introduction to the case given by the Committee Rapporteur, each member of the Committee in turn has the

---

[77] Twentieth Report on Competition, at point 4.

[78] Art. 10(5) of Reg. 17. There are similar provisions in the transport regulations.

[79] *Ibid.* In the case of a meeting to consider a draft regulation relating to a block exemption, the relevant period is one month. See, *e.g.* Art. 6(2) of Reg. 19/65.

[80] See the opinion of A.G. Warner in Case 30/78, *Distillers* v. *Commission*: [1980] E.C.R. 2229, [1980] 3 C.M.L.R. 121 where the question whether certain documents were "important" and the implications of the Advisory Committee deciding not to adjourn to study them when produced later than the notice convening the meeting are discussed.

[81] Art. 10(5) of Reg. 17. In the U.K. the OFT, on receipt of the draft decision, will canvas the views of relevant Whitehall departments. Inglese, *op. cit.*, n. 11.

[82] Case 44/69, *Buchler* v. *Commission*: [1970] E.C.R. 733, at para. 17, discussed at para. 4.27 above.

[83] Case T–69/89, *Radio Telefis Eireann* v. *Commission*: [1991] 4 C.M.L.R. 586, at paras. 24–25. If a plea of procedural irregularity, that the Committee only had draft minutes, is to succeed, the parties must demonstrate that there are material discrepancies *and that* the draft was actually misleading. See also A.G. Vesterhof in Case T–7/89, *SA Hercules NV* v. *Commission*: [1992] 4 C.M.L.R. 84, where the plea also failed.

[84] *Radio Telefis Eireann*, above, at para. 27.

opportunity to make any points, express any views, and put any questions he may have on the subject-matter of the preliminary draft decision. The Commission usually responds and there may be further free discussion between the members of the Committee and the Commission prior to members of the Committee determining among themselves what should be contained in their opinion (*avis*). The Committee determines its own procedure. The practice is for one of its members (appointed in rotation) to act as the Committee Rapporteur for a particular case to co-ordinate and assist in the preparation of the opinion. It is usual to deal with two or three cases during a two-day meeting.

5.24   Article 10(6) provides that a "report of the outcome of the consultative proceedings shall be annexed to the draft decision" which goes before the Commissioners. In practice, the opinion (*avis*) of the Advisory Committee accompanies this report. Article 10(6) has two things to say about the opinion. First the Advisory Committee may deliver an opinion notwithstanding that some of its members of their alternatives are not present. There is, however, no fixed quorum. Second, the opinion "shall not be made public."

Secrecy of the opinion

5.25   The opinion is not shown to the undertakings concerned who are therefore unaware of its contents and cannot reply to it. Nor is the opinion automatically provided to the Court in the event of an appeal being brought against the Commission's decision by the undertakings concerned. There have, however, been two cases where details of the consultative proceedings have been made available to the Court. In the *Quinine* case,[85] extracts of the minutes of the consultation were apparently made available to the Court of Justice for the purpose of determining certain questions relating to the regularity of the procedure before the Advisory Committee. Again, in the *Distillers*,[86] case, a copy of the report was supplied to the Court of Justice although it is clear that the Committee's opinion was not shown to the applicant undertaking. The question of disclosure to the undertakings concerned was mentioned but did not fall to be determined by the Court.

5.26   The secrecy of the opinion has been the subject of comment and criticism from academics, legal practitioners and industry alike.[87] The argument has been put forward that the opinion should be made available to the undertakings directly concerned in order to protect the rights of the defence. But the Court of Justice has not accepted

---

[85] Case 41/69, *ACF Chemiefarma* v. *Commission*: [1970] E.C.R. 661, 709–711.

[86] Above, n. 80. But see the comments of A.G. Warner who was most uneasy about the secrecy surrounding the procedure of the Advisory Committee. In his view, the risks of injustice that it entails made it imperative that the procedure should be carried out with scrupulous care.

[87] See, for example, Steindorff, "Die Durchsetzung des Wettbewerbsrecht in der EWG—Wirksamkeit und Rechtstaatlichkeit", Aufgaben der Wettbewerbspolitik im Gemeinsamen Markt, Heft 14d. Schriftenreihe der Europa Union Deutschland (Dusseldorf, 1963); Van Bael "EEC Antitrust Enforcement and Adjudication as seen by Defence Counsel" (1979) 7 *Revue Suisse du Droit International de la Concurrence* 1; UNICE Memorandum of February 21, 1980, *EEC Procedures in Competition Cases*. The House of Lords Select Committee (above n. 12) is also in favour of the opinion being communicated to the undertakings concerned (see para. 20 of the Report).

this. In the *Pioneer*[88] case the Court rejected the argument that Article 10(6) of Regulation 17 should be construed in such a way as to allow the Committee's opinion to be disclosed to the undertakings. To give the undertakings the opportunity of making their views known on the opinion and therefore on the draft decision would, the Court said, amount to re-opening the previous stage of the procedure, which would be contrary to the system intended by the regulation. Non-disclosure of the opinion is not contrary to the right to a fair hearing. Whatever may be the Committee's opinion, the Commission may base its decision only on facts on which the undertakings have had the opportunity of making known their views. The position under the Merger Control Regulation, Regulation 4064/89, is different. Express provision is made for publication of the Committee's opinion in certain circumstances.[89]

Irregularities in procedure

5.27 A failure on the part of the Commission to consult the Advisory Committee may constitute a breach of an essential procedural requirement such as to vitiate the Commission's decision. In the *Quinine*[90] case, Advocate General Gand, in the context of a discussion of questions concerning the regularity of the Committee's procedure, said:

> "it cannot be excluded that, if a procedural requirement to consult a body is laid down by a provision prior to taking a decision, the omission or the improper completion of that formality may in certain cases constitute an infringement of an essential procedural requirement invalidating the decision."

In the *Distillers*[91] case, Advocate General Warner went further and dealt with irregularities in the Committee's own procedures. He said "disregard of procedural requirements by the Committee is just as capable of vitiating the Commission's Decision as disregard of them by the Commission itself." This statement was made in the context of a discussion of the Committee's own decision when told of the contents of documents submitted by the undertaking concerned after the notice convening the meeting of the Committee, not to adjourn to study them further.

5.28 The Commission's decision will usually recite the fact of consultation. But if the undertaking does not have access to the Commission's complete file and/or the report of the consultation prepared pursuant to Article 10(6) of Regulation 17 it is unlikely to know whether there has been any irregularity such as may invalidate the decision and on which to base an appeal to that end under Article 173 of the Treaty.

[88] Cases 100–103/80, *Musique Diffusion Française et al.* v. *Commission*: [1983] E.C.R. 1823, [1983] 3 C.M.L.R. 221, at paras. 34–36, A.G. Reischl had reached a similar conclusion in the *FEDETAB* case (Cases 209–215 & 218/78: [1980] E.C.R. 3125 at 3129, [1981] 3 C.M.L.R. 134 at 164).

[89] Art. 19(7). For an example of a published opinion see *Nestlé/Perrier*: [1992] O.J. C319/3. The form of the opinion is similar to that in cases under Reg. 17. The 1993 House of Lords Report (above, n. 58) recommended that the Advisory Committee's opinion under Regulation 17 should be available to the parties and, as under the Merger Control Regulation, be given wider publication.

[90] Above, n. 85.

[91] Above, n. 80. More generally on failure to consult making an instrument void see Case 130/79, *Roquette Fréres* v. *Council*: [1980] E.C.R. 3333 and Case 165/87, *Commission* v. *Council*: [1988] E.C.R. 5545, [1990] 1 C.M.L.R. 457. Note: Case C–65/93, *European Parliament* v. *Council*, presently before the Court of Justice, addressing the question of the effect of failure to consult in urgent situations.

This has not stopped parties raising such arguments before the Court of Justice as already mentioned. But, as a general principle, it is far from satisfactory that a party should have to make an appeal in order to be able to ascertain (or for the Court to ascertain) whether there are grounds for such an appeal.[92] There should be some way of checking that the Advisory Committee has been properly consulted.

EEA

5.29 Article 55 of the Agreement of the European Economic Area (EEA) places a duty on the E.C. Commission and the EFTA Surveillance Authority to ensure the application of the competition rules in Articles 53 and 54 in accordance with the jurisdiction and division of responsibility laid down in Article 56. Article 55, like Article 89 of the E.C. Treaty, provides a skeleton procedure for this.[93] The Agreement contemplates that the detailed procedural rules of the EEA's competition authorities, the Commission and the EFTA Surveillance Authority, will mirror those of the Commission in application of Articles 85 and 86, *i.e.* Regulation 17 and the other implementing regulations.[94] Protocol 4 of the EFTA Surveillance Agreement does just this. In particular Chapter II mirrors Regulation 17 and provides the general procedural rules to implement Articles 53 and 54 of the EEA Agreement. The relationship between the EFTA Surveillance Authority and the competent authorities of the EFTA States should therefore follow that described above *mutatis mutandis*.

5.30 Reference was made in Chapter 1 to the Agreement on the European Economic Area making provision for co-operation between the two enforcement authorities, the Commission and the EFTA Surveillance Authority. Article 58 imposes an obligation to co-operate:

> "with a view to developing and maintaining a uniform surveillance throughout the European Economic Area in the field of competition and promoting a homogeneous implementation, application and interpretation of the provisions of this Agreement to this end."

So far as the application of substantive rules in Articles 53 and 54 (the equivalent of Articles 85 and 86) is concerned the detail of the co-operation is set out in Protocol 23. First, there is a general obligation on each authority to exchange information and consult each other on general policy issues at the request of the other.[95] Second, as regards "mixed" cases, that is those cases where the effect of the agreement or practice, etc., in question is not restricted to the Community or to the EFTA States,[96] there are rules

---

[92] See the discussion of the *Hoffmann-La Roche* case at para. 4.11.
[93] Art. 55 EEA contemplates the investigation of cases by the competent surveillance authority in co-operation with the competent national authorities and with the other surveillance authority. It can take appropriate measures to bring any infringement to an end. If the infringement is not brought to an end the competent surveillance authority shall record the infringement in a reasoned decision and may authorise States within its territory to take measures necessary to remedy the situation. It may also request the other surveillance authority to authorise States within its territory to take such measures.
[94] Protocol 21, Arts. 1–3.
[95] Protocol 23, Art. 1. The obligation to consult experts on legislative changes is contained in Art. 99 EEA, see para. 1.34C.
[96] The jurisdictional division of cases between the Commission and the EFTA Surveillance Authority is discussed at para. 1.34A–B.

providing for assistance and cooperation between the Commission and the EFTA surveillance Authority throughout and at the key states in the proceedings:

(i) *Notifications and complaints*

Copies of these have to be forwarded without due delay to each other except where it is apparent that they have been addressed to both surveillance authorities. The recipient authority may comment within 40 working days.[97]

(ii) *Ex officio proceedings*

The two authorities must inform each other when opening *ex officio* proceedings. The recipient authority may comment within 40 working days.[98]

(iii) *Supply of documents between authorities*

A surveillance authority may at all stages in the proceedings request from the authority having jurisdictional responsibility (under the rules in Article 56 EEA) to decide on a case copies of the most important documents lodged with that authority for the purposes of establishing an infringement of Articles 53 and 54 EEA or obtaining negative clearance or exemption.[99]

(iv) *Information gathering, investigations*

When sending a request for information to an undertaking located in the territory of the other authority, the competent surveillance authority must at the same time forward a copy of that request to the other authority. If it becomes necessary to require the information by decision, a copy of the decision must be sent to the other authority. Where a competent surveillance authority carries out investigations within its own territory it shall inform the other authority of the fact of such investigations and, on request, send to the other authority the relevant results of the investigations. A competent authority can request the other authority to carry out investigations within the territory of that authority where it considers that such investigation is necessary. The requested authority must undertake the investigation and permit the competent surveillance authority to be represented and take an active part in the investigation. All information obtained during such investigations on request shall be sent to the authority which requested the investigation immediately after its completion.[1]

(v) *Negative clearance, exemptions*

Where one authority publishes its intention to give a negative clearance or take a decision in application of Article 53(3) EEA it must consult the other who may deliver its comments within the time-limits set out in the publication. Observations received from the undertakings concerned or third parties shall be sent to the other authority.[2]

---

[97] Protocol 23, Art. 2
[98] *Ibid.*
[99] Protocol 23, Art. 7.
[1] Protocol 23, Art. 8.
[2] Protocol 23, Art. 3.

(vi) *Statement of objections*

When addressing to undertakings a statement of objections the competent surveillance authority must consult the other who can comment within the time-limits set out in the statement of objections. Observations received from the undertakings concerned shall be sent to the other authority.[3]

(vii) *Comfort letters, rejection of complaint*

The competent surveillance authority must send to the other authority a copy of the administrative letters by which a file is closed or a complaint rejected.[4]

(viii) *Hearings*

The competent surveillance authority must invite the other authority to be represented at hearings of the undertakings concerned. The invitation shall also extend to the States falling within the competence of the other surveillance authority.[5]

(ix) *Advisory Committees*

The competent surveillance authority must in due time inform the other authority of the date of the meeting of the Advisory Committee and send it all the relevant documentation. Any documents given in response must be presented to the Advisory Committee. Each surveillance authority and the States falling within its competence shall be entitled to be present at the Advisory Committee of the other authority and to express their views therein. They do not, however, have the right to vote.[6]

(x) *Right to make observations*

At any stage in the proceedings before a final decision is taken, a surveillance authority may make any observations it considers appropriate on a case to the authority having competence under Article 56 EEA to decide on the case.[7]

---

[3] *Ibid.*
[4] Protocol 23, Art. 4.
[5] Protocol 23, Art. 5.
[6] Protocol 23, Art. 6
[7] Protocol 23, Art. 7.

6

Commission Decisions

Introduction

6.01   This chapter is principally concerned with the different types of decision taken by the Commission under Regulation 17 and the other implementing regulations and their formal requirements. Before dealing with final decisions, *i.e.* those which require infringements to be terminated or grant negative clearance or exemption, some consideration is given to interim measures (including the special provisions relating to air transport) and provisional decisions under Article 15(6). But it would be wrong to imagine that every case ends in a formal decision. In fact very few decisions are made each year. Many more cases are dealt with informally. Some of the legal issues involved with less formal arrangements, settlements and undertakings, are therefore also discussed.

I. INTERIM MEASURES

Generally

6.02   By its order in *Camera Care* v. *Commission*,[1] the Court of Justice settled the long-standing debate as to whether or not the Commission had powers to take interim measures in relation to infringements of Articles 85 and 86. The position under the ECSC Treaty had been made clear in *National Carbonising Co.* v. *Commission*,[2] but it was by no means certain whether the Commission had similar powers in connection with the application of Articles 85 and 86 of the EEC Treaty, given, in particular, the general necessity for implementing regulations under Article 87. Moreover, Regulation 17, the first and principal implementing regulation, is apparently silent on the

---

[1] Case 792/79R: [1980] E.C.R. 119, [1980] 1 C.M.L.R. 334. See Henderson, "The Camera Care Case and the European Court's Role as Praetor" (1980) 77 L.S.Gaz. 575, Ferry, "Interim Relief under the Rome Treaty–The European Commission's Powers" (1980) 3 E.I.P.R. 330, and Temple Lang, "The Powers of the Commission to order Interim Measures in Competition Cases" (1981) 18 C.M.L.Rev. 49.

[2] Cases 109 & 114/75R: [1975] E.C.R. 1193, [1975] 2 C.M.L.R. 457. The Commission has express power to adopt interim measures under Art. 66(5) ECSC in connection with mergers. In Cases 160, 161 & 170/73R, *Miles Druce & Co. Ltd.* v. *Commission*: [1973] E.C.R. 1049, [1974] 1 C.M.L.R. 224, the Court decided that this power could be used before the Commission had adopted its definitive position. In the *National Carbonising* case, the President of the Court found that the Commission also had an implied power to order interim measures to protect an enterprise claiming to be a victim of an abuse of a dominant position contrary to Art. 66(7) while the Commission was considering the merits of the claim.

matter—it nowhere refers expressly to the possibility of the Commission taking interim measures. Indeed Regulation 17, and in particular Article 3, suggests that the only measure which the Commission can take short of a decision, finding an infringement, is a recommendation. Advocate General Warner took this view. The Court, however, clearly rejecting any literal approach and choosing to interpret Regulation 17 in such a way as to give it maximum practical effectiveness, held that the powers in Article 3 to take decisions terminating infringements included the power to take interim measures:

> "The Commission must also be able, within the bounds of its supervisory task conferred upon it in competition matters by the Treaty and Regulation 17, to take protective measures to the extent to which they might appear indispensable in order to avoid the exercise of the power to make decisions given by Article 3 from becoming ineffectual or even illusory because of the action of certain undertakings. The powers which the Commission holds under Article 3(1) of Regulation 17 therefore include the power to take interim measures which are indispensable for the effective exercise of its functions and, in particular, for ensuring the effectiveness of any decisions requiring undertakings to bring to an end infringements which it has found to exist."[3]

The Court considered that there might be a need to adopt such measures:

> "when the practice of certain undertakings in competition matters has the effect of injuring the interests of some Member States, causing damage to other undertakings, or of unacceptably jeopardising the Community's competition policy."[4]

For some time it seemed as though the Commission was never going to exercise its new-found powers. The *Camera Care* complaint resulted in a final decision,[5] no interim decision was taken. In other instances either the Commission has rejected the application for interim relief[6] or the firms under attack have given in and no measures have had to be taken.[7] The Commission has in fact taken six decisions imposing interim measures: five under Regulation 17 and one under Regulation 4056/86: *Ford*,[8]

---

[3] Above, n. 1, at para. 18. The power to take interim measures is also, it is submitted, implied in the transport regulations: Reg. 1017/68, Art. 11(1); Reg. 4056/86, Art. 11(1); Reg. 3975/87, Art. 4(1). Indeed the special fast track procedure provided by Reg. 1284/91 (see para. 6.11A) is stated expressly to be without prejudice to Art. 4(1) of Reg. 3975/87. *Cf.* the concept of implied powers adopted by the Court in such cases as Case 8/55, *Fédération Charbonnière de Belgique* v. *High Authority*: [1954–56] E.C.R. 292, and Case 22/70, *Commission* v. *Council*: [1971] E.C.R. 263, [1971] C.M.L.R. 335.

[4] *Ibid.* at para. 14.

[5] *Hasselblad*: [1982] O.J. L161/18, [1982] 2 C.M.L.R. 233.

[6] In its recent decision, *Sea Containers* v. *Stena Sealink*: [1994] O.J. L15/8, the Commission took a formal decision rejecting the application for interim measures.

[7] See, *e.g.* the cases of *IGR Stereo Television* and *Amicon/Fortici* and *Wright Scientific*, described in the Eleventh Report on Competition Policy, at points 94 and 112.

[8] *Ford Werke AG–Interim Measure*: [1982] O.J. L256/20, [1982] 3 C.M.L.R. 267, later annulled by the Court, Cases 228 & 229/82, *Ford of Europe Inc., and Ford Werke AG* v. *Commission*: [1984] E.C.R. 1129, [1984] 1 C.M.L.R. 649.

ECS/AKZO,[9] *BBI/Boosey and Hawkes,*[10] *Eco-System/Peugeot,*[11] *Mars*[12] and *Sea-link/B&I.*[13] In a number of cases it has accepted an undertaking instead.[14]

Infringement of Article 85 or 86

6.03   The Court considered that the power to take decisions given by Article 3(1) of Regulation 17 should be exercised "in the most efficacious manner best suited to the circumstances of each given situation." It continued:[15]

> "To this end the possibility cannot be excluded that the exercise of the right to take decisions conferred on the Commission should be linked in successive stages so that a decision finding that there is an infringement may be preceded by any preliminary measures which may appear necessary at any given moment."

From this it may be concluded that a grant of interim measures is not dependent on a finding of infringement. Indeed, if it were, the word "interim" would hardly seem appropriate. The question, however, remains to what extent the granting of interim measures is dependent on evidence or proof of infringement of Article 85 or 86. The Court's own rule and practice is to require a prima facie case on the substantive issues (in the main action) to be shown before interim measures can be taken.[16] Following the Court's order in *Camera Care*, the Commission made it clear in a statement given to the parties prior to the oral hearing in its administrative proceedings that it would look for a prima facie case of violation of the competition rules.[17] In the later *Ford* case,[18] Advocate General Slynn said that at least a prima facie case must be shown to justify the Commission's power to order interim measures. There must be a sufficient substratum of facts, and a sufficiently clear case in law, to justify the order. Where there is an active complainant seeking relief, the burden of showing that there is a prima facie case may well fall on it, although the Commission may use its own powers

---

[9] *ECS/AKZO–Interim Measures*: [1983] O.J. L252/13, [1983] 3 C.M.L.R. 694.

[10] [1987] O.J. L286/36.

[11] *Ecosystem SA* v. *Peugeot SA*: [1990] 4 C.M.L.R. 449.

[12] Decision of March 25, 1992, not yet reported.

[13] *Sealink/B&I — Holyhead–Interim Measures*: [1992] 5 C.M.L.R. 255.

[14] *E.g. Hilti*: [1985] 3 C.M.L.R. 619; *Napier Brown* v. *British Sugar*: [1986] 3 C.M.L.R. 594; *Eurofix–Bauco* v. *Hilti*: [1988] O.J. L65/19, and *Napier Brown–British Sugar*: [1988] O.J. LA284/41, [1990] 4 C.M.L.R. 196.

[15] Above, n. 1, at para. 17. Emphasis added.

[16] Art. 83(2) of the Court's Rules of Procedure refers to the application for interim measures including the legal and factual grounds which establish a prima facie case. Interim measures before the Court are discussed in Chap. 9. See paras. 9.38–43. It will be remembered that on an application for an interim injunction an English court has merely to be satisfied that there is a serious question to be tried (*i.e.* that the claim is not frivolous or vexatious) before proceeding to consider whether the balance of convenience lies in favour of granting or refusing interlocutory relief: *American Cyanamid Co.* v. *Ethicon Ltd.*: [1975] A.C. 396.

[17] The full text of the Commission's statement is set out in Appendix I. In its decisions in *BBI/Boosey and Hawkes*, above, n. 10, and *Sealink/B & I*, above, n. 13, the Commission refers to the need for a "reasonably strong prima facie case establishing an infringement."

[18] Above, n. 8.

of investigation and resources to this end.[19] In both *Peugeot* and *La Cinq*,[20] the Court of First Instance condemned the Commission for applying too stringent a test. The requirement of a finding of a prima facie infringement did not make the adoption of interim measures conditional of proof of "a clear, flagrant infringement". The requirement of certainty demanded of a final decision was not needed to satisfy the condition relating to the probable existence of an infringement in interim measures proceedings. The undertaking complained of has a right to be heard and will no doubt submit evidence to contradict that of the complainant and/or the Commission. The argument could easily become protracted and the Commission's difficulty in balancing the evidence at a preliminary stage is not to be underestimated.[21] The Commission's finding that there is a prima facie case should not prejudice its final decision in the matter.

Urgency

6.04   In the *Camera Care* case, the Court of Justice said that: "it is essential that interim measures be taken only in cases proved to be urgent in order to avoid a situation likely to cause serious and irreparable damage to the party seeking their adoption, or which is intolerable for the public interest."[22]

The requirement that the case should be "urgent" means that it must be one calling for immediate action on the part of the Commission. Time might be a critical factor and a complainant might reasonably be expected to act without delay in bringing the matter to the attention of the Commission. In *Mars*, the urgency of the request was related to the seasonal nature of the product, ice-cream.[23] The date (if later) when the irreparable damage appears likely is probably more relevant than that of the alleged breach of Article 85 or 86.[24] The Commission may assume urgency whenever the occurrence of serious and irreparable damage needs to be prevented.[25]

Serious and irreparable damage

6.05   The applicant must show that the conduct complained of is likely to cause "serious and irreparable damage."[26] The Court of Justice has emphasised a similar criterion in cases under Articles 185 and 186.[27] Whether or not damage is or is likely to be serious is essentially a question of fact to be determined in the circumstances of the

---

[19] In *Ecosystem/Peugeot*, above, n. 11, the Commission used its powers under Article 11 of Reg. 17.

[20] Case T–31/89, *Peugeot* v. *Commission*: [1990] II E.C.R. 265; Case T–44/90, *La Cinq* v. *Commission*: [1992] II E.C.R. 1, [1992] 4 C.M.L.R. 449, at para. 61.

[21] Para. 15 of the Commission's statement (App. I) refers to the possibility that the parties may produce an agreed statement of facts and submit any evidence by means of signed statements. It is clear from *Sealink/B & I-Holyhead–Interim Measures:* [1992] 5 C.M.L.R. 255, that the Commission may work hard to reach a settlement between the parties. Note also the involvement of the Hearing Officer in *Ecosystem/ Peugeot:* [1990] 4 C.M.L.R. 449.

[22] Case 792/79R: [1980] E.C.R. 119, [1980] 1 C.M.L.R. 334, at para. 19. This closely follows the approach of the Court in cases under Articles 185 and 186, and Art. 85(2) of the Rules of Procedure. See, *e.g.* Case 23/86R, *U.K.* v. *European Parliament:* [1986] 3 C.M.L.R. 82, at para. 39.

[23] Above n. 12. Note also the importance of the advent of the holiday season in *Sealink/B & I*, above.

[24] Ferry, *op. cit.*, at p. 334.

[25] *Mars*, above n. 12.

[26] Case 792/79R: [1980] E.C.R. 119, [1980] 1 C.M.L.R. 334, at para. 19.

[27] See paras. 9.38–43.

particular case. The applicant should present as much evidence as he can when applying for relief. Whether or not damages are "irreparable" may involve questions of law. In the *Camera Care* case, the Court said: "it is important to ensure that, whilst enquiries are being carried out no irreparable damage is caused such as could not be remedied by any decision which the Commission might take at the conclusion of the administrative procedure."[28] The Court of First Instance, in *La Cinq*,[29] made it clear that this does not mean that only damage which could not be remedied by a subsequent decision can be regarded as irreparable. The Commission cannot award damages or compensation in any decision it makes, but the effect of a decision declaring certain conduct unlawful, prohibiting it and, in appropriate circumstances, requiring positive action to correct the default may go some way to make good the situation, at least prospectively. So in ECS/AKZO,[30] where there was an allegation of discriminatory and predatory pricing, the Commission made an order prohibiting the supply of products below specified prices and restricting the offer or supply of products at prices or terms different from those offered or given to other comparable buyers. It is uncertain to what extent damage is "irreparable" if compensation might be awarded in a national court for breach of Article 85 or 86 once proven either on the basis of the final decision of the Commission or independently on evidence produced to the national court.[31] Even if a national court did so, it may not be easy to quantify damages where commercial reputation is damaged or a business loses potential sales as a result, for example, of a refusal to supply or a collective boycott. In *Mars*,[32] the Commission looked not only at the likely financial loss to the company but also the loss of Mars' competitive advantage. The Commission is unlikely to stand by where an undertaking may be driven out of business.[33] The threat to the continued existence of the undertaking is not, however, a precondition for the adoption of interim measures. The Commission has said that damage may be serious when the applicant for relief may suffer considerable competitive disadvantage likely to have a lasting effect on its position.[34] Nevertheless the Commission often asks whether national remedies have been tried and may increasingly look to national courts and authorities to deal with complaints.[35]

Public interest

6.06 The Court of Justice said that interim measures might be taken to avoid a situation "which is intolerable in the public interest."[36] The "public interest criterion is an alternative to 'serious and irreparable damage.'" The case must still be an urgent one. The Court did not elaborate on what it meant by the public interest and its previous practice in cases under Articles 185 and 186 gives little assistance in this respect. As

[28] Case 792/79R: above, at para. 14.
[29] Case T–44/90, *La Cinq v. Commission*: [1992] II E.C.R. 1, [1992] 4 C.M.L.R. 449, at paras. 79 and 80.
[30] *ECS/AKZO–Interim Measures*: [1983] O.J. L252/13, [1983] 3 C.M.L.R. 694. And see the positive orders in *BBI/Boosey and Hawkes*, above, n. 10; *Ecosystem/Peugeot*, above, n. 11 and *Sealink/B & I*, above, n. 13.
[31] See the discussion of this in *Sealink/B & I*, above, at para. 50, and, generally, paras. 10.15–24.
[32] Decision of March 25, 1992, not yet reported.
[33] *BBI/Boosey and Hawkes*, above, n. 10, and *Ecosystem/Peugeot*, above, n. 11. *Cf. Sea Containers v. Stena Sealink*, above, n. 6.
[34] *Mars*, above.
[35] Notice on co-operation between national courts and the Commission in applying Articles 85 and 86 of the EEC Treaty: [1993] O.J. C39/6, at paras. 14 and 15.
[36] Case 792/79R, *Camera Care v. Commission*: [1980] E.C.R. 119, [1980] 1 C.M.L.R. 334, at para. 19.

already mentioned, the Court said that interim measures may be suitable "when the practice of certain undertakings in competition matters has the effect of injuring the interests of some Member States, causing damage to other undertakings, or of unacceptable jeopardising the Community's competition policy."[37] Accordingly, the "public interest" might involve, at least in part, the protection of the interests of the Member States (and thereby the citizens of those States) and the Community's competition policy.[38] The situation must be "intolerable". This, it is submitted, imports a degree of magnitude, seriousness or severity sufficient to justify the taking of the exceptional measures contemplated by the Court. Not every breach of Article 85 or 86 can be said to "unacceptably jeopardise" the Community's competition policy.

Protection of the interest of the undertaking concerned

6.07   The Court held that the Commission could not take interim measures "without having regard to the legitimate interests of the undertaking concerned."[39] These interests are protected in four ways:

(a) by the requirements of "urgency" and "serious and irreparable damage" or injury to the "public interest";
(b) by the temporary and conservatory nature of the measures;
(c) by the "essential safeguards guaranteed" by Regulation 17 and in particular Article 19; and
(d) by the requirement that the measures be in such a form that an action may be brought on them before the Court by any party who considers that it has been injured.

(a) has already been discussed. (b), (c) and (d) are dealt with below.

Nature of the measures

6.08   The measures are temporary and conservatory in nature.[40] In effect they should not go further than is necessary at any given moment to preserve the status quo ante. Therefore a complainant cannot require his position to be made better than it was before the conduct in question. Thus an undertaking which has cut off supplies to another might reasonably be expected to recommence supplying at a level and on terms equivalent to that in a representative period before the termination, but the recipient should not be put in any better position merely as a result of the interim measures taken.[41] Whilst it is, of course, the Commission who will decide on the appropriate measures, applicants for interim measures should indicate as precisely as possible the

---

[37] *Ibid.* at para. 14. The Commission spoke of preserving the public interest in *Ecosystem/Peugeot* (above n. 11), in terms of Ecosystem being allowed to continue to serve its customers until the final decision. See para. 21 of the decision.

[38] See Ferry, *op. cit.*, at pp. 333–334. He concludes: "It is clear from the application of the phrase and its cousin phrases in the national arenas that it enables the courts to override a particular unwanted result by reference to (often unspoken) value judgments. In the establishment of policy (and therefore in the application of value judgments) in competition matters, the policy making body is the Commission."

[39] *Camera Care*, above, at para. 19.

[40] *Ibid.*

[41] See *BBI/Boosey and Hawkes*: [1987] O.J. L286/36., where the Commission considered it inappropriate in the circumstances to require Boosey and Hawkes to extend credit to the complainants.

nature of the measures they expect the Commission to order. The legal basis of interim measures is Article 3 of Regulation 17 and, therefore, the Court of Justice held in *Ford* that interim measures must come within the framework of the final decision which may be adopted under that Article. The Court found that Ford's refusal to supply certain right-hand-drive vehicles was not itself an infringement of Article 85 or 86, and that the Commission's powers were limited to the distribution agreement notified. The Court refused to accept that the two were related and that, as the Commission had argued, the interim measures ought to be interpreted as allowing Ford to maintain its refusal to supply on condition that it ceased to operate the dealer agreement.[42] It is therefore doubtful whether in an interim order the Commission can ever order that which it could not in terms order in a final decision.[43]

Procedure

6.09 The Commission is required "to maintain the essential safeguards guaranteed to the parties concerned by Regulation 17, in particular by Article 19."[44] There seems to be no room for any form of *ex parte* application by a complainant. Proceedings must be formally initiated. The request for relief must be related to and accompanied by a complaint which the Commission may require to be a formal one.[45] The undertaking likely to be the subject of the measures must be informed of the Commission's objections and given the opportunity to reply to them and make known its point of view. It is doubtful whether the provisions of Regulation 99/63 apply in these circumstances. The undertaking concerned should nevertheless be given the opportunity of an oral hearing to the extent that this is required by the general principles of natural justice, evidenced as applicable in Community law by the *Transocean Marine Paint* case.[46] It is also clear that the interests of third parties who show "sufficient interest" to be heard must not be overlooked.[47] In application of Article 11 of Regulation 99/63, the Commission should balance the time required for preparation of comments and the urgency of the case. There may be cases of such urgency that a truncated procedure, with short time-limits, may be justified.[48] If an oral hearing takes place, the complainant may be present, in which event the proceedings could take on, if they have

---

[42] *Ford Werke AG–Interim Measure*: [1982] O.J. L256/20, [1982] 3 C.M.L.R. 267, later annulled by the Court: Cases 228 & 229/82, *Ford of Europe Inc. and Ford Werke AG* v. *Commission*: [1984] E.C.R. 1129, [1984] 1 C.M.L.R. 649, at para. 21.

[43] The Commission view in *Sea Containers* v. *Stena Sealink*, above, n. 6. But see A.G. Slynn in *Ford, ibid.* who considered that it could not absolutely be said that the Commission may not do so, since in order to preserve the Commission's power to make a final order it may be necessary temporarily to forbid acts or to require steps to be taken which could not be included in a final order, provided what is ordered does not exceed in substance what could be done in a final order.

[44] Case 792/79R, *Camera Care* v. *Commission*: [1980] E.C.R. 119, [1980] 1 C.M.L.R. 334, at para. 19.

[45] Para. 4 of the Commission's statement (App. I).

[46] Case 17/74: [1974] E.C.R. 1063, [1974] 2 C.M.L.R. 459. Oral hearings are allowed by the Commission, see, *e.g. Ecosystem SA* v. *Peugeot SA*: [1990] 4 C.M.L.R. 449.

[47] Per A.G. Slynn in *Ford*. He found that the interests of two British Ford dealers had been overlooked and considered this a breach of an essential requirement sufficient to annul the decision. In *Sea Containers* v. *Stena Sealink*, above, n. 6, the complainant was invited to the oral hearing.

[48] *Ibid.*

not done so already, and adversarial nature. There must be liaison with the Member States[49] and the Advisory Committee has to be consulted.[50]

The *ECS/AKZO* case,[51] gives a useful example of the likely timetable involved. The request for interim relief was made on May 13, 1983 (the original complaint being earlier), the statement of objections on June 8 and oral hearing on June 23, the Advisory Committee on July 4, and the decision made on July 29, 1983. So the procedure appears to take at least two months (other cases have taken longer) and should be contrasted with the speed with which interim relief can be obtained in national courts.

The balance of interests

6.10 Any measures taken by the Commission must be limited to the needs of the given situation and the Commission should take into consideration the implications for the undertaking to whom the measures are addressed.[52] The principle of proportionality is relevant here.[53] The Commission should not go beyond what is necessary in the circumstances. In so deciding the Commission will have to balance the interests of the two sides. So in *Sealink/B&I*,[54] the Commission weighed the additional costs incurred by Sealink by having to reschedule its services against the potential damage to B&I due to loss of traffic and commercial standing. In *Mars*, the President of the Court of First Instance thought that the Commission had erred too much in favour of the complainant Mars, finding that the interim measures would in part cause substantial injury to the two manufacturers' distribution systems concerned whose terms excluded Mars. That injury, and the effect on the market, might not be reversible. The President therefore granted interim relief against the interim measures ordered by the Commission.[55]

The decision

6.11 The measures must be made in such a form that they may be the subject of an action before the Court.[56] They will therefore be decisions within the meaning of Article 189 and hence must be fully reasoned and will take effect upon notification. This does not mean that the Commission has to comment on all the arguments addressed by the complainant. It is sufficient, the Court of First Instance has said,[57] to set out the facts and legal considerations of primary importance in the general scheme of the decision. A fine under Article 15(2)(a) is not available because no infringement has been proven. The Commission is, however, able to impose a periodical penalty payment

---

[49] Art. 10 of Reg. 17.
[50] Per A.G. Slynn in *Ford* rejecting the Commission's argument that consultation was necessary only when a periodical penalty payment was to be imposed. *Cf.* A.G. Roemer in Cases 8–11/66, *Cimenteries* v. *Commission*: [1967] E.C.R. 75, [1967] C.M.L.R. 77. See para. 6.14.
[51] *ECS/AKZO–Interim Measures*: [1983] O.J. 252/13, [1983] 3 C.M.L.R. 694.
[52] *Ecosystem/Peugeot system*, above, at para. 21.
[53] See generally paras. 8.25–27.
[54] *Sealink/B&I — Holyhead–Interim Measures:* [1992] 5 C.M.L.R. 255, at paras. 52 and 53.
[55] Cases T 24 & 28/92R, *Langnese-Iglo and Schöller Lebensmittel* v. *Commission*: Order of June 16, 1992.
[56] Case 792/79R, *Camera Care* v. *Commission*: [1980] E.C.R. 119, [1980] 1 C.M.L.R. 334, at paras. 19 and 20. But where the Commission refuses interim measures this does not mean the Court can, under Article 186, simply step into the Commission's shoes and itself grant such relief; see Case T–131/89R, *Cosimex GmbH* v. *Commission*: [1990] II E.C.R. 1, [1992] 4 C.M.L.R. 395.
[57] *La Cinq*, above n. 29, at para. 41.

under Article 16(1)(a) which refers to decisions taken pursuant to Article 3 of Regulation 17. Such a sanction has been imposed in five of the interim measures decisions taken to date.[58]

Although no express reference was made to it by the Court of Justice in the *Camera Care* case, the Commission may require the complainant in whose favour the interim measures are taken to give some form of guarantee indemnifying the party the subject of the measures in the event that no infringement of Article 85 or 86 is ultimately established. This was especially mentioned by the Court in the *National Carbonising* case[59] under the ECSC Treaty and there is no reason to suppose that a similar requirement should not be possible under the EEC Treaty. The Commission has indicated that the party requesting interim measures may be ordered to give a suitable bond or guarantee to indemnify the party against whom the interim measures are ordered.[60] Undertakings may also be used to support decisions. In *BBI/Boosey and Hawkes*,[61] the Commission took an undertaking from the complainants (potential competitors of Boosey and Hawkes) to deal fairly with Boosey and Hawkes and not to denigrate them or use them as a bait or loss leader.

Finally, if not themselves expressly limited in time,[62] the interim measures will last until such time as the Commission takes a formal decision[63] or discharges them or takes further measures or they are annulled by the Court, whichever is the sooner.[64]

Air Transport—Regulation 1284/91

6.11A The Council and Commission have recognised that in a liberalised market smaller airlines offering new services may be highly vulnerable when they have to compete with established, sometimes dominant airlines.[65] Regulation 1284/91 therefore amends Regulation 3975/87, the principal implementing regulation for air transport, by giving an additional power, in a new Article 4a, to take interim measures in certain circumstances by a shortened procedure. The Commission must have "clear prima facie evidence" of practices contrary to Article 85 or 86 which "have the object or effect of directly jeopardizing the existence of an air service." Only experience will

---

[58] No periodical penalty payment was imposed in *B&I/Sealink*, above.

[59] Above, n. 2; and note the conditions on which the Court granted relief in the *Ballbearings* cases (Cases 113 & 118/77R: [1977] E.C.R. 1721; Case 119/77R: [1977] E.C.R. 1867; and Case 121/77R: [1977] E.C.R. 2107).

[60] Para. 13 of the Commission's statement (App. I). There has been no instance under EEC rules yet. But see, for example, the form of guarantee required by the Commission in the *National Carbonising* case *NCB-NSF-Nat. Carbonising*: [1976] O.J. L35/6, [1976] 1 C.M.L.R. D82. *Cf.* the general requirement in English civil procedure whereby an applicant for injunctive relief must give cross-undertakings in damages. This may place a serious obstacle in the way of a small complainant relying on Article 85 or 86 in an English court.

[61] [1987] O.J. L286/36. The Commission reserved the right to amend or cancel the interim measures decision in the event of any breach of the undertaking.

[62] As was part of the measure ordered in *BBI/Boosey and Hawkes*, above. See also *Sealink/B&I — Holyhead–Interim Measures*: [1992] 5 C.M.L.R. 255 where the decision was limited in time subject to being terminated earlier if the parties reached a new scheduling agreement.

[63] See *Ecosystem SA v. Peugeot SA*: [1990] 4 C.M.L.R. 449.

[64] See the *Ford* case. The interim measures were formally terminated by the Commission's final decision, *Ford Werke AG (Distribution System)*: [1983] O.J. L327/31, [1984] 1 C.M.L.R. 596, and later annulled by the Court, Cases 228 & 229/82, *Ford of Europe Inc. and Ford Werke AG v. Commission*: [1984] E.C.R. 1129, [1984] 1 C.M.L.R. 649.

[65] Twenty-first Report on Competition Policy, at point 39.

show what additional burden this may place on a complainant beyond that which is required in "ordinary" interim measures cases.[66] The intention[67] is to allow the Commission to act speedily to aid, for example, a small airline against anti-competitive practices such as predatory pricing[68] or excessive capacity which if not checked quickly could lead to irreversible damage to the competitive structure. The advantage given of the new Article 4a is that it enables the Commission to take interim measures to ensure the practices in question are stopped or not commenced (the Commission can also give instructions to prevent the occurrence) without having to consult the Advisory Committee in the usual way. The Committee can be consulted at very short notice and on the basis of an oral report only from the Commission. A decision under Article 4a may last up to six months but may be renewed for a further three months. Before renewal the Committee must be consulted in the usual way.

II. PROVISIONAL DECISIONS

Generally

6.12   Immunity from fine, which is the principal benefit arising from notification,[69] may be lost. Article 15(6) provides that the Commission may withdraw it: "where the Commission has informed the undertakings concerned that after preliminary examination it is of opinion that Article 85(1) of the Treaty applies and that the application of Article 85(3) is not justified."[70] This is the legal basis for what has become known as the provisional or preliminary decision. Any doubts as to the legal status of the measure taken under Article 15(6) were swept away by the Court of Justice in the *Cimenteries* case. The Court said:

> "This measure deprived [the undertakings] of the advantages of a legal situation which Article 15(5) attached to the notification of the agreement, and exposed them to a grave financial risk. Thus the said measure affected the interests of the

---

[66] See Soames, *Butterworths Competition Law Encyclopedia*, para. 51–55.

[67] Introducing the new provisions the Commission gave, as examples of practices used to threaten competitors unfairly: (1) providing so much capacity or such high frequencies on a route that other airlines find it difficult to sell their service, *e.g.* laying on an 8.45 flight and a 9.15 flight without good reason when a competitor has just introduced a new 9.00 service; (2) charging fares appreciably below the carrier's own fully allocated costs; (3) granting benefits such as "override" commission to travel agents which make it difficult for other airlines to compete; (4) granting loyalty benefits to passengers which artificially maintain their loyalty to a specific airlines. Commission press release P26, May 2, 1990.

[68] Predatory pricing may be extremely difficult in practice to establish to the necessary standards. Refusal to allow interlining—as in *British Midland/Aer Lingus*—being more in the nature of a refusal to supply case may be a more typical/better example.

[69] See para. 2.18.

[70] In the transport sector there are equivalent provisions in Reg. 4056/86, Art. 19(4) and Reg. 3975/87, but not in Reg. 1017/68 (which was drafted on the basis that notification would be very much the exceptional case).

undertakings by bringing about a distinct change in their position. It is unequivocally a measure which produces legal effects touching the interests of the undertakings concerned and which is binding on them. It thus constitutes not a mere opinion but a decision."[71]

The Court was clearly influenced by the fact that Article 15(6) involved the Commission making rulings on the applicability of Article 85(1) and (3) and thought that neither the absence of any express reference to a decision in Article 15(6) nor the provisional nature of the Commission's examination were sufficient grounds for discarding the notion of decision. It was also concerned that the measure should not be excluded from all judicial control. The essential feature of a decision under Article 15(6) is the termination of immunity of fine. As the Court of First Instance said in *Prodifarma II* this produces two legal effects for the parties to the agreement in question.[72] First, it lays them open to being fined if they continue to implement the agreement. Second, it excludes the parties' good faith as regards the compatibility of their agreement with Article 85, so that thereafter they can scarcely deny that any infringement was committed intentionally or, at the least, negligently.[73] Strictly the decision itself does not have the effect of preventing the parties from implementing the agreement. The risk of fine could well deter them although the President of the Court of First Instance in *Vichy* considered that such a risk was the same as that incurred by any undertaking which has failed to notify to the Commission an agreement falling within the scope of Article 85(1).[74]

The possibility of a provisional decision under Article 15(6) does not exclude the possibility of interim measures.[75] The two procedures differ in a number of respects as the judgments in *Prodifarma II*[76] and *Vichy*[77] demonstrate. A decision under Article 15(6) is possible only where an agreement has been notified. For Article 15(6) to apply the test is whether the agreement notified appears, after a preliminary assessment has been made, incompatible with Article 85(1). The infringement should be sufficiently clear and serious that an exemption is unjustified. For the adoption of interim measures it is necessary, as described above, that there be a prima facie infringement and that other conditions are satisfied, in particular that urgency and risk of irreparable harm are established. The effect of a decision under Article 15(6) is more limited. It merely lifts the immunity from fine. As already mentioned the risk of fine may deter

[71] Cases 8–11/66, *Cimenteries v. Commission*: [1967] E.C.R. 75, [1967] C.M.L.R. 77, at para. 4. The Court confirmed its view that Art. 15(6) involved a decision, when in the *Portelange* case it said: "If the Commission considers that the implementation of an agreement notified infringes the competition rules, it is open to it to adopt, within the appropriate time, a decision under Article 85(3) of the Treaty or under Article 15(6) of Regulation No. 17." Case 10/69, *Portelange SA v. Smith Corona Marchant International SA*: [1969] E.C.R. 309, [1974] 1 C.M.L.R. 397, at para. 17.
[72] Case T–3/90, *Vereniging Prodifarma v. Commission*: [1991] II E.C.R. 1, at paras. 40–42.
[73] See para. 7.13–15.
[74] Case T–19/91, *Societe d'Hygiène Dermatologique de Vichy v. Commission*: [1991] II E.C.R. 265, at para. 18
[75] In the *Ford* case, above n. 64, it was argued that the order in question went beyond what was necessary because the same effect could have been achieved by a decision under Article 15(6). A.G. Slynn rejected this argument. He did not accept that if the agreement is notified interim measures cannot be ordered if a fine is less severe. He noted that in the *Camera Care* case itself the agreement had been notified. The Court in *Ford*, whilst annulling the interim measures, pointed out that a decision under Art. 15(6) had been available.
[76] Above, n. 72, at paras. 15, 42 and 43.
[77] Above, n. 74, at para. 20.

the parties from implementing their agreement but unlike interim measures a decision under Article 15(6) does not itself contain any injunction and requires no enforcement. This said, in some cases the deterrent effect of Article 15(6) may in practice produce the same result, *i.e.* the termination of an infringement. The Court of First Instance has said that, as opposed to interim measures, a decision under Article 15(6) cannot *directly* benefit complainants.[78] This is a procedural point. Although complainants have an interest in seeing the possible deterrent effect of Article 15(6) this interest is not sufficient to enable a complainant, by means of the procedure under Article 175, to compel the Commission to take a decision under Article 15(6) . The Court of First Instance has recognised that a decision under Article 15(6) must satisfy considerations of expediency which require that the Commission enjoy wide freedom of action.[79] Whilst the entitlement of a complainant under Regulation 17 to a decision rejecting the complaint is yet to be made certain by the Court of Justice, it is to be noted that in *La Cinq*[80] the Court of First Instance, on the application of the complainant, annulled the Commission's refusal to take interim measures.

6.13 Decisions under Article 15(6) are relatively rare. There are five reported examples. Article 15(6) was probably used in the *Cimenteries* case, because the Commission sought an expeditious end to what it saw as a serious anti-competitive agreement. In two cases, *Sirdar/Phildar*[81] and *Bronbemaling/Heidemaatschappij*[82] proceedings in national courts may have precipitated its use. The decision in *SNPE/ Leafields Engineering*[83] was published very shortly after an announcement that a greater use would be made of the Article 15(6) procedure.[84] The more recent case of *Vichy* is the only other example.[85] In practice, it is not so simple or so quick for the Commission to make a preliminary decision. There can be informal indications to the same effect which bring infringements to an end or lead to modifications. Where a decision is necessary there are certain procedural safeguards which must be observed and the complex internal procedures of the Commission may not be suited to an expeditious solution.

Procedure

6.14 Regulation 17 does not lay down a particular procedure for cases involving decisions under Article 15(6). In the *Cimenteries* case,[86] the Court described the Commission's decision under Article 15(6) as being the final step in a special procedure. Advocate General Roemer considered that the peculiarities inherent in the Article 15(6) decision and its very function allowed a reasonable interpretation of Regulation

---

[78] *Prodifarma II*, above, n. 72, at para. 42

[79] *Ibid.* at para. 43.

[80] Case T–44/90, *La Cinq v. Commission*: [1992] II E.C.R. 1, [1992] 4 C.M.L.R. 449.

[81] [1975] O.J. L125/27, [1975] 1 C.M.L.R. D93.

[82] [1975] O.J. L249/27, [1975] 2 C.M.L.R. D67. And see (1979) 4 E.L.Rev. 413 for a brief account of what took place in the Dutch courts subsequent to the Commission's decision.

[83] [1978] O.J. L191/41, [1978] 2 C.M.L.R. 758.

[84] Reported by Korah in (1979) J.B.L. 67.

[85] [1991] O.J. L75/57. But the procedure was commenced in *P. & I. Clubs*: [1985] O.J. L376/2, [1989] 4 C.M.L.R. 178 and in *Decca Navigation System*: [1989] O.J. L43/27, [1990] 4 C.M.L.R. 627.

[86] Above, n. 71, at para. 9.

17 and the other competition regulations, making it possible to a certain extent to depart from the normal procedure. He thought it might not be necessary for the Commission to hear third parties or to involve the Advisory Committee or the national authorities.[87] With regard to the undertaking's right to be heard, he thought that the normal rules, which could provide for a short time-limit and the renunciation of oral observations, left the Commission with sufficient discretionary powers to ensure that the hearing did not delay the procedure substantially.

The basic requirements seem therefore to be that the Commission must make its case known to the undertaking (or undertakings) involved[88] and the undertaking must be given the right to reply (to be heard). The four decisions, *Sirdar/Phildar*, *Bronbemaling*, *SNPE/Leafields* and *Vichy*, all recite the fact that the undertakings concerned had been heard as required by Article 19(1) of Regulation 17 and by Regulation 99/63.[89] But in none of these cases did the undertakings have a formal oral hearing[90] and the question has been raised whether a party is entitled to one. It has been argued that Regulation 99/63 does not apply to a decision under Article 15(6) and that consequently the Commission has maximum flexibility in the procedure to be taken in these cases.[91] An undertaking should nevertheless be afforded all necessary procedural protection which, it is submitted, should include the availability of an oral hearing, particularly if circumstances were such as to make the denial of an oral hearing an infringement of the requirements of natural justice.[92] Third parties have no right to be heard in the procedure.[93] It has not been the Commission's practice to consult the Advisory Committee. The point was taken in *Vichy* where the Court of First Instance has held that such consultation is not necessary.[94]

Decision

6.15 Article 15(6) decisions, being decisions within the meaning of Article 189 of the Treaty, must be properly reasoned. In the *Cimenteries* case,[95] the Court held that even though the Commission's assessment in the decision of the applicability of Article 85(1) and Article 85(3) may be expressed succinctly by reason of the provisional character of the procedure, the Commission's reasoning should nonetheless appear

[87] He thought consultation of the Advisory Committee would mean an intolerable delay in the procedure.
[88] So there will be a statement of objections: see, e.g. *P. & I. Clubs*, above.
[89] The Commission may refuse to hear witnesses—see *Bronbemaling*, above, n. 82.
[90] In the proceedings in the High Court, Sirdar claimed that the Commission's decision under Art. 15(6) was a nullity because it had not been given an oral hearing in accordance with the provisions of Art. 19 of Reg. 17 and Art. 7(1) of Reg. 99/63. See *Sirdar Ltd.* v. *Les Fils de Louis Mulliez and Orsay Knitting Wools Ltd.*: [1975] 1 C.M.L.R. 378, 380. Graham J. did not find it necessary to determine the issue or, for that matter, to give any opinion on the validity of the agreement in Community law. He refused Sirdar's application for interlocutory relief on the balance of convenience, taking the view that there was not a serious likelihood of confusion between the two marks which could not be adequately compensated by damages.
[91] Leigh, "Resurrection of the Provisional Decision" (1977) 2 E.L.Rev. 91.
[92] Leigh, *op. cit.*, and see Case 17/74, *Transocean Marine Paint Association* v. *Commission*: [1974] E.C.R. 1063, [1974] 2 C.M.L.R. 459.
[93] *Per* the Court of First Instance in *Prodifarma II*: Case T-3/90, *Vereniging Prodifarma* v. *Commission*: [1991] II E.C.R. 1, at para. 44
[94] Case T-19/91, *Vichy* v. *Commission*: [1992] II E.C.R. 415.
[95] Cases 8–11/66, *Cimenteries* v. *Commission*: [1967] E.C.R. 75, [1967] C.M.L.R. 77, at para. 14, and see para. 6.41.

from the decision itself with sufficient clarity to allow the Court and all concerned to determine whether the provisions have been applied properly.

III. PROCEDURAL DECISIONS

6.16   Decisions made in pursuance of Articles 11 and 14 of Regulation 17 in connection with the Commission's powers of investigation have already been described in Chapter 3. The imposition of fines for procedural infringements is discussed in Chapter 7. There is no requirement on the Commission to delay making a decision imposing a fine for a procedural infringement until the final decision on the substance is taken. For example, in the *Sugar* case, Raffinerie Tirlemontoise[96] was fined for incomplete submission of business records in advance of the Commission's decision on the cartel. Similarly, in the Commission's inquiries into the European — West African shipping conferences fining decisions were taken for misleading the Commission and failure to submit to investigations.[97] On the other hand, it may be convenient to deal with all matters at the same time. Thus in *Theal/Watts*,[98] the Commission imposed a fine for supplying incorrect or misleading information in connection with a notification for exemption of an exclusive distribution agreement at the same time as imposing a fine for the substantive infringement relating to the prohibition on exports from the United Kingdom. In large investigations, however, the Commission may not want to await a final decision and the threat or actuality of a procedural decision may encourage a settlement or the giving of undertakings.

IV. FINAL DECISIONS

Termination of infringement

Cease and desist orders

6.17   Article 3 of Regulation 17 provides that where the Commission finds that there is an infringement of Article 85 or 86, "it may by decision require the undertakings or associations of undertakings concerned to bring such infringement to an end." The Commission may therefore order that the undertakings terminate the infringement forthwith.[99] Such an order is sometimes referred to as a "cease and desist order". This may be particularly relevant where the parties vigorously deny the infringements and

---

[96] [1971] 11 E.C. Bull. 55.
[97] *Secrétama*: [1991] O.J. L35/23, [1992] 5 C.M.L.R. 76; *Ukwal* [1992] O.J. L121/45, and *Mewac:* [1993] O.J. L20/6.
[98] [1977] O.J. L39/19, [1977] 1 C.M.L.R. D44. See also *Peugeot*: [1986] O.J. L295/19, [1989] 4 C.M.L.R. 371, where the Commission fined under Art. 15(1)(b) for incorrect replies to requests under Art. 11(3), but did not fine for the breach of Art. 85(1).
[99] See, for example, *Sugar*: [1973] O.J. L140/17, [1973] C.M.L.R. D65; *Brooke Bond Liebig*: [1978] O.J. L53/20, [1978] 2 C.M.L.R. 116; *White Lead* [1979] O.J. L21/16, [1979] 1 C.M.L.R. 464; *AEG-Telefunken*: [1982] O.J. L117/15, [1982] 2 C.M.L.R. 386; *Ford Werke AG (Distribution System)*: [1983] O.J. L327/31, [1984] 1 C.M.L.R. 596.

it is not certain that they have in fact ceased.[1] The Commission may also order termination of the infringement in so far as it has not already been terminated.[2] In a number of cases, the Commission has sought to restrain further acts of the parties and has included in its decision what may be described as a "like effects" order.[3] Where however, the infringement has been terminated[4] (perhaps voluntarily) before the decision, the Commission may limit itself to a declaration that the conduct in question constituted an infringement and need not include a cease and desist order.[5]

The legality of issuing declaratory decisions was upheld by the Court of Justice in the *GVL* case.[6] The Court considered the question not to be one of competence or jurisdiction but of whether the Commission had a legitimate interest in declaring conduct which had already been terminated by the undertaking concerned to be an infringement. The power to take decisions requiring termination of infringements and fining implied a power to make a finding that an infringement exists. The Court held that in the circumstances the Commission had been entitled to take the view that there was a real danger of the resumption of the abusive practice if GVL's obligation to terminate it were not expressly confirmed and that consequently it was necessary to confirm the legal position. In a number of instances the Commission has taken declaratory decisions to clarify the position for the benefit of the public, or complainants in particular, and in order to prevent future infringements.[7] A finding of an infringement may

---

[1] *Polypropylene*: [1986] O.J. L230/1, [1988] 4 C.M.L.R. 347; *Building and Construction industry in the Netherlands*: [1992] O.J. L92/1; *PVC*: [1989] O.J. L74/1, [1990] 4 C.M.L.R. 345 and *LdPE*: [1989] O.J. L74/21, [1990] 4 C.M.L.R. 382.

[2] See *IM-Rules*: [1980] O.J. L318/1, [1981] 2 C.M.L.R. 498; *British Telecommunications*: [1982] O.J. L360/36, [1983] 1 C.M.L.R. 457; *Hudson's Bay*: [1988] O.J. L316/43, [1989] 4 C.M.L.R. 340 and *Eurofix–Hilti*: [1988] O.J. L65/19, [1989] 4 C.M.L.R. 677.

[3] See, *e.g. Grundig–Consten*: [1964] J.O. 2545/64, [1964] C.M.L.R. 489; *Theal/Watts*, above, n. 64; *Distillers*: [1978] O.J. L50/16, [1978] 1 C.M.L.R. 400; *Maize Seed*: [1978] O.J. L286/23, [1978] 3 C.M.L.R. 434; *Pioneer Hi-fi*: [1980] O.J. L60/21, [1980] 1 C.M.L.R. 457; *SSI*: [1982] O.J. L232/1, [1982] 3 C.M.L.R. 703; *Peroxygen Products*: [1985] O.J. L35/1, [1985] 1 C.M.L.R. 481; *Sperry New Holland*; [1985] O.J. L376/21, [1988] 4 C.M.L.R. 306; *Sandoz*: [1987] O.J. L222/28, [1989] 4 C.M.L.R. 628; *Welded Steel Mesh*: [1989] O.J. L260/1, [1991] 4 C.M.L.R. 13; *UK Agricultural Tractor Registration Exchange*: [1992] O.J. L68/19, [1993] 4 C.M.L.R. 358 and *Viho/Parker Pen*: [1992] O.J. L233/27. The use of "like effects" orders in the transport sector can be seen in *French-West African Shipowners' Committees*: [1992] O.J. L134/1, and *Cewal, Cowac and Ukwal*: [1993] O.J. L34/20.

[4] As to when an infringement is terminated, see *Zinc Producer Group*: [1984] O.J. L220/27, [1985] 2 C.M.L.R. 108, at para. 92, where in the absence of clear evidence as to when exactly an infringement ended, the Commission exercised a presumption in the firm's favour that the infringement ended when the last recorded instance of the effect of the relevant agreement or practice occurred.

[5] See, for example, *Pabst and Richarz–BNIA*: [1976] O.J. L331/24, [1976] 2 C.M.L.R. D63; *Video-Cassettes*: [1978] O.J. L47/42, [1978] 2 C.M.L.R. 160; *Michelin*: [1981] O.J. L353/33, [1982] 1 C.M.L.R. 643, and *Fatty Acids*: [1987] O.J. L3/17. The legality of taking decisions after infringements have been terminated was established in Case 8/72, *Cementhandelaren* v. *Commission*: [1972] E.C.R. 977, [1973] C.M.L.R. 7.

[6] Case 7/82, *GVL* v. *Commission*: [1983] E.C.R. 483, [1983] 3 C.M.L.R. 645, at paras. 16–28. Applied by the Commission in *Roofing Felt*: [1986] O.J. L232/15, [1991] 4 C.M.L.R. 130; *Sugarbeet*: [1990] O.J. L31/32, [1991] 4 C.M.L.R. 629; *Bayer Dental*: [1990] O.J. L351/46, [1992] 4 C.M.L.R. 61; *Scottish Salmon Board*: [1992] O.J. L246/37, and *Zera/Montedison* and *Hinkers/Stähler*: [1993] O.J. L272/28.

[7] *Breeders' Rights: Roses*: [1985] O.J. L369/9, [1988] 4 C.M.L.R. 193; *Wood Pulp*: [1985] O.J. L85/1, [1985] 3 C.M.L.R. 474; *Decca Navigation System*: [1989] O.J. L43/27, [1990] 4 C.M.L.R. 627; *Auditel*: [1993] O.J. L306/50. In *Tetra Pak I (BTG licence)*: [1988] O.J. L272/27, [1990] 4 C.M.L.R. 47, the Commission made it clear that a declaratory decision may be used to warn the addressee and other firms who might undertake similar lines of conduct.

also be necessary for the imposition, by decision, of a fine.[8] It is also increasingly the Commission's policy to encourage actions before national courts to enforce the competition rules.[9] There is therefore a further public interest in producing declaratory infringement decisions.

6.18 There is some doubt whether the Commission can take a decision against a threatened or likely breach of the competition rules. Article 3 appears, by its terms, to be limited to cases where the Commission "finds that there is infringement."[10] It has therefore been argued that the Commission cannot take a decision against undertakings who have not yet concluded an agreement albeit that if it were concluded it might have the effect, or likely effect, on inter-State trade and competition required by Article 85(1). In *Polypropylene*, Advocate General Vesterdorf concluded that there is no place within the ambit of Article 85 for the introduction of a separate concept of attempt.[11] Could the Commission, for example, prohibit undertakings from entering into a joint venture agreement the terms of which had been submitted in draft to the Commission for comment? Advocate General Vesterdorf thought that the Commission had no power to break into the undertakings negotiations before an agreement is concluded. If the undertakings have already put the agreement into effect although it has not been formally signed then the Commission may take a decision.[12] But where there is in fact no agreement or practice, the Commission, it would appear, has no power to take a final decision under Article 3 to enjoin the parties from entering into the agreement. Even if interim measures might not be available in such a case, the Commission, having warned the parties, might fine heavily if they went ahead.

Positive measures

6.19 It is well established that the powers given to the Commission by Article 3 of Regulation 17 to require an infringement to be brought to an end, include the power to order, in appropriate circumstances, positive measures to be taken by the undertakings concerned.[13] In *Commercial Solvents*,[14] the Court of Justice said:

> "[Article 3] must be applied in relation to the infringement which has been established and may include an order to do certain acts or provide certain advantages

[8] *Napier Brown–British Sugar*: [1988] O.J. L284/41, [1990] 4 C.M.L.R. 196; *British Dental Trade Association*: [1988] O.J. L233/15, [1989] 4 C.M.L.R. 1021; *Building and Construction Industry in the Netherlands*: [1992] O.J. L92/1 and *Distribution of package tours during the 1990 World Cup*: [1992] O.J. L326/31.

[9] Thirteenth Report on Competition Policy, at point 218, and see *Aluminium*: [1985] O.J. L92/1, [1987] 3 C.M.L.R. 813 (para. 18.1 and 2). Most recently, see the Commission's Notice on co-operation between national courts and the Commission in applying Articles 85 and 86 of the EEC Treaty: [1993] O.J. C39/6

[10] But note the construction given to Art. 3 by the Court in *Camera Care Ltd.* v. *Commission* (Case 792/79R: [1980] E.C.R. 119, [1980] 1 C.M.L.R. 334).

[11] Case T–7/89, *Hercules* v. *Commission:* [1992] 4 C.M.L.R. 84, at p. 164.

[12] See, for example, *WANO–Schwarzpulver*: [1978] O.J. L322/26, [1979] 1 C.M.L.R. 403. Or if an agreement has been made but not yet implemented, see *Ansac:* [1991] O.J. L152/54.

[13] Cases 56 & 58/64, *Consten and Grundig* v. *Commission:* [1966] E.C.R. 299, [1966] C.M.L.R. 418.

[14] Cases 6 & 7/73: [1974] E.C.R. 223, [1974] 1 C.M.L.R. 309, at para. 45. Cited in *ECS/AKZO*: [1985] O.J. L374/1, [1986] 3 C.M.L.R. 273, at para. 99.

which have been wrongfully withheld as well as prohibiting the continuation of certain actions, practices or situations which are contrary to the Treaty."

The Court upheld the Commission's decision which having established a refusal to sell incompatible with Article 86, ordered the dominant undertaking to supply certain quantities of raw materials to the complainant and to submit proposals to prevent a repetition of the conduct complained of. Similarly, in the *Continental Can* case,[15] the Commission, having found the takeover to be contrary to Article 86, ordered a scheme for divestiture to be submitted within six months. Although the *Continental Can* decision was set aside by the Court of Justice for want of reasoning, the Court in the *Commercial Solvents* case clearly endorsed the type of remedial action ordered by the Commission in the earlier case, when it was said that: "the Commission may, if necessary, require the undertaking concerned to submit to it proposals with a view to bringing the situation into conformity with the requirements of The Treaty."[16] This may be particularly useful in cases where the agreement or abuse in question involves in whole or in part the creation or transfer of proprietary interests.

Whilst Article 85(2) declares the agreement to be automatically void, it does not appear to affect proprietary rights which may have accrued or been transferred under the agreement.[17] Under Article 86 nothing is rendered void automatically. It may, however, be necessary where, for example, a licence of industrial property or a joint venture falls foul of Article 85 or 86, for the proprietary interests to be readjusted in order to eliminate any anti-competitive effects and re-establish the pro-competitive situation. As Article 85(2) appears not to, and Article 86 certainly does not, involve automatic divestiture of interests or annulment of property transactions, then the Commission's order may, where necessary, order action to be taken to that end. In its recent decision in *Gillette*,[18] the Commission ordered the disposal by Gillette of its equity interest in Eemland and its interest as a creditor of Eemland within a specified period, failing which an independent third party had to be appointed, on terms approved by the Commission, to effect the disposal. Certain trademarks had also to be reassigned to Eemland. It has been suggested that in the case of joint ventures, the Commission would normally make the order which is least onerous for the undertakings concerned and which gives them the opportunity to choose between different possible ways of putting an end to the infringement.[19]

In *Automec II*, the complainant was refused an injunction requiring BMW to supply it with vehicles for distribution. The Court of First Instance started from the premise that freedom of contract remains the basic rule and therefore the "Commission cannot

---

[15] Case 6/72, *Europemballage Corp. and Continental Can Co. Inc.* v. *Commission*: [1973] E.C.R. 215, [1973] C.M.L.R. 199.

[16] Above, n. 77. And see the form of order used by the Commission in *GEMA*: [1971] J.O. L134/15, [1971] C.M.L.R. D35; *Hugin/Liptons*: [1978] O.J. L22/23, [1978] 1 C.M.L.R. D19, and *IJsselcentrale*: [1991] L28/32, [1992] 5 C.M.L.R. 154.

[17] See Case 40/70, *Sirena* v. *Eda and others*: [1971] E.C.R. 69, [1971] C.M.L.R. 260, and *Consten and Grundig* v. *Commission*, above, n. 13. There is no suggestion in either case that the applicability of Art. 85(1) (with consequent nullity under Art. 85(2)) affected the trade mark licences involved. And see Temple Lang, "Joint Ventures under the EEC Rules on Competition—1" (1977) *Irish Jurist* 15, 34, 35.

[18] *Warner-Lambert/Gillette and Others and BIC/Gillette and Others*: [1993] O.J. L116/21.

[19] Temple Lang, *op. cit.*, and see *St. Gobain/Pont a Mousson and Boussois-Souchon-Neuvesel*, Fourth Report on Competition Policy, at point 79. In the recent case of *Astra*: [1993] O.J. L20/23, the parties had themselves effected termination agreements during the proceedings. The Commission had however to address the question of what to do with contracts existing between the joint venture and third parties. See text to n. 28.

in principle be acknowledged to possess a power to order a party to enter into a contractual relationship where as a general rule the Commission has suitable means at its
disposal for compelling an enterprise to end an infringement".[20] Those means are presumably the finding of an infringement, the withdrawal where appropriate of the benefit of an exemption (block or individual) and a fine. On the other hand requiring
undertakings to refrain from conduct,[21] to amend terms of supply and to publish such
information specifically[22] or generally may not be objectionable as they are less positive in character. And as the Commission argued in *Automec II*, the position as between Article 85 and 86 may be different. Under Article 86 orders to supply may be
more justifiable, *e.g.* as in *British Midland* v. *Aer Lingus* where the Commission ordered Aer Lingus to authorise British Midland to issue and change air tickets and
other documentation in order to enable British Midland to interline on the Heathrow-
Dublin route.[23] Indeed in the *Magill* case,[24] the Court of First Instance, following
Commercial Solvents, upheld the Commission's decision requiring the BBC and
other broadcasting companies to make available to each other and to third parties their
listings and to permit their reproduction, such supply being subject to the payment of
reasonable royalties and compliance with any conditions needed to ensure comprehensive coverage of all their programmes, including those of sectional or sectorial
interest.

An undertaking may be required to bring matters to the notice of other parties. For
example, in *Hasselblad*,[25] the Commission ordered the undertakings concerned to inform other parties, including the public generally, of remedial steps. An order may be
policed by the use of a reporting obligation. So, in *ECS/AKZO*,[26] in addition to the restriction on future pricing behaviour and terms of supply, AKZO was asked to inform
customers that tying obligations were not binding and to produce compliance reports
(each year for five years) relating to prices offered and supplied. Similar requirements
were imposed in *Tetra Pak II*.[27] In *Astra*,[28] the Commission had to go further and address the question of contracts of third parties with a condemned joint venture. Article

---

[20] Case T–24/90, *Automec Srl* v. *Commission*: [1992] 5 C.M.L.R. 431, at para. 51. See also Subiotto, "The
Right to Deal with Whom One Pleases under EEC Competition Law: A Small Contribution to a Necessary Debate" [1992] 6 E.C.L.R. 234.

[21] See, *e.g. Soda-ash Solvay:* [1991] O.J. L152/21 and *Eco System/Peugeot:* [1992] O.J. L66/1.

[22] See *Hudson's Bay:* [1988] O.J. L316/43, [1989] 4 C.M.L.R. 340, where special notice had to be given to
two expelled members.

[23] [1992] O.J. L96/34, [1993] 4 C.M.L.R. 596. The decision recognises that the duty to interline is limited in
time to enable British Midland to develop its service.

[24] Case T–70/89, *British Broadcasting Corporation:* [1991] 4 C.M.L.R. 669, at paras. 71 and 72.

[25] [1982] O.J. L161/18, [1982] 2 C.M.L.R. 233. Similar requirements were imposed in *Chiquita:* [1976]
O.J. L95/1, [1976] 1 C.M.L.R. D28; *Gerofabriek:* [1977] O.J. L16/8, [1977] 1 C.M.L.R. D35 and *Johnson & Johnson:* [1980] O.J. L377/16, [1981] 2 C.M.L.R. 287. See also *FEDETAB:* [1978] O.J. L224/29,
[1978] 3 C.M.L.R. 524; *Bundesverband Deutscher Stahlhandel:* [1980] O.J. L62/34, [1980] 3 C.M.L.R.
193 (ECSC); *VBBB/VBVB:* [1982] O.J. L54/36, [1982] 2 C.M.L.R. 344, and *NAVEWA/ANSEAU:* [1982]
O.J. L167/39, [1982] 2 C.M.L.R. 193, *Publishers Association–Net Book Agreements:* [1989] O.J. L22/12
and *CNSD:* [1993] O.J. L203/27.

[26] Above, n. 14. AKZO challenged the fairness of certain of the measures imposed, in particular those relating to its ability to fix different prices. The Court of Justice rejected this plea, upholding the Commission's decision in this respect. See Case C–62/86, *AKZO* v. *Commission:* [1991] I E.C.R. 3359, [1993] 5
C.M.L.R. 215, at paras. 155–157.

[27] [1992] O.J. L72/1, [1992] 4 C.M.L.R. 551.

[28] Above n. 19.

3 of Regulation 17, the Commission said, "implies not only the termination of restrictive agreements between the parties, but also the elimination of restrictive effects agreements." The parties to the joint venture concerned were ordered not only to inform those third parties that the joint venture had been prohibited by the Commission but also to offer them a renegotiation of the terms of their contracts or the possibility of terminating their contracts subject to a reasonable period of notice. The Commission were prepared to allow, in the circumstances, the customer contracts to run under the original terms at the choice of the customer, recognising that the contracts would not necessarily have a foreclosing effect on the relevant market. If new elements appeared and foreclosure seemed likely, the Commission could take further independent proceedings relating to the contracts in question.

6.20 A decision finding an infringement may also impose a fine[29] in respect of the infringement and/or a periodical penalty payment[30] as a measure of compulsion to put an end to the infringement[31] or to compel performance of a positive obligation.[32]

Relationship with the statement of objections

6.21 Article 4 of Regulation 99/63 provides that the Commission: "shall in its decision deal only with those objections raised against undertakings and associations of undertakings in respect of which they have been afforded the opportunity of making known their views." But this does not mean that the decision must be a replica of the statement of objections. As the Court of Justice indicated in the *Quinine* case:[33]

> "In fact the Commission must take into account the factors emerging from the administrative procedure in order either to abandon such complaints as have been shown to be unfounded or to supplement and redraft its arguments both in fact and in law in support of the complaints which it maintains.
>
> The latter does not contradict the rights of the defence protected by the above-mentioned Article 4.
>
> This provision is observed if the decision does not allege that the persons concerned have committed infringements other than those referred to in the notice of complaints and only takes into consideration facts on which the persons concerned have had the opportunity of making known their views."

In the *GVL* case,[34] the Court of Justice said that Regulation 99/63 does not require the Commission to discuss all the observations on the statement of objections in the statement of reasons in the decision if those reasons are, of themselves, sufficient to

---

[29] Under Art. 15 of Reg. 17.
[30] Under Art. 16 of Reg. 17.
[31] On fines and penalties, see generally Chap. 7.
[32] As in *ECS/AKZO*: [1985] O.J. L374/1, [1986] 3 C.M.L.R. 273.
[33] Case 41, 44 & 45/69, *ACF Chemiefarma and others* v. *Commission*: [1970] E.C.R. 661, at paras. 92–94. See also the *FEDETAB* case: Cases 209–215 & 218/78, *Heintz van Landewyck and others* v. *Commission*: [1980] E.C.R. 3125, [1981] 3 C.M.L.R. 134, at paras. 67–74; Cases 96–102, 104, 105, 108 & 110/82, *NV I.A.Z. International Belgium SA and others* v. *Commission*: [1983] E.C.R. 3369, [1984] 3 C.M.L.R. 276, at paras. 9–11; Cases 142 and 156/84, *BAT and Reynolds* v. *Commission*: [1987] E.C.R. 4487, [1988] 4 C.M.L.R. 24, at para. 72, and, more recently, the Court of First Instance in Case T–66/89, *Publishers Association* v. *Commission*: [1992] 5 C.M.L.R. 120, at para. 65.
[34] Above, n. 6, at para. 12.

justify the Commission's conclusions. But the grounds for a decision must be sufficiently stated to allow the Court to check the legality and provide the party concerned with the information necessary for ascertaining whether the decision is justified.[35] Similarity between the statement of objections and the decision (*e.g.* as to the facts found) does not imply that the Commission has ignored the parties' contentions. Moreover, the Court will not, as a general rule, order an examination of internal Commission documents in order to verify whether the decision was influenced by factors other than those indicated in the statement of objections.[36] Such an examination would, in the Court's eyes, constitute an exceptional measure of inquiry. On the other hand this did not deter the Court of First Instance in *PVC*[37] ordering, by way of measures of inquiry, the Commission to produce minutes of a meeting of the Commission and the text of the decision adopted by the full Commission, where discrepancies were apparent on the face of the decisions as notified to the different parties.

The arguments of the parties

6.22   The decision should set out clearly and logically the essential legal and factual reasons upon which it relies. This may be done concisely. Although Article 190 of the Treaty requires the Commission to mention the factual circumstances justifying the decision and the considerations which led to its adoption, the Commission is not required to discuss all the points of fact or law which the parties may have raised in the administrative procedure.[38] The Commission has to make findings of fact rather than necessarily to set out all the arguments and evidence. But there may be cases where fairness requires that both versions are set out and analysed.[39] In fact the Commission often follows the good practice of responding, albeit sometimes briefly, to the parties' principal contentions.[40]

---

[35] *Dutch Books: VBBB & VBVB* v. *Commission*: (Cases 43 & 63/82) [1984] E.C.R. 19, [1985] 1 C.M.L.R. 27, at paras. 21 and 22. As has been pointed out, with the advent of the Court of First Instance, the Commission cannot afford to be economical with its reasons. Joshua, "The Right to be heard in EEC Competition Procedures" 15 Fordham Int. L.J. 16, at p. 87.

[36] Cases 142 & 156/84, *BAT and Reynolds* v. *Commission*: (Order of the Court on application for discovery) [1987] 2 C.M.L.R. 551 and Case 212/86, *ICI* v. *Commission*: [1987] 2 C.M.L.R. 500.

[37] Cases T 79, 84–86, 91–92, 94, 96, 98, 102 & 104/89, *BASF AG and others* v. *Commission*: [1992] 4 C.M.L.R. 357. The Court justified its stance by saying that the plea of non-existence is a matter of public interest which can be raised by the parties at any time and by the Court on its own motion.

[38] *Quinine*, above, n. 33. In Case 41/69, at para. 77, the Court said: "the Commission is not required to discuss all the issues of fact and of law which have been touched on by every interested person in the course of the administrative procedure". And see also Cases 56 & 58/64, *Consten and Grundig* v. *Commission*: [1966] E.C.R. 299, [1966] C.M.L.R. 418, at paras. 6 and 7; *Dyestuffs:* Cases 48, 49, 51–57/69, *ICI and others* v. *Commission*: [1972] E.C.R. 619, [1972] C.M.L.R. 557, Cases 55 & 59/69, at para. 22; Case 6/72, *Europemballage Corp. and Continental Can Co. Inc.* v. *Commission*: [1973] E.C.R. 215, [1973] C.M.L.R. 199, at para. 6; the *FEDETAB* case, above, n. 33, at para. 66; Case 86/82, *Hasselblad (GB) Ltd.* v. *Commission*: [1984] E.C.R. 883, [1984] 1 C.M.L.R. 559, at para. 17; Case 322/81, *Michelin* v. *Commission*: [1983] E.C.R. 3461, [1985] 1 C.M.L.R. 282, at para. 14; Case 41/83, *Italy* v. *Commission*: [1985] E.C.R. 873, [1985] 2 C.M.L.R. 368, at para. 46; the *Ford* case (25–26/84), at paras. 38–42; *BAT and Reynolds* v. *Commission*, above, n. 33, at para. 72, and Case 246/86, *Société coopérative des asphalteurs belges (Belasco) and others* v. *Commission*: [1989] E.C.R. 2181, [1991] 4 C.M.L.R. 96, at para. 55.

[39] Per A.G. Slynn in the *Hasselblad* case, above.

[40] See, *e.g. PVC*, above, n. 1 and LdPE, *ibid.*

Finding of infringement

6.23   In *Consten and Grundig*, it was argued that there was an infringement of an essential procedural requirement, because the finding that an infringement of Article 85 had been committed should have been included solely in the preamble to and not in the operative part (the dispositif) of the decision. The Court of Justice replied: "That finding constitutes the basis of the obligation of the parties to terminate the infringement. Its effects on the legal situation of the undertakings concerned do not depend on its position in the decision."[41] As regards the need to identify and assess every restrictive provision in the agreement, the Court has held that the Commission must make a finding on sufficient clauses to justify a finding of infringement. This does not require it necessarily to rule on each and every provision, provided the Commission has considered the agreement as a whole.[42] There are, however, some matters which the Commission must address fully in the decision. So, as the Court of First Instance said in *Italian Flat Glass*, a definition of the relevant market is a necessary precondition of any judgment concerning allegedly anti-competitive behaviour.[43]

Operative part of the decision

6.24   The operative part (the *dispositif*) of the decision is usually brief. It will identify the undertakings concerned, the nature of any infringement and, for example, order its termination and impose any fine or penalty. It is necessarily concise and where there may be doubt as to what conduct is in issue and should be terminated the Court of Justice has said that reference should be made to the preamble containing the statement of reasons.[44] Only if there remains insufficient clarity may the decision be annulled in this respect.

Number of infringements

6.25   In the *Sugar* case,[45] the Court of Justice said that there was no reason why the Commission should not make a single decision covering several infringements, even if some of the undertakings to which it is addressed are not involved in some of the infringements, provided each addressee is able to obtain from the decision a clear picture of the complaints and findings made against it. But the Commission is not necessarily obliged to deal with all infringements in one decision. A selective approach is permissible provided the rights of defence are not adversely affected by

---

[41] Above, n. 13, at paras. 10 and 11.
[42] *Ford*, above, n. 38, at paras. 10 and 11.
[43] Cases T 68 & 77–78/89, *Societa Italiano Vetro SpA and others* v. *Commission:* [1992] II E.C.R. 1403, [1992] 5 C.M.L.R. 302, at para. 159.
[44] Cases 40–48, 50, 54–56, 111 & 113–114/73, *Cooperatieve Vereniging "Suiker Unie" UA and others* v. *Commission:* [1975] E.C.R. 1663, [1976] 1 C.M.L.R. 295, at paras. 122 and 123. See also *NAVEWA/ ANSEAU*: [1982] O.J. L167/39, [1982] 2 C.M.L.R. 193, as to the positive measures to be taken. The *dispositif* does not state what has to be done, other than a duty to bring the infringement to an end. Para. 69, however, contemplates the publication of the change to non-discriminatory terms of issue of conformity labels.
[45] *Ibid.* at para. 111. See also the *FEDETAB* case, above, n. 33, at paras. 75–78. *Rolled Zinc:* [1982] O.J. L362/40, [1983] 2 C.M.L.R. 285, is an example of a decision concerning a number of infringements.

dealing with the infringements in separate procedures.[46] And indeed matters may be left on the Commission's file.

Negative clearance

6.26 The substance of a decision giving negative clearance is that "on the basis of the facts in its possession, there are no grounds under Article 85(1) or Article 86 of the Treaty for action on its part" in respect of the agreement, decision[47] or practice in question.[48] The decision is usually considered to be one which is favourable to the undertakings concerned. But it may not give the parties complete legal protection. First, the validity of the agreement under Article 85 might be challenged in a national court and although the latter might follow the Commission's decision, it is probably not bound by it and could take a different view, particularly if new or further facts were presented to it.[49] Secondly, the decision does not stop the Commission itself from reconsidering the agreement. The principle of *res judicata* does not apply to decisions of the Commission.[50] The Commission might, for example, be prompted into reexamining the agreement if a complainant were to put forward new evidence or to show that circumstances had changed or that the parties had not told the Commission the whole story in their application for clearance.[51] Finally, a decision of negative clearance will not prevent a national court or competition authority from applying national competition law (perhaps stricter than Community law) to the agreement.[52]

Article 7 of Regulation 17 enables the Commission to negate retroactively the prohibitions in Article 85(1) in the case of duly notified old and accession agreements which have been modified in order to be given negative clearance. Article 7 is discussed in more detail below.[53]

---

[46] See *Dutch Books*, above, n. 35, at paras. 28–31, dealing with the argument that the Commission should not have acted against the trans-national agreement without also dealing with the national agreements. Note the problems which arose at the earlier stage of the Commission's procedures in Cases T 10, 11, 12 & 15/92, *SA Cimetaries and others* v. *Commission*: [1993] 4 C.M.L.R. 243.

[47] Of an association of undertakings.

[48] Art. 2 of Reg. 17. Neither Reg. 1017/68 nor Reg. 4056/88 expressly give the Commission negative clearance decision making power. But Art. 3(2) of Reg. 3975/87 does so in relation to air transport.

[49] The Commission appears to agree with this view. See its answer to Written Question No. 1508/81: [1982] O.J. C85/6. And see A.G. Van Gerven in Case C–128/92, *H.J. Banks & Co. Ltd.* v. *British Coal Corporation*: Opinion of October 27, 1993, at para. 60. The new Notice on co-operation with national courts (above n. 35) urges the need to avoid conflicting decisions but does not deal with the problems described above. And, more generally, on the legal nature and effects of negative clearances, see Waelbroeck, "Judicial Review of Commission Action in Competition Matters," 1983 Proceedings of Fordham Corporate Law Institute 179, at 203.

[50] Lewis and Kemp, *Registration of Commercial and licence Agreements in the Common Market* (1962), p. 5.

[51] The effects of negative clearance as against third parties who lodge complaints are thus comparable to those of a decision rejecting their complaint. *Prodifarma I*: Case T–116/86, *Vereniging Prodifarma and others* v. *Commission*: [1990] II E.C.R. 843, at para. 70.

[52] *Perfumes* cases: Cases 253/78, 1–3, 37 & 99/79: [1980] E.C.R. 2327, [1981] 2 C.M.L.R. 99.

[53] See paras. 6.29–31. Note also the implications for the EEA, para. 6.31A.

A decision may at the same time give negative clearance to one agreement and exemption for another, or, for example, give negative clearance to one part of a distribution system whilst granting exemption for the remainder.[54]

Exemption

Generally

6.27   A decision granting exemption under Article 85(3) declares inapplicable the prohibition in Article 85(1). The agreement being exempted must satisfy the four conditions specified in Article 85(3) and, as the Court of Justice has indicated, this "necessarily implies complex evaluations on economic matters."[55] The Commission's reasoning in its decision must not only show how the agreement falls within Article 85(1) but must also set out the facts and considerations on which such evaluations are based.[56] The requirement has not prevented the Commission from producing on one occasion what has been termed the "short form" exemption.[57] An exemption decision will be for a fixed period of time and may be subject to conditions and impose obligations on the undertakings concerned.

Date of exemption—possible retroactive effect

6.28   Article 6(1) of Regulation 17 provides that a decision granting exemption under Article 85(3) must specify the date from which it shall take effect. Such date shall not be earlier than notification.[58] The fact that the agreement has been amended subsequent to the notification is no objection to fixing that date, provided the provision

---

[54] See *Schlegel/CPIO*: [1983] O.J. L351/20, [1984] 2 C.M.L.R. 179; *SABA's EEC Distribution System*: [1983] O.J. 376/41, [1984] 1 C.M.L.R. 676; *ABI*: [1987] O.J. L43/51, [1989] 4 C.M.L.R. 238; *X/Open Group*: [1987] O.J. L35/36, [1988] 4 C.M.L.R. 542; *Charles Jourdan*: [1989] O.J. L35/31, [1989] 4 C.M.L.R. 591; *Uniform Eurocheques*: [1989] O.J. L36/16, [1989] 4 C.M.L.R. 907 and *Dutch Banks*: [1989] O.J. L253/1, [1990] 4 C.M.L.R. 768. Contrast *Pronuptia*: [1987] O.J. L13/39, [1989] 4 C.M.L.R. 355, where the Commission in its exemption decision simply disregarded the "services" restrictions, considering them to be of little economic significance. See also *D'Ieteren materials*: [1991] O.J. L20/42, [1992] 4 C.M.L.R. 399, where the Commission gave negative clearance as an alternative to a declaration that the agreement was covered by a block exemption.

[55] Cases 56 & 58/64, *Consten and Grundig* v. *Commission*: [1966] E.C.R. 299, [1966] C.M.L.R. 418, at para. 53.

[56] *Ibid.*

[57] See *BP/Kellogg*: [1985] O.J. L369/6, [1986] 2 C.M.L.R. 619, where the legal assessment is comprised of just four short paragraphs. For the background, see the Eleventh Report on Competition Policy, at point 15. There remains, of course, a need to comply with Art. 190 of the Treaty. See para. 6.41. *BP/Kellogg* is the only example of the "short form" exemption. But the evaluations and justifications in others have not, on occasion, been overly long.

[58] See, *e.g. Langenscheidt/Hachette*: [1982] O.J. L39/25, [1982] 1 C.M.L.R. 181 where the agreements were made on March 31, 1977, came into force on January 1, 1978, but were not notified until November 6, 1979. The exemption could only run from the last date. But see *KSB/Goulds/Lowara/ITT*: [1991] O.J. L19/25, [1992] 5 C.M.L.R. 55 where the exemption appears to have been given from date of agreements (July 22) and not the notification (August 4). See also *Rich Products/Jus-rol*: [1988] O.J. L69/21, [1988] 4 C.M.L.R. 527 where the date of commencement of the exemption is neglected but the 10-year term computed from the date of the agreement, not the later notification date. Generally where agreements have to be modified the exemption commences from the date of amendment; see *Computerland*: [1987] O.J. L222/12, [1989] 4 C.M.L.R. 259 where certain agreements are only exempted from the time their adaptation (to the standard form agreement) has been confirmed to the Commission. For a more recent example, see *UIP*: [1989] O.J. L226/25, [1990] 4 C.M.L.R. 749.

which has been amended was of no practical importance (and therefore no bar to exemption) before the amendment was made.[59] Modification of an agreement to comply with the Commission's new standards and so obtain exemption does not exclude the possibility of the earlier unamended agreement being judged against the former standards and also being exempted.[60] There are two cases where exemption may be made retrospective to a date earlier than notification. First, agreements exempted from notification under Article 4(2) may be granted exemption under Article 85(3) retrospectively to the date of making the agreement.[61] Second, "old" agreements which have been notified within the time specified in Regulation 17 may be granted exemption from the date of making the agreement. Accession agreements which have been notified within the time specified in Regulation 17 may be granted exemption as from the date they became subject to the prohibition of Article 85(1), *i.e.* the relevant date of accession.[62] As will be explained below, both these exceptions have been carried over into the EEA, the second to deal with the case of agreements in existence at the date of entry into force of the EEA.

Retroactive validation—Article 7

6.29   Article 7 of Regulation 17 entitled "Special provisions for existing agreements, decisions and practices," enables the Commission to negate retroactively the prohibitions in Article 85(1) in the case of "old" agreements (and also "accession" agreements) provided they have been notified within the specified time. Article 7(1) provides as follows:

> "Where agreements, decisions and concerted practices in existence at the date of entry into force of this Regulation and notified before 1 August 1962 do not satisfy the requirements of Article 85(3) of the Treaty and the undertakings or associations of undertakings concerned cease to give effect to them or modify them in such manner that they no longer fall within the prohibition contained in Article 85(1) or that they satisfy the requirements of Article 85(3), the prohibition contained in Article 85(1) shall apply only for a period fixed by the Commission. A decision by the Commission pursuant to the foregoing sentence shall not apply as against undertakings and associations of undertakings which did not expressly consent to the notification."

Whilst the validity of the power given to the Commission by Article 7 is not beyond question,[63] its function and value have been acknowledged by the Court of Justice in relation to the so-called provisional validity of agreements.[64] An agreement which in its notified form satisfies the criteria of Article 85(3) can be exempted from the date of

---

[59] *ACEC/Berliet*: [1968] J.O. L201/7, [1968] C.M.L.R. D35. *Cf. Delta Chemical/DDD*: [1988] O.J. L309/34, [1989] 4 C.M.L.R. 535.
[60] *Grundig's EEC Distribution System*: [1985] O.J. L233/1, [1988] 4 C.M.L.R. 865. 61 Art. 6(2) of Reg. 17.
[61] Art. 6(2) of Reg. 17.
[62] *Ibid.* referring to Arts. 5(1), 25(2) and 25(5) of Reg. 17.
[63] See Oberdorfer, Gleiss, Hirsch, *Common Market Cartel Law* (2nd ed., 1971), p. 190 and the commentators referred to therein.
[64] Case 48/72, *Brasserie de Haecht* v. *Wilkin (No. 2)*: [1973] E.C.R. 77, [1973] C.M.L.R. 287. Provisional validity is discussed at paras. 10.04–11.

notification,[65] but a decision establishing nullity under Article 85(2) will have complete retroactive effect.[66] The power given to the Commission by Article 7(1) and which can only be exercised where the agreement in its notified form cannot be given negative clearance or be exempted under Article 85(3), gives recognition to the principle of legal certainty[67] and alleviates the otherwise automatic sanction of nullity.

6.30   Article 7 applies only in relation to "old" agreements (*i.e.* those in existence at the effective date of Regulation 17) and "accession" agreements (*i.e.* those in existence at the relevant date of accession and to which Article 85 applies by virtue of accession). Moreover such agreements must be notified within the specified time. For agreements in existence when Regulation 17 came into force, the relevant date is August 1, 1962 with the exception of agreements exempted from notification (*i.e.* those listed in Article 4(2) of Regulation 17[68]) which should have been notified before January 1, 1967.[69] "Accession" agreements should have been notified before July 1, 1973,[70] July 1, 1981[71] or January 1, 1986[72] as the case may be. Article 7 also requires that the undertakings must, either at their own initiative or at the request of the Commission, amend the agreement so that it is no longer caught by Article 85(1) or else satisfies the criteria of Article 85(3). In practice, therefore, Article 7(1) is applied by the Commission only in the context of a favourable decision, *i.e.* granting negative clearance[73] or an exemption.[74] Finally, it is important to note that Article 7(1) does not apply automatically but in the discretion of the Commission.[75] Co-operation with the Commission and a willingness to amend the agreement to comply are necessary.[76] It would appear that there can be a number of amendments on several occasions before a position is accepted where the agreement qualifies for Article 7.[77] Article 7 may not be applicable where the old agreement has been terminated and immediately replaced by a new agreement, even if it contains the same kind of restrictions on competition.[78]

---

[65] Art. 6(1) of Reg. 17. See previous para.; exemption may be retrospective.

[66] *Brasserie de Haecht (No. 2)*, above, at para. 27.

[67] *Ibid.* at para. 6. Parties to "old" agreements were not able to ascertain whether their agreement satisfied the criteria of Art. 85(3). On legal certainty generally, see paras. 8.22–24.

[68] Discussed at paras. 2.09–15.

[69] Art. 7(2) of Reg. 17 as amended by Reg. 118/63.

[70] In the case of the accession of Denmark, Ireland and the United Kingdom. Art. 25 of Reg. 17.

[71] In the case of the accession of Greece. Art. 25 of Reg. 17.

[72] In the case of the accession of Spain and Portugal. Art. 25 of Reg. 17.

[73] For example, *Zanussi*: [1978] O.J. L322/26, [1979] 1 C.M.L.R. 81, and *Industrieverband Solnhofener Natursteinplatten eV*: [1980] O.J. L318/32, [1981] 2 C.M.L.R. 308.

[74] For example, *Campari*: [1978] O.J. L70/69, [1978] 2 C.M.L.R. 397; *National Sulphuric Acid Association*: [1980] O.J. L260/25, [1980] 3 C.M.L.R. 429 renewed [1989] O.J. L190/22, [1980] 3 C.M.L.R. 429 and *SMM & T Exhibition Agreement*: [1983] O.J. L376/1, [1984] 1 C.M.L.R. 611.

[75] For an example of a case where the Commission considered it would not be able to exercise its discretion favourably, see *Dutch Bicycles*: [1978] O.J. L20/18, [1978] 2 C.M.L.R. 194.

[76] *Belgian Central Heating Agreement*: [1972] J.O. L264/22, [1972] C.M.L.R. D130. *Cf. Fine Papers*: [1972] J.O. L182/24, [1972] C.M.L.R. D94.

[77] *Cobelaz (No. 2)*: [1968] J.O. L276/13, [1968] C.M.L.R. D45.

[78] *VVVF*: [1969] J.O. L168/22, [1970] C.M.L.R. D1, and see *ASPA*: [1970] J.O. L148/9, [1970] C.M.L.R. D25.

Before taking any decision applying Article 7 the Commission must give the undertakings concerned the opportunity of being heard on any matter to which the Commission has taken objection.[79] Decisions taken in application of Article 7 must be published.[80]

6.31 The second sentence of Article 7(1) preserves the position of undertakings which did not expressly consent to the notification of the agreement. Thus a party to an agreement having refused or declined to perform its obligations on the ground that to do so would be contrary to Article 85(1) will be protected, for example, from an action for damages for breach of contract if the obligations are later validated by the Commission pursuant to Article 7(1).[81] It is, however, uncertain whether retroactive validation under Article 7(1) is effective as against third parties. Little help may be derived from the text in this respect; but it has been argued that it was the recognised intention of the Council that Article 7 should be effective as against third parties, wiping the slate clean of past illegality being the quid pro quo for conformity with the Treaty thereafter.[82]

EEA-Exemptions

6.31A The basic rule is that the competitive surveillance authority (*i.e.* the Commission or the EFTA Surveillance Authority, in accordance with the jurisdictional rules set out in Article 56 EEA)[83] shall specify in its decisions in application of Article 53(3) EEA the date from which the decision shall take effect. The general rule is that the date will not be prior to the date of notification of the agreement in question.[84] As under Regulation 17 agreements exempted from the notification obligation (*i.e.* those agreements which fall within the categories listed in Article 4(2) of Protocol 21—the mirror image of Article 4(2) of Regulation 17)[85] are excepted from this rule. There are also special transitional arrangements for agreements in existence at the date of entry into force of the EEA. The general rule that the date of an exemption decision cannot precede the date of notification does not therefore apply to an agreement in existence at the date of entry into force of the EEA and which is notified within six months of that date.[86] The EEA also contains a special rule modelled on Article 7 of Regulation 17 whose purpose and operation has been described above. Where agreements in existence at the date of entry into force of the EEA and notified within a six-month period thereafter are abandoned or modified in such a way that they no longer fall under the prohibition contained in Article 53 EEA or that they satisfy the requirements of Article 53(3) EEA, the prohibition contained in Article 53(1) shall apply only for a

---

[79] Art. 19(1) of Reg. 17, and see also Case 17/74, *Transocean Marine Paint Association* v. *Commission:* [1974] E.C.R. 1063, [1974] 2 C.M.L.R. 459.

[80] Art. 21(1) of Reg. 17.

[81] If the action is brought in a national court which is invited to proceed on the basis that the agreement is provisionally valid, the party seeking to rely on the illegality under Art. 85(2) might apply for the proceedings to be stayed pending the Commission's decision.

[82] Deringer, *The Competition Law of the European Economic Community* (1968), at para. 2116. But see *Hummel/Isbecque:* [1965] J.O. L2581/65, [1965] C.M.L.R. 242 where the Commission expressly reserved the rights of third parties.

[83] See para. 1.34A and B

[84] Protocol 21, Art. 6.

[85] See para 2.09–16.

[86] Protocol 21, Art. 6.

period fixed by the competent surveillance authority.[87] As in the case of Article 7 of Regulation 17, a decision by a competent surveillance authority using this power does not apply as against undertakings which did not expressly consent to the notification. Where parties to an existing agreement which is, under Article 4(2) of Protocol 21, exempt from notification, wish to take advantage of this rule they must notify the agreement within six months of the entry into force of the EEA, *i.e.* before July 1, 1994.

Conditions and obligations attached to exemption

6.32 Article 8(1) of Regulation 17 provides that conditions and obligations may be attached to a decision in application of Article 85(3).[88] This stems from Article 87(2) (b) of the Treaty which provides for regulations designed "to lay down detailed rules for the application of Article 85(3), taking into account the need to ensure effective supervision . . ." The Court of Justice in the *Transocean Marine Paint* case explained the purpose of conditions and obligations as follows:[89]

> "Since Article 85(3) constitutes, for the benefit of undertakings, an exception to the general prohibition contained in Article 85(1) the Commission must be in a position at any moment to check whether the conditions justifying the exemption are still present."

As will be explained in more detail below, it is not unusual for an exemption to be made subject to the obligation periodically to furnish specified particulars concerning the operation of the agreement and the effect on the market to the Commission.

Article 8(1) refers to both "conditions" and "obligations" and although the two terms may be used indiscriminately by both Commission and Court there is a difference between them as regards both meaning and legal effect.[90] A condition, which presumably may be either precedent or subsequent, is something upon whose fulfilment depends the exemption. Breach of or failure to satisfy the condition will result in the loss of the exemption and consequent nullity of the restrictions under Article 85(2). The fulfilment of an obligation is independent of the validity of the exemption. Although an undertaking which intentionally or negligently commits a breach of any obligation imposed pursuant to Article 8(1) may be fined,[91] the breach of an obligation does not automatically remove the exemption and trigger off the nullity under Article 85(2). A breach of an obligation may justify the revocation or amendment of the exemption but, if so, it has to be done by positive act of the Commission under Article

---

[87] Protocol 21, Art. 7.

[88] There are similar provisions in the transport regulations

[89] Case 17/74: [1974] E.C.R. 1063, [1974] 2 C.M.L.R. 459, at para. 16. It is not finally settled to what extent a party is entitled to have an offending agreement considered for a conditional exemption. See Cases 56 & 58/64, *Consten & Grundig* v. *Commission*: [1966] E.C.R. 299, 350, [1966] C.M.L.R. 418, 480. But in Case T–24/90, *Automec Srl* v. *Commission*: [1992] C.M.L.R. 431, at para. 75, the Court of First Instance said: "It follows that the Commission cannot be required to give a ruling . . . unless the subject matter of the complaint is within its exclusive remit, such as the withdrawal of an exemption granted pursuant to Article 85(3)." The grant of an exemption is, of course, also within the Commission's exclusive remit.

[90] The term "condition" is frequently used when "obligation" is legally correct. See, *e.g. Carbon Gas Technologie*: [1983] O.J. L376/17, [1984] 2 C.M.L.R. 275, or *SABA's EEC Distribution System*, above, n. 54, where the reporting conditions are merely misdescribed obligations. Contrast the recent decision under Reg. 1017/68, *Tariff structures in the combined transport of goods*: [1993] O.J. L73/38, where the *dispositif* refers to obligations when the preamble describes them as conditions.

[91] Art. 15(2)(b) of Reg. 17.

8(3) of Regulation 17. By contrast an exemption will not apply if and to the extent that a condition is not satisfied,[92] but may only be withdrawn in pursuance of, and on the grounds stated in, Article 8(3).[93] An example of the imposition of both conditions and obligations can be seen in the Commission's decision in *Bayer/BP Chemicals*.[94]

6.33   Any conditions or obligations imposed by the Commission must be within the ambit of Article 85, and, in particular, must be directed towards the purpose and objects of Article 85(3) as a means of exemption from the prohibition in Article 85(1) and towards the need to ensure effective supervision of the exemption. In *Transocean Marine Paint*, the Court of Justice said:[95] "in relation to the detailed rules to which it may subject the exemption, the Commission enjoys a large measure of discretion, while at the same time having to act within the limits imposed upon its competence by Article 85." Advocate General Warner considered that where the Commission imposed an obligation to supply information during the period of exemption then as a matter of law the Commission's powers were limited in two respects. First, the information must be relevant to competition in the relevant product within the Community and second, "the requirement should not be oppressive, in the sense of imposing on the [undertakings concerned] a burden disproportionate to the value of the information the Commission may obtain from it." The first limitation relates to competence in relation to Article 85, whilst the second is an application of the principle of proportionality which is part of the general Community legal order.

In practice, it is common for the Commission to impose an obligation on the undertakings benefiting from an exemption to supply information to the Commission periodically during the term of the exemption. The need for reporting obligations is not solely related to the time the exemption is to run (*i.e.* shortness) but also the nature of the agreement and the perceived potential detrimental effects on competition during that term.[96] In the case of an agreement between undertakings, the parties may be required to inform the Commission of any amendments, additions, etc., to the agreement or where they enter into new agreements.[97] Note the obligation to notify amendments, etc., does not dispense with the need to notify changes under Article 4(1) of Regulation 17 if the agreement is to continue to have the benefit of exemption.[98] The Commission also commonly requires the parties to notify it of the results of

---

[92] See, for example, *Vacuum Interrupters*: [1977] O.J. L48/32, [1977] 1 C.M.L.R. D67.

[93] See paras. 6.37–40. If a condition is not complied with, the prohibition in Art. 85(1) will apply, and the Commission could in theory fine under Art. 15(2)(a).

[94] [1988] O.J. L150/35, [1989] 4 C.M.L.R. 24. See also *Optical Fibres*: [1986] O.J. L236/30. *Cf.* the position under the ECSC Treaty. Both Arts. 65 and 66 speak only of conditions being attached to authorisations although in practice both types of "condition" are employed. See, for example, *Creusot/Loire/Ugine*: [1978] O.J. L242/10, [1979] 1 C.M.L.R. 349.

[95] Above n. 89, at para. 16.

[96] So no reporting obligations were imposed in *ARG/Unipart*: [1988] O.J. L45/34, [1988] 4 C.M.L.R. 513 (joint venture — 7 years) or *IVECO/Ford:* [1988] O.J. L230/39, [1989] 4 C.M.L.R. 40 (joint venture — 9 years), the Commission taking the view that further notification on renewal of exemption would suffice. See also *Scottish Nuclear, Nuclear Energy Agreement*: [1991] O.J. L178/31 (15 years). *Cf. Parfums Givenchy system of selective distribution*: [1992] O.J. L236/11 (5 years with reporting obligations).

[97] For example, *Beecham/Parke Davis*: [1979] O.J. L70/11, [1979] 2 C.M.L.R. 157 and *VW/MAN*: [1983] O.J. L376/11, [1984] 1 C.M.L.R. 621. And see *Campari*: [1978] O.J. L70/69, [1978] 2 C.M.L.R. 397, where the parties had to inform the Commission of the effects of certain clauses on exports.

[98] *P. & I. Clubs*: [1985] O.J. L376/2, [1989] 4 C.M.L.R. 178.

any arbitrations relating to the terms of the agreement.[99] In the case of a joint venture or specialisation agreement, the Commission may require the parties to submit reports on their activities in the field covered by the decision, on the working of the agreement and the development of the factual situations and market conditions in which the agreement is being applied.[1] In one decision the Commission went so far as to reserve the right to ask the parties to supply any other information that it deemed necessary to check that competition was not restricted more than the decision allowed.[2] Parties to such agreements may also be required to inform the Commission of the taking up of shares, the establishing of links between the managements of the parties, and any proposal for mergers (or takeovers) between the parties or one or more of them and a third party in the relevant sector.[3] Where a trade association is involved, the association may be required to keep the Commission informed of changes in the membership and to submit an annual report on the activities of the association including, for example, volumes of production and sales of members, and improvements in marketing and production or other statistical information.[4] Where the exempted agreement may give the parties the power, for example, to control or regulate participation in a distribution system, purchasing pool or trade exhibition, then the parties may be required to give details (for example, copy letters of expulsion or refusal) of the operation of such exclusionary powers, including the reasons given in particular cases.[5] It used to be less

---

[99] For example, *Kabelmetall/Luchaire*: [1975] O.J. L222/34, [1975] 2 C.M.L.R. D40; *GEC/Weir*: [1977] O.J. L327/26, [1978] 1 C.M.L.R. D42 and *Internationale Dentalschau*: [1987] O.J. L293/58 and *UIP*: [1989] O.J. L226/25, [1990] 4 C.M.L.R. 749. *Cf.* Reg. 4056/86, Art . 5 where the block exemption for liner conferences is made subject to a number of obligations including notification to the Commission of arbitration awards.

[1] For example, *ACEC/Berliet*: [1968] J.O. L201/7, [1968] C.M.L.R. D35; *MAN/SAVIEM*: [1972] J.O. L31/29, [1974] 2 C.M.L.R. D123; *United Reprocessors*: [1976] O.J. L51/7, [1976] 2 C.M.L.R. D1; *Sopelem/Vickers*: [1978] O.J. L70/47, [1978] 2 C.M.L.R. 146; *BPCL/ICI*: [1984] O.J. L212/1, [1985] 2 C.M.L.R. 330; *Olivetti/Cannon*: [1988] O.J. L52/51, [1989] 4 C.M.L.R. 940; *KSB/Goulds/Lowara/ITT*: [1991] O.J. L19/25, [1992] 5 C.M.L.R. 55. And see *Henkel/Colgate*: [1972] J.O. L14/14, where the Commission required the parties to inform it of all licences granted by the joint research subsidiary. The Commission has acknowledged that information so supplied may be treated as business secrets; see *Vacuum Interrupters*: [1977] O.J. L48/32, [1977] 1 C.M.L.R. D67 (technical reports).

[2] *ENI/Montedison*: [1987] O.J. L5/13, [1989] 4 C.M.L.R. 444. It will be interesting to see whether this becomes a standard clause.

[3] For example, *Henkel/Colgate*, above; *Fine Papers*: [1972] J.O. L182/24, [1972] C.M.L.R. D94; *Bayer/Gist Brocades*: [1976] O.J. L30/13, [1976] 1 C.M.L.R. D98; *Transocean Marine Paint*: [1974] O.J. L19/18, [1974] 1 C.M.L.R. D11, and Case 17/74: [1974] E.C.R. 1063, [1974] 2 C.M.L.R. 459, and *De Laval/Stork*: [1977] O.J. L215/11, [1977] 2 C.M.L.R. D69. *Cf. Enichem/ICI:* [1988] O.J. L50/18 where the Commission went further and imposed a condition not to maintain either directly or indirectly any interest in competing producers or distribution undertakings of a kind whereby they could influence the commercial conduct of such undertakings. **Note:** There have been a good number of ECSC authorisations where the Commission has imposed restrictions relating to interlocking directorships, management links, exercising of voting rights and acquisition of shares in competing undertakings. See, for example, *Société Française des Minerais Préréduits SA*: [1975] O.J. L277/22 (Art. 65) and *Thyssen/Rheinstahl*: [1974] O.J. L84/36, [1974] 2 C.M.L.R. D1, and *ARBED/Rodanger Athus*: [1978] O.J. L164/14, [1978] 2 C.M.L.R. 767 (Art. 66).

[4] *Transocean Marine Paint Association*, above; *Nuovo CEGAM*: [1984] O.J. L99/29, [1984] 2 C.M.L.R. 484.

[5] See *Omega*: [1970] J.O. L242/22, [1970] C.M.L.R. D49; *BMW*: [1975] O.J. L29/1, [1975] 1 C.M.L.R. D44; *Cematex*: [1971] J.O. L227/26, [1973] C.M.L.R. D135; *BPICA*: [1977] O.J. L299/18, [1977] 2 C.M.L.R. D43; *National Sulphuric Acid Association*, above, n. 74; *SMM & T Exhibition Agreement*, above, n. 74; *UNIDI*: [1984] O.J. L322/10, [1985] 2 C.M.L.R. 38; *Grundig's EEC Distribution System*: [1985] O.J. L233/1, [1988] 4 C.M.L.R. 865; *VIFKA*: [1986] O.J. L291/46, and *EMO*: [1989] O.J. L37/11, [1990] 4 C.M.L.R. 231.

common for the Commission to impose conditions (as opposed to obligations) under Article 8(1) of Regulation 17. Control of patents and know-how may cause their use,[6] or the need to limit the exchange of information between the parties.[7] In *Optical Fibres*,[8] a condition relating to the disclosure of prices and other sensitive information was imposed to reduce the risk of collusion between the joint venturers exempted. In *Ford/Volkswagen*,[9] a number of conditions (concerning the nature and range of products of the joint venture, the safeguarding of sensitive information, marketing strategies of the parents, and licensing of technology) were attached in order to ensure that a measure of product differentiation is maintained so that the partners should be able actively to compete with each other at the distribution level. In other cases conditions have been imposed relating to the closure of industrial plant,[10] levels of purchasing commitments[11] and the taking up of interests in competing undertakings.[12]

6.34   Before any such conditions or obligations can be imposed and particularly in the case where they may be far-reaching in their effect, the undertakings concerned must be informed of them and their views canvassed. This is so notwithstanding that Regulation 99/63, the "hearing regulation," does not expressly provide for it.[13] Finally, in some cases the Commission has avoided the need to impose formal conditions or obligations, preferring to rely on undertakings from the parties concerned and/or monitoring the agreements in question.[14] The Commission would closely monitor the working of the agreement before the exemption expires in order to assess whether a renewal could be granted, if it were requested.

Period of exemption

6.35   Article 8(3) of Regulation 17 provides that an exemption under Article 85(3) "shall be issued for a specified period." There is no stipulated minimum period and a variety of periods up to 20 years have been granted. As a general rule, the Commission grants exemption for a period which will allow the parties a reasonable time in which to realise the objectives of the agreement.[15] This is particularly so in relation to joint venture agreements where a considerable amount of investment is involved.[16] A long

---

[6] In *De Laval/Stork*, above, n. 3, the Commission exempted a joint venture imposing conditions on the exercise of patents and know-how both during the joint venture and following its dissolution in order that there should remain opportunities for the parties to the joint venture to compete. See, in particular, Art. 1 of the decision. *Cf. Rockwell/IVECO*: [1983] O.J. L224/19, [1983] 3 C.M.L.R. 709, "obligations" relating to the use by the undertakings of the patent rights and know-how vested in the joint venture company in the event of its dissolution.

[7] *Synthetic Fibres*: [1984] O.J. L207/17, [1985] 1 C.M.L.R. 787.

[8] [1986] O.J. L236/30.

[9] [1993] O.J. L20/14.

[10] *Bayer/BP Chemicals*: [1988] O.J. L150/35, [1989] 4 C.M.L.R. 24, but the Commission reserved the power to defer the closure. The Commission has since published a notice under Art. 19(3) of Reg. 17 seeking third party views on the postponement of closure of two LdPE plants: [1990] O.J. C44/11, [1993] 5 C.M.L.R. 86.

[11] *Jahrhundertvertrag*: [1993] O.J. L50/14.

[12] *Enichem/ICI* described above, n. 3.

[13] Case 17/74, *Transocean Marine Paint* v. *Commission*: [1974] E.C.R. 1063, [1974] 2 C.M.L.R. 459.

[14] *IATA Passenger Agency Programme*: [1991] O.J. L258/18, [1992] 5 C.M.L.R. 496 and *IATA Cargo Agency Programme*: [1991] O.J. L258/29, [1992] 5 C.M.L.R. 796.

[15] *Sopelem/Langen*: [1972] J.O. L13/47, [1972] C.M.L.R. D77; *Beecham/Parke Davis*: [1979] O.J. L70/11, [1979] 2 C.M.L.R. 157; *Carlsberg*: [1984] O.J. L207/26, [1985] 1 C.M.L.R. 735.

[16] *Beecham/Parke Davis*, above.

term may be necessary to enable the parties to rely on the enforceability of the agreement and to obtain a satisfactory return on capital. A longer term may also be justified where a market is highly competitive and there are no barriers to entry. On the other hand a short term only may be given for certain activities, such as a crisis cartel.[17] Exemption for a term over 10 years used to be the exception rather than the rule but is now more common. It has been granted in relation to some joint ventures,[18] exhibition agreements,[19] and specialisation/co-operation agreements.[20] On the other hand, the Commission has granted terms of only five years in the case of certain sensitive distribution agreements.[21] Terms of 10 years have become more standard in relation to franchising assignments[22] and standard terms etc in the insurance sector.[23] In a case falling outside a block exemption, it may still be relevant to set as the duration of the industrial exemption the same period as would have been given under the block exemption.[24] Each case will, of course, depend on its own particular circumstances, the type of business and nature of the transaction and the ascertainment of a "norm" or "average" would have only academic value as a statistic.

Renewal of an exemption under Article 85(3)

6.36   Article 8(2) of Regulation 17 provides that a decision granting exemption may on application be renewed provided that the requirements of Article 85(3) continue to be satisfied and the Commission considers the agreement suitable still for exemption. There is no special application form but it would seem sensible to make a request in writing accompanied by any requisite authorisation to act.[25] In *Metro II*,[26] the Court of Justice held that it is not necessary to use Form A/B. A simple application (by letter) with communication of amendments suffices where the "new" agreement does not

---

[17] *Synthetic Fibres*, above, n. 7. See also *Enichem* v. *ICI*, above, n. 3, 5 years for a restructuring agreement.

[18] *United Reprocessors*, above, n. 1 (15 years); *KEWA*: [1976] O.J. L51/15, [1976] 2 C.M.L.R. D15 (15 years); *GEC/Weir*, above, n. 99 (12 years); *BPCL/ICI*, above, n. 1 (15 years); *Optical Fibres*: [1986] O.J. L236/30 (15 years); *De Laval-Stork*: [1988] O.J. L59/33, [1988] 4 C.M.L.R. 714 (20 years); *Olivetti/Canon*: [1988] O.J. L52/51, [1989] 4 C.M.L.R. 940 (12 years); *Continental/Michelin*: [1988] O.J. L305/33, [1989] 4 C.M.L.R. 920 (20 years); *Eirpage*: [1991] O.J. L306/22, [1993] 4 C.M.L.R. 64 (11 years); *Fiat/Hitachi*: [1993] O.J. L20/10 (13 years), and *Ford/Volkswagen*: [1993] O.J. L20/14 (13 years).

[19] *Cematex*, above, n. 5 (12 years); *Internationale Dentalschau*: [1987] O.J. L293/58 (15 years); *British Dental Trade Association*: [1988] O.J. L233/15 (10 years); *EMO*: [1989] O.J. L37/11, [1990] 4 C.M.L.R. 231 (15 years), and *Sippa*: [1991] O.J. L60/19, [1992] 5 C.M.L.R. 528 (10 years).

[20] *ENI/Montedison*, above, n. 2 (15 years) and *BBC Brown Boveri*: [1988] O.J. L301/68, [1989] 4 C.M.L.R. 610.

[21] *Yves Saint Laurent Parfums*: [1992] O.J. L12/24, [1993] 4 C.M.L.R. 120 and *Parfums Givenchy*, above n. 96.

[22] *Computerland*: [1987] O.J. L222/12, [1989] 4 C.M.L.R. 259; *ServiceMaster*: [1988] O.J. L332/38, [1989] 4 C.M.L.R. 581; *Charles Jourdan*: [1989] O.J. L35/31, [1989] 4 C.M.L.R. 591.

[23] *P. & I. Clubs*: [1985] O.J. L376/2, [1989] 4 C.M.L.R. 178; *ABI*: [1987] O.J. L43/51, [1989] 4 C.M.L.R. 238; *TEKO*: [1990] O.J. L13/34, [1990] 4 C.M.L.R. 957; *Concordato Incendio*: [1990] O.J. L15/25, [1991] 1 C.M.L.R. 199 and *Assurpol*: [1992] O.J. L37/16, [1993] 4 C.M.L.R. 338.

[24] *KSB/Goulds/Lowara/ITT*: [1991] O.J. L19/25, [1992] 5 C.M.L.R. 55.

[25] Proof of a representative's authority to act is normally required in applications to the Commission. See Forms A/B and C. Community law may apply such rules strictly: see Case 289/83, *G.A.A.R.M.* v. *Commission*: [1984] E.C.R. 2789, [1986] 1 C.M.L.R. 602 (action before the Court dismissed because applicant failed to produce evidence of advocate's authorisation to act).

[26] Case 75/84: [1986] E.C.R. 3021, [1987] 1 C.M.L.R. 118, a paras. 30 and 31. But see *ARG/Unipart*: [1988] O.J. L45/34, [1988] 4 C.M.L.R. 513, where a further notification is expressly contemplated (para. 48).

differ in principle from the earlier, properly notified one. It will be necessary to make sure that the Commission is informed about the current status[27] of the agreement and to show that the criteria set out in Article 85(3) are still satisfied.[28] The undertakings might be expected to show that the two positive conditions (improvement in production/distribution of goods, etc.: fair share of resulting benefit to consumers) have materialised in the period since the initial grant of the exemption and continue to do so after renewal, and that the two negative conditions (indispensability of restrictions: competition not eliminated) have been and will remain satisfied. The Commission must verify whether the competitive situation on the relevant market has not changed to such an extent that the preconditions for the grant of an exemption are no longer fulfilled.[29] The Commission should, for example, have regard to any increases in the concentration ratio to see how it affects the competitive structure of the relevant market.[30] If the way in which the agreement is actually implemented differs significantly from the conditions originally notified and from the terms of the "new" agreement, this could affect renewal or even justify withdrawal of the existing exemption.[31] The degree of scrutiny on renewal required largely depends on the intervening changes in the legal and economic situation. Where the arrangements are substantially unchanged then, as the Court has indicated,[32] the Commission could take it as highly probable that the conditions of exemption were still fulfilled. The Commission must however pay particular attention to any material changes in the facts or circumstances of a given case since the initial exemption was granted. The entry into force of the EEA, for example, could be significant in certain cases. The Commission will also want to check that any conditions or obligations attached to the original exemption have been met and properly complied with.[33] Before taking a decision applying Articles 6 and 8 of Regulation 17 the Commission must give the undertakings concerned the opportunity of being heard on any matter to which the Commission has taken objection.[34] If conditions are to be attached to the exemption then the undertakings must be clearly informed, in good time, of the essence of the conditions in order that they may have the opportunity to submit their observations to the Commission.[35] Before any decision renewing the exemption can be taken, the Commission must publish a summary of the relevant application and invite all interested third parties to submit their observations within a time-limit of not less than one month.[36] The Advisory Committee must also be consulted.[37]

---

[27] The Commission will, of course, have the original Form A/B together with any other information acquired prior to the original decision or following it in pursuance of any reporting obligations attached to it. It is advisable (see Art. 8(3)(c), discussed below) to point out the extent, if any, to which any relevant terms or facts have changed.

[28] Useful reference may be made to the reasons given for exemption in the original decision.

[29] *Metro II*, above, n. 26, at para. 39.

[30] Case 43/85, *ANCIDES* v. *Commission*: [1987] E.C.R. 3131, [1988] 4 C.M.L.R. 821, at para. 13. See, *e.g. National Sulphuric Acid Association*: [1989] O.J. L190/22, [1990] 4 C.M.L.R. 612.

[31] *Metro II*, above, n. 26, at para. 32.

[32] *ANCIDES*, above, at para. 18.

[33] *De Laval-Stork*: [1988] O.J. L59/33, [1988] 4 C.M.L.R. 714.

[34] Art. 19(1) of Reg. 17.

[35] Case 17/74, *Transocean Marine Paint*: [1974] E.C.R. 1063, [1974] 2 C.M.L.R. 459.

[36] Art. 19(3) of Reg. 17. The minimum period of one month is usually specified. Respondents do not have a right to be heard under Art. 19(1). If they have a sufficient interest they may apply to be heard under Art. 19(2)—see *ANCIDES* v. *Commission*, above, n. 30, at paras. 7–10.

[37] Art. 10(3) of Reg. 17. One would expect this to be after the period specified in the Art. 19(3) notice in order that any relevant observations by third parties might be brought to the Committee's attention. But see

It would appear that an exemption can be renewed more than once[38] and also that different conditions or obligations may be attached to take account of any changed circumstances or deficiencies revealed since the earlier decision.[39] So far as timing is concerned, it is obviously desirable to apply for renewal before the expiry of the original exemption in order that the renewal can commence immediately thereafter, although a late application does not appear to be inadmissible.[40] While there are no special provisions for bridging the gap between the expiry of one decision and the commencement of another, a renewal decision is one taken "pursuant to Article 85(3)" and it may therefore be possible under Article 6(1) to make the renewal operative from a date earlier than its making[41] and thus avoid any period between the decisions when the status of the agreement under Article 85 might be uncertain.[42] A comfort letter may be used to bridge the gap whilst the Commission is reconsidering an agreement[43] or even as a substitute for a new exemption. Decisions taken in application of Article 8 must be published.[44]

Revocation of exemptions

6.37 Article 8(3) of Regulation 17 provides as follows:

> "The Commission may revoke or amend its decision or prohibit specified acts by the parties:
>
> (a) where there has been a change in any of the facts which were basic to the making of the decision;
>
> (b) where the parties commit a breach of any obligation attached to the decision;
>
> (c) where the decision is based on incorrect information or was induced by deceit;
>
> (d) where the parties abuse the exemption from the provisions of Article 85(1) of the Treaty granted to them by the decision.
>
> In cases to which sub-paragraphs (b), (c) or (d) apply, the decision may be revoked with retroactive effect."

The list of circumstances in which an exemption may be revoked or amended appears to be exhaustive and it is generally agreed to be so.[45] Having said this, the exhaustive

---

the Commission's decision in *Jaz-Peter*: [1978] O.J. L61/17, [1978] 2 C.M.L.R. 186.

[38] See the Commission's decision in *Transocean Marine Paint (No. 4)*: [1980] O.J. L39/73, [1980] 1 C.M.L.R. 694.

[39] See *EMO*: [1989] O.J. L37/11, [1990] 4 C.M.L.R. 231 and the earlier decision, *CECIMO*: [1979] O.J. L11/16, [1979] 1 C.M.L.R. 419.

[40] *Jaz-Peter*, above.

[41] On the retroactive effect of decisions, see Art. 6(1) of Reg. 17, above, para. 6.28.

[42] This appears to have been done in *Transocean Marine Paint (No. 4)*, above, and *SABA's EEC Distribution System*: [1983] O.J. 376/41, [1984] 1 C.M.L.R. 676. See also *De Laval-Stork*: [1988] O.J. L59/33, [1988] 4 C.M.L.R. 714; *Grundig's EC Distribution System*: [1994] O.J. L20/15 and *International Energy Agency*: [1994] O.J. L68/35. Cf. *Jaz-Peter*, above, n. 37 and *UNIDI*: [1984] O.J. L322/10, [1985] 2 C.M.L.R. 38.

[43] *Eurocheque: Helsinki Agreement*: [1992] O.J. L95/50.

[44] Art. 21(1) of Reg. 17.

[45] Deringer, *The Competition Law of the European Economic Community* (1968), at para. 2124; Goldman, *European Commercial Law* (1973), para. 616; Oberdorfer, Gleiss, Hirsch, *Common Market Cartel Law*

nature of the list should not prove a stumbling block to the Commission, as the grounds listed are sufficiently comprehensive to cover the vast majority of situations where such action may be desired. There are, however, no reported cases where an individual exemption has been revoked or amended in pursuance of Article 8(3). Withdrawal of the benefit of its block exemptions has however been considered on a number of occasions.[46] In its interim measures decision in *Mars*[47] the Commission withdrew the benefits of the block exemption in Regulation 1984/83 (exclusive purchasing) in so far as it was necessary to enable Mars to sell its ice-cream products to retailers who had exclusive contracts with Mars competitors on the German market. The benefit of the block exemption was formally withdrawn in the final decision.[48]

6.38   Ground (a) deals with the situation where there has been a change of facts. Not *any* change of facts is sufficient—there must be a change in the facts "which were basic to the making of the decision." A fact is presumably "basic" if it is material in relation to the satisfaction of one or more of the four conditions set out in Article 85(3). There is no requirement that the change be in any way brought about by the undertakings concerned or by the operation of the agreement or practice exempted. The structure of the market may change through a variety of causes such as natural and political crises, technical innovation or development, environmental costs, mergers, bankruptcies, etc. None of these need, in any sense, be caused by the undertakings concerned, but each may have an impact on the competitive structure of the relevant market. Factors which make it more competitive rather than less are unlikely to bring about the revocation of an exemption under ground (a). Where the undertakings concerned change the ambit of their agreement or the operation of their activities then this may amount to a change of facts within Article 8(3)(a). Much will depend on the circumstances and, as indicated above, the four conditions in Article 85(3) are the relevant marker. Where the terms of an agreement are amended, then it is a question of looking to see whether the agreement as amended is still substantially the same agreement as exempted or whether it contains further restrictions falling within the prohibition of Article 85(1). If the latter, and the restrictions are not severable, the agreement may no longer benefit from the exemption as it ceases to come within the terms of exemption. In short, it is a different agreement. If the new restrictions are severable, then their effects (*ex hypothesi*, contrary to Article 85(1)) may constitute a change of facts within the meaning of Article 8(3)(a) depending on their relationship with the reasons for the original exemption.[49]

   With reference to ground (b), mention has already been made of the nature and purpose of obligations imposed under Article 8(1) of Regulation 17. The failure to comply with the obligation must be serious. There is an alternative remedy available to the Commission to compel compliance with such an obligation in the form of a fine under Article 15(2)(b) and it is arguably a general principle of Community law that where there are several means available to an administrative authority, the least stringent if it

---

   (2nd ed., 1971), at para. 393.

[46] See, *e.g. Tetra-Pak I (BTG licence):* [1988] O.J. L272/27, [1990] 4 C.M.L.R. 47 and *Ecosystem/Peugot:* [1992] O.J. L66/1, [1993] 4 C.M.L.R. 42.

[47] Decision of March 25, 1992, not yet reported.

[48] *Langnese-Iglo GmbH:* [1993] O.J. L183/19.

[49] And see Oberdorder, Gleiss, Hirsch, *op. cit.*, at paras. 389–393.

is appropriate must be employed.[50] In any event, it must be doubtful whether the Commission can revoke an exemption for breach of an obligation which is designed simply to keep the Commission informed of the present state of play. Whilst lack of information may be disadvantageous to the Commission, it does not imply that the criteria of Article 85(3) are no longer satisfied or that the agreement does not have the beneficial effects contemplated by Article 85(3).

An exemption may be revoked where it is based on incorrect information or was induced by deceit. As in the case of ground (a), the information must, it is submitted, have been material to the granting of the exemption. There is no requirement that the incorrect information must have been supplied by the undertakings benefiting from the exemption. It is submitted that even if the information was incorrect the exemption should not be revoked or amended except where it can be shown that one or more of the conditions necessary for exemption would not be satisfied on the basis of the "correct" information. This should be so even if the incorrect information has been supplied by the undertakings concerned. If they have done so intentionally or negligently they may be liable to a fine under Article 15(1)(a) or (b) depending on the circumstances in which the incorrect information was supplied, and this may constitute sufficient action on the part of the Commission in connection with the default. When the exemption has been induced by deceit, then this may justify the revocation of the exemption being made retroactive in effect.

Ground (d) introduces the concept of abuse of an exemption.[51] This term is nowhere defined and some guidance may be sought from the definition of abuse within the context of Article 86. An example might be where an undertaking uses an "exempted" system of selective distribution to facilitate the maintenance of resale prices or to police an undisclosed export ban or where a joint pricing arrangement led to the fixing of extremely low prices which dissuaded new entrants or competitors in the market.[52] Where the undertaking concerned does not have a dominant position then the mere exercise of the exemption can hardly be an abuse. The Court of Justice has, however, taken the view that the fact that an agreement may benefit from exemption under Article 85(3) does not prevent it from being an abuse within the meaning of Article 86.[53]

6.39 Article 8(3) expressly provides that where ground (b), (c) or (d) apply, the exemption may be revoked with retroactive effect. As mentioned above in connection with ground (c), this may be appropriate where some element of fraud or deceit has been employed in connection with the original decision. Beyond this, it is submitted that the circumstances must be particularly serious to justify the taking of such a measure. The general principle of legal certainty[54] should be respected except where the public interest in retrospectively enforcing the competition rules clearly outweighs it. The Commission also has the option under Article 8(3) of taking a decision

---

[50] On the principle of minimum intervention, see para. 8.27.

[51] *Cf.* s. 12(1), No. 1 of the German Act against Restraints of Competition (Gesetz gegen Wettbewerbsbeschränkungen).

[52] See the example given in *Scottish Nuclear, Nuclear Energy Agreement*, above, n. 96, at para. 41.

[53] See Case 85/76, *Hoffmann-La Roche* v. *Commission*: [1979] E.C.R. 461, [1979] 3 C.M.L.R. 211, at para. 116, and, more recently and in some detail, the Court of First Instance in Case T–51/89, *Tetra Pak Rausing* v. *Commission*: [1990] II E.C.R. 309, [1991] 4 C.M.L.R. 334, at para. 21.

[54] In particular, the principle of the security of legal transactions. See Oberdorfer, Gleiss, Hirsch, *op. cit.*, at para. 393. On the principle of legal certainty, see, generally, paras. 8.22–24.

prohibiting specified acts and can enforce such order by sanctions under Articles 15 and 16.

6.40 Before the Commission takes a decision under Article 8(3), it must make its objections known to the undertakings concerned and give them the opportunity of being heard on the matters to which the Commission has taken objection.[55] Unlike the case of the renewal of an exemption, where the undertakings concerned might reasonably be expected to show that the conditions necessary for an exemption will continue to be satisfied, the burden of proof in revocation proceedings would appear to be on the Commission, not merely to show that there are "grounds" but also that such grounds give sufficient reason to justify revocation, prospectively or retrospectively as the case may be. The Advisory Committee must also be consulted.[56] The Commission's decision must be published.[57] The decision takes effect on notification to the undertakings concerned and may be the subject of appeal before the Court.[58] It has been suggested that the Commission may not be entitled to exercise its powers under Article 8(3) where there is undue delay on its part.[59] But, it is submitted, the disadvantage to the parties in the Commission's acting after a delay must be balanced against the public interest in restoring competition. Revocation without retroactive effect might be appropriate in some circumstances.

General points on decisions

Decisions must give reasons

6.41 Article 190 of the Treaty requires the Commission to state the reasons on which its decisions are based. The purpose of this requirement was most clearly stated by the Court of Justice in *Germany* v. *Commission*:[60]

> "In imposing upon the Commission the obligation to state reasons for its decisions, Article 190 is not taking mere formal considerations into account, but seeks to give an opportunity to the parties of defending their rights, to the Court of exercising its supervisory function and the Member States and all interested nationals of ascertaining the circumstances in which the Commission has applied the Treaty."

The Commission must therefore set out in its decision "in a concise but clear and relevant manner, the principles of law and fact upon which it is based and which are necessary in order that the reasoning which led the Commission to its decision may be understood."[61] Article 190 does not require the Commission to discuss all the matters of fact and of law which may have been raised by every party or dealt with during the administrative proceedings. The statement of reasons must, as indicated, be sufficient

---

[55] Art. 19(1) of Reg. 17.
[56] Art. 10(3) of Reg. 17.
[57] Art. 21(1) of Reg. 17.
[58] Arts. 191 and 173 of the Treaty.
[59] Deringer, *op. cit.*, at para. 2128 and the commentators cited therein.
[60] Case 24/62: [1963] E.C.R. 63, 69, [1963] C.M.L.R. 347, 367. For a more recent statement of the principle, see Case 42/84, *Remia and Nutricia* v. *Commission:* [1985] E.C.R. 2545, [1987] 1 C.M.L.R. 1, at para. 26.
[61] See n. 60, above.

to allow the Court to exercise its power of review of the decision's legality, and to provide the undertakings concerned with the information necessary to enable them to decide whether or not the decision is well founded.[62] The Court has held that the Commission is not obliged to provide lengthy explanations of an anti-competitive feature of an agreement where the effects on competitors are obvious.[63] But, as the Court of First Instance has indicated, a definition of the relevant market is a necessary precondition of any judgment concerning allegedly anticompetitive behaviour.[64] The length and amount of detail required in relation to a particular decision will depend not only on the nature of the circumstances and facts of the case, but also on the type of decision and its novelty. Thus a procedural decision (*i.e.* a decision ordering the supply of information or the inspection of books and business records under Articles 11 and 14 of Regulation 17 respectively) need not be as lengthy or detailed in its reasoning as a final decision finding infringement of Article 85 or 86.[65] As regards novelty, in the *Papiers Peints* case,[66] the Court said:

> "Although a decision which fits into a well-established line of decisions may be reasoned in a summary manner, for example by a reference to those decisions, if it goes appreciably further than the previous decisions, the Commission must give an account of its reasoning."

If the Commission's decision breaks new ground, its legal reasoning must therefore be fuller.[67] When rejecting a complaint it is sufficient that the Commission should state the reasons for which it did not consider it possible to hold that an infringement of the competition rules had occurred. The Commission is not under a duty to explain any differences between its final assessment and the provisional assessment in its statement of objections.[68]

---

[62] *Dutch Books*: Cases 43 & 63/82, *VBBB & VBVB* v. *Commission*: [1984] E.C.R. 19, [1985] 1 C.M.L.R. 27, at para. 22. See also Cases 240–242, 261, 262, 268 & 269/82, *Stichting Sigarettenindustrie (SSI)* v. *Commission*: [1985] E.C.R. 3831, [1987] 3 C.M.L.R. 661, at para. 88; Cases 96–102, 104, 105, 108 & 110/82, *NV I.A.Z. International Belgium SA and others* v. *Commission*: [1983] E.C.R. 3369, [1984] 3 C.M.L.R. 276, para. at 37; Cases 142 & 156/84, *BAT and Reynolds* v. *Commission*: [1987] E.C.R. 4487, [1988] 4 C.M.L.R. 24, at para. 72; *Remia and Nutricia*, above, at para. 26; Case T–66/89, *Publishers Association* v. *Commission*: [1992] 5 C.M.L.R. 120, at para. 75 and Case T–44/90, *La Cinq* v. *Commission*: [1992] II E.C.R. 1, [1992] 4 C.M.L.R. 449, at para. 42.

[63] Case 272/85, *ANTIB* v. *Commission*: [1987] E.C.R. 2201, [1988] 4 C.M.L.R. 677 at para. 23. The Court seems to be echoing its approach in Case 2/56, *Geitling* v. *High Authority*: [1957–58] E.C.R. 3, at 15 where it said that it is not necessary "to state independent and exhaustive reasons" for each part of a decision where "sufficient reason can be deduced from the context of all the findings stated in support of the decision as a whole."

[64] Case T 68 & 77–78/89, *Società Italiano Vetro Spa and others* v. *Commission*: [1992] II E.C.R. 1403, [1992] 5 C.M.L.R. 302, at para. 159.

[65] See, generally, Case 31/59, *Acciaierie e Tubificio di Brescia* v. *High Authority*: [1960] E.C.R. 71, and Case 136/79, *National Panasonic* v. *Commission*: [1980] E.C.R. 2033, [1980] 3 C.M.L.R. 169, discussed at paras. 3.24–26.

[66] Case 73/74, *Groupement des Fabricants de Papiers Peints de Belgique* v. *Commission*: [1975] E.C.R. 1491, [1976] 1 C.M.L.R. 589, at para. 31. Distinguished in *BAT and Reynolds,* above, n. 62, at para. 71.

[67] Lack of reasoning or inadequate or defective reasoning may amount to an infringement of an essential procedural requirement or an infringement of the Treaty within the meaning of Art. 173. See paras. 9.15 and 9.17.

[68] Cases 142 & 156/84R, *BAT and Reynolds* v. *Commission*: (Order of the Court) [1987] 2 C.M.L.R. 551, at para. 15.

Statement of the right to appeal the Commission's decision

6.42 Regulation 17 expressly provides that a procedural decision under Article 11 or 14 must specify the right to have the decision reviewed by the Court.[69] There is no such express requirement in the case of final decisions.[70] In the *Quinine* case,[71] an applicant complained that "the Commission violated a general principle of law to the effect that persons concerned must be made aware of their rights of action and of the limits fixed for this purpose." The Court of Justice held that the submission was irrelevant because the application had in fact been lodged within the prescribed time. The Court therefore did not rule on whether such a general principle existed as part of Community law. Advocate General Gand thought not.

Errors, formal and clerical

6.43 In the *Sugar* case,[72] the name of one of the undertakings concerned was left out of one article in the operative part (the *dispositif*) of the Commission's decision through inadvertence. The Court of Justice held that the article in question could not apply to that undertaking and therefore the undertaking could not be said to have committed the infringement the subject of the article notwithstanding that the main body of the decision may have indicated its possible involvement. The Court said:[73] "For the purpose of determining the persons to whom a decision, which finds that there has been an infringement, applies, only the operative part of the decision must be considered, provided that it is not open to more than one interpretation."

The fact that some undertakings are clearly named may be sufficient to indicate that others (not named) are not the subject of the decision. By contrast, the mere fact that the decision is given under a title in the *Official Journal* which differs from that used in the version notified to the undertakings concerned will not affect the validity of the decision. In the *Continental Can* case,[74] the Court of Justice rejected an argument to the contrary based on the fact that the decision published in the *Official Journal* had been entitled "Continental Can Company" whilst the decision notified to the undertakings (and therefore binding) had been entitled "Europemballage Corporation." Similarly, the Court may not allow a party to rely on a clerical error in the text of a decision. In the *Sugar* case,[75] the French version of the decision referred by mistake at one point to "1969/70" when the correct date should have been "1968/69". One undertaking claimed that it was entitled to rely on the date in the French version being the version of the decision which had been notified to him. The Court rejected this argument, saying that it was clear both from the Commission's statement of objections and

---

[69] See Arts. 11(5) and 14(3) of Reg. 17.
[70] Or in the case of interim decisions and provisional decisions.
[71] Case 41, 44 & 45/69, *ACF Chemiefarma and others* v. *Commission*: [1970] E.C.R. 661, at paras. 97 and 98.
[72] Cases 40–48, 50, 54–56, 111 & 113–114/73, *Cooperatieve Vereniging "Suiker Unie" UA and others* v. *Commission*: [1975] E.C.R. 1663, [1976] 1 C.M.L.R. 295, at paras. 311–317.
[73] *Ibid.* at para. 315.
[74] Case 6/72, *Europemballage Corp. and Continental Can Co. Inc.* v. *Commission*: [1973] E.C.R. 215, [1973] C.M.L.R. 199, at para. 10. And see Cases 56 & 58/64, *Consten and Grundig* v. *Commission*: [1966] E.C.R. 299, [1966] C.M.L.R. 418, at paras. 1 and 2, where the Court rejected the complaint that the decision was defective because it had been referred to as a directive in the *Official Journal*. The text addressed to the parties referred to a decision and this text, the Court said, was the authentic one.
[75] Above, n. 72, at paras. 227–232.

from the undertaking's own pleading before the Court that "1968/69" was the correct date. There was also a clerical error in the Commission's decision in *Hasselblad* (a reference to clauses 22 and 27 of an agreement, instead of 23 and 26) but, the Court of Justice held, that error could not have had any material effect on the applicant's understanding of the Commission's objections.[76]

Notification of decisions

6.44 Article 191 of the Treaty provides that decisions shall be notified to those to whom they are addressed and shall take effect upon such notification. The essential features of such notification were set out by the Court of Justice in the *Continental Can* case,[77] as follows: "A decision is duly served within the meaning of the Treaty if it is communicated to its addressee and the addressee has been enabled to take notice of it."[78] The Court held that if in fact a decision has been served on an undertaking then it cannot invoke its own refusal to take notice of the decision to make such service invalid. In this respect it does not seem to matter that the addressee is situate outside the Community.[79] The date of receipt may become critical; for example, for computing the time-limit for proceedings under Article 173. In *Bayer*,[80] the decision was sent by registered letter and Bayer's post-room acknowledged receipt by completing and sending off the tear-off label. But with the decision the Commission enclosed a separate acknowledgement of receipt form which was completed by Bayer's legal office some five days later. The Court of First Instance held that a registered letter with an advice of delivery slip was a suitable method of giving notice of a Commission decision as it enabled the date from which time runs to be determined. The inclusion in the envelope of the acknowledgement of receipt form was in no way irregular and, the Court held, did not detract from the decision having been validly notified by completion of tear-off advice of delivery slip. The Commission was not obliged to alert the firm to the discrepancy between the two receipts.

In the *Dyestuffs* case,[81] the Court of Justice held that irregularities in the procedure of notification of a decision cannot invalidate the decision itself. The Court described

---

[76] Case 86/82, *Hasselblad (GB) Ltd.* v. *Commission*: [1984] E.C.R. 883, [1984] 1 C.M.L.R. 559, at para. 40.

[77] Above, at para. 10. Applied in Case 374/87, *Orkem* v. *Commission*: [1989] E.C.R. 3283, [1991] 4 C.M.L.R. 502, where there was confusion between a parent company and its subsidiary and a question as to whether there had been an adequate prior request under Art. 11(1) of Reg. 17 to the party concerned. The Court declined to take the "unity of undertakings" route (see para 1.07), relying on the fact that both companies had replied to requests addressed by the Commission to one or other of them.

[78] It is a nice question, therefore, whether a decision may be addressed to an unnamed party who may at some time in the future fall within a given class. See Art. 4 of the decision in *International Energy Agency*: [1983] O.J. L376/30, [1984] 2 C.M.L.R. 186, which purports to apply the decision to any oil company which may later be asked to participate in an emergency oil allocation system by the IEA, by any government or by the NESO, and to a holding company, a fellow subsidiary or a subsidiary company of such an oil company.

[79] *Continental Can*, above, n. 74, and *Dyestuffs*: Cases 48, 49, 51–57/69, *ICI and others* v. *Commission*: [1972] E.C.R. 619, [1972] C.M.L.R. 557.

[80] Case T–12/90, *Bayer* v. *Commission*: [1991] II E.C.R. 219, [1993] 4 C.M.L.R. 30.

[81] Above, (Case 48/69). ICI had argued that the Commission, by providing in its decision that notification could be made at the registered office of its subsidiaries in the Common Market, and by proceeding accordingly, had infringed the Treaty, or at least an essential procedural requirement. The plea was rejected. Not only did the Court make the point set out in the text above, it went on to say that ICI had complete knowledge of the text of the decision and had exercised its rights to bring an action within the prescribed time-limits. The question of any irregularity was, therefore, in the opinion of the Court, immaterial.

the notification as being "external to the legal act." It acknowledged, however, that although the validity of the decision was not impaired by some irregularity in notification, the irregularity might prevent the time for bringing an action (for example, for annulment under Article 173 of the Treaty) from starting to run. In *NAVEWA/ ANSEAU*, the decision was published before it was communicated to the parties. The Court of Justice said that however regrettable such a procedure may be, when a decision has been adopted measures taken after its adoption cannot affect its validity.[82]

Amendment of decisions

6.45 Article 8 of Regulation 17 expressly provides for the renewal, amendment and revocation of decision granting exemption under Article 85(3). The provisions of Article 8 are described above.[83] It seems, however, that decisions under Article 3 also may be renewed or amended although there is no express provision in Regulation 17 dealing with this. Interim decisions will be made for a limited period of time and, as the Court of Justice has suggested, there may be successive decisions[84] tailored to the needs and circumstances of the case. In this respect, such decisions can therefore be renewed or amended. Final decisions under Article 3 are not limited in time and therefore renewal is hardly appropriate. It does seem, however, that they can be amended. In its decision in *GEMA*,[85] the Commission required the German authors' rights society to take certain specified measures in relation to its constitution and contracts to remedy the abuse found by the Commission. The measures were required to be taken within six months of the decision. By its later decision, *GEMA (No. 2)*,[86] the Commission accepted an alternative solution suggested by the society in relation to one of the measures ordered by the Commission and replaced the article of the original decision. It is important to note that the amendment concerned the method by which the abuse could be remedied and did not affect the legal reasoning and findings in the decision. The Commission is unlikely to accept any change here, and the undertaking's best course is to appeal the decision to the Court. Having said this, it is clear that the Commission is prepared to and can, by a further decision, amend a decision based on an error of fact. In *NAVEWA/ANSEAU*,[87] it amended its earlier decision of the same name[88] by removing Bosch from the list of those undertakings fined. The Commission accepted the evidence adduced by Bosch that it did not become a party as early as the Commission had first found.[89]

---

[82] Above, n. 62, at para. 16. Followed in Case 85/87, *Dow Benelux* v. *Commission*: [1989] E.C.R. 3137, [1991] 4 C.M.L.R. 410, at para. 49. The conduct of officials acting outside their powers under Art. 14(3) of Reg. 17 (see para 3.31–37) cannot affect the validity of the decision itself.

[83] See para. 6.36.

[84] Case 792/79R: *Camera Care*: [1980] E.C.R. 119, [1980] 1 C.M.L.R. 334.

[85] [1971] J.O. L134/15, [1971] C.M.L.R. D35.

[86] [1972] J.O. L166/22, [1972] C.M.L.R. D115.

[87] [1982] O.J. L325/20.

[88] [1982] O.J. L167/39, [1982] 2 C.M.L.R. 193.

[89] The result was that the Commission still found Bosch a party but no longer liable to a fine. The Commission later fined IPTC Belgium for its participation in the agreement which it had originally ascribed to Bosch. See *IPTC Belgium*: [1983] O.J. L376/7, [1984] 2 C.M.L.R. 131.

Delegation of powers

6.46 As indicated in Chapter 1, competition policy is only one part of the Commission's overall responsibility and, as a practical matter, not every procedural step in every case could be dealt with by the Commissioners personally. Community regulations[90] provide for the delegation of powers[91] in order to facilitate the day to day working of the Commission. The Court has recognised the need to prevent the rule of discussion in full session from leading to complete paralysis.[92] Accordingly, certain tasks have been delegated to the Commissioner responsible for competition who in turn may sub-delegate to the Director-General of DG IV and the Directors of the different directorates within DG IV. Such delegation is limited in its extent both by regulation and by the general principles of Community law laid down by the Court,[93] and the principle of collective responsibility safeguarded in practice by the Commission's use of certain procedural checks.[94] Decisions taken by delegation are nevertheless decisions taken on behalf of the Commission and are subject to judicial review by the Court in just the same way as if they had been discussed by the full Commission.[95]

Certain matters therefore either cannot or have not been delegated and remain to be dealt with by the Commissioners. Perhaps most important among these are decisions under Articles 2 (negative clearance), 3 (termination of infringements and interim measures), 6, 7, 8 (exemptions), 15 and 16 (fines and penalties, including preliminary decisions under Article 15(6)). This issue was central to the ruling by the Court of First Instance in *PVC* that the Commission's decision was non-existent. The full Commission had only agreed the supposed authentic text in three languages (English, French and German) and not in Dutch or Italian, the languages of certain of the undertakings to whom the decision was addressed. The decision, with some alterations, was later adopted in these languages by the Commissioner for Competition. The Court of

---

[90] Reglement Interieur de la Commission: [1967] J.O. L147/1, as amended by Commission decision of July 23, 1975: [1975] O.J. L199/43. Art. 27 of the Rules of Procedure provides as follows: "Subject to the principle of collegiate responsibility being respected in full the Commission may empower its members to take, in its name and subject to its control, clearly defined measures of management or administration. Officials may also be empowered to take such measures if this is indispensable for the Commission properly to be able to fulfil its tasks. Unless they have been delegated to him personally powers vested in an official shall be valid for his deputy. Power conferred in this way may not be sub-delegated except to the extent expressly laid down in the enabling decision. The provisions of this article shall not affect the rules concerning delegation in respect of financial matters and staff administration." The principle of collegiate responsibility, *i.e.* that the Commission must act collectively and that decisions are taken by a majority of votes, is found in Art. 17 of the Merger Treaty.

[91] See, generally, the House of Lords Select Committee on the European Communities, Commission's Powers of Investigation and Inspection, Session 1983–84, 18th Report, at paras. 30, 31 and 55.

[92] Case 5/85, *AKZO Chemie BV and AKZO Chemie U.K. Ltd.* v. *Commission*: [1986] E.C.R. 2585, [1987] 3 C.M.L.R. 716, at para. 30. And see Art. 16 of the Merger Treaty which requires the Commission to adopt its rules of procedure so as to ensure that both it and its departments operate.

[93] See Case 9/56, *Meroni* v. *High Authority*: [1957–58] E.C.R. 133, discussed at para. 9.10, and the other cases mentioned by Schermers, *Judicial Protection in the European Communities*, at paras. 257–263.

[94] In *AKZO* (above, at para. 32), the Commission informed the Court that decisions on delegation are taken at meetings of the full Commission and authority is delegated only to certain persons and for certain types of measures of routine management or administration. The person to whom authority is delegated may take a decision only with the agreement of all the Commission departments concerned and having assured himself that the decision does not, for whatever reason, have to be discussed by the full Commission. Finally, any decisions taken by delegation are forwarded the day after their adoption to all the members of the Commission and all the Commission departments.

[95] *Ibid.* at para. 35.

First Instance held that the adoption of a decision applying Article 85(1) was not a measure of management which could be delegated within the terms of the Commission's Rules of Procedure.[96]

The Commissioners also make recommendations under Article 3(3), open and close sector inquiries under Article 12, and decide on any refusal to hear a third party under Article 19(2). Broadly speaking all other matters concerning the preparation and execution of such decisions are delegated to the Commissioner responsible for competition. By an habilitation of November 5, 1980 the Commissioner was given the power to take decisions under Articles 11 and 14 (information and inspections).[97] None of these decisions granting delegation have been published although the Court of Justice has said that the principle of legal certainty and the need for transparency in administrative decisions require this to be done.[98]

The Commissioner for competition has in turn sub-delegated a considerable number of the day to day tasks to the Director-General or the Directors. Reference has been made in Chapter 4 to the appointment of a hearing officer to conduct hearings pursuant to Article 19 and Regulation 99/63. In practice, therefore, an official exercises this function on behalf of the Commission.[99] Similarly, a Director usually chairs the meeting for the consultation with the Advisory Committee. Certain tasks are, however, specifically reserved for the Commissioner for competition. These include the initiation of proceedings,[1] the determination of the statement of objections sent to the parties and of the draft decision (and accompanying note) which goes to the Advisory Committee, and the determination of the contents of the publications made under Articles 19 and 21.

6.47 A distinction is drawn between the delegation of powers (discussed above) and the delegation of signature. A task may be the responsibility of one person but another may be able to sign any necessary measure on his behalf. Thus, while the Commissioner for competition has responsibility for statements of objections, in practice they will be sent to the undertakings concerned in a letter signed by the Director-

---

[96] Cases T 79, 84–86, 89, 91–92, 94, 96, 98, 102 & 104/89, *BASF AG and Others* v. *Commission*: [1992] 4 C.M.L.R. 357, at paras. 56–59. The Commission has appealed the ruling of the Court of First Instance (Case C–137/92). In his opinion to the Court of Justice, A.G. Van Gerven has said that the judgment should be set aside. On the question of delegation of the right to adopt the decision, the Advocate General has said it is lawful to delegate the adoption of a decision which has already been adopted by the full Commission in another language version. The task is essentially one of practical execution or internal organisation.

[97] In *AKZO* (above, at paras. 35–37) the Court of Justice upheld this delegation as it relates to decisions under Art. 14(3), considering such decisions not to have the effect of removing authority from the Commission, and to be mere measures of management. Further, the Court held that it was no misuse of authority for the Commissioner to take the decision when he knew that the undertaking would not submit voluntarily. Art. 14(3) decisions are taken when the Commission expects the undertakings to refuse to submit, whatever their reasons (*ibid.* at para. 40). Followed by the Court of Justice in Cases 46/87 & 227/88, *Hoechst AG* v. *Commission*: [1989] E.C.R. 2859, [1991] 4 C.M.L.R. 410, at para. 44, where the Court rejected the further argument that the delegation contravened the principle *nulla poena sine lege* because the failure to comply with Art. 14(3) might lead to a fine under Art. 15 of Reg. 17.

[98] *Ibid.* at para. 38. Nor have the delegation arrangements for the opposition procedure (see, generally, paras. 2.40–52) been publicised. But see Venit (1985) 22 C.M.L.Rev. 167.

[99] Of the rank of conseiller (A3).

[1] There was, until recently, a distinction between, on the one hand, initiation of a procedure on the basis of a complaint or a notification and, on the other, initiation by the Commission of its own motion. The latter power was reserved to the Commissioners acting collegiately. Now, the Commissioner responsible for competition can initiate proceedings in all three circumstances.

General of DG IV. The Court of Justice recognised and upheld this practice in the *Dyestuffs* case.[2] Again in the *Dutch Books* case, the Court acknowledged that delegation of the authority to sign is the normal means by which the Commission exercises its powers.[3] More recently the Court held in *Dow Chemical Iberica*[4] that there is no requirement that the copy of a decision notified to an undertaking (*in casu* a decision under Article 14(3)) must be signed by the Commissioner.

As mentioned above, any decision under Regulation 17 to terminate an infringement, or grant negative clearance or exemption, is taken by the Commissioners. It seems, quite sensibly, that they need not have read the complete file on the case. In *Buchler* v. *Commission*,[5] the applicant argued that the decision was invalidated because the complete file had not been sent to each Commissioner. The Court considered it sufficient that the Commissioners had "received complete and detailed information regarding the essential points of the case and had access to the entire file."

V. RECOMMENDATIONS TO TERMINATE INFRINGEMENTS

6.48   Article 3(3) of Regulation 17[6] provides: "Without prejudice to the other provisions of this Regulation, the Commission may, before taking a decision under paragraph (1), address to the undertakings or associations of undertakings concerned recommendations for termination of the infringement."

In *Camera Care*,[7] the Court of Justice considered that the object of the Commission's powers to make recommendations under Article 3(3) was to: "enable the Commission to inform the undertakings concerned of its assessment of the situation with regard to the Community law in order to persuade them to comply with its point of view without immediately resorting to legal enforcement." Whilst a decision is binding in its entirety upon those to whom it is addressed, a recommendation has no binding force.[8] The legality of recommendations cannot be reviewed by the Court under Article 173 of the Treaty.[9] Therefore an undertaking to whom a recommendation is addressed may only go back to the Commission with fresh factual evidence and/or legal arguments if it disagrees with or objects to the terms of the recommendation.[10]

Recommendations should be specific.[11] It is, however, doubtful to what extent they need to contain a fully reasoned statement of the facts and arguments as to the applicability of Article 85(1) of the Treaty. This would only seem necessary where the rights

---

[2] Above, n. 79. A similar point arose in Case 8/72, *Vereniging van Cementhandelaren* v. *Commission*: [1972] E.C.R. 977, [1973] C.M.L.R. 7, and see para. 9.11.

[3] Cases 43 & 63/82, *VBBB and VBVB* v. *Commission*: [1984] E.C.R. 19, [1985] 1 C.M.L.R. 27, at para. 14.

[4] Cases 97, 98 & 99/87, *Dow Chemical Iberica SIA and others* v. *Commission*: [1989] E.C.R. 3165, [1991] 4 C.M.L.R. 410, at para. 59. The Court accepted that the contested decisions were duly certified as authentic by signature of the Secretary General of the Commission.

[5] Case 41, 44 & 45/69, *ACF Chemiefarma and others* v. *Commission*: [1970] E.C.R. 661. Case 44/69, at paras. 21–23.

[6] There are similar provisions in the transport implementing regulations.

[7] Case 792/79R: [1980] E.C.R. 119, [1980] 1 C.M.L.R. 334, at para. 16.

[8] Art. 189 of the Treaty.

[9] Art. 173 provides: "The Court of Justice shall review the legality of acts of the Council and the Commission *other than recommendations* and opinions" (emphasis added).

[10] Re-examination may, of course, strengthen the Commission's resolve to take a decision.

[11] Per A.G. Warner in Cases 6 & 7/73, *Commercial Solvents*: [1974] E.C.R. 223, [1974] 1 C.M.L.R. 309. He thought that a recommendation in general terms to cease and desist would be pointless. This observation was made in the context of a discussion of the Commission's powers to make specific orders (includ-

of defence might be prejudiced by their absence.[12] But a recommendation has no binding force and the undertaking has not foregone any of its rights which it would have if the Commission were to proceed to take a decision. On the other hand, a recommendation might have some persuasive effect, for example, in a national court, if the agreement in question were in issue before it.[13] Failure to comply with a recommendation might also be influential on the Commission with regard to the imposition of a fine in any final decision.

6.49   Where an undertaking fails to comply with the terms of a recommendation and, for example, continues to give effect to a restriction on competition or fails to take the remedial action recommended, the Commission may proceed to take a decision against the undertaking. The power to make a recommendation in Article 3(3) is expressed to be without prejudice to the other provisions of Regulation 17, including the power to take a decision to terminate an infringement under Article 3(1). Where, however, an undertaking complies with the recommendation and the Commission nevertheless proceeds to take a decision, that decision might be challenged before the Court, having regard to the doctrine of proportionality.[14] The Commission may, however, be justified in taking a decision notwithstanding the fact that an undertaking is willing and proposes to adhere to the terms of a recommendation. Where there is a formal complaint and the proceedings have been initiated on application of the complainant, the Commission's general discretion to use a recommendation may still apply. If the Commission fails to proceed to take a decision in relation to an alleged infringement it cannot be subjected to an action for failure to act brought by the complainant under Article 175 of the Treaty.[15]

There is no obligation on the Commission to publish recommendations.[16] The recommendation may therefore have the benefit of lack of publicity, but not necessarily.[17] In practice the Commission has made extremely little use of recommendations under Article 3(3).

---

[12] See, generally, para. 4.01. And note that Goldman (*European Commercial Law* (1973), para. 595) takes the view that a recommendation can be made at any stage in the procedure: "In particular, it may send it without waiting for the submissions, if it finds that the evidence which it has gathered is sufficient to establish the offence."

[13] Cf. the *Perfumes* cases: Cases 253/78, 1–3, 37 & 99/79: [1980] E.C.R. 2327, [1981] 2 C.M.L.R. 99, where the Court considered that a national court should at least have regard to an opinion given by the Commission when considering the applicability of Art. 85 to an agreement the subject of proceedings before it.

[14] See, generally, paras. 8.25–26.

[15] Case 125/78, *GEMA v. Commission*: [1979] E.C.R. 3173, [1980] 2 C.M.L.R. 177. See, generally, paras. 9.26–35.

[16] Art. 21(1) of Reg. 17.

[17] See, for example, the *Convention Faience* case: J.O. 1167/64, EEC Bulletin, 1964/5, Annex 11. Note also the Commission's practice of occasionally publishing details of "settled" cases, see para. 6.55.

VI. PUBLICITY

Decisions

6.50 Article 21(1) of Regulation 17 requires the Commission to publish the decisions which it takes pursuant to Articles 2 (negative clearance), 3 (termination of infringements), 6, 7 and 8 (exemptions and renewed revocation of exemptions). This is done in the *Official Journal* ("L" series). The publication must state the names of the parties and the main content of the decision. It is expressly provided that the publication shall have regard to the legitimate interest of undertakings in the protection of their business secrets. So it is common practice for the Commission to delete the details of an undertaking's turnover in the relevant products.[18]

6.51 There are several points to note. First, there are some decisions which the Commission is not obliged to publish. Most important in this category are the procedural decisions under Articles 11, 12 and 14 of Regulation 17. Here the Commission has a discretion whether to publish, and it has chosen to do so only in cases of general interest.[19] The Court of Justice has indicated that whilst the Commission may not be obliged to publish certain decisions, there is nothing either in the wording or spirit of Article 21 which prevents publication provided it does not involve the disclosure of the business secrets of the undertakings.[20] Furthermore, the Court has pointed out that the publication of Commission decisions can even contribute to ensuring respect for the competition rules of the Treaty.[21] Second, Article 20(2), restricting disclosure of professional secrets, is stated to be "without prejudice to the provisions of Articles 19 and 21." But Article 21(2) provides that regard must be had to the legitimate interest of undertakings in the protection of their business secrets and the Court has recently indicated that this provision is an expression of a general principle restricting access to business secrets by third parties.[22] They may not be disclosed in any circumstances. The Commission must therefore take the greatest care[23] to avoid disclosure of business secrets in its administrative procedure, including the publication of decisions under Article 21. The Commission has on occasion deleted the name of a party (but not an addressee of the decision), presumably to protect it against retaliatory action.[24] Finally, the date of publication may be important as regards the time limit for bringing an action under Article 173.[25]

---

[18] For a recent example see *Ecosystem/Peugeot*: [1992] O.J. L66/1.

[19] See Answer to Written Question No. 133/80: [1980] O.J. C183/35. Examples of published procedural decisions are *CSV*: [1976] O.J. L192/31; *Fides*: [1979] O.J. L57/33, [1979] 1 C.M.L.R. 650, and *A.M. & S.*: [1979] O.J. L199/31, [1979] 3 C.M.L.R. 376.

[20] See Francolor's complaint in the *Dyestuffs* case: Cases 48, 49, 51–57/69, *ICI and others* v. *Commission*: [1972] E.C.R. 619, [1972] C.M.L.R. 557, Case 54/69, at paras. 29–32.

[21] Case 41/69, *ACF Chemiefarma* v. *Commission*: [1970] E.C.R. 661, at para. 104.

[22] Case 53/85, *AKZO Chemie* v. *Commission*: [1986] E.C.R. 1965, [1987] 1 C.M.L.R. 231, at paras. 26–28.

[23] The Court of Justice has laid down a strict procedure for the Commission. See *AKZO*, above, at para. 29, described at para. 8.20.

[24] For example, in *BPB Industries Plc:* [1989] O.J. L10/50, [1990] 4 C.M.L.R. 464, at para. 128.

[25] See generally Lasok, *op. cit.*, pp. 126–133.

Generally

6.52 The work of antitrust authorities is frequently newsworthy and the investigation by the Commission of a particular undertaking or product market seldom escapes the notice of such persons as the press, legal commentators, etc. Moreover, it is the practice of the Commission occasionally to issue press releases during the investigation of a case, sometimes at an early stage. These releases may be of great value, *e.g.* to stifle rumour, to encourage people with information to come forward and generally to inform the public of what the Commission is doing. There is, however, a need for the Commission to exercise great care in such circumstances because there is a danger of giving the impression that it may have already made up its mind on the question of any infringement and that the party's guilt is presumed to be a fact from the outset.[26]

Premature announcements may be extremely prejudicial to the interests of the undertakings under investigation. But it is doubtful whether such conduct will found an action for damages against the Commission or constitute a sufficient ground for the overturning of any subsequent decision made by the Commission. In the *United Brands* case,[27] UBC claimed that it had suffered moral damage because a Commission official had made certain denigrating comments to a newspaper about UBC's commercial conduct. This was reproduced by the world press and gave the impression that the alleged infringements had been proved, when in fact the parties concerned had not yet delivered their defences. UBC argued that as a result the Commission was no longer able to evaluate impartially the facts of the case and the arguments it put forward. The Court of Justice thought that the statements were "regrettable"[28] but that there was nothing to justify the presumption that the contested decision would not have been adopted or would have been different had it not been for the statements. There was nothing to indicate that the Commission's conduct was such as to have an adverse effect on the way the procedure was normally carried out.[29]

Press announcements made after the final decision in a case may also call into question the reasons stated in the decision and suggest that the Commission has taken other factors into account. The Court has refused to order[30] the production of the Commission's internal documents relating to press releases and has indicated that press statements and interviews given by officials cannot reflect the institution's own position, which remains that laid down in the decision itself. The general issue is presently before the Court.[31]

---

[26] The International Chamber of Commerce has, amongst others, indicated concern over this. See note to the Commission Doc. No. 205/206 (1975).

[27] Case 27/76, *United Brands* v. *Commission*: [1978] E.C.R. 207, [1978] 1 C.M.L.R. 429, at paras. 280–288.

[28] *Ibid.* at para. 286. See also the Court of First Instance's criticism of the Commission's press release in T–30/89, *Hilti AG* v. *Commission*: [1991] II E.C.R. 1439, [1992] 4 C.M.L.R. 16, at para. 136.

[29] See also the *Sugar* case: Cases 40–48, 50, 54–56, 111 & 113–114/73, *Cooperatieve Vereniging "Suiker Unie" UA and others* v. *Commission*: [1975] E.C.R. 1663, [1976] 1 C.M.L.R. 295, at paras. 89–93.

[30] Order of the Court of December 11, 1986 in Case 212/86, *ICI* v. *Commission*: [1987] 2 C.M.L.R. 500.

[31] In the *Polypropylene* cases, of which the ICI case, above, is one.

VII. INFORMAL SETTLEMENTS

6.53   There are relatively few formal decisions. The Commission makes about a dozen or more substantive[32] decisions a year with as many as twice that number in a highly exceptional year. Between two and three hundred agreements are notified to the Commission each year,[33] and it is, of course, administratively impracticable to take a formal decision in every case. Leaving aside complaint cases,[34] policy considerations will largely dictate which cases are pursued and when.[35] But the point to note here is that the Commission is dealing with many cases at any one time[36] and each year a large number of cases are settled without formal decision being taken.[37] In its Fifth Report on Competition Policy,[38] the Commission stated: "Although this procedure is less well known and has less legal value than a formal decision, its importance should not be underestimated, as it enables some cases to be settled with a minimum of administrative intervention." It has become a feature of the Commission's annual Report on Competition Policy to indicate the number of informal settlements achieved. In the past, many involved distribution agreements, the cases generally being terminated after amendments were made to conform to the relevant block exemption.[39]

6.54   A considerable number of cases[40] are, following a preliminary examination, dealt with by so-called "comfort letters." The letter, which is usually signed by a Director or other senior official of DG IV, states the Commission's intention of closing the file on the case. A reason may be given. For example, the agreement may be considered not to fall within the prohibition of Article 85(1) or might be thought to come within the terms of a block exemption or of one of the Commission's notices, or to be eligible for an exemption under Article 85(3). Or the letter may simply say that in view of amendments made by the parties no further action is to be taken by the Commission. In short, the letter amounts to a declaration that the agreement poses no problem from the point of view of the competition rules. In some cases the Commission may issue what has been termed a "discomfort letter". Here the Commission indicates

---

[32] *I.e.* decisions finding infringements of the competition rules, granting exemption, negative clearance, etc., as distinct from "procedural" decisions requiring information or ordering investigations. In 1990, there were 15 such decisions, see the Twentieth Report on Competition Policy, point 90; and in 1991, 13 decisions, see the Twenty-first Report on Competition Policy, point 73.

[33] 246 in 1992. The impact of the Single Market may cause this to increase, as companies become less robust about relying on the limited domestic effect of their agreements.

[34] Where the possibility of an action for failure to act under Art. 175 of the Treaty may sometimes act as a spur. Sometimes, because even with complaints the Commission may have some discretion when to act. See Case T–24/90, *Automec Srl* v. *Commission*: [1992] 5 C.M.L.R. 431, at para. 76.

[35] The Court of Justice has recognised the Commission's discretion to determine priorities: see *Dutch Books*: Cases 43 & 63/82, *VBBB & VBVB* v. *Commission*: [1984] E.C.R. 19, [1985] 1 C.M.L.R. 27, at para. 27. The Court of First Instance similarly in *Automec,* above, at para. 77.

[36] See Answer to Written Question No. 1740/79: [1980] O.J. C140/14. Some 300 cases may be under investigation at a time.

[37] In 1990, 710 cases settled and a further 158 procedures closed by comfort letter. In 1991, 676 cases settled and a further 146 closed by comfort letter.

[38] Fifth Report on Competition Policy, p. 9.

[39] In the past, many agreements fell under the terms of Reg. 67/67, now replaced by Regs. 1983/83 and 1984/83. For an example of a case closed by a comfort letter relating to Reg. 1984/83 see Scholler, Fifteenth Report, at point 22.

[40] As already mentioned, figures for informal settlements and comfort letters are published in the Commission's annual report.

the agreement is caught by Article 85(1) and is not suitable for exemption, but declines to take a formal decision because of the agreement's weak impact on competition.[41] The Commission may expressly reserve its rights to reconsider the matter. The content of comfort letters (and "discomfort letters") is not regulated and probably the only common feature is the closing of the file.

The Commission has sought to distinguish cases where the file is closed by a comfort letter from those where there has been a settlement or a suspension.[42] The Commission has not defined what comprises such a settlement but one commentator has suggested that it might be restricted to where something is actually "settled" in return for concessions that are made.[43] Settlements may cover a wide variety of cases and circumstances, not just those in which there are complaints or which deserve a press release or a separate note in the annual Report on Competition Policy. It is clear however that it regards the IBM case as a suspension, not a settlement.[44]

6.55   An informal settlement, by whatever name, may be desirable on all sides, saving time, energy and resources in connection with the procedures required where a formal decision was taken. But there are several features which deserve comment.

Publicity

The informal nature of the settlement does not necessarily mean that it will not be made public in some way by the Commission. Although there is clearly no obligation to publish, the Commission may do so. The Commission pointed out in its Sixth Report: "In cases of particular importance, either because of the points of law which were raised or because of the economic power of the firms involved, the Commission issued press releases."[45] A brief description of some informal settlements may also appear in the *Bulletin of the European Communities* (published monthly) and the annual Report on Competition Policy. Whilst the position of the undertakings concerned is no worse in this respect than if a formal decision is taken,[46] an undertaking should not enter into discussions and negotiations with the Commission with a view to an informal settlement be' ¸ving that in this way all publicity will be avoided. Numerically very few settlements receive any publicity and even that is, as already indicated, quite modest. In only one case, *IBM*, have the full terms of a settlement been published.

Lack of legal security

6.56   The Commission has for a long time acknowledged that an informal settlement may have "less legal value than a formal decision."[47] Informality as such is not necessarily decisive as regards the question of legal status. The general principle is that merely because an act does not have the appearance of a formal decision does not mean that it is not a decision within the meaning of Article 189 of the Treaty. The test

---

[41] See the helpful analysis in Brown, "Notification of Agreements to the EC Commission: Whether to submit to a flawed system" (1992) E.L.Rev. 323.

[42] The Commission's annual reports now regularly separate the figures for cases closed by comfort letters and those settled.

[43] Van Bael, "The Antitrust Settlement Practice of the E.C. Commission" (1986) 23 C.M.L.Rev. 61.

[44] Fifteenth Report, point 1. *IBM* is reported at [1984] 3 C.M.L.R. 147.

[45] Sixth Report on Competition Policy, p. 11.

[46] Certain decisions have to be published—Art. 21 of Reg. 17, discussed at paras. 6.50–51.

[47] Fifth Report, above, n. 38.

is one of substance rather than form, the essential feature of a decision being that it produces legal effects with regard to the persons to whom it is addressed. This is most clearly shown by the *Cimenteries* case.[48] It is doubtful, however, whether "informal" statements or communications[49] from the Commission amount to decisions or otherwise bind the Commission.

6.57 The question has been considered by the Court of Justice on a number of occasions,[50] but most significantly in the *Perfumes* cases.[51] In brief, a number of standard-form bilateral agreements relating to the distribution of perfumes had been notified to the Commission which, following a more detailed examination of a selected two or three,[52] suggested to the undertakings concerned that the agreements be modified by the deletion or amendment of certain clauses. This having been done, the Commission sent a comfort letter to each undertaking stating that it had no grounds for action under Article 85(1) and intended to treat the case as closed. The question of the status of some of these agreements was raised in the course of proceedings in several national courts which referred the matter to the Court under Article 177. The Court was clearly of the opinion that the letters were not decisions within the meaning of Articles 2 and 6 of Regulation 17 if only because the publication requirements of Articles 19 and 21 had not been complied with.[53] They were, the Court said, simply letters (*lettres administratives*) informing the undertakings concerned of the Commission's views on the agreements. Such a letter did not restrict a national court from coming to a different view, on the basis of the information before it, of the applicability of Article 85(1) to the agreement, although the Court directed the national court at least to have regard to the Commission's letter as an element of fact before coming to any decision on the matter.[54] Moreover, the Court said, such a letter did not in the circumstances restrict a

---

[48] Cases 8–11/66, *Cimenteries* v. *Commission*: [1967] E.C.R. 75, [1967] C.M.L.R. 77. See, generally, paras. 9.06–09.

[49] See, *e.g.* the Court of First Instance's treatment of Sir Leon Britten's letter to Ministers in the Dutch Government in *Prodifarma I*: Case T–116/89, *Vereniging Prodifarma and Others* v. *Commission:* [1990] II E.C.R. 843.

[50] In Case 71/74, *Frubo* v. *Commission*: [1975] E.C.R. 563, [1975] 2 C.M.L.R. 123, the applicants sought to rely on a letter in which the Director of DG IV had said that, in his view, having regard to certain proposals made by the undertakings to amend their agreement, it could be the subject of an exemption under Art. 85(3). The Commission later found that the agreement infringed Art. 85(1) and could not be exempted. The applicants challenged the validity of the Commission's decision and argued, *inter alia*, that the Commission's failure to take account of the assurances given by the Director in his letter constituted a breach of an essential procedural requirement. The Court rejected this. It did not think that the terms in the letter could convey any impression that it committed the Commission. Moreover, the Director, the Court said, had no authority to bind the Commission in such a way. In the later Case 59/77, *De Bloos* v. *Bouyer*: [1977] E.C.R. 2359, [1978] 1 C.M.L.R. 511, a question was raised by a Belgian court on a reference under Art. 177 of the Treaty relating to the status of an informal statement made by the Commission to the parties that it had decided to take no action pursuant to the notification of the agreement in question because it appeared to the Commission that the agreement fell within the terms of the group exemption in Reg. 67/67. In the event the Court did not find it necessary to give a ruling but A.G. Mayras expressed the view that the letter was not an act of the Commission which constituted a decision. It was in his opinion a provisional instruction for the Commission which left the responsibility and the freedom of assessment of the Belgian court unaffected.

[51] Cases 253/78, 1–3, 37 & 99/79: [1980] E.C.R. 2327, [1981] 2 C.M.L.R. 99. See also Case 31/80, *NV L'Oréal (Brussels), L'Oréal SA (Paris)* v. *De Nieuwe AMCK*: [1980] E.C.R. 3775, [1981] 2 C.M.L.R. 235.

[52] See the Fourth Report on Competition Policy, points 93–97, and the Fifth Report, point 57–59.

[53] Above, n. 51: Case 253/78, at paras. 11 and 12.

[54] *Ibid.* at para. 13.

national court from applying national competition law to the agreement, even if more strict than Community law.[55]

The question has been raised whether a comfort letter can have any binding effect on the Commission. In *L'Oréal*,[56] Advocate General Reischl said:

> "it must be accepted ... that, having regard to the principle that legitimate expectation must be upheld, the Commission may depart from the judgment arrived at by its officers only if the factual circumstances change or its finding was reached on the basis of incorrect information."

Thus a former judge of the Court has expressed the view that it will not be open to the Commission to reopen the file in the absence of any new facts which came to its attention after the comfort letter or unless a judgment of the Court indicated that the Commission had been acting under a misapprehension as to the law.[57] In the *Mars* case, the Commission did not consider itself bound by a comfort letter where the factual circumstances had changed in the meantime, including the entry of five new players in the market.[58]

There is, however, an added complication. In one of the *Perfumes* cases, *Lancôme*,[59] the Court of Justice held that the Commission's letter had the effect of withdrawing any provisional validity which the agreement might have. This, of course, will only be relevant in the case of "old" agreements[60] (and almost certainly accession agreements[61]), as it is well established that new agreements cannot benefit from provisional validity.[62] (The detailed implications of this are discussed further in Chapter 10.) But in this respect it is necessary to distinguish between old and new agreements when considering the effects of comfort letters.

6.58   Shortly after the *Perfumes* cases, the Commission acknowledged[63] the limited effect of comfort letters, and spoke of "upgrading the legal status", saying it proposed: "to make improvements in administrative letters of this kind both from a factual and from a legal point of view so as to prevent court judgments at variance with them, if not in law, at least in practice." It saw added legal value coming from prior publication of a notice in the *Official Journal* giving interested parties the opportunity to comment.[64] The Commission then formally issued two notices announcing its intention to

---

[55] *Ibid.* at para. 18. The Court took the view that the letters indicated that the agreements had been judged by the Commission as not coming within the prohibition of Art. 85(1) and therefore there could be no conflict between Community law and national law. See para. 10.28.

[56] Above, n. 51.

[57] See Lord Mackenzie Stuart, "Legitimate Expectations and Estoppel in Community Law and English Administrative Law" (1983) 1 L.I.E.I. 53.

[58] *Langnese-Iglo GmbH*: [1993] O.J. L183/19. A further point made by the Commission was that only the addressee of the comfort letter might be able to support a claim that it should stand.

[59] Above, n. 51: Case 99/79, at para. 17.

[60] *I.e.* agreements in existence at the time Reg. 17 came into force.

[61] *I.e.* agreements in existence at the time of accession of the new Member States (in 1972, 1981 or 1986, as the case may be) and which become subject to Art. 85 by reason of accession.

[62] Case 48/72, *Brasserie de Haecht* v. *Wilkin (No. 2)*: [1973] E.C.R. 77, [1973] C.M.L.R. 287.

[63] See the Answer to Written Question No. 1508/81: [1982] O.J. C85/6.

[64] Eleventh Report on Competition Policy, point 15. An example quickly followed: *Europages*: [1982] O.J. C343/5, [1985] 1 C.M.L.R. 97. The opportunity for third parties to comment may be particularly important if a national court has to decide what weight to give a comfort letter: see *Inntrepreneur Estates Ltd.* v *Mason*: [1993] 2 C.M.L.R. 293, at paras. 46–48.

use the comfort letter procedure to close both cases of application for negative clearance[65] and exemption.[66] The principal means of enhancing the legal value remains publicity in the *Official Journal*, but the formality of the procedure may also add some weight. In the light of any comments from third parties, the Commission may send a comfort letter stating that the Director-General for Competition, in agreement with the undertakings concerned, does not consider it necessary to pursue the formal procedure through to the adoption of a decision. Further procedural steps involve liaison with the Advisory Committee.[67] There have been a number of cases where such notices have been published.[68] Such a notice does not prevent the procedure moving towards a formal decision of exemption,[69] a comfort letter only being sent if the undertakings concerned agree to the procedure being closed in this way. Few undertakings appear to have taken advantage of this "upgraded" comfort letter procedure, presumably preferring the lack of publicity of an ordinary comfort letter to any enhanced legal value.

6.59   The position, it is submitted, is broadly as follows. Strictly speaking, comfort letters have little legal value or effect. The Court of Justice has taken a view that where a regulation (*in casu*, Regulation 17) prescribes that a formal decision be taken by the Commission following certain specified procedures, then such decision cannot be replaced by any other measure taken by a Commission official, whether or not acting with authority[70] on behalf of the Commission. Thus a letter indicating the likelihood of an agreement being exempted (as in the *Frubo* case)[71] or that an agreement does not come within the prohibition of Article 85(1) (as in the *Perfumes* cases)[72] has not been considered by the Court to be a decision under Article 2 or 6 of Regulation 17. This said most companies are prepared to tick the box in Form A/B indicating that they will be satisfied with a comfort letter. A likelihood is that less publicity will be given to the agreement and the time-scale may be shorter. There will be little or no liaison with the Member States. Comfort letters may be relevant as guidance to a national court if it is called upon to consider the position of the agreement under Article 85.[73] A comfort letter which amounts to a negative clearance, *i.e.* a statement from the Commission that an agreement does not fall within Article 85(1), may well be influential before a national court, especially where judges may have little if any experience of applying Article 85. It will be difficult in practice for a third party to mount a challenge where the Commission has been confident enough of the facts to conclude, albeit informally,

[65] See the Notice from the Commission on the procedures concerning applications for negative clearance pursuant to Art. 2 of Council Reg. 17/62: [1982] O.J. C343/4.
[66] See the Notice from the Commission on procedures concerning notifications pursuant to Art. 4 of Council Reg. 17/62: [1983] O.J. C295/6.
[67] Twelfth Report on Competition Policy, point 30.
[68] Recent examples include *Infonet*: [1992] O.J. C7/3, [1992] OJ C7/3, [1992] 4 C.M.L.R. 493 and *United Technologies (Pratt & Whitney) and NITU*: [1992] O.J. C279/2, [1993] 4 C.M.L.R. 84 and *Acriss*: [1993] O.J. C149/9.
[69] *BPCL/ICI*: [1984] O.J. C20/9, [1984] 1 C.M.L.R. 257, and above, n. 1.
[70] The Court has been reluctant to develop a doctrine of ostensible authority. But see above, n. 57 and para. 8.30, dealing with the application of the doctrine of estoppel in Community law.
[71] Above, n. 50.
[72] Above, n. 51, and see also *L'Oréal* v. *De Nieuwe AMCK*, *ibid.*
[73] See the Commission Notice on co-operation between national courts and the Commission in applying Articles 85 and 86 of the EEC Treaty: [1993] O.J. C39/6, at para. 20. Even letters short of being comfort letters may be taken account of by the national court: see *Inntrepreneur Estates Ltd.* v. *Mason*, above, n. 64.

that Article 85(1) is not infringed. As regards comfort letters indicating eligibility for an Article 85(3) exemption, if a third party attempts to take action in the national court it would be relatively straightforward to respond by making a formal request to the Commission for a decision, and inviting the national court to stay proceedings pending the outcome. A national court might conceivably give greater weight to a comfort letter which follows the "upgraded" procedure. Comfort letters do not appear to be binding on the Commission.[74] In practice, however, the Commission is unlikely to go back on a comfort letter without good reason (for example, if there is a substantial change in the facts or it appears the Commission has issued the letter without having had access to all the relevant facts). Finally, the position of comfort letters relating to old agreements which have provisional validity is more complex and much may depend on the precise terms of the letter. In some circumstances provisional validity may be withdrawn by the letter.[75]

6.60   Settlements, it is submitted, can give no greater legal security than comfort letters, and may in fact give less. They will not bind national courts or third parties. They may not even bind the Commission, if only because many will be made at official level,[76] and, particularly important, the Commission remains free to reopen the case if new facts emerge or the circumstances change.[77] Even this limited legal effect may be excluded by the terms of the settlement. In *IBM*, the firm's undertaking stated:[78]

> "This undertaking is made without prejudice and may not be used in any way by IBM or the Commission in this or any other proceeding and does not constitute in any way an admission by IBM or the Commission. It is fundamental to this undertaking that it should not be enforceable by any other natural or legal person or any national authority or agency. IBM understands and asks the Commission to confirm that the Commission will rely exclusively upon Articles 85 and 86 of the Treaty and not upon this undertaking in this or any other proceeding."

For its part, the Commission expressly reserved its position to reopen the case: "the suspension of a particular proceeding cannot preclude the Commission, as a public authority, from terminating this suspension or from initiating a new proceeding in respect of IBM's conduct." Whatever the precise legal effect *vis-à-vis* the Commission, the practical effect is that the proceedings against IBM were suspended. There is apparently no formal finding or admission which a third party could rely on in proceedings before a national court.

---

[74] For cases reopened after a comfort letter, see *British Dental Trade Association*: [1988] O.J. L233/15, [1989] 4 C.M.L.R. 1021 and *Sippa*: [1991] O.J. L60/19.

[75] See para. 10.10.

[76] See *Frubo*, above, n. 50. Only exceptionally, it appears, will the Commissioners be involved (as in the *IBM* case).

[77] For this reason the settlement has been likened in legal effect to negative clearance. See Van Bael, *op. cit.* The position is the same for comfort letters, see the decisions cited at n. 74.

[78] Above, n. 44. See also the Eighteenth Report on Competition, at point 78. The implementation of the agreement is kept under review.

Undertakings

6.61   A constituent element in the settlement (or suspension) in the *IBM* case was the undertaking as to its future conduct given by IBM.[79] Undertakings have become an important feature in various aspects of the Commission's procedure. Brief mention has already been made of their use in lieu of interim measures decisions.[80] This has the advantage of enabling the Commission to respond and react to complaints in a shorter time. Such undertakings are, however, merely preservative measures and do not prejudice the outcome of the main proceedings. Indeed they may formally recite that they are without prejudice to any subsequent objections being issued by the Commission or any argument on the statement of objections from the undertaking concerned. The Court of Justice has acknowledged the role and validity of undertakings in the Commission's procedure. The Court has accepted that the Commission may use undertakings to reinforce its general power of surveillance and control, and that it is legitimate to use them to prevent agreements having effects contrary to Article 85.[81] Undertakings have therefore been used to avoid the need to take decisions,[82] to support decisions ordering positive measures,[83] to underpin an exemption[84] and to remove the need for attaching conditions or obligations.[85] Where an undertaking supports a formal decision ordering positive measures, that undertaking will, as the Court of Justice indicated in *Wood Pulp II*,[86] stand or fall with the terms of the decision itself. The Court rejected the Commission's plea that an undertaking is a unilateral act which is not subject to annulment under Article 173. Where, as in *Wood Pulp II* only parts of the decision are annulled, the Court may annul the provisions in the undertaking in so far as they impose obligations other than those resulting from findings of infringements made by the Commission which have not been declared void by the Court.

Plea-bargaining

6.62   In a reply to a question in the European Parliament,[87] the Commission has explained its attitude to co-operation by undertakings in its procedure. Plea-bargaining, as used to describe the negotiations which may take place between the public prosecutor and the accused in criminal cases, is not appropriate in E.C. competition cases, given the non-criminal nature of fines.[88] But the Commission has said that in cases where undertakings do not contest the facts found against them by the Commission there would be no reason for the Commission to oppose requests by the undertakings to shorten the duration of the procedure, for example, by relinquishing the right to be

---

[79] Above, n. 44. IBM undertook to change certain products in a way which satisfied the main objectives of the Commission. The reader is referred to the report for the details.

[80] Above, para. 6.02, n. 14.

[81] Cases 142 and 156/84, *BAT and Reynolds* v. *Commission*: [1987] E.C.R. 4487, [1988] 4 C.M.L.R. 24, at paras. 57 and 58.

[82] See, *e.g. BA/BCal*: Eighteenth Report on Competition, at point 821.

[83] *Tetra Pak II*: [1992] O.J. L72/1, [1992] 4 C.M.L.R. 551, at para. 180 and annex 7.

[84] *UIP*: [1989] O.J. L226/25, [1990] 4 C.M.L.R. 749; *Eirpage*: [1991] O.J. L306/22, [1993] 4 C.M.L.R. 64 and *Fiat/Hitachi*: [1993] O.J. L20/10.

[85] *IATA Passenger Agency Programme:* [1991] O.J. L258/18, [1992] 5 C.M.L.R. 496.

[86] Cases C 89, 104, 114, 116, 117 & 125–129/85, *A. Åhlström Osakeyhtio and others* v. *Commission*: [1993] 4 C.M.L.R. 407, at paras. 178–185.

[87] See Answer to Written Question No. 2006/82: [1983] O.J. C118/21.

[88] See Art. 15(4) of Reg. 17.

heard, in writing or orally, or both. As regards the suggestion that where firms actively assist the Commission in establishing the facts in the case against them, thereby saving time and expense for all concerned, a reduction of any fine might be justified, the Commission replied that whilst this was not explicitly provided for in Regulation 17, it did not wish to reject the possibility as a matter of principle, in particular in view of the fact that similar arrangements are allowed in the legal systems of Member States, for example in the case of tax law. But the Commission said that it would only contemplate introducing a procedure of this type within the framework of Regulation 17 and its established fining policy.

It is doubtful whether plea-bargaining as such is compatible with the procedure laid down in Regulation 17 and although the approach of offering a reduced fine in consideration for the help of the undertaking concerned to establish the facts was tried in at least one case,[89] it appears that the practice was discontinued shortly thereafter following objections in the Advisory Committee.[90] But as noted elsewhere, the co-operation of the parties during the procedure and the giving of undertakings as to the future conduct may be taken into account when fixing any fine.[91]

Lobbying

6.63 Concern has been expressed over the apparently developing practice of lobbying in competition cases. A question in the European Parliament[92] suggests that leading political figures, ex-Commissioners and former high-ranking Commission officials have been employed for this purpose. The Commission has taken the view that "undertakings are at liberty to decide who will act on their behalf and the Commission is not required within the framework of the procedure established by Regulation No. 17/62 to question the reasons why a particular representative is acting in a given case."[93] It considers that there are sufficient safeguards of independence and objectivity in the procedure and special rules or procedures on lobbying are therefore not necessary. In particular, as regards complaints, there is adequate protection for persons with legitimate interests to make their views known to the Commission, formally or informally, and to appeal to the Court.[94] Whatever one's views on the subject of lobbying,[95] the reality of the practice cannot be ignored.

---

[89] *Zinc Producer Group*: [1984] O.J. L220/27, [1985] 2 C.M.L.R. 108.
[90] Van Bael, *op. cit.*
[91] See para. 7.36.
[92] See Answer to Written Question No. 306/84: [1984] O.J. C225/20.
[93] *Ibid.*
[94] But a plea based on the Commission being unduly influenced may be difficult to substantiate. In Cases 142 and 156/84, *BAT and Reynolds* v. *Commission*: [1987] E.C.R 4487, [1988] 4 C.M.L.R. 24, the applicants complained that during the negotiations between the Commission and the undertakings pressure was placed on the Commission by one of its former members. The Court of Justice rejected this: the applicants had produced no evidence to support this plea (para. 25).
[95] For a strong criticism, see Van Bael, "Comment on the EEC Commission's Antitrust Settlement Practice: The Shortcircuiting of Regulation 17?" (1984) 22 *Revue Suisse du Droit International de la Concurrence* 67.

7

Fines and Penalties

Preliminary points

7.01   (a) The Commission's powers to impose fines and periodic penalty payments are contained in Articles 15 and 16 respectively.[1] There are equivalent provisions in the transport implementing regulations.[2] Both Articles are directed against undertakings and not individuals. Under some antitrust laws individuals, such as the directors of undertakings or other officers responsible, may be subject to fines and even imprisonment.[3] This is not the case with regard to the Community rules where only undertakings may be fined or made subject to penalties.[4] This said, the Commission has made it clear that it considers that management has the responsibility to establish effective internal rules for compliance with EEC competition law.[5] It is however possible that an individual may be an undertaking.[6] A sole trader is an undertaking for the purposes of Article 85 and, at least in theory, Article 86. Inventors may be undertakings, as may be artistes, where they commercially exploit the product of their talents.[7]

---

[1] See, generally, Deringer, *The Competition Law of the European Economic Community* (1968); Harding, "The use of fines as a sanction in EEC competition law" (1979) 16 C.M.L.Rev. 591; Temple Lang, "EEC fines for restrictive practices and abuses of dominant position" (1978) 75 L.S.Gaz. 1094.

[2] See Reg. 1017/68, Arts. 22 and 23; Reg. 4056/86, Arts. 19 and 20; Reg. 3975/87, Arts. 12 and 13. There are no special rules for transport cases and already there have been fining decisions.

[3] For example, under U.S. and German law. See Neale and Goyder, *The Antitrust Laws of the USA* (3rd ed., 1980), Chaps. XIII and XIV, and Riesenkampff/Gres, *Law Against Restraints of Competition* (1977).

[4] *Cf.* Art. 66(6) of the ECSC Treaty. The Merger Control Regulation, Reg. 4064/89, also contemplates individuals being fined but as owners of shares etc not as directors of undertakings as such.

[5] *Viho/Toshiba*: [1991] O.J. L287/39, [1992] 5 C.M.L.R. 180, at para. 30. The nature and extent of such rules will vary from one enterprise to another and even from one part of an enterprise to another. The Commission regards effective implementation and monitoring as essential to achieve compliance. See generally Marks, "Setting up an Antitrust Compliance Programme" [1988] E.C.L.R. 88, and Stanbrook and Ratliff, "EEC Antitrust Audit" [1988] E.C.L.R. 334.

[6] It would appear that A.G. Mayras did not countenance this possibility in Case 7/72, *Boehringer Mannheim GmbH* v. *Commission*: [1972] E.C.R. 1281, [1973] C.M.L.R. 864. Discussing whether the set-off rule for a previous conviction was a general principle of law and a part of Community law applicable to its competition rules, he said of the sanctions imposed by Arts. 15 and 16 of Reg. 17: "they are not directed against individuals, but exclusively against the assets of undertakings, who are bodies corporate. The concern to protect the individual from proceedings under two different penal sanctions, especially when it is a question of custodial sanctions, is of no relevance here." The question of what is an "undertaking" is discussed briefly at para. 1.05.

[7] *Reuter/BASF*: [1976] O.J. L254/40, [1976] 2 C.M.L.R. D44; *AOIP/Beyrard*: [1976] O.J. L6/8, [1976] 1 C.M.L.R. D14; *RAI/UNITEL*: [1978] O.J. L157/39, [1978] 3 C.M.L.R. 306. And note the position of Mr. de Rooij in Case 42/84, *Remia and Nutricia* v. *Commission*: [1985] E.C.R. 2689, [1987] 1 C.M.L.R. 1, at

Undertakings which entrust third parties with the task of implementing their restrictive agreements still remain responsible for them. An undertaking may be responsible for the activities of its subsidiaries and required to pay the fine.[8] Where a company takes over the defence of a related company it may find itself the addressee of the decision and fined.[9] Moreover, third party undertakings who help to implement cartels run the risk of being fined along with the principals.[10] There are no special rules for transport cases and there have already been fining decisions.[11]

7.02   (b) Article 15(4) provides that decisions taken pursuant to Article 15(1) and (2) "shall not be of a criminal law nature." Fines under Article 15 are often described as having an "administrative" nature or character and have been likened to the French *sanctions administratives* or the penalties imposed under the German *Gesetz über Ordnungswidrigkeiten*.[12] Article 15(4)[13] was most probably included in order to avoid the legal and political arguments relating to sovereignty which might have arisen had the Commission been given the power to apply criminal sanctions.[14] This may give little comfort to the party being fined. In practical terms fines under Article 15 may be closely likened to criminal or penal sanctions.[15] The so-called "administrative" nature of the fines should not result in any less legal protection for the undertaking concerned in the exercise of its rights of defence.[16]

---

paras. 49–51.
[8] *Moët et Chandon (London) Ltd.*: [1982] O.J. L94/7, [1982] 2 C.M.L.R. 166; *Cast Iron and Steel Rolls*: [1983] O.J. L317/1, [1984] 1 C.M.L.R. 694. Note that a parent may not always be liable, see the position of Asahi in *Benelux Flat Glass*: [1984] O.J. L212/13, [1985] 2 C.M.L.R. 350.
[9] *Fatty Acids*: [1987] O.J. L3/17, [1989] 4 C.M.L.R. 445.
[10] See *Italian Cast Glass*: [1980] O.J. L383/19, [1982] 2 C.M.L.R. 61. Note the position of Fides, a firm providing management and accountancy services. (Fides features in other Commission decisions—see n. 38, below, *Wood Pulp*: [1985] O.J. L85/1, [1985] 3 C.M.L.R. 474, and *Fatty Acids*, above). See also *Roofing Felt*: [1986] O.J. L232/15, [1991] 4 C.M.L.R. 130, where a fine was imposed on the trade association, Belasco, for its involvement in actually running the cartel. Cf. the position of NAC in *Building and Construction Industry in the Netherlands*: [1992] O.J. L92/1, not fined because only played administrative role.
[11] See, *e.g. Cewal, Cowac & Ukwal*: [1992] O.J. L34/20.
[12] Deringer, *op. cit.*, para. 2279. Note that in *Société Stenuit* v. *France*: (1992) 14 E.H.R.R. 509, the European Commission on Human Rights classified the procedures under French competition law leading to a penalty (up to 5 per cent. of turnover) as criminal for the purposes of Art. 6(1) of the European Convention, being influenced, *inter alia*, by the potential size and therefore deterrent effect of the penalty.
[13] There is no equivalent in Art. 16.
[14] In *Boehringer Mannheim GmbH* v. *Commission*, above n. 6, A.G. Mayras said: "While there can be no doubt that the Member States have transferred to the Community institutions the right to exercise certain of their sovereign prerogatives in economic matters, it is equally certain that they had no intention to relinquish their penal jurisdiction."
[15] *Ibid.* and see also A.G. Warner in Case 19/77, *Miller International Schallplatten GmbH* v. *Commission*: [1978] E.C.R. 131, [1978] 2 C.M.L.R. 334.
[16] See A.G. Mayras in Cases 40–48, 50, 54–56, 111, 113 & 114/73, *Co-operatieve Vereniging "Suiker Unie" UA and others* v. *Commission*: [1975] E.C.R. 1663, 2119–2120, [1976] 1 C.M.L.R. 295, 396. The Commission's decision is reported at [1973] O.J. L140/17, [1973] C.M.L.R. D65. See also A.G. Vesterdorf in *Polypropylene*: Case T–7/89, *Hercules NV* v. *Commission*: [1992] 4 C.M.L.R. 84, at p. 101, re-

7.03   (c) Both Articles 15(3) and 16(3) provide that "Article 10(3) to (6) shall apply." This means that before any decision imposing a fine or penalty can be taken the
Commission must consult the Advisory Committee on Restrictive Practices and
Monopolies.[17] The members of the Committee will have before them a preliminary
draft decision and will be informed of the amount of the fine or penalty the Commission is proposing.[18] In the opinion it gives, the Committee may comment on such matters as the justification for, desirability of and level of the fine.[19]

7.04   (d) There appears to be no restriction on the Commission imposing a fine (under Article 15) and a periodic penalty payment (under Article 16) at the same time.
Article 15 basically covers past violations whilst Article 16 deals with continuing and
future violations. The Commission should be entitled and be able to punish an undertaking for its wrongdoing before the decision and seek to discourage or prevent continuing or recurrent infringements. It is, however, unclear whether the Commission can
impose a fine in respect of conduct for which a periodic penalty payment has already
been imposed (*i.e.* where the Commission has imposed a penalty under Article 16, can
it at a later date and by a further decision impose a fine under Article 15 for the "future" violation once committed?).[20] It might be argued that the principle of *non bis in
idem*[21] should apply in such circumstances. The applicability of this principle is however uncertain in this context, having regard to the administrative nature of the two
types of sanction and also their different purpose.[22] The Court might nevertheless consider that in fairness and equity the amount of any periodic penalty payment should be
taken account of in any fine imposed.[23]

---

ferring to the Court of Human Rights in *Öztürk* ((1985) 6 E.H.R.R. 409) and concluding that fines under
Regulation 17 (Art. 15(4)) have a criminal law character. But in Case 374/87, *Orkem* v. *Commission*:
[1989] E.C.R. 3283, [1991] 4 C.M.L.R. 502, the Court proceeded on the basis that the Commission's procedure was not criminal in concluding that the privilege against self-incrimination had but limited scope
in relation to investigations under Regulation 17. This may have to be revisited by the Court in the light of
the decision in *Stenuit*, above, n. 12 and judgment of the European Court of Human Rights in *Funke* v.
France: [1993] 1 C.M.L.R. 897.

[17] For a more detailed account of the Advisory Committee see paras. 5.21–28.

[18] In the *Quinine* case: Cases 41, 44 & 45/69, *ACF Chemiefarma and Others* v. *Commission*: [1970] E.C.R.
661, Boehringer complained that the Commission did not indicate to the Advisory Committee the
amount of the fine envisaged. Details of the Advisory Committee's discussions were made available to
the Court (see n. 19 below and para. 5.25) and the Court found (at p. 798) that the members of the Committee had acquired details of the proposed fines and were able to give their opinion thereon. The opinion
of the A.G. reveals (at p. 711) that "a member of the Committee was moreover critical of the figures."

[19] The opinion is not a public document (Art. 10(6) of Reg. 17). It is annexed to the draft decision placed before the Commissioners. On the question of the disclosure of the Advisory Committee's opinion, see
paras. 5.25–26.

[20] Deringer, *op. cit.*, at para. 2040 takes the view that the Commission should be able to do so.

[21] The principle was applied in the staff case, Cases 18 & 35/66, *Gutman* v. *Commission*: [1966] E.C.R.
103.

[22] *Boehringer Mannheim GmbH* v. *Commission*, above, n. 14, at para. 4.

[23] See Case 14/68, *Walt Wilhelm and Others* v. *Bundeskartellamt*: [1969] E.C.R. 1, [1969] C.M.L.R. 100, at
para. 9. The Commission has acknowledged that a principle of equity may apply in the assessment of a
fine. See *Johnson & Johnson*: [1980] O.J. L377/16, [1981] 2 C.M.L.R. 287.

I. PROCEDURAL INFRINGEMENTS

Article 15(1)

7.05 Under Article 15(1) the Commission may by decision impose on undertakings[24] fines of from 100 to 5,000 units of account where, intentionally or negligently:

(a) *They supply incorrect or misleading information in an application for negative clearance or in a notification for an exemption.*

In *Tepea* v. *Commission*,[25] the Court of Justice upheld the Commission's decision[26] to impose a maximum fine for the failure in 1963 by Tepea, a Dutch undertaking, when notifying particulars of an oral exclusive distributorship agreement between itself and an English manufacturer, to notify certain additional facts relating to its exclusive use of trade marks in the Netherlands. This infraction was, in the opinion of the Court, "if not intentional, at least negligent"[27] because the notification form[28] clearly drew attention to the duty to inform the Commission of the provisions of the agreement and to state whether it "involved a sharing of markets or a restriction of freedom to purchase from or sell to third parties or might in any other way have as its object or effect the restriction or distortion of competition." The joint effect of the two agreements (distribution and trade marks) was found by the Court to have prevented parallel imports between the United Kingdom and the Netherlands in violation of Article 85(1). The Court thought that the maximum fine was completely justified in view of the gravity of the infraction which led to the misapprehension under which the Commission laboured for 11 years. Although as long as the United Kingdom was not a Member State any restrictions on competition arising out of the application of the agreements only affected trade within the Netherlands and did not interfere with the pattern of trade between Member States, the period between notification in 1963 and the accession of the United Kingdom in 1973 could nevertheless be taken into account under Article 15(1). The Court of Justice did not expressly say that the infraction existed during this time but it seems reasonable to conclude that the Court considered that it did. The implication is clear. There can be an infringement under Article 15(1)(a) even if there is no infringement of Article 85 or 86, or none proven. This also seems to follow logically from the reference in Article 15(1)(a) to applications for negative clearance. The granting of an exemption under Article 85(3) is not prohibited by an infringement of Article 15(1)(a) although it must be remembered that an exemption can only be granted pursuant to a valid notification.[29] Whether to proceed under Article 15(1)(a) isof course a matter of discretion for the Commission.[30] The Commission has recognised that the completion of Form A/B involves a matter of judgment as to how much

---

[24] "Or associations of undertakings."

[25] Case 28/77: [1978] E.C.R. 1391, [1978] 3 C.M.L.R. 392.

[26] *Theal/Watts*: [1977] O.J. L39/19, [1977] 1 C.M.L.R. D44.

[27] Harding, *op. cit.*, at p. 605, takes the view that Tepea's failure to mention certain features of the agreement, such as the grant by Watts of the exclusive trade mark rights, was deliberate so that it was more properly an intentional rather than a negligent infringement.

[28] Form A/B was not in use at the time. Form A/B replaced Form B in 1968 and was itself revised in 1986. Form A/B is presently under review, see para. 2.28.

[29] Case 30/78, *Distillers* v. *Commission*: [1980] E.C.R. 2229, [1980] 3 C.M.L.R. 121.

[30] See *Sperry New Holland*: [1985] O.J. L376/21, [1988] 4 C.M.L.R. 306, at para. 65, where the Commission did not fine under Art. 15(1)(c) although the notification was apparently defective.

detail is relevant. Moreover, estimates and opinions, as well as facts, may be comprised in the information supplied. The Commission has said that it will use its Article 15(1)(a) powers only where the applicants or notifiers have, intentionally or negligently, provided false information of grossly inaccurate estimates or suppressed readily available information or estimates, or have deliberately expressed false opinions in order to obtain negative clearance or exemption.[31]

7.06   (b) *They supply incorrect information in response to a request made pursuant to Article 11(3) or (5) or to Article 12, or do not supply information within the time fixed by a decision taken under Article 11(5).*

In five cases, the Commission has fined undertakings for supplying incorrect replies to Article 11(3) requests for information.[32] There has also been one case under Regulation 4056/86, maritime transport.[33] The decisions reveal that in at least four of them the defect was discovered by later investigations under Article 14. In only one case was less than the maximum (5,000 ECUs) fine imposed.[34] In that case (*Peugeot*) the Commission seems to have given the undertaking the benefit of the argument that two letters of request may constitute only one request under Article 11 where they put a series of questions in a single context, and because the second letter referred to the first. The Commission also accepted that the offence had been committed partly intentionally and partly negligently. The persons who drafted the replies were not fully acquainted with the facts. The Commission nevertheless found that the company did not exercise sufficient supervision within the group to prevent false statements being made, with the result that the offence was "at the very least, the result of negligence."

It is noteworthy that Article 15(1)(b) relates only to incorrect information supplied under Article 11 (or 12) and does not cover false replies to requests for oral explanations on the spot during an investigation under Article 14. This is not to say that incorrect information can be given with impunity in such a context. See the discussion of Article 15(1)(c) which follows.

7.07   (c) *They produce the required books or other business records in incomplete form during investigations under Article 13 or 14, or refuse to submit to an investigation ordered by decision under Article 14(3).*

During its investigation of the glass market in Italy, the Commission fined two undertakings for producing books, etc., in incomplete form. Both had voluntarily submitted to an investigation without decision, their attention having been expressly drawn to the provisions of Article 15(1). In *Fabbrica Pisana*,[35] Pisana had said that it was unaware of any agreements of the type which the inspectors asked to see but

---

[31] See Complementary Note to Form A/B, set out in Appendix F.
[32] See *Telos*: [1982] O.J. L58/19, [1982] 1 C.M.L.R. 267; *National Panasonic (Belgium) NV*: [1982] O.J. L113/18, [1982] 2 C.M.L.R. 410; *National Panasonic (France) SA*: [1982] O.J. L211/31, [1982] 3 C.M.L.R. 623; *Comptoir Commercial d'Importation*: [1982] O.J. L27/31, [1982] 1 C.M.L.R. 440 and *Peugeot*: [1986] O.J. L295/19, [1989] 4 C.M.L.R. 371.
[33] *Secrétama*: [1991] O.J. L35/23, [1992] 5 C.M.L.R. 76.
[34] Peugeot, fined 4,000 ECUs.
[35] [1980] O.J. L75/30, [1980] 2 C.M.L.R. 354, and see also *Raffinerie Tirlemontoise*: [1971] 11 Bull. E.C. 55.

agreed to make available all its documents and files.[36] In *Fabbrica Sciarra*,[37] the inspectors asked about Sciarra's relations with another undertaking Fides[38] and requested production of all correspondence with it or other glass manufacturers. In both cases very little was forthcoming from the undertakings. A later investigation of Fides disclosed the shortcomings of Pisana and Sciarra. The Commission found that the infringements were committed "intentionally", indicating that the nature of the inspectors' request could not have left the undertakings in any doubt about what matters concerned the Commission. Moreover both undertakings could be reasonably supposed to have been informed by Fides of its refusal to submit to an investigation at about the same time.[39] The Commission also drew attention to the fact that each had ample time in the period following the investigation to demonstrate its good faith by informing the Commission of its intention to produce all the documents which had been requested.[40] In *FNICF*,[41] the Commission fined a French trade association for the footwear industry for refusing to produce minutes or records of meetings of its management bodies. The association claimed that such documents were confidential and beyond the investigators' terms of reference. All three decisions describe the infringements as being "serious" because the failure to produce the documents made more difficult the Commission's task of ensuring compliance with the competition rules.[42] Maximum fines were imposed.

7.08 Article 15(1)(c) specifies two separate types of infringement. Because they are alternatives (note the "or") it is arguable that the incomplete production of books does not amount to a refusal to submit to an investigation where ordered by decision.[43] But in *CSM-NV*,[44] the undertaking's refusal to hand over documents for inspection (until placed under the threat of a periodic penalty payment) was treated as a refusal to submit to the investigation. A denial of entry to the authorised Commission officials is a

---

[36] This reply was not considered sufficient to satisfy the undertaking's obligations under Art. 14 of Reg. 17. This aspect is discussed further at para. 3.16.

[37] [1980] O.J. L75/35, [1980] 2 C.M.L.R. 362.

[38] See the Commission's decision. *Fides*: [1979] O.J. L57/33, [1979] 1 C.M.L.R. 650.

[39] The two decisions do not exhibit any facts or other evidence to show that there was in fact any such communication from Fides to Pisana or Sciarra at the relevant time.

[40] In the case of Pisana, the Commission rejected any suggestion that Pisana's subsequent authorisation of Fides to present its papers to the Commission's inspectors should they renew their request at a later date (which they did and thereby discovered the "omissions" of both Pisana and Sciarra) demonstrated Pisana's good faith.

[41] [1982] O.J. L319/12, [1983] 1 C.M.L.R. 575.

[42] Unless the Commission can obtain the same information elsewhere and immediately, any infringement of Art. 15(1)(c) seems likely to have this effect and therefore, presumably, will be "serious".

[43] FNICF could not, for example, have been fined for refusing to submit because the inspection was merely by mandate under Art. 14(1). But the lesson of FNICF, above, n. 41, seems to be that once having voluntarily submitted, it may be impossible to withdraw from or terminate the inspection without risk of a fine for incomplete production of books. It has been suggested that undertakings should formally refuse to submit and at the same time inform the inspectors that if they request any documents within the mandate they are likely to be produced: see Korah, "Inspections under the EEC competition rules: Danger of voluntary submission" (1983) 4 *Business Law Review* 23. But this is an artificial device which may find little sympathy with the Court, and there must be a danger that the Commission will consider there to be an implied submission by conduct in such circumstances and put the matter to the test.

[44] [1992] O.J. L305/16. CSM had disputed whether certain documents were relevant. Some were released on reconsideration by the firm — this was regarded as "negligent". The remainder were released upon the threat of penalty under Art. 16(1) decision — this was regarded as intentional. A fine of 3,000 ECUs was imposed.

clear breach of the obligations imposed by Article 14 of Regulation 17[45] and may attract a maximum fine.

Acts short of a total or complete refusal may constitute an infringement of Article 15(1)(c). Unduly delaying the commencement of an inspection will be treated as a refusal to submit to the investigation. In *Mewac*,[46] a shipping case, the Commission said that it is not for the undertaking concerned to decide the date and time of the investigation. The exact commencement of an inspection is particularly important where simultaneous investigations take place of parties suspected of having collectively infringed the competition rules. Where an investigation is ordered by decision, the terms of the decision will make it clear what in relation to the provisions of Article 14(1)(a) to (d) the Commission requires of the undertaking concerned. It may, for example, require the undertaking to produce certain documents and permit the Commission to take copies. Any failure by the undertaking concerned to comply with the terms of the decision in full may constitute a refusal to submit to the investigation ordered. It is extremely doubtful whether there can be any conditional or partial submission to an investigation.[47]

Whilst it is recognised that Article 15(1)(c) is a penal provision and is therefore liable to be construed narrowly, it may nevertheless be sufficient to deal with at least some cases where an undertaking either refuses to give oral explanations under Article 14(1)(c) or gives a false explanation. An outright refusal may constitute a refusal to submit to the investigation ordered. A false denial of the existence of papers or files, or a false indication as to their whereabouts may constitute a failure to produce the required books or records.[48] The greatest care should always be taken in replying to requests for explanations made during investigations. There may be a risk of fine where the effect of the reply, if false, is totally or even partially to frustrate the production of relevant documents or otherwise the conduct of the investigation.

II. SUBSTANTIVE INFRINGEMENTS

Article 15(2)

7.09 Under Article 15(2) the Commission may by decision impose on undertakings[49] fines where, either intentionally or negligently:

(a) they infringe Article 85(1) or Article 86 of the Treaty; or
(b) they commit a breach of any obligation imposed pursuant to Article 8(1) of Regulation 17 in connection with the grant of an exemption under Article 85(3).

---

[45] Or the equivalent provisions in the transport regulations, *e.g.* Art. 18 of Reg. 4056/86 as in *Ukwal*: [1992] O.J. L121/45.

[46] *Mewac*: [1993] O.J. L20/6. Mewac in fact consented to the investigation the following day and this was taken into account when fixing the fine at 4,000 ECUs.

[47] See Kreis, "EEC Commission investigation procedures in competition cases" (1983) 17 *The International Lawyer* 14, and Joshua, "The element of surprise: EEC competition investigations under Article 14(3) of Regulation 17" (1983) 3 E.L.Rev. 3.

[48] But Kreis, *op. cit.*, at p. 43 acknowledges a lacuna where all relevant documents have been produced and the incorrect explanations relate to the content or meaning of the documents. Joshua, *op. cit.*, at p. 18 appears to consider this as a refusal, if the conduct amounts to an obstruction or an attempted obstruction of the due execution of the decision.

[49] "Or association of undertakings."

There have been no instances of the Commission imposing fines in respect of conduct within category (b) and what follows concentrates on substantive infringements within category (a).

Infringement already terminated

7.10 The Commission can impose a fine notwithstanding that the infringement has terminated prior to the Commission's investigation or decision. In the *Quinine* case,[50] Boehringer complained that the Commission had imposed a fine on it for an infringement which had come to an end and that, by failing to take that fact into consideration, at least for the purpose of fixing the amount of the fine, the Commission was guilty of an abuse of its powers. The Court of Justice rejected this argument:[51] "The Commission's power to impose penalties is in no way affected by the fact that the conduct constituting the infringement has ceased and that it can no longer have detrimental effects." Distinguishing periodic penalty payments, the Court said that the object of fines under Article 15 was "to suppress illegal activities and to prevent any recurrence." This could not be achieved if the Commission was limited to fining only in cases where the infringement was extant at the time of the decision. The statement made by the Court in the *Quinine* case must be qualified in the light of the limitation regulation (Regulation 2988/74)[52] which provides that infringements against the substantive rules are subject to a limitation period of five years.[53] As far as U.K. firms or firms from other "new" Member States are concerned, there seems to be nothing to prevent the Commission fining such a firm in respect of unlawful conduct prior to accession in 1973, 1980 or 1986, as the case may be, provided the Commission had jurisdiction over the firm at that time, the criteria for infringement are established and the matter is not time-barred under Regulation 2988/74.[54]

Legal and economic predecessors — undertaking identity

7.11 As already indicated, a parent company may be liable for its subsidiaries.[55] An undertaking may also be responsible for the conduct of its legal or economic predecessors. The fact that the undertaking being fined is a different legal person from that whose conduct wholly or in part is the subject of the infringement will not be any defence. The competition rules are concerned with "undertakings" — essentially a functional and economic concept and one which is not necessarily identical with that of legal personality under national company laws. So a change in the legal form and name of an undertaking does not create a new undertaking free of liability for the anti-

---

[50] Above, n. 18 (Case 45/69).

[51] *Ibid.*, at para. 53.

[52] Limitation is dealt with generally at paras. 8.28–29. Reg. 2988/74 is discussed at paras. 7.46–49.

[53] Provided the Commission brings its procedure within the limitation period, it seems to have the power to fine for the whole period of the infringement even if it exceeds five years. See Temple Lang, *op. cit.*

[54] See the position of the U.K. firms in *Dyestuffs*: Cases 48, 49, 51–57/69, *ICI and Others* v. *Commission*: [1972] E.C.R. 619, [1972] C.M.L.R. 557 (the Commission's decision is reported at [1969] J.O. L195/11, [1969] C.M.L.R. D23); *Theal/Watts*: [1977] O.J. L39/19, [1977] 1 C.M.L.R. D44, and *Zinc Producer Group*: [1984] O.J. L220/27, [1985] 2 C.M.L.R. 108 (Note the position of RTZ). *Cf. Sperry New Holland*: [1985] O.J. L376/21, [1988] 4 C.M.L.R. 306.

[55] See, for example, *Benelux Flat Glass*: [1984] O.J. L212/13, [1985] 2 C.M.L.R. 350.

competitive behaviour of its predecessor when, from an economic point of view, the two are identical.[56]

In the *Sugar* case,[57] the Court of Justice refused to accept the argument that Suiker Unie, a company formed by the merger of four co-operatives, was not responsible for the conduct of the co-operatives when carrying on business as an association under the same name. The Court noted that the new company had assumed all the rights and liabilities of the four co-operatives, the same name had been used throughout and for the most part the business had been carried on by the same persons from the same office. The Court said: "the main feature of the conduct of the applicant and its predecessor was its obvious continuity, which means that the whole of this behaviour must be attributed to the applicant."

The Commission has taken a similar approach in a number of cases where there have been mergers or reorganisations of the corporate structure of the parties involved.[58] Where a party effects a transfer of its business activities in the relevant sector to another undertaking the transferor undertaking continuing in existence remains liable to be fined.[59] Where the business has been transferred or merged with that of another undertaking, the original undertaking having ceased to exist, the question is whether responsibility for the infringement has followed and attached to the new or merged entity. The determining factor is whether there is an economic and functional continuity between the original undertaking and its successor.[60] This is a question of Community law and the outcome therefore is not necessarily dependent on the particular legal form adopted or changes in organisation under national law.[61] National company laws may, however, come back into play when it comes to enforcement and collection of the fine.[62]

---

[56] *Rolled Zinc*: Cases 29 & 30/83, *Compagnie Royale Asturienne* v. *Commission*: [1984] E.C.R. 1679, [1985] 1 C.M.L.R. 688, at paras. 8 and 9.

[57] Cases 40–48, 50, 54–56, 111, 113 & 114/73, *Co-operatieve Vereniging "Suiker Unie" UA and others* v. *Commission*: [1975] E.C.R. 1663, [1976] 1 C.M.L.R. 295, at paras. 75–88. Again in the *Rolled Zinc* case, the Court drew attention to the fact that Rheinzink was not only the legal successor of Rheinisches Zinkenwalzwerk but had continued the economic activities of the latter.

[58] See the Commission's decisions in *Quinine*: [1969] J.O. L192/5, [1969] C.M.L.R. D41; *Floral*: [1980] O.J. L39/51, [1980] 2 C.M.L.R. 285, and *Zinc Producer Group*: [1984] O.J. L220/27, [1985] 2 C.M.L.R. 108.

[59] See the position of AMC and Rhône Poulenc in *Polypropylene*: [1986] O.J. L230/1, [1988] 4 C.M.L.R. 347.

[60] See *Welded steel mesh*: [1989] O.J. L260/1, [1991] 4 C.M.L.R. 13, at paras. 194 and 195 where there is an extensive consideration of this subject. See also *Aluminium*: [1985] O.J. L92/1, [1987] 3 C.M.L.R. 813. The Commission considered the continuance in employment of senior officers as an indication of continuance of policy after acquisition: see the position of *Kaiser*: [1985] O.J. L92/1, [1987] 3 C.M.L.R. 813, at para. 19.1.

[61] In *Peroxygen Products*: [1985] O.J. L35/1, [1985] 1 C.M.L.R. 481, Atochem was held responsible for infringement by PCUK, having taken over the assets and adopted the economic objectives of PCUK. Again in *PVC*: [1989] O.J. L74/1, [1990] 4 C.M.L.R. 345, Atochem was held responsible for the activities of Chloe and ATO Chemie. See also the position of Statoil in *Polypropylene*, above. It absorbed the business of SAGA but did not liquidate the assets. The activities and functions were retained, management and employment continued. The position of Statoil was considered again in *LdPE*: [1989] O.J. L74/21, [1990] 4 C.M.L.R. 382.

[62] See para. 7.50.

No fines or lower fines in previous cases

7.12   The fact that in some cases the Commission has not imposed any fine will not be a bar to the Commission imposing a fine on a subsequent occasion in a similar case. In *BMW Belgium and Others* v. *Commission*,[63] the Court of Justice rejected the plea of certain dealers who had accepted an export ban proposed by the distributor, BMW Belgium, that in comparable situations before the Commission had not imposed fines on dealers[64] and therefore the Commission was infringing the principle of non-discrimination by fining them. The Court said:

> "The fact that in similar previous cases the Commission did not consider that there was a reason to impose fines on resellers as well cannot deprive it of such a power expressly granted to it by [Reg. 17] where the conditions required for the exercise thereof are satisfied."[65]

But the Commission's practice is to have regard to the fact that it may be a "first" decision when assessing the gravity of the infringement and the amount of any fine.[66] Dealers, for example, who accept contracts containing export bans may be guilty of infringing Article 85(1), but the Commission has had regard to whether it has previously taken decisions in the relevant sector[67] before imposing a fine.

In the *Pioneer* case,[68] the Court of Justice upheld the Commission's policy of increasing the level of fines. The fact that the Commission, in the past, imposed fines of a certain level for certain types of infringement does not mean that it is estopped from raising the level (within the limits indicated in Regulation 17) if that is necessary to ensure the implementation of Community competition policy. On the contrary, the proper application of the competition rules requires that the Commission may at any time adjust the level of fines to the needs of policy.[69]

---

[63] Cases 32/78 & 36–82/79: [1979] E.C.R. 2435, [1980] 1 C.M.L.R. 370.

[64] For example, in *Kawasaki*: [1979] O.J. L16/9, [1979] 1 C.M.L.R. 448. The Commission will have close regard to what is the purpose of the export ban or other anti-competitive practice. Thus if the dealers are only the vehicle for the protective policy which may indeed be contrary to their interests, they will not be joined in the proceedings although formally parties to the agreements contrary to Art. 85(1). See *Johnson & Johnson*: [1980] O.J. L377/16, [1981] 2 C.M.L.R. 287 and *Sandoz*: [1987] O.J. L222/28, [1989] 4 C.M.L.R. 628.

[65] Above, n. 63, at para. 53. See also Case 322/81, *Michelin* v. *Commission*: [1983] E.C.R. 3461, [1985] 1 C.M.L.R. 282, at para. 107.

[66] See *AEG-Telefunken*: [1982] O.J. L117/15, [1982] 2 C.M.L.R. 386; *Toltecs/Dorcet*: [1982] O.J. L379/19, [1983] 1 C.M.L.R. 412, (fine quashed on appeal); *Windsurfing*: [1983] O.J. L229/1, [1984] 1 C.M.L.R. 1; *Fatty Acids*: [1987] O.J. L3/17, [1989] 4 C.M.L.R. 445; *British Dental Trade Association*: [1988] O.J. L233/15, [1989] 4 C.M.L.R. 1021; *London European–Sabena*: [1988] O.J. L317/47, [1989] 4 C.M.L.R. 662 and *Flat Glass*: [1989] O.J. L33/44, [1990] 4 C.M.L.R. 535. See also para 7.19.

[67] *E.g.* agricultural machinery, as in *John Deere*: [1985] O.J. L35/58, [1985] 2 C.M.L.R. 554, and *Sperry New Holland*: [1985] O.J. L376/21, [1988] 4 C.M.L.R. 306; banking as in *Eurocheque Helsinki Agreement*: [1992] O.J. L95/50, distribution of tickets at sporting events, as in *Distribution of package tours during 1990 World Cup*: [1992] O.J. L326/31.

[68] Cases 100–103/80, *Musique Diffusion Française and Others* v. *Commission*: [1983] E.C.R. 1823, [1983] 3 C.M.L.R. 221.

[69] *Ibid.* at para. 109.

Intentionally or negligently

7.13 Article 15 provides that the infringement must have been committed "intentionally or negligently". Both the Commission and the Court of Justice have taken a fairly robust line in relation to the application of this criterion. Whilst there have been cases where the Commission has found the infringement to have been committed "intentionally"[70] and others where "negligently,"[71] in practice the Commission has not restricted itself to finding one or the other and has on occasion found infringements to have been committed "intentionally or negligently"[72] or "intentionally, or at least negligently."[73] The Court of Justice has not condemned or been critical of this approach. There are, however, potential pitfalls for the Commission whichever formula it chooses. If it finds that the infringement was committed "intentionally" but the Court on appeal concludes that the infringement was not intentional but negligent, then it has been suggested that the Court must annul the decision and cannot substitute a finding of negligence.[74] If on the other hand the Commission uses the "alternative" formula, "intentionally or negligently", then assuming that an intentional infringement merits a greater fine than a mere negligent infringement[75] it is submitted that the Commission cannot impose a fine greater than it would for the (lesser) negligent infringement without fear of offending the principle of proportionality.[76]

Intentionally

7.14 "Intentionally" probably connotes an awareness by the undertaking that the conduct in question is or is reasonably likely to be restrictive of competition, coupled with a desire or preparedness to carry it out.[77] It will readily be appreciated that explicit evidence of such "intention" may be extremely rare or hard to come by. In practice, therefore, the Commission and the Court have been content to impute such intention

---

[70] For example, in *Kawasaki*: [1979] O.J. L16/9, [1979] 1 C.M.L.R. 448.

[71] For example, in *Deutsche Philips*: [1973] O.J. L293/40, [1973] C.M.L.R. D241 and see *Michelin*: [1981] O.J. L353/33, [1982] 1 C.M.L.R. 643, where the Commission found that NBIM had infringed Art. 86 by its discount policy "at least negligently."

[72] For example, *Pittsburgh Corning Europe*: [1972] J.O. L272/35, [1973] C.M.L.R. D2.

[73] For example, *Pioneer Hi-fi*: [1980] O.J. L60/21, [1980] 1 C.M.L.R. 457, or more recently *Polistil/Arbois*: [1984] O.J. L136/9, [1984] 2 C.M.L.R. 594 or *Hudson's Bay–Dansk Pelsdyravlerforening*: [1988] O.J. L316/43, [1989] 4 C.M.L.R. 340.

[74] Per A.G. Mayras in Case 26/75, *General Motors Continental BV* v. *Commission*: [1975] E.C.R. 1367, [1976] 1 C.M.L.R. 95, *sed quaere* whether the Court is so restricted in the exercise of its "full" or "unlimited" jurisdiction. And see A.G. Warner in Cases 32/78 & 36–82/79, *BMW Belgium* v. *Commission*: [1979] E.C.R. 2435, [1980] 1 C.M.L.R. 370.

[75] *Quinine* case: Cases 41, 44 & 45/69, *ACF Chemiefarma and Others* v. *Commission*: [1970] E.C.R. 661, Case 45/69, at para. 58.

[76] Harding, "The use of fines as a sanction in EEC competition law" (1979) 16 C.M.L.Rev. 591, at p. 603 appears to advocate the "alternative" approach: "If an intentional infringement cannot be established, the Commission may be able to prove more easily a negligent infringement, but it must be careful in its decision to make sure of its options by using the 'intentional, or at least negligent' formula."

[77] See, for example, the *Pioneer* case: Cases 100–103/80, *Musique Diffusion Francaise and Others* v. *Commission*: [1983] E.C.R. 1823, [1983] 3 C.M.L.R. 221, at para. 221. In Case 26/75, *General Motors Continental BV* v. *Commission*: [1975] E.C.R. 1367, [1976] 1 C.M.L.R. 95, A.G. Mayras said that "intentionally" "necessarily implies that the author of the infringement has acted intentionally with the will to commit an act which he knew was unlawful and prohibited by the Treaty and conscious of the unlawful consequences of his behaviour."

to undertakings on the basis of the facts and circumstances relating to their infringement. The *Vitamins* case[78] provides a good example. The Court of Justice, dealing with Roche's use of requirements contracts and fidelity rebates, said:[79]

> "The suggestions and instructions contained in *Management Information* and the other internal documents relating to the importance and the anticipated effects of entering into contracts, which provided for the purchaser obtaining his requirements exclusively from Roche and for a system of fidelity rebates, in relation to the retention by Roche of its market shares prove that the applicant intentionally pursued a commercial policy designed to bar the access to the market of new competitors. The increase from 1970 onwards of contracts under which the purchaser obtains his supplies exclusively from Roche or is induced to do so confirms this intention."

But even this sort of evidence may not be necessary in all cases. The Court has consistently held that it is sufficient that the undertaking could not have been unaware that the contested conduct had as its object the restriction of competition.[80] Thus in both *Miller International Schallplatten* v. *Commission*[81] and *BMW*,[82] the Court of Justice has made it clear that the mere imposition of a clause prohibiting exports in a contract or trade circular may be sufficient to indicate an intentional infringement.[83] The Court considered it irrelevant in such cases whether or not the undertaking knew that there was an infringement of the competition rules. The Court of First Instance has followed the Court of Justice. In its recent judgment in *Plasterboard* the Court of First Instance held that it was apparent from the very nature of the conduct in question, which was characterised by the imposition of a requirement not to deal in plasterboard other than that manufactured by the applicants, that the latter could not have been unaware that such conduct contravened the competition rules of the Treaty. Accordingly the conduct, the Court said, must be regarded as having been pursued intentionally.[84] In practice the state of development of the law, by reference to both Commission decisions

---

[78] Case 85/76, *Hoffmann-La Roche & Co. AG* v. *Commission*: [1979] E.C.R. 461, [1979] 3 C.M.L.R. 211. The Commission's decision is at: [1976] O.J. L223/27, [1976] 2 C.M.L.R. D25.

[79] *Ibid.* at para. 139.

[80] Case 246/86, *Société coopérative des asphalteurs Belges (Belasco) and others* v. *Commission*: [1989] E.C.R. 2117, [1991] 4 C.M.L.R. 96, at para. 41; Case 279/87, *Tipp-ex* v. *Commission*: [1990] I E.C.R. 261 and see also the Commission's decision in *London European–Sabena*: [1988] O.J. L317/47, [1989] 4 C.M.L.R. 662.

[81] Case 19/77, *Miller International Schallplatten GmbH* v. *Commission*: [1978] E.C.R. 131, [1978] 2 C.M.L.R. 334.

[82] Cases 32/78 & 36–82/79: [1979] E.C.R. 2435, [1980] 1 C.M.L.R. 370. And see *Johnson & Johnson*: [1980] O.J. L377/16, [1981] 2 C.M.L.R. 287, where the Commission indicated that it expected undertakings outside the Community (*in casu*, Swiss and American companies) to know that export bans are contrary to Community law.

[83] A principle applied in, for example, *Moët et Chandon (London) Ltd.*: [1982] O.J. L94/7, [1982] 2 C.M.L.R. 166; *Fisher Price/Quaker Oats Ltd.—Toyco:* [1988] O.J. L49/19, [1989] 4 C.M.L.R. 553 and *Viho/Parker Pen*: [1992] O.J. L233/27.

[84] Case T–65/89, *B.P.B. Industries Plc and British Gypsum Ltd.* v. *Commission*: not yet reported, at para. 166

and Court rulings, appears to be relevant in the Commission's finding whether an infringement was committed intentionally or otherwise.[85] Knowledge may still be significant in this context. Thus in *Konica*,[86] the Commission, in finding that Article 85(1) had been "deliberately" infringed, drew attention to the fact that the evidence revealed that Konica UK knew that an export ban constituted a serious violation of the Treaty. Active concealment of the agreement or practice by the parties may be considered strong evidence of an intentional infringement.[87]

Negligently

7.15 The fact that the infringement must be committed intentionally or negligently indicates that some degree of culpability is required and mere inadvertence or accident should not be punished. In *Deutsche Philips*,[88] the Commission found that Deutsche Philips had negligently infringed Article 85(1) when, having removed certain export prohibitions from a number of its agreements following an earlier proceeding brought by the Commission, it maintained an export ban in its electric shaver agreement for a further period of four years. The Commission apparently accepted that this was "the result of an error" within the undertaking but nevertheless considered that it was bound to impose a fine in respect of the infringement. While it is probably true to say that parties do not fall accidentally into price-fixing cartels,[89] collective boycotts[90] or arrangements insulating national markets,[91] blameworthiness may be less apparent in the borderline or grey areas of antitrust. So, for example no joint ventures have attracted fines.[92] This may to some extent be true in cases under Article 86 where an undertaking concerned may not only have difficulty in ascertaining whether or not it is dominant but also in determining whether its conduct may constitute an abuse, given that the boundaries of "abuse" are not definitely settled. The Court of Justice has, however, taken a firm line and requires dominant firms to exercise a standard of care commensurate with the size, capabilities and experience. Thus in the *United Brands* case, the Court said:[93]

---

[85] *Napier Brown/British Sugar*: [1988] O.J. L284/41, [1990] 4 C.M.L.R. 196. See also paras. 7.12 and 7.19.
[86] [1988] O.J. L78/34, [1988] 4 C.M.L.R. 848, at para. 52. See also *WEA-Filipachi*: [1972] J.O. L303/52, [1973] C.M.L.R. D43, and *National Panasonic*: [1982] O.J. L354/28, [1983] 1 C.M.L.R. 497.
[87] *Quinine*: [1969] J.O. L192/5, [1969] C.M.L.R. D41, and see *Cast Iron and Steel Rolls*: [1983] O.J. L317/1, [1984] 1 C.M.L.R. 694, where the Commission drew evidence of intentional infringement from the existence of an alarm system to warn members in the event of a sudden inspection by a competition authority, and a code system for communications between members routed via a neutral office in Switzerland. In *French-West African shipowners' committees*: [1992] O.J. L134/1, the Commission took account of the concealment of the practices in question by authorities in third countries beyond the Commission's jurisdiction.
[88] [1973] O.J. L293/40, [1973] C.M.L.R. D241, and see also *Floral*: [1980] O.J. L39/51, [1980] 2 C.M.L.R. 285, and Cases 240–242, 261, 262, 268 & 269/82, *Stichting Sigarettenindustrie* v. *Commission*: [1985] E.C.R. 3831, [1987] 3 C.M.L.R. 661, at paras. 65–68.
[89] For example, *Quinine*, above.
[90] For example, *Groupement des Fabricants de Papiers Peints de Belgique*: [1974] O.J. L237/3, [1974] 2 C.M.L.R. D102.
[91] For example, *Preserved Mushrooms*: [1975] O.J. L29/26, [1975] 1 C.M.L.R. D83.
[92] Indeed only two have been condemned by decision. See *WANO-Schwarzpulver*: [1978] O.J. L322/26, [1979] 1 C.M.L.R. 403, and *Astra*: [1993] O.J. L20/23.
[93] Case 27/76, *United Brands Co. and United Brands Continental BV* v. *Commission*: [1977] E.C.R. 207, [1978] 1 C.M.L.R. 429, at paras. 298–301.

"The applicant submits that it did not know that it was in a dominant position, still less that it had abused it, especially as, according to the case law of the Court to date, only undertakings which were pure monopolies or controlled an overwhelming share of the market have been held to be in a dominant position. UBC is an undertaking which, having engaged for a very long time in international and national trade, has special knowledge of antitrust laws, and has already experienced their severity. UBC by setting up a commercial system combining the prohibition of the sale of bananas while still green, discriminatory prices, deliveries less than the amounts ordered, all of which was to end in strict partitioning of national markets, adopted measures which it knew or ought to have known contravened the prohibition set out in Article 86 of the Treaty."

The Court of Justice concluded that the Commission therefore had good reason to find that UBC's infringements were "at least very negligent." Similarly in *Vitamins*,[94] the Court of Justice expected Roche, a multinational experienced in antitrust, to exercise a high standard of care in its dealings. But it is not only multinationals who must take care. In *Miller*,[95] Advocate General Warner said: "I think that traders in the Community ought to be presumed to know the law as laid down by the Treaties, by Regulations made thereunder and perhaps by decisions of this Court."[96] The Commission certainly expects firms, including those based outside the Community, to be correctly informed of the legal position in their major markets.[97] It expects parties to know of the Court's rulings[98] and its own decisions,[99] and of the existence of block exemptions and if their agreements go beyond what is permitted, the need for them to be notified.[1]

Amount of the fine

7.16 In fixing the amount of the fine, Article 15(2) requires the Commission to have regard to both the gravity and the duration of the infringement.

Gravity of the infringement

7.17 In *Pioneer*,[2] the Court of Justice said that in assessing the gravity of an infringement regard must be had to a large number of factors, the nature and importance of which vary according to the type of infringement in question and the circumstances of the case. These factors may include the conduct of each of the undertakings, the

---

[94] Above, n. 78, at paras. 128–137.

[95] Case 19/77, *Miller International Schallplatten GmbH* v. *Commission*: [1978] E.C.R. 131, [1978] 2 C.M.L.R. 334. Note that A.G. Warner makes no reference to Commission decisions.

[96] See Cases 32/78 & 36–82/79, *BMW Belgium* v. *Commission*: [1979] E.C.R. 2435, [1980] 1 C.M.L.R. 370, where the Court upheld the findings of negligent infringement on the part of several dealers.

[97] *Wood Pulp*: [1985] O.J. L85/1, [1985] 3 C.M.L.R. 474.

[98] *Polistil/Arbois*: [1984] O.J. L136/9, [1984] 2 C.M.L.R. 594, at para. 60, and *British Leyland*: [1984] O.J. L207/11, [1984] 3 C.M.L.R. 92, at para. 31, and *Distribution of railway tickets by travel agents:* [1992] O.J. L366/47.

[99] See *Johnson & Johnson*: [1980] O.J. L377/16, [1981] 2 C.M.L.R. 287, at para. 22.

[1] *Siemens/Fanuc*: [1985] O.J. L376/29, [1988] 4 C.M.L.R. 945, where the agreement fell outside Reg. 67/67.

[2] Cases 100–103/80, *Musique Diffusion Francaise and Others* v. *Commission*: [1983] E.C.R. 1823, [1983] 3 C.M.L.R. 221, at paras. 120 and 129. For a brief statement of the Commission's approach, see the Reply to Written Question No. 2002/86: [1987] O.J. C133/52.

role played by each of them, the profit which they were able to derive from the infringements, the volume and value of goods concerned, the size and economic power of the undertaking and, consequently, the influence which the undertaking was able to exert on the market, and the threat that infringements of the type concerned pose to the objectives of the Community. A variety of factors[3] may therefore be relevant in this context. The analysis below broadly follows the Court's categorisation.

Nature of the infringement

7.18　It is clear that the Commission regards the nature of the infringement, and in particular the purpose and effects of the condemned restriction on the competitive position, as a most important factor concerning the gravity of the infringement. The Commission has repeatedly[4] said that export bans constitute a grave infringement of Article 85 preventing the attainment of a single market, the attainment of a fundamental objective of the Treaty, and *Pioneer*[5] indicates that fines may be very substantial in relation to such activities. The Court of Justice has taken a similar view on export bans. In *Miller* it said:[6] "With regard to the gravity of the infringement, the clause prohibiting exports constitutes a form of restriction on competition which by its very nature jeopardises trade between Member States."

Infringements of the classic type, in particular horizontal agreements fixing prices and market sharing, will almost certainly attract a fine.[7] Irreversibly removing a competitor from the market may attract a heavy fine.[8] The Commission will look to see if the agreement has produced significant effects on the market.[9] In *British Midland* v.

---

[3] In the *Sugar* case: Cases 40–48, 50, 54–56, 111, 113 & 114/73, *Co-operatieve Vereniging "Suiker Unie" UA and others* v. *Commission*: [1975] E.C.R. 1663, [1976] 1 C.M.L.R. 295, the Court referred (at para. 612) to the "legislative background and economic context" of the conduct in question.

[4] For other examples, see *National Panasonic*: [1982] O.J. L354/28, [1983] 1 C.M.L.R. 497; *John Deere*: [1985] O.J. L35/58, [1985] 2 C.M.L.R. 554; *Sperry New Holland*: [1985] O.J. L376/21, [1988] 4 C.M.L.R. 306; *Sandoz*: [1987] O.J. L222/28, [1989] 4 C.M.L.R. 628; *Konica*: [1988] O.J. L78/34, [1988] 4 C.M.L.R. 848; *Fisher Price/Quaker Oats Ltd. – Toyco*: [1988] O.J. L49/19, [1989] 4 C.M.L.R. 553 and *Viho/Toshiba*: [1991] O.J. L287/39, [1992] 5 C.M.L.R. 180. In the case of an export ban, the very nature of the infringement may in the mind of the Commission outweigh its effectiveness—see *Johnson & Johnson*: [1980] O.J. L377/16, [1981] 2 C.M.L.R. 287, at para. 46, dealing with the German export ban.

[5] Above, n. 2.

[6] Case 19/77, *Miller International Schallplatten GmbH* v. *Commission*: [1978] E.C.R. 131, [1978] 2 C.M.L.R. 334, at para. 19. And see also Cases 32/78 & 36–82/79: *BMW Belgium and Others* v. *Commission*: [1979] E.C.R. 2435, [1980] 1 C.M.L.R. 370; Case 279/87, *Tipp-ex* v. *Commission*: [1990] I E.C.R. 261 and Case C–277/87, *Sandoz* v. *Commission*: [1990] I E.C.R. 45.

[7] See, for example, *Zinc Producer Group*: [1984] O.J. L220/27, [1985] 2 C.M.L.R. 108; *Benelux Flat Glass*: [1984] O.J. L212/13, [1985] 2 C.M.L.R. 350 and *MELDOC*: [1986] O.J. L348/50, [1989] 4 C.M.L.R. 853. In Cases 240–242, 261, 262, 268 & 269/82, *Stichting Sigarettenindustrie* v. *Commission*: [1985] E.C.R. 3831, [1987] 3 C.M.L.R. 661, the Court noted the seriousness of price-fixing agreements. See also *PVC*: [1989] O.J. L74/1, [1990] 4 C.M.L.R. 345; *LdPE*: [1989] O.J. L74/21, [1990] 4 C.M.L.R. 382 and *Solvay/ICI*: [1991] O.J. L152/1.

[8] *Tetra Pak II*: [1992] O.J. L72/1, [1992] 4 C.M.L.R. 551. See also *Eurofix-Bauco* v. *Hilti*: [1988] O.J. L65/19, [1989] 4 C.M.L.R. 677 (upheld by Court of First Instance — Case T–30/89, *Hilti AG* v. *Commission*: [1991] II E.C.R. 1439, [1992] 4 C.M.L.R. 16).

[9] *Polypropylene*: [1986] O.J. L230/1, [1988] 4 C.M.L.R. 347. Note also let the Court of Justice in Case C–62/86, *AKZO* v. *Commission*: [1991] I E.C.R. 3359, [1993] 5 C.M.L.R. 215 described as "particularly serious" attempts to prevent a competitor from extending its activity into the market. See also *Hudson's Bay–Dansk Pelsdyravlerforening*: [1988] O.J. L316/43, [1989] 4 C.M.L.R. 340 where the Commission considered that the restriction had resulted in an almost total elimination of competition in the relevant market (fur sales in Denmark).

Aer Lingus, the Commission took into account the fact that Aer Lingus' conduct had been intended to affect the structure of competition by penalising a competitor entering an important market and therefore was particularly serious.[10] Even where there may not be significant effects on the market the Commission may still impose a fine where the parties have the intention of insulating or dividing markets.[11]

Knowledge of the parties

7.19 The Commission will also have regard to whether the undertaking knew or ought to have known[12] that the conduct in question involved a breach of Article 85 or 86. In *Floral*,[13] the Commission fined three leading French manufacturers of fertilisers in relation to their participation in an export cartel (Floral) dealing with the supply of certain compound fertilisers to Germany. There had been a considerable amount of activity by the Commission in relation to fertiliser cartels and the Commission pointed out that the French manufacturers knew that it regarded fertiliser export cartels within the Community as prohibited by Article 85 and as not capable of exemption.[14] The fact that the undertakings in question have been found guilty of previous infringements may be particularly relevant. But as the Court of First Instance said in *Polypropylene* "the absence of any previous infringement is a normal circumstance which the Commission does not have to take into account as a mitigating factor", especially if the case involves a particularly clear infringement of the competition rules.[15] But whilst the illegality of certain infringements of Article 85 (such as those mentioned in the previous paragraph) is well established and known, where the Commission's decision breaks new ground or there was previously some doubt or uncertainty as to the status of the conduct in question then the likelihood of a fine is less great,[16] and even where one is imposed it may be "moderate."

This is how the Commission described its fine in *United Brands*[17] relating to UBC's pricing policy. The Commission recognised that account should be taken of the fact that its decision was the first occasion on which such a policy had been fully considered by it in the light of Article 86. In *AKZO*,[18] the Court of Justice reduced the fine taking into account, *inter alia*, "that abuses of this kind [unreasonably low prices]

---

[10] [1992] O.J. L96/34, [1993] 4 C.M.L.R. 596.

[11] See *Preserved Mushrooms*: [1975] O.J. L29/26, [1975] 1 C.M.L.R. D83; *London European–Sabena*: [1988] O.J. L317/47, [1989] 4 C.M.L.R. 662 and *French-West African shipowners' committees*: [1992] O.J. L134/1.

[12] As to what the Commission expects, see para. 7.15.

[13] [1980] O.J. L39/51, [1980] 2 C.M.L.R. 285.

[14] Joint selling agencies in the fertiliser industry had been the subject of the Commission's scrutiny for some time. See *Cobelaz*: [1968] J.O. L276/13, [1968] C.M.L.R. D45; *CFA*: [1968] J.O. L276/29, [1968] C.M.L.R. D57, and *SEIFA*: [1969] J.O. L173/8. And note the Commission's "second thoughts" in its First Report on Competition Policy, points 11–18, Third Report, points 50–52, and Fourth Report, points 144–145. The Commission had given the French manufacturers full information on the position of export cartels under Art. 85 in its proceedings against CFA shortly before Floral was formed.

[15] Case T–7/89, *SA Hercules NV* v. *Commission*: [1992] 4 C.M.L.R. 84, at para. 348.

[16] See *Vegetable Parchment*: [1978] O.J. L70/54, [1978] 1 C.M.L.R. 534. The lack of legal precedents was noted in *Decca Navigation System*: [1989] O.J. L43/27, [1990] 4 C.M.L.R. 627. See also the analysis of the state of development of the law relating to abuses under Art. 86 in *Napier Brown/British Sugar*: [1988] O.J. L284/41, [1990] 4 C.M.L.R. 196.

[17] *Sub. nom. Chiquita*: [1976] O.J. L95/1, [1976] 1 C.M.L.R. D28, at para. 119.

[18] Above n. 9, at para. 163.

come within a field of law in which the rules of competition had never been determined precisely". In *Peugeot*, the Commission declined to fine Peugeot for a systematic refusal of supplies within a distribution system. The necessary clarification of the obligations on dealers was not given until the Court of Justice's judgment in the *Ford* case.[19] Novelty is not, however, a bar to the Commission imposing a fine, especially where the law is well-known even if it has not been the subject of an earlier Commission decision. So in *Cewal, Cowac and Ukwal*,[20] a case under Regulation 4056/86, the Commission fined certain members of a shipping conference. They were treated as knowing the unacceptable nature of their behaviour both in relation to the terms of Regulation 4056/86 and to other benchmarks such as the UNCTAD Code of Conduct.

Behaviour of the parties

7.20 Where, for example, undertakings have striven to keep secret and concealed their anti-competitive agreement or practice, the infringement will be aggravated. In *Johnson & Johnson*,[21] the Commission referred to the "determined and vigorous manner" in which the undertaking had sought to prevent exports and to the means employed to identify and dissuade exporters. Conversely the publicity and transparency of an agreement may go to mitigation of a fine.[22] The institutionalised nature of the cartel may however be an aggravating factor.[23] The Commission will also have regard to the reaction of undertakings when the position under Community law is brought to their attention either by customers, complainants or the Commission. Persistence in the infringement may increase the gravity of the infringement as in *WEA-Filipachi*,[24] where the distributor concerned continued to impose an export ban despite being warned by retailers of its illegality under Community law, or in *Newitt/Dunlop Slazenger International*[25] where it appears that the infringements continued notwithstanding formal warnings from the Commission. Obstructing the Commission's investigation by trying to influence or co-ordinate responses may be an aggravating factor.[26] On the other hand, voluntary termination of an infringement and co-operation with the Commission may be mitigating factors.[27] The Commission will also take into account any remedial action taken by the undertakings concerned; for example, the partial repayment of the alleged excessive charges in the *General Motors* case.[28]

---

[19] [1986] O.J. L295/19, [1989] 4 C.M.L.R. 371. See the Sixteenth Report on Competition Policy, p. 64. Notification also precluded a fine in respect of part of the conduct in question. Peugeot also got the benefit in *Eco System/Peugeot:* [1992] O.J. L66/1, [1993] 4 C.M.L.R. 42, where the decision was of an explanatory nature, the first of its type clarifying the position of authorised agents under Reg. 123/85.

[20] [1993] O.J. L34/20. In *French-West African shipowners' committees*, above, n. 11, the Commission took the same approach to the publicity surrounding Reg. 4056/86. See also *British Midland* v. *Aer Lingus*, above, n. 10, where the Commission fined Aer Lingus under Art. 86 but not under Art. 85(1), having regard to the relationship of the timing of the infringement and the introduction of Reg. 84/91.

[21] *Johnson & Johnson*: [1980] O.J. L377/16, [1981] 2 C.M.L.R. 287.

[22] *Building and construction industry in the Netherlands*: [1992] O.J. L92/1.

[23] *PVC*: above n. 7 and *LdPE, ibid.*

[24] [1972] J.O. L303/52, [1973] C.M.L.R. D43, and note the position of Theal in *Theal/Watts*: [1977] O.J. L39/19, [1977] 1 C.M.L.R. D44.

[25] [1988] O.J. L284/41 and see also *Peroxygen Products*: [1985] O.J. L35/1, [1985] 1 C.M.L.R. 481. *AROW/BNIC*: [1982] O.J. L379/1, [1983] 2 C.M.L.R. 240; *ECS/AKZO*: [1985] O.J. L374/1, [1986] 3 C.M.L.R. 273 and *Eurofix-Bauco* v. *Hilti*, above, n. 8.

[26] See *Bayo-n-ox*: [1990] O.J. L21/71, [1990] 4 C.M.L.R. 930, and *Newitt/Dunlop*: [1992] O.J. L131/32.

[27] See para. 7.36.

[28] [1974] O.J. L29/14, [1975] 1 C.M.L.R. D20.

Nature and value of the product

7.21   The Commission, in fixing the level of the fine, may have regard to the volume and value of the product or services involved and to the impact of the agreement on consumers.[29] The Court of Justice has also recognised this. In the *Sugar* case,[30] it noted that: "The damage which the users and consumers suffered as a result of the conduct to which exception is taken was limited." The nature of the product and its importance to consumers may be relevant in this context. In *Theal/Watts*,[31] the Commission took into account the fact that the product, a record cleaning device, was not one that could be regarded as necessary for the consumer or as forming an essential part of his expenditure. On the other hand, in *Hasselblad*,[32] the Commission noted that the products concerned (expensive high-quality cameras) were not in mass production but had a high unit value and the impact even on a small number of users might be considerable. It is of course difficult to gauge precisely the direct economic consequences of particular infringements. However, the Commission has in a number of cases emphasised the effect of the alleged infringements on consumers and consumer prices in particular. "Consumer" here does not necessarily mean the ultimate consumer. The impact on industry in the Community may be relevant. So in *Siemens/Fanuc*,[33] the Commission noted that the exclusive distribution denied the Community machine-tool industry access at the best possible prices to a development of modern technology of the utmost importance. In *Konica*,[34] on the other hand the Commission noted that the actual economic impact on trade between Member States was not very great and that Konica's market was very small.[35]

Number and size of the parties

7.22   The Commission will have regard to the number and size of the undertakings and the economic impact of the agreement on the market. The position and number of the parties concerned may be an indication of the economic power possessed and the influence the undertakings were able to exert on the market. This may have an effect on the seriousness of the restriction on competition, and hence the gravity of the infringement. In *PVC*,[36] the Commission noted that PVC was a major industrial product with sales of over 3,000 million ECUs annually in Western Europe, and that the undertakings concerned accounted for almost the whole of this market. The Commission will consider what the market is worth and what is the economic significance of the

---

[29] This may also influence whether to impose any fine at all. See the view taken by the Commission in *Vegetable Parchment*, above, n. 16, as to the conduct of Wiggins Teape and the French and German manufacturers in relation to the British market.

[30] Cases 40–48, 50, 54–56, 111, 113 & 114/73, *Co-operatieve Vereniging "Suiker Unie" UA and others* v. *Commission*: [1975] E.C.R. 1663, [1976] 1 C.M.L.R. 295, at para. 621.

[31] [1977] O.J. L39/19, [1977] 1 C.M.L.R. D44, and note the similar approach taken by the Court of Justice in Case 28/77, *Tepea* v. *Commission*: [1978] E.C.R. 1391, [1978] 3 C.M.L.R. 392.

[32] [1982] O.J. L161/18, [1982] 2 C.M.L.R. 233.

[33] [1985] O.J. L376/29, [1988] 4 C.M.L.R. 945.

[34] [1988] O.J. L78/34, [1988] 4 C.M.L.R. 848.

[35] See also *Quantel International – Continuum/Quantel SA*: [1992] O.J. L235/9. Most of the products concerned had not been placed on the market by the time of the (late) notification. Therefore the restrictions in question had a very limited effect on trade in the relevant products.

[36] [1989] O.J. L74/1, [1990] 4 C.M.L.R. 345. See also *Floral*:. [1980] O.J. L39/51, [1980] 2 C.M.L.R. 285; *LdPE*: [1989] O.J. L74/21, [1990] 4 C.M.L.R. 382, and *Viho/Toshiba*: [1991] O.J. L287/39, [1992] 5

relevant product market. It will also look at the structure of the market,[37] whether it is competitive and what, for example, is the effect of the agreement on the level of prices.[38] The Commission will assess what share of the market the undertakings have.[39] The turnovers achieved may give indications of the relevant market positions of the undertakings involved, and thereby indicate the gravity of their involvement in the infringement.[40]

Extent of participation in infringement

7.23 The Commission will take into account in fixing the amount of the fine to be imposed on each undertaking concerned any difference in the roles played by the undertakings in the infringement as well as any difference in the degree or length of participation. The Court of Justice has endorsed this approach. For example, in *BMW*,[41] the Court upheld the Commission's fining the members of the Dealers' Advisory Committee more heavily than the signatory dealers. The ringleaders can expect to get the much heavier fines.[42] But if there is equal participation then there will be equal fines.[43] If more than one undertaking is being fined, the Commission must consider the position of each undertaking separately.[44] When on appeal fines have been reduced, the Court of First Instance has retained the principle that the fines, their amounts reduced, must remain proportionally the same.[45] Where an undertaking has played only

C.M.L.R. 180. Compare *Vaessen/Moris*: [1979] O.J. L19/32, [1979] 1 C.M.L.R. 511, where the Commission referred to the very small nature of the undertaking and the very little financial benefit from the restrictive agreement in question as reasons for not imposing a fine.

[37] See *MELDOC*: [1986] O.J. L348/50, [1989] 4 C.M.L.R. 853, where the Commission recognised the difficult market situation that the undertakings faced, in particular the concentration of market power on the side of the big retailers, consolidation by way of take-overs and mergers, the important change in the composition of the product range and vulnerability to exports.

[38] See, *e.g. Wood Pulp*: [1985] O.J. L85/1, [1985] 3 C.M.L.R. 474.

[39] See, *e.g. Polistil/Arbois*: [1984] O.J. L136/9, [1984] 2 C.M.L.R. 594. *Viho/Toshiba*, above.

[40] Recognised by the Court of Justice in the *Pioneer* case: Cases 100–103/80, *Musique Diffusion Francaise and Others* v. *Commission*: [1983] E.C.R. 1823, [1983] 3 C.M.L.R. 221, at paras. 119–120.

[41] Cases 32/78 & 36–82/79: [1979] E.C.R. 2435, [1980] 1 C.M.L.R. 370, at para. 51. See also the treatment of Fincell in *Wood Pulp II*: Cases C 89, 104, 114, 116, 117 & 125–129/85, *A. Åhlström Osakeyhtio and Others* v. *Commission*: [1993] 4 C.M.L.R. 407, at para. 189. It works in the other direction too. See *SSI*, above, n. 88, at para. 100, where the Court reduced the fine on Reynolds because of its "less active participation", and Case 279/87, *Tipp-ex* v. *Commission:* [1990] I E.C.R. 261, where the Court considered it normal for the fine on the local distributor, Beiersdorf, to be lower in view of its secondary role.

[42] For example, in *Pioneer Hi-fi*: [1980] O.J. L60/21, [1980] 1 C.M.L.R. 457, Pioneer Electronics (Europe) was fined most heavily as "the dominant economic partner." Note the position of Montepolimeri and ICI in *Polypropylene*: [1986] O.J. L230/1, [1988] 4 C.M.L.R. 347. And see the distinction drawn in *LdPE*: [1989] O.J. L74/21, [1990] 4 C.M.L.R. 382 between those who were full members of the cartel and those who operated only on the periphery.

[43] All other things being equal: *Siemens/Fanuc*: [1985] O.J. L376/29, [1988] 4 C.M.L.R. 945.

[44] In the *Quinine* case: Cases 41, 44 & 45/69, *ACF Chemiefarma and Others* v. *Commission*: [1970] E.C.R. 661, Case 45/69, at para. 55, the Court of Justice said that the fixing of an aggregate fine which is then apportioned among the undertakings concerned is not incompatible with this approach. See also *Dyestuffs*: Cases 48, 49, 51–57/69, *ICI and Others* v. *Commission*: [1972] E.C.R. 619, [1972] C.M.L.R. 557. Where, however, an undertaking has been guilty of several infringements, it does not appear to be necessary for the Commission to stipulate a separate fine for each infringement. See the *Sugar* case: Cases 40–48, 50, 54–56, 111, 113 & 114/73, *Co-operatieve Vereniging "Suiker Unie" UA and others* v. *Commission*: [1975] E.C.R. 1663, [1976] 1 C.M.L.R. 295.

[45] *Italian Flat Glass* on appeal: Cases T 68 & 77–78/89, *Società Italiano Vetro SpA and others* v. *Commission*: [1992] II E.C.R. 1403, [1992] 5 C.M.L.R. 302, at para. 373.

a very minor role compared with the other undertakings who were the principal parties in and beneficiaries of the unlawful activity or where parties have acted under duress or unwillingly or against their own economic interests then the Commission may decide to impose no fine at all on that undertaking.[46]

This is not always the case. As the Commission noted in *French–West African Shipowners Committees*,[47] an undertaking which is under strong pressure to associate itself with practices contrary to the Treaty rules always has the possibility of appealing to the Commission or to the national courts to request that such practices be brought to an end.

Legislative and economic context

7.24 The infringement has to be considered in the light of its legislative and economic context.[48] This may be particularly important where there is interaction between the Community's competition rules and other Community policy and legislation. Thus, in the *Sugar* case,[49] the Court of Justice acknowledged that the Community's common organisation of the market in sugar left very little room for competition and "helped to ensure that sugar producers continue to behave in an uncompetitive manner." This, the Court said, did not justify the anti-competitive conduct but meant that it should not be judged as rigorously as it would otherwise have been. The Commission appears to have taken a similar approach where the structure of the market has been affected by Community legislation.[50] On the other hand, in *Pioneer*,[51] the Court of Justice rejected the argument that the Commission's authorisation under Article 115 of the Treaty for France to exclude from Community

[46] See, for example, the position of Firma Schiffer in *Floral*: [1980] O.J. L39/51, [1980] 2 C.M.L.R. 285, the dealers in *Sperry New Holland*: [1985] O.J. L376/21, [1988] 4 C.M.L.R. 306 and in *Konica*: [1988] O.J. L78/34, [1988] 4 C.M.L.R. 848, the unwilling non-members in *Roofing Felt*: [1986] O.J. L232/15, [1991] 4 C.M.L.R. 130; Toyco in *Fisher Price/Quaker Oats Ltd.—Toyco*: [1988] O.J. L49/19, [1989] 4 C.M.L.R. 553; Herlitz in *Viho/Parker Pen*: [1992] O.J. L233/27; the smaller exclusive distributors in *Tipp-Ex*: [1987] O.J. L222/1, [1989] 4 C.M.L.R. 425 the position of NAC in *Building and construction industry in the Netherlands*: [1992] O.J. L92/1.

[47] [1992] O.J. L134/1, referring to the position of the cross-traders.

[48] Again, this may be relevant not only at the stage of fining, but also at the stage of finding any infringement. See *Cane Sugar*: [1980] O.J. L39/64, [1980] 2 C.M.L.R. 559.

[49] Cases 40–48, 50, 54–56, 111, 113 & 114/73, *Co-operatieve Vereniging "Suiker Unie" UA and others* v. *Commission*: [1975] E.C.R. 1663, [1976] 1 C.M.L.R. 295, at paras. 619 and 620.

[50] See *SSI*: [1982] O.J. L232/1, [1983] 3 C.M.L.R. 702 where the Commission took into account the relevant E.C. directive on taxes affecting the consumption of tobacco and the Dutch excise and price laws. See also *MELDOC*: [1986] O.J. L348/50, [1989] 4 C.M.L.R. 853. See also *Welded steel mesh*: [1989] O.J. L260/1, [1991] 4 C.M.L.R. 13 where account was taken of the effect of the Commission's crisis measures for the steel industry during the relevant period. *Cf.* the rejection of its arguments relating to the Community's directives on public procurement in *Building and construction industry in the Netherlands*, above, n. 46.

[51] Cases 100–103/80, *Musique Diffusion Francaise and Others* v. *Commission*: [1983] E.C.R. 1823, [1983] 3 C.M.L.R. 221, at paras. 99 and 100. See also *Preserved Mushrooms*: [1975] O.J. L29/26, [1975] 1 C.M.L.R. D83, where the Commission held that even if the undertakings concerned believed that there would be a serious disturbance on the market by dumping (later recognised by the Commission in Reg. 2107/74) that did not permit an infringement of the Treaty in order to alleviate the position. *Cf. BPB Industries PLC*: [1989] O.J. L10/50, [1990] 4 C.M.L.R. 464 where the Commission, whilst noting that no formal dumping complaint had been made, took into account when fixing the level of the fine the fact that BPB's conduct had been directed at countering Spanish imports at a time when Spain was outside the Community.

treatment Japanese hi-fi products justified a cancellation or reduction of the fine. The position of the agreement in relation to the national law of the relevant Member States may also have to be considered. Undertakings cannot be expected to disregard totally the local law where they reside or carry on business and whilst national law cannot, of course, authorise or render permissible conduct prohibited by Article 85 or 86[52] the domestic legislative context, and in particular the legality of conduct under national law,[53] may be a factor to be taken into consideration by the Commission when fining, particularly where the illegality under Community law is not clear or well established.[54]

Duration of the infringement

7.25   In fixing the amount of the fine the Commission is required to have regard not only to the gravity of the infringement but also its duration.[55] In practice it may be difficult to keep the two considerations separate because the time-factor will often be relevant to the circumstances and other matters which make up the gravity of the infringement. But generally speaking, the longer the infringement the greater will be the fine. In *Pioneer*, for example, the Court of Justice had regard to the shorter duration resulting from the partial annulment of the decision (which had purported to deal with infringements of a longer duration than those mentioned in the statement of objections) when considering the claims for a reduction of the fines.[56] But, as the Court indicated in *SSI*, the fact that an infringement operates for only a fairly short period does not necessarily exclude a fine or operate as an extenuating circumstance.[57] In

---

[52] National statutory price controls cannot, for example, justify export bans. See Case 15/74, *Centrafarm* v. *Sterling Drug:* [1974] E.C.R. 1183, [1974] 2 C.M.L.R. 480, and *Johnson & Johnson:* [1980] O.J. L377/16, [1981] 2 C.M.L.R. 287. But see *AROW/BNIC:* [1982] O.J L379/1, [1983] 2 C.M.L.R. 240, where the Commission appeared to recognise the special legal context in which BNIC's decisions were extended by Ministerial order. See also the Court of First Instance in Case T–16/91, *Rendo NV* v. *Commission:* not yet reported; the Commission could not compel undertakings to act in a manner which was contradictory to a national law for the purpose of terminating a breach of Art. 85, without assessing the national law in the light of Community law.

[53] In *Welded steel mesh:* [1989] O.J. L260/1, [1991] 4 C.M.L.R. 13 the Commission took account of the fact that the German central authority had authorised the foundation of a structural crisis cartel in Germany. The Commission found that this did not justify illegal measures taken in other Member States but it was an element of mitigation.

[54] Case 73/74, *Groupements des Fabricants de Papiers Peints de Belgique* v. *Commission:* [1975] E.C.R. 1491, [1976] 1 C.M.L.R. 589, *per* A.G. Trabucchi.

[55] In *Johnson & Johnson:* [1980] O.J. L377/16, [1981] 2 C.M.L.R. 287, the Commission described the four years during which an export ban operated in the U.K. as a "considerable period". Similarly in *Hilti,* above, n. 98, the Court of First Instance (at para. 134) described four years as "an appreciable period". In *Distribution of railway tickets by travel agents:* [1992] O.J. L366/47 the recommendation in question dated back to 1952, and in *Hudson's Bay – Dansk Pelsdyravlerforening:* [1988] O.J. L316/43, [1989] 4 C.M.L.R. 340 infringement lasted 12 years but still overall only a low fine was imposed. Short periods were noted in *Konica:* [1988] O.J. L78/34, [1988] 4 C.M.L.R. 848 (five months) and *London European – Sabena:* [1988] O.J. L317/47, [1989] 4 C.M.L.R. 662 (two months). For cases where duration was affected by accession see *Hugin/Liptons:* [1978] O.J. L22/23, [1978] 1 C.M.L.R. D19 and *Soda-ash Solvay, ICI:* [1991] O.J. L152/1. In the latter case the Commission treated the infringement as regards ICI as commencing on the date of U.K. accession; 1992, although the Commission held that the relevant period for the fine could have run from 1962 (when Reg. 17 came into effect).

[56] Cases 100–103/80, *Musique Diffusion Française and Others* v. *Commission:* [1983] E.C.R. 1823, [1983] 3 C.M.L.R. 221, at paras. 123 and 124.

[57] Cases 240–242, 261, 262, 268 & 269/82, *Stichting Sigarettenindustrie* v. *Commission:* [1985] E.C.R. 3831, [1987] 3 C.M.L.R. 661, at para. 95. Particularly when the agreement operated precisely in the

Commercial Solvents,[58] the Court of Justice reduced the fine on account of the delay by the Commission in acting on the complaint. The Court considered that the infringement might have been shorter had the Commission intervened more quickly.

On the other hand, as indicated above, where conduct persists after Commission intervention (for example, an interim decision[59]) this will be an aggravating factor. It should also be remembered that where an agreement or practice has been notified to the Commission no fines can be imposed in respect of acts taking place after notification and before its decision in application of Article 85(3).[60] Finally, the duration of the infringement may be relevant not simply to the question of the amount of the fine but also to whether to fine at all[61] or to fine a particular party.[62]

Fines imposed

7.26 Article 15(2) provides that the Commission may impose fines of "from 1,000 to 1,000,000 units of account [now ECUs], or a sum in excess thereof but not exceeding 10 per cent. of the turnover in the preceding business year of each of the undertakings participating in the infringement."[63] The Commission did not exercise its powers of fining until 1969 but has done so on many occasions since then.[64] In practice the Commission will specify the amount of the fine in European Currency Units (ECUs), although formerly fines were specified in both ECUs and a national currency. The value of the ECU is computed daily by the Commission and published in the *Official Journal*. The monies provided by fines form a part of the revenues of the Community and are included in the general budget of the Community.[65]

Fining policy

7.27 In its Twenty-first Report on Competition Policy (1991) the Commission made the following statement:[66]

> "In the Tetra Pak decision the Commission imposed a very heavy fine, which reflected the serious nature and the long duration of the abuse in that case. That decision is indicative of the Commission's intention to make fuller use of the

---

period when some competition was possible.

[58] Cases 6 & 7/73: [1974] E.C.R. 223, [1974] 1 C.M.L.R. 309, at para. 51. Note the Court of Justice rejected a similar plea in Cases 32/78 & 36–82/79, *BMW*: [1979] E.C.R. 2435, [1980] 1 C.M.L.R. 370, at para. 45.

[59] *ECS/AKZO*: [1985] O.J. L374/1, [1986] 3 C.M.L.R. 273.

[60] Art. 15(5) of Reg. 17. And note Art. 15(6). See para. 7.33.

[61] In *Italian Flat Glass*: [1981] O.J. L326/32, [1982] 3 C.M.L.R. 366, the Commission took the view that it was not necessary to fine as the agreements were applied for a relatively short time (but it seems to have been 1½–2½ years) and that while the agreements were in existence the restrictions were only implemented partially. Contrast *Rolled Zinc*: [1982] O.J. L362/40, [1983] 2 C.M.L.R. 285, where the infringement was of short duration ("began at the latest on 21 October 1976 and persisted until 29 October 1979") but the infringement was a serious one.

[62] See the position of Condellis in *Sperry New Holland*: [1985] O.J. L376/21, [1988] 4 C.M.L.R. 306.

[63] A literal construction would give the result that a firm which has a turnover of less than 10 million units of account (now ECUs) can be fined in excess of 10 per cent. But see A.G. Warner in Case 19/77, *Miller International Schallplatten GmbH* v. *Commission*: [1978] E.C.R. 131, [1978] 2 C.M.L.R. 334.

[64] Readers wishing to see a complete list of fines should refer to Jones, Van der Woude and Lewis, *EEC Competition Law Handbook* (published annually).

[65] Answer to Written Question No. 715/80: [1980] O.J. C245/15.

[66] Point 139 of the Report.

possibility offered by Regulation No 17 to impose fines of up to 10% of the annual turnover of the companies involved, in order to reinforce the deterrent effect of penalties under Community competition law.

In assessing the fine, the Commission takes into account all the relevant facts of the case. The financial benefit which companies infringing the competition rules have derived from their infringements will become an increasingly important consideration. Wherever the Commission can ascertain the level of this ill-gotten gain, even if it cannot do so precisely, the calculation of the fine may have this as its starting-point. When appropriate, that amount could then be increased or decreased in the light of the other circumstances of the case, including the need to introduce an element of deterrence or penalty in the sanction imposed on the participating companies."

No tariff of fines

7.28   Article 15(2) does not prescribe a tariff of fines. It merely specifies an upper and a lower limit and requires the Commission when fixing the amount to have regard to the gravity and duration of the infringement. Until relatively recently, few fines have been at the level of or above 1,000,000 ECUs and most probably none had come anywhere near the 10 per cent. of turnover level. Before *Pioneer* the Commission had not imposed fines exceeding 2 per cent. of the total turnover of the undertaking, even in serious cases. In *Pioneer*,[67] the original fines ranged from 2 to 4 per cent. of turnover. Although the fines were reduced because of the question of "duration" (see paragraph 7.25 above) the Court of Justice clearly gave the Commission the green light for its new policy increasing the general level of fines. There have been some heavy fines in recent cases. Fines in millions of ECU are no longer rare.[68] The highest fine to date, 75 million ECU, was imposed in *Tetra Pak II* in 1992.[69]

What meaning, if any, then should be given to the limits fixed by Article 15(2)(a)? As the Court of Justice has indicated[70] the limits are fixed to prevent fines from being disproportionate to the size of the undertaking.[71]

Turnover in preceding year

7.29   One problem in determining the upper limit specified in Article 15(2)(a) lies in the ascertainment of "the turnover in the preceding business year" of the undertaking concerned.[72] Article 15 does not specify whether it is the total (possibly worldwide)

---

[67] Cases 100–103/80, *Musique Diffusion Francaise and Others* v. *Commission*: [1983] E.C.R. 1823, [1983] 3 C.M.L.R. 221.

[68] *Eurofix-Bauco* v. *Hilti* (1988), 6 million ECUs (see n. 8, above); *Flat Glass* (1989), 8 million ECUs on Pisanna, (see n. 66 above); *Soda-ash* (1991), 20 million ECUs on Solvay and 10 million ECUs on ICI (see n. 77, above); *Newitt/Dunlop* (1992), 5 million ECUs on Dunlop (see n. 25, above); *French-West African shipowners' committees*, 11.6 million ECUs on Delmas (see n. 11, above).

[69] [1992] O.J. L72/1, [1992] 4 C.M.L.R. 551.

[70] *Pioneer*, above, at para. 119. See also Case 19/77, *Miller International Schallplatten GmbH* v. *Commission*: [1978] E.C.R. 131, [1978] 2 C.M.L.R. 334, where A.G. Warner preferred a scale for fixing fines within the limits.

[71] On the principle of proportionality, see generally, paras. 8.25–26.

[72] Where the infringement is committed by an association of undertakings it may be appropriate to look at the total of the turnovers of its members rather than the association's turnover. See Cases T 39 & 40/92, *Groupement des cartes bancaires "CB" and Europay International SA* v. *Commission*: judgment of February 24, 1994, not yet reported, where the Court of First Instance rejected the plea that Art. 15(2) did not

turnover in all products that is pertinent or whether it is only turnover in the relevant products in the Community or in that part of the Community affected by the infringement. In *Pioneer*,[73] the Court of Justice confirmed that it is the total turnover of the undertaking concerned:

> "the limit [1 million ECUs] seeks to prevent fines from being disproportionate in relation to the size of the undertaking and, since only the total turnover can give an approximate indication of that size, the aforementioned percentage [10 per cent.] must . . . be understood as referring to the total turnover."

No territorial limit need be taken into account when calculating an undertaking's turnover.[74] Turnover in the relevant products may concern the question of gravity. So it is permissible, for the purpose of fixing the fine, to have regard both to the total turnover of the undertaking (which indicates, albeit imperfectly, the size and economic power of the undertaking) and to the proportion of the turnover accounted for by the goods in respect of which the infringement was committed (which indicates the scale of the infringement).[75] Where turnover is inappropriate (*e.g.* in the case of a trade association) another criterion, such as annual expenditure, will be considered.[76]

Profits of the infringement

7.30 As the policy statement quoted above[77] indicates the Commission in fixing the amount of the fine will take into account any profits or other financial benefits achieved by this undertaking as a result of the infringement. An undertaking cannot and should not expect to profit from the infringement and the difficulty of computing the "unlawful" profits has not deterred the Commission.[78] Thus in *Eurocheque: Helsinki Agreement*,[79] the Commission calculated the annual gains for the French banks concerned in terms of the commissions obtained by the operation of the agreement, taking an average amount of a Eurocheque, the approximate annual number of Eurocheques used and the average commission applied. The Commission also considered indirect profits, through the suppression of the development of Eurocheques which

allow the Commission to look beyond the turnover of CB, a French *groupement* (similar to an EEIG) where the members were liable to third parties for the debts of the grouping.

[73] *Pioneer*, above, at para. 119.

[74] Case 279/87, *Tipp-ex* v. *Commission:* [1990] I E.C.R. 261.

[75] *Ibid.* at paras. 120 and 121. See, *e.g. Soda-ash Solvay, ICI:* [1991] O.J. L152/1, where Solvay and ICI were each fined 7 million ECUs—"while ICI's soda ash sales are less than one third of those of Solvay, its turnover for all products is three times greater than that of Solvay".

[76] See *Roofing Felt:* [1986] O.J. L232/15, [1991] 4 C.M.L.R. 130. Upheld by the Court of Justice in Case 246/86, *Société coopérative des asphalteurs Belges (Belasco) and others* v. *Commission:* [1989] E.C.R. 2117, [1991] 4 C.M.L.R. 96, at para. 66.

[77] See para. 7.27.

[78] Temple Lang, "EEC fines for restrictive practices and abuses of dominant position" (1978) 75 L.S.Gaz. 1094, says: "It would clearly be a guarantee of an ineffectual antitrust law if fines were consistently less than the profits derived from clearly unlawful behaviour. Therefore, in cases where it is reasonably clear that the companies knew that they were acting contrary to the EEC Treaty, it seems reasonable that the fine on each company should (subject to all other relevant factors) be approximately equal to the profit it made from the unlawful behaviour, when that can be estimated. Restrictive practices are not crimes, but they should not be allowed to pay, either."

[79] [1992] O.J. L95/50. For an earlier example see *Kawasaki:* [1979] O.J. L16/9, [1979] 1 C.M.L.R. 448 where the Commission linked closely the amount of the fine with the higher prices paid by consumers as

would have competed with the banks' own cards.[80] Finally when considering different levels of fine for parties to the same infringement, the extent to which one party may have benefited more than another will be considered.[81]

Fines as deterrents

7.31 In the *Dyestuffs* case, BASF argued that the purpose of Article 15 was not to punish or to expiate activities in the past, but to prevent repetition of infringements and therefore it was sufficient for the Commission to take a decision against it. The Court of Justice replied:[82]

> "Article 15 of Regulation 17 does not limit the imposition of fines exclusively to cases of recurrence of infringements already found to have taken place and forbidden by the Commission under Article 3. Such limitation of Article 15 would considerably reduce the deterrent effect of fines."

In *Pioneer*,[83] the Court of Justice said that the Commission must ensure that its action has the necessary deterrent effect, especially as regards those types of infringement which are particularly harmful to the objectives of the Community. The Court pointed out that it may be appropriate to raise the level of fines to reinforce their deterrent effect.[84] The deterrent is not directed solely towards the undertakings the subject of the decision to the exclusion of other undertakings which might be considering similar activities contrary to Article 85 or 86. The Commission continues to set high fines as deterrents. In *ECS/AKZO*,[85] the Commission imposed an exemplary fine of 10 million ECUs. The 75 million ECU fine in *Tetra Pak II* will also not go unnoticed.

Ability to pay/economic circumstances

7.32 In *BMW*,[86] the Commission stated that it considered reference to an undertaking's turnover "important for the purposes of determining the degree to which the undertakings are affected by the fines imposed." This would suggest that the

---

the result of the export ban imposed on distributors.

[80] The Commission ended up fining Group CB 5 million ECUs and Eurocheque International 1 million ECUs. In *Groupement des cartes bancaires "CB" and Europay International SA* v. *Commission*, above, n. 72, the Court of First Instance reduced the fine on CB on the grounds that the Commission had erred in finding one aspect of the agreement in question to have infringed Art. 85 and therefore the assumption on which the calculation of unlawful profits had been made was no longer correct. Eurocheque's fine was quashed on the grounds of the Commission's failure to respect the rights of defence.

[81] See the position of Martell in *Gosme/Martell – DMP*: [1991] O.J. L185/23, [1992] 5 C.M.L.R. 586.

[82] Cases 48, 49, 51–57/69, *ICI and Others* v. *Commission*: [1972] E.C.R. 619, [1972] C.M.L.R. 557, (Case 49/69), at para. 38.

[83] Cases 100–103/80, *Musique Diffusion Francaise and Others* v. *Commission*: [1983] E.C.R. 1823, [1983] 3 C.M.L.R. 221., at para. 106.

[84] *Ibid.* at para. 108.

[85] [1985] O.J. L374/1, [1986] 3 C.M.L.R. 273. The fine was reduced to 7.5 million ECUs on appeal, but not on this ground. Case C–62/86, *AKZO* v. *Commission*: [1991] I E.C.R. 3359, [1993] 5 C.M.L.R. 215. Provided the recitals to the decision justify the fine imposed, the Commission's description, *e.g.* in a press release, of the fine as being "exemplary" will not be grounds for reduction or quashing the fine, although it may, as the Court of First Instance said in Case T–30/89, *Hilti AG* v. *Commission*: [1991] II E.C.R. 1439, [1992] 4 C.M.L.R. 16, be regrettable. Description of a fine as examplary does not mean it is excessive.

[86] [1978] O.J. L46/33, [1978] 2 C.M.L.R. 126.

Commission may take account of an undertaking's ability to pay any fine when assessing its amount.[87] The Commission has in fact shown that it is prepared to recognise particular difficulties undertakings may have. In *Cast Iron and Steel Rolls*,[88] the Commission took account of the persistent losses suffered by the parties, the declining market and the steps being taken by the parties in consultation with the Commission to restructure and reduce the size of their operations in an attempt to restore their economic health. Elsewhere the Commission has also had regard to the impact of the recession, difficult economic circumstances and declining markets.[89] But the Court of First Instance indicated in *Polypropylene* that the fact that the Commission has in previous cases taken into account crisis or other difficulty in the relevant economic sector does not oblige it do so in later cases where the Commission has proved to the requisite legal standard the commission of a serious infringement of the competition rules.[90] Finally, it has also been suggested that where an undertaking has genuine difficulty in paying a large fine, the Commission may give it time to pay or allow the fine to be paid by way of instalments.[91]

Effect of notification

7.33 Article 15(5)(a) provides that fines shall not be imposed in respect of acts taking place after notification to the Commission and before its decision in application of Article 85(3)[92] provided they fall within the limits of the activity described in the notification. To obtain such benefit[93] there must be a notification[94] and it must be a valid

---

[87] See also Case 19/77, *Miller International Schallplatten GmbH* v. *Commission*: [1978] E.C.R. 131, [1978] 2 C.M.L.R. 334, at paras. 20 and 21, where the applicant argued that the amount of the fine was extremely burdensome for an undertaking of its nature. The Court did not have to rule on the question because the applicant refused to produce its accounts when requested by the Court and thus prevented verification of the applicant's statement. And in Case 279/87, *Tipp-ex* v. *Commission*: [1990] I E.C.R. 261, the Court rejected the plea that the amount of the fines endangered Tipp-Ex's competitive capacity.

[88] [1983] O.J. L317/1, [1984] 1 C.M.L.R. 694.

[89] See *Benelux Flat Glass*: [1984] O.J. L212/13, [1985] 2 C.M.L.R. 350; *Zinc Producer Group*: [1984] O.J. L220/27, [1985] 2 C.M.L.R. 108; *Polistil/Arbois*: [1984] O.J. L136/9, [1984] 2 C.M.L.R. 594; *John Deere*: [1985] O.J. L35/58, [1985] 2 C.M.L.R. 554 and *Roofing Felt*: [1986] O.J. L232/15, [1991] 4 C.M.L.R. 130; *PVC*: [1989] O.J. L74/1, [1990] 4 C.M.L.R. 345; *LdPE*: [1989] O.J. L74/21, [1990] 4 C.M.L.R. 382 and *Flat Glass*: [1989] O.J. L33/44, [1990] 4 C.M.L.R. 535. In the maritime transport sector, see the treatment of CMC in *Cewal, Cowac and Ukwal*: [1993] O.J. L34/20. In *PVC*, above, the Commission even took account of the fact that the majority of the firms had already been the subject of substantial fines for participation in another cartel in the same sector in the same period. In this context, see also the comments of the Court of Justice in an ECSC case, Cases 154, 205–206, 226–228, 263–264/78 & 31, 39, 83 & 85/79, *Re Concrete Reinforcement Bars: Spa Ferriera Valsabbia and Others* v. *Commission*: [1980] E.C.R. 907, [1981] 1 C.M.L.R. 613.

[90] Case T–13/89, *ICI* v. *Commission*: [1992] II E.C.R. 1021, at para. 372.

[91] Temple Lang, *op. cit.* But even this will not guarantee payment, see n. 216, below.

[92] An application for negative clearance does not constitute a notification for the purpose of Art. 15(5). See *John Deere*, above.

[93] For a recent example, see *Auditel*: [1993] O.J. L306/50. There are similar provisions in relation to maritime and air transport but not under Reg. 1017/68. For other benefits of notification, see para. 2.18.

[94] Even if the agreement is exempt from notification under Art. 4(2), see Cases 240–242, 261, 262, 268 & 269/82, *Stichting Sigarettenindustrie* v. *Commission*: [1985] E.C.R. 3831, [1987] 3 C.M.L.R. 661, at para. 77. See also the Court of Justice in *Pioneer*: Cases 100–103/80, *Musique Diffusion Francaise and Others* v. *Commission*: [1983] E.C.R. 1823, [1983] 3 C.M.L.R. 221, at paras. 92–93. An undertaking cannot claim, on being fined, that there was a hypothetical possibility that notification might have led to exemption.

notification.[95] But there is no requirement that notification must be made before the agreement takes effect (although this may be the wisest course) and, at least in theory, an agreement can be notified at any time during its lifetime or before a decision is taken against it under Article 85(1). An agreement may, for example,[96] be in existence and have operated for 10 years before it is notified and still the period of time after notification has to be disregarded pursuant to Article 15(5). The proviso in Article 15(5)(a) is most important. The infringement must not involve acts which do not come within the notification. Thus in *BMW*,[97] the Court of Justice rejected the argument that on their proper construction the circulars to dealers containing the alleged export bans merely reminded the dealers of the prohibition of sales to non-approved dealers laid down in the standard form dealership agreement previously notified to the Commission. The Commission is entitled to construe any notification restrictively,[98] and a party will not be able to rely on any ambiguity.[99] Although exemption cannot be granted in respect of Article 86 of the Treaty, if the abuse relates to a notified agreement Article 15(5) may still operate to prevent a fine being imposed for acts within the notification.[1] Article 15(5)(b) provides that in the case of "old" agreements and "accession" agreements fines shall not be imposed in respect of acts before notification provided notification is made within the time specified in Articles 5(1) and 7(1) or Regulation 17.[2] The immunity from fine conferred by Article 15(5) can be withdrawn by a provisional decision of the Commission under Article 15(6).

Possible mitigating factors

(i) *Reliance on legal advice*

7.34 The fact that an undertaking has relied on legal advice in connection with the course of action found contrary to Articles 85 and 86 does not appear to be a mitigating factor. This was raised by the applicant during the course of the appeal in *Miller*.[3]

---

[95] Art. 4 of Reg. 27 must be complied with. A defective notification may not confer immunity from fine. See *Sperry New Holland*: [1985] O.J. L376/21, [1988] 4 C.M.L.R. 306.

[96] See *Floral*: [1980] O.J. L39/51, [1980] 2 C.M.L.R. 285. In *Cafeteros de Colombia*: [1982] O.J. L360/31, [1983] 1 C.M.L.R. 703 notification was a year after a Commission inspection and there was even a supplementary notification a further year later. In *Quantel International – Continuum/Quantel SA*: [1992] O.J. L235/9 notification was some four years after the agreements came into force and when, it would appear, relations had broken down.

[97] Cases 32/78 & 36–82/79: [1979] E.C.R. 2435, [1980] 1 C.M.L.R. 370, at paras. 41 and 42. See, also, *AEG-Telefunken*: [1982] O.J. L117/15, [1982] 2 C.M.L.R. 386, where the Commission held that the anti-competitive application of the distribution system, *i.e.* the whole distribution system, had not been notified.

[98] See *Sperry New Holland*, above, where the Commission was in fact generous.

[99] *Hasselblad*: [1982] O.J. L161/18, [1982] 2 C.M.L.R. 233, and *Aluminium imports from Eastern Europe*: [1985] O.J. L92/1, [1987] 3 C.M.L.R. 813.

[1] Case 27/76, *United Brands Co. and United Brands Continental BV* v. *Commission*: [1977] E.C.R. 207, [1978] 1 C.M.L.R. 42, at para. 291.

[2] "Old" and "accession" agreements are defined and discussed at paras. 10.04 and 10.07.

[3] Case 19/77, *Miller International Schallplatten GmbH* v. *Commission*: [1978] E.C.R. 131, [1978] 2 C.M.L.R. 334. A.G. Warner said: "I do not doubt that, whilst the fact that a layman has acted on the advice of a qualified lawyer is in general no defence either to a civil claim or to a criminal charge, it must, in the absence of bad faith, be a strong mitigating circumstance when it comes to the assessment of any penalty, even though expressed not to be 'of a criminal law nature' (Art. 15(4) of Reg. 17)." As the plea had not been made to the Commission in the administrative proceedings, A.G. Warner considered that the correct course of action for the Court was to remit the case to the Commission to reconsider the amount of the fine

The Court of Justice took the view that the applicant could not have been unaware that the export bans it imposed had the object of restricting competition between its customers and considered that it was irrelevant whether or not the applicant knew it was infringing Article 85. The Court said: "In this connection the opinion of a legal advisor, on which it relies, is not a mitigating factor."[4] Indeed, in some circumstances, legal advice may constitute an aggravating factor.[5]

(ii) *Effect of Commission Notice*

7.35 Mention[6] has already been made of the fact that from time to time since 1962 the Commission has issued notices giving its point of view on particular subject-matters. Strictly speaking they have no legal force and compliance with the provisions of a relevant notice does not prohibit the Commission from finding an infringement in the circumstances of a particular case. It may, however, be sufficient to avoid a fine. In the *Sugar* case,[7] one applicant argued that a particular infringement was not such as to justify a fine because the Commission's notice on Commercial Agents had given it the impression that its practices in this respect were lawful. The Court of Justice said:

> "Although the applicant must have known that the organisation of its marketing network on the basis of agency agreements entered into by it with commercial undertakings which were not simply ordinary auxiliaries was likely to restrict competition, the possibility that the wording of the said communication could induce the belief that such a practice was accepted as being compatible with the Treaty nevertheless cannot be ruled out. Therefore, this infringement cannot be taken into consideration for the purpose of fixing the amount of the fine."[8]

---

in the light of the new evidence put forward.

[4] *Ibid.* at para. 18. The advice did not relate to or refer to Community law. The Court took the same view in the *BMW* case: Cases 32/78 & 36–82/79: [1979] E.C.R. 2435, [1980] 1 C.M.L.R. 370, at paras. 43 and 44. And see *Polistil/Arbois*: [1984] O.J. L136/9, [1984] 2 C.M.L.R. 594, where the Commission followed *Miller*. In Case 279/87, *Tipp-ex* v. *Commission*: [1990] I E.C.R. 261, the Court of Justice was unmoved by the plea that the undertaking had acted on the basis of wrong legal advice.

[5] In *BMW* (Cases 32/78 & 36–82/79: [1979] E.C.R. 2435, [1980] 1 C.M.L.R. 370), A.G. Warner said: "Here the opinion of Counsel was, to my mind, if anything, an aggravating factor. It conveyed that Counsel thought the circulars contrary to Art. 85 but hoped that, with the emendations he had made, their incompatibility would not be 'too flagrant'." And see the Commission decision in *John Deere*: [1985] O.J. L35/58, [1985] 2 C.M.L.R. 554 and in *London European – Sabena*: [1988] O.J. L317/47, [1989] 4 C.M.L.R. 662. On mistakes of law, see A.G. Reischl in Case 85/76, *Hoffmann-La Roche & Co. AG* v. *Commission*: [1979] E.C.R. 461, [1979] 3 C.M.L.R. 211.

[6] See para. 1.03.

[7] Cases 40–48, 50, 54–56, 111, 113 & 114/73, *Co-operatieve Vereniging "Suiker Unie" UA and others* v. *Commission*: [1975] E.C.R. 1663, [1976] 1 C.M.L.R. 295. See also, *Franco-Japanese Ballbearings Agreement*: [1974] O.J. L343/19, [1975] 1 C.M.L.R. D8. As to the possibility of reliance on a notice raising a sort of estoppel precluding the Commission from fining, see A.G. Warner in the *Miller* case, above, n. 3.

[8] *Ibid.* at para. 556.

It therefore seems that the Court will give the undertaking the benefits of the doubt where the terms of the notice are ambiguous or uncertain and no fine should be imposed. *A fortiori* no fine should be imposed where there is strict compliance with a notice whose terms are clear and incontrovertible.[9] If compliance with a notice may mitigate or even exclude a fine, reliance on a comfort letter should also be an extenuating factor.[10]

(iii) *Voluntary termination of infringement/co-operation with Commission*

7.36 The Commission will take into account the fact that the undertakings concerned have, without waiting for the Commission's decision, taken steps to bring an infringement to an end. No *ex post facto* co-operation can alter the fact that an infringement has occurred.[11] However, since the Commission's decision in *National Panasonic*,[12] where allowance was made for the undertaking's "constructive attitude" and adoption of a comprehensive antitrust compliance programme, it is noteworthy that Commission decisions have drawn attention to the existence or absence of co-operation on the part of undertakings.[13] The Court of Justice has recognised this factor.[14] But in *Polypropylene*, the Court of First Instance held that the Commission is not obliged to take co-operation into account in the same way in all cases, nor to indicate precisely how such mitigating facts have been weighed.[15] In cases involving a serious infringement of the competition rules, some degree of co-operation out of the ordinary

---

[9] The position is far less certain where the terms of a Notice may have been overtaken (at least in part) by later decisions of the Commission. Clearly where a notice is withdrawn or replaced the undertaking cannot rely on it for any period after its withdrawal or replacement. Although it is accepted that there may be difficulties in renegotiating agreements in this event (contracts could be drafted to provide expressly for renegotiation) transitional provisions are hardly suitable in such circumstances.

[10] But see *Hasselblad*: [1982] O.J. L161/18, [1982] 2 C.M.L.R. 233. It may all depend on the circumstances, degree of disclosure, etc.

[11] See, for example, *Floral*: [1980] O.J. L39/51, [1980] 2 C.M.L.R. 285. *Cf. British Telecommunications*: [1982] O.J. L360/36, [1983] 1 C.M.L.R. 457 and *Benelux Flat Glass*: [1984] O.J. L212/13, [1985] 2 C.M.L.R. 350; *Hudson's Bay*: [1988] O.J. L316/43, [1989] 4 C.M.L.R. 340 and *Distribution of railway tickets by travel agents*: [1992] O.J. L366/47.

[12] [1982] O.J. L354/28, [1983] 1 C.M.L.R. 497. Regard was also had to the introduction of compliance programmes in *Fisher Price/Quaker Oats Ltd. – Toyco*: [1988] O.J. L49/19, [1989] 4 C.M.L.R. 553 and *Viho/Toshiba*: [1991] O.J. L287/39, [1992] 5 C.M.L.R. 180.

[13] See, *e.g. Polistil/Arbois*: [1984] O.J. L136/9, [1984] 2 C.M.L.R. 594; *British Leyland*: [1984] O.J. L207/11, [1984] 3 C.M.L.R. 92; *Zinc Producer Group*: [1984] O.J. L220/27, [1985] 2 C.M.L.R. 108; *John Deere*: [1985] O.J. L35/58, [1985] 2 C.M.L.R. 554; *Sperry New Holland*: [1985] O.J. L376/21, [1988] 4 C.M.L.R. 306; *Siemens/Fanuc*: [1985] O.J. L376/29, [1988] 4 C.M.L.R. 945; *British Dental Trade Association*: [1988] O.J. L233/15, [1989] 4 C.M.L.R. 1021 and *Welded steel mesh*: [1989] O.J. L260/1, [1991] 4 C.M.L.R. 13.

[14] Case 226/84, *British Leyland plc v. Commission*: [1986] E.C.R. 3263, [1987] 1 C.M.L.R. 184, at para. 44. See also Case C–277/87, *Sandoz v. Commission*: [1990] I E.C.R. 45 and *Wood Pulp II*: Cases C 89, 104, 114, 116, 117 & 125–129/85, *A. Åhlström Osakeyhtio and Others v. Commission*: [1993] 4 C.M.L.R. 407, at para. 194.

[15] Case T–7/89, *SA Hercules NV v. Commission*: [1992] 4 C.M.L.R. 84, at paras. 357–359.

may be necessary.[16] In *Wood Pulp*,[17] the Commission took into account the undertakings given by the parties as to their future behaviour which was likely to improve the competitive conditions of the market and to lessen future infringements. This, the Commission said, justified a substantial reduction in the fine.

(iv) *Delay by the Commission*

7.37   In *Commercial Solvents*,[18] the Court of Justice reduced the fine by half because of the time taken by the Commission in dealing with the complaint and taking its decision. It took the view that the duration of the infringement (more than two years) "might have been shorter if the Commission, which had been put on enquiry by the complaint of Zoja on 8 April 1971, that is six months after the first refusal by CSC—Istituto, had intervened more quickly."[19] The Court also drew attention to the fact that Commercial Solvents had resupplied Zoja following and in accordance with the Commission's decision. Whereas conduct after a decision can hardly be used to mitigate a fine for an infringement before the decision, it may, as in the *Commercial Solvents* case, go some way in support of the argument that had the Commission acted more quickly the infringement would have been of shorter duration and therefore, all other things being equal, the fine should be that much less.[20] The Commission cannot be accused of delay for the period of time before the infringement came to its attention.[21] Moreover the Commission will not accept that, because it may have known some of what was going on, it must have known all the facts.[22] But it may take into account the failure to object to known terms and restrictions in the past.[23]

---

[16] In Case T–13/89, *ICI* v. *Commission*: [1992] II E.C.R. 1021, the Court reduced the fine from 10 million ECUs to 9 million ECUs on account of the very detailed replies given by ICI about its and others involvement in the conduct in question. This enabled the Commission to understand the significance of certain documents. See para. 393 of the judgment.

[17] [1985] O.J. L85/1, [1985] 3 C.M.L.R. 474. The Annex to the decision gives the terms of the undertakings "voluntarily" given. Much of the decision and the undertakings were in fact quashed on appeal — see *Wood Pulp II*, above, n. 14. Cf. *Eurofix-Bauco* v. *Hilti*: [1988] O.J. L65/19, [1989] 4 C.M.L.R. 677 where the Commission took into account as "co-operation" the temporary undertakings in response to interim measures, a compliance programme, permanent undertakings and admissions made in response to the statement of objections. The fine was still 6 million ECUs.

[18] Cases 6 & 7/73: [1974] E.C.R. 223, [1974] 1 C.M.L.R. 309.

[19] *Ibid.* at para. 51. Contrast Case 322/81, *Michelin* v. *Commission*: [1983] E.C.R. 3461, [1985] 1 C.M.L.R. 282, at para. 110, where the Court rejected an argument based on the lack of speed of the Commission in bringing the infringement to an end, the Court having regard to the difficulties faced by the Commission in dealing with the subject matter (an unwritten discount system whose application in practice was unclear) of the particular case.

[20] In *Eurocheque: Helsinki Agreement*: [1992] O.J. L95/50, the Commission acknowledged as a mitigating factor the fact that it had not at an earlier time sought to investigate more vigorously the scope and impact of the agreement in question.

[21] Cases 32/78 & 36–82/79, *BMW Belgium and Others* v. *Commission*: [1979] E.C.R. 2435, [1980] 1 C.M.L.R. 370, at para. 45.

[22] *Zinc Producer Group*: [1984] O.J. L220/27, [1985] 2 C.M.L.R. 108.

[23] *E.g.* the form of evergreen contracts and certain competition classes in *Soda-ash Solvay*: [1991] O.J. L152/21, and the tolerance by the Commission of Ford's claims to benefit from Reg. 123/85 in *Ford Agricultural*: [1993] O.J. L20/1.

(v) *Tax implications*

7.38 In the *Quinine* case,[24] the Court said that in fixing the amount of fines under Article 15 the Commission was not required to take into account the differences existing between national revenue laws. Buchler had complained that the Commission should have treated it, a German undertaking, more favourably than another undertaking concerned, a Dutch firm, because whereas fines were deductible for tax purposes in the Netherlands this was not the case in Germany.

(vi) *Special circumstances*

7.38A The *Aluminium* decision[25] demonstrates that parties may avoid fines where there are "special circumstances" (the decision does not, however, say what this means). Special consideration has been given to the legal form of an undertaking[26] and to public safety.[27] The involvement or knowledge of national governments will not however necessarily be a defence[28] but in some cases may go to mitigation.[29]

Double jeopardy

7.39 Double jeopardy may arise where an anti-competitive agreement or practice may be the subject of proceedings in more than one jurisdiction. An undertaking may thus be penalised more than once in relation to the same act or conduct. In dealing with the potential problem of double jeopardy, the Court of Justice has differentiated between the situation where such parallel proceedings exist on the one hand, before the Commission and before a court or tribunal in a Member State and, on the other hand, before the Commission and before a court or tribunal of a non-Member State.

In *Wilhelm* v. *Bundeskartellamt*,[30] the Court considered several questions relating to the possible conflict of Community and national law arising out of the German cartel authority's prosecution of the international quinine cartel whilst the Commission was also seised of the same matter. The Court of Justice held that the principle of the supremacy of Community law does not have the effect of prohibiting such parallel proceedings under national competition law, and that possibility of more than one sanction does not affect their lawfulness.

But on the question of a possible double sanction, the Court said:[31]

---

[24] Cases 41, 44 & 45/69, *ACF Chemiefarma and Others* v. *Commission*: [1970] E.C.R. 661, Case 44/69, at paras. 50 and 51.
[25] [1985] O.J. L92/1, [1987] 3 C.M.L.R. 813, at para. 17.2.
[26] So in *Hudson's Bay – Dansk Pelsdyravlerforening*: [1988] O.J. L316/43, [1989] 4 C.M.L.R. 340, the Commission gave special allowance for the fact that DPF was a co-operative association. Upheld by the Court of First Instance in Case T–61/89, *Dansk Pelsdyravlerforening* v. *Commission*: [1992] II E.C.R. 1931. The Court confirmed that the particular obligations of a co-operative do not preclude the application of Art. 85. The fine was, however, reduced because of other inadequacies in the Commission's decision. It is unlikely that being a co-operative will be a special factor in future.
[27] *Distribution of package tours during the 1990 World Cup:* [1992] O.J. L326/31.
[28] See *Zinc Producer Group*, above, n. 22.
[29] *Building and construction industry in the Netherlands*: [1992] O.J. L92/1.
[30] Case 14/68, *Walt Wilhelm and Others* v. *Bundeskartellamt*: [1969] E.C.R. 1, [1969] C.M.L.R. 100.
[31] *Ibid.* at para. 11.

"If, however, the possibility of two procedures being conducted separately were to lead to the imposition of consecutive sanctions, a general requirement of natural justice, such as that expressed at the end of the second paragraph of Article 90 of the ECSC Treaty, demands that any previous punitive decision must be taken into account in determining the sanction which is to be imposed."

The Commission should therefore take account of any fine or penalty imposed on the undertaking by the authorities in the Member States when considering the question of imposing a fine on it in its own proceedings in respect of the same act or conduct. In *Welded steel mesh*,[32] the Commission took account of the fact that the French producers had been fined earlier by the French authorities. Where, peculiarly, the same conduct involves the infringement of both Article 85 and 86, the Commission has recognised the principle that fines should not be applied cumulatively in respect of the same set of facts.[33] Only the fines for the more serious infringement should be imposed.

7.40 Where the parallel proceedings involve the authorities of a non-Member State, it is not sufficient that the proceedings arise from the same act. In *Boehringer Mannheim* v. *Commission*,[34] the Court of Justice said:

"It is only necessary to decide the question whether the Commission may also be under a duty to set a penalty imposed by the authorities of a third State against another penalty if in the case in question the actions of the applicant complained of by the Commission, on the one hand, and by the American authorities, on the other hand, are identical.

Although the sanctions on which the two convictions in question are based arise out of the same set of agreements they nevertheless differ essentially as regards both their object and their geographical emphasis."

The Court of Justice rejected the applicant's plea that the Commission, when considering the fines to be imposed on the applicant in respect of its participation in the international quinine cartel, should have taken into account fines totalling $80,000 which it had paid to a federal court in the United States in respect of violations of section 1 of the Sherman Act. The Court considered that the mischief lay not in the agreement itself but in its application and whilst the Community decision only penalised the applicant in respect of acts done which were likely to affect trade between Member States and to distort competition within the Common Market, the applicant had produced no evidence to suggest that the fines imposed by the federal court extended to acts done and effects outside the United States. The Court therefore acknowledged, as a matter of Community law, the equity of a set-off to avoid or mitigate such double jeopardy but did not consider it applicable in the circumstances of the case. Whilst coincidence of purpose and effect appears to be to a great extent assumed where the parallel proceedings are before the authority of a Member State (indeed, the territorial impact in such circumstances will most likely overlap), the stricter approach adopted

---

[32] [1989] O.J. L260/1, [1991] 4 C.M.L.R. 13. See also *Cast Iron and Steel Rolls:* [1983] O.J. L317/1, [1984] 1 C.M.L.R. 694 where a majority of the undertakings had been fined earlier by the German Cartel Office.

[33] [1989] O.J. L33/44, [1990] 4 C.M.L.R. 535, at para. 84A.

[34] Case 7/72, *Boehringer Mannheim GmbH* v. *Commission*: [1972] E.C.R. 1281, [1973] C.M.L.R. 864, at paras. 3 and 4.

in the second category of case imposes a considerable burden of proof on an undertaking seeking to invoke the equity.

Joint and several liability

7.41 Where more than one undertaking is involved in the infringement it may be possible for the Commission to make the liability for a fine a joint and several one. It did this in the *Commercial Solvents* case[35] where the two undertakings fined were an American parent company and its 51 per cent. Italian subsidiary. The Court of Justice substantially upheld the Commission's decision,[36] taking the view that the two undertakings should be treated as one economic unit and were jointly and severally responsible for the infringement.[37] The Court did not comment specifically on the appropriateness of imposing a joint and several liability in respect of the fine. There are obvious advantages to the Commission in being able to extract the total fine from one party, leaving it free to seek contributions from the others as best it can. In the event of any default in payment, the Commission need only seek to enforce its decision once, presumably against the one most convenient and/or best able to pay.[38]

Joint and several liability may not, it is submitted, be appropriate in all cases where more than one undertaking is involved. The Commission cannot, by imposing joint and several liability, increase an undertaking's liability to fine under Article 15 of Regulation 17. One practical result of this is that the total fine on all parties subject to the joint and several liability cannot exceed 10 per cent. of the smallest turnover of any of the parties. Moreover, even if this limit is not exceeded, the general principle of proportionality requires that a party should not be responsible for a fine disproportionate to the gravity and duration of the infringement and in particular to the extent of its participation in it, its size[39] and turnover.[40]

Payment of fines

7.42 The decision will specify the amount of any fine, and when and where it is to be paid.[41] It will usually provide that the fine should be paid within a period of three months from the date of notification to the undertakings to which it is addressed. If

---

[35] Cases 6 & 7/73: [1974] E.C.R. 223, [1974] 1 C.M.L.R. 309.

[36] [1972] J.O. L299/51, [1973] C.M.L.R. D50.

[37] Above, at para. 41.

[38] So, in *Commercial Solvents*, the Commission might have been able to collect all its fine inside the Community and thereby avoid any problems of trying to enforce the decision against the American company. And see *Hugin/Liptons*: [1978] O.J. L22/23, [1978] 1 C.M.L.R. D19, where a joint and several fine was imposed on a Swedish parent company and an English subsidiary. The decision was, for other reasons, quashed by the Court (Case 22/78) [1979] E.C.R. 1869, [1979] 3 C.M.L.R. 345.

[39] Case 27/76, *United Brands Co. and United Brands Continental BV* v. *Commission*: [1977] E.C.R. 207, [1978] 1 C.M.L.R. 42, at para. 302.

[40] Cases 32/78 & 36–82/79: [1979] E.C.R. 2435, [1980] 1 C.M.L.R. 370, at para. 47.

[41] It is the Commission's practice to nominate a bank account usually in the Member State where the undertaking is situate. Where the undertaking is outside the Community, an account within the Community may be nominated—see *Polypropylene*: [1986] O.J. L230/1, [1988] 4 C.M.L.R. 347, where a Norwegian undertaking was ordered to pay the fine into a British bank account. In *Wood Pulp*: [1985] O.J. L85/1, [1985] 3 C.M.L.R. 474, all the undertakings (American and Canadian) were ordered to pay into a Belgian account. Where there has been joint and several liability, the Commission has nominated one account for payment within the Community (see *Commercial Solvents*, above, n. 36 and *Hugin/Liptons*, above, n. 38) or a number of accounts (see *Johnson & Johnson*: [1980] O.J. L377/16, [1981] 2 C.M.L.R. 287, where four accounts were nominated, two of which were outside the Community).

there is an appeal against the decision, the Commission will not automatically defer enforcement of the fine but may agree to do so where the undertaking agrees to pay interest and provides a bank guarantee covering both the sum due and the interest thereon.[42] In *AEG-Telefunken* v. *Commission*,[43] the Court of Justice rejected AEG's claim that there was no legal basis in Community law for a requirement to pay debt interest. It was not disputed that, particularly in a situation where higher interest rates exist, an undertaking might derive considerable advantage from delaying payment of a fine for as long as possible. If measures could not be taken under Community law to counterbalance such advantage, it could lead to the bringing of obviously ill-founded appeals where the sole aim was to delay the payment of the fine. The Court took the view that such a position could not have been intended by the provisions of the Treaties concerning appeals against measures adopted by Community institutions.[44] The Commission has taken this a step further. Typically decisions provide that if after three months (the time within which the fine is ordered to be paid) the fine is unpaid interest shall automatically be payable at a specified rate.[45] To date undertakings concerned have generally respected their obligation to pay the fines imposed upon them.[46] Where an undertaking is in a poor financial situation the Commission may allow it to pay by instalments.[47]

7.43 It was formerly the Commission's practice to specify the fine in ECUs and also in the currency of the Member State in which the undertaking concerned is situate or is most closely connected. In this event the important figure is the one in the national currency. It is this figure which fixes the amount of the debt arising out of the fine although the Commission is entitled to accept payment in a national currency of the Community other than the one specified in the decision. This was made clear in an interpretation judgment[48] of the Court of Justice in the *Sugar* case.[49] The Court went on to say that the Community was entitled to accept payment in a national currency of the Community other than that in which the debt has been determined. But if so, the Commission must see that the actual value of the payments made in the alternative currency corresponds to that fixed in the national currency in the Commission's decision or the Court's judgment. The conversion of the two currencies involved must therefore be effected at the exchange rate on the foreign exchange market applicable on the

---

[42] See the answer to Written Question No. 1406/81: [1982] O.J. C47/28. The practice has been upheld by the Court. See the Orders of the President of the Court in Case 107/82R, *AEG-Telefunken* v. *Commission*: [1982] E.C.R. 1179 and Case 86/82R, *Hasselblad* v. *Commission*: [1982] E.C.R. 1555.

[43] Case 107/82: [1983] E.C.R. 3151, [1984] 3 C.M.L.R. 325.

[44] *Ibid.* at paras. 139–143.

[45] The rate is that charged by the European Monetary Co-operation Fund on its ECU operations on the first working day of the month in which the decision is adopted plus 3.5 percentage points.

[46] Answer to Written Question No. 715/80: [1980] O.J. C245/15.

[47] This was done in *Preserved Mushrooms*: [1975] O.J. L29/26, [1975] 1 C.M.L.R. D83. But even this did not mean that the Commission received payment by the time the last instalment fell due. In the event two undertakings went into liquidation and the Commission lodged claims with the liquidators. In respect of the other three undertakings the Commission had to commence enforcement proceedings.

[48] Art. 40 of the Protocol on the Statute of the Court of Justice of the European Economic Community.

[49] Cases 41, 43 & 44/73, *SA Général Sucrière and Société Béghin-Say* v. *Commission*: (interpretation) [1977] E.C.R. 445. The Court considered that there was no requirement to fix the fine in terms of [then] units of account but that the *Commission*: was bound to fix the amount of the fine in national currency since the unit of account was not a currency in which payment could be made.

day of payment. Nowadays the Commission adopts the procedure of specifying the amount of the fine in ECUs alone.[50]

III. PERIODIC PENALTY PAYMENTS

7.44   Article 16(1) of Regulation 17 empowers the Commission to impose periodic penalty payments in the range of 50 to 1,000 ECUs per day.[51] They may be imposed to compel undertakings:

    (a) to put an end to an infringement of Article 85 or 86, in accordance with a decision taken pursuant to Article 3 of Regulation 17;[52]

    (b) to refrain from any act prohibited under Article 8(3) of Regulation 17 in connection with an exemption under Article 85(3);[53]

    (c) to supply complete and correct information requested by decision of the Commission under Article 11(5) of Regulation 17;[54]

    (d) to submit to an investigation ordered by decision of the Commission under Article 14(3) of Regulation 17.[55]

7.45   In practice, two decisions are involved.[56] The first "threatens" the imposition of the penalty, *i.e.* says "they will be imposed unless". The second determines how long the infringement of the first continued and how much the penalty should amount to. The total payment is calculated from the date fixed by the first decision.[57] There is no requirement that the Commission show that the undertaking has acted "intentionally or negligently" in relation to the obligation in respect of which the penalty is imposed. However, the Commission has a certain discretion when fixing the total amount due. Where the undertaking has satisfied the obligation in respect of which the

---

[50] Having regard to the reasoning in the *Sugar* case, above, n. 49, the Commission apparently takes the view that the ECU is a currency in which payment can be made. The ECU is not yet, however, a currency of last resort.

[51] Contrast the figures in Art. 15 of Reg. 4064/89, the Merger Control Regulation.

[52] On the question of the Commission's power to impose penalties to enforce compliance with interim decisions, see para. 6.10. In its decisions imposing interim measures, *Ford Werke AG*: [1982] O.J. L256/20, [1982] 3 C.M.L.R. 267; *ECS/AKZO*: [1983] O.J. L252/13, [1983] 3 C.M.L.R. 694; *BBI/Boosey and Hawkes*: [1987] O.J. L286/36, [1988] 4 C.M.L.R. 67 and *Mars/Langnese and Schöller*: (December 23, 1992) not yet published, the Commission has attached a periodic penalty payment to compel performance of the relevant measures.

[53] On Art. 8(3) of Reg. 17, see paras. 6.37–40.

[54] For decisions under Art. 11(5), see paras. 3.08–09. For an example of the imposition of a periodic penalty payment to compel performance, see *CSV*: [1976] O.J. L192/72 and *Baccarat*: [1991] O.J. L97/16, [1992] 5 C.M.L.R. 189.

[55] *E.g.* the Commission imposed a 1,000 ECUs per day penalty on Hoechst AG to compel the company to submit to an investigation into price fixing for PVC and polyethylene (Press Release IP(87)58) and the Report for the hearing in Cases 46/87 & 227/88, *Hoechst* v. *Commission*: [1989] E.C.R. 2859, [1991] 4 C.M.L.R. 410. *Cf. CSM-NV*: [1992] O.J. L305/16, where there was a decision under Article 16(11)(d) but a fine under 15(1)(c). Although the decision under Article 16 produced the documents sought the next day, there was still a delay overall in the conduct of the enquiry due to the failure to furnish the documents at the earlier inspection. For decisions under Art. 14(3), see paras. 3.24–26.

[56] The clearest analysis of this two stage process is in *Hoechst*, above, at para. 55.

[57] Art. 16(1) of Reg. 17. See *Commercial Solvents*, above, n. 36, where different dates were used for the different obligations in respect of which penalties were imposed, both fixed by reference to the receipt of the decision by the parties.

penalty was imposed, the Commission may fix the total amount of the periodic penalty payment at a figure which is less than the amount due under the original decision.[58] As already mentioned, the Advisory Committee must be consulted prior to the imposition of any periodic penalty payment,[59] *i.e.* before the second decision fixing the definitive amount of the penalty.

An example of the imposition of such a payment can be seen in the Commission's decision in the *Commercial Solvents* case.[60] The Commission required Commercial Solvents and its subsidiary company, Istituto, jointly and severally (a) under penalty of 1,000 units of account per day of delay to resupply the complainant Zoja with stipulated amounts of product in order to satisfy its immediate needs, and (b) under a further penalty of 1,000 units of account per day to submit to the Commission, within two months, proposals[61] for the further supply of Zoja. In order to terminate the infringement the Commission thus imposed two obligations each with the maximum penalty to compel performance. The Court of Justice *sub silentio* upheld that. Whilst there may be little doubt that the Commission can impose more than one obligation in order to compel the termination of an infringement, it is perhaps surprising and at least noteworthy that the Commission may be able, by the use of more than one obligation, to impose a daily penalty in excess of 1,000 ECUs.[62]

IV. LIMITATION PERIODS

7.46 Regulation 2988/74 fixes limitation periods in respect of the Commission's powers to impose fines and penalties ("limitation periods in proceedings") and to enforce the collection of fines and penalties ("limitation period for the enforcement of sanctions").

(i) *Limitation periods in proceedings*

Article 1 of Regulation 2988/74 provides that no fines or penalties can be imposed after:

    (a) three years in the case of infringements of provisions concerning applications or notifications, requests for information, or the carrying out of investigations; and

    (b) five years in the case of all other infringements.

---

[58] Art. 16(2) of Reg. 17.

[59] Art. 16(3) of Reg. 17. See generally paras. 5.21–28. In *Hoechst*, above, n. 55, the Court of Justice held that the Committee need not be consulted where the decision only concerns the first "threatening" stage. Consulting the Committee, the Court said at para. 57, would entail delaying the date of adoption of the decision and therefore jeopardise the effectiveness of the decision ordering the investigations.

[60] Above, n. 36. That is an old but instructive case. For other examples see *United Brands*: above, n. 17 in para. 7.19; *Hugin/Liptons*: [1978] O.J. L22/23, [1978] 1 C.M.L.R. D19; *IM-Rules*: [1980] O.J. L318/1, [1981] 2 C.M.L.R. 498; *ECS/AKZO*: [1985] O.J. L374/1, [1986] 3 C.M.L.R. 273 and more recently *Baccarat*, above, n. 54.

[61] *Quaere* whether a penalty could be enforced against the undertaking if it made good the infringement (*e.g.* by resupplying in full) but refused to discuss the matter with the Commission.

[62] The two parties were made jointly and severally liable in respect of the penalties but this, it is submitted, cannot increase the maximum liability fixed by Reg. 17 for any one undertaking. See para. 7.41.

Time starts to run on the day the infringement is committed. Where the infringement continues or is repeated, time starts to run on the day on which the infringement ceases.[63] It should be noted that the Commission is not prohibited from taking action in relation to any agreements, etc., after these periods have elapsed but is merely prohibited from imposing fines.[64] In the case of applications or notifications these are made at the "effective date"[65] for the purposes of Article 3 of Regulation 27. But if incorrect or misleading information has been intentionally or negligently supplied does time begin to run from the effective date or only from such time as the defect is rectified? Similarly in the case of requests for information or investigations, does the infringement continue until the correct information is supplied or the required books, etc., produced in a complete form? It will clearly be advantageous to the Commission to be able to treat these as "continuing" infringements and it appears that it may do so.[66]

7.47   Any action taken by the Commission for the purpose of the preliminary investigation or proceedings in respect of an infringement will interrupt the limitation period with effect from the date on which it is notified to at least one of the undertakings concerned in the infringement.[67] The following are included in the category of actions which have such interruptive effect:

(a)   written requests for information,[68] or a Commission decision requiring the requested information;[69]

---

[63] Art. 1(2) of Reg. 2988/74. See, *e.g. Toltecs/Dorcet*: [1982] O.J. L379/19, [1983] 1 C.M.L.R. 412, where the Commission found that for the purposes of Art. 1(2) the infringement (a no-challenge clause relating to a BAT trade mark) did not terminate, at the earliest, until BAT declared at the oral hearing that it attached no further importance to the continuation of the relevant agreement. See also *LdPE*: [1989] O.J. L74/21, [1990] 4 C.M.L.R. 382. For examples of "repeated"/continuing infringements, see *Cast Iron and Steel Rolls*: [1983] O.J. L317/1, [1984] 1 C.M.L.R. 694; *Zinc Producer Group*: [1984] O.J. L220/27, [1985] 2 C.M.L.R. 108 and *Welded steel mesh*: [1989] O.J. L260/1, [1991] 4 C.M.L.R. 13. The Commission will look to the facts and circumstances to see if there is any relationship between the earlier and later infringements: see *Polypropylene*: [1986] O.J. L230/1, [1988] 4 C.M.L.R. 347. In Case T–7/89, *SA Hercules NV* v. *Commission*: [1992] 4 C.M.L.R. 84, at para. 301, the Court of First Instance held that, at least as regards Hercules involvement in *Polypropylene*, the infringement had been a single continuing one for the purposes of Reg. 2988/74.

[64] This may be important for a number of reasons. First, the Commission may still take a decision declaring that an infringement has taken place. This could affect the liability of the parties before a national court, either *inter se* or in relation to third parties, subject of course to the national rules relating to *res judicata* for past proceedings and to limitation for future proceedings. Second, Reg. 2988/74 does not appear to prohibit the Commission from ordering positive action to remedy an infringement, *e.g.* the divestiture of a merger (Art. 86) or a joint venture (Art. 85) or the reassignment or adjustment of industrial property rights (Art. 85 or 86).

[65] Normally the date of receipt by the Commission or, where sent by registered post, the date shown one the postmark of the place of posting.

[66] *Theal/Watts*: [1977] O.J. L39/19, [1977] 1 C.M.L.R. D44, and Case 28/77, *Tepea* v. *Commission*: [1978] E.C.R. 1391, [1978] 3 C.M.L.R. 392, *sub silentio*. Contrast *Aluminium*: [1985] O.J. L92/1, [1987] 3 C.M.L.R. 813, where the deficiencies in the notification were time-barred.

[67] Art. 2(1) of Reg. 2988/74. The action may also be taken by a Member State acting at the Commission's request. The action need not apparently be taken by a competent authority for the purposes of Reg. 17. Although the list of actions set out in Art. 2(1) refers to the competent authority it is a non-exhaustive list.

[68] Under Art. 11(3) of Reg. 17.

[69] Under Art. 11(5) of Reg. 17.

(b) written authorisations to carry out investigations,[70] or a Commission decision ordering an investigation;[71]

(c) the commencement of proceedings by the Commission;[72] and

(d) notification of the Commission's statement of objections.[73]

Such an interruption, once notified to at least one of the undertakings concerned, affects all the undertakings concerned.[74] Each interruption starts the time running afresh.[75] However, in order to protect undertakings from inordinately protracted proceedings and to be an incentive to the Commission to expedite its work,[76] it is expressly provided that the limitation period shall expire at the latest on the day on which a period equal to twice the limitation period has elapsed without the Commission having imposed a fine.[77] In short, even where there are interruptions, the Commission can impose fines only within a six year period in the case of a procedural infringement and a 10 year period in other cases.

7.48 The limitation period is suspended for as long as the Commission's decision is subject to proceedings pending before the Court.[78] The Commission has said:

> "This provision is to ensure that the Commission can resume proceedings in respect of an infringement, if its original decision to impose a fine is set aside by the Court of Justice for procedural reasons. It is based on the general legal principle that the parties concerned should not benefit from prescription rules in respect of periods for which the authority responsible for instituting proceedings is prevented from taking action for justifiable reasons and on grounds beyond its control."[79]

Although an action before the Court will suspend the limitation period as indicated it will not suspend the effect of the decision in question.[80]

---

[70] Under Art. 14(2) of Reg. 17. It appears sufficient that authorisations are issued and their existence notified to one undertaking concerned. Peculiarly, there seems to be no requirement that an investigation take place. The written authorisation is, however, always drafted so as to require an inspection visit to begin on or about a specified date and once the Commission has decided to have an inspection, it will always carry it out without delay. See the submissions and argument of the Commission in Case 136/79, *National Panasonic (UK) Ltd.* v. *Commission*: [1980] E.C.R. 2033, [1980] 3 C.M.L.R. 169.

[71] Under Art. 14(3) of Reg. 17. For an example of interruption by investigation decision see *Cast Iron and Steel Rolls*, above, n. 63 and *Welded steel mesh, ibid.*

[72] What amounts to the commencement of proceedings is discussed at paras. 2.38–39.

[73] In practice, the commencement of proceedings and the statement of objections may be notified at the same time.

[74] Art. 2(2) of Reg. 2988/74. So, *e.g.* in *PVC*: [1989] O.J. L74/1, [1990] 4 C.M.L.R. 345, the first investigations by the Commission interrupted the limitation period for all participants in the suspected infringement, not just the firms visited at the time.

[75] Art. 2(3) of Reg. 2988/74.

[76] Commission's Fourth Report on Competition Policy, p. 32.

[77] Art. 2(3) of Reg. 2988/74. The "double" period can be extended by the time during which limitation is suspended (pursuant to Art. 3) when the decision in question is the subject of proceedings before the Court.

[78] Art. 3 of Reg. 2988/74.

[79] Fourth Report on Competition Policy, p. 33.

[80] Art. 185 of the Treaty. Separate application should be made to the Court for the decision to be suspended. See paras. 9.38–42.

(ii) *Limitation period for the enforcement of sanctions*

7.49　Article 4 of Regulation 2988/74 stipulates a limitation period of five years in respect of the Commission's power to enforce any decision imposing a fine and/or periodic penalty payment under Regulation 17. Time starts running on the day on which the decision becomes final.[81] The five-year period is interrupted[82] by a decision which varies the original amount of the sanction or refuses an application for such variation,[83] or by any action to enforce payment.[84] Time starts running afresh after each interruption.[85] The limitation period is suspended for so long as time to pay is allowed or enforcement of payment is suspended pursuant to a decision of the Court.[86]

V. ENFORCEMENT OF DECISIONS IMPOSING FINES

7.50　Article 192 of the Treaty provides as follows:

> "Decisions of the Council or of the Commission which impose a pecuniary obligation on persons other than States shall be enforceable.
>
> 　　Enforcement shall be governed by the rules of civil procedure in force in the State in the territory of which it is carried out. The order for its enforcement shall be appended to the decision, without other formality than verification of the authenticity of the decision, by the national authority which the Government of each Member State shall designate for this purpose and shall make known to the Commission and to the Court of Justice
> 　. . ."

In the United Kingdom, the European Communities (Enforcement of Community Judgments) Order[87] enables Commission decisions imposing fines to be registered in the High Court[88] and enforced in the same way as if they were judgments or orders of

---

[81] Art. 4(2) of Reg. 2988/74. "Becomes final" is not defined. It presumably means made by the Commission and properly notified to the persons to whom it is addressed in accordance with Art. 191 of the Treaty. "Becomes final" does not, it is submitted, imply that the decision must be upheld by the Court on appeal (*e.g.* under Art. 172 or 173 of the Treaty) or time-barred in respect of such an appeal. Such an interpretation would be inconsistent with Art. 6 of Reg. 2988/74 and Art. 185 of the Treaty.

[82] Art. 5 of Reg. 2988/74.

[83] There are no express provisions in Reg. 17 or the other implementing regulations dealing with applications for variation of a fine and consequent decisions by the Commission. There have been two cases where a decision has been varied. See *GEMA (No. 2)*: [1972] O.J. L166/22, [1972] C.M.L.R. D115 and *ANSEAU/NAVEWA*: [1982] O.J. L325/20, [1983] 1 C.M.L.R. 470.

[84] Taken by the Commission or a Member State at its request. Art. 5(2)(b) of Reg. 2988/74. The action by a Member State will not necessarily be taken by the competent authority for the purposes of Reg. 17 but a national authority within the meaning of Art. 197 of the Treaty.

[85] Art. 5(2) of Reg. 2988/74.

[86] Art. 6 of Reg. 2988/74. An example of the Commission's allowing time to pay can be found in the reply to Written Question No. 584/76: [1977] O.J. C27/15. Actions brought before the Court do not have suspensory effect (Art. 185 of the Treaty). Separate applications should be made to the Court for the decision to be suspended. See paras. 9.38–42.

[87] S.I. 1972 No. 1590, made under the European Communities Act 1972.

[88] The "High Court" means in England and in Northern Ireland the High Court, and in Scotland the Court of Session. Art. 2(1) of the Order.

that Court.[89] Effective enforcement may well depend on a clearly identifiable entity. Although, as has been pointed out above,[90] the concept of "undertaking" is not dependent on national company law, for the purposes of the enforcement and collection of fines it is necessary for the Commission to identify an entity possessing legal personality. In the case of a large industrial group it is therefore the Commission's practice to address the decision to the group holding company or headquarters company where the undertaking itself consists of the unit formed by the parent and subsidiaries.[91]

Article 110 of the EEA provides for the enforcement of decisions of the Commission and the EFTA Surveillance Authority which impose pecuniary obligations. Enforcement shall be governed by the rules of civil procedure in the territory of the State in which it is carried out.

---

[89] The Order gives effect to the obligations imposed by Art. 192 of the EEC Treaty, Arts. 44 and 92 of the ECSC Treaty and Arts. 18, 159 and 164 of the Euratom Treaty.
[90] See para. 7.11
[91] *E.g. Welded steel mesh*, above, n. 63; *PVC*, above, n. 74, and *LdPE*, above, n. 63.

8

General Legal Rules

Jurisdiction

Generally

8.01 Article 85 only applies "to agreements … which may affect trade *between Member States* and which have as their object or effect the prevention, restriction or distortion of competition *within the common market* …" Article 86 prohibits any "abuse … *within the common market* or in a substantial part of it … in so far as it may affect trade *between Member States*."[1] Provided these criteria are satisfied it does not seem to matter whether the undertaking or undertakings involved have, in Community terms, a seat in the territory of one of the Member States. As will be seen it is not just the wording of these Articles which has to be taken into account but the wider legal order, including the position under international law. The fact that an undertaking has its registered office or centre of operations outside the Community does not necessarily exclude it from the jurisdiction of Community competition law. In a number of cases the Commission has applied the competition rules to undertakings outside the Community.[2] But where not only the undertakings concerned are situated but also the acts or conduct complained of take place entirely outside the Community, it is not certain whether the Commission is entitled to proceed against such undertakings for infringement of Community law, albeit that there may be some anti-competitive impact on the Community and, in particular, effects felt on trade between Member States.[3]

---

[1] Emphasis added.

[2] See generally Lowe, *Extraterritorial Jurisdiction* (1983); Bellis, "International Trade and the Competition Law of the European Economic Community" (1979) 16 C.M.L.Rev. 647; Rosenthal and Knighton, *National Laws and International Commerce: The Problem of Extraterritoriality* (1982); Slot and Grabandt, "Extraterritoriality and Jurisdiction" (1986) 23 C.M.L.Rev. 545; Lange and Born, *The Extraterritorial Application of National Laws* (1987) and Roth, "Reasonable Extraterritoriality: correcting the 'Balance of Interests' " (1992) 41 I.C.L.Q. 245. For a recent example of the competition rules being applied against (and a fine being imposed on) an undertaking from a non-Member State, see *PVC*: [1989] O.J. L74/1, [1990] 4 C.M.L.R. 345 and *LdPE*: [1989] O.J. L74/21, [1990] 4 C.M.L.R. 382.

[3] The Commission has argued that such an agreement might be caught by Art. 85—see Case 51/75, *EMI Records Ltd.* v. *CBS United Kingdom Ltd.*: [1976] E.C.R. 811, [1976] 2 C.M.L.R. 235. But the Court did not clearly accept this—see paras. 29 and 30 of its judgment. Note that it expressly refers to an agreement between traders within the Common Market and competitors in third countries at para. 29, and to a proprietor of a trade mark which has within the Community various subsidiaries established in different Member States at para. 30.

8.02 The basis of a State's jurisdiction over subject matter is the territorial principle.[4] A State can regulate foreign firms in respect of their activities which take place wholly or in part within its territory. This basic jurisdiction is generally extended in a manner recognised by international law to include jurisdiction over things done outside the territory as a result of conduct within the territory (subjective territorial jurisdiction) and things done within the territory as a result of conduct outside the territory (objective territorial jurisdiction). Under the latter, for example, jurisdiction may be exercised where an agreement is made outside the territory but it is implemented, at least as to an essential part, within the territory. Things may be done in the Community either by the undertaking itself (possibly through a branch) or by an agent, whether a subsidiary or an unrelated body, on its behalf.[5] In some circumstances it may be legitimate for a State to assert jurisdiction on the basis of nationality, and therefore over companies established in (*i.e.* formed under the law of) that State.[6] But the suitability of nationality as a basis for exercising jurisdiction in competition cases is extremely doubtful.[7] There is also, most notably in the present context, the so-called "effects doctrine". This has been described as "that territorial jurisdiction over conduct which occurred wholly outside a State but which may be justified because of effects within the State."[8] It is a controversial principle of jurisdiction, particularly in relation to competition law. Perhaps the best known example of its use is in United States antitrust law.[9] The Community has itself recognised the controversial nature of the effects doctrine, classifying it as one of the bases of jurisdiction which have found less than general acceptance under international law.[10]

---

[4] This discussion of the general principles of jurisdiction is necessarily abbreviated and simplified. For a more detailed analysis of the subject, see Mann, "The Doctrine of Jurisdiction in International Law" in *Studies in International Law* (1973), and Akehurst, "Jurisdiction in International Law", 46 B.Y.I.L. 145.

[5] See, *e.g. Polypropylene*: [1986] O.J. L230/1.

[6] For an application of this principle, see *Aluminium Imports from Eastern Europe*: [1985] O.J. L92/1, [1987] 3 C.M.L.R. 813, at para. 14.4. But even the nationality principle is not unrestricted in relation to its assertion and exercise by States. See Rosenthal and Knighton, *op. cit.*

[7] See Brittan, "Jurisdictional Issues in EEC Competition Law", Hersch Lauterpacht Memorial Lectures, February 8, 1990, "competition law should be applied only in order to deal with competition laws in one's own market and not to make sure one's own companies behave in a certain way abroad."

[8] Wertheimer, quoted by Allen in "The Development of European Economic Community Antitrust Jurisdiction over Alien Undertakings" [1974] 2 L.I.E.I. 35, 43.

[9] See *United States* v. *Aluminium Co. of America*, 148 F. 2d 416 (2d Cir. 1945) and, recently, *Hartford Fire Insurance Co* v. *California et al*, judgment of U.S. Supreme Court, February 23, 1993. The Sherman Act applies to foreign conduct that was meant to produce and does in fact produce some substantial effect in the United States. Earlier decisions of U.S. courts had indicated that their application of the effects doctrine may be qualified by a test based on the concept of comity and the balancing of the conflicting interests of the sovereign states involved. See *Timberlane Lumber Co*. v. *Bank of America*, 549 F. 2d 597 (9th Cir. 1976); *Mannington Mills* v. *Congoleum Corp.*, 595 F. 2d 1287 (3d Cir. 1979); *Montreal Trading Ltd.* v. *Amax Inc.*, 661 F. 2d 864 (10th Cir. 1981); *National Bank of Canada* v. *Interbank Card Association and Bank of Montreal*, 666 F. 2d 6 (2d Cir. 1981) and *Industrial Development Corp.* v. *Mitsui Ltd.*, 671 F. 2d 876 (5th Cir. 1982). But not all U.S. courts had adopted this approach. See, generally, Griffin, "The impact of reconsideration of US Antitrust policy intended to protect US exporters" (1992) IS W. Comp. 4, at p. 5. In the recent *Hartford Fire Insurance* case the majority of the Supreme Court robustly rejected the notion that comity precluded the exercise of jurisdiction against the London re-insurers: "the only substantial question in this case is whether there is in fact a true conflict between domestic and foreign law." Comity is discussed further, at para. 8.08.

[10] The context was the Siberian pipeline affair. See the Community's Note and Comments on the Amendments of June 22, 1982 to the Export Administration Act, described and set out in Lowe, *op. cit.*, at p. 197.

The Commission' view

8.03   The Commission has asserted jurisdiction on the basis of the so-called "effects doctrine" on a number of occasions,[11] its decision in *Dyestuffs*[12] being historically the most significant. As will be explained, when the jurisdiction was challenged, the Court of Justice did not expressly endorse the Commission's approach but upheld the Commission's decision as regards the English and Swiss parties on the grounds that they had acted within the Community via their respective subsidiaries, *i.e.* applying the territoriality principle. Whilst the Commission has on occasion[13] followed the Court's judgment in *Dyestuffs*, it has never conceded its position as regards the application of the effects doctrine. Indeed, in *Franco-Japanese Ballbearings Agreement*,[14] four years after *Dyestuffs*, it clearly reaffirmed its views on the matter. See, also, the Eleventh Report on Competition Policy.[15] Later, there was the suggestion that its decisions in both *Wood Pulp* and *Aluminium* were examples of the application of the effects doctrine.[16]

8.04   It must be acknowledged that the Commission has not been alone in asserting the position of the effects doctrine in Community law. In the *Dyestuffs* case,[17] Advocate General Mayras reached the view after a consideration of the laws of both Member States and non-Member States (in particular, of the United States and also, he said, the United Kingdom), of public international law and of Community law that the principal criterion for the applicability of competition law was territorial effect. But he thought that the criterion of effect was in Community law subject to certain conditions and limitations. In particular, the effect must be a direct and immediate restriction on the market, must be reasonably foreseeable and substantial, and must be a constituent element, and probably even the essential element, of the infringement. The Commission too has recognised that any "effects doctrine" must be qualified.[18] In the later *Commercial Solvents* case,[19] Advocate General Warner referred to the effects doctrine although he said that it was not necessary for him to express a "concluded opinion" having taken the view that the parties, an Italian subsidiary and an American parent company, constituted one "single undertaking" for the purposes of Article 86.

[11] For early examples, see *Grosfillex*: [1964] J.O. 915/64, [1964] C.M.L.R. 237, and *Mertens and Straet*: [1964] J.O. 1426/64, [1964] C.M.L.R. 416.

[12] [1969] J.O. L195/11, [1969] C.M.L.R. D23, D33.

[13] *Vitamins*: [1976] O.J. L223/27, [1976] 2 C.M.L.R. D25, where the Commission relied on Roche's numerous subsidiaries in the EEC. See also *Aluminium*, above, n. 6, at para. 14.5. *Siemens/Fanuc*: [1985] O.J. L376/29, [1988] 4 C.M.L.R. 945 can also be justified on this basis.

[14] [1974] O.J. L343/19, [1975] 1 C.M.L.R. D8. And see the Notice on imports of Japanese products: [1972] J.O. C111/13.

[15] Particularly paras. 34–37.

[16] See the Fourteenth Report on Competition Policy, at point 60.

[17] Cases 48, 49, 51–57/69, *ICI and Others* v. *Commission*: [1972] E.C.R. 619, [1972] C.M.L.R. 557.

[18] See *Zinc Producer Group*: [1984] O.J. L220/27, [1985] 2 C.M.L.R. 108 and Commissioner Andriessen in *Competition Law in the European Communities*, Vol. 5, No. 1 at p. 8. *Cf.* Title IV of the U.S. Foreign Trade Antitrust Improvements Act of 1982 which relates to import trade. But in practice the test may be the same for both imports and exports. See Griffin, *op. cit.*

[19] Cases 6 & 7/73, *Istituto Chemioterapico Italiano and Commercial Solvents Corp.* v. *Commission*: [1974] E.C.R. 223, [1974] 1 C.M.L.R. 309. It may be going too far, however, to say that Mr. Warner adopted the "effects doctrine". At an A.B.A. symposium in 1979, he said: "So far as the European Court is concerned, although there has been flirtation with the effects doctrine by my French colleague, and though I said something about it in the Commercial Solvents case, the Court has not yet committed itself to that doctrine." *Enterprise Law of the 80s* (A.B.A. 1980), p. 234.

Commenting on the Commission's pleading, he said: "This is a reference to the 'effects doctrine' which was adopted by the Court in the *Béguelin* case and discussed by Mr. Advocate General Mayras in his Opinion in the *Dyestuffs* cases."

In *Wood Pulp*,[20] Advocate General Darmon in a full opinion reviewed the effects doctrine in the light of international law, the relevant principles of U.S. law and the various jurisdictional bases in antitrust suggested by academics. He concluded that the criterion of effects was a legitimate one and provided the effects of the conduct alleged by the Commission were substantial, direct and foreseeable the Commission was right in exercising jurisdiction over the foreign parties in the case.

8.05 Whilst the Court of Justice did not apply the effects doctrine in either of the leading cases, *Dyestuffs* and *Wood Pulp*, or in the *Continental Can*[21] or *Commercial Solvents* cases where questions of jurisdiction were discussed, it has arguably referred to it on at least two occasions. In the *Béguelin* case,[22] the Court of Justice said: "The fact that one of the undertakings which are parties to the agreement is situated in a third country does not prevent application of [Article 85] since the agreement is operative[23] on the territory of the Common Market." The Commission has frequently cited *Béguelin* to support its views on jurisdiction. But *Béguelin's* authority on this point is dubious. The question was not raised before the Court and, it is submitted, the Court was saying no more than that the criterion of "effects" expressly required by Article 85(1) was met.

The other oft-quoted reference by the Court to the effects doctrine is not in a competition case but in a case involving the Community rules against discrimination on the grounds of nationality (*in casu*, Articles 7, 48 and 59 of the Treaty). In *Walgrave* v. *Union Cycliste Internationale*,[24] the Court said that the rule against such discrimination "applies in judging all legal relationships in so far as these relationships, by reason either of the place where they are entered into or of the place where they take effect, can be located within the territory of the Community." It has been argued that there is no reason to assume that the territorial scope of application of Articles 85 and 86 should be any more limited than that of Articles 7, 48 and 59.[25] But neither *Walgrave* nor the later case of *Prodest*[26] (citing *Walgrave*) is an instance of extra-territoriality. They are applications of the territoriality and nationality principles.

Territoriality—the Court's reply

8.06 It remains the position that the Court of Justice has not adopted and applied the effects doctrine in any competition case although at least twice invited to do so. The Court has held firm to the territoriality principle albeit with certain developments or nuance. So in *Dyestuffs* it extended the traditional territorial principle by the theory of enterprise entity. It held that the four non-Member States undertakings concerned had

---

[20] Cases 89, 104, 114, 116–117 & 125–129/85, *A Åhlström Oy and Others* v. *Commission*: [1988] E.C.R. 5193, [1988] 4 C.M.L.R. 901.

[21] Case 6/72, *Europemballage Corp,. and Continental Can Co. Inc.* v. *Commission*: [1973] E.C.R. 215, [1973] C.M.L.R. 199.

[22] Case 22/71, *Beguelin Import Co.* v. *G.L. Import Export*: [1971] E.C.R. 949, [1972] C.M.L.R. 81, at para. 11.

[23] In the French text, "produit ses effets", and in the C.M.L.R. translation, "produces its effects".

[24] Case 36/74: [1974] E.C.R. 1405, [1975] 1 C.M.L.R. 320.

[25] Bellis, *op. cit.*, at p. 649.

[26] Case 237/83, *Sarl Prodest* v. *Caisse Primaire d'Assurance Maladie de Paris*: [1984] E.C.R. 3153.

acted within the Community through their respective subsidiaries in the Community. The Court said:[27]

> "The fact that a subsidiary has separate legal personality is not sufficient to exclude the possibility of imputing its conduct to the parent company. Such may be the case in particular where the subsidiary, although having separate legal personality, does not decide independently upon its own conduct on the market, but carries out, in all material respects, the instructions given to it by the parent company. Where a subsidiary does not enjoy real autonomy in determining its course of action in the market, the prohibitions set out in Article 85(1) may be considered inapplicable in the relationship between it and the parent company with which it forms one economic unit. In view of the unity of the group thus formed, the actions of the subsidiaries may in certain circumstances be attributed to the parent company."

Thus, by finding that the parent had acted through the subsidiary and that the conduct had been carried on directly in the Community, the Court of Justice did not depart from the territorial approach to jurisdiction. The Court followed *Dyestuffs* in both *Continental Can* and *Commercial Solvents*, relying on the concept of economic entity/unity and thereby showing, where the parent decided or determined the subsidiary's activities, how the parent had acted in the Community via the subsidiary.

This clearly has implications for the theory of the separate legal personalities of the holding and subsidiary company.[28] Indeed it is noteworthy what little evidence the Court of Justice has required to show that the subsidiary has not acted autonomously and that there is unity of conduct on the market.[29] In *Commercial Solvents*, for example, apart from a 51 per cent. shareholding which it was strongly argued did not imply any control of market behaviour, the evidence was largely inferential and circumstantial.[30] The Court nevertheless concluded that the conduct of the two companies involved was "characterised by an obviously united action", at least on the matter in question.[31] Advocate General Warner had even suggested that there is a presumption that a subsidiary will act in accordance with the wishes of its parents and that accordingly parent and subsidiary companies should be treated as a single undertaking unless this presumption could be rebutted by their showing that the subsidiary had in fact conducted its business autonomously. The Court of Justice did not go this far and indeed it has later stated that: "the bond of economic dependence existing between a parent company and the subsidiary does not preclude a divergence in conduct

---

[27] Above, n. 17, Case 48/69, at paras. 132–135.
[28] For a vigorous criticism of, *inter alia*, this aspect of the Court's judgment in *Dyestuffs*, see Mann, "The Dyestuffs Case in the Court of Justice of the European Communities" (1973) 22 I.C.L.Q. 35, 48. See also Goyder, *EEC Competition Law* (2nd ed., 1993) at pp. 461–464.
[29] Above, n. 17, Case 48/69, at paras. 136–139. The Court was satisfied, in the case of ICI, by evidence of a majority shareholding, of the ability to influence the subsidiary's sales policy, and of one example which showed that ICI had in fact determined the subsidiary's selling prices and by the absence of any contrary evidence.
[30] Allen, *op. cit.*, at p. 73, and see the judgment of the Court, above, n. 17, at paras. 37 and 39. The Court's analysis in *Continental Can* is described in Goyder, *op. cit.*
[31] Above, n. 17, at para. 41.

or even a divergence of interests between the two companies."[32] Nonetheless in practice, the burden of proof on the companies concerned may well be substantial.

8.06A In *Wood Pulp*,[33] the Court of Justice again turned its back on the effects doctrine, at least in the sense that it did not accept the advice proffered by Advocate General Darmon and spoke only in terms of territoriality. But the Court's judgment is short and not free from debate as to its precise meaning. The relevant part of the judgment starts with a brief analysis of Article 85(1) itself, considering the business of the undertakings concerned and their sales to consumers in the Community in relation to competition within the Common Market. The Court concludes that "by applying the competition rules in the Treaty in the circumstances of the case to undertakings whose registered offices are situated outside the Community, the Commission has not made an incorrect assessment of the territorial scope of Article 85."[34]

The Court by these words is not endorsing a finding of infringement but is merely saying that *prima facie* the alleged conduct in question falls within the wording of Article 85(1).

The Court then moves on to the key issue, the plea that the decision was incompatible with public international law because it was founded exclusively on the economic repercussions within the Common Market of conduct outside the Community. The Court observes that an infringement of Article 85 is made up of two elements; first, the formation of the agreement, decision or concerted practice, and second, its implementation. Because parties could simply avoid the prohibition by forming their agreements outside the Community, the decisive factor, the Court concludes, is the place where it is implemented. The Court proceeds:

> "The producers in this case implemented their pricing agreement within the Common Market. It is immaterial whether or not they had recourse to subsidiaries, agents, sub-agents, or branches within the Community in order to make their contracts within the Community.
>
> Accordingly the Community's jurisdiction to apply its competition rules to such conduct is covered by the territoriality principle as universally recognised in public international law."[35]

8.06B Both sides, "effects" and territoriality, have laid claim to these words as justifying their position.[36] Like many national courts the Court of Justice rarely goes further than is necessary in the instant case. What is paramount therefore, it is submitted, is the factual position in the case. Regrettably the Court does not go into this in the detail which may be required to comprehend fully its findings. It has been suggested that

---

[32] Cases 32 & 36–82/78, *BMW Belgium and others* v. *Commission*: [1979] E.C.R. 2435, [1980] 1 C.M.L.R. 370, at para. 24. See also Case 107/82, *AEG-Telefunken* v. *Commission*: [1983] E.C.R. 3151, [1984] 3 C.M.L.R. 325, at paras. 47–53, and Case 75/84, *Metro-SB-Grossmarkte GmbH & Co. KG* v. *Commission*: [1986] E.C.R. 3021, [1987] 1 C.M.L.R. 118, at para. 84.

[33] Above, n. 20

[34] *Ibid.* at para. 14

[35] *Ibid.* at paras. 17 and 18

[36] Indeed as Goyder, *op. cit.*, at p. 467 comments: "what is unclear from the Court's judgment is the degree to which the analysis of 'formation' and 'implementation' reaches the same result as the 'effects doctrine'. The end result may only be significant in borderline cases."

the judgment is authority for the proposition that selling directly from outside the Community to purchase inside is sufficient to comprise "implementation within" the Community. But it is unclear (and the Court ruling does not make express findings on this) whether any of the undertakings in question engaged in such conduct without some presence or activity, whether directly or through an agent, within the Community. What is noteworthy in this context is the way the Court dealt with the KEA, an export association permitted under U.S. law, of which a number of North American parties were members. The KEA was in effect merely a legal mechanism by which certain parties could come together consistently with U.S. antitrust law as an export association. As such the KEA did nothing within the Community. The Court sidesteps the question of the Community's jurisdiction over the KEA by finding that its activities (its price recommendations, etc.) cannot be distinguished from the agreements concluded by the association's member undertakings.[37] The Court thereby avoided addressing the case where on the facts there was no activity by an undertaking concerned in the Community. The Court, as mentioned above, concluded that the conduct of the undertakings was "covered by territoriality principle as universally recognised in public international law." *Wood Pulp* is an example, as regards conduct implemented within the Community, of the objective territoriality principle.

There remains, however, some uncertainty as to what factual contact between the undertaking concerned and the Community is necessary in order to satisfy the need for "implementation within" the Community, and in particular whether direct selling to customers in the Community from and at prices agreed outside is caught. In legislative mode, the Council has adhered to the territorial approach. The Merger Control Regulation, when touching on the issue of jurisdiction for when a concentration will have a Community dimension and therefore fall within the ambit of Regulation, expressly contemplates that undertakings should have substantial operations in the Community.[38] However, not unexpectedly, the Commission takes the view that direct selling is sufficient to give it jurisdiction although it is unclear in recent reported decisions how much activity existed, or was considered necessary, in the Community to justify taking jurisdiction on the basis of "implementation within" the Community.[39]

Investigation and enforcement

8.07 So far the discussion has concerned "subject matter" (or "legislative") jurisdiction; that is the power under international law to enact laws, regulations and other rules, *e.g.* whether there can be an infringement of Community law where the parties are situated and the activities take place outside the Community. Enforcement jurisdiction relates, *inter alia*, to the exercise of powers to compel discovery of information during the investigation of an alleged infringement and, if necessary, to compel termination of an infringement once found. The distinction may not always be realistic, as Advocate General Darmon recognised in *Wood Pulp*:[40] the imposition of a fine constitutes the exercise of prescriptive jurisdiction and to deny the power to make such an order renders the prescriptive jurisdiction nugatory.

---

[37] *Ibid.* at paras. 24 to 28. *Cf.* the Commission's decision in *ANSAC*: [1991] O.J. L152/54.

[38] Reg. 4064/89, preamble para. 11. See Cook and Kerse, *EEC Merger Control* (1991), para. 1.8.

[39] See *PVC*: [1989] O.J. L74/1, [1990] 4 C.M.L.R. 345 and *LdPE*: [1989] O.J. L74/21, [1990] 4 C.M.L.R. 382.

[40] Above n. 20.

The formal exercise of investigatory powers or action on foreign territory is generally unacceptable in the absence of an international agreement between the States concerned.[41] Thus, under the EEA, where investigations by one surveillance authority are required in the other, the first authority shall request the other authority to undertake the investigations in accordance with its internal rules.[42] Although prepared to adopt the effects doctrine as part of the legislative jurisdiction of the Community, in *Dyestuffs* Advocate General Mayras took a more restrictive approach to enforcement:[43]

> "Whether it be criminal law or, as in the present cases, administrative proceedings that are involved, the courts or administrative authorities of a State—and, *mutatis mutandis*, of the Community—are certainly not justified under international law in taking coercive measures or indeed any measure of inquiry, investigation or supervision outside their territorial jurisdiction where execution would inevitably infringe the internal sovereignty of the State on the territory of which they claimed to act."

He thought, however, that it would be possible to impose a fine for substantive infringement, drawing a very fine distinction between the imposition of a fine and its recovery and "a true injunction which would result, for example, from a decision for the production, under pain of periodic penalty payments, of certain documents, or which would constitute a means of applying pressure to obtain the revocation of certain clauses considered illegal."

But experience would suggest that the Court of Justice may not be so reticent although it is not clear to what extent it has addressed the international law implications. In *Continental Can*,[44] the Court did not doubt that the Commission had power to issue the challenged decision against the American company or to address to it the demand to put an end to the infringement and for this purpose to submit proposals to the Commission by a specified date. The Commission's decision was, however, annulled on other grounds and hence no problem of enforcement in fact arose. But in *Commercial solvents*[45] the Court clearly contemplated the Commission's decision operating extraterritorially and unhesitatingly upheld it. The Court held that the Commission was entitled to require CSC, the American parent, and Ist.C.I., the Italian subsidiary, to resupply the complainant Zoja with a sufficient product to take account of its trade not only within the Community but also by way of export (which amounted to 90 per cent. of its business) in as much as it was necessary to maintain its position in the Community. Although the Commission's decision imposed a joint and several liability on CSC and Ist.C.I. the Court could not have been unaware that, in order to comply with the decision, measures would have to be taken by CSC outside the Community with regard to the production of the supplies ordered for Zoja. It should also be noted that the

[41] See, *e.g.* Slot and Grabandt, *op. cit.*, and Maesen, "Antitrust Jurisdiction under Customary International Law" (1984), 78 Am. J. Int'l. L. 783.

[42] Protocol 23, Art. 8(3).

[43] Cases 48, 49, 51–57/69, *ICI and Others* v. *Commission*: [1972] E.C.R. 619, [1972] C.M.L.R. 557. Attempts under U.S. law to exercise enforcement jurisdiction extraterritorial have not met with great success and indeed have encountered opposition (*e.g.* blocking statutes)—see, generally, Griffin, *op. cit.*

[44] Case 6/72, *Europemballage Corp. and Continental Can Co. Inc.* v. *Commission*: [1973] E.C.R. 215, [1973] C.M.L.R. 199, at para. 14.

[45] Cases 6 & 7/73, *Istituto Chemioterapico Italiano and Commercial Solvents Corp.* v. *Commission*: [1974] E.C.R. 223, [1974] 1 C.M.L.R. 309, at paras. 42–50.

Court, admittedly *sub silentio*, endorsed the use by the Commission of periodic penalty payments to compel performance by CSC and Ist.C.I. Having gone this far, it seems to be not inconceivable that, notwithstanding the restraints of international law, the Court might uphold the Commission's use of Article 11 of Regulation 17 to obtain information from undertakings outside the Community. Indeed, it arguably suggested the Commission do this in the *United Brands* case.[46] Dealing with the allegation of excessive pricing, the Court said that "the Commission was at least under a duty to require UBC to produce particulars of all the constituent elements of its production costs." On the facts, the Court was referring to UBC's costs in Latin America, information most probably in UBC's possession outside the EEC.

Comity

8.08   The Commission has recognised the applicability of the principle of comity in relation to the enforcement of the competition rules. In *Aluminium* it said:

> "There are no reasons of comity which militate in favour of self-restraint in the exercise of jurisdiction by the Commission. The exercise of jurisdiction by the Commission does not require any of the undertakings concerned to act in a way contrary to the requirements of their domestic laws, nor would the application of Community law adversely affect important interests of a non-Member State."[47]

Comity is one means of the resolution of jurisdictional conflicts which is receiving greater recognition and acceptance internationally. It can be seen in the practice of the courts, both here and across the Atlantic.[48] It can also be seen in Community competition legislation. Article 9 of Regulation 4056/86, the implementing regulation for maritime transport, is entitled "Conflicts of international law" and provides for consultation with the competent authorities for third countries where the application of the regulation may conflict with the law, regulation or administrative action of those third countries. More widely comity is embodied in an OECD recommendation.[49] In

---

[46] Case 27/76: [1978] E.C.R. 207, [1978] 1 C.M.L.R. 429, at para. 256. But UBC had a subsidiary within the Community which could have been required to produce the information albeit that it was outside the Community.

[47] *Aluminium Imports from Eastern Europe*: [1985] O.J. L92/1, [1987] 3 C.M.L.R. 813, at para. 14.7.

[48] The need to have regard to foreign jurisdictional interests can be seen in *Lonrho Ltd.* v. *Shell*: [1981] 2 All E.R. 456; *R.* v. *Grossman*: (1981) 17 Cr.App.R. 302, and in *MacKinnon* v. *Donaldson Lufkin Corp.*: [1986] 2 W.L.R. 453, [1987] *European Commercial Cases* 139. In Canada, in *Frischke* v. *Royal Bank*: (1977) 17 Ont. 2d 388. In the U.S.A., in the cases listed in n. 9, above.
    As the minority in the *Hartford Fire Insurance* case (above, n. 9) said, "it is important to distinguish between the comity of courts, whereby judges decline to exercise jurisdiction over matters more appropriately adjudged elsewhere, and 'prescriptive comity', ie the respect sovereign nations afford each other by limiting the reach of their laws. That comity is exercised by legislatures when they enact laws, and courts assume that it has been exercised when they come to implement the scope of laws their legislatures have enacted." See also the Restatement (Third) of the Foreign Relations Law of the United States. Comity is also recognised, for example, in the U.S./Australia Co-operation Agreement on Antitrust Matters and in the U.S./E.C. Co-operation Agreement. The latter is discussed at para. 8.08A.

[49] OECD Council Recommendation concerning co-operation between Member Countries on Restrictive Business Practices Affecting International Trade, September 25, 1979, set out in Lowe, op. cit., at p. 251. In the context of OECD the Commission has pointed out its record of moderation and restraint in seeking to reconcile the Community's interest in a proper enforcement of its internal rules with major interests of third countries: Fifteenth Report on Competition Policy, at point 11. Brittan, *op. cit.*, sees comity as an

Wood Pulp, the Court of Justice noted the compliance by the Commission with the OECD recommendation but did not, because it would in the Court's view have amounted to calling into question the Community's jurisdiction which it had found to exist in the case, consider the nature or application of the principle of comity. This approach is disappointing, notwithstanding the Court's ruling that jurisdiction in the case was "covered by the territoriality principle as universally recognised in public international law." There is still a place and room for comity.[50] *A fortiori* the exercise of controversial jurisdiction (that is to say on a basis not internationally accepted, such as "effects") particularly requires a proper consideration of the interests of the other States involved, and consultation and forbearance if necessary. Comity is a material consideration to which the Commission should have regard before it exercises jurisdiction where non-Member States may be concerned.

E.C./U.S. Co-operation Agreement

8.08A In September 1991, the Commission concluded[51] a non-binding agreement with the United States government for co-operation in and co-ordination of their respective competition laws. This is a Commission, not a Community, agreement. Nor are Member States otherwise parties or bound by it. The full text is set out in Appendix K. The agreement provides for each party to notify the other where its enforcement activities may affect the interests of the other (Article 2). This includes notifying remedies which may require or prohibit conduct in the other party's territory. The practice, which has existed for some time, of the parties exchanging information and meeting to discuss matters of mutual interest is formalised (Article 3). The parties agree to render assistance to each other in their enforcement activities (Article 4). Somewhat controversially, because it appears to be aimed at certain third States including Japan, the parties agree to co-operate regarding anti-competitive activities in the territory of one party that adversely effect the interests of the other (Article 5). This has been described as "positive" comity. The agreement provides for the avoidance of conflicts over enforcement activities; each party undertakes to take into account the important interests of the other (Article 6). This is an important practical statement of the more traditional comity principle.[52] The confidentiality of information is required to be maintained (Article 7) and, most importantly, nothing in the agreement is to be interpreted in a manner inconsistent with the existing laws of the parties or as requiring any change in those laws (Article 9). It is understood that the Commission has also drafted a similar co-operation agreement with the Canadians.[53]

---

expression of the obligations of states to exercise moderation and restraint.

[50] Above, n. 20, at para. 22.

[51] The ability of the Commission to conclude the agreement has been challenged, principally on the ground of the Commission's lack of competence having regard to Arts. 228 and 229 of the Treaty; see Case C–327/91, *France* v. *Commission*, A.G. Tesauro has opined that the Commission exceeded its powers in purporting to conclude the agreement (Opinion of December 16, 1993). On the agreement generally see Ham, *International cooperation in the anti-trust field and in particular the Agreement between the United States of America and the Commission of the European Communities* (1993) 30 C.M.L.Rev. 571

[52] See in particular the matters listed in Art. 6(3).

[53] It is not expected to be signed until the French challenge to the E.C./U.S. Agreement (above, n. 51) has been determined by the Court of Justice.

General principles of law and fundamental rights

8.09   Community law is not constituted solely by the Treaties and the regulations, etc., made thereunder. It is well established that in the performance of its duty under Article 164 of the Treaty to ensure that "the law" is observed the Court of Justice may have regard to and apply general principles of law.[54] Such principles may be distilled from the laws of the Member States and in this respect national law may have a dynamic impact on the application and development of Community law. In the ascertainment of applicable general principles of law, the Court is not bound to look for the lowest common denominator from the laws of the Member States but may be selective and may adopt the best and most progressive solution having regard to the objects of the Treaty.[55] The laws of the Member States have thus provided a fruitful source of Community law, in particular in the area of administrative law.[56]

Transocean Marine Paint[57] provides one example. The Court of Justice held that despite the absence of any express provision in Regulation 99/63, an undertaking on whom conditions or obligations are to be imposed[58] in connection with the grant of exemption under Article 85(3) has a right to be heard on the matter. Advocate General Warner analysed the position in the laws of the different Member States in relation to the rule which in English law is known as *audi alteram partem* and reached the conclusion that whilst not all Member States had such or a similar rule nevertheless the right to be heard should form part of "the law" within the meaning of Article 164. The Court did not repeat such analysis in its judgment but referred simply to "the general rule that a person whose interests are perceptibly affected by a decision taken by a public authority must be given the opportunity to make his point of view known."

The *Hoechst* litigation provides another good example. The Court of Justice found, in the context of its examination of the Commission's powers of investigation under Article 14, that it was common for all legal systems to provide protection against arbitrary or disproportionate intervention and recognised the need for that protection as a general principle of Community law governing the Commission's investigatory powers.[59] On the other hand the comparative analysis of the laws of Member States undertaken in *Orkem* failed to show that the privilege against self-incrimination was a general principle in the area of competition law.[60]

---

[54] See, generally, Brown and Jacobs, *The Court of Justice of the European Communities* (3rd ed., 1989), Chap. 15.

[55] Per A.G. Lagrange in Case 14/61, *Hoogovens* v. *High Authority*: [1962] E.C.R. 253, 283–284, [1963] C.M.L.R. 73, 85–86.

[56] See Usher, "The Influence of National Concepts on Decisions of the European Court" [1976] 1 E.L.Rev. 359.

[57] Case 17/74, *Transocean Marine Paint Association* v. *Commission*: [1974] E.C.R. 1063, [1974] 2 C.M.L.R. 459.

[58] Under Art. 8(1) of Reg. 17. See paras. 6.32–34.

[59] Cases 46/87 & 227/88, *Hoechst AG* v. *Commission*: [1989] E.C.R. 2859, [1991] 1 C.M.L.R. 410, at para. 19.

[60] Case 374/87, *Orkem* v. *Commission*: [1989] E.C.R. 3282, [1991] 4 C.M.L.R. 502, at para. 29. Nevertheless the Court held that there should be a limited degree of protection—see para. 3.44. As mentioned there, the scope of any privilege in Community Law might usefully be reviewed in the light of the judgment of the European Court of Human Rights in *Funke* v. *France*: [1993] 1 C.M.L.R. 897.

8.10 Fundamental rights also form part of the law within the meaning of Article 164 of the Treaty. In the *Internationale Handelgesellschaft* case,[61] the Court of Justice said:

> "Respect for fundamental rights forms an integral part of the general principles of law protected by the Court of Justice. The protection of such rights, whilst inspired by the constitutional traditions common to the Member States, must be ensured within the framework of the structure and objectives of the Community."

This was reaffirmed in the second *Nold* case[62] where the Court went further and held that in the identification and protection of such rights the Court may also have regard to international treaties on which Member States have collaborated or to which they are signatories: *in casu*, the European Convention on Human Rights.[63] The special importance of the European Convention has been also expressly recognised in the preamble to the Single European Act[64] and now in the Treaty on European Union. Article F(2) states:

> "The Union shall respect fundamental rights, as guaranteed by the European Convention for the Protection of Human Rights and Fundamental Freedoms signed in Rome on 4 November 1950 and as they result from the constitutional traditions common to the Member States, as general principles of Community law."[65]

8.11 The protection given to natural persons by fundamental (or human) rights is not necessarily to be denied to legal persons, including undertakings within the meaning of Articles 85 and 86. In *National Panasonic* v. *Commission*,[66] the applicant argued that its fundamental rights had been infringed by the Commission's failure to give it prior notice of the decision ordering an investigation under Article 14 of Regulation 17, thus rendering it unable to take advice as to its rights and obligations in relation to the investigation, to ascertain whether any documents were outside the Commission's power of inspection and to prepare itself to collaborate fully in the investigation. Reliance, at least in part, was placed on Article 8(1) of the European Convention on Human Rights whereby "everyone has the right to respect for his private

---

[61] Case 11/70: [1970] E.C.R. 1125, [1972] C.M.L.R. 255. And see also Case 29/69, *Stauder* v. *Ulm*: [1969] E.C.R. 419, [1970] C.M.L.R. 112. On the subject generally, see Dauses, "The Protection of Fundamental Rights in the Community Legal Order" (1985) 6 E.L.Rev. 398.

[62] Case 4/73, *Nold KG* v. *Commission*: [1974] E.C.R. 491, [1974] 2 C.M.L.R. 338, and see Case 44/79, *Hauer* v. *Land Rheinland-Pfalz*: [1979] E.C.R. 3727, [1980] 3 C.M.L.R. 42, at paras. 14 and 15.

[63] See generally, Jacobs, *The European Convention on Human Rights* (1975), and van Dijk and van Hoof, *Theory and Practice of the European Convention on Human Rights* (2nd ed., 1990).The Community is not a signatory to the Convention and the European Commission of Human Rights has held that proceedings cannot be brought before it against the Community or its institutions. See App. No. 8030/77, *Confédération Française Démocratique de Travail* v. *European Communities or the Member States*.

[64] See also the Joint Declaration of April 5, 1977 of the European Parliament, the Council and the Commission: [1977] O.J. C103/1.

[65] There is also mention of the Convention in the context of co-operation in the fields of justice and home affairs (Article K2). See generally Krogsgaard, "Fundamental Rights in the European Community after Maastricht" [1993] 1 L.I.E.I. 99.

[66] Case 136/79: [1980] E.C.R. 2033, [1980] 3 C.M.L.R. 169.

and family life, his home and his correspondence."[67] The Court of Justice examined the provisions of Article 8 of the European Convention (and in particular Article 8(2)[68] which contemplates interference by public authorities in the exercise of the rights set out in Article 8(1)) and the purpose of the investigatory powers of Article 14 of Regulation 17 in relation to the functions of the competition rules of the Treaty. It concluded that the Commission's power to carry out investigation without previous notification did not infringe the right invoked by the applicant.[69] In the *AKZO* case,[70] the Court held that provided the conditions contained in Article 14(3) of Regulation 17 are fulfilled a decision ordering inspections is not a breach of Article 8 of the Convention. However, in *Hoechst* the Court took a different approach to this Article of the Convention. It held that the fundamental right to the inviolability of the home does not apply to undertakings. The protective scope of Article 8(1), the Court said, is concerned with the development of man's personal freedom and may not therefore be extended to business premises.[71]

8.12 In the *FEDETAB* case,[72] the argument was put forward that the Commission's procedures violated Article 6(1)[73] of the European Convention because they did not provide the safeguard of the right to be heard by an independent tribunal. The Court of Justice's response concentrated on the question whether the Commission constituted

---

[67] These guarantees, it was argued, should be provided *mutatis mutandis* to legal persons. Whilst the Court left open the question whether, and to what extent, Art. 8 of the European Convention applies to persons other than natural persons (it was not necessary for the Court to determine this), its general approach did not appear to exclude undertakings from the protection given by fundamental rights in appropriate circumstances. Companies would appear to have the right to a fair trial under Art. 6 of the Convention. See Jacobs, *op. cit.*, p. 228 and the cases cited therein. The inapplicability of Art. 8(1) was however determined in *Hoechst*. See text to n. 71, below.

[68] Art. 8(2) of the Convention provides: "There shall be no interference by a public authority with the exercise of this right except such as is in accordance with the law and is necessary in a democratic society in the interests of national security, public safety or *the economic well-being of the country*, for the prevention of disorder or crime, for the protection of health or morals, or for the protection of the rights and freedoms of others" (emphasis added).

[69] Above, n. 66, at para. 20.

[70] Case 5/85, *AKZO Chemie BV (Netherlands) and AKZO Chemie U.K. Ltd.* v. *Commission*: [1986] E.C.R. 2585, [1987] 3 C.M.L.R. 716, at paras. 24–26.

[71] Above, n. 59, at paras. 17–18.

[72] Cases 209–215 & 218/78, *Heintz van Landewyck and others* v. *Commission*: [1980] E.C.R. 3125, [1981] 3 C.M.L.R. 134, at paras. 78–81.

[73] Art. 6(1) provides: "In the determination of his civil rights and obligations or of any criminal charge against him, everyone is entitled to a fair and public hearing within a reasonable time by an independent and impartial tribunal established by law. Judgment shall be pronounced publicly but the press and public may be excluded from all or part of the trial in the interests of morals, public order and national security in a democratic society, where the interests of juveniles or the protection of the private life of the parties so require, or to the extent strictly necessary in the opinion of the court in special circumstances where publicity would prejudice the interests of justice". In *Société Stenuit* v. *France* (1992) 14 E.H.R.R. 509, the European Commission on Human Rights proceeded on the basis that the French competition law procedures, leading to an administrative penalty, were criminal in character and that the French procedures (whereby the decision was taken by the Competition Commission with a right of appeal to the Conseil d'Etat) contravened Art. 6(1). But it appears that the European Commission would not have so found had the Conseil d'Etat been prepared to conduct a full judicial review of such decisions. The French procedures have subsequently been changed by the introduction of a Competition Council). Does this suggest that the E.C. Commission's procedures might be similarly characterised as criminal (notwithstanding that Art. 15(4) of Reg. 17 says that fining decisions shall not be of a criminal law nature)? It is debatable and noteworthy that in *Polypropylene*: Case T–7/89, *Hercules* v. *Commission*: [1992] 4 C.M.L.R. 84, at p. 101 A.G. Vesterdorf took the view that fines under Art. 15 of Reg. 17 "have a criminal law character".

a tribunal for this purpose. Having considered certain case law of the European Court of Human Rights, the Court took the view that the Commission was not a tribunal within the meaning of Article 6(1).[74] In the *Pioneer* case,[75] the Court rejected the contention that the Commission's decision was unlawful because it had been adopted under a system in which the Commission combines the functions of judge and jury, contrary to Article 6(1). The Court, referring to *FEDETAB*, reiterated that the Commission was not a "tribunal". But whether the Commission is a tribunal is not necessarily the question for Article 6. In both these cases however the Court stressed that the Commission nevertheless had to respect the procedural guarantees provided for by Community law. The Commission, it is submitted, cannot neglect the standards of Article 6, especially when fines are in question. In *Orkem*, the Court also rejected Article 6 as authority for the right of an undertaking not to give evidence against itself,[76] but, as already mentioned, this question may need to be revisited in the light of recent jurisprudence of the European Court of Human Rights.

It has also been argued that the application of the competition rules may itself be contrary to the Convention in certain circumstances. So in *Dutch Books*,[77] it was suggested that the abolition of the system of resale price maintenance on books was contrary to the freedom of expression guaranteed by Article 11 of the European Convention. The Court rejected this. There was no restriction on the freedom of publication by submitting the production and trade in books to rules whose sole purpose was to ensure freedom of trade between the Member States.

Notwithstanding the apparent lack of success by applicants so far, the evidence is that the Court is concerned to rationalise the express provisions of Community law (and in particular Regulations 17 and 99/63) with fundamental rights and will not be content merely to pay lip-service to their existence.[78] Indeed in order to ensure compliance with the standards of the European Convention, and Article 6 in particular, the Court of First Instance should be especially vigilant when looking at the facts and issues of a case and should not be loath to interfere with the Commission's exercise of its discretion and judgment of economic matters.

On the other hand it must not be forgotten that the Court of First Instance and the Court of Justice can and do exercise a full supervisory jurisdiction over the Commission. They may be looked to in order to provide the safeguards required by the Convention.

[74] See also *Polypropylene*: Case T–11/89, *Shell* v. *Commission*: and Case T–14/89, *Montedipe* v. *Commission*: not yet reported.

[75] Cases 100–103/80, *Musique Diffusion Française et al.* v. *Commission*: [1983] E.C.R. 1823, [1983] 3 C.M.L.R. 221, at paras. 6–8.

[76] Above, n. 60, at para. 30. The Court also rejected a similar argument based on Art. 14 of International Convention on Civil and Political Regulations 1966. But there remains some limited protection against self-incrimination. See para. 3.44.

[77] Cases 43 & 63/82, *VBBB and VBVB* v. *Commission*: [1984] E.C.R. 19, [1985] 1 C.M.L.R. 27, at paras. 33 and 34.

[78] *National Panasonic* v. *Commission*, above, n. 66 (the result was, in the author's opinion, the correct one). And see Case 117/76, *Firma Albert Ruckdeschel & Co.* v. *Hauptzollamt Hamburg-St. Annen*: [1977] E.C.R. 1753, [1979] 2 C.M.L.R. 445.

The principle of equality

8.12A   The principle of equality or non-discrimination has long been accepted by the Court of Justice as one of the fundamental principles of Community law. The principle requires that similar situations shall not be treated differently unless differentiation is objectively justified.[79] Particular focus has been placed on the principle in relation to the Commission's fining policy. In *Belasco*,[80] the plea that the Commission had infringed the principle by treating members of the trade association (Belasco) differently from the non-members involved failed. On examination the Court of Justice found that the respective position of members and non-members was not comparable. They were not party to the same infringements and therefore the Commission was justified in imposing different levels of fine. More recently in the *Polypropylene* case,[81] Hercules complained that the Commission had infringed the principle of equal treatment by treating Hercules differently from Amoco and BP, undertakings who were not included amongst the addressees of the decision. The Court of First Instance held on the facts that Hercules situation had been different from the other two undertakings, Hercules having taken part in the system of regular meetings in the framework of which target prices and sales volume targets were fixed and extensive information was exchanged between competitors about their future conduct. For there to be a breach of the principle of equal treatment comparable situations must have been treated differently. It should be noted that the principle of equality prohibits not only different treatment of situations which are identical but also identical treatment of situations which are different.[82] So, for example, if more than one undertaking is being fined, the Commission must consider the position of each undertaking separately.

Legal professional privilege/legal confidence

Introduction

8.13   Regulation 17 contains no special provision dealing with the position of lawyer–client communications. In this respect the Council arguably did not follow the recommendation contained in the Report of the Committee of the European Parliament[83] that documents and information protected by "secret professionel" should be immune from disclosure.[84] This does not mean, however, that the confidentiality of lawyer–client communications which, under English law, would be safeguarded by legal professional privilege (and under Scots law by "confidentiality") is

---

[79] Cases 117/76 & 16/77, *Ruckdeschel* v. *Hauptzollamt Hamburg St Annen*: [1977] E.C.R. 1753, [1979] 4 C.M.L.R. 445.

[80] Case 246/89, *Société coopérative des asphalteurs belges (Belasco) and others* v. *Commission*: [1989] E.C.R. 2181, [1991] 4 C.M.L.R. 96, at paras. 46–48. And see para. 7.12 discussing the *BMW Belgium* case.

[81] *Hercules* v. *Commission*, above, n. 73, at para. 295. See also *Wood Pulp II*: Cases C 89, 104, 114, 116, 117, & 125–129/85, *A Åhlström Osakeyhtio and Others* v. *Commission*: [1993] 4 C.M.L.R. 407, at paras. 145–147.

[82] Case 58/86, *Coopérative Agricole d'approvisionnement des avirons* v. *Receveur des douanes de Saint Denis*: [1987] E.C.R. 1525, [1988] 2 C.M.L.R. 30, at para. 15.

[83] Doc. 104/1960–61, the Deringer Report. But see the interpretation of the Report given by A.G. Warner in his Opinion in the *A.M. & S.* case, below, n. 86.

[84] *Cf.* Art. 20(2) of Reg. 17 which protects information covered by the obligation of professional secrecy from disclosure by (not to) the Commission. See paras. 8.18–21.

denied protection in Community law. There exists a general principle of law, applicable in Community law as part of "the law" within the meaning of Article 164 of the Treaty: the protection of confidentiality of certain communications between lawyer and client. This protection is assured not only in proceedings before the Court of Justice[85] but also in the administrative proceedings of the Commission under Regulation 17. The matter came before the Court in the now famous *A.M. & S.* case.[86] The Court has acknowledged that a person must be able, without constraint, to consult a lawyer whose profession entails the giving of independent legal advice to all those in need of it.[87] Regulation 17, the Court has said, must be interpreted in such a way as to protect the confidentiality of lawyer–client communications subject to two conditions: first, the communications must be made for the purposes and in the interests of the client's right of defence; and secondly, the communications must emanate from independent lawyers.[88] But whilst the Court identified the existence of the protection and its basic conditions, it did not define its full scope. Inevitably, many questions remain unanswered, although few problems seem to have arisen in practice.

Communications protected

8.14   The relevant communications must be made "for the purposes and in the interests of the client's right of defence." The rights of defence must be exercisable in full and the protection of lawyer–client communications is, the Court of Justice said, "an essential corollary" to those rights.[89] This prompts the question as to when such rights of defence arise. In particular, will only communications which are made after the Commission has commenced proceedings against the undertaking, or will earlier correspondence, written advices, etc., be protected? The Court has made it clear that the protection covers all communications exchanged after the initiation[90] of proceedings by the Commission under Regulation 17 but has accepted that it must also be possible to extend it to earlier written communications which have a *relationship* to the subject-matter of that procedure.[91] This is important bearing in mind that inquiries, formal and informal, may be made by the Commission before such initiation of proceedings

---

[85] To a certain extent such privilege is contained in Art. 32(2) of the Court of Justice's Rules of Procedure which provides that the privileges of agents, advisers and lawyers includes the exemption from both search and seizure of "papers and documents relating to the proceedings". The Court of First Instance has a similar rule—see Art. 38(2) of its Rules of Procedure.

[86] Case 155/79, *A.M. & S. Europe Ltd.* v. *Commission*: [1982] E.C.R. 1575, [1982] 2 C.M.L.R. 264. An account of the history of the case can be found in the first edition of and supplements to the present book. Much has been written on the case and its implications: see, *e.g.* Boyd (1982) 7 E.L.Rev. 493; Forrester (1983) 20 C.M.L.Rev. 75; Faull (1983) 8 E.L.Rev. 411; Pagone (1984) 33 I.C.L.Q. 663; Faull (1985) 10 E.L.Rev. 1991 and Christoforou (1985–86) 9 Fordham Int. L.J. 1.

[87] *Ibid.* at para. 18.

[88] *Ibid.* at paras. 21 and 22.

[89] *Ibid.* at para. 23. In Case T–30/89A, *Hilti AG* v. *Commission*: [1990] 4 C.M.L.R. 602, in the context of an application to exclude documents being shown to interveners, the Court of First Instance described the protection as being an essential principle (para. 11).

[90] It seems likely that the Court is not here referring to the formal initiation of proceedings (see paras. 2.38–39) but to the factual commencement of the Commission's procedure. See Christoforou, *op. cit.* In Cases 46/87 & 227/88, *Hoechst AG* v. *Commission*: [1989] E.C.R. 2859, [1991] 4 C.M.L.R. 410, the Court of Justice speaks of the need for the privileged nature of lawyer client communications to be respected as from the preliminary inquiry stage (para. 16). The rights of undertakings during investigations was the point at issue and the Court is not, it is submitted, saying that correspondence, etc., originating at an earlier time will not be protected.

[91] Above, n. 86, at para. 23 (emphasis added).

and there should be no discouragement from taking legal advice at the earliest opportunity. In the instant case the Court held that communications made in 1972 and 1973 were protected. The investigations under Article 14 of Regulation 17 did not take place until 1978 and 1979. The relevant documents originated at the time of the United Kingdom's accession to the Community and were, the Court said, "concerned with how far it might be possible to avoid conflict between the applicant and the Community authorities on the applicant's position, in particular with regard to the Community provisions on competition."[92]

It is not clear over what period of time the alleged cartel in zinc investigated by the Commission existed, but the Court's general words and its ruling on the facts give support to the view that "early" communications between lawyer and client will be protected. Thus it appears that preliminary advice as to the status of an agreement or practice under the competition rules, the need to notify, the likelihood of prosecution and fine, etc., is protected under Community law. Advice given at this stage would seem to be clearly related to the subject-matter of a later procedure, whether or not that procedure concerns the termination of an infringement or the granting of an exemption.[93] Advice given in relation to interim measures would also be covered.

The Court of Justice lays down no restrictions on the type of undertakings who may claim the protection. It is not restricted to natural persons but will apply to all undertakings, whatever their legal form, which may be subject to the Commission's procedures. Further, the Court imposes no qualifications as to where the documents are; whether in the hands of the client, the lawyer or a third party. On the facts the protection was not lost because the documents had circulated within the group of companies and in *Hilti*,[94] the Court of First Instance took the view that when advice is reproduced in an internal note distributed within the undertaking concerned so that it can be considered by relevant staff it is protected provided such notes are confined to reporting the text or the content of the lawyer–client communications. But if the documents are in the hands of a third party this may raise doubts as to whether they are confidential to the lawyer–client relationship.

It is significant moreover that the Court of Justice in *A.M. & S.* refers to lawyer–client communications having a relationship with the subject-matter of a procedure under Regulation 17. The existence of the protection is not dependent on there being an investigation under Article 14, nor is the extent of the protection necessarily limited to the scope of any such investigation. A Commission procedure under Regulation 17 or the likelihood of such a procedure is the key factor. Thus a document dealing with widgets would be protected from disclosure during a Commission investigation into blodgets. Indeed it would be inconsistent with the purpose and rationale of the protection if legal advice on the subject of widgets could be seen by the Commission during an investigation into blodgets and vice versa.

Finally, the Court speaks of the communications "emanating" from independent lawyers. At first sight this might be taken to mean that only letters, etc., from such lawyers are protected. But it is clear from an examination of the list of documents in A.M.

---

[92] *Ibid.* at para. 34.
[93] The Court refers to "a decision on the application of Arts. 85 and 86" which should, it is submitted, include a decision under Art. 85(3)—it has been established that the rights of defence (in particular the right to be heard) are relevant to the granting of exemption: see Case 17/74, *Transocean Marine Paint Association* v. *Commission*: [1974] E.C.R. 1063, [1974] 2 C.M.L.R. 459.
[94] Above, n. 66. This decision seems at variance with how the Court of Justice treated a similar document (Doc No. 12) in *A.M. & S.*, above, n. 63, but the Court of First Instance's decision seems preferable.

& S. (they are described and classified in the opinion of Advocate General Slynn) that the protection extends to communications between lawyer and client, *i.e.* to and from the lawyer.

Independent lawyer

The documents must emanate from an "independent lawyer", *i.e.* one who is not bound to his client by a relationship of employment.[95] Communications between the undertaking, its executives and other staff, and its own group or in-house lawyers will not be protected. This limitation is a little surprising given the underlying rationale: the requirement is:

> "based on a conception of the lawyer's role as collaborating in the administration of justice by the court and as being required to provide, in full independence, and in the overriding interests of that cause, such legal assistance as the client needs. The counterpart of that protection lies in the rules of professional ethics and discipline which are laid down and enforced in the general interest by institutions endowed with the requisite powers for that purpose."[96]

Commission officials, as well as many others, had considered that the relevant criterion should be liability to professional ethics and discipline.[97] Advocate General Slynn had taken this view. The Court, however, whilst recognising the importance of this professional responsibility, has drawn the line by reference to the relationship of employment.[98]

There is yet another important qualification. The lawyer must be entitled to practise his profession in one of the Member States. Communications with lawyers qualified in third states (*e.g.* the United States or Commonwealth countries) will not be protected whether or not the lawyer is based within or outside the Community (the latter was the case in relation to a number of documents in *A.M. & S.*).[99] As to whether a lawyer is entitled to practise in one of the Member States, this is to be determined by reference to the Directive on legal services.[1] The reference to the Directive causes some

---

[95] Above, n. 89, at para. 27.

[96] *Ibid.* at para. 24. The rationale follows very much that of the common law, see *Greenough* v. *Gaskell*: (1833) 1 My. & K. 98.

[97] Many realised however that this would produce disparity between the professions in the different Member States.

[98] Much has been said about the lot of the in-house lawyer, much less about what is meant by the relationship of employment. But see Christoforou, *op. cit.* What is probably the case is that you cannot avoid this qualification by setting up a "firm" within the undertaking or its group. Following comment by and discussion with those concerned, the Commission after due consideration has decided not to extend the principle of confidentiality to in-house lawyer communications. For the Commission to do this spontaneously would in its opinion be a breach of the Treaty and the Commission does not envisage any amendment to Reg. 17 in this respect. In the Commission's view, extension of legal privilege to in-house lawyers in certain Member States, in accordance with the various rules of professional ethics in force, would create differences in the legal systems within the Community and would also be manifestly incompatible with the ratio of the Court's ruling.

[99] The English text, "entitled to practise", might give some room for argument that an American lawyer, for example, lawfully carrying on his practice in the EEC might qualify for protection. But any doubt about this is made clear by the French text, *avocat inscrit au barreau*, the phrase used in Art. 17 of the Protocol on the Statute of the Court and translated "a lawyer entitled to practise before a court of a Member State".

[1] Council Dir. 77/249: [1977] O.J. L78/17, as amended by the Treaties of Accession of Greece, Spain and Portugal. As regards the EEA, Annex VII adds to the list in the directive the languages from the relevant

uncertainty.[2] But whilst the qualification excludes non-Community lawyers by the restriction of the named categories of lawyers (*e.g.* United Kingdom advocates, barristers and solicitors) it is submitted that there should be no further restriction (the lawyer's nationality)[3] because of the reference to the Directive. It is clear, however, that the client need not be situated in the same Member State as the lawyer. The Court has paid regard to both the freedom of establishment and the freedom to provide services,[4] most probably wishing to go no further than to avoid discrimination between lawyers of the different Member States.[5]

8.15 *Verification.* The Court of Justice rejected any idea that the question whether any particular document is protected should be determined by the Commission or by a third party, whether an expert or arbitrator, or by a national court. The Court's solution is based on the current institutional structure of the Community. The Court itself will in the final outcome determine the question pursuant to an application under Article 173 challenging a Commission decision requiring production of the document(s) in issue under Article 14(3) of Regulation 17. Such a procedure should cause little or no delay. An appeal under Article 173 has no suspensory effect—the burden will be shifted to the applicant undertaking which can make application for interim measures (under Articles 185 and 186) to suspend the production of the documents ordered. The Court appears to contemplate that the issue of the protection will be capable of determination during such preliminary proceedings. The Court touched upon the practical procedures at the earlier stage of the investigation. The undertaking must provide the inspector "with *relevant material* of such a nature as to demonstrate that the communications fulfil the conditions for being granted legal protection as defined above, although it is not bound to reveal the contents of the communications in question."[6] If doubt remains after this, the Commission can take a decision under Article 14(3) requiring the undertaking either to supply such additional evidence as the Commission considers necessary or to produce the communications in question whose confidentiality, in the Commission's view, is not protected in law.[7]

EFTA States.

[2] The question has been raised (see Usher [1982] J.B.L. 400) whether communications from a lawyer qualified in one Member State, but practising in another Member State not under the terms of the Services Directive but by pursuing activities to which access is not restricted, would be protected.

[3] Christoforou, *op. cit.*, notes the apparent contradiction on the facts—protection was accorded to documents prepared pre-accession by then non-Community lawyers.

[4] Above, n. 86, at paras. 25 and 26.

[5] As regards independent lawyers from non-Community countries (such as the U.S.) the Commission has considered negotiating agreements based on reciprocity with certain countries so as to extend legal privilege to their independent lawyers. In the mid 1980s the Commission submitted appropriate proposals to the Council so that such negotiations might be opened, but the matter has not proceeded further. In practice there does not seem to have been any major problems.

[6] Above, n. 86, at para. 29 (emphasis added).

[7] It is not clear whether this decision is only available where the investigation has not been ordered by decision under Art. 14(3). If there is already a decision under Art. 14(3) ordering the investigation, requiring the production of books and giving of explanations, etc., then any subsequent decision of the kind envisaged by the Court, although it may be more specific than the first, will most probably only duplicate the earlier decision in effect. Arguably, the first decision should suffice, but a second would not be invalid merely because of the existence of the first and might be preferable given the opportunity it would present to define the issues for the parties and the Court if applications were to be made under Arts. 173, 185 and 186.

As was suggested in the argument before the Court in *A. M & S.*, it may be possible to identify a document as protected by exhibiting part of it; for example, a letter heading and signature or a backsheet to counsel's opinion. but will this be sufficient? It may be possible for the Commission inspector so to establish that the communication was to or from an independent lawyer, but how can he check that the document satisfied the Court's first condition, *i.e.* that it was made for the purposes and in the interests of the client's right of defence? If as is suggested above a fairly liberal interpretation of his condition is taken, both as to the temporal and subject-matter aspects of the scope of the protection, then probably little more than a short explanation of the nature of the subject-matter of the document and the circumstances of its coming into being should be necessary. There is nothing however to suggest that this has been a practical problem in inspections carried out since *A.M. & S.*

8.16 *Surrender or loss of protection.* The Court of Justice has indicated that the protection belongs to the undertaking, not the lawyer. The principle of confidentiality, the Court said, does not prevent a lawyer's client from disclosing the written communications between them if he considers that it is in his interests to do so.[8] This suggests that it is the client's, not the lawyer's, right to claim or waive[9] the protection. Can the protection be lost unintentionally or accidentally? For instance, the document is left on the file being examined by the Commission inspector. Once seen, can protection for that document still be claimed? Indeed, if it is on an "open" file could it be argued that "confidentiality" is missing? Some firms keep separate files for lawyers' advice. Prevention is of course better than cure. The undertaking under investigation would be wise to examine all documents before their submission to the inspector. Can an undertaking lawfully claim to do this or is the Commission inspector entitled to a first run at the files? If the principle of legal protection described by the Court is to have any value then the undertaking must be able to exercise effectively any rights it has to protect relevant documents from (accidental) disclosure. It need not, it is submitted, consent to the Commission's inspector going through its books, etc., without the undertaking first examining them itself to determine which, if any, are protected from disclosure. The question of which documents are protected may well be complex and a lawyer's advice on the matter might itself be necessary. (This is another good reason for having a lawyer present to assist the undertaking during the investigation.) In *National Panasonic*,[10] the Court of Justice indicated that an undertaking was not entitled to delay the start of the investigation pending the arrival of its lawyer, but in *Hoechst* the Court indicated that the right to legal representation must be respected as from the preliminary enquiry stage (*i.e.* the investigation).[11] Therefore if an investigation has commenced an undertaking would be well advised to put to one side (not necessarily out of total sight of the inspector so there can be no question of its getting "lost") any document which it thinks might possibly come within the protected class until the undertaking's lawyer has arrived.

---

[8] Above, n. 86, at para. 28.
[9] Can waiver be partial? The common law does not allow this.
[10] Case 136/79: [1980] E.C.R. 2033, [1980] 3 C.M.L.R. 169.
[11] Above, n. 90, at para. 16.

It seems unlikely, however, that any protection would be given where the lawyer is involved in or assists his client in the infringement of Community law.[12] It is, for example, well established in English law that there is no privilege where the lawyer participates in a crime or fraud with his client or executes work which furthers the commission of a crime or fraud by the client.[13] Protection from disclosure, reflecting the public interest in the lawyer–client relationship, cannot be justified in such circumstances. It might also be excluded where the communication is made other than in the context of the lawyer–client relationship. A communication should be protected not because the sender or recipient happens to be a lawyer but only if he is acting *qua* lawyer in the circumstances. Thus, for example, minutes of a company's board meeting should not be protected from disclosure simply because one of the directors is a lawyer entitled to practise in the Community.

8.17 Although concerned primarily with Article 14 inspections, the principle of protection enunciated by the Court would seem to be equally applicable to Article 11 of Regulation 17. It would be a nonsense if the Commission's inspector could not see the document when exercising his powers of inspection under Article 14 but could require its production or disclosure of its contents by a suitably worded request or decision under Article 11.

Professional secrecy

8.18 Undertakings dealing with the Commission, whether notifying an agreement or practice, making a formal complaint, or answering an allegation of infringement, will naturally wish to ensure that confidential information given to the Commission is protected from disclosure. Article 214 of the Treaty prohibits the disclosure by members of the institutions of the Community, the members of committees, and the officials and other servants of the Community of "information of the kind covered by the obligation of professional secrecy, in particular information about undertakings, their business relations or their cost components."[14] To this end Article 20(2) of Regulation 17,[15] implementing that general rule in respect of the competition rules, provides that "the Commission and the competent authorities of the Member States, their officials and other servants shall not disclose information acquired by them as a result of the application of this Regulation and of the kind covered by the obligation of professional secrecy."

In addition to Article 20(2), Article 19(3) provides that publication of proposed decisions (negative clearances and exemptions) and of final decisions under Article 21 "shall have regard to the legitimate interest of undertakings in the protection of their business secrets." As will be seen, the position of business secrets, a different concept, is special. Finally, Article 9(3) of Regulation 99/63 provides: "Hearings shall not be

[12] See Ehlermann and Oldekop, "Due Process in Administrative Procedure", F.I.D.E. Conference 1978.
[13] See the examples and authorities cited at para. 82 of Halsbury's Laws of England (4th ed.), Vol. 13.
[14] Art. 47(2) of the ECSC Treaty is in the same terms. *Cf.* Art. 194 of the Euratom Treaty which goes further, requiring Member States to treat infringement as prejudicial to its rules on secrecy and to the security of the State (see also Arts. 24–27 of the Euratom Treaty). Documents in the archives of the E.C. are released for public inspection under a 30-year rule. These which were subject to commercial or professional secrecy are listed in advance so that interested parties may have an opportunity to object. Decision 90/631/EEC: [1990] O.J. L340/24.
[15] And the equivalent provisions in the transport implementing regulations.

public. Persons shall be heard separately or in the presence of other persons summoned to attend. In the latter case, regard shall be had to the legitimate interest of the undertakings in the protection of their business secrets."

Article 17 of the Commission's Staff Regulations should also be noted:[16]

> "Le fonctionnaire est tenu d'observer la plus grande discretion sur tout ce qui concerne les faits et informations qui viendraient à sa connaissance dans l'exercice ou à l'occasion de l'exercice de ses fonctions; il ne doit communiquer, sous quelque forme que ce soit, a une personne non qualifée pour en avoir connaissance, aucun document ni aucune information qui n'auraient pas été rendus publics. Il reste soumis à cette obligation après la cessation de ses fonctions."

An official may be required to pay for any damage suffered by the Commission as a result of his serious misconduct in the performance of his duties. The Commission may be liable to injured third parties under Article 215 of the Treaty.[17] As the *Stanley Adams* case shows, that provision may impose a duty to take reasonable steps to avoid any disclosure (*e.g.* of the identity of an informant) which might cause a party harm.[18]

The requirement not to disclose information of the kind covered by professional secrecy is also mirrored in the provisions of the EEA.[19] The EFTA Surveillance Authority and EFTA States are subject to equivalent obligations of the Commission at the Member States under the E.C. Treaty and competition regime.

8.19   Whereas the existence of the obligation not to disclose is thus clearly stated, its extent is somewhat uncertain, in particular as regards the types of information, facts, etc., which are protected. The Court of Justice has not yet had to rule generally on the question of what information is "of the kind covered by the obligation of professional secrecy." In some Continental legal systems the obligation may arise from the relationship in which information is transferred rather than the character of the information itself. There is probably no real equivalent to the Continental *secret professionel* in English or Scots law. In the United Kingdom secrets are protected to a greater or lesser extent by, *inter alia*, the Official Secrets Act, contract, the law relating to breach of confidence and the rules of evidence as they apply for example to legal professional privilege. In the original six Member States the notion of professional secrecy is well established. In France, Belgium and Luxembourg, for example, it has its roots firmly in the Penal Code which provides that it is an offence to reveal another person's "secret". A useful summary of the different laws of the Member States has been prepared by the CCBE in the Edward Report.[20] As to the meaning of professional secret, the Report under the heading of the position in France, Belgium and Luxembourg states: "A 'secret' has been defined as 'tout ce qui a un caractére intime que le client a un interet

---

[16] Statut des Fonctionnaires des Communautes Europeennes: [1972] J.O. C100.

[17] See, generally, Schermers, "The Law as it stands on the Appeal for Damages", [1975] 1 L.I.E.I. 113. And see the opinion of A.G. Reischl in Cases 209–215 & 218/78, *Heintz van Landewyck and others* v. *Commission*: [1980] E.C.R. 3125, [1981] 3 C.M.L.R. 134.

[18] Case 145/83, *Stanley Adams* v. *Commission*: [1985] E.C.R. 3534, [1986] 1 C.M.L.R. 506, analysed by Hunnings in "The Stanley Adams Affair or the Biter Bit" (1987) 24 C.M.L.Rev. 65.

[19] Article 9 of Protocol 23 to the EEA Agreement, Article 122 of the EEA Agreement, and Article 20 and 21 of Chapter II of Protocol 4 to the Agreement between the EFTA States on the establishment of a Surveillance Authority and of a Court of Justice.

[20] "The Professional Secret, Confidentiality, and Legal Professional Privilege in the Nine Member States of the European Community" (1975), By D. A. O. Edward Q.C.

moral et matèriel á ne reveler', but the question of whether an item of information is a 'secret' is a pure question of fact in each case. The obligation of professional secrecy applies even where the facts are susceptible of being known by others."[21]

In Italy, the essential elements are that the facts should not be generally known (*la non-notorieta del dato*) and the existence of a judicially appreciable interest in its concealment (*la sussistenza di un interesse giuridicamente apprezzabile al suo occultamento*).[22] The Report says the law in the Netherlands is substantially the same as in France, Belgium and Luxembourg and that in Germany what is protected is a secret (*Geheimnis*).[23] Whilst the national laws lay stress on the "professional" relationship, in the context of the Community rule, the concept is probably wider to cover all information received by Community officials in the course of their duties.[24] Moreover, although confidentiality is frequently, if not regularly, widely requested by parties dealing with the Commission, it most probably does not have to be expressly requested for the Community rules to apply. The obligation of professional secrecy is not restricted to business secrets. The Commission starts from the position that all commercial documentation which it obtains from undertakings is prima facie confidential and is covered by Article 20(2) irrespective of whether it is a business secret or confidentiality has expressly been requested.[25] The Commission has also expressed the view that it regards the names of undertakings being investigated as subject to the obligation of professional secrecy.[26] The position of complainants may also have special protection. In the *Stanley Adams* case the Court held that where information is supplied on a voluntary basis and accompanied by a request for confidentiality to protect anonymity, if the Commission accepts such information it is bound to comply with such a condition.[27] Indeed there is a case for saying that the obligation of professional secrecy covers all information received by the Commission in the exercise of its functions under the Competition Rules, and in particular Regulation 17 and the other implementing regulations, with the exception of material which is in the public domain. The question then turns to the special position of business secrets.

It is clear from the Treaty and the relevant regulations that Article 20(2) will cover "business secrets" as well as information about "business relations" and "cost components". In practice therefore confidential know-how and other technical information[28] will be covered as well as financial and other information relating to costs and

---

[21] *Ibid.* para. 23.

[22] *Ibid.* para. 24.

[23] *Ibid.* paras. 25 and 26.

[24] In Case 53/85, *AKZO Chemie BV and AKZO Chemie U.K. Ltd.* v. *Commission*: [1986] E.C.R. 1965, [1987] 1 C.M.L.R. 231, A.G. Lenz thought the designation "official security" might be more appropriate as, at least in German law, the obligation of professional secrecy covers only that imposed on the liberal professions by the terms of the professional rules.

[25] Joshua, *Treatment of Business Secrets*, Seminar on Competition Procedures, Brussels, September 27–28, 1993.

[26] Answer to Written Question No. 1740/79: [1980] O.J. C140/14. Also, it seems, reports of inquiries and discussions with particular undertakings: see *Hoffmann-La Roche*, above, n. 29, at para. 18. **Note:** *Tipp-Ex*: [1987] O.J. L222/1, [1989] 4 C.M.L.R. 425, where the name of a party to the concerted practice is not disclosed in the published decision. This is remarkable given the Commission's concern for transparency and general desire to assist third parties to take action against parties to condemned cartels. No explanation is given for the non-disclosure and it is not clear how it fits with Art. 21(2). Presumably "party" there means party to whom the decision is addressed.

[27] Above, n. 18, at para. 34.

[28] See *Vacuum Interrupters*: [1981] O.J. L383/1, [1981] 2 C.M.L.R. 217. And see *Boussois/Interpane*: [1987] O.J. L50/30, [1988] 4 C.M.L.R. 124, where the Commission considered certain unpatented know-

turnover.[29] The Commission has taken the view that whilst a competitor's prices and other trading conditions can often be found out by inquiry or own customer feedback, accurate information on quantities sold and market share is normally considered a trade secret which confers legitimate competitive advantages and thus not to be revealed or shared with competitors.[30] The details of contracts, for example, with customers or suppliers (whom, how much and at what price, etc.) should also be protected as well as such matters as business forecasts, plans and sales programmers.[31] Information which has been published or is publicly available (for example, in the United Kingdom, on the public registers, etc., maintained under the Companies Acts, Consumer Credit Act, Restrictive Trade Practices Act and Patents Act) can hardly be termed "secrets" or warrant protection as such under Community law.[32] On the other hand the fact that information has been disclosed to one party does not mean that it loses its confidential character *vis-à-vis* all other parties.[33] Information given, for example, to banks, professional advisers, the Inland Revenue, etc., probably remains "secret" as regards third parties. Technical information disclosed to a licensee or subcontractor should also remain a "secret".[34] On the other hand, information given to customers where there is no obligation to maintain its confidentiality would probably not be protected.[35]

8.20 Article 20(2) is, however, expressly stated to be "without prejudice to the provisions of Articles 19 and 21" (Article 19 deals with a party's right to be heard and Article 21 with the publication of decisions). Regulation 17 appears to contemplate that there may be circumstances where the public interest may justify the Commission disclosing information subject to the obligation of professional secrecy. Such disclosure may be to particular parties (for example, to undertakings charged by the Commission with infringement, and complainants with sufficient interest to be heard[36]) under Article 19 or to the public generally under Article 21. The obligation of professional

how secret where, although individual parts of it were not totally unknown or unobtainable, particularly for experts in the sector, the know-how package as a whole was not readily available or in the public domain. See also the treatment of know-how in *Delta Chemie/DDD*: [1988] O.J. L309/34, [1989] 4 C.M.L.R. 535, "knowledge, information and experience, all of which has not yet entered the public domain", and *Rich Products/Jus-rol*: [1988] O.J. L69/21, [1988] 4 C.M.L.R. 527, "a body of complex technical knowledge in several areas (formulas, manufacturing process, marketing etc)".

[29] Note the Commission's practice in relation to decisions published under Art. 21 of Reg. 17. Contrast the lack of disclosure under the ECSC Treaty, noted by Hunnings, *op. cit.*

[30] *UK Agricultural Tractor Registration Exchange*: [1992] O.J. L68/19, [1993] 4 C.M.L.R. 358.

[31] Also sales figures, estimates of market shares, etc. See Case 85/76, *Hoffmann-La Roche* v. *Commission*: [1979] E.C.R. 461, [1979] 2 C.M.L.R. 211, at paras. 12–17. See also Case T–57/91, *National Association of Licensed Opencast Operators* v. *Commission*: [1993] 5 C.M.L.R. 124, at paras. 9–11 (details of production figures and correspondence from members to their trade association dealing with personal circumstances and business relations).

[32] The fact that information may in due course have to be supplied to an authority for publication on a register does not, it is submitted, prevent it from being "secret" in the meantime. For example, financial information about a company which ultimately may form part of the accounts under the Companies Acts.

[33] Cases 209–215 & 218/78, *Heintz van Landewyck and others* v. *Commission*: [1980] E.C.R. 3125, [1981] 3 C.M.L.R. 134, at para. 46. For example, statistical information such as sales figures, terms of payment supplied to a trade association by its members.

[34] See the Commission's Notice on Subcontracting: [1979] O.J. C1/2.

[35] Temple Lang, CBI Conference December 1977. He also expressed the view that "any general information which could legitimately be obtained by an outsider who took a reasonable amount of trouble would not be secret."

[36] *FEDETAB*, above, n. 31, at para. 46.

secrecy is not intended to frustrate the enforcement of the Treaty. This said, the disclosure without consent of business secrets to complainants appears never to be permissible.[37] The "business secret", as mentioned, is a special category. It is protected by virtue of its very nature, not just the circumstances in which it is obtained by the Commission. The relationship between Article 19 and Article 20(2) has come before the Court of Justice on a number of occasions. In the *AKZO* case, the Court, balancing the duty of confidentiality against the right to be heard, came down firmly on the side of maintaining business secrecy.[38] The Court held that a complainant was not in any circumstances to be given access to documents containing business secrets.[39] Other information subject to the obligation of professional secrecy could be disclosed in so far as it is necessary to do so for the proper conduct of the procedure.[40] The Court was not prepared to permit any exceptions in the case of business secrets,[41] or to accept that business secrets could be disclosed subject to conditions (*e.g.* to use only for the Commission's procedures, or to legal advisers). Nor apparently did the Court accept that documents which constitute evidence of infringement can never be subject to the obligation not to disclose.[42] Most importantly, the Court requires the Commission to take a decision on whether a document contains a business secret, which can be reviewed by the Court before disclosure.[43] Such a safeguard will inevitably delay the Commission's procedure and could well have the consequence that the Commission will disclose fewer documents to third parties. But disclosure without the possibility of a prior check could cause irremediable damage to the proprietor of the business secret.

8.21 The absolute prohibition laid down in *AKZO* was directed against disclosure to complainants. It is necessary to consider the position of the defendant undertaking. In a number of cases the Court of Justice has rejected arguments that parties have been prejudiced in the exercise of their rights of defence because they have not seen certain documents, which the Commission has refused to disclose on the grounds of confidentiality. In *Vitamins*,[44] the Court stated that the rule against disclosure contained in

---

[37] *AKZO*, above, n. 24. And see the approach of the Court of Justice in the ECSC case: Case 27/84, *Wirtschaftsvereinigung Eisen- und Stahlindustrie* v. *Commission*: [1987] 1 C.M.L.R. 171, where the Court refused to treat Art. 47 as an absolute rule prohibiting disclosure. The Court will protect confidential information from being disclosed in its own proceedings—see Case 273/85, *Silver Seiko Ltd. and Silver Read International GmbH* v. *Council*: [1985] E.C.R. 3475, [1986] 1 C.M.L.R. 214.

[38] Following *FEDETAB*, above, n. 31.

[39] *AKZO*, above, n. 24, at para. 28. See also Cases 142 & 156/84, *BAT and Reynolds* v. *Commission*: [1987] E.C.R. 4487, [1987] 2 C.M.L.R. 551, at para. 21.

[40] *Ibid.* at para. 27.

[41] A.G. Lenz had been prepared to permit a very limited exception, where it would be impossible to determine whether or not there had been an infringement without such disclosure.

[42] A.G. Lenz was clearly not able to accept such an exception, on the basis that until the Commission's decision there is no infringement.

[43] Above, n. 24, at para. 29. The procedure for dealing with questions of business secrets is as follows. It is for the Commission in the first place to assess whether or not a particular document contains business secrets. The undertaking must then be given an opportunity to give its views on the question. If the Commission continues to maintain that the document does not contain business secrets, the Commission must adopt a decision which contains an adequate statement of reasons and which must be notified to the undertaking concerned. The Commission must then, before implementing its decision, give the undertaking an opportunity to bring an action before the Court in order to have the Commission's assessment reviewed and to prevent disclosure of the documents in question.

[44] Above, n. 29, at paras. 7–19. See also the *Quinine* case: Case 41/69, *ACF Chemiefarma* v. *Commission*: [1970] E.C.R. 661, at paras. 31–43, and the *Sugar* case: Cases 40–48, 50, 54–56, 111, 113 & 114/73,

Article 20(2) "must, as the express reference to Article 19 confirms, be reconciled with the right to be heard"[45] and that it did not allow the Commission:

> "to use, to the detriment of the undertakings involved . . . facts, circumstances or documents which it cannot in its view disclose if such a refusal of disclosure adversely affects that undertaking's opportunity to make known effectively its views on the truth or implications of those circumstances on those documents or again on the conclusion drawn by the Commission from them."[46]

In short the Commission cannot use Article 20(2) as a shield if to do so would undermine an undertaking's right to be heard. As already pointed out,[47] this may place the Commission in an extremely difficult position. If it is not possible to communicate the substance of the business secrets or other confidential material to the undertaking accused of infringement in a way which does not breach Article 20(2), then the Commission may be substantially restricted in its enforcement of the competition rules. The Commission has said that the:

> "recognition of extensive protection of confidential information is, however, subject to an important exception justified by the public interest in the enforcement of the EEC competition rules. The confidential nature of documents does not preclude their disclosure where the infringement."[48]

Even where confidential information is permitted to be disclosed, the Commission will have to determine whether the public interest is best served by enforcing the competition rules at the expense of the disclosure of such material. The Commission has recognised that when deciding whether such disclosure should occur it will take into account the legitimate interests of the undertaking providing the information and the rights of defence of the parties who are the subject of the proceedings. The latter course of action, even where consistent with the public interest in the enforcement of the Community's competition rules, may well have the practical result of drying up voluntary sources of information on which the Commission places much reliance.[49]

Legal certainty

8.22 The principle of legal certainty, that "the application of the law to a specific situation must be predictable",[50] is basic to many legal systems and has an established place as part of the general principles of Community law.[51]

Cooperatieve Vereniging "Suiker Unie" and others v. *Commission*: [1975] E.C.R. 1663, [1976] 1 C.M.L.R. 295, at para. 425.

[45] *Ibid.* at para. 13.

[46] *Ibid.* at para. 14. See also Case 107/82, *AEG-Telefunken* v. *Commission*: [1983] E.C.R. 3151, [1984] 3 C.M.L.R. 325, at paras. 23–25.

[47] See para. 4.10. Particular problems may arise where there are multi-party proceedings.

[48] Eighteenth Report on Competition Policy, at point 43.

[49] And see Korah, "The Rights of the Defence in Administrative Proceedings under Community Law" [1980] *Current Legal Problems* 73, 89.

[50] Schermers and Waelbroeck, *Judicial Protection in the European Communities* (5th ed., 1992), at paras. 86–89, and see, generally, Wyatt and Dashwood, *European Community Law* (3rd ed., 1993), pp. 91–95.

[51] And see Usher, *op. cit.,* at p. 366.

A good example of its application in Community competition law can be seen in the Court's creation of the doctrine of "provisional validity".[52] In a series of cases referred from national courts to the Court of Justice under Article 177 of the Treaty, the Court has had to consider the problems surrounding the application of Article 85 by national courts to agreements in dispute between the parties before them. The difficulty has been to reconcile the automatic nullity provided for in Article 85(2), which the national courts must apply to agreements found to fall within Article 85(1), with the Commission's exclusive power to grant exemptions under Article 85(3). In *Brasserie de Haecht (No. 2)*,[53] the Court drew a distinction between so-called "old" and "new" agreements. In the case of old agreements (*i.e.* agreements which came into existence prior to the entry into force of Regulation 17) the Court said:[54]

> "the general principle of contractual certainty requires, particularly when the agreement has been notified in accordance with the provisions of Regulation 17, that the Court may only declare it to be automatically void after the Commission has taken a decision by virtue of that Regulation."[55]

The Court was influenced by the absence of transitional provisions to deal with old agreements and the powers given to the Commission in Regulation 17, and in particular Article 7, which enabled the Commission to take into consideration the general principle of legal certainty. But the Court did not consider the principle to be similarly applicable in the context of new agreements. Here the parties could have regard to Regulation 17 and in particular to the fact that notification under Article 4(1) does not have any suspensory effect. New agreements can only be implemented at the parties' own risk.[56] The doctrine of provisional validity remains important, not just for the case of the case of the accession of new Member States, but now also for the EEA.

8.23 In the later case of *B.R.T.* v. *S.A.B.A.M.*,[57] the Court of Justice was asked whether national courts were "authorities of the Member States . . . competent to apply Article 85(1) and Article 86" within the meaning of Article 9(3) of Regulation 17. If so, it was argued, a national court only remains competent to apply Article 85(1) and Article 86 until such time as the Commission has initiated a procedure under Article 2, 3 or 6 of Regulation 17. The Court said:[58]

> "The fact that the expression 'authorities of the Member States' appearing in Article 9(3) of Regulation 17 covers such courts cannot exempt a court before which the direct effect of Article 86 is pleaded from giving judgment.
>
> Nevertheless, if the Commission initiates a procedure in application of Article 3 of Regulation 17 such a court may, if it considers it necessary for reasons of legal certainty, stay the proceedings before it while awaiting the outcome of the Commission's action."

---

[52] Provisional validity is discussed in more detail post, at paras. 10.04–11.
[53] Case 48/72, *Brasserie de Haecht* v. *Wilkin (No. 2)*: [1973] E.C.R. 77, [1973] C.M.L.R. 287.
[54] *Ibid.* at para. 9.
[55] And note the effect of the Court's ruling in Case 99/79, *Lancôme* v. *Etos and Albert Heijn Supermart BV*: [1980] E.C.R. 2511, [1981] 2 C.M.L.R. 164, discussed at para. 10.10.
[56] *Brasserie de Haecht (No. 2)*, above, n. 53, at para. 10.
[57] Case 127/73: [1974] E.C.R. 51, [1974] 2 C.M.L.R. 238.
[58] *Ibid.* at paras. 20 and 21. Relied on by the Commission in *Bloemenveilingen Aalsmeer*: [1988] O.J. L262/27, [1989] 4 C.M.L.R. 500.

Here the application of the principle of legal certainty is directed towards the elimination of possible conflict arising from the concurrent jurisdiction of the national court and the Commission.[59]

8.24 It is not intended to give an exhaustive account of the application of the principle of legal certainty in Community law. The two examples given above indicate its practical utility and importance. One further example of its application should, however, be noted. It is recognised that the need for legal certainty is one reason for the making of block or group exemptions by the Commission. This was acknowledged by the Court in *Italy* v. *Council and Commission*:[60]

> "Article 85(3) of the Treaty provides that the exemption in question may be granted to categories of agreements. The need of undertakings to know their legal position with certainty could justify giving priority to the use of this power [Article 87 of the Treaty], which does not require the Council to adopt rules simultaneously for applying the other provisions of the said Article."

But in *Tetra Pak*, the Court of First Instance, whilst acknowledging the position of the principle of legal certainty in the Community's legal order, rejected the argument that legal certainty prohibited the application of Article 86 to conduct exempt under Article 85(3). The Court recognised that one of the main purposes of block exemptions is to secure legal certainty for the parties to an agreement as regards its validity under Article 85 so long as the Commission has not withdrawn the benefit of the block exemption. But that did not, in the Court's view, discharge undertakings in a dominant position from the obligation to comply with Article 85.[61]

Proportionality

8.25 The principle of proportionality is well established in Community law.[62] It has been applied by the Court of Justice in a number of cases involving a variety of different subject matters.[63] In *Denkavit Nederland BV* v. *Hoofdproduktschap voor Akkerbouwprodukten*,[64] the Court of Justice said: "By virtue of the principle of

---

[59] The problems surrounding the exercise of the concurrent jurisdictions of national authorities and the Commission are discussed in Chap. 10.

[60] Case 32/65: [1966] E.C.R. 389, [1969] C.M.L.R. 39.

[61] Case T–51/89, *Tetra Pak Rausing SA* v. *Commission*: [1990] II E.C.R. 309, [1991] 4 C.M.L.R. 334, at paras. 32–38.

[62] See, generally, Schermers and Waelbroeck, *op. cit.*, at para. 127, Wyatt and Dashwood, *op. cit.*, and Schmitthoff "The Doctrines of Proportionality and Non-Discrimination" (1977) 2 E.L.Rev. 329.

[63] For example, Case 8/55, *Fédération Charbonnière de Belgique* v. *High Authority*: [1954–56] E.C.R. 292; Case 122/78, *Buitoni* v. *FORMA*: [1979] E.C.R. 677, [1979] 2 C.M.L.R. 665, and Case 66/82, *Société Fromançais* v. *FORMA*: [1983] E.C.R. 395, [1983] 3 C.M.L.R. 453.

[64] Case 15/83: [1984] E.C.R. 2171, at para. 25. See also A.G. Capotorti in Case 114/76, *Bela-Mühle* v. *Grows-Farm*: [1977] E.C.R. 1211, 1232, [1979] 2 C.M.L.R. 83. In *Regina* v. *Goldstein*: [1983] 1 W.L.R. 151, at 155, Lord Diplock referred to the need "to show that the measures were not disproportionately severe having regard to the gravity of the mischiefs against which they were directed. This last mentioned consideration involves the concept in Community Law (derived principally from German law) called 'proportionality'. In plain English it means you must not use a steam hammer to crack a nut if a nut cracker will do."

proportionality, according to well-established case law of the Court, measures adopted by Community institutions must not exceed what is appropriate and necessary to attain the objective pursued."

Proportionality has been said to be guaranteed both by the general principles of Community law and by express provision of the Treaty.[65] The Court has found legislative expression of the principle of proportionality in provisions of the Treaty such as Article 40[66] (common agricultural policy) and Article 115[67] (common commercial policy) where the Commission is enabled to take such measures only as "required" and "necessary" respectively. In *Buitoni* v. *FORMA*,[68] the Court again spoke of the need to determine whether the "provision exceeds what is appropriate and necessary to attain the objective sought."

8.26 The principle of proportionality is clearly applicable in relation to the enforcement of the Community competition rules. In the *United Brands* case,[69] the Court of Justice considered whether the amount of the fine imposed by the Commission was proportionate to the duration and gravity of the infringement as well as the size of the undertaking concerned. And in *BMW Belgium and others* v. *Commission*,[70] the amount of the fines on certain dealers was held not to be disproportionate to their turnovers. The application of the principle in relation to fining is but one example of its general applicability to the administrative actions or conduct of the Commission in competition cases. Proportionality is also relevant to the exercise of investigatory powers under Articles 11 and 14 of Regulation 17 and also to decisions, whether interim or final, taken in relation to infringements.[71] As regards investigations, in *Hoechst* the Court of Justice expressly regarded as a general principle of Community law the need for protection against arbitrary or disproportionate intervention.[72] The principle may be applicable to the degree of precision in the identification of subject-matter in the mandate given to the Commission's inspectors[73] and also to the question

[65] Per A.G. Dutheillet de Lamothe in Case 11/70, *Internationale Handelsgesellschaft mbH* v. *Einfuhr- und Vorratsstelle für Getreide und Futtermittel*: [1970] E.C.R. 1125, [1972] C.M.L.R. 255.

[66] *Internationale Handelsgesellschaft*, above.

[67] Case 62/70, *Bock* v. *Commission*: [1971] E.C.R. 897, [1972] C.M.L.R. 160.

[68] Above, n. 63, at para. 16.

[69] Case 27/76: [1978] E.C.R. 207, [1978] 1 C.M.L.R. 429, at para. 302.

[70] Cases 32 & 36–82/78, *BMW Belgium and others* v. *Commission*: [1979] E.C.R. 2435, [1980] 1 C.M.L.R. 370, at para. 47.

[71] *I.e.* decisions under Art. 3 of Reg. 17. Indeed proportionality may be reflected in the application of Articles 85(1) and 85(3). See the Commission's analysis of the restrictions and the question of safety in *Distribution of package tours during the 1990 World Cup*: [1992] O.J. L326/31. The world exclusive rights granted were considered disproportionate to the objective pursued and therefore could not be justified by the need to maintain safety. In Case T–19/91, *Vichy* v. *Commission*: [1992] II E.C.R. 415, the Court of First Instance, upholding the Commission's decision under Art. 15(6), appeared to apply a proportionality test to the assessment under Art. 85(1) of the conditions of Vichy's selective distribution system.

[72] Cases 46/87 & 227/88, *Hoechst AG* v. *Commission*: [1989] E.C.R. 2859, [1991] 4 C.M.L.R. 410. This was followed by the Court of First Instance in Case T–39/90, *S.E.P* v. *Commission*: [1992] 5 C.M.L.R. 33, where that Court held that the principle of proportionality was not violated by the Commission's asking for the disclosure of a document under Art. 11 even though it was particularly confidential and the undertaking concerned perceived a risk that the document would come into the hands of another party (the Dutch State) with whom it had separate contractual dealing which might be affected by knowledge of the document in question. In Cases 97, 98 & 99/87, *Dow Chemicals Iberica* v. *Commission*: [1989] E.C.R. 3165, [1991] 4 C.M.L.R. 410, the Court of Justice held that the principle of proportionality does not require Article 14 to be construed in accordance with national contractual provisions (paras. 37 and 38).

[73] It can be argued that a fair degree of precision is required to ensure the respect of the principle of proportionality.

whether the inspection is made with or without a decision, is announced or made by surprise.[74] As regards decisions concerning infringements, proportionality may be relevant in the nature and extent of the order prohibiting certain conduct or activities and any conditions attached thereto. It may also be relevant to conditions attached to an exemption.[75] The Court has already indicated that proportionality is applicable in relation to fines.[76] It should therefore apply to periodic penalty payments.[77] But the burden of upsetting any measure on the ground of proportionality is substantial. As the Court has said:[78] "the legality of a measure can be adversely affected only if the measure is manifestly unsuitable for achieving the aim pursued by the competent Community institution."

8.27   Article 5 of the ECSC provides that the Community shall carry out its task "with a limited measure of intervention." There is no similar expression of the principle of limited intervention in the EEC Treaty. This does not exclude the possibility of its being a part of the general principles of law applied by the Court of Justice. The principles of proportionality and of minimum or limited intervention are not the same thing but are not mutually exclusive.[79] Thus, where several means are available, each being justifiable in relation to the end sought (proportionality), the least stringent which will be effective must be employed (minimum intervention). It is submitted that the principle of limited intervention, if applicable in EEC law, might be relevant, for example, to whether information was obtained under Article 11 or Article 14. Another application might be in relation to the disclosure of technical (often highly valuable) know-how to the Commission. Here there is an obvious need to minimise any risk of accidental disclosure to a third party. It is submitted that it might be sufficient, for example, in response to a request for information under Article 11[80] simply to show material (such as specifications, formulae, technical reports, etc.) to the Commission without supplying copies for retention by it. This might be done by making the material available for examination by the Commission in Brussels. It is by no means a foregone conclusion that such action would be considered a default of Article 11 and it is at least arguable that the Article should be permissively construed, at least to this extent, in application of the principle of least stringent means.

---

[74] It may, however, be dangerous to place too much weight in practice on the importance of the principle here—see Case 136/79, *National Panasonic UK Ltd.* v. *Commission*: [1980] E.C.R. 2033, [1980] 3 C.M.L.R. 169, at paras. 28–30. *Cf.* A.G. Roemer in Case 31/59, *Acciaieria e Tubificio di Brescia* v. *High Authority*: [1960] E.C.R. 71, 88–89.

[75] See A.G. Warner in Case 17/74, *Transocean Marine Paint Association* v. *Commission*: [1974] E.C.R. 1063, [1974] 2 C.M.L.R. 459.

[76] See Cases 32 & 36–82/78, *BMW Belgium and others* v. *Commission*: [1979] E.C.R. 2435, [1980] 1 C.M.L.R. 370 and Case 27/76, *United Brands* v. *Commission*: [1978] E.C.R. 207, [1978] 1 C.M.L.R. 429 and also Case 1/59, *Dalmas* v. *High Authority*: [1959] E.C.R. 199.

[77] Art. 16 of Reg. 17. In *Hoechst*, above, n. 72, the claim that the definitive amount of the periodic penalty payment was disproportionate was rejected (paras. 62–64).

[78] Case 59/83, *SA Biovilac NV* v. *Community*: [1984] E.C.R. 4057, at para. 17. Lavoie supports this view. "The Investigative Powers of the Commission with respect to Business Secrets under Community Competition Rules" (1992) E.L.Rev. 20.

[79] See A.G. Roemer in *Acciaieria e Tubificio di Brescia* v. *Commission*, above, n. 73.

[80] See generally, para. 3.07.

Subsidiarity

8.27A   Whilst subsidiarity has been on the periphery of discussion on European integration for a good many years only relatively recently has it taken on special significance. As a concept its pedigree has been linked to the Roman Church and Papal encyclicals aimed at redressing the balance in favour of the individual against the state.[81] Subsidiarity has been defined as "the principle that a central authority should have a subsidiary function, performing only those tasks which cannot be performed effectively at a more immediate or local level."[82] It has not been a basic principle of Community law but with the entry into force of the Maastricht Treaty it becomes so.[83] Title II of the Treaty on European Union provides for the following Article to be inserted into the E.C. Treaty:

> "*Article 3b*
>
> The Community shall act within the limit of the powers conferred on it by this Treaty and of the objectives assigned to it therein. In areas which do not fall within its exclusive competence, the Community shall take action, in accordance with the principle of subsidiarity, only if and in so far as the objectives of the proposed action cannot be sufficiently achieved by the Member States and can therefore, by reason of the scale or effects of the proposed action, be better achieved by the Community. Any action by the Community shall not go beyond what is necessary to achieve the objectives of this Treaty."

Whilst at the time of negotiation there was considerable debate both in political and legal circles as to whether subsidiarity was justiciable and should be given legislative expression in the body of the Treaty, that debate is past and the Court of Justice will, as necessary and no doubt in the fullness of time, have to construe the meaning of the new Article 3b. This may not be as formidable as task as some have predicted. The Court is well experienced in determining what is or is not within Community competence and in the application of tests, such as "proportionality"[84] and "necessity",[85] which are similar in character to the tests contained in the second and third sentences of Article 3b.

8.27B   In the context of competition law and policy attention has already focused on the implications of subsidiarity. The debate on decentralisation, the respective roles of the Commission and national competent authority and national courts in the application and enforcement of Community law, and the relationship between Community competition laws and national competition laws, has been revived. Already ideas have emerged from the Commission aimed at refining further the balance between the Commission and national authorities with the aim of ensuring that each case is dealt

---

[81] See Lasok, "Subsidiarity and the occupied field" (1992) New L.J. 1228 and Emilou, "Subsidiarity: An effective barrier against 'the Enterprises of Ambition' " [1992] E.L.Rev. 383.

[82] O.E.D.

[83] See Conclusions of European Council in Lisbon June 26–27, 1992 and Edinburgh December 11–12, 1992.

[84] See paras 8.25–27. Emilou op at points out that subsidiarity is similar to but goes beyond proportionality.

[85] See, e.g. Case 62/70, *Bock* v. *Commission*: [1971] E.C.R. 897.

by the body best placed to handle it.[86] It has been noted that many of the complaints the Commission receive relate solely to a single Member State. The question is whether these can be adequately dealt with by national authorities or national courts, either applying Articles 85 and 86 or national competition laws. The Commission has issued a Notice on co-operation between national courts and the Commission in applying Articles 85 and 86.[87] This provides a number of positive ways in which the Commission can assist a national court faced with an issue concerning the application of Article 85 or 86. Equally importantly it gives an indication of the Commission's likely future policy on complaints. Where there is no important Community interest at stake either in political or economic terms or in relation to important questions or legal precedent, and adequate redress is available at national level, the complainant will be referred to the national authorities.[88] National courts, as Chapter 10 explains, apply Articles 85 and 86 by virtue of their direct effect and national competition authorities derive certain competence via Article 88 of the Treaty. The scheme of Regulation 17 and the other implementing regulations is to maintain the ability of national competent authorities to apply the Community rules until such time as the Commission has formally initiated proceedings.[89] It is therefore fully compatible with the Commission's approach to subsidiarity and decentralisation. There is however one area where only the Commission can presently act, namely as regards the granting of individual exemptions under Article 85(3). It appears that the Commission has considered carefully the question of whether national competent authorities should also have the power to grant exemptions. The conclusion is that it is not yet the right time to do this. There is too greater risk that this would encourage the divergent application of Community law and might lead to "forum shopping".[90] The Commission's monopoly on the application of Article 85(3) is broken by the use of block exemptions. They offer considerable scope for decentralisation as once the terms of the block exemption are set national courts have jurisdiction to decide whether an agreement is covered by the regulation. At the same time they preserve the benefits of notification and individual exemption for other agreements.[91]

Limitation, estoppel, legitimate expectations

8.28 The fixing of limitation periods is a particular example of the application of the principle of legal certainty in Community law. In both the *Quinine* case[92] and the *Dyestuffs* case,[93] the Court of Justice rejected the argument that in the absence of an express provision fixing limitation periods as regards the Community competition rules, a principle common to the national legal systems should be applied in Community law. The Court took the view that in order to fulfil its function of ensuring legal certainty a limitation period should be fixed in advance and that the fixing of a limitation

---

[86] Sir Leon Brittan. Speech December 7, 1992 to the Centre for European Policy Studies.
[87] [1993] O.J. C39/6. The Notice is discussed further in Chap. 10.
[88] *Ibid.* at para. 14.
[89] Art. of Reg. 17. See paras. 1.26 and 10.02.
[90] Sir Leon Brittan, *op. cit.* See also the comments of Dr. Ehlermann as reported in the House of Lords Select Committee's Report, Enforcement of Community Competition Rules, at para. 75.
[91] See Siragusa, "Notification of Agreements in the EEC—to notify or not to notify" (1986) Fordham Corp. L. Inst. 243, at 284 and 285.
[92] Case 44/69, *Buchler* v. *Commission*: [1970] E.C.R. 733, at paras. 5–7.
[93] Cases 48, 49, 51–57/69, *ICI and Others* v. *Commission*: [1972] E.C.R. 619, [1972] C.M.L.R. 557, Case 48/69 at para. 45–50.

period and its method of application was a matter for the Community legislator. In November 1974 the Council adopted Regulation 2988/74 "concerning limitation periods and the enforcement of sanctions under the rules of the European Economic Community relating to transport and competition."[94]

Regulation 2988/74, which came into force on January 1, 1975, fixes limitation periods for the imposition of fines ("limitation periods in proceedings") and in relation to the enforced collection of fines and periodic penalty payments ("limitation period for the enforcement of sanctions"). It sets out the limitation periods to be applied, the time when such periods commence and the actions which interrupt or suspend the running of the periods. Regulation 2988/74 is discussed in detail in Chapter 7 dealing with fines. It is important to note that Regulation 2988/74 does not stop the Commission taking a decision finding an infringement notwithstanding that it might be time-barred from imposing a fine in respect of that infringement.

8.29   However, in *Dyestuffs*[95] the Court of Justice clearly contemplated that in the absence of a statutory limitation period the fundamental requirement of legal certainty might prevent the Commission from delaying indefinitely the exercise of its power to impose fines. Furthermore, it is noteworthy that in the *Commercial Solvents* case[96] the Court reduced the amount of the fines imposed on account of the delay by the Commission in its procedure. Although Regulation 2988/74 will serve generally to meet the requirements of legal certainty in this context, it remains open whether the Court, bearing in mind the fundamental requirement of legal certainty as it was expressed in the *Dyestuffs* case, the principle of fairness as it was exercised in the *Commercial Solvents* case and the added difficulty a long lapse of time may bring to the exercise of the right of defence,[97] might admit a plea of laches or undue delay in suitable circumstances.[98]

8.30   Where time does not bar the Commission proceeding, the principle of estoppel or non venire contra factum proprium may nevertheless apply.[99] There is evidence to suggest that it forms part of "the law" within the meaning of Article 164 of the Treaty. In *Boizard* v. *Commission*,[1] Advocate General Warner saw the emergence of such a general principle from the legal heritage of the Member States. In an ECSC case, *Klockner* v. *High Authority*,[2] the applicant argued that the High Authority should not

---

[94] Reg. 2988/74 is set out in App. E. and discussed at paras. 7.46–49.

[95] Above, Case 48/69, at para. 49.

[96] Cases 6 & 7/73, *Istituto Chemioterapico Italiano and Commercial Solvents Corp.* v. *Commission*: [1974] E.C.R. 223, [1974] 1 C.M.L.R. 309. For other cases where fines have been less because of delays on the part of the Commission, see para. 7.37.

[97] Documents may be destroyed or lost, witnesses die or disappear, and memories may fade.

[98] The Commission could not be barred by laches if the conduct is still continuing. If it has stopped, and the limitation period has elapsed (and so no fine is possible), the Commission may be unlikely to bring a procedure although it would still appear possible.

[99] See generally, Lord Mackenzie Stuart, "Legitimate Expectations and Estoppel in Community Law and English Administrative Law" (1983) 1 L.I.E.I. 53.

[1] Cases 63 & 64/79: [1980] E.C.R. 2975, [1982] 1 C.M.L.R. 157, although it is sometimes suggested that the Court impliedly rejected the principle in Case 230/81, *Luxembourg* v. *European Parliament*: [1983] E.C.R. 255, [1983] 2 C.M.L.R. 726.

[2] Cases 17 & 20/61: [1962] E.C.R. 325, 342. See also A.G. Warner in Case 19/77, *Miller International Schallplatten* v. *Commission*: [1978] E.C.R. 131, [1978] 2 C.M.L.R. 334, where he suggested that a Commission Notice may create "a sort of estoppel" in relation to the imposition of fines under Art. 15 of Reg. 17. But the Commission's statement that it was prepared to delay implementation of an investigation be-

be allowed to go back on what it had said and which had led the applicant to believe it shared the same view on the question of what constituted an undertaking. Whilst rejecting the applicant's plea in the particular circumstances, the Court of Justice said: "Moreover the administrative authority is not always bound by its previous actions in its public activities by virtue of a rule which, in relations between the same parties, forbids them to venire contra factum proprium."

The doctrine of legitimate expectations may also be relevant.[3] At least one context in which it may be applicable is the so-called "comfort letter". It has been submitted that where the Commission has closed its file following a comfort letter that no action will be taken, it would not be open to the Commission to re-open the file in the absence of any new facts which came to its attention after the comfort letter or unless a judgment of the Court indicated that the Commission had been acting under a misapprehension as to the law.[4] There may however be a number of relevant factors in practice. First, as regards the conduct on which a party may rely, the Court has taken the view that where a regulation (*in casu*, Regulation 17) prescribed that a formal decision be taken following specified procedures then such a decision cannot be replaced by any other measure taken by a Commission official. Thus a letter indicating the likelihood of an agreement being exempted[5] or that an agreement does not come within the prohibition of Article 85(1)[6] is not a decision which is binding on the Commission. Similarly where Regulation 17 specifies that the completion of Form A/B is necessary before exemption can be granted, that requirement must be observed to the letter and it will not matter that the Commission may have all the necessary information (copies of the agreement, etc.) and may have discussed the question of exemption with the parties over a period of years if the form has not been properly submitted.[7] Second, the Court has been reluctant to develop any doctrine of ostensible authority in relation to the actions of Commission officials.[7a] Third, the Commission's failure or slackness in enforcing the law cannot make lawful an infringement.[8] Fourth, the Commission's failure to enforce the law cannot give rise to a legitimate expectation or estoppel where the Commission has no discretion in relation to enforcement.[9] Finally, how far

---

fore the Court does not stop the Commission fixing the definitive amount of a periodic penalty payment from the date of the first decision under Art. 16. See Cases 46/87 & 227/88, *Hoechst AG* v. *Commission*: [1989] E.C.R. 2859, [1991] 4 C.M.L.R. 410, at paras. 60 and 61.

[3] See, generally, Lord Mackenzie Stuart, *op. cit.*, and Sharpston, "Legitimate Expectations and Economic Reality" (1990) E.L.Rev. 103.

[4] *Ibid.* at p. 64, relying for support on the opinion of A.G. Reischl in Case 31/80, *L'Oréal* v. *De Nieuwe AMCK*: [1980] E.C.R. 3775, 3803, [1981] 2 C.M.L.R. 235, 246. The point is in issue in Case T–7/93, *Langnese-Iglo GmbH* v. *Commission*: [1993] O.J. L54/6. In its decision, *Langnese-Iglo GmbH*: [1993] O.J. L183/19, the Commission said it was not bound by a comfort letter sent to SLG in 1985, Langnese-Iglo was not the addressee of the letter and the factual circumstances had changed in the meantime.

[5] Case 71/74, *Frubo* v. *Commission*: [1975] E.C.R. 563, [1975] 2 C.M.L.R. 123. In the *Welded Steel Mesh* case, at least two undertakings are pleading infringement of legitimate inspections in relation to the fines imposed: Case T–141/89, *Trefilarbed Luxembourg–Saarbrucken Sarl* v. *Commission*: and Case T–145/89, *Baustahlgewebe GmbH* v. *Commission*:.

[6] *Perfumes* (Cases 253/78, 1–3, 37 & 99/79) [1980] E.C.R. 2327, [1981] 2 C.M.L.R. 99, [1980] E.C.R. 2511, [1981] 2 C.M.L.R. 164. But it may affect the level of any fine. See para. 7.

[7] Case 30/78, *Distillers* v. *Commission*: [1980] E.C.R. 2229, [1980] 3 C.M.L.R. 121.

[7a] *Frubo*, above n.5.

[8] Case 1252/79, *Lucchini* v. *Commission*: [1980] E.C.R. 3753, [1981] 3 C.M.L.R. 487, at para. 9.

[9] Cases 303 & 312/81, *Klockner Werke AG* v. *Commission*: [1983] E.C.R. 1549, [1984] 2 C.M.L.R. 714, at para. 34. Failure and laxity on the part of the Commission may however be relevant in fixing a fine. See Case 344/85, *Ferriere San Carlo SpA* v. *Commission*: [1987] E.C.R. 4435.

in Community law the principle that an administrative authority should not be able to bind itself so as to fetter its discretion in relation to the exercise of its powers in the public interest has yet to be determined.[10]

Language

8.31 The official languages and the working languages of the institutions of the Community are Danish, Dutch, English, French, German, Greek, Italian, Portuguese and Spanish.[11]

Notifications

Article 2(3) of Regulation 27 provides that applications (for negative clearance) and notifications (for exemption) must be in one of the official languages of the Community. Supporting documents must be submitted in their original language. Where that language is not one of the official languages, a translation in one of the official languages must also be attached. Regulation 3666/93 amended Article 2 of Regulation 27 in order to facilitate notifications under E.C. and/or EEA competition rules. This enables, as explained below, the use of the official languages of the EFTA States in certain cases. The Commission recommends, "in order to ensure rapid proceedings", the use, in notifications to the Commission, of one of the official languages of the E.C. or the working language of the EFTA Surveillance Authority (which is English).

Communications between Commission and undertaking

Article 3 of Council Regulation 1 requires that documents which an institution of the Community sends to a person subject to the jurisdiction of a Member State shall be drafted in the language of that State.[12] The statement of objections will therefore be in an official language related to the undertaking concerned. In most cases the choice of that language will be clear if not self-evident from the communications which have already taken place between the Commission and the undertaking. Where the Commission relies on documentary evidence in support of the statement of objections then that evidence should, if not in the appropriate official language, be accompanied by a suitable translation. A translation may not, however, be necessary where the document emanates from the undertaking concerned. An undertaking does not need a translation of a document of which it is the author. But merely because a document is found on the premises of the undertaking will not necessarily absolve the Commission from the responsibility to provide a translation. However, an undertaking is most probably not entitled to a translation of all the documents to which it may be given access when it inspects the Commission's file. Where a complaint is made in a language other than that of the undertaking the subject of the complaint it is the Commission's practice when sending a copy of the complaint to the undertaking for its reactions to attach a summary in the appropriate official language. Complaints can be voluminous,

[10] See A.G. Warner in Case 81/72, *Commission* v. *Council*: [1973] E.C.R. 575, [1973] C.M.L.R. 639. *Cf.* his opinion in *Boizard* v. *Commission*, (above, n. 1), quoted above.

[11] Council Reg. 1: [1958] J.O. 385/58, as amended by the Acts of Accession of 1972, 1979 and 1985.

[12] *Cf.* Art. 6(3)(a) of the European Convention on Human Rights.

especially where detailed evidence is attached, and the Commission cannot be expected to provide a complete translation at this preliminary stage. But any statement of objections based on the complaint would, as mentioned, have to be in the (official) language of the undertaking concerned.

In *ACF Chemiefarma* v. *Commission*,[13] the applicant claimed that the Commission's failure to submit the minutes of the oral hearing to it in Dutch infringed the principles contained in Articles 217 and 248 of the Treaty and Regulation No. 1 of the Council. The Court considered that, although this failure constituted an irregularity capable of affecting the validity of the minutes, such irregularity was not in the circumstances sufficient to vitiate the administrative procedure. The applicant had been able to acquaint itself with the contents of the minutes and no allegation had been made that the failure to supply a Dutch text resulted in the minutes containing any substantial inaccuracies or omissions.

Regulations, decisions, etc.

8.32   Article 155 of the Act of Accession of 1972 as amended by Article 30 of the Adaptation Decision of the first Act of Accession provides:

> "The texts of the acts of the institutions of the Community adopted before accession and drawn up by the Council or the Commission in the Danish and English languages shall, from the date of accession, be authentic under the same conditions as the texts drawn up in the four original languages. They shall be published in the *Official Journal of the European Communities* if the texts of the original languages were so published."

The Acts of Accession of 1979 and of 1985 similarly provide for texts in the Greek, Portuguese and Spanish languages.[14] As the Court of Justice said in the *Sugar* case: "Community institutions are under a duty to send an undertaking to which a decision is addressed a copy of that decision in the language of the Member State to which this undertaking belongs."[15] The Court held that an undertaking cannot complain if in addition to its own language version it also receives the text of the decision in other languages without an indication which was the authentic language as regards the undertaking. The Court has been robust and not too formalistic, including as regards the position of undertakings from third States. In the *Continental Can* case,[16] the applicants, an American company and its subsidiary, argued that the Commission had contravened Article 3 of Council Regulation 1 because it had designated the French version of its decision as binding instead of the German version. The Court said:

> "since the applicant companies have their seats in a non-Member country the choice of an official language for the decision had to depend in the present case on the connection existing within the Common Market between the applicant companies and any of the Member States of the Community."

---

[13] Above, n. 44, at paras. 47–52.

[14] See Art. 147 of the Act of Accession of 1979 and Art. 397 of that of 1985.

[15] Above, n. 44, at para. 114.

[16] Case 6/72, *Europemballage Corp. and Continental Can Co. Inc.* v. *Commission*: [1973] E.C.R. 215, [1973] C.M.L.R. 199, at paras. 11–13.

Europemballage, the subsidiary, had an office in Brussels and had replied to the Commission's statement of objections in French; therefore the Court did not consider that there had been any contravention of Article 3 of Council Regulation 1. Where the undertaking has itself chosen the language it can hardly complain. In the absence of such choice it seems that the Commission will have to decide on the basis of the circumstances of the case. If that decision is made in good faith and with commonsense, it is most doubtful that the Court of Justice would overturn it.[17]

The need to have the decision ready for adoption in the language of all the addressees arose in the *PVC* case. The Court of First Instance held that where the Commission intends to adopt by a single measure a decision which is binding on a number of legal persons for whom different languages might be used, the decision must be adopted in each of the languages in which it is binding in order to avoid making authentication impossible.[18] According to the Commission's Rule of Procedure the Commission could not delegate to one of its members authority to adopt a decision in an authentic language version, as opposed to one where the text is not authentic. The latter is permissible since the version of the decision in question does not produce any legal effect and is not enforceable against any of the undertakings mentioned in the operative part of the decision.[19] In *PVC*, the decision had been adopted by the full Commission only in English, German and French, but not in Dutch and Italian the language of two undertakings each.

EEA

8.33 Article 12 of Protocol 24 to the EEA specifically addresses the question of languages to be used by undertakings concerned and third parties in their communications with the surveillance authorities. The starting point is that, provided it uses an official language of an EFTA state or the Community, an undertaking concerned or a third party may address the surveillance authority in a language of its choice. Where however that language is not one of the official languages of the States falling within the competence of that authority, or a working language of that authority, all documentation supplied must be simultaneously supplemented by a translation into an official language of that authority. The choice of the language used in the translation is an important one for the party concerned. This is because, as Article 12 provides, the language chosen for the translation will determine the language in which the undertakings may be addressed by the competent authority.

As regards applications and notifications to the Commission pursuant to Articles 53 and 54 of the EEA. The Commission has amended[20] Regulation 27 (and the equivalent provisions of the subordinate legislation under the transport regulations: Regulations 1629/69, 4260/88 and 4261/88) to allow the use of the official languages of the EFTA

---

[17] See Marenco, *Aspects linguistiques des droits de la défense*, Seminar on Competition Procedures, Brussels, September 27–28, 1993.

[18] Joined Cases T 78, 84–86, 89, 71–92, 94, 96, 98, 102 & 104/89, *BASF AG and others* v. *Commission*: [1992] 4 C.M.L.R. 357, at paras. 54–55.

[19] *Ibid.* at paras. 56–59. The Commission has appealed; see Case C–137/92, *Commission* v. *BASF and others*. Advocate General Van Gerven gave his opinion on June 29, 1993, saying that the judgment of the Court of First Instance should be set aside. On the question of delegation and language, he thought it permissible for the Commission to delegate to a commissioner the adoption of a text of a decision which had already been adopted by the full Commission in another language version. The task was essentially one of practical execution or internal organisation.

[20] See Reg. 3666/93, Arts. 1–4.

States or the working language of the EFTA Surveillance Authority (which is English).

9

Judicial Review by the European Court of Justice

9.01 The Court of Justice is the guardian of Community law and has the duty to en-sure that in the application and interpretation of the Treaty the law is observed.[1] As mentioned in Chapter 1, the Court of Justice has a wide jurisdiction and competition matters may be brought before the Court in various circumstances. The Court of First Instance has, by contrast, a less extensive jurisdiction[2] but one in which natural or legal persons can challenge the Commission's implementation of Articles 85 and 86. This chapter describes three basic ways in which the legality of the Commission's ap-plication and enforcement of the competition rules can be subjected to judicial control:

- (a) under Article 172, an application can be made under the 'unlimited' jurisdic-tion of the Court where a fine or periodic penalty payment is imposed;
- (b) under Article 173, an application can be made to annul a decision of the Com-mission on the basis of one or more of four specified grounds;
- (c) under Article 175, an application can be made for the Court to rule on the legal-ity of the Commission's failure to act.

There follows a brief description of the position of third parties in the Court's proced-ure and of the Court's powers to grant interim relief.

---

[1] Art. 164 of the Treaty. On the role and work of the Court, see generally; Brown, *The Court of Justice of the European Communities* (3rd ed., 1989); Lasok, *The European Court of Justice Practice and Procedure* (1984); Schermers and Waelbroeck, *Judicial Protection in the European Communities* (5th ed., 1992); Usher, *European Court Practice* (1983).

[2] By a decision of the Council of Ministers of June 8, 1993 the Court was given jurisdiction to hear all direct actions brought by a material or legal person. See [1993] O.J. L144/21 (anti-dumping and subsidy cases were added in March 1994). It has no jurisdiction, *e.g.* to take references from national courts under Art. 177. As regards the Court's approach to competition cases, see generally van der Woude, "The Court of First Instance: The First Three Years" 16 Fordham Int.L.J. 412.

I. ARTICLE 172—THE COURT'S "UNLIMITED" JURISDICTION

9.02   Article 172 of the Treaty provides that regulations made by the Council pursuant to the provisions of the Treaty may give the Court unlimited jurisdiction in regard to the penalties provided for in such regulations.[3] Thus, in the context of competition, Article 17 of Regulation 17 provides:

> "The Court shall have unlimited jurisdiction within the meaning of Article 172 of the Treaty to review decisions whereby the Commission has fixed a fine or periodic penalty payment; it may cancel, reduce or increase the fine or periodic penalty imposed."

There are similar provisions in the implementing regulations governing the transport sector.[4]

The concept of unlimited jurisdiction comes from French administrative law where the distinction is drawn between *recours de pleine jurisdiction* and *recours de la lègalitè*, the former enabling the administrative court to go further than the annulment of the act in question and, with the powers of an ordinary civil court, to deal fully with the matter inter partes awarding compensation where appropriate. Articles 172 and 173 of the Treaty are based on this distinction but have developed independently.

Article 172 almost certainly does not go so far. The words "in regard to the penalties" in Article 172 restrict the extent and exercise of the "unlimited jurisdiction" to the consideration of the fine or other penalty imposed by the Commission[5] and do not, for example, permit the Court to annul the decision on grounds other than those in Article 173 or if application is not made under that Article.[6] As the Court of First Instance opined in *Italian Flat Glass*, although a Community court may, as part of the judicial review of the community administration, partially annul a Commission decision in the field of competition, that does not mean that it has jurisdiction to remake the contested decision.[7] Nonetheless, the Court can, when looking at the fine imposed by the Commission, consider all aspects of the case and all relevant questions of law and fact.

9.03   In the matter of remedies Article 172 enables the Court to go further than does Article 173 and, as mentioned above, to cancel, reduce or increase fines or penalties imposed by the Commission in competition decisions. In practice the Court has not been reluctant to reduce fines,[8] especially where the Commission has not proved all its case or there has been some defect in reasoning in the Commission's decision which is

---

[3] Useful introductions to the plenary or full jurisdiction of the Court are contained in Brown, *op. cit.*, Chap. 7 and Lasok and Bridge, *The Law and Institutions of the European Communities* (5th ed., 1991), Chap. 9. In the *Commercial Solvents* case (below, n. 13), A.G. Warner said: "I do not doubt that in exercising that jurisdiction the Court is entitled to take into account considerations of common justice."

[4] Reg. 1017/68, Art. 24; Reg. 4056/86; Art. 21; Reg. 3975/87, Art. 14.

[5] *Italian Flat Glass*: Cases T 68 & 77–78/89, *Società Italiano Vetro SpA and others* v. *Commission*: [1992] II E.C.R. 1403, [1992] 5 C.M.L.R. 302, at para. 318.

[6] The fact that the Court's jurisdiction under Art. 172 does not enable it to annul a decision on grounds other than those in Art. 173 most probably involves no hardship to an applicant because the Court has adopted a most flexible approach in relation to its interpretation and application of the grounds set out in Art. 173. In practice, an application is normally made under both Arts.

[7] Above, at para. 319.

[8] The Court has however been reluctant to change measures other than fines and penalties. See Case 46/72, *De Greef* v. *Commission*: [1973] E.C.R. 543, at para. 46, discussed by Schermers and Waelbroeck, *op. cit.*, at para. 646.

not sufficient to justify complete annulment. Thus in *Windsurfing*,[9] the Court of Justice referring expressly to its jurisdiction under Article 172,[10] reduced WSI's fine by half[11] on the grounds that some of the findings of infringement were not ultimately upheld by the Court, the seriousness of the infringements was found to be diminished appreciably having regard to the size of the market in the earlier years, and the failure to prove beyond doubt the impact on the licensees of the prohibition on the sale of separate rigs.

More recently, in *Wood Pulp II*,[12] the Court of Justice substantially reduced the fines on four of the parties following the Court partially annulling the Commission's finding of infringements involving concertation on prices. The Court upheld the Commission's decision as regards the imposition of export and resale bans and, in fixing the level of fine, had regard to the nature of the infringement, the reactions of the parties and the argument, uncontested by the Commission, that the infringement had been committed negligently. Reduction of the fine is not necessarily dependent on the Court's partial annulment of the decision in question. In *Commercial Solvents*,[13] the Court upheld the Commission's decision but nevertheless reduced the fine by half because although there was a serious infringement (a refusal to supply) its duration might have been shorter if the Commission had acted more quickly in the prosecution of its case. The Court drew attention to the fact that the undertaking concerned had complied promptly with the Commission's decision once made.

II. ARTICLE 173—ACTION FOR ANNULMENT

Generally

9.04 Article 173 is the basic provision in the Treaty dealing with the right to judicial review of the acts of the Council and the Commission:

> "The Court of Justice shall review the legality of acts of the Council and the Commission ... on the grounds of lack of competence, infringement of an essential procedural right, infringement of this Treaty or of any rule of law relating to its application, or misuse of powers."

The four "grounds" thus stated are perhaps unfamiliar to the English lawyer as they derive principally from French administrative law.[14] Differences in terminology do not necessarily, however, reflect differences of substance. The four grounds of annulment in Article 173 are similar to the grounds on which English courts have for many

---

[9] Case 193/83, *Windsurfing International Inc.* v. *Commission*: [1986] E.C.R. 611, [1986] 3 C.M.L.R. 489, at paras. 110–114.

[10] *Ibid.* at para. 110, and note the Court's reference at para. 114 to "setting" the fine.

[11] From 50,000 to 25,000 ECUs.

[12] Cases C 89, 104, 114, 116, 117 & 125–129/85, *A Åhlström Osakeyhtio and Others* v. *Commission*: [1993] 4 C.M.L.R. 407. The fines on Canfor, MacMillan, St Anne and Westar were reduced to 20,000 ECUs each, see paras. 190–198.

[13] Cases 6 & 7/73, *Istituto Chemioterapico Italiano SpA and Commercial Solvents Corp.* v. *Commission*: [1974] E.C.R. 223, [1974] 1 C.M.L.R. 309, at para. 51.

[14] See, generally, Brown and Bell, *French Administrative Law* (4th ed., 1993) and Lasok and Bridge, *op. cit.*, Chap. 9.

years quashed decisions of administrative authorities and inferior tribunals.[15] Although the grounds will be considered separately, it is noteworthy that the Court has been most flexible in its approach under Article 173 and that the grounds have gradually lost their individual importance.[16] They can be pleaded in the alternative or in addition to each other as the circumstances of the case may require.[17] And the Court may not go into the legal classification of the grounds of annulment in its judgment.

In contrast to the position under Article 172 where the Court can substitute its own judgment for that of the Commission so far as the fine is concerned, the Court under Article 173 is concerned to see that the limits of the Commission's discretion have not been exceeded. Competition cases frequently involve complicated economic assessments and it is recognised that the Commission enjoys a considerable measure of discretion. The Court will therefore be concerned to verify whether the relevant procedural rules have been complied with, whether the facts have been accurately stated and whether there has been a manifest error of appraisal or a misuse of powers.[18]

Who can sue

9.05   Proceedings under Article 173 may be brought by a Member State,[19] the Council or the Commission. The Article also expressly provides that:

> "Any natural or legal person may . . . institute proceedings against a decision addressed to that person or against a decision which, although in the form of a regulation or a decision addressed to another person, is of direct and individual concern to the former."

In *B.P.* v. *Commission*,[20] the Court of Justice held that the absence of pecuniary sanctions (*i.e.* a fine[21] or periodic penalty payment[22]) in a decision applying Articles 85 and 86 does not preclude the addressee from having an interest in obtaining a review by the Court of the legality of the decision under Article 173. With regard to the position of third parties (*i.e.* non-addressees) it is a question of whether the party has a "direct and individual concern."

---

[15] Kahn-Freund, "Common Law and Civil Law—Imaginary and Real Obstacles to Assimilation" in M. Cappelletti (ed.), *New Perspectives for a Common Law of Europe* (1978), at p. 159.

[16] See Schermers, "The Law as it stands on the Appeal for Annulment" (1975) 2 L.I.E.I. 95. Schermers suggests that the Court has become less concerned with the specific ground of illegality and that most "logical" reasons for illegality are accepted as "infringement of the Treaty or of any rule of law relating to its application." See para. 9.19.

[17] Indeed it may be sufficient for the grounds to be expressed in terms of their substance rather than their legal classification provided it is sufficiently clear from the application which grounds are being invoked: Cases 19 & 21/60, 2–3/61, *Societe Five Lille Cail* v. *High Authority*: [1961] E.C.R. 281, [1962] C.M.L.R. 251.

[18] Case 42/84, *Remia and others* v. *Commission*: [1985] E.C.R. 2545, [1987] 1 C.M.L.R. 1, at para. 34.

[19] For an example of a Member State attacking a Commission decision under Reg. 17, see Case 41/83, *Italy* v. *Commission*: [1985] E.C.R. 873, [1985] 2 C.M.L.R. 368, the decision in question being *British Telecommunications*: [1982] O.J. L360/36, [1983] 1 C.M.L.R. 457.

[20] Case 77/77: [1978] E.C.R. 1513, [1978] 3 C.M.L.R. 174, at para. 13.

[21] Under Art. 15 of Reg. 17.

[22] Under Art. 16 of Reg. 17.

The Court of Justice has recognised that a related company is sufficiently concerned for these purposes.[23] But in a general context the Court of Justice has said that the mere fact that a measure may exercise an influence on the competitive relationships existing on the market in question is not sufficient to allow any trader in any competitive relationship whatsoever with the addressee of the measure to be regarded as directly and individually concerned by that measure.[24] The decision must affect such persons by reason of certain attributes which are peculiar to them, or by reason of circumstances in which they are differentiated from all other persons, and by virtue of those factors distinguish them individually just as in the case of the person addressed.[25] If a person is entitled to bring a complaint[26] under Article 3(2)(b) of Regulation 17, then he will be entitled to sue under Article 173. In *Metro* v. *Commission*,[27] the Court of Justice said:

> "It is in the interests of a satisfactory administration of justice and of the proper application of Articles 85 and 86 that natural or legal persons who are entitled, pursuant to Article 3(2)(b) of Regulation 17, to request the Commission to find an infringement of Articles 85 and 86 should be able, if their request is dismissed either wholly or in part, to institute proceedings in order to protect their legitimate interests. In those circumstances, the applicant must be considered to be directly and individually concerned, within the meaning of the second paragraph of Article 173, by the contested decision."

The Court had previously taken a more narrow approach to Article 173(2) and had shown a reluctance to admit actions by persons other than those to whom it could clearly be shown the act being challenged was addressed.[28] But as the Court of Justice went on to say in *Metro II*,[29] it will not restrict the class of persons who are "directly and individually concerned" to formal complainants (like Metro) adopted by the Commission, *i.e.* to cases of decisions adopted pursuant to an application under Article 3(2)(b). The Court held Metro's application admissible, drawing attention to the fact that it had been refused admission to the SABA distribution system, it had participated in the Commission's proceedings (its objections being made both before and

---

[23] Cases 113 & 118–121/77, *NTN Toyo Bearings and others* v. *Council*: [1979] E.C.R. 1185, [1979] 2 C.M.L.R. 257 (parent and subsidiary), and Cases 228 & 229/82, *Ford of Europe Inc. and Ford Werke AG* v. *Commission*: [1984] E.C.R. 1129, [1984] 1 C.M.L.R. 649 (fellow subsidiaries).

[24] Cases 10 & 18/68, *Società Eridania Zuccherifici* v. *Commission*: [1969] E.C.R. 459, at para. 7. The mere fact that a measure may affect the relations between different shareholders of a company does not of itself mean that any individual shareholder can be regarded as directly and individually concerned by that measure: Case T–83/92, *Zunis Holding SA and others* v. *Commission*: judgment of the Court of First Instance, October 28, 1993, not yet reported.

[25] Case 169/84, *COFAZ and others* v. *Commission*: [1986] E.C.R. 391, [1986] 3 C.M.L.R. 385. See also Case 253/89, *Sociedade Agro-Pecuaria Vincente Nobre Lda* v. *Council*: [1990] 1 C.M.L.R. 105.

[26] As to whether a person has a "legitimate interest" under Art. 3(2)(b) of Reg. 17, see para. 2.29.

[27] Case 26/76: [1977] E.C.R. 1875, [1978] 2 C.M.L.R. 1, at para. 13. See, generally Dinnage, "Locus Standi and Article 173 EEC: the Effect of *Metro-SB-Grossmarkte* v. *Commission*" (1979) 4 E.L.Rev. 177, and Waelbroeck, "Judicial Review of Commission Action in Competition Matters" (1983) *Annual Proceedings of the Fordham Corporate Law Institute*.

[28] A.G. Mancini has said that the formula employed in *Metro* introduces an exception of a special nature, which is justified by the overriding interest of verifying in Court proceedings whether the competition rules have been properly applied. "Access to Justice: International Undertakings and EEC Antitrust Law-Problems and Pitfalls" (1989) 12 Fordham Int. L.J. 189.

[29] Case 75/84, *Metro-SB-Grossmarkte GmbH & Co. KG* v. *Commission*: [1986] E.C.R. 3021, [1987] 1 C.M.L.R. 118, at paras. 21–23.

after the Article 19(3) notice), the Commission had recognised that it had a "legitimate interest" under Article 19(3), and the agreement in question still contained the special features which Metro had criticised. The class, it is submitted, should not be too narrowly drawn, nor necessarily by reference to formal criteria of participation in the Commission's proceedings.[30] The Court should admit any person who might suffer direct loss or injury as a consequence of the act in question.[31]

Acts which may be challenged

9.06 Article 173 expressly provides that the Court can review the legality of "acts of the Council and the Commission other than recommendations or opinions." Of the measures described in Article 189 of the Treaty, regulations, directives and decisions therefore appear to be "acts" within the meaning of Article 173 and there are in fact many instances of the legality of, in particular, regulations and decisions being considered by the Court in this way.[32] For example, in *Italy* v. *Council and Commission*,[33] the validity of Regulation 19/65 empowering the Commission to make certain block or group exemptions was unsuccessfully challenged on the grounds, *inter alia*, that it purported to give the Commission powers to exempt agreements under Article 85(3) which could not fall within the prohibition of Article 85(1). The *Metro* cases,[34] mentioned above, are examples of an individual exemption decision being challenged before the Court. And there are many cases where decisions of the Commission under Regulation 17 finding an infringement of Article 85 or 86 have been appealed under this provision. Some of these are discussed in the following pages.

9.07 The meaning of "acts" is, however, not restricted to regulations and decisions. In the *AERT* case,[35] the Court said: "Article 173 treats as open to review by the Court all measures adopted by the institutions which are intended to have legal force." And in *IBM*:[36]

---

[30] See Waelbroeck, *op. cit.*, at p. 201 who considers that this may be a justifiable condition in relation to decisions of exemption or negative clearance where there are publication requirements. Mancini, *op. cit.* on the other hand, formulates a broader test—a person may be held to have standing, although he was not involved in the action taken by the Commission, if he maintains that the Commission's action would prejudice a legal position of his that is directly protected by Community antitrust rules. He must therefore demonstrate the possible repercussions to his legal position.

[31] In dumping cases, where the challenged act is a regulation and not a decision, the Court has recognised the position of producers and exporters named in the measure or who have participated in the investigation (Cases 239 & 275/82, *Allied Corporation and Others* v. *Council*: [1984] E.C.R. 1005) but not necessarily importers (Case 307/81, *Alusuisse Italia* v. *Commission and Council*: [1982] E.C.R. 3463, but see Cases C 133 & 150/87, *Nashua Corporation and Others* v. *Commission and Council*: [1990] 2 C.M.L.R. 6). Complainants have also been admitted: see Case 191/82, *FEDIOL* v. *Commission*: [1983] E.C.R. 2913, [1984] 3 C.M.L.R. 244, and Case 264/82, *Timex* v. *Council and Commission*: [1985] E.C.R. 849, [1985] 3 C.M.L.R. 550.

[32] See, generally, Schermers and Waelbroeck, *op. cit.*, at paras. 267–384.

[33] Case 32/65: [1966] E.C.R. 389, [1969] C.M.L.R. 39.

[34] Above, nn. 27 and 29.

[35] Case 22/70, *Commission* v. *Council*: [1971] E.C.R. 263, [1971] C.M.L.R. 335, at paras. 39–42.

[36] Case 60/81, *IBM* v. *Commission*: [1981] E.C.R. 2639, [1981] 3 C.M.L.R. 635, at para. 9.

"Any measure the legal effects of which are binding on, and capable of affecting the interests of, the applicant by bringing about a distinct change in his legal position is an act or decision which may be the object of an action under Article 173 for a declaration that it is void."

An individual cannot, however, challenge a regulation unless it is a "disguised decision".[37] As already mentioned, if not addressed to him the applicant must show that the decision is of direct and individual concern to him. There are, as has been described in earlier chapters, a number of circumstances where Regulation 17 requires the Commission to act by way of a formal decision. There are also instances where Regulation 17 does not expressly provide that a formal decision be taken but the Commission's act may affect the legal position of the parties to whom it is addressed. In such cases it will be important to determine whether the act in question is a decision or otherwise such as to permit the possibility of judicial review under Article 173 by the party concerned.

9.08　The Court is prepared to construe the notion of measures having legal effects broadly. In each case regard must be had to the substance rather than the form[38] of the measure in question. The nature of a measure will depend largely on its content and scope. Thus a negative clearance given under Article 2 of Regulation 17 on application by the undertakings concerned gives satisfaction to the undertakings and therefore cannot be challenged by them. The Court of First Instance has held that such a decision is not, by its nature, capable of altering their legal problem or giving them cause for complaint.[39] It is also important to look at the circumstances and facts of each case.[40] So a letter from a Commission official merely saying that the matter is being considered[41] or advising that it will be concluded shortly[42] will not be challengeable. Letters which go more into the substance may cause more difficulty. In *Prodifarma I*,[43] the Court of First Instance had to consider a letter from the Competition Commissioner to the Dutch Government. The background was an arrangement aimed at trying to curb the costs in the supply of medicinal products in the Netherlands by way of an agreement providing for a reduction in the level of the prices at which medicinal products were supplied to chemists coupled with an amendment to the Netherlands rules on chemists profit margins. The agreement had been concluded between all the organisations in the Netherlands concerned in the supply of medicinal products except Prodifarma. The letter suggested that certain amendments be made to the agreement and that a monitoring system be set up before a favourable decision

---

[37] For an example of this principle, see Case 101/76, *Koninklijke Scholten Honig NV* v. *Council and Commission*: [1977] E.C.R. 797, [1980] 2 C.M.L.R. 669.

[38] See the general statement of the Court of Justice in Cases 53 & 54/63, *Lemmerz-Werke* v. *High Authority*: [1963] E.C.R. 239, [1964] C.M.L.R. 384.

[39] *Dutch Banks*: Case T–138/89, *Nederlandse Bankiersvereniging and Nederlandse Vereniging Van Banken* v. *Commission*: [1993] 5 C.M.L.R. 436, at para. 32. On the other hand, a negative clearance may affect the economic interests of a third party who, provided he has a sufficient legitimate interest, could sue under Article 173.

[40] See A.G. Roemer in Cases 8–11/66, *Cimenteries* v. *Commission*: [1967] E.C.R. 75, [1967] C.M.L.R. 77.

[41] Cases 42 & 49/59, *Snupat* v. *High Authority*: [1961] E.C.R. 53; Case 40/71, *Richez-Parise* v. *Commission*: [1972] E.C.R. 73.

[42] Case 79/70, *Mullers* v. *Economic and Social Committee*: [1971] E.C.R. 689.

[43] Case T–116/89, *Vereniging Prodifarma and Others* v. *Commission*: [1990] II E.C.R. 843. See also Case T–113/89, *Nefarma* v. *Commission*: [1990] II E.C.R. 797 and Case T–114/89, *V.N.Z.* v. *Commission*: [1990] II E.C.R. 827.

could be given by the Commission. In reaction to the letter the Dutch Government amended the domestic rules. Prodifarma challenged the legality of the arrangements under Article 85, requesting the Commission to take action against it. The Court of First Instance looked to see whether the letter produced binding legal effects. It was not, the Court said, an exemption under Article 85(3) as it was merely the starting point of an examination of the agreement to see whether such an exemption could be granted. Nor did it, upon examination, have the features of a decision of negative clearance or of interim measures. The procedural rights of the parties to the agreement in question and third parties were reserved.[44] Nor did the letter impose a decision on the Dutch Government as there was no power under Article 85 or Regulation 17 to address a binding decision to a Member State as regards the conduct to be adopted by national authorities in connection with an agreement between undertakings falling under Article 85.[45] Neither the wording nor the content of the letter indicated that it was intended to produce any legal effects. There was no collegiate decision of the Commission. Moreover the letter was not in the form either of a communication of a decision taken by the Commission or something written in the name of the Commission or by virtue of a delegated power. As the Court said: "It appears rather to have been written by Sir Leon Brittan in his own name and in the context of an exchange of views between politicians."[46]

Preliminary steps in a procedure do not generally constitute challengeable acts. As the Court of Justice explained in *IBM*,[47] where there is a procedure involving several stages, then it is necessary to distinguish the final decision from provisional measures which pave the way for such a decision. An act is open to review only if it is a measure definitively laying down the position of the Commission on the conclusion of the procedure. Measures adopted in the course of preliminary proceedings will only be reviewable under Article 173 if they have all the legal characteristics described above and also are the culmination of a special procedure distinct from that of the final substantive decision or, in exceptional circumstances, lack even an appearance of legality.[48] In *IBM*, the Court of Justice held that the initiation of a procedure by the Commission and the statement of objections[49] are not acts challengeable under Article 173. They do not have the necessary adverse legal effects. Nor, as is shown by the recent *Cement* case in the Court of First Instance, does the refusal to give access to the Commission file.[50] The Court said:

---

[44] *Prodifarma I*, above, at paras. 68–73.

[45] *Ibid*. at para. 82.

[46] *Ibid*. at para. 87.

[47] Above, n. 36, at para. 10. Followed by the Court of First Instance in Case T–64/89, *Automec Srl* v. *Commission*: [1990] II E.C.R. 367, [1991] 4 C.M.L.R. 177, at para. 42, and Cases T 10–12 & 14–15/92R, *Cimenteries CBR SA and Others* v. *Commission*: [1993] 4 C.M.L.R. 243, at para. 45.

[48] The Court of Justice thus left a door open. At para. 23 it said: "It is not necessary for the purposes of this case to decide whether, in exceptional circumstances, where the measures concerned lack even the appearance of legality, a judicial review at an early stage . . . might be considered compatible with the system of remedies provided for in the Treaty." It is difficult to envisage what steps would be sufficient to justify such an early intervention by the Court. In the recent *Cement* case, the Court of First Instance recognised the exception provided by the Court of Justice in *IBM* but did not consider it applicable on the facts. See *Cement*, above, n. 47, at para. 49.

[49] In *Cement*, above, n. 47, the Court of First Instance held that the Commission's failure, in a multiparty case, to disclose the entirety of the statement of objections to all the parties was not admissible.

[50] *Per* the Court of First Instance in *Cement*, above, n. 47.

"Commission measures refusing access produce in principle only limited effects, characteristic of a preparatory measure forming part of a preliminary administrative procedure. Only measures immediately and irreversibly affecting the legal situation of the undertakings concerned would be of such a nature as to justify before completion of the administrative procedure, the admissibility of an action for annulment."[51]

The Court considered that the Commission could rectify any procedural irregularities by subsequently granting access to the file so that the undertakings concerned would have a further opportunity, in full knowledge of the facts, to express their views. On the other hand, in the (1967) *Cimenteries* case the Court of Justice held that a letter signed by a Commission official in application of Article 15(6) of Regulation 17 informing the undertakings concerned that their agreement had been preliminarily examined and found to fall within Article 85(1) but to be unsuitable for exemption was a decision.[52]

"The undertakings ceased to be protected by Article 15(5) which exempted them from fines, and came under the contrary rules of Article 15(2) which thenceforth exposed them to the risk of fines. This measure deprived them of the advantages of a legal situation which Article 15(5) attached to the notification of the agreement, and exposed them to a grave financial risk. Thus the said measure affected the interests of the undertakings by bringing about a distinct change in their position. It is unequivocally a measure which produces legal effects touching the interests of the undertakings concerned and which is binding on them. It thus constitutes not a mere opinion but a decision."

The decision was annulled for lack of reasoning.[53]

There are other measures which the Commission may take which may similarly be decisions albeit not expressly referred to as such in Regulation 17 or the other implementing regulations and in practice frequently taking the form of a letter. In *Camera Care Ltd.* v. *Commission*,[54] for example, Advocate General Warner thought that a letter signed by a Commission official which simply said, "I regret that I cannot comply with your proposal to make an interim decision. There is no legal basis in Community law for such procedure", was a decision of the Commission. In *C.I.C.C.E.* v. *Commission*,[55] the Court of Justice proceeded on the basis that a letter from the Director-General of DG IV affirming the Commission's intention to discontinue the procedure on a complaint after it had considered the complainant's comments pursuant to Article 6 of Regulation 99/63 was a decision. In *BAT and Reynolds* v. *Commission*, the Court of Justice noted that the Commission had drawn letters rejecting the complaint in "decision" form: they closed the investigation, contained an assessment of all agreements in question and prevented the complainants requiring the re-opening of

[51] *Ibid.* at para. 42.
[52] Above, n. 40. In *Prodifarma II*: Case T–3/90, *Vereniging Prodifarma* v. *Commission*: [1991] II E.C.R. 1, the Court of First Instance recognised that whilst an Art. 15(6) decision constitutes the culmination of a special procedure, it is one concerning only the parties to the agreement. The Art. 15(6) procedure is, the Court said, distinct from a complaint by a third party who has no procedural rights capable of being affected by a decision taken at the end of the Art. 15(6) procedure (para. 44).
[53] See para. 9.15.
[54] Case 792/79R: [1980] E.C.R. 119, [1980] 1 C.M.L.R. 334.
[55] Case 298/83: [1985], E.C.R. 1105 [1986] 1 C.M.L.R. 486, at para. 18.

the case unless they put forward new evidence.[56] In *Automec I*, the Court of First Instance held that a letter lacking those features, containing both definitive and provisional assessments in response to a complaint and sent before any formal communication under Article 6 of Regulation 99/63 was not a decision or otherwise challengeable before the Court.[57] The refusal to hear a third party may constitute a decision.[58] The category is not closed. The Court may well be influenced by the importance which an affirmative or negative response may have in the particular circumstances for the individual's legal protection.

9.09 The status of the comfort letter has been questioned. In the *Perfumes* cases,[59] the Court of Justice described them as *lettres administratives* informing the undertakings concerned of the Commission's opinion that the agreements did not fall within Article 85(1).[60] They were not decisions under Article 2 or 6 of Regulation 17 because the publicity requirements of Articles 19 and 21 had not been fulfilled.[61] The Court made it clear that the opinions of the Commission expressed in the letters did not bind the Commission and that they left a national court free to come to a different conclusion as to the applicability of Article 85(1).[62] All this would seem to negate any idea of decision. But the Court of Justice also held that the effect of such a letter from the Commission indicating that the file on a notified agreement is to be closed (*classée*) will be to withdraw any provisional validity the agreement may have.[63] The position of the parties to the agreement may be affected as a result and it might be argued that therefore the letter may constitute a decision. There is however no hint of this in the Court's judgments and no consideration is given to the possible implications as to formal requirements and delegation of powers.[64] There is an element of uncertainty. Comfort letters generally imply that a decision has been made to close the file,[65] but as *lettres administratives* they may have no binding character.

---

[56] Cases 142 & 156/84: [1986] E.C.R. 1899, [1987] 2 C.M.L.R. 551, at para. 12. In *Automec I*, above, n. 47, the Court of First Instance considered that these three factors characterised a decision rejecting a complaint (para. 57).

[57] Above, n. 47, at paras. 52–58.

[58] But not a refusal to hear the undertakings concerned, who could undoubtedly challenge any final decision on this ground. See Waelbroeck, *op. cit.*

[59] Cases 253/78, 1–3, 37 & 99/79: [1980] E.C.R. 2327, [1980] E.C.R. 2481, [1980] E.C.R. 2511, [1981] 2 C.M.L.R. 99, [1981] 2 C.M.L.R. 143, [1981] 2 C.M.L.R. 164. See Korah, "Comfort Letters—Reflection on the Perfumes Cases" (1981) 6 E.L.Rev. 14.

[60] *Ibid.* Case 253/78, at para. 12.

[61] *Ibid.* Case 253/78, at para. 11.

[62] *Ibid.* Case 253/78, at para. 13. The Court expected the national court at least to have regard to the Commission's opinion.

[63] *Ibid.* Case 99/79, at para. 17, and see para. 10.10.

[64] It is arguable that, if decisions, they might be annulled for lack of reasoning (see in particular the letter used in *Lauder*, Case 37/79) or considered to be non-existent acts because neither the Director-General nor the Director who signed the letters had the necessary power to take decisions. The Commission had itself pointed out their lack of powers and drew a distinction with the *Cimenteries* case (above, n. 40) where although the letter had been signed by the Commissioner for competition it had been considered by the Commissioners acting collegiately.

[65] See, *e.g.* Waelbroeck, *op. cit.*, at p. 212.

Grounds for annulment

(i) *Lack of competence*

9.10   This ground is concerned with the absence or lack of powers. The Community institutions are creatures of the Treaties and if therefore they act outside the powers given thereby their acts are liable to be declared invalid through lack of competence. Further, where powers are given to an institution which purports to delegate them then that delegation must not only be legally possible but also properly executed. The leading case is *Meroni* v. *High Authority*,[66] where the Court of Justice drew the following distinction:

> "The consequences resulting from a delegation of powers are very different depending on whether it involves clearly defined executive powers the exercise of which can, therefore, be subject to strict review in the light of objective criteria determined by the delegating authority, or whether it involves a discretionary power, implying a wide margin of discretion which may according to the use which is made of it make possible the execution of actual economic policy.
>
> A delegation of the first kind cannot appreciably alter the consequences involved in the exercise of the powers concerned, whereas a delegation of the second kind, since it replaces the choices of the delegation by the choices of the delegate, brings about an actual transfer of responsibility."

The Court declared unlawful the purported transfer by the High Authority of certain discretionary power relating to levies of scrap iron to specified organisations based in Brussels.

9.11   On a number of occasions parties have challenged the validity of measures on the basis that they have been taken unlawfully by delegation. In *AKZO*,[67] the Court of Justice upheld the delegation of the power to take decisions under Article 14 of Regulation 17 (to order inspections) to the Commissioner responsible for competition. On the other hand in *PVC*, the Court of First Instance held that it was not legitimate within the Commission's rules of procedure or consistent with the principle of collegiate responsibility for the Commission to delegate authority to one of its members to adopt a decision finding an infringement of Article 85 alone or after his mandate had expired.[68] Further, the Court of Justice has recognised a distinction between the delegation of powers and delegation of signature and acknowledged that delegation of authority to sign is the normal means by which the Commission exercises its powers.[69] Accordingly it has upheld the validity of instruments (such as the statement of objections) signed by officials.[70]

[66] Case 9/56: [1957–58] E.C.R. 133.
[67] Case 5/85, *AKZO Chemie BV and AKZO Chemie U.K. Ltd.* v. *Commission*: [1986] E.C.R. 2585 [1987] 3 C.M.L.R. 716. See, generally, para. 6.46.
[68] Cases T 79, 84–86, 89, 91–92, 94, 96, 98, 102 & 104/89, *BASF A.G. and Others* v. *Commission*: [1992] 4 C.M.L.R. 357 at paras. 51–65.
[69] *Dutch Books*: Cases 43 & 63/82, *VBVB and VBBB* v. *Commission*: [1984] E.C.R. 19, [1985] 1 C.M.L.R. 27. at para. 14.
[70] Cases 48, 49, 51–57/69, *ICI and others* v. *Commission*: [1972] E.C.R. 619, [1972] C.M.L.R. 557.

Perhaps more important in relation to competition cases has been the attempted use of the ground of lack of competence to challenge the Commission's purported extraterritorial application of the competition rules.[71] In *Dyestuffs*,[72] *Continental Can*[73] and *Commercial Solvents*,[74] undertakings which had their seats outside the Community alleged lack of competence on the part of the Commission to apply the competition rules against them. As has already been mentioned, through its development of the enterprise or economic entity concept the Court of Justice ruled that the practices in question had been carried out by the undertakings through the actions of subsidiaries situated in the Community and that therefore they had acted within the Community. The plea of lack of competence was thus rejected.

(ii) *Infringement of an essential procedural requirement*

9.12   Not every procedural irregularity will be sufficient to vitiate a decision. The Court of Justice has classified the Commission's procedure in competition cases as "administrative" and "non-judicial"[75] and, as a general principle of Community law, a person seeking the annulment of an administrative decision on the grounds of procedural irregularity must be able to show at least a possibility that the outcome would have been different but for the irregularity complained of.[76] So in the *AEG* case,[77] whilst the Court accepted that the undertaking's right to be heard had been infringed it did not consider the infringement in question sufficient to vitiate the decision. The ground is nevertheless far from being a dead letter.[78]

9.13   *Consultation and hearings.* Where, for example, the Treaty requires one Community institution to consult with another before taking an act, then failure to do so may violate a procedural requirement and may be attacked under Article 173.[79] In *Quinine*,[80] ACF Chemiefarma challenged the legality of Regulation 99/63, the "hearings" regulation, claiming, *inter alia*, that the draft of Regulation 17 which had been submitted to the Parliament did not provide for power to be conferred on the Commission to make such a regulation. The Court of Justice rejected this argument on the basis that the draft which had been approved by the Parliament contained a provision

---

[71] See paras. 8.01–08. The question of the jurisdictional reach of the competition rules was further considered by the Court in *Wood Pulp*: Cases 89, 104, 114, 116, 117 & 125–129/85, *A Åhlström Oy and Others v. Commission*: [1988] E.C.R. 5193, [1988] 4 C.M.L.R. 901.

[72] Case 48/69, above, n. 70, at para. 142.

[73] Case 6/72, *Europemballage Corporation and Continental Can Co. Inc. v. Commission*: [1973] E.C.R. 215, [1973] C.M.L.R. 199, at para. 14.

[74] Cases 6 & 7/73, *Istituto Chemioterapico Italiano SpA and Commercial Solvents Corp. v. Commission*: [1974] E.C.R. 223, [1974] 1 C.M.L.R. 309, at para. 41.

[75] Cases 56 & 58/64, *Consten Sarl and Grundig-Verkaufs GmbH v. Commission*: [1966] E.C.R. 299, [1966] C.M.L.R. 418, at para. 5.

[76] For a clear statement of this principle, see A.G. Warner in Case 30/78, *Distillers v. Commission*: [1980] E.C.R. 2229, [1980] 3 C.M.L.R. 121.

[77] Case 107/82, *AEG-Telefunken v. Commission*: [1983] E.C.R. 3151, [1984] 3 C.M.L.R. 325.

[78] But see Joshua, "The Right to be heard in EEC Competition Procedures" (15) Fordham Int.L.J 16, at p. 28, where he notes the short shrift given to procedural arguments in some cases by the Court of Justice. He suggests that procedural points may have been perceived by the Court as an attempt to divert attention away from the weakness of the case on the merits.

[79] Art. 43 of the Treaty requires the Council to consult the Parliament before taking certain measures. A regulation may be annulled if this essential formality is disregarded. See Case 138/79, *Maizena Gesellschaft mbH v. Council*: [1980] E.C.R. 3333.

[80] Case 41/69, *ACF Chemiefarma v. Commission*: [1970] E.C.R. 661, at paras. 68 and 69.

substantially identical to Article 24 of Regulation 17. Consultation provisions in Community regulations may similarly have to be respected. It will be remembered that, before taking certain decisions under Regulation 17, the Commission is required to consult the Advisory Committee.[81] Failure to do so would, it is submitted, be an infringement of an essential procedural requirement.[82]

9.14 The procedural requirement in issue need not necessarily be set out in the Treaty or in the express provisions of regulations made thereunder. In *Transocean Marine Paint*,[83] the Court of Justice held that a party may have a right to be heard notwithstanding that the relevant Community legislation does not expressly confer it. The case concerned the attachment of an onerous condition to an exemption under Article 85(3). The Court said:[84]

> "It is clear however both from the nature and objective of the procedure for hearings, and from Articles 5, 6 and 7 of Regulation 99/63, that this Regulation, notwithstanding the cases specifically dealt with in Articles 2 and 4, applies the general rule that a person whose interests are perceptibly affected by a decision taken by a public authority must be given the opportunity to make his point of view known."

The Court found that the views of the undertaking concerned had not been canvassed and concluded that "the condition ... was imposed in breach of procedural requirements."[85] On the other hand in *ANCIDES*, the Court rejected the plea that a third party had not been given a fair hearing because it had not been heard orally. Article 19(1) of Regulation 17 was not concerned with third parties who had to make application under Article 19(2). This the third party had not done. Moreover it had been heard in writing.[86]

9.15 *Lack of reasoning.* Lack of reasoning in a decision may also amount to an infringement of an essential procedural requirement.[87] The statement of reasons required by Article 190 of the Treaty must, as the Court of Justice has said, disclose in a clear and unequivocal fashion the reasoning followed by the Community authority

---

[81] See Arts. 10(3), 15(3) and 16(3) of Reg. 17. But the Committee does not have to be consulted before the (first) decision subjecting a party to a periodic penalty payment. See Cases 46/87 & 227/88, *Hoechst A.G.* v. *Commission*: [1989] E.C.R. 2859, [1991] 4 C.M.L.R. 410. Or a decision under Art. 15(6), see Case T–19/91, *Vichy* v. *Commission*: [1992] II E.C.R. 415.

[82] In the *Quinine* case, above, n. 80, at p. 710, A.G. Gand, with the Advisory Committee specifically in mind, said: "it cannot be excluded that, if a procedural requirement to consult a body is laid down by a provision prior to taking a decision, the omission, or the improper completion, of that formality may in certain cases constitute an infringement of an essential procedural requirement invalidating the decision"—cited by A.G. Warner in *Distillers*, above, n. 76. A.G. Warner also considered that the failure of the Advisory Committee itself to observe procedural requirements might be sufficient to vitiate the Commission's decision. And see paras. 5.27–28.

[83] Case 17/74, *Transocean Marine Paint Association* v. *Commission*: [1974] E.C.R. 1063, [1974] 2 C.M.L.R. 459.

[84] *Ibid.* at para. 15.

[85] *Ibid.* at para. 20.

[86] Case 43/85, *Ancides* v. *Commission*: [1987] E.C.R. 3131, [1988] 4 C.M.L.R. 821, at paras. 7–9.

[87] *Meroni* v. *High Authority*, above, n. 66, at p. 143.

which adopted the measure in question in such a way as to make the persons concerned aware of the reasons[88] for the measure and thus enable them to defend their rights, and to enable the Court to exercise its supervisory jurisdiction.[89] Thus, in *Cimenteries,*[90] the Court held that the act whereby the Commission gave a ruling under Article 15(6) of Regulation 17 constituted a decision within the meaning of Article 190. The Commission had taken the view that no decision was involved. On the facts, the "decision" had taken the form of a letter to the undertakings concerned which briefly identified the relevant restrictions on competition, stated simply that the Commission had subjected the agreement to a provisional examination and concluded that the conditions for the application of Articles 85(1) and 85(3) were not met. Finally it informed the parties that the provision of Article 15(5) of Regulation 17 would cease to apply to the agreement as from the receipt of the letter. The Court had little hesitation in annulling the decision for lack of reasoning. Subsequent decisions under Article 15(6) have been more formal and lengthy and have contained detailed reasoning as to the applicability of Article 85(1) and as to why the application of Article 85(3) is not justified in the circumstances.[91]

9.16 Three points should be noted here. First, as has already been mentioned, Article 85(2) renders void only those parts of the agreement which fall within the prohibition of Article 85(1), provided they are severable from the rest of the agreement. The implications of this for the reasoning in the decision were made clear by the Court of Justice in *Consten & Grundig*:[92]

> "The Commission should, therefore, either have confined itself in the operative part of the contested decision to declaring that the infringement lay in those parts only of the agreement which came within the prohibition, or else it should have set out in the preamble to the decision the reasons why those parts did not appear to it to be severable from the whole agreement."

The Court held that not all the clauses of the exclusive distribution agreement between Consten and Grundig fell within Article 85(1) but only certain clauses when coupled with a further agreement relating to the use of the GINT trade mark. The Court therefore annulled the Commission's decision to this extent.

---

[88] The person concerned must have the necessary information to enable him to decide whether or not the decision is well founded. Case 42/84, *Remia and others* v. *Commission*: [1985] E.C.R. 2545, [1987] 1 C.M.L.R. 1, at para. 26. The adequacy of reasoning in "procedural" decisions (*i.e.* under Arts. 11 and 14 of Reg. 17) is discussed at paras. 3.09 and 3.25–26.

[89] See also Case 258/84, *Nippon Seiko KK* v. *Council*: [1987] E.C.R. 1923, [1989] 2 C.M.L.R. 76, at para. 28.

[90] Cases 8–11/66: [1967] E.C.R. 75, [1967] C.M.L.R. 77, at para. 14. For a further example, see Cases 19–20/74, *Kali und Salz/Kali Chemie* v. *Commission*: [1975] E.C.R. 499, [1975] 2 C.M.L.R. 154.

[91] See paras. 6.12–15.

[92] Cases 56 & 58/64, *Consten Sarl and Grundig-Verkaufs GmbH* v. *Commission*: [1966] E.C.R. 299, [1966] C.M.L.R. 418.

9.17   Second, where a Commission decision breaks new ground, the Court expects more detailed reasoning. In *Papiers Peints*,[93] the Court of Justice said:

> "Although a decision which fits into a well-established line of decisions may be reasoned in a summary manner, for example by a reference to those decisions, if it goes appreciably further than the previous decisions the Commission must give an account of its reasoning."

The Court annulled part of the Commission's decision on the grounds that the Commission had not explained how the restriction in question was liable to affect trade between Member States. Assertions are not sufficient for the requirements of Article 190 of the Treaty. Nor must there be any gaps in the reasoning.

9.17A   Finally it is to be noted that the procedural requirement to state the reasons upon which the Commission's decision is based can be confused with questions of substantive law. In *Polypropylene*, Advocate General Vesterdorf explained the distinction as follows:

> "It is therefore important to stress that the requirement to state reasons, even though its scope is determined by the nature of the case, is purely procedural. So if a statement of reasons is based on an incorrect legal view or a wrong assessment of the evidence, this is not therefore a defect in the statement of reasons but, on the contrary, a defect in the legal and factual assessment on which the decision in the case is based."[94]

9.18   *Failure to adduce evidence.* The Court of Justice has treated failure to adduce sufficient evidence as an infringement of an essential procedural requirement.[95] In *Quinine*,[96] the Court said:

> "The applicant maintains that the Commission has not established its powers through its failure to provide the necessary evidence to prove the existence of the conditions necessary for the application of Article 85. The submission related to the infringement of an essential procedural requirement and not to the powers of the Commission."

---

[93] Case 73/74, *Groupement des Fabricants de Papiers Peints de Belgique and others* v. *Commission*: [1975] E.C.R. 1491, [1976] 1 C.M.L.R. 589, at para. 31. But see *BAT & Reynolds* v. *Commission* (above, n. 56) where the Court sought to distinguish *Papiers Peints*. Although the decisions concerned agreements of a type which the Commission had not dealt with before, they did not lay down new principles but were "limited essentially to an examination of the special features of the agreements in question" (paras. 71–72).

[94] Case T–7/89, *Hercules NV* v. *Commission*: [1992] 4 C.M.L.R. 84, at p. 125.

[95] Equally it may be treated as a defect of substance, as in the *Sugar* case, below, n. 97, at paras. 439–440. See, generally, Lasok, "Judicial Review of Issues of Fact in Competition Cases" [1983] E.C.L.R. 85. Lasok makes the point that errors of fact result in errors of law and it is wrong to assume that error of fact itself constitutes a ground for annulment or that it can be subsumed under one particular ground. And see Joshua, "Proof in Contested EEC Competition Cases" (1987) 12 E.L.Rev. 315.

[96] Case 41/69, above, n. 80, at p. 683. The Court held that there was insufficient proof as regards the application of the "gentleman's agreement" on the system of sales quotas between 1962 and 1965, and on the fixing of prices in relation to the export of quinine to Belgium, Luxembourg and Italy in 1964 and 1965, and therefore annulled the Commission's decision to this extent, reducing the fines accordingly.

An example may serve to show the practical application.

In *Continental Can*,[97] a case before the Merger Control Regulation, the Court of Justice held that if the Commission wished to contend that there is an abuse within the meaning of Article 86 where an undertaking in a dominant position strengthens that position by means of a merger so that actual or potential competition in the relevant products is almost eliminated in a substantial part of the Common Market, then it must give reasons that are sufficient in law to justify it or at least must prove that the competition was so substantially impaired that the remaining competition would not constitute an adequate counterweight. Through Europemballage, its wholly-owned subsidiary, Continental Can had a controlling interest in Schmallbach, a company which the Commission alleged to have a dominant position in Germany in the market for meat and fish tins and for metal caps other than crown corks. The Commission held that Europemballage's acquisition of about 80 per cent. of the shares of Thomassen, the largest producer in the Netherlands of such tins and caps, was an infringement of Article 86. Whilst agreeing with the Commission that Article 86 may be applicable to mergers, the Court quashed the decision because it did not sufficiently explain the facts and appraisals on which it was based. In particular the Commission's decision did not contain data relating to the special characteristics of meat and fish tins and of metal caps (distinguishing crown corks) sufficient to justify the view that they constituted separate markets. The Commission had not shown that competitors making other types of tins could not adapt their production and enter the market, so forming a serious counterweight. The lack of such factual data struck at the basis of any finding that actual or potential competition would be almost eliminated.

(iii) *Infringement of the Treaty or of any rule of law relating to its application*

9.19   This ground may well be wide enough to encompass the other three. The Court has held that lack of reasoning may constitute an infringement of an essential procedural requirement. But a requirement that a decision must state the reasons on which it is based comes direct from a provision of the Treaty, Article 190, and therefore "lack of reasoning" could equally well be classified as an infringement of the Treaty. Similarly, because Community institutions are creatures of the Treaties and their powers are derived from and circumscribed by them, then "lack of competence" and "misuse of power" could also be included under this head. Further, in *Topfer* v. *Commission*,[98] the Court held that a failure to observe a general legal principle which forms part of the Community legal order (*in casu*, the principle of the protection of legitimate expectation) can be treated as an "Infringement of the Treaty or of any rule of law relating to its application". Thus, breach of the "general rule" enunciated in *Transocean*

---

[97] Case 6/72, *Europemballage Corporation and Continental Can Co. Inc.* v. *Commission*: [1973] E.C.R. 215, [1973] C.M.L.R. 199, at paras. 28–37. For other examples: see Case 27/76, *United Brands* v. *Commission*: [1978] E.C.R. 207, [1978] 1 C.M.L.R. 429, at paras. 235–269 relating to the allegation of excessive or unfair pricing; the *Sugar* case: Cases 40–48, 50, 54–56, 111, 113 & 114/73, *Cooperative Vereniging "Suiker Unie" and others* v. *Commission*: [1975] E.C.R. 1663, [1976] 1 C.M.L.R. 295, at paras. 403–420, relating to the allegations against SV and CSM concerning the importation of sugar for the Dutch milk processing industry, and at paras. 494–498, relating to the alleged discrimination by SZV as regards the direct supply of certain large consumers; and *Woodpulp II*: Cases C 89, 104, 114, 116, 117 & 125–129/85, *A Åhlström Osakeyhtio and Others* v. *Commission*: [1993] 4 C.M.L.R. 407, at paras. 66–127 relating to allegation of concertation on announced prices.

[98] Case 112/77: [1978] E.C.R. 1019.

Marine Paint[99] would be likely to come within this ground. "Due process" arguments, it has been said, may be presented either as a procedural irregularity or as a breach of a fundamental rule of law.[1] Failure to comply with the principle of proportionality or with any other general principle of Community law would also appear capable of being subsumed in the concept of infringement of the Treaty.

9.20   There have been a number of cases where the Court of Justice has annulled the Commission's decision because it has disagreed with the Commission's interpretation of the facts or of the law or both. For example, in *General Motors* v. *Commission*,[2] the Court had to consider whether GMC had infringed Article 86 by charging excessive prices in respect of the inspection of vehicles imported into Belgium. The Court said:[3]

> "The applicant has given an adequate explanation of the circumstances in which in order to meet a new responsibility transferred from the State testing-stations to the manufacturers or authorised agents of the different makers of motor car in Belgium, it applied, for an initial period, to European cars a rate which was normally applied to vehicles imported from America. The absence of any abuse is also shown by the fact that very soon afterwards the applicant brought its rates into line with the real economic cost of the operation, that it bore the consequences of doing so by reimbursing those persons who had made complaints to it and that it did so before any intervention on the part of the Commission."

In short, the Court took an entirely different view of the facts and consequently annulled the Commission's decision.

As Advocate General Vesterdorf said in *Polypropylene*:[4]

> "It is important first to point out that the activity of the Court of Justice and thus also that of the Court of First Instance is governed by the principle of the unfettered evaluation of evidence, unconstrained by the various rules laid down in the national legal systems. Apart from the exceptions laid down in the Communities' own legal order, it is only the reliability of the evidence before the Court which is decisive when it comes to its evaluation."

In competition cases documentary evidence is often crucial. Therefore the reliability of records of meetings, notes, etc., has to be carefully examined by the Commission. Evidence has to be marshalled purposefully but objectively. In *Italian Flat Glass*,[5] the Court of First Instance has shown that it is prepared to examine most thoroughly the documentary evidence on which the Commission had based its allegations that three Italian manufacturers had conspired on prices. The Court critically examined that

[99] Above, n. 83.
[1] Joshua, "The Right to be heard in E.E.C. Competition Procedures" [1991–92] Fordham Int. L.J. 16, at p. 27. Characterisation of the ground of annulment is largely an academic exercise and frequently it is unclear on which ground the court is relying.
[2] Case 26/75, [1975] E.C.R. 1367, [1976] 1 C.M.L.R. 95.
[3] *Ibid.* at paras. 21 and 22.
[4] Above, n. 94, at p. 172.
[5] Cases T 68 & 77–78/89, *Società Italiano Vetro SpA and others* v. *Commission*: [1992] II E.C.R. 1403, [1992] 5 C.M.L.R. 302.

evidence and whilst there were some instances where the Court found the Commission had provided proof to the requisite standard, there were other instances where it had not. The Court found defects in the Commission's methodology preparing statistics relevant to the assessment of market shares and in its methodology in the classification of the main customers by category or level.[6] It found instances where the evidence was partial or inaccurate,[7] or was insufficient to support the allegations of consultation.[8] There were also instances where the Commission had failed to analyse correctly the documents in its possession[9] As a result the Court partially annulled the Commission's decision, reducing the fine imposed on two of the undertakings, and cancelling the fine imposed on the third.

9.21 The *Sugar* case,[10] provides a useful example of a decision partially quashed because of an erroneous interpretation of the law. The Commission held that SZV had committed an abuse of its dominant position by requiring wholesalers to purchase from its agents and by not supplying them direct. The Court of Justice said:[11]

> "If the producer avails himself of an agent who is an auxiliary organ forming an integral part of his undertaking, purchases from his representative are in fact direct purchases from his principal. Therefore such conduct can neither be an abuse nor evidence thereof."

The Court clearly held that as a matter of law the conduct complained of by the Commission could not constitute an abuse within the meaning of Article 86.

Another example can be seen in the Court of First Instance's judgment in *La Cinq*.[12] Quashing the Commission's decision refusing La Cinq interim measures, the Court held that the Commission had committed manifest errors of law both in respect of the test it had applied in determining what was necessary to establish a prima facie infringement of Article 85(1)[13] and also what was necessary to show "irreparable damage".[14]

It may not, however, always be easy to discern whether the Court has annulled a decision because of an incorrect or incomplete assessment of the facts or an erroneous interpretation of the law on the part of the Commission.[15]

---

[6] *Ibid.* at paras. 164 and 205.

[7] *Ibid.* at para. 193.

[8] *Ibid.* at paras. 223, 271 and 281.

[9] *Ibid.* at para. 238, error as to attendance of VP director at meeting in Milan.

[10] Above, n. 97.

[11] *Ibid.* at paras. 492 and 493. The allegation that SZV had also abused its dominant position by placing a restriction on its agents not to resell sugar from other sources without consent failed on the facts. The Court took a different view of the circumstances of the relevant market and, in particular, noted the considerable number of persons importing and exporting sugar (see paras. 473–489).

[12] Case T–44/90, *La Cinq SA* v. *Commission*: [1992] II E.C.R. 1, [1992] 4 C.M.L.R. 449.

[13] *Ibid.* at paras. 61 and 62. See generally para. 6.03.

[14] *Ibid.* at paras. 79–83. See generally para. 6.05.

[15] See, for example, Case 77/77, *B.P.* v. *Commission*: [1978] E.C.R. 1513, [1978] 3 C.M.L.R. 174.

(iv) *Misuse of powers*

9.22   The ground is not concerned with the absence of powers but with the exercise of a lawful power for a purpose other than that for which it was conferred. The test is a strict one. A decision is vitiated by a misuse of powers only if it appears, on the basis of objective, relevant and consistent indications, to have been adopted in order to achieve purposes other than those for which it was intended.[16] Hence it is exceptional that the Court will accept this plea.

There have not been any competition cases where the Court has annulled a decision of the Commission on this ground although it has been pleaded on a number of occasions.[17] For example, in the *AKZO* case it was alleged that the contested decision (ordering an inspection under Article 14(3) of Regulation 17) was taken to punish the applicants for disputing the statement of objections in another proceeding.[18]

Remedies

9.23   Article 174 provides that "if the action is well founded, the Court of Justice shall declare the act concerned to be void." It is well established that such annulment need not be total but may, in appropriate circumstances, be partial.[19] Thus, in *Quinine*,[20] where the Commission failed to adduce adequate evidence in respect of part of the alleged infringement, the Court annulled:

> "so much of Article 1 of the decision . . . as records that the applicant applied the clauses of the gentlemen's agreement of 9 April 1960 on the system of quotas and compensation during the period from November 1962 to February 1965, and the fixing of prices and rebates for the export of quinine and quinidine during the period from May 1964 to February 1965."

9.24   The criterion for partial annulment is severability. At a basic level this entails the Court looking to see if the article in question can be separated from the rest of the decision and of considering the consequences of its annulment as regards the remainder. In *Transocean Marine Paint*,[21] for example, the Court of Justice held that a condition attached to an exemption under Article 85(3) had been imposed in breach of a fundamental procedural requirement and said:

> "Notwithstanding the importance of the subject matter of this part of the decision, it is nevertheless capable of being severed, for the time being, from the

---

[16] Case 198/87, *Kerzmann* v. *Court of Auditors*: [1989] E.C.R. 2083. For an example of a case where the Court has annulled a decision on this ground, see Case 105/75, *Giuffrida* v. *Commission*: [1976] E.C.R. 1395.

[17] For example, Cases 6 & 7/73, *Istituto Chemioterapico Italiano SpA and Commercial Solvents Corp.* v. *Commission*: [1974] E.C.R. 223, [1974] 1 C.M.L.R. 309.

[18] Case 5/85, *AKZO Chemie BV and AKZO Chemie U.K. Ltd.* v. *Commission*: [1986] E.C.R. 2585 [1987] 3 C.M.L.R. 716, at paras. 13 and 15.

[19] See, *e.g.* Case 66/63, *Netherlands* v. *High Authority*: [1964] E.C.R. 533, [1964] C.M.L.R. 522.

[20] Above, n. 80, at p. 704. For recent examples of partial annulment, see *Wood Pulp II*: Cases C 89, 104, 114, 116, 117 & 125–129/85, *A Åhlström Osakeyhtio and Others* v. *Commission*: [1993] 4 C.M.L.R. 407 and *Italian Flat Glass*: Cases T 68 & 77–78/89, *Società Italiano Vetro SpA and others* v. *Commission*: [1992] II E.C.R. 1403, [1992] 5 C.M.L.R. 302.

[21] Above, n. 83, at para. 21.

other provisions, and a partial annulment is therefore possible and justified by the fact that, taken as a whole, the decision is favourable to the interests of the undertaking concerned."

Advocate General Warner had pointed out that if it was only possible to declare the whole decision void this "would involve inflicting upon the Association, as a result of its forensic success, an order wholly adverse to its interest." It was therefore both just and practical to annul the offending article in the decision. But, as the Court of First Instance said in *Italian Flat Glass*, although the Court may partially annul the Commission's decision that does not mean it has the jurisdiction to remake the contested decision. So where the Court finds that some conclusions are not proven, it is not open to the Court to carry out a comprehensive reassessment of the evidence and draw fresh conclusions. It can only establish whether the conditions for partial annulment are met. This may be quite a complex task. As the Court of First Instance said:

> "It is thus necessary to determine whether the scope of the operative part of the decision, read in the light of the decision, can be limited *ratione materiae*, *ratione personae* or *ratione temporis* in such a way that its effects are restricted but its substance remains unaltered; whether the proof of the infringement so limited is accompanied by an adequate assessment of the market in the reasoning of the decision; and whether the undertaking or undertakings concerned were given an opportunity of replying effectively to the object so defined."[22]

In the instant case, the Court looked carefully at what was left having discarded those parts of the decision where for one reason or another[23] the Commission's evidence or argument had not reached the requisite legal standard. Having examined the residue from the position of the substance of the infringement (*materiae*), the position of each of the undertakings concerned (*personae*) and the time factor (*temporis*) the Court was left with a decision against two, rather than three, undertakings and a finding of a less serious infringement, and consequently reduced the fine.

9.25 Article 176 provides that "the institution whose act has been declared void . . . shall be required to take the necessary measures to comply with the judgment of the Court." In *Transocean Marine Paint*, the Commission argued that this should be construed as empowering the Court where necessary to refer matters back to the Commission. Advocate General Warner agreed. "Otherwise," he said, "the Court would be powerless to do justice in a case such as this." He thought that it would have been unjust for the Association to have lost its exemption by the Court's declaring the whole decision void, but equally unjust to declare the particular clause in the decision void because, he said, "it is obvious that the Commission must have at least some of the information envisaged in that provision if it is properly to perform its duty under Regulation 17." The Court of Justice also considered that the Commission should be given the opportunity to reach a fresh decision on the point after hearing the observations and suggestions of the undertakings concerned. The case was therefore referred back to the Commission.[24]

---

[22] Cases T 68 & 77–78/89, *Società Italiano Vetro SpA and Others* v. *Commission*: [1992] II E.C.R. 1403, [1992] 5 C.M.L.R. 302, at paras. 319 and 320.

[23] See text to nn. 6–9 above.

[24] *Ibid.* at para. 22.

III. ARTICLE 175—ACTION FOR FAILURE TO ACT

9.26　Whereas Articles 172 and 173 are directed towards challenging the positive acts of the Commission, Article 175 enables action to be taken against the Commission's failure to act.[25] It provides:

> "Should the Council or the Commission, in infringement of this Treaty, fail to act, the Member States and other institutions of the Community may bring an action before the Court of Justice to have the infringement established. The action shall be admissible only if the institution concerned has first been called upon to act. If, within two months of being so called upon, the institution concerned has not defined its position, the action may be brought within a further period of two months.
>
> Any natural or legal person may, under the conditions laid down in the preceding paragraphs, complain to the Court of Justice that an institution of the Community has failed to address to that person any act other than a recommendation or opinion."

Infringement of the Treaty

9.27　The failure to act must involve "an infringement of the Treaty." This would include an infringement of any subordinate legislation made under the Treaty such as a regulation, and therefore Regulation 17. The fact that the failure must involve an infringement implies however that the Commission must be under a specific obligation to act in the circumstances.[26] The Court has held that the general duty imposed on the Commission by Article 155 to ensure that the provisions of the Treaty are applied is insufficient for this purpose.[27] It therefore seems unlikely that the Court would take the view that the duty imposed on the Commission by Article 89 "to ensure the application of the principles laid down in Articles 85 and 86" confers on natural or legal persons an enforceable legal right at large to require the Commission to take certain measures such as a decision to terminate an infringement or grant an exemption. In the *Lord Bethell* case,[28] the Court of Justice held that an individual complainant under Article 89 was not a potential addressee of a legal measure which the Commission has a duty to adopt with regard to him. The Court of Justice has also considered whether certain provisions of Regulation 17 create a sufficient obligation for these purposes. In

---

[25] See, generally, Toth, "The Law as it stands on the Appeal for Failure to Act" [1975] 2 L.I.E.I. 65. And see Waelbroeck, *op. cit.*, at pp. 191–198. The breakdown and discussion of Art. 175 which follows has its emphasis on actions brought by natural or legal persons against the Commission in the context of competition cases.

[26] See A.G. Gand's analysis of the Commission's position under Art. 169 of the Treaty in Case 48/65, *Lutticke* v. *Commission*: [1966] E.C.R. 19, [1966] C.M.L.R. 378.

[27] Case 15/71, *Mackprang* v. *Commission*: [1971] E.C.R. 797, [1972] C.M.L.R. 52.

[28] Case 246/81, *Lord Bethell* v. *Commission*: [1982] E.C.R. 2277, [1982] 3 C.M.L.R. 300, at para. 16. Art. 89 contains no express provision conferring on a complainant an entitlement to demand that the Commission initiate an inquiry into allegations of unlawful agreements, practices, etc., and the Court was not prepared to accept the argument that the entitlement made explicit in Art. 3(2) of Reg. 17 is implicit in Art. 89. But in *Automec II*: Case T–24/90, *Automec Srl* v. *Commission*: [1992] 5 C.M.L.R. 431, the Court of First Instance suggests that Member States may as complainants under Art. 89 be able to oblige the Commission to investigate complaints they refer to it (para. 76).

GEMA v. *Commission*,[29] the Court held that Article 3 which provides that the Commission upon the application, *inter alia*, of "natural or legal" persons "may by decision require" undertakings to terminate infringements of Articles 85 or 86, does not entitle such applicants to require the Commission to take a final decision on the existence of an alleged infringement. The Court of Justice said:[30]

> "In fact the Commission cannot be obliged to continue the proceedings whatever the circumstances up to the stage of a final decision. The interpretation put forward by the applicant would remove all meaning from Article 3 of Regulation 17 which in certain circumstances allows the Commission the opportunity of not adopting a decision to compel the undertakings concerned to put an end to the infringement established."

The Court considered that it followed from "the nature of the procedure to establish an infringement laid down by Article 3" that a complainant was not entitled to demand a final decision on the question of any infringement. It is however clear that Article 6 of Regulation 99/63 requires the Commission to give a complainant a provisional communication of its reasons where there are insufficient grounds for granting its application.[31] If no answer is received within two months, the complainant can bring an action for failure to act.[32]

9.28   *GEMA* is authority for the view that the Commission is not obliged to take a final decision at the request of a complainant under Article 3(2)(b). It would appear from the generality of the statements made by the Court in relation to Article 3 that the Commission is similarly under no obligation *vis-á-vis* the parties to the agreement. It might at first sight seem unlikely that an undertaking would seek to require the Commission to take such a decision, but it is possible, for example, that one party might wish to avoid his obligations under an agreement and so ask the Commission to rule on its legality under Article 85(1).[33] It is more probable that an undertaking might request the Commission to give a negative clearance under Article 2 of Regulation 17 or to grant or renew an exemption under Articles 4, 6 and 8. Here again the language of the relevant Articles uses "may" rather than "shall" and arguably empowers rather than obliges the Commission to take such decisions. Having regard to the approach taken by the Court in GEMA it might seem unlikely that the Court would find that the Commission was under an obligation to take such decisions at the request of the undertakings concerned.[34] But different Articles of Regulation 17 are applicable and different considerations may apply. Parties to an agreement under which, say, ancillary

---

[29] Case 125/78: [1979] E.C.R. 3173, [1980] 2 C.M.L.R. 177.

[30] *Ibid.* at para. 18. Followed by the Court of First Instance in *Automec II*, at para. 76.

[31] See paras. 2.34–37. It is a separate question whether a complainant is entitled to a formal decision rejecting his complaint. See, generally, Dinnage, *op. cit.*, at p. 31, and Temple Lang, *op. cit.*, at pp. 180–182, and note the views of A.G. Warner in Case 792/79R, *Camera Care* v. *Commission*: [1980] E.C.R. 119, [1980] 1 C.M.L.R. 334 and A.G. Mancini in Cases 142 & 156/84, *BAT and Reynolds* v. *Commission*: [1986] E.C.R. 1899, [1987] 2 C.M.L.R. 551.

[32] Case T–28/90, *Asia Motor France* v. *Commission*: [1992] 5 C.M.L.R. 431, at para. 30.

[33] See, *e.g.* the dispute between the parties underlying the Commission's decision in *Quantel International—Continuum/Quantel SA*: [1992] O.J. L235/9.

[34] For a discussion of the question of the possible existence of duties of the Commission to deal with individual requests for favourable rulings, see Temple Lang, "Community Antitrust Law—Compliance and Enforcement" [1981] C.M.L.Rev. 335, at pp. 343–350.

restraints relating to valuable know-how are accepted, and who may need to know their legal position with certainty should, if they are prepared to come openly to the Commission and to notify their agreement, be entitled to a decision on the matter.[35] (Remember that there is no provisional validity for new agreements.) Similarly, where a notified agreement is the subject of proceedings in a national court and the judge is required to apply Article 85(1) but cannot apply Article 85(3), it is at least arguable that the parties to the agreement should be entitled to a ruling from the Commission on the question of Article 85(3). This might be critical in relation to the enforceability of the agreement and also might, for example, constitute a defence to an action for damages brought by a third party, or, possibly, to proceedings under national competition law. Certainly the Court of First Instance appears to be prepared to move in this direction. In *Automec II*, the Court of First Instance thought that where the subject matter of the complaint was within the Commission's exclusive remit (*e.g.* the withdrawal of an exemption) the Commission could be compelled to pursue the complaint.[36] As regards individual decisions of exemption under Article 85(3) the Commission, in its recent Notice on co-operation between national courts and the Commission in applying Articles 85 and 86, has implicitly accepted an obligation to give a decision in application of Article 85(3) where this is necessary for the proceedings before the national court.[37]

Addressed to the applicant

9.29 The third paragraph of Article 175 (quoted above) requires that the Commission must have failed to address to the potential applicant the act in question. Whereas under Article 173 a person may institute proceedings "against a decision which, although in the form of a regulation or a decision addressed to another person, is of direct and individual concern to the former" it is most probably the position that under Article 175 a person cannot initiate proceedings for a failure to take an act which, whilst of direct and individual concern to it within the meaning of Article 173, would not if taken be addressed to it.[38] This lack of parallelism has been noted by the Court of First Instance.[39] A complainant may therefore commence proceedings under Article 173 in respect of the Commission's final decision as in *Metro*,[40] but cannot take proceedings under Article 175 for the failure to take a final decision on the alleged infringement because even if there was an obligation on the Commission to take such a decision, it would not be one addressed to the complainant. So, for example, in the *Lord Bethell* case, Lord Bethell could not complain under Article 175 that the Commission had failed to find an infringement of the competition rules by the airlines because any such finding would be addressed to the airlines, and not to him.[41] Similarly

---

[35] Note that in Case 85/76, *Hoffmann-La Roche* v. *Commission*: [1979] E.C.R. 461, [1979] 3 C.M.L.R. 211, the Court said that had Roche wanted to know its position under Arts. 85 and 86 it should have made an application to the Commission under Art. 2 of Reg. 17 (negative clearance). See paras. 129–134.

[36] Above, n. 28, at para. 76.

[37] [1993] O.J. C39/6, at para. 30: "if it takes the view that individual exemption is possible, the national court should suspend the proceedings while awaiting the Commission's decision."

[38] *Mackprang*, above, n. 27 and see the opinion of A.G. Capotorti in *GEMA*, above, n. 29.

[39] Case T–3/90, *Vereniging Prodifarma* v. *Commission*: [1991] II E.C.R. 1, at para. 39.

[40] Case 26/76: [1977] E.C.R. 1875, [1978] 2 C.M.L.R. 1.

[41] See the opinion of A.G. Slynn, above, n. 28.

in *Prodifarma II*, the Court of First Instance held that a complainant could not use Article 175 to compel the Commission to take a decision under Article 15(6) of Regulation 17, removing the immunity from fine of a notified agreement, because a decision under Article 15(6) is not addressed to the complainant but only the parties to the agreement in question.[42] The Court went on to say that even if Article 175 could extend to acts which were of direct and individual concern to the complainant, this would not assist a complainant because in relation to Article 15(6) the complainant's interest is only an indirect one and complainants have no legitimate interest in having the benefit of the immunity from fine withdrawn from the parties to the agreement.[43] This is remarkably formalistic given, in practice, the deterrent effect of Article 15(6).

Acts

9.30   The Commission must have failed to address to the applicant an "act" other than a recommendation or an opinion. The only measure under Article 189 which can be addressed to a private party other than a recommendation or an opinion is a decision, regulations and directives being measures of general application. It is, however, arguable that "act" within Article 175 is not restricted in meaning to decisions under Article 189 but is wider and includes other measures which have legal effects as between the Commission and the person to whom the measure is addressed. In *GEMA*,[44] Advocate General Capotorti took the view that the term "act" should be interpreted widely to include "measures which cannot be identified with the formal structure of a decision."[45] He gave as examples the measure whereby the Commission permits persons having an interest to be heard under Article 19(2) of Regulation 17 and Article 5 of Regulation 99/63, permits persons to supplement their written observations orally under Article 7 of Regulation 99/63, summons persons to be heard on a certain date under Article 8 of Regulation 99/63 and communicates information to a complainant under Article 6 of Regulation 99/63. In *Asia Motor France*, the Court of First Instance proceeded on the basis that the provisional communication from the Commission to the complainant under Article 6 of Regulation 99/63 is an act for the purpose of Article 175(3).[46]

---

[42] Above, at paras. 35–37.

[43] *Ibid.* at paras. 42 and 43.

[44] Above, n. 29.

[45] A.G. Capotorti thought a wide interpretation was justifiable on "both lexicographical and logical grounds." He said: "From the literal point of view it is significant that the Treaty prefers this word to the technical expression 'decision' which has a clear position in the system of sources of law. It is indeed reasonable to suppose that, if the Community legislature had wished to permit individuals to initiate proceedings on grounds of failure to act in relation to decisions only it would have used the appropriate technical expression and not a word like 'act' bearing a number of meanings. From a logical point of view, then, it appears to me important that in the first paragraph of Article 175 the omission of the Council or of the Commission is described in words having a wide meaning ('should the Council or the Commission, in infringement of the Treaty, fail to act . . .'). In its turn the request which, pursuant to the second paragraph, must be addressed to the institution in question is described as a request 'to act', not 'to decide'."

[46] Above, n. 32, at para. 29.

Request to act

9.31   The Commission must be called upon to act. The potential applicant should put the Commission on notice by clearly indicating the act which it requires the Commission to take and by informing the Commission of its intention to commence proceedings under Article 175 if the Commission fails to act as requested. The Commission then has two months in which to act or define its position. If the Commission acts as requested within the two months then, as there is no "failure", there is no cause of action under Article 175. If the Commission acts outside the two-month period and after the application has been commenced under Article 175, the Court may decline to give a ruling but require the Commission to pay the applicant's costs.[47] If the Commission defines its position within the two months, then any action under Article 175 would be inadmissible. If the Commission defines its position (other than by a formal act) outside the two months the action under Article 175 is still admissible[48] and, it is submitted, the Court may rule on the failure to act. But where the Commission has not merely defined its position but taken all such procedural steps which in effect conclude the proceedings *vis-á-vis* the applicant in the Article 175 proceedings (and that conclusion is itself amenable to judicial review, *e.g.* under Article 173) those proceedings become devoid of purpose and a ruling from the Court is unnecessary.[49]

Definition of position

9.32   Following the party's request to act, the Commission has two months in which to act or define its position. It is not sufficient for the Commission merely to say that it is considering or looking into the matter. The definition of its position requires it to act or to take a view on the act requested to be taken. Thus, for example, in *GEMA*, GEMA, the German performing right society, had complained to the Commission in 1971 about an alleged abuse of a dominant position by Radio Luxembourg in connection with certain contracts which the latter, through its subsidiaries, had made with music publishers and which had the result of giving it an excessive share of the royalties distributed through GEMA. The Commission investigated the complaint and in 1974 issued a statement of objections and heard the undertakings concerned. GEMA was not informed of any outcome and in 1978 called upon the Commission to adopt "a formal decision in the inquiry into the proceedings" within two months failing which it would commence proceedings under Article 175. The Commission replied by letter within two months and expressed the view that on the basis of the most recent information in its possession a decision by way of Article 86 would not be justified and set out in detail the facts and the reasons for such views. In accordance with Article 6 of Regulation 99/63 the Commission gave GEMA the opportunity to submit any further comments within two months. The Court of Justice held that a complainant under Article 3 of Regulation 17 was not entitled to have the Commission take a final decision on the existence of the alleged infringement but was, under Article 6, entitled to

---

[47] Case 75/69, *Ernest Hake & Co.* v. *Commission*: [1970] E.C.R. 535, [1970] C.M.L.R. 426.
[48] Cases 7 & 9/54, *Groupement des Industries Sidèrurgiques Luxembourgeoises* v. *High Authority*: [1954–56] E.C.R. 175.
[49] *Asia Motor France*, above, n. 32, where a complainant had brought proceedings under Art. 175 to get a reaction from the Commission but in the meantime the Commission had fulfilled its obligations under Art. 6 of Reg. 99/63 and made a final decision rejecting complaint.

be informed by the Commission "that on the basis of the information in its possession there are insufficient grounds for granting the application." The Commission had done this in its letter in reply to GEMA's request to act and therefore had "addressed to the applicant an act which constitutes a definition of its position within the meaning of the second paragraph of Article 175 of the Treaty."[50]

9.33   The fact that the Commission has taken a measure different from that desired or considered necessary by the person concerned does not mean necessarily that there has been a failure to act or to take a position. In *Deutscher Komponistenverband* v. *Commission*,[51] the German Composers' Association requested that it be heard in the proceedings taken by the Commission against GEMA,[52] arguing that it was a legal person having a "sufficient" interest within the meaning of Article 19(2) of Regulation 17 and Article 5 of Regulation 99/63. When the Association insisted on being heard orally, the Commission replied that, without prejudice to the question whether it was a person having a sufficient interest within the above-mentioned provisions, it could have the opportunity to make known its views in writing. The period for submitting such written observations was in fact extended by the Commission on two occasions. The Court of Justice said:[53]

> "It is clear from the context [of Article 175], especially from the first paragraph, that by its use of the phrase 'has failed to address to that person any act', the Article refers to failure to act in the sense of failure to take a decision or to define a position, and not the adoption of a measure different from that desired or considered necessary by the persons concerned."

The Court considered that the Commission had acted under Article 5 of Regulation 99/63 on the subject of the hearings provided for in Article 19 of Regulation 17 and in the circumstances had not refrained from acting when called upon to do so.

9.34   It appears that the "definition of position" does not necessarily have to take the form of an act which is binding on the Commission and which would therefore be capable of annulment on application under Article 173.[54] It may simply involve the taking of a view or attitude by the Commission. For example, in *Lutticke* v. *Commission*,[55] the applicant had requested the Commission to institute infraction proceedings under Article 169 against Germany in relation to its imposition of a turnover equalisation tax on dairy products which was alleged by the applicant to be contrary to Article 95 of the Treaty. The Commission replied that in its opinion there was no infringement of

---

[50] Above, n. 29, at para. 21.
[51] Case 8/71: [1971] E.C.R. 705, [1973] C.M.L.R. 902.
[52] See the Commission's decisions in *GEMA*: [1971] J.O. L134/15, [1971] C.M.L.R. D35, and [1972] J.O. L166/22, [1972] C.M.L.R. D115.
[53] Above, at para. 2.
[54] *Lutticke*, above, n. 28; Case 42/71, *Firma Nordgetreide* v. *Commission*: [1972] E.C.R. 105, [1973] C.M.L.R. 177. And see A.G. Slynn in Case 64/82, *Tradax* v. *Commission*: [1984] E.C.R. 1359.
[55] Above, n. 28.

Article 95 on the part of Germany justifying such proceedings. The applicant commenced proceedings under both Articles 173 and 175. The Court of Justice held that the Commission's reply constituted a definition of position sufficient for the purposes of Article 175 although it was not a measure having binding force which could be the subject of annulment under Article 173. Both applications (Articles 173 and 175) were therefore rejected. Where therefore the measure taken to "define a position" is not an "act" capable of annulment under Article 173, the person concerned may find itself without an effective remedy under either Article 173 or 175 in respect of the Commission's conduct.[56] The request made under Article 175 will not *ex hypothesi* have produced the act desired and yet the position taken by the Commission whilst sufficient to render any application under Article 175 inadmissible may not constitute an act capable of being the subject of an action for annulment under Article 173.[57]

Remedy

9.35   Article 176 provides that:

> "the institution . . . whose failure to act has been declared contrary to this Treaty shall be required to take the necessary measures to comply with the judgment of the Court of Justice."

The essence of the Court's judgment is a declaration that the Commission has failed to act and that such failure constitutes an infringement of the Treaty.[58] The Court does not order the Commission to take the necessary measures to rectify that infringement nor can it take such measures itself. Article 176 itself requires the Commission to take the necessary measures to make good the infringement and the way will in effect be shown by the Court in its judgment when by defining the Commission's failure it indicates what should have been done.[59] A failure to take such necessary measures may give grounds for a further action under Article 175.[60]

---

[56] In *Camera Care* (Case 792/79R) A.G. Warner stated clearly that an aggrieved person should not find himself in the predicament of being denied both remedies.

[57] Toth (*op. cit.*, at p. 83) is critical of this possible gap in the system of remedies contained in the EEC (and Euratom) Treaty (The position is different in the ECSC Treaty where the actions for annulment and failure to act completely dovetail.) He suggests that the defect could be corrected by the Court simply construing "definition of position" as meaning definition of position by a formal (*i.e.* binding) act which would be subject to annulment proceedings in the usual way under Art. 173. See also Waelbroeck, *op. cit.* and Shaw, "Competition complainants: a comprehensive system of remedies?" (1993) 18 E.L. Rev. 427.

[58] In *Deutscher Komponistenverband*, above, n. 119, A.G. Roemer said (at p. 714): "Article 175 of the EEC Treaty is concerned with an action to obtain a declaration." *Cf.* the position under the ECSC Treaty where the Court's judgment annuls the implied decision of refusal.

[59] A.G. Roemer, *ibid.* at p. 715, said: "in the event of the action's being well-founded a ruling to the effect that the Commission has infringed the Treaty would mean that the measures to be taken by the Commission in accordance with Article 176 would thus be unequivocally discerned in the judgment; the result attained in practice would therefore be equivalent to a direct order to perform a specific action."

[60] The necessary procedure (*i.e.* the request to act, etc.) would, of course, have to be followed.

Interventions

9.36   Article 37 of the Statute of the Court enables Member States and the institutions of the Communities to intervene in cases before the Court.[61] The same right is granted to "any other person establishing an interest in the result of any case."[62] The existence of such an interest must be assessed in relation to the particular action.[63] The submissions contained in the application to intervene must be limited to supporting the case of one of the parties.[64] The procedure for intervention involves two separate stages: the first deals with the obtaining of an order from the Court on the question of the admissibility of the intervention,[65] the second deals with the position of the intervener once the intervention has been allowed. An application to intervene must be made within three months of the appearance in the *Official Journal* of the notice relating to the case.[66]

---

[61] The right of a Member State to intervene should not be confused with its right (under Art. 20 of the Protocol) to make observations in references for preliminary rulings under Art. 177. The U.K. intervened, for example, in *A.M. & S.* (Case 155/79: [1982] E.C.R. 1575, [1982] 2 C.M.L.R. 264). It has submitted observations in a number of competition cases including the *Perfumes* cases (Cases 253/78, 1–3, 37 & 99/79: [1980] E.C.R. 2327, [1980] E.C.R. 2481, [1980] E.C.R. 2511, [1981] 2 C.M.L.R. 99, [1981] 2 C.M.L.R. 143, [1981] 2 C.M.L.R. 164); *Woodpulp* (Cases C 89, 104, 114, 116, 117 & 125–129/85, *A Åhlström Osakeyhtio and Others* v. *Commission*: [1993] 4 C.M.L.R. 407) and *Italian Flat Glass* (Cases T 68 & 77–78/89, *Società Italiano Vetro SpA and Others* v. *Commission*: [1992] II E.C.R. 1403, [1992] 5 C.M.L.R. 302). See, generally, Everling, "The Member States of the European Community before their Court of Justice" (1984) 9 E.L.Rev. 215.

[62] Whilst a Member State or Community institution is presumed to have a legitimate interest in intervening, any other person must give reasons for and establish its interest—see examples in nn. 67–72, below. The right of a third party to intervene cannot be exercised in cases between Member States, between institutions of the Community or between Member States and institutions of the Community: Art. 37 of the Protocol. See, *e.g.* Case 154/85R, *Commission* v. *Italy*: [1986] 2 C.M.L.R. 159. On the question of the third party being a "person", the Court held in the *Sugar* case, admitting the intervention of an Italian consumers association, that "bodies which do not enjoy personality may be admitted as intervening parties so long as they possess those characteristics which constitute the basis for such personality, particularly a degree of autonomy and of responsibility for their actions, even if to a limited extent"—see Cases 41, 43–48, 111, 113–114/73, *Société Générale Sucrière*: [1973] E.C.R. 1465, [1974] 1 C.M.L.R. 215, at para. 2.

[63] See Cases 197–200, 243, 245 & 247/80, *Ludwigshafener Waltzmuhle Erlenz KG* v. *EEC*: [1981] E.C.R. 3211, where the Court of Justice refused to admit the intervention of a trade union in an action brought by certain firms to recover losses from the Community's having fixed an inappropriate price for durum wheat. The union had, the Court said, no specific interest, only an indirect and remote one—if the proceedings were successful that would affect the wellbeing of the firms and therefore the number of persons employed. *Cf.* the approach of the Commission in *B.P./TGWU—Llandarcy Refinery*: Sixteenth Report on Competition Policy, at point 43.

[64] Art. 37 of the Protocol. See Case 71/74R, *Frubo* v. *Commission*, below, n. 67, at paras. 7 and 8.

[65] A potential intervener should show that he has an interest not in relation to the submissions or arguments of the parties but in relation to the conclusions advocated, *i.e.* the interest must relate to the operative part of the final judgment which the parties ask the Court to deliver—see Case 111/63, *Lemmerz-Werke*: [1965] E.C.R. 677, [1968] C.M.L.R. 280, and Cases 116, 124 & 143/77, *Amylum NV and others* v. *Council and Commission*: [1978] E.C.R. 893. To what extent this applies in cases of "representative" interveners, e.g. as in the *Sugar* case: Cases 40–48, 50, 54–56, 111, 113 & 114/73, *Cooperatieve Vereniging "Suiker Unie" and others* v. *Commission*: [1975] E.C.R. 1663, [1976] 1 C.M.L.R. 295, is uncertain.

[66] Art. 93(1) of the Rules. The notice in the *Official Journal* is that required by Art. 16(6) of the Rules.

9.37 Interventions, other than by Member States or Community institutions, have been made in a number of competition cases. In *Frubo*,[67] for example, the Court of Justice allowed the intervention of an independent Dutch fruit importer whose business, it argued, was likely to suffer serious damage by the continuance (even if only temporary) of the agreement between the Dutch Fruit Importers Association and the Dutch Fruit Wholesalers Association which the Commission had found to infringe Article 85(1) and to be unsuitable for exemption under Article 85(3). Complainants and parties complained of have been admitted as interveners. Thus in *Commercial Solvents*,[68] the complainant was allowed to intervene where the Commission's decision had upheld the complaint and ordered resupplies to be made to it and in *Camera Care*,[69] intervention by the party the subject of the complaint was admitted where the complainant challenged the Commission's refusal or failure to act on the complaint. In *Consten & Grundig*,[70] the Court allowed two firms being sued by Consten in the French courts for unfair competition and trade mark infringement to intervene in Consten's appeal against the Commission's decision finding infringements of Article 85(1) relating to the sole agency agreement and trade mark licence which formed the basis of the actions in the national courts.

In all the examples given above the intervener's interest in the outcome of the proceedings before the Court is readily apparent. The Court of Justice has, however, admitted parties with a less immediate interest. So in a number of cases it has allowed representative bodies to intervene. In *Sugar*,[71] an Italian association which had the object of representing and protecting the interests of consumers was admitted as intervener because it had an interest "in the correct application of the Community provision" and in the solution of the case in so far as it involved a concerted practice which had the object or effect of protecting the Italian market. In *A.M. & S. Europe Ltd.* v. *Commission*,[72] concerning the verification of legally privileged documents during Commission investigations under Article 14 of Regulation 17, the Court allowed the intervention of the C.C.B.E. acting in effect on behalf of the legal profession in the Community. In the *Ford* case, the Court allowed an intervention by the BEUC, an organisation representing consumers, whilst refusing two British Ford distributors who in the Court's view did not have "a sufficiently defined interest."[73] More recently the Court of First Instance permitted BEUC to intervene in *Automobiles Peugeot* v. *Commission*.[74]

---

[67] Case 71/74, *Nederlandse Vereniging voor de Fruit en Groentenimporthandel and Frubo* v. *Commission*: [1974] E.C.R. 1031, [1975] 1 C.M.L.R. 646. The Court then proceeded to suspend the decision under Art. 185. See para. 9.40.

[68] Cases 6 & 7/73, *Istituto Chemioterapico Italiano SpA and Commercial Solvents Corp.* v. *Commission*: [1974] E.C.R. 223, [1974] 1 C.M.L.R. 309.

[69] Case 792/79R: [1980] E.C.R. 119, [1980] 1 C.M.L.R. 334.

[70] Cases 56 & 58/64, *Consten Sárl and Grundig-Verkaufs GmbH* v. *Commission*: [1966] E.C.R. 299, [1966] C.M.L.R. 418.

[71] Above, n. 65, at paras. 3 and 4.

[72] Case 155/79, above, n. 61. A note in the Law Society's Gazette (for June 25, 1980, at p. 644) states: "The CCBE has intervened because the result of this case will have a direct bearing on the rights and duties of individual lawyers throughout the Community, as well as upon the definition, interpretation, application and enforcement of the rules of professional conduct by the CCBE and the national professional authorities." Legal professional privilege is discussed at paras. 8.13–17.

[73] See Leaver, "The Ford case: The Right of Intervention" (1982) Law Soc.Gaz. 1557.

[74] Case T–23/90, *Automobiles Peugeot SA* v. *Commission*: not yet reported.

Interim relief

9.38 Article 185 of the Treaty provides that "actions brought before the Court of Justice shall not have suspensory effect." Thus where, for example, a decision of the Commission is challenged under Article 172 or 173, the application does not operate automatically to stay the operation and effect of the decision in question. The Court has a discretion in such circumstances. Article 185 goes on to say: "The Court of Justice may, however, if it considers that circumstances so require, order that application of the contested act be suspended." Article 186 is also relevant in this context. It provides: "The Court of Justice may in any cases before it prescribe any necessary interim measures." It is thus for the Court to determine what "circumstances so require" (Article 185) and what interim measures are "necessary" (Article 186), and whilst it is apparent from the Court's decisions and practice in relation to interim measures that certain general criteria must be satisfied, the major factor influencing the Court's decision on the award of interim measures under Articles 185 and 186 may be the type of case involved. Perhaps surprisingly, the chances of success in competition cases are, at least statistically, quite good.[75]

Basic requirements and criteria

9.39 It is important to note at the outset that an application under Article 185 or 186 cannot be made unless there is a main action in existence before the Court. This is an important procedural requirement which cannot be neglected even, for example, in cases involving procedural decisions where the inspectors might be standing on the doorstep! If the main action is itself inadmissible the application for interim relief must also fail.[75a] The application for interim relief must, as Article 83(2) of the Rules provides, "state the subject matter of the dispute, the circumstances giving rise to urgency and the factual and legal grounds establishing a prima facie case for the interim measures applied for." This points to the criteria which the Court has applied in relation to the granting of interim relief. In *IBM*, the President of the Court said:[76]

> "It is clear from the consistent case law of the Court that measures cannot be considered unless the factual and legal grounds relied on to obtain them establish a prima facie case for granting them. In addition there must be urgency in the sense that it is necessary for the measures to be issued and to take effect before the decision of the Court on the substance of the case in order to avoid serious and irreparable damage to the party seeking them; finally they must be provisional in the sense that they do not prejudice the decision on the substance of the case."

[75] See, generally, Gray, "Interim Measures of Protection in the European Court" (1979) 4 E.L.Rev. 80, 102, Borchardt, "The Award of Interim Measures by the European Court of Justice" (1985) 22 C.M.L.Rev. 203; Oliver, "Interim Measures: Some recent developments" [1992] 29 C.M.L.Rev. 7 and Lasok, *op. cit.*, Chap. 8.
[75a] Case 117/91R, *Jean-Marc Bosman* v. *Commission*: order of the Court of Justice, June 27, 1991.
[76] Cases 60 & 190/81R, *International Business Machines Corp.* v. *Commission*: [1981] E.C.R. 1857, [1981] 3 C.M.L.R. 93, at para. 4.

Failure to satisfy any of these requirements, and in particular urgency, may result in the Court's refusal to grant the relief sought. A party requesting the suspension of the operation of a contested decision of the Commission must therefore adduce evidence to show that it cannot await the outcome of the proceedings without having to sustain personally damage which would result in serious and irreparable consequences for it.[77] The Court will balance the relevant interests, *i.e.* balance those to be protected by the measures requested and the interest of the Commission in attaining the aims of its measures which are at issue in the proceedings.[78]

Article 185

9.40 Whilst it has acknowledged that it will grant a stay of execution under Article 185 only in exceptional circumstances,[79] the Court of Justice has in fact ordered the suspension[80] of the Commission's decision in a number of competition cases. For example, in the *United Brands* case,[81] the Court suspended the operation of those parts of the Commission's decision requiring United Brands to refrain from charging discriminatory and unfair prices and from prohibiting the resale of green bananas. The Court may have been impressed by the argument that United Brands would suffer serious financial damage if it had to comply with the first provision and the fact that it had voluntarily given up the second. Moreover, the Commission did not object to the measures requested. In the *Magill*[82] case, the Court suspended part of the Commission's decision which would have required the broadcasters to grant compulsory licences of their programme schedules, recognising that the case raised delicate questions concerning the scope of Article 86 and to allow the Commission's decision to be enforced would lead to developments in the market which would be difficult, if not impossible, to reverse. But that part of the decision which required the parties to discuss with the Commission the conditions under which licences should be granted to third parties remained.

In the *Net Book Agreements* case,[83] the Court again suspended part of the Commission's decision which would have required substantial amendments to the agreements in question. The Court recognised that the changes which the decision would bring about in a marketing system as extensive and complex as the "net book" system on the U.K. and Irish markets might cause serious and irreparable damages to the operators concerned. On the other hand, in *AKZO*,[84] the Court did not accept that the applicant would suffer serious and irreparable damage, by loss of business, if it complied with

---

[77] Case 111/88R, *Greece* v. *Commission*: [1989] 3 C.M.L.R. 454, at para. 15.

[78] Case 246/89R, *Commission* v. *U.K.*: [1989] 3 C.M.L.R. 601, at para. 39. See, *e.g.* Case 56/89R, *Publishers Association* v. *Commission* [1989] 4 C.M.L.R. 816, at para. 35.

[79] Case 45/71R, *GEMA* v. *Commission*: [1971] E.C.R. 791, [1972] 1 C.M.L.R. 694, and see also Case 20/74R, *Kali Chemie AG* v. *Commission*: [1974] E.C.R. 337, 387.

[80] In practice, only parts of the challenged decision may need to be suspended.

[81] Case 27/76R: [1976] E.C.R. 425, [1976] 2 C.M.L.R. 147.

[82] Cases 76–77 & 91/89R, *Radio Telefis Eireann and Others* v. *Commission*: [1989] 4 C.M.L.R. 749.

[83] Above, n. 78. See also *Dutch Books*: Cases 43 & 63/82R, *VBVB and VBBB* v. *Commission*: [1982] E.C.R. 1241.

[84] Case 62/86R, *AKZO Chemie BV* v. *Commission*: [1987] 1 C.M.L.R. 225. Contrast the *FEDETAB* case: Cases 209–215 & 218–78R, *Heintz van Landewyck and Others* v. *Commission*: [1978] E.C.R. 2111, when the Court granted relief recognising the possibility that certain traders would be driven out of the market.

the prohibition in the challenged decision not to reduce its prices ad hoc where it was competing with the complainant.

In *Peugeot*,[85] the Court of First Instance refused to order the suspension of the Commission's interim order requiring in effect supplies of cars to remain available for purchase by Eco-system for its customers. The Court looked at the respective volumes of transactions of the two parties and concluded that these did not show a risk of destroying the Peugeot network. Nor did the Court find sufficient evidence that Peugeot's brand image would be seriously and irreparably harmed. Finally it should be noted that in *Frubo*,[86] the Court of Justice said:

> "It is outside the jurisdiction of the Court, within the context of an interim procedure, to substitute its own appraisal for that of the Commission and render provisionally valid an agreement which has been annulled on the basis of Article 85(1) with the consequences prescribed by Article 85(2)."

The Court proceeded to order the suspension of the operation of the Commission's decision but expressly forbade the parties to enforce certain clauses under which penalties might be imposed on parties to the agreement.[87]

9.41   An application for suspension under Article 185 may relate to procedural decisions as well as substantive decisions. In the *Brescia* case,[88] the applicant sought the suspension of the decision ordering an investigation under Article 47 of the ECSC Treaty pending the determination of the validity of the decision by the Court in the main action. The Court of Justice refused the application on the basis that the applicant had failed to show that serious damage could result. It rejected the argument that once the information was obtained under the decision, the application for annulment would become purposeless.

Similarly in *Hoechst*,[89] the Court of First Instance refused to suspend a decision of the Commission under Article 14(3) of Regulation 17 ordering an investigation and imposing a periodical penalty payment of 2,000 ECUs per day. Hoechst claimed that the decision under Article 14(3) was not only illegal but manifestly unconstitutional on the ground that it violated a fundamental right which was part of the general principles of law, namely the inviolability of its premises. The Court refused to consider this plea in the context of an application for interim relief on the grounds that to address the problems which the applicant raised in the context of the summary proceeding would be tantamount to prejudicing the main issue in the case. Looking at whether Hoechst had shown necessity and urgency of its application the Court concluded that there would be no irreparable damage if the investigation was carried out. If the Commission's decision under Article 14(3) was ultimately found to be unlawful the Commission would be prevented from using all the papers etc which it may have

---

[85] Case T–23/90R, *Automobiles Peugeot SA* v. *Commission*: [1990] 4 C.M.L.R. 674.
[86] Above, n. 67, at para. 5, and see *FEDETAB*, above, at para. 5.
[87] For other examples of reservations on clauses relating to penalties or exclusions, see *FEDETAB*, above, and *VBVB*, above.
[88] Case 31/59R, *Acciaieria e Tubificio di Brescia* v. *High Authority*: [1960] E.C.R. 98.
[89] Case 46/87R, *Hoechst AG* v. *Commission*: [1988] 4 C.M.L.R. 43. See also Case 87/87R, *Dow Chemical* v. *Commission*: [1988] 4 C.M.L.R. 439 where the Court of First Instance adopted a similar approach to the request for suspension of the Commission's investigation decision.

obtained in the course of the investigation on pain of exposing itself to risk of annulment of the decision concerning infringement insofar as it might be based on such
evidence.[90] As regards the periodical penalty payment the Court had substantial
doubts as to whether the potential sum of the penalty could be regarded as serious
when regard was had to the size and turnover of a company like Hoechst. Moreover
the Commission would have to return to the amount of the penalty if the decision was
later annulled by the Court in the main action. In these circumstances, the Court said,
such damage was not irreparable.[91]

Article 186

9.42   In application of Article 186, the Court has made orders in connection with the
competition rules of the ECSC and in relation to Articles 85 and 86. In *Miles Druce
and Co. Ltd.* v. *Commission*,[92] the Court of Justice, on the application of Miles Druce,
the subject of a takeover bid from GKN, ordered the Commission to take all necessary
measures to ensure neutral behaviour on the part of those concerned in the bid and that
no prejudicial action be taken. Whilst the Court had previously[93] considered that
GKN's undertaking and the Commission's declaration to the same effect were sufficient to eliminate the criterion of urgency, the Court changed its view on the second
application stressing that it was important that no change should take place in the status quo and no irreparable harm should be done. The Court in *National Carbonising
Co. Ltd.* v. *Commission*[94] and later in *Camera Care*[95] has refused to grant interim relief
itself to the applicant and held that the Commission has, in the first case, power under
the ECSC Treaty and, in the second, power by virtue of Article 3 of Regulation 17, to
take necessary interim measures to preserve the status quo and to ensure the effectiveness of any final decisions required to terminate any infringements of the competition
rules in the two Treaties. The practical implications of the Court's decision in *Camera
Care* are discussed in Chapter 6 under the heading "Interim Measures".
   Where the Commission has itself refused interim measures the Court cannot itself
give interim relief without first having declared void the act embodying the Commission's refusal. The Court cannot take over the Commission's role under the Treaty and
the relevant implementory regulations.[96]

Third parties

9.43   A third party (such as, for example, a complainant) may apply for interim relief under Article 185 or 186 as appropriate provided, of course, he is a party to the litigation. For example, in the *Metro* case,[97] the complainant having made an application
under Article 173 challenging the Commission's decision granting exemption under
Article 85(3) to SABA's distribution system, applied to the Court under Article 185

[90] *Ibid.* at para. 34
[91] *Ibid.* at para. 35
[92] Cases 160, 161 & 170/73RII: [1974] E.C.R. 281, [1974] 2 C.M.L.R. D22.
[93] Cases 160 & 161/73R: [1973] E.C.R. 1049, [1974] 1 C.M.L.R. 224.
[94] Case 109/75R: [1975] E.C.R. 1193, [1975] 2 C.M.L.R. 457.
[95] Case 792/79R: [1980] E.C.R. 119, [1980] 1 C.M.L.R. 334.
[96] Case T–131/89R, *Cosimex GmbH* v. *Commission*: [1992] 4 C.M.L.R. 395.
[97] Case 26/76R: [1976] E.C.R. 1353.

for the Commission's decision to be suspended pending the outcome of its main application. The Court in fact refused to grant the relief sought by Metro on the grounds that the decision affected not only the applicant's relationship with SABA but also that of all its distributors in the Community and the suspension of all these relationships "would be outside the scope of an urgent interim measure intended to safeguard temporarily the interests of the applicant."[98] A third party might also seek interim relief under Article 186 where, for example, it was taking action against the Commission for failure to act under Article 175 and it considered it necessary to protect itself from damage pending the outcome of such proceedings.

[98] The Court also rejected Metro's alternative request for the adoption of measures to enable it to obtain provisionally supplies of SABA equipment and to resell it in its capacity as a wholesale supermarket. The Court said: "it has not been established that it would be impossible for the applicant to comply, even temporarily, with the conditions imposed by SABA for the purposes of recognition as a SABA wholesaler or that compliance with those conditions until the decision of the Court giving judgment in the main action would cause it irreparable damage."

10

National Courts and National Law

10.01 It is a well-established principle of Community law that provisions of the Treaty may produce direct effects and create individual rights which national courts must protect. In the famous *Van Gend en Loos* case,[1] the Court of Justice spoke of Community law, independently of the legislation of the Member States, not only imposing obligations on individuals but also conferring rights upon them which become part of their legal heritage. It is equally well established that in the event of a conflict between Community law and national law Community law is supreme and has primacy over national law, irrespective of the date of that law.[2] Both these principles have practical applications in the field of competition law. That the Community competition rules contained in Articles 85 and 86 are directly applicable and may have direct effect has been acknowledged by the Court of Justice on several occasions. In *B.R.T.* v. *S.A.B.A.M.*,[3] the Court said: "As the prohibitions of Articles 85(1) and 86 tend by their nature to produce direct effects in relations between individuals, these Articles create direct rights in respect of the individuals concerned which the national courts must safeguard." That their application may defeat a claim based on national law is clearly shown by the Court's decision in *Consten and Grundig* v. *Commission*.[4] As regards the question of the supremacy of Community law, in *Walt Wilhelm* v. *Bundeskartellamt*[5] the Court proclaimed: "conflicts between the rules of the Community and national rules in the matter of the law on cartels must be resolved by applying the principle that Community law takes precedence."

Furthermore the Court of Justice has consistently held[6] that in the absence of Community rules on the subject it is for the domestic legal system to determine the procedural conditions governing actions at law intended to ensure the protection of the rights which individuals derive from the direct effect of Community law, provided that those

---

[1] Case 26/62 *Van Gend en Loos* v. *Nederlandse Administratie der Belastingen*: [1963] E.C.R. 1, [1963] C.M.L.R. 105.
[2] Case 6/64 *Costa* v. *ENEL*: [1964] E.C.R. 585, [1964] C.M.L.R. 425. See also Case 106/77, *Italian Finance Administration* v. *Simmenthal*: [1978] E.C.R. 629, [1978] 3 C.M.L.R. 263.
[3] Case 127/73: [1974] E.C.R. 51, [1974] 2 C.M.L.R. 238, at para. 16. Restated by the Court in Case C–234/89, *Delimitis* v. *Henninger Bräu AG*: [1991] I E.C.R. 935, [1992] 5 C.M.L.R. 210, at para. 45.
[4] Cases 56 & 58/64: [1966] E.C.R. 299, [1966] C.M.L.R. 418.
[5] Case 14/68: [1969] E.C.R. 1, [1969] C.M.L.R. 100.
[6] Case 33/76, *Rewe-Zentralfinanz eG and Rewe-Zentral AG* v. *Landwirtschaftskammer für das Saarland*: [1976] E.C.R. 1899, [1977] 1 C.M.L.R. 533; Case 199/82, *Amministrazione delle Finanze dello Stato* v. *San Giorgio Spa*: [1983] E.C.R. 3595. [1985] 2 C.M.L.R. 658. Referred to by the Commission in its recent Notice on co-operation between national courts and the Commission in applying Articles 85 and 86 of the EEC Treaty: [1993] O.J. C39/6, at para. 10.

conditions are not less favourable than those relating to similar actions of a domestic nature nor framed so as to render virtually impossible the exercise of rights conferred by Community law. As the *Factortame* litigation demonstrates Community law may require national courts to give remedies not available in a domestic context where the full effectiveness of Community law may be jeopardised without such remedy.[7]

This chapter is concerned with some of the implications of the direct applicability of Articles 85 and 86 in relation to proceedings in national courts and also in relation to the application of national competition laws. The first part concentrates on the enforceability of agreements in national courts and with the question whether breach of Article 85 or 86 gives rise to an action for damages in English law. The second part deals briefly with some of the problems involved in the concurrent application of Community and national competition laws.

I. PROCEEDINGS IN NATIONAL COURTS

Authorities of the Member States

10.02   At first sight it would appear that the commencement of proceedings by the Commission will exclude any activity by a national court in relation to an agreement. Article 9(3) of Regulation 17 provides that as long as the Commission has not initiated any procedure under Article 2, 3 or 6 of that regulation, the authorities of the Member States remain competent to apply Articles 85 and 86 of the Treaty in accordance with Article 88.[8] The significance of this provision has already been mentioned in relation to possible proceedings under Articles 85 and 86 brought by national competition authorities.[9] The present question is to what extent, if any, Article 9(3) has an effect on proceedings in a national court involving a dispute between private parties where the applicability of the Community competition rules, and in particular nullity under Article 85(2), is pleaded. There has been considerable academic discussion on the question of the position of national courts in relation to Article 9(3) and it was some time before the Court of Justice made the position clear.[10] In *Bilger* v. *Jehle*,[11] the Court had simply said that the phrase "authorities of the Member States" encompassed national courts but did not indicate whether this included ordinary courts applying Articles 85 and 86 indirectly in the context of private disputes or whether it was limited to national courts which had a function in the direct enforcement of competition law. The question remained undecided even after *Brasserie de Haecht (No. 2)*[12] where the Court considered that it was not necessary to re-examine the question whether Article

---

[7] Case C-213/89, *R.* v. *Secretary of State for Transport, ex p. Factortame Ltd.*: [1990]I E.C.R. 2423, [1990] 3 C.M.L.R. 1.

[8] Initiation of a procedure is discussed at paras. 2.38–39. Where the Commission closes the file the Member States' authorities' jurisdiction may return. See A.G. Mancini in Cases 142 & 156/84, *BAT and Reynolds Industries* v. *Commission*: [1987] E.C.R. 4487, [1987] 2 C.M.L.R. 551.

[9] See para. 1.26.

[10] See generally Gijlstra and Murphy, "EEC Competition Law after the Brasserie de Haecht and S.A.B.A.M. cases," [1974] L.I.E.I. 2 and Faull and Weiler, "Conflicts of Resolution in European Competition Law," (1978) 3 E.L.Rev. 116.

[11] Case 43/69: [1970] E.C.R. 127, [1974] C.M.L.R. 382.

[12] Case 48/72, *Brasserie de Haecht* v. *Wilkin-Janssen (No. 2)*: [1973] E.C.R. 77, [1973] C.M.L.R. 287.

9(3) covered ordinary national courts applying Article 85(2) in a case. Eventually, in *B.R.T.* v. *S.A.B.A.M.*,[13] the Court of Justice went into the matter in some detail:

> "It must thus be examined whether the national courts before which the prohibitions contained in Articles 85 and 86 are invoked in a dispute governed by private law, must be considered as 'authorities of the Member States.'
>
> The competence of those courts to apply the provisions of Community law, particularly in the case of such disputes, derives from the direct effect of those provisions.
>
> As the prohibitions of Articles 85(1) and 86 tend by their very nature to produce direct effects in relations between individuals these articles create direct rights in respect of the individuals concerned which the national courts must safeguard.
>
> To deny, by virtue of the aforementioned Article 9, the national courts' jurisdiction to afford this safeguard would mean depriving individuals of rights which they hold under the Treaty itself.
>
> The fact that Article 9(3) refers to 'the authorities of the Member States' competent to apply the provisions of Articles 85(1) and 86 'in accordance with Article 88' indicates that it refers solely to those national authorities whose competence derives from Article 88.
>
> Under that article the authorities of the Member States—including in certain Member States courts especially entrusted with the task of applying domestic legislation on competition or that of ensuring the legality of that application by the administrative authorities—are also rendered competent to apply the provisions of Articles 85 and 86 of the Treaty.
>
> The fact that the expression 'authorities of the Member States' appearing in Article 9(3) of Regulation 17 covers such courts cannot exempt a court before which the direct effect of Article 86 is pleaded from giving judgment."

The Court reconfirmed this definition of "authorities of the Member States" in the *Air Tariffs* case.[14]

The Court has thus drawn a distinction between national courts applying Articles 85 and 86 by virtue of their direct effect (*soit à titre incident*) and those courts especially entrusted to apply domestic competition law or to ensure its proper application by domestic authorities and which apply Articles 85 and 86 qua authorities deriving competence from Article 88 of the Treaty (*soit à titre principal*).[15] The latter category does not on this basis include, for example, the criminal courts whose task is to punish breaches of the law.[16] It may include certain courts in France and Germany[17] and, it

---

[13] Above, n. 3, at paras. 14–20.

[14] Cases 209–213/84, *Ministère Public* v. *Lucas Asjes and others*: [1986] E.C.R. 1425, [1986] 3 C.M.L.R. 173, at para. 55, also known as *Nouvelles Frontières*.

[15] The position under the EAA is less clear. Art. 89 EEC is reflected in Art. 55 EEA. The detailed procedural rules of the EFTA Surveillance Agreement follow as expected, Reg. 17 including Art. 9(3) of the Reg. The EEA will therefore have "competent authorities" for the EFTA States. But whilst the EFTA States have adopted Community law as laid down by the Court of Justice at the date of the EEA it is unclear to what extent and how this will include the notion of national authorities deriving competence from Arts. 88 and 89 to apply competition rules.

[16] *Ibid.* at para. 56.

[17] See the examples given by A.G. Mayras in the *S.A.B.A.M.* case, above, n. 3.

has been suggested, the Restrictive Practices Court in the United Kingdom.[18] Although other courts in the United Kingdom (for example, the High Court and County Court in England and Wales) may have jurisdiction in proceedings based on section 35(2) of the Restrictive Trade Practices Act 1976 or section 26 of the Resale Prices Act 1976 brought by third parties injuriously affected by a breach of those Acts, it is doubtful whether they can be said to be "*especially* entrusted with the task of applying domestic legislation on competition" in the sense indicated by the Court in *B.R.T.* v. *S.A.B.A.M.*[19] Whilst the initiation of proceedings by the Commission under Regulation 17 will operate to oust the jurisdiction of authorities deriving competence from and applying Articles 85 and 86 by virtue of Article 88 of the Treaty, proceedings before national courts *à titre incident* are not affected thereby and there is no general obligation on a national court to stay its proceedings pending the outcome before the Commission. The Court of Justice made it clear in *B.R.T.* v. *S.A.B.A.M.*, that Article 9(3) of Regulation 17 should not operate to deprive individuals of rights they have by virtue of the direct effect of Articles 85 and 86 of the Treaty.

Enforceability of agreements

10.03   The enforceability of an agreement between its parties is essentially a matter of national law (including its rules of conflict of laws where a foreign element is involved) but where the agreement falls within the prohibition of Article 85(1) the court is bound to apply Community law, including Article 85(2) which provides for automatic nullity. That is so notwithstanding that the Commission has the primary responsibility for the enforcement of the competition rules and a national court may be ill-equipped to deal with the economic analysis which may be necessary to determine the applicability of Article 85(1). Furthermore because a national court cannot positively apply Article 85(3)—only the Commission has the power to grant exemptions—a national court may be left with little room for manoeuvre when Article 85 is pleaded. It will also be appreciated that the likelihood of a conflict not only of jurisdiction but also of resolution[20] is not remote in such circumstances.

Provisional validity

10.04   The Court of Justice has held that in the case of certain agreements the general principle of legal certainty[21] requires that the direct effectiveness of the prohibition of Article 85(1) may not be invoked until such time as the Commission has pronounced on the question of exemption under Article 85(3). The Court has drawn a distinction between the position of "old" and "new" agreements. "Old" agreements are those which came into existence prior to the entry into force of Regulation 17, and

---

[18] In Case T–66/89, *Publishers Association* v. *Commission*: [1992] 5 C.M.L.R. 120, the Court of First Instance referred (para. 19) to the R.P. Court as "the competent body in the United Kingdom in competition matters".

[19] Above n. 3, emphasis added.

[20] See generally Faull and Weiler, *op. cit.*

[21] The general principle is discussed at paras. 8.22–24.

"new" agreements those made after such time. In its decision in *Brasserie de Haecht (No. 2)*,²² the Court said:

> "In the case of old agreements, the general principle of contractual certainty requires, particularly when the agreement has been notified in accordance with the provisions of Regulation No. 17, that the court may only declare it to be automatically void after the Commission has taken a decision by virtue of that Regulation. In the case of new agreements, as the Regulation assumes that so long as the Commission has not taken a decision the agreement can only be implemented at the parties' own risk, it follows that notifications in accordance with Article 4(1) of Regulation No. 17 do not have suspensive effect."

In short, old agreements may benefit from provisional validity, new agreements cannot. In the case of standard form contracts however, the doctrine of provisional validity will benefit contracts concluded after the date of entry into force of Regulation 17 (March 15, 1962) where they are exact reproductions of the standard form contract concluded before that date and duly notified.²³

10.05 In developing this doctrine the Court of Justice appears to have been influenced by the fact that whilst Article 85(3) provides for exemption, the Treaty contains no transitional provisions to deal with the effect of Article 85(2) on agreements existing prior to the commencement date of the Treaty or of Regulation 17. In previous decisions, the Court has also emphasised the indivisible unity of Article 85(1) and 85(3).²⁴ There being no possibility of getting a speedy ruling from the Commission on the applicability of Article 85(3), the application of Article 85(2) had to be reconciled with the principle of legal certainty requiring undertakings to be able to enforce their contracts. The solution was therefore to permit the principle of legal certainty to operate to secure the validity of old agreements until such time as the Commission intervened and by decision²⁵ declared them contrary to Article 85(1) and incapable of exemption under Article 85(3). The Court noted that Regulation 17 itself made special provision for old agreements and enabled the Commission to take into consideration the principle of legal certainty when dealing with them. In particular, Article 7 permits the retroactive regularisation of provisions in notified old agreements which are contrary to Article 85(1) on condition that such provisions are amended as to the future to the satisfaction of the Commission.²⁶

---

²² Above, n. 2, at paras. 9 and 10. This case gave rise to a considerable amount of academic comment and discussion. See, for example, Dashwood, "A New Look at Provisional Validity," [1974] C.L.J. 116; Gijlstra and Murphy, *op. cit.*; Vogelaar and Guy, "The Second Brasserie de Haecht Case: a Delphic Oracle" (1973) 22 I.C.L.Q. 648; Wertheimer, "The Haecht II Judgment and its Repercussions" (1973) 10 C.M.L.Rev. 386. These articles should now be read subject to the decision of the Court in the *Perfumes* case, discussed below.

²³ Case 1/70, *Parfums Marcel Rochas* v. *Bitsch*: [1970]I E.C.R. 515, [1971] C.M.L.R. 104. This special rule was restated recently in the *Delimitis* case, above, n. 3, at para. 49, although the contracts in question did not benefit.

²⁴ See Case 13/61., *Bosch* v. *de Geus*: [1962] E.C.R. 45, [1962] C.M.L.R. 1; Case 10/69, *Portelange SA* v. *Smith Corona Marchant International*: [1969] E.C.R. 309, [1974] 1 C.M.L.R. 397, and *Air Tariffs*, above, n. 14, at para. 61.

²⁵ The Court has held that provisional validity may be terminated by a measure less than a decision. See the *Perfumes* cases, discussed below, at para. 10.10.

²⁶ Art. 7 of Reg. 17 is discussed at paras. 6.29–31.

10.06   The doctrine of provisional validity as stated in *Brasserie de Haecht (No. 2)* was reaffirmed by the Court of Justice in the later case of *de Bloos* v. *Bouyer*.[27] The Court made it clear that provisional validity applies to old agreements duly notified or exempt from notification and that the effect of provisional validity is that the agreements should be treated by the national court as being fully valid (at least inter partes) from the standpoint of Article 85 during the period before the Commission has pronounced on the question of Article 85(3). The Court said:[28]

> "Courts before which proceedings are brought relating to an old agreement duly notified or exempted from notification must give such an agreement the legal effects attributed thereto under the law applicable to the contract, and those effects cannot be called into question by any obligation which may be raised concerning its compatibility with Article 85(1)."

The national court should therefore treat the agreement as valid and enforceable notwithstanding that it falls within the prohibition of Article 85(1).[29] Any theory that provisional validity only implies some form of limited or restricted validity which as a matter of Community law does not allow the agreement to be fully enforced between the parties would appear to be no longer maintainable after the Court's decision in *de Bloos*.[30]

Accession agreements and the EEA

10.07   The Court of Justice has not yet had to rule on the question whether "accession agreements" have the benefit of provisional validity in the same way as old agreements. Accession agreements are "agreements, decisions and concerted practices to which Article 85 of the Treaty applies by virtue of accession."[31] The agreement must therefore have been in existence before the relevant date of accession of the "new" Member States (including, of course, the United Kingdom) to the Community and must not have restricted competition or have affected inter-state trade in the Common Market[32] before accession. An agreement is not an accession agreement if it fell within the scope of Article 85 before accession.[33] The Commission has taken the view[34] that:

> "the principles applicable to old agreements could also be applied by analogy to agreements which became subject to Article 85 following the Accession of the

---

[27] Case 59/77: [1977] E.C.R. 2359, [1978] 1 C.M.L.R. 511. Confirmed recently in *Delimitis*, above, n. 3, at para. 48.

[28] *Ibid.* at para. 15.

[29] This was the approach of the French and Dutch courts as reported in the Commission's decision in *Velcro/Aplix* [1985] O.J. L233/21, [1989]4 C.M.L.R. 157, at para. IV(b).

[30] For a useful summary of the different theories of the effect of provisional validity, see Gijlstra and Murphy, *op. cit.*

[31] Art. 25(1) of Reg. 17.

[32] *I.e.*, of the Six, the Nine, the Ten or the Twelve, as the case may be.

[33] For example, *Sirdar/Phildar*: [1975] O.J. L126/27, [1975] 1 C.M.L.R. D93. The question of the extraterritorial effect of Arts. 85 and 86 may be relevant in this context. See generally paras. 8.01–08.

[34] Third Report on Competition Policy, p. 19, point 5(a).

new Member States, provided they were already in force before the date of accession (1 January 1973)[35] and were notified[36] before the end of the six month period following accession."[37]

An English court has taken the same view.[38] But this view was not universally held.[39] As mentioned above, in *Brasserie de Haecht (No. 2)*, the Court of Justice appeared to be influenced by the absence from the Treaty of transitional rules to deal with the effect of Article 85(2) and the impossibility of getting a speedy ruling from the Commission on the applicability of Article 85(3). The situation which existed at the times of accession with regard to the Commission's position in relation to the enforcement of the Community competition rules, and in particular its ability to grant exemptions, was different from that which existed between the commencement date of the Treaty and that for Regulation 17. The position in relation to accession agreements has yet to be clarified by the Court of Justice but it is likely that they would be treated by the Court in the same way as old agreements.

A similar case can be made for existing agreements under the EEA. Provided the agreement did not fall within the scope of Article 85 E.C. before the date of entry into force of the EEA and it is notified to the competent surveillance authority[40] within 6 months of that date, the agreement should have the benefit of provisional validity for the purpose of Article 53(2) EEA.

Termination of provisional validity

10.08 Provisional validity will be brought to an end by a decision of the Commission under Regulation 17 in application of Article 85(3). Such a decision may be one granting exemption or refusing it and declaring the agreement null and void under Article 85(2). A decision under Article 15(6) of Regulation 17 may also terminate provisional validity.[41] It is, however, uncertain whether an interim decision will necessarily terminate provisional validity but it is thought that it may do so. Although such decisions will not normally involve any assessment or finding by the Commission on the applicability of Article 85(3) and are directed primarily to the preservation of the status quo pending the Commission's determining the position under Article 85

[35] January 1, 1981 in the case of Greece, and January 1, 1986 in the case of Spain and Portugal.
[36] This should presumably be qualified by such words as "if not exempt from notification:" see *de Bloos* v. *Bouyer*, above, n. 27.
[37] Art. 25(2) of Reg. 17 provides that accession agreements "shall be notified pursuant to Article 5(1) or Article 7(1) or (2) within six months from the date of accession."
[38] In *Esso Petroleum Co. Ltd.* v. *Kingswood Motors (Addlestone) Ltd.*: [1974] 1 Q.B. 142, [1973] C.M.L.R. 665, Bridge J. treated a solus agreement entered into in 1969 for a period of five years between two U.K. companies as an old agreement. He said: "Earlier Articles of that Regulation, i.e., Reg. 17, classify agreements in two ways. First, they are classified into what are conveniently referred to as 'old' and 'new' agreements. In the original regulation that meant agreements which had been entered into before the making of the Regulation in 1962 and after, but as that Regulation is adapted to apply to the countries who entered into the Community on January 1, 1973, the Regulation has the effect of treating pre-1973 agreements as old agreements and post-1973 agreements as new agreements. We are therefore concerned here with an old agreement." Having considered the cases of *Bilger* v. *Jehle* and *Brasserie de Haecht (No. 2)*, Bridge J. reached the conclusion that as the time for notification of the agreement had not expired, a national court could not treat the agreement as null and void under Art. 85(2).
[39] See Waelbroek in [1974] *Cahiers de droit europeèn* 169.
[40] For the division of responsibility between the Commission and the EFTA Surveillance Authority, see para. 1.34A–B. On notification of agreements, see para. 2.28A.
[41] *Portelange* v. *Smith Corona*, above, n. 24.

or 86, it would surely be unwise and inappropriate, if not actually illegal, to order interim measures if an exemption was likely. The Commission has indicated that it will order interim measures only if there is a sufficiently strong prima facie case.[42]

10.09   Under Article 9(3) of Regulation 17 the authorities of the Member States remain competent to apply Articles 85 and 86 in accordance with Article 88 of the Treaty, as long as the Commission has not initiated a procedure under Article 2, 3 or 6.[43] A finding of infringement of Article 85 by such authority would, it is submitted, terminate any provisional validity and the consequent nullity under Article 85(2) would have retroactive effect. To deny the ability of the competent authorities to make such a finding would be contrary to the express wording of Article 9(3) ("remain competent") and to deny the above-mentioned effect would be to render such finding to a great extent practically meaningless.

10.10   Provisional validity may be lost by action of the Commission less than a decision. In *Perfumes*,[44] the Court of Justice held that a comfort letter from the Commission may have the same effect. In the case in question, the letter had informed the parties that in the opinion of the Commission the agreement did not appear to come within the prohibition in Article 85(1) and therefore, there being no reason for the Commission to intervene, the file was being closed. The Court considered that in such circumstances the Commission was unlikely to take an individual decision relating to the agreement in question and therefore it was improbable that it would exercise its powers, given by Article 6 of Regulation 17 when granting an exemption, to make the exemption retroactive to a date before notification. The Court thought that in these circumstances the justification for the retention of the provisional validity no longer subsisted.

Comfort letters[45] are sent in a wide variety of circumstances and although nearly all may expressly or impliedly refer to the fact that the Commission intends to take no further action at the present time (*e.g.* to close the file) their contents may differ considerably. The question is therefore whether every comfort letter has the same effect of withdrawing provisional validity. It is thought probably not. The important thing, it is submitted, is that the letter should give some indication as to the likely application of Article 85(3) and, therefore, the probable retroactive effect by virtue of Article 6 of Regulation 17. It may also be significant whether, as in the *Perfumes* case, the agreement has been examined by the Commission. Thus a letter which merely refers to the fact that the file is being closed because of lack of priority or which simply says that in the light of the information available the Commission proposes to take no further steps in the matter, should not affect any provisional validity. There is in such cases no indication one way or the other either of the applicability of Article 85(1) or the application of Article 85(3) (and exercise of the powers in Article 6). Contrast the letters in the *Perfumes* case, which informed the parties that in the Commission's opinion the

---

[42] Interim decisions are discussed at paras. 6.02–11.

[43] See generally paras 5.02–03.

[44] Case 99/79, *Lancôme* v. *Etos and Albert Heijn Supermart*: [1980] E.C.R. 2511, [1981] 2 C.M.L.R. 164, at paras. 12–18.

[45] See generally paras. 6.53–59.

agreement did not fall within Article 85(1).[46] There was no express reference to Article 85(3) but if the agreement did not come within Article 85(1) an individual decision under Article 85(3) was out of the question. Another type of comfort letter may refer to the applicability of a block exemption to the relevant agreement (in past practice, often the block exemption for exclusive distribution agreements, as in the *de Bloos* case[47]). Again it is thought unlikely that any provisional validity is affected—it would, of course, only be relevant if the national court considered that the agreement fell within Article 85(1) and took a different view on the applicability of the block exemption. The fact that an agreement comes within the terms of a block exemption does not prejudice the question of the applicability of Article 85(1).[48] It may therefore be necessary to see whether the Commission has made an examination of the agreement to determine the applicability of Article 85(1) and to what extent the Commission's position is set out in the letter. Even so, the Commission's opinion on the applicability of a block exemption does not imply any view by it as to the possible application of Article 85(3) by individual decision. Any provisional validity should accordingly remain unaffected.

Finally, it may be noted that in the *Hasselblad* case,[49] Advocate General Slynn took the view that provisional validity might be lost by a Commission letter objecting to a term in the agreement. But neither the Court of Justice nor the Commission has gone this far.[50]

Effect of termination

10.11 The effect of the termination of provisional validity depends on the nature of the measure effecting the termination. Where a decision grants exemption under Article 85(3) then it may, by Article 6 of Regulation 17, be retroactive to the date of notification (or earlier, in the case of agreements exempt from notification) and consequently the provisional validity may be converted into absolute validity. Where the decision refuses exemption and finds that the agreement contravenes Article 85(1), nullity under Article 85(2) has retroactive effect[51] and the provisional validity will be replaced by absolute nullity. Where exemption can only be given to the agreement in an amended form agreed with the Commission, Article 7 of Regulation 17 may nevertheless enable the Commission in the case of old agreements duly notified[52] to regularise the agreement retroactively and again the provisional validity may be

---

[46] With the exception of that in Case 37/79, *Estée Lauder*: [1980] E.C.R. 2481, [1981] 2 C.M.L.R. 143, which was more generally worded.

[47] Above, n. 27. Reg. 67/67 has now been replaced by Regs. 1983/83 and 1984/83.

[48] Case 32/65, *Italy* v. *Council and Commission*: [1966] E.C.R. 389, [1969] C.M.L.R. 39.

[49] *Hasselblad (G.B.) Ltd.* v. *Commission*: [1984] E.C.R. 883, [1984] 1 C.M.L.R. 559.

[50] See, in particular, *Velcro/Aplix*, above, n. 29, where the Commission proceeded on the basis that it is the decision, and not any earlier letter or instrument, which has the effect of terminating the provisional validity of the agreement.

[51] *Brasserie de Haecht (No. 2)*, above, n. 12, at para. 27. It is, however, arguable that nullity under Art. 85(2) is not retroactive where an agreement has provisional validity but only operates from the date of the measure terminating it. First, it is not certain whether the Court at this part of its judgment is intending to cover both "old" and "new" agreements. Secondly, the interests of legal certainty are hardly well served if the enforceability of contracts may be lost retroactively at some unknown future date. But such an interpretation appears to render otiose the provisions of Art. 7 of Reg. 17 which are specially designed to regularise infringements retroactively. See, however, Korah's note on *Velcro/Aplix* (1985) 10 E.I.P.R. 296.

[52] Agreements exempt from notification have to be duly notified in order to benefit under Art. 7 of Reg. 17.

converted into absolute validity. In *de Bloos* v. *Bouyer*,[53] Advocate General Mayras pointed out that there could be no question of amending an agreement between parties who had ceased doing business with each other (and, in the *de Bloos* case, might be in litigation with each other on the agreement). Clearly, the party arguing that the agreement is null and void under Article 85(2) is unlikely to agree with the other party and with the Commission to an amendment which will heal any infringement with retroactive effect under Article 7 of Regulation 17. For this reason Advocate General Mayras considered that "there can no longer be any question of provisional validity or nullity but merely of absolute validity or nullity."[54]

Position of new agreements

10.12   New agreements are not provisionally valid.[55] Nor are notifiable old or accession agreements which have not been properly notified. In these cases the national court may apply the prohibition of Article 85(1) and consequently declare an agreement (or such parts of it as fall within the prohibition) null and void. But, as already mentioned, the likelihood of a conflict between the Commission and the national court is not remote. A national court may apply Article 85(1) and (2) to an agreement but the Commission take a later decision granting negative clearance or an exemption under Article 85(3). The former may occur because the national court and the Commission may not have all or the same facts before them, even if they were to take the same approach as regards the economic and legal arguments involved. In the latter case, the Commission's exclusive power to grant exemptions may hamstring the national court, particularly in interlocutory proceedings where the question of immediate relief may be critical and in practice often decisive.[56] The Court of Justice has therefore developed a number of principles aimed at avoiding contradictory decisions between Commission and national court. In its recent Notice on co-operation between national courts at the Commission and Commission seeks in practical ways to augment those principles.

10.13   In *Brasserie de Haecht (No. 2)*,[57] the Court of Justice gave the following guidance to the national court:

> "Whilst the principle of legal certainty requires that, in applying the prohibitions of Article 85, the sometimes considerable delays by the Commission in exercising its powers should be taken into account, this cannot, however, absolve the court from the obligation of deciding on the claims of interested parties who invoke the automatic nullity."

More recently, in *Delimitis* v. *Henninger Bräu*, the Court of Justice warned also of the risk of national courts taking decision which might conflict with those taken by the Commission in application of Articles 85 and 86. Whilst the national court always has

---

[53] Above, n. 27.
[54] See Korah in [1978] J.B.L. 73.
[55] Case 48/72, Brasserie de Haecht (No. 2): [1973] E.C.R. 77. [1973] C.M.L.R. 287.
[56] See Faull and Weiler, *op. cit.*, at p. 137.
[57] Above, at para. 11.

the power to suspend proceedings and make a reference to the Court of Justice for a preliminary ruling under Article 177[58] the Court has identified three basic situations:

(a) where it is clear that the conditions for the application of Article 85(1) are not satisfied in relation to the agreement, the national court may continue the proceedings and rule on the agreement in issue;[59]
(b) where it is clear that Article 85(1) does apply, and the agreement has not been notified (or is exempt from notification), but having regard to the block exemption regulations and the Commission's previous decisions the agreement may on no account be exempted under Article 85(3), the national court cannot give effect to the agreement in so far as it infringes Article 85;[60] and
(c) where the position of the agreement is uncertain (*i.e.* it could be the subject of an exemption decision) the national court may decide to stay the proceedings pending a decision of the Commission or to adopt interim measures pursuant to its national rules of procedure.[61]

This implies that the national court can apply Article 85 negatively, at least in clear cases. Although a national court cannot apply Article 85(3) positively,[62] it can, however, rule on the applicability of a block exemption. The Court in *Delimitis* confirmed that where an agreement may be covered by a block exemption, the national court has jurisdiction to determine whether the block exemption applies. But the direct applicability of those provisions may not however lead the national court to modify the scope of the block exemption regulations by extending their scope of application to agreements not covered by them.[63] The fact that an agreement has the benefit of an individual or block exemption does not, at least in theory, prevent a national court applying Article 86.

The Commission may be in a position to assist the national court faced with a question of the applicability of Articles 85 and 86. Within the limits of the relevant national procedural rules of the national court and subject to Article 214 of the Treaty (the protection of confidentiality) the national court can obtain from the Commission information as to the state of play of the Commission's own procedures in relation to the agreement in question, including the likelihood of its giving an official ruling on the agreement pursuant to Regulation 17.[64] The Commission's Notice on Cooperation indicates that the national court may in particular ask the Commission to say how long it will be before the decision granting or refusing exemption will be taken. For its part, the Commission states, it will try to give priority to cases suspended in this way before

---

[58] Case C–234/89, *Delimitis* v. *Henninger Bräu AG*: [1991] I E.C.R. 935, [1992] 5 C.M.L.R. 210, at para. 54. See also Van Bael, "The Role of National Courts" (1994) 15 E.C.L.R. 3.
[59] *Ibid.* at para. 50.
[60] *Ibid.* at paras. 50 and 51.
[61] *Ibid.* at para. 52. See, *e.g.* the approach of the Dutch court in *Bloemenveilingen Aalsmeer*: [1988] O.J. C262/27, [1989] 4 C.M.L.R. 500, at paras. 15 and 16.
[62] But see Kon, "Article 85(3): A Case for Application by National Courts" (1982) 19 C.M.L.Rev. 541. Contra, Steindorff, "Article 85(3): No Case for Application by National Courts" (1982) 20 C.M.L.Rev. 125.
[63] Above, n. 58, at para. 46. See also *De Bloos* v. *Bouyer*, above n. 23, at para. 11.
[64] Above, n. 58, at para. 53.

national courts.[65] Similarly the national court may ask the Commission for what is described as "economic and legal information" relating to the agreement in question.[66] The Notice indicates that the Commission is willing to give its view on points of law relating to the applicability of Articles 85 and 86, including an interim opinion on eligibility for exemption under Articles 85(3).[67] The Notice points out that the Commission's answers are not binding on the national court. Nor are the Commission's replies definitive—the national court, as mentioned above, may always seek a preliminary ruling of the Court of Justice under Article 177.[68] The Commission adds that it may also be able to supply the national court with factual data: for example, statistics, market studies and economic analyses.[69] The Commission's Notice on cooperation with national courts is potentially of some considerable practical importance. It is a manifestation and example of the Commission's general duty to cooperate with national courts to ensure that Community law is applied and respected.[70]

Approach of English courts

10.14   A number of cases have already come before the English courts. In *Esso Petroleum* v. *Kingswood Motors (Addlestone)*,[71] the High Court was asked to consider the compatibility of a petrol solus agreement with Article 85(1), but, the agreement being an "accession agreement" and the time for notification not having expired, the court proceeded on the basis that it was provisionally valid. Euro-defences are now not uncommon.[72] Article 85 has been raised, for example, as a defence in actions to recover payment of royalties under a patent licence.[73] See, for example, *Chemidus Wavis* v. *TERI*[74] where the Court of Appeal had little difficulty in applying Article 85(1) to the terms of the licence in question. It is, however, by no means certain that an English court would feel bound to apply Article 85(1) (and the automatic nullity in Article 85(2)) in the context of an interim application where immediate relief may have to be given. In *Sirdar* v. *Les Fils de Louis Mulliez and Orsay Knitting Wools*,[75] Graham J. seemed prepared to grant an interlocutory injunction and so enforce the agreement which the Commission had declared contrary to Article 85(1), had the balance of convenience (under the *American Cyanamid*[76] rule) been in favour of so doing. On the other hand there is some evidence of the courts' preparedness to stay

---

[65] [1993] O.J. C39/6, at para. 37.

[66] *Delimitis*, above, n. 58, at para. 53.

[67] Notice, above, at para. 38.

[68] *Ibid.* at para. 39. For an example of the English Court's approach to the Notice, see *Inntrepreneur Estates Ltd.* v. *Mason*: [1993] 2 C.M.L.R. 293.

[69] *Ibid.* at para. 40. The national court may choose not to do so, *e.g.* where it considers it unnecessary because the Commission has already issued a decision covering the same issues in the same product market albeit in another Member State. See the approach of the Irish High Court in *Masterfoods Ltd. T/A Mars Ireland* v. *H.B. Ice Cream Ltd.*: [1992] 3 C.M.L.R. 830.

[70] *Delimitis*, above, n. 58, at para. 53 and Case C–2/88 Imm, *Zwartfeld*: [1990] I E.C.R. 3365, [1990]3 C.M.L.R. 457.

[71] Above, n. 38.

[72] See para. 10.15 and the cases cited at n. 88.

[73] *J. F. Dymond* v. *G. B. Britton and Sons (Holdings) Ltd.*: [1976] 1 C.M.L.R. 133, and *Chemidus Wavin* v. *TERI*: [1978] 3 C.M.L.R. 514.

[74] *Ibid.* and see the approach of the Northern Ireland High Court applying Art. 85(1) in a trade mark infringement case, *Tayto (Northern Ireland) Ltd.* v. *McKee*: [1991] 3 C.M.L.R. 269.

[75] [1975] 1 C.M.L.R. 378, discussed by Faull and Weiler, *op. cit.*, at pp. 135–137.

[76] [1975] A.C. 396.

proceedings in suitable circumstances. For example, in *British Leyland* v. *Wyatt Interpart*,[77] Graham J. stayed proceedings in an action for infringement of the plaintiff's design copyright in certain motor vehicle spare parts pending the Commission's decision on the defendant's allegation that the plaintiff had abused its dominant position. The party relying on the Community defence in such circumstances will be expected to give an undertaking to pursue its complaint expeditiously before the Commission and may be required to deposit with the court a sufficient sum to cover the costs in the proceedings and also any damages likely to be awarded if the other party succeeds in the action. As was indicated in *Aero Zipp Fasteners* v. *YKK*[78] any delay while a matter is being dealt with by the Commission may justify inactivity by a party in the domestic proceedings, provided the determination by the Commission is important for the domestic proceedings. But, as Whitford J. pointed out, the determination of the matter by the Commission may not necessarily dispose of the case before the national court. The Commission may consider that a party has cleansed himself of any default by subsequent remedial action whereas before the national court the relevant consideration may well be only as to whether or not during any relevant period there was, in fact, some breach of the Community competition rules.

Damages for breach of Articles 85 and 86

Community or national solution

10.15   The question whether an injured party can sue for damages for breach of Article 85 or 86 cannot, at least at the present time, receive a simple answer.[79] Neither the Treaty nor the Regulations deal expressly with the subject.[80] The Deringer Report considered that the question of remedies for breach of Articles 85 and 86 should have been included in Regulation 17 but thought that no uniform rule should be proposed

---

[77] [1979] 3 C.M.L.R. 79. Note the delay which may then ensue. Two years in the Dutch case of *Centraal Bureau voor Rijwielhandel* v. *Firma Donck en Zonen*, reported in (1977) 2 E.L.Rev. 474. For an example of a German court's preparedness to stay proceedings, see *Grundig AG* v. *Firma Heinrich Bolte Georgsmartienhütte*: [1980] 3 C.M.L.R. 641.

[78] [1978] 2 C.M.L.R. 88. For a case where the English High Court carried on whilst acknowledging that the matter was being considered in the two tribunals, see *Apple Corp. Ltd.* v. *Apple Computers Inc.*: [1992] 1 C.M.L.R. 969.

[79] See generally van den Heuvel, "Civil Law Consequences of Violation of the Antitrust Provisions of the Rome Treaty" (1963) 12 A.J.C.L. 172; Temple Lang, *The Common Market and Common Law* (1966), Chap. 17; Rew, "Actions for Damages by Third Parties under English Law for Breach of Article 85 of the EEC Treaty" (1971) C.M.L.Rev. 462; Staines, "The Right to Sue in Ireland for Violation of the EEC Rules on Competition" [1977] 2 L.I.E.I. 53; Paines, "Enforcing EEC Competition Law in English Courts" [1983] L. S. Gaz. 272; Picanol, "Remedies in National Law for Breach of Articles 85 and 86 of the EEC Treaty: A Review" [1982] 2 L.I.E.I. 1; Davidson, "Action for Damages in the English Courts for Breach of EEC Competition Law" (1985) 34 I.C.L.Q. 178; Temple Lang, "EEC Competition Actions in Member States' Courts—Claims for Damages, Declarations and Injunctions for Breach of Community Antitrust Law" Annual Proceedings of Fordham Corporate Law Institute 1984; Steiner, "How to make the Action suit the Case: Domestic Remedies for Breach of EEC Law" (1987) 12 E.L.Rev. 102; and Hoskins "Garden Cottage Revisited: The Availability of Damages in the National Courts for Breaches of EEC Competition Rules" (1992) 13 E.C.L.R. 257 and Whish, "The Enforcement of E.C. Competition Law in the Domestic Courts of Member States" (1994) 5 E.B.L. Rev. 3.

[80] But see Art. 4(3) of Reg. 19/65. And note that A.G. Mayras made several references to actions for damages in Case 127/73, *B.R.T.* v. *S.A.B.A.M.*: [1974] E.C.R. SI, [1974] 2 C.M.L.R. 238.

until a study of the laws of the Member States had been made.[81] A study[82] was made for the Commission by a team of experts. It concluded:

> "Les consultants sont parvenus à la conclusion qu'une violation des règles de concurrence instituées par le Traité ouvre aux personnes lesées par cette infraction des voies judiciaires de droit interne leur permettant d'obtenir réparation sous toutes les formes reconnues par les droits nationaux des six Etats membres; indemnité, action en cessation, astreinte, publication du jugement.
> Ce principe s'applique cependant suivant des modalités différentes suivant les Etats membres et, parfois, sous certaines restrictions."

This positive, albeit qualified, result of the study may have deterred the Commission from taking any legislative initiative in the matter. The Commission has proceeded on the basis that action for damages are available to injured parties.[83] Indeed, it is the Commission's policy to encourage actions before national courts for enforcement of the competition rules.[84] The Commission's Notice on cooperation points out some potential advantages to proceeding via the national court: the possibility of recovering compensation for any loss suffered; speedier adoption of interim measures; the possibility of combining a claim under Community law with one under national law; and, the national court's power to award costs.[85] The Commission has however taken no legislative initiative. Indeed although a uniform Community solution may be thought desirable, there is much to be said for waiting until inadequacies or shortcomings of national law are clearly demonstrated.

In the absence of an express Community rule, reference must therefore be made to the laws of the Member State where the action is to be maintained. The relevant case law of the national courts is increasing and developing.[86] A number of significant landmarks have been passed,[87] particularly in the United Kingdom. The present discussion concentrates on the position under English law. Articles 85 and 86, being directly applicable provisions, may be pleaded in English courts and have in fact been so in a number of cases to date. It is clear that they may be used as a defence. This was established in the *Application des Gaz* case and there are a good number of examples in

---

[81] Report of the Committee of the European Parliament. Doc. 104/1960–61.

[82] Ètudes de la CEE (Sèrie Concurrence No. 1), La rèparation des consèquences dommageables d'une violation des articles 85 et 86. It is understood that the Commission has updated this study to deal with the enlarged Community.

[83] See the Commission's statement on Interim Measures, set out in App. 1.

[84] See the Fifteenth Report on Competition Policy, at point 38; *Aluminium*: [1985] O.J. L92/1, [1987] 3 C.M.L.R. 813, at para. 18.2, and the Sixteenth Report on Competition Policy, at point 41. Occasionally the policy has manifested itself in individual decisions: see, *e.g. Building and construction industry in the Netherlands*: [1992] O.J. L92/1, where the Commission observed that the complainant might have fared better by going to the national court.

[85] [1993] O.J. C39/6, at para. 16.

[86] For a useful and comprehensive historical exposition, see Picanol, *op. cit.*

[87] For example, in Germany, by the *BMW* case, below, n. 10; in Ireland, by *Cadbury Ireland Ltd.* v. *Kerry Co-operative Creameries Ltd.*: [1981] Dublin U.L.J. 94; in Belgium, by the *GB-INNO* case, below, n. 10; in the Netherlands, by *Van Gelderen Import* v. *Impressum Nederland*: [1981] N.J. 129, and in the U.K., by *Garden Cottage Foods Ltd.* v. *Milk Marketing Board*: [1983] 2 All E.R. 770, [1983] 3 C.M.L.R. 43.

the law reports of Articles 85 and 86 being pleaded by way of defence, not always successfully.[88] But it does not automatically follow that because Articles 85 and 86 may be used as a shield that they can be used as a sword.[89]

Injunctive relief

10.16   It is now well established that interim injunctive relief can be obtained to restrain a breach of the competition rules.[90] Interlocutory injunctions have been granted to restrain breaches of Article 86. In *Budgett* v. *British Sugar*,[91] the High Court granted an injunction restraining BSC from refusing to accept orders from Budgett, a large sugar merchant, for the supply of its named regular customers. Budgett produced an affidavit by one of its customers to the effect that it sold a considerable amount of product made with the sugar in other Member States and that it was concerned lest merchants be eliminated from the trade who had shown themselves capable of purchasing on the Continent and resupplying in the United Kingdom in order to satisfy any shortfall in the supply of sugar from the United Kingdom producers (principally BSC and Tate & Lyle). The parties ultimately reached a settlement so no judgment was delivered on the merits of the case.

Another example can be seen in the *AKZO* case. As the Commission's decision reveals,[92] in December 1979 ECS obtained an *ex parte* interim injunction in the High Court to restrain AKZO from reducing its selling prices contrary to Article 86. As regards Article 85, in *Cutsforth* v. *Mansfield Inns*[93] an interim injunction was granted to restrain the defendant, who had taken over a number of tied public houses in Humberside where the plaintiff's juke-boxes and other amusement machines were installed, from interfering in the relationship between the plaintiff and his customers who formed a part of the tied house system. The defendant had introduced a policy of permitting only approved machine suppliers to be used, and had refused to put the plaintiff on the list. It was argued that such a provision fell within Article 8 of Regulation 1984/83 and therefore could not benefit from that block exemption. There is, of course, no right to an injunction. It is a matter of discretion for the judge who may, as the *Garden Cottage Foods* case shows, take the view that the *American Cyanamid* criteria are not satisfied (for example, because a remedy in damages is available and an

---

[88] *Application des Gaz SA* v. *Falks Veritas Ltd.*: [1974] 2 C.M.L.R. 75. And see, for example, *Lerose Ltd.* v. *Hawick Jersey International Ltd.*: [1973] C.M.L.R. 83; *Aero Zipp Fasteners* v. *YKK*: [1973] C.M.L.R. 819; *Sirdar Ltd.* v. *Les Fils de Louis Mulliez and Orsay Knitting Wools Ltd.*, above, n. 75; *J. F. Dymond* v. *G. B. Britton and Sons (Holdings) Ltd.*, above, n. 73; *Chemidus Wavin* v. *TERI*, above, n. 56; *British Leyland* v. *Wyatt Interpart*, above, n. 77; *British Leyland* v. *T.I. Silencers*: [1980] 2 C.M.L.R. 332, reversed on appeal: [1981] 2 C.M.L.R. 75; *ICI Ltd.* v. *Berk Pharmaceuticals Ltd.*: [1981] F.S.R. 1, [1981]2 C.M.L.R. 91; *Hoover plc* v. *George Hulme (Stockport) Ltd. and George Hulme*: [1982] 3 C.M.L.R. 186; *Lansing Bagnall Ltd.* v. *Buccaneer Lift Parts Ltd.*: [1984] 1 C.M.L.R. 224; *Ransburg-Gema AG* v. *Electrostatic Plant Systems Ltd.*: [1989] 2 C.M.L.R. 712; *Pitney Bowes Inc.* v. *Francotyp-Postalia GmbH*: [1990] 3 C.M.L.R. 466; *Chiron Corp* v. *Organon Teknika Ltd.*: [1992] 3 C.M.L.R. 813; *Inntrepreneur Estates Ltd.* v. *Mason*, above, n. 68; and *Chiron Corporation* v. *Murex Diagnostics Ltd.* (No. 2): [1994] 1 C.M.L.R. 410.
[89] Various unsuccessful attempts have been made to use Arts. 85 and 86 positively. See, for example, *Felixstowe Dock and Railway Company and European Ferries Ltd.* v. *British Transport Docks Board*: [1976] 2 C.M.L.R. 655, and *Chelmkarm Motors Ltd.* v. *Esso Petroleum Co. Ltd.*: [1979] 1 C.M.L.R. 73.
[90] *Garden Cottage Foods*, above, n. 87.
[91] Not fully reported. There is a note of the case given by Korah in (1979) 4 E.L.Rev. 417.
[92] *ECS/AKZO*: [1983] O.J. L252/13, [1983] 3 C.M.L.R. 694.
[93] [1986] 1 C.M.L.R. 1. See also *Holleran and Evans* v. *Thwaites plc*: [1989] 2 C.M.L.R. 917.

adequate remedy in the circumstances) and refuse to grant an injunction.[94] Finally, it should be noted that in no case yet has a final injunction been granted, although such a remedy would, it is submitted, be available in an appropriate case.

Damages

10.17 Recent decisions of the Court of Justice in such cases as *Factortame*[95] and *Francovich*[96] show the Court's concern that national courts should ensure the effective application of Community law by granting appropriate relief, including remedies which may not be available in a purely domestic context. In the *Bourgoin* case,[97] the Court of Appeal held that a breach of Article 30 by a State-imposed prohibition on imports does not in itself give rise to liability in damages but the House of Lords has recently indicated that, in the light of *Francovich*, there must now be doubt whether *Bourgoin* was correctly decided.[98] As already mentioned, enforcement of rights conferred by directly effective Articles is generally a matter for the national court, particularly as regards procedural conditions.[99] Against this background, as regards Articles 85 and 86, it seems most unlikely that the English courts will restrict the "rights" described by the Court in such cases as *B.R.T.* v. *S.A.B.A.M.*[1] to the obtaining of an injunction or declaration.

10.18 Commentators have generally tended to concentrate on whether a violation of Article 85 or 86 constitutes a breach of statutory duty. Whilst the tort of breach of statutory duty is well established, it is by no means an easy task to predict whether the courts will find that the breach of a particular statute involves tortious liability. The whole statute must be looked at together with the circumstances in which it was enacted in order to discern the legislator's intention.[2] It may be particularly important to determine whether the duty created by the statute is one which is owed primarily to the public at large or to individuals or to an identifiable group of individuals.[3] Although it is certainly true that the Treaty is primarily concerned with macro-economic policies and objectives, the Court of Justice has been loath to deny the position and importance of the individual in the enforcement of Community law. The Court has acknowledged on several occasions that the Treaty not only imposes obligations but also confers rights. Both the *Van Gend en Loos* case[4] and *B.R.T.* v. *S.A.B.A.M.*[5] have already been

---

[94] An interim injunction was refused in *Garden Cottage Foods*. So, too, in the Scottish case, *Argyll Group plc and others* v. *The Distillers Company plc*: [1986] 1 C.M.L.R. 764, and in *Plessey Co plc* v. *General Electric Co plc and Siemens*, unreported, judgment of December 20, 1988; *Megaphone* v. *British Telecom*, unreported, judgment of February 28, 1989; *Macarthy* v. *Unichem*, unreported, judgment of November 24, 1989 and *Leyland Daf Ltd.* v. *Automotive Products plc*, The Times, April 6, 1993.
[95] Case C-213/89, *R.* v. *Secretary of State for Transport, ex p. Factortame Ltd.*: [1990] I E.C.R. 2423, [1990] 3 C.M.L.R. 1.
[96] Cases C 6 & 9/90, *Francovich and Bonifaci* v. *Italy*: [1991]I E.C.R. 5357, [1993] 2 C.M.L.R. 66, where the Court held that a Member State may in certain circumstances be liable to pay damages to an individual who suffers loss where the Member State has failed to implement a directive.
[97] *Bourgoin SA* v. *Ministry of Agriculture, Fisheries and Food*: [1986] 1 C.M.L.R. 267.
[98] See the judgment of Lord Goff in *Kirklees B.C.* v. *Wickes Building Supplies Ltd.*: [1992] 2 C.M.L.R. 765.
[99] See para. 10.01.
[1] Above, n. 80.
[2] *Cutler* v. *Wandsworth Stadium Ltd.*: [1949] A.C. 398, *per* Lord Simonds at p. 407.
[3] *Phillips* v. *Britannia Hygienic Laundry Co.*: [1923] 2 K.B. 832, *per* Bankes C.J. at p. 838.
[4] Case 26/62, Van Gend en Loos: [1963] E.C.R. 1, [1963] C.M.L.R. 105.
[5] Above, n. 80.

mentioned. In *Sacchi*,[6] the Court said: "Even within the framework of Article 90, the prohibitions of Article 86 have a direct effect and confer on interested parties rights which the national courts must safeguard." The Court's order in the *Camera Care* case[7] also shows that Articles 85 and 86 are to protect individual private interests. If the Commission's power to grant interim measures must be used to protect such interests, it should follow that the rules of substantive law must be intended to protect those interests. The part to be played by the individual in the enforcement of Community competition law is also acknowledged in the Treaty and the regulations.[8] In *Garden Cottage Foods*,[9] the House of Lords (as indeed have courts in other Member States[10]) recognised that Articles 85 and 86 are laws for the protection of individual interests and that breach of those rules may constitute a breach of statutory duty.

Garden Cottage Foods

10.19　*Garden Cottage Foods* alleged a breach of Article 86 on the part of the Milk Marketing Board and sought, *inter alia*, an injunction to restrain it. The alleged abuse concerned the Board's decision to restrict sales of bulk butter for export to only four companies. Garden Cottage Foods had been one of some 20 or more firms which had previously bought bulk butter direct from the Board for resale abroad. It claimed that if it had to buy from one of the four chosen distributors, and not direct from the Board, it would go out of business, its previous profit margin being very small (1/4 per cent.). The judge, Parker J., refused to exercise his discretion in favour of Garden Cottage Foods, considering that there was a cause of action for breach of Article 86 and that damages would be an adequate remedy. But the Court of Appeal granted an injunction[11]—the plaintiff had a cause of action, but it was not clear that it sounded in damages, and the only certain remedy being an injunction and there being sufficient evidence to grant one, that relief would be given.

The House of Lords (Lord Wilberforce dissenting) reversed the Court of Appeal and discharged the injunction. Parker J. had not misunderstood the law and was entitled to take the view that a remedy in damages was available and an adequate remedy in the circumstances. There was no ground which would justify the Court of Appeal in

---

[6] Case 155/73, *Italy* v. *Sacchi*: [1974] E.C.R. 409, [1974] 2 C.M.L.R. 177; and see also the *Perfumes* case: *Estee Lauder*, above, n. 46, at para. 13.

[7] Case 792/79R, *Camera Care Ltd.* v. *Commission*: [1980] E.C.R. 119, [1980] 1 C.M.L.R. 334. Moreover at para. 14 of the judgment, the Court emphasised that it was important that whilst the Commission was carrying out its inquiries in a case "no irreparable damage is caused such as could not be remedied by any decision which the Commission might take at the conclusion of the administrative procedure." The Commission cannot, of course, award damages. The Court, it is submitted, must be contemplating compensation being available in the national courts. Otherwise the requirement of irreparable damage before interim measures can be taken by the Commission would be largely meaningless in practice because all damage would be irreparable once it occurred.

[8] As to the position of third parties, see para. 2.29. Art. 3 of Reg. 17 provides that any person who shows a legitimate interest may request the Commission to terminate an infringement of Art. 85 or 86.

[9] Above, n. 87.

[10] See the decision of the *Bundesgerichtshof* (German Federal Supreme Court) in the *BMW* case: [1980] E.C.C. 213, where it ruled that Arts. 85 and 86 are laws for the protection of individual rights. Note also *NV Club and NV GB-INNO-BM* v. *NV Elsevier-Sequoia*: [1980] 3 C.M.L.R. 258 (Commercial Court, Brussels).

[11] At [1983] 2 All E.R. 292.

interfering with the way Parker J. had exercised his discretion. In his judgment (with which Lords Keith, Bridge and Brandon concurred), Lord Diplock said:[12]

> "This article [86] of the Treaty was held by the Court of Justice of the European Communities in *Belgische Radio en Televisie* v. *SV SABAM* Case 127/73 [1974] E.C.R. 51 at 62 to produce direct effects in relations between individuals and to create direct rights in respect of the individuals concerned which the national courts must protect. The decision of the Court of Justice as to the effect of Article 86 is one which s. 3(1) of the European Communities Act 1972 requires your Lordships to follow. The rights which the article confers on citizens in the United Kingdom accordingly fall within s. 2(1) of the 1972 Act. They are without further enactment to be given legal effect in the United Kingdom and enforced accordingly.
>
> A breach of the duty imposed by article 86 not to abuse a dominant position in the Common Market or in a substantial part of it can thus be categorised in English law as a breach of statutory duty that is imposed not only for promoting the general economic prosperity of the Common Market but also for the benefit of private individuals to whom loss or damage is caused by a breach of that duty."

And later:[13]

> "My Lords, in the light (a) of the uniform jurisprudence of the Court of Justice of the European Communities, of which it is sufficient to mention the *Belgische Radio* case (which I have already cited) and the subsequent case of *Rewe-Zentralfinanz eG* v. *Landwirtschaftskammer für das Saarland* Case 33/76 [1976] E.C.R. 1989, which was to the same effect as respects the duty of national courts to protect rights conferred on individual citizens by directly applicable provisions of the Treaty, and (b) of ss. 2(1) and 3(1) of the European Communities Act 1972, I, for my own part, find it difficult to see how it can ultimately be successfully argued, as the Board will seek to do, that a contravention of Article 86 which causes damage to an individual citizen does not give rise to a cause of action in English law of the nature of a cause of action for breach of statutory duty; but since it cannot be regarded as unarguable that is not a matter for final decision by your Lordships at the interlocutory stage that the instant case has reached."

Lord Wilberforce, dissenting on the procedural issues and favouring the grant of an injunction, agreed however that an injured party can sue in this country for a breach of Article 86 and, since prohibited conduct is sanctioned by an injunction, obtain such relief. But, whilst Lord Diplock thought it "quite unarguable" that if breach of Article 86 gives rise to a cause of action at all, the only remedy was by way of injunction to prevent future loss, Lord Wilberforce did not share the confidence of the others that an injured party could recover damages. He drew attention to the scheme of Regulation

---

[12] Above, n. 87, at p. 775 of the All E.R. report, p. 49 of the C.M.L.R. report.
[13] *Ibid.* at p. 777 and p. 49 respectively.

17 and the Commission's powers in Articles 3 and 15 and added that there was no way under Community law by which such persons can get damages:

> "So the question is whether the situation is changed, and the remedy extended, by the incorporation of article 86 into our law by s. 2 of the European Communities Act 1972. To say that thereby that what is prohibited action becomes a tort or 'breach of statutory duty' is, in my opinion, a conclusionary statement concealing a vital and unexpressed step. All that s. 2 says (relevantly) is that rights arising under the EEC Treaty are to be available in law in the United Kingdom, but this does not suggest any transformation or enlargement of their character. Indeed the section calls them 'enforceable Community rights' not rights arising under United Kingdom law."

Lord Wilberforce did not, however, contend that a remedy in damages was unarguable. He did not think that the House could take a position on the point, which was only skeletally argued in interlocutory proceedings.

10.20   All their Lordships were of the view that a private person can sue in this country to prevent a breach of Article 86.[14] Whilst conceding that the matter was not to be finally decided in the instant context of appeal in interlocutory proceedings, the majority took the view that a remedy in damages is available for breach of the Community competition rules by way of an action for breach of statutory duty. But still as yet there has been no case where damages have been awarded[15] although it is understood that a number of cases have been settled. There is, as indicated above, strong authority that damages are available and in subsequent cases both the Court of Appeal and the High Court have recognised this.[16] However, one should not be too optimistic about the position of the injured party even if English courts hold that Articles 85 and 86 create a duty breach of which gives rise to an action for compensation. The plaintiff would still have to establish a breach of the duty. It is probable that he would have to show some degree of culpability or fault: the nature of the liability may be qualified and not absolute.[17] He would also have to show that the loss or injury suffered was of the type contemplated by the Treaty[18] and that it was caused by the breach. The difficulty of discharging the burden of proof in such cases should not be underestimated. Alternative routes are worthy of consideration and, as will be explained, it is possible that the Court of Justice may resolve some of the complex issues from a Community standpoint.

---

[14] On injunctive relief, see para. 10.16.

[15] In *Merson* v. *Rover Group*, unreported, judgment of May 22, 1992, the English High Court refused to give summary judgment with damages to be assessed under RSC Order 14A procedure. The infringement of the E.C. competition rules behind the case was upheld by the Court of Justice in Case 226/84, *British Leyland* v. *Commission*: [1986] E.C.R. 3263 [1987] 1 C.M.L.R. 185.

[16] In the *Bourgoin* case, above, n. 97, in *Cutsforth* v. *Mansfield Inns*, above, n. 93 and in *Plessey Co plc* v. *General Electric Co plc and Siemens*: [1990] E.C.C. 384 (granting *ex parte* injunction which was later lifted, above, n. 94).

[17] See Rew, *op. cit.*, at p. 472 referring to *Ministry of Housing and Local Government* v. *Sharp*: [1970] 1 W.L.R. 802. But see Steiner, *op. cit.*

[18] *Gorris* v. *Scott*: [1874] L.R. 9 Ex. 125.

A new tort

10.21 Whilst much academic discussion has concentrated on the breach of statutory duty, and the *Garden Cottage Foods* case suggested that this was the way, other remedies have been considered, including the torts of causing loss by unlawful means and of conspiracy and should not necessarily be neglected.[19] Another approach was proposed by Lord Denning in *Application des Gaz* v. *Falks Veritas*.[20] Having referred to *B.R.T.* v. *S.A.B.A.M.*[21] he said:

> "that the judgment of the European Court shows that Articles 85 and 86 create rights in private citizens which they can enforce in the national courts and which the national courts are bound to uphold. Furthermore ... the European Court held that it is for the national courts to assess the facts so as to see if they amount to an infringement. So we reach this important conclusion. Articles 85 and 86 are part of our law. They create new torts or wrongs. Their names are 'undue restriction of competition within the Common Market;' and 'abuse of dominant position within the Common Market.' Any infringement of those Articles can be dealt with by the English courts. It is for our courts to find the facts, to apply the law, and to use the remedies which we have available."

It must be said that this statement was most probably obiter—the case concerned the availability of the Articles as a defence to an action for copyright infringement. The textbook writers have not treated Lord Denning's new torts too enthusiastically.[22] Nor have other members of the Court of Appeal.[23] A new tort or torts might at least have the advantage that the difficulties associated with the attempts to find the remedy in the action for breach of statutory duty might be avoided.[24] It would also avoid the need to treat the Treaty as if it were a statute and despite *Garden Cottage Foods*, there is scope for treating the particular Community rights as *sui generis* and enforcing them accordingly.[25] But the desire, from the Community's position, to ensure, so far as possible, the uniform and effective enforcement of Community law and the forward movement of the Court of Justice in recent judgments to guarantee legal protection to those to whom Community law gives rights by directly effective measures may point

---

[19] These were discussed in the first edition of this book. See paras. 10.19–10.22, where some of these remedies were discussed. The ruling of the House of Lords in *Lonrho* v. *Shell*: [1981] 2 All E.R. 456 appeared to curtail severely the opportunities these torts could provide. But the more recent judgment of the Court of Appeal in *Lonrho* v. *Fayed*: [1989] 2 All.E.R. 65 and dicta in the House of Lords in that case have revived interest in the tort of causing loss by unlawful means and the author still considers that they may have potential in some cases. And see Steiner, *op. cit.* and Hoskins, *op. cit.*

[20] Above, n. 88.

[21] Case 127/73: [1974] E.C.R. 51, [1974] 2 C.M.L.R. 238.

[22] On the subject matter in the tort textbooks. See, for example, *Winfield and Jolowicz on Tort* (13th ed., 1989), p. 495.

[23] See *Valor International Ltd.* v. *Application des Gaz SA and E.P.I. Leisure Ltd.*: [1978] 3 C.M.L.R. 87, where Roskill L.J. said: "Obviously there are many questions which will have to be argued in this Court or elsewhere in this country or at Luxembourg, before it can be stated categorically, as is stated there by the Master of the Rolls, that Articles 85 and 86 create new torts or wrongs ... There are many arguments which can be advanced on both sides on this question and I would not want it thought, if this litigation continues over the next five or 10 years as it has over the past five years, that the passage represents the decision of this Court." But Lord Denning was, characteristically, not deterred and reiterated his view in the *Garden Cottage Foods* case, above, n. 11.

[24] See, *e.g.* Staines, *op. cit.*, at p. 64.

[25] See Davidson, *op. cit.*

the way for the nature and extent, if not every formal detail, of an action for damages being determined in Luxembourg rather than in London. The issue is presently before the Court of Justice.

10.21A In *Banks*[26] Advocate General Van Gerven has opined that a national court is obliged under Community law to award damages for loss sustained as a result of breach of a directly effective competition rule laid down by ECSC Treaty. Although *Banks* is an ECSC case it is clear from the argument and reasoning employed that the result would be the same under the E.C. Treaty. The Advocate General builds on the Court of Justice's jurisprudence ensuring that Community law is fully effective and also on the obligation in Article 5 of the Treaty requiring national courts to safeguard the legal protection which persons derive from the direct effect of provisions of Community law. He would extend the *Francovich* principle, that Member States may be liable to make good loss or damage caused by breaches of Community law for which they are responsible, to the case of an individual infringing a provision of Community law to which he is subject thereby causing loss and damage to another individual. Additional arguments, he says, justify this conclusion in the field of competition law; namely, the only effective way whereby national courts can fully safeguard provisions such as Articles 85 and 86 in a situation governed by private law where a party has suffered loss or damage is to restore the rights of the injured party by an award for damages, and such a rule of reparation would play a significant role in making the Community rules of competition more operational.

Advocate General Van Gerven argues that it is for the Court of Justice to lay down detailed rules for bringing actions of this kind. This is logical for if the very basis of the action is Community law there would be serious risks for the uniform and effective application of Community law if too many details are left to national law. Whilst recognising that the present state of Community law is not sufficient to fill in all the details, he proceeds, by drawing on the existing jurisprudence of the Court of Justice under Article 215 of the Treaty (which in itself, as regards non-contractual liability, draws "on the general principles common to the laws of the Member States"), to set out a number of rules. Essentially, a party invoking liability must prove that it has suffered damage. This must be actual and not speculative, although the latter requirement should not stop a party coming to the national court to restrain imminent forseeable damage. There must be a direct causal connection between the wrongful act or omission and the damage sustained. As regards the illegality of the conduct alleged the Advocate General concludes that it is sufficient if an undertaking infringes the directly affected provisions of Community competition law. The claimant does not therefore have to show any other element of fault nor can national law introduce any rule to limit or exclude such liability. Compensation must be made in full and interest would be payable on damages. Such a solution is far-reaching and at least as regards the issue of the strict advice of the liability, likely to be controversial. The response of the Court is awaited.

[26] Case C–128/92, *H.J. Banks & Co. Ltd.* v. *British Coal Corporation.*

Standard of proof—relevance on Commission decisions

10.22   In *Shearson Lehman Hutton Inc.* v. *Mclaine Watson*,[27] the English High Court took the view that the court should apply "a high degree of probability" in determining whether there had been an infringement of Article 85 or 86. Webster J. was influenced by the fact that an infringement of those rules renders the parties responsible liable to being fined. He therefore appeared to set a standard of proof higher than that normally appropriate to civil proceedings, namely the balance of probabilities. But in *Masterfoods Ltd. T/A Mars Ireland* v. *HB Ice Cream Ltd.*,[28] the Irish High Court held that the potential penal sanction for infringement of Article 85 or 86 did not alter the standard of proof from that required in civil cases to that in criminal proceedings. Whether the standard proposed by the English Court amounts to that of criminal cases is doubtful—it is probably somewhere between the normal civil and criminal standards. How far a plaintiff and a national court is entitled to rely on a related decision of the Commission must also receive a qualified answer at present. It has been suggested that the principle of constant and sincere co-operation in Article 5 of the Treaty and the Court of Justice's ruling in *Walt Wilhelm* v. *Bundeskartellamt*[29] should not permit a case already decided by the Commission to be re-litigated in the domestic court on issues concerning the application of Articles 85 and 86.[30] This is also consistent with the Court of Justice's guidance in *Delimitis*[31] that national courts should stay proceedings to allow the Commission to act where the position under Article 85(1) is not clear. There can be no doubt about this as regards an individual exemption decision under Article 85(3)—the Commission has exclusive jurisdiction and its decisions must be respected unless and until set aside by the Court. But in other cases the position is less clear. Decisions of negative clearance are probably not binding on a national court and the position as regards comfort letters is, as described more fully in Chapter 6, that a national court is not required to follow them although they are factors which that court may and should take into account. The extent to which a national court must follow a Commission decision finding an infringement should not, of course, be less than the case of a comfort letter and Article 5 of the Treaty may well imply a duty on the national court to mitigate as far as possible the risks of a ruling which conflicts with the Commission's decision. For the moment, as Advocate General Van Gerven said in *Banks*[32], the national court should follow the Court of Justice's guidance in *Delimitis*. He added that in the case of a finding which carried no weight in the Commission's final decision the national court is free to adopt a different interpretation. But in the case of findings which have an influence on the final decision the national court would be advised "to suspend the proceedings and to seek the necessary information from the Commission or to make a direct reference to the Court for a preliminary ruling concerning the validity of the decision in question[33] or the interpretation of the relevant competition rules". This may provide a way to a practical

[27] [1989] 3 C.M.L.R. 429.
[28] [1992] 3 C.M.L.R. 830.
[29] Case 14/68: [1969] E.C.R. 1, [1969] C.M.L.R. 100.
[30] Hoskins, *op. cit.*
[31] Case C–234/89, *Delimitis* v. *Henninger Bräu*: [1991] I E.C.R. 935, [1992] 5 C.M.L.R. 210.
[32] Above n. 26.
[33] It is unclear exactly what the A.G. had in mind here. Proceedings under Article 177 are not the same as and therefore cannot be substituted for Article 173. It is difficult to see how the Court of Justice could, in the context of Article 177 proceedings, resolve factual differences in the circumstances of a particular case. See, in this general context, the approach of the Berlin Court of Appeal in *Verband Sozialer Wett-*

solution but one should not underestimate the problems where the facts before the two bodies may not be identical.

Jurisdiction

10.23 It is a somewhat remarkable fact that in the vast majority of cases where Article 85 or 86 has been used as a sword, both plaintiff and defendant were resident in the same Member State.[34] Whilst it is not intended to treat the question of jurisdiction in detail,[35] it may be useful to point to the opportunities provided by the Convention of September 27, 1968 on Jurisdiction and the Enforcement of Judgments in Civil and Commercial Matters.[36] Its rules may be applicable to claims (tortious or delictual) for damages for breach of the competition rules. The basic rule is that a defendant who is domiciled in a Member State may be sued there,[37] irrespective of where the tort was committed or damage suffered. Where there are a number of defendants, they may be sued in the courts of a Member State in which any one of them is domiciled.[38] Article 5(3) provides an additional special rule for tort actions, allowing such actions to be brought in the courts for "the place where the harmful event occurs." The Court of Justice, in *Bier* v. *Mines de Potasse d'Alsace*,[39] has construed this as meaning either the place of the event causing damage or the place where damage occurred. Finally it should be noted that if the dispute arises out of the operations of a branch, agency or other establishment of the defendant, the defendant may be sued where it (the branch, agency, etc.) is situated.[40] The above list of jurisdictional bases may well give a plaintiff the opportunity for forum shopping, and legal advisers will no doubt consider and contrast the substantive and procedural rules (including discovery) in the available fora. As regards the recognition and enforcement of judgments in another Member State, the Convention provides a uniform procedure with limited grounds of review.[41]

Self-incrimination

10.24 Whilst the privilege against self-incrimination has a somewhat limited application in the context of the Commission's procedure[42] (as described in Chapter 3 it may be an answer to certain types of questions in requests and decisions under Article

---

bewerb v. *F. Berlin KG*: [1987] 3 C.M.L.R. 418. Moreover the Court of Justice has recently ruled that parties who do not take up their rights to challenge Commission decisions directly under Article 173 cannot later challenge them by way of a reference from a national court under Article 177: see Case C–188/92, *TWD Textilwerke Degendorf GmbH* v. *Germany*: judgment of March 9, 1994, not yet reported.

[34] See Picanol, *op. cit.*, at pp. 33–35.

[35] For this, as regards the position under English law, the reader is referred to *Supreme Court Practice* (the *White Book*).

[36] Implemented in the U.K. by the Civil Jurisdiction and Judgments Act 1982.

[37] Art. 2. The rules for determining domicile are contained in Arts. 52–53. And see ss. 41–46 of the 1982 Act.

[38] Art. 6(1).

[39] Case 21/76: [1976] E.C.R. 1735, [1977] 1 C.M.L.R. 284. See R.S.C. Ord. 11 r. 1(1)(b).

[40] Art. 5(5). And see Case C–439/93, *Lloyds Register of Shipping* v. *Société Companon Bernard*, before the Court of Justice.

[41] See Arts. 27 and 28.

[42] [1978] 1 All E.R. 434. S. 14 provides: "(1) The right of a person in any legal proceedings other than criminal proceedings to refuse to answer any question or produce any document or thing if it would tend to expose that person to proceedings for an offence or for the recovery of a penalty—(a) shall apply only as

11 of Regulation 17 requiring information) it seems that it may have greater impact in relation to proceedings before English courts, at least where the court is applying Articles 85 and 86 *à titre incident*. In *Rio Tinto Zinc* v. *Westinghouse Electric*, the House of Lords held that the privilege against self-incrimination contained in section 14 of the Civil Evidence Act 1968 extended to the discovery of documents by companies which might expose them to the risk of a fine by the Commission under Article 15 of Regulation 17. It held that such a fine was a penalty for the purposes of section 14 of the 1968 Act.[42] The practical effect may be a party alleging infringement of Article 85 or 86, whether by way of attack or defence, may be prevented by the plea of self-incrimination from gaining access (for example, by way of discovery) to the relevant documents and other materials which may be necessary to prove his case. The decision of the House of Lords in the *RTZ* case was followed and applied by Graham J. in *British Leyland* v. *Wyatt Interpart*.[43] Although, as mentioned at the beginning of this chapter, it is for Member States to designate procedural conditions governing legal actions intended to safeguard rights which derive from the direct effect of Community law, it is also clear, as the Court of Justice has said, that these conditions should not be such as to make it impossible in practice to exercise these rights. The *Factortame* case shows that national rules may have to be amended to secure the effectiveness of Community law. Moreover, quite independently of Community law, domestic law may be moving to according less protection in such circumstances.[44] The privilege against self-incrimination in national litigation may therefore come under attack. On the other hand the Court of Justice has recently held, in *Otto* v. *Postbank*,[45] that where privilege against self-incrimination does not exist in national proceedings Community law does not require the national court to apply the *Orkem* principle that an undertaking is not obliged to answer questions the answers to which might involve an admission of the existence of an infringement of Article 85 or 86. National procedural rules prevail. The Court of Justice recognised however that information so obtained might come to the knowledge of the Commission. In this event, the Court held, the Commission cannot use such information as evidence of a breach of the competition rules or even as evidence justifying the initiation of an inquiry prior to such proceedings.

II. CO-EXISTENCE OF COMMUNITY AND NATIONAL COMPETITION LAWS

10.25 Community competition law and national competition laws may overlap in their fields of application.[46] Whilst national laws may be designed to deal with the same sorts of circumstances (*i.e.* restrictive practices, cartels, dominant positions) as

regards criminal offences under the law of any part of the United Kingdom and penalties provided for by such law."

[43] [1979] 3 C.M.L.R. 79.

[44] See *A.T. & T Istel Ltd. and another* v. *Tully and another*: [1992] 3 W.L.R. 344.

[45] Case C–60/92, *Otto BV* v. *Postbank NV*: judgment of November 10, 1993, not yet reported.

[46] See generally, Goldman, *European Commercial Law* (1973), Chap. 31; Jacobs, "The Application of the EEC Rules on Competition in the U.K. after Accession" (1972) 88 L.Q.R. 487; Markert, "Some Legal and Administrative Problems of the Co-existence of Community and National Competition Law in the EEC" (1974) 11 C.M.L.Rev. 92, Verstrynge, "The Relationship between National and Community Antitrust Law: An Overview after the Perfume Cases" (1981) 3 Northwestern J. of Int'l Law and Business 358, and Stockmann, "EEC Competition Law and Member State Competition Laws" (1987) Fordham

Community law, their purposes will, generally, be specific to the Member State in question and may not however necessarily reflect the same interests and objectives as the Community's.[47] The application of two or more concurrent systems of competition law need not necessarily give rise to conflicts. A good example is the *GKN/Sachs* merger.[48] The Commission was concerned first for the market of iron and steel products under the ECSC competition rules and following an examination of the case gave authorization under Article 66 of the ECSC Treaty. The German Cartel Office was concerned for the market of automotive components, particularly clutches, which were outside the ECSC rules but might have come within the E.C. rules. However, the Commission did not consider that there were any grounds for action under Article 86 against the merger. The non-ECSC market was therefore free for the Cartel Office to deal with and there was therefore no conflict in the circumstances. The Cartel Office decided that section 24 of the Restraint of Competition Act was applicable to the case and prohibited the merger.[49]

The broad jurisdictional demarcation line between the E.C. rules and national competition law is said to be "the effect upon trade between Member States." Thus in *Consten and Grundig* v. *Commission*, the Court said:[50] "The concept of an agreement 'which may affect trade between Member States' is intended to define, in the law governing cartels, the boundary between the areas respectively covered by Community law and national law." Only if an agreement affects trade between Member States is it capable of falling within the prohibition of Article 85(1). In practice the different fields of application, whether territorial or substantive, of national and Community law may be blurred and as a consequence there is, at least potentially, always a possibility of conflict.

Precedence of Community Law

10.26   Article 87(2)(e) empowers the Council, acting on a proposal from the Commission, to determine by means of regulations or directives the relationship between national laws and the Community rules on competition and their application.[51] No such regulation or directive has been made and, in the absence of such measures, the

---

Corp.L.Inst. 265.

[47] Community law is not obliged to follow the precepts and policies of Member States' laws. Cases 43 & 63/82, *VBVB and VBBB* v. *Commission*: [1984] E.C.R. 19, [1985] 1 C.M.L.R. 27, at paras. 38–40. The Court rejected the argument that because r.p.m. for books was accepted in Member States' laws, the Commission ought therefore to accept this convergent practice as a mandatory guideline for its own policy on the subject. See also Case 298/83, *C.I.C.C.E.* v. *Commission*: [1985] E.C.R. 1106, [1986] 1 C.M.L.R. 486, at paras. 26–28. Similarity between national competition law and the Community rules cannot restrict the Commission's freedom of action and compel it to adopt the same assessment of the situation.

[48] Sixth Report on Competition Policy, points. 110–113. A more recent example of peaceful co-existence can be seen in *Eurocheque Helsinki Agreement*: [1992] O.J. L95/50.

[49] The *Bundesgerichtshof* (German Federal Supreme Court) ultimately upheld the Cartel Office's decision to prohibit the merger—Eighth Report on Competition Policy, point 58.

[50] Cases 56 & 58/64: [1966] E.C.R. 299, 341, [1966] C.M.L.R. 418, 472, and see Cases 6 & 7/73, *Commercial Solvents* v. *Commission*: [1974] E.C.R. 223, [1974] 1 C.M.L.R. 309, at para. 31; Case 22/78, *Hugin* v. *Commission*: [1979] E.C.R. 1869, [1979] 3 C.M.L.R. 345, at para. 17; and the *Perfumes* cases: Cases 253/78 & 1–3/79, *Procureur de la République* v. *Giry and Guerlain SA*: [1980] E.C.R. 2327, [1981] 2 C.M.L.R. 99, at para. 15. *Quaere* whether the principle of subsidiarity will be considered by the Court of Justice as cause for redefining this boundary between Community and national law.

[51] Art. 87 is discussed at para. 1.24.

Court of Justice has ruled that conflicts must be resolved on the basis of the general principles of Community law. The leading case is *Walt Wilhelm* v. *Bundeskartellamt*.[52] The German Cartel Office took proceedings, under German law, against a number of German companies which had participated in alleged concerted practices relating to the prices of aniline dyes. On appeal to the Kammergericht, the companies claimed that because the same matter was the subject of proceedings brought by the Commission,[53] the Cartel Office could not proceed against them. The Kammergericht referred the question of the compatibility of parallel proceedings under Community law to the Court of Justice under the Article 177 procedure. The Court explained the position as follows:

"3. . . . Community and national law on cartels consider cartels from different points of view. Whereas Article 85 regards them in the light of the obstacles which may result for trade between Member States, each body of national legislation proceeds on the basis of the considerations peculiar to it and considers cartels only in that context. It is true that as the economic phenomena and legal situations under consideration may, in individual cases, be interdependent, the distinction between Community and national aspects could not serve in all cases as the decisive criterion for the delimitation of jurisdiction.However, it implies that one and the same agreement may, in principle, be the object of two sets of parallel proceedings, one before the Community authorities under Article 85 of the EEC Treaty, the other before the national authorities under national law.

4. Moreover this interpretation is confirmed by the provision in Article 87(2) (e), which authorises the Council to determine the relationship between the national laws and the Community rules on competition; it follows that in principle the national cartel authorities may take proceedings also with regard to situations likely to be the subject of a decision by the Commission. However, if the ultimate general aim of the Treaty is to be respected, this parallel application of the national system can only be allowed in so far as it does not prejudice the uniform application throughout the Common Market of the Community rules on cartels and of the full effect of the measures adopted in implementation of those rules.

5. Any other solution would be incompatible with the objectives of the Treaty and the character of its rules on competition. Article 85 of the EEC Treaty applies to all the undertakings in the Community whose conduct is governed either by prohibitions or by means of exemptions, granted—subject to conditions which it specifies—in favour of agreements which contribute to improving the production or distribution of goods or to promoting technical or economic progress. While the Treaty's primary object is to eliminate by this means the obstacles to the free movement of goods within the common market to confirm and safeguard the unity of that market, it also permits the Community authorities to carry out certain positive, though indirect, action with a view to promoting a harmonious development of economic activities within the whole

[52] Above, n. 29.
[53] *Dyestuffs*: [1969] J.O. L195/11, [1969] C.M.L.R. D23.

Community in accordance with Article 2 of the Treaty. Article 87(2)(e), in conferring on a Community institution the power to determine the relationship between national laws and the Community rules on competition, confirms the supremacy of Community law.

6. The EEC Treaty has established its own system of law, integrated into the legal systems of the Member States, and which must be applied by their courts. It would be contrary to the nature of such a system to allow Member States to introduce or to retain measures capable of prejudicing the practical effectiveness of the Treaty. The binding force of the Treaty and of measures taken in application of it must not differ from one state to another as a result of internal measures, lest the functioning of the Community system should be impeded and the achievement of the aims of the Treaty placed in peril. Consequently, conflicts between the rules of the Community and national rules in the matter of law on cartels must be resolved by applying the principle that Community law takes precedence.

7. It follows from the foregoing that should it prove that a decision of a national authority regarding an agreement would be incompatible with a decision adopted by the Commission at the culmination of the procedure initiated by it, the national authority is required to take proper account of the effect of the latter decision.

8. Where, during national proceedings, it appears possible that the decision to be taken by the Commission at the culmination of a procedure still in progress concerning the same agreement may conflict with the effects of the decision of the national authorities, it is for the latter to take the appropriate measures.

9. Consequently, and so long as a regulation adopted pursuant to Article 87(2) (e) of the Treaty has not provided otherwise, national authorities may take action against an agreement in accordance with their national law, even when an examination of an agreement from the point of view of its compatibility with Community law is pending before the Commission, subject however to the condition that the application of national law may not prejudice the full and uniform application of Community law or the effects of measures taken or to be taken to implement it."

The Court clearly confirmed the co-existence of Community law and national laws on competition and rejected the argument that Community competition law might in some respect be exclusive. The parallel application of national competition law is, however, permissible only in so far as it does not impinge upon the uniform application, throughout the Common Market, of the Community rules on restrictive agreements and of the full effect of measures taken in implementation of the rules. The Court repeated this general principle in the *Perfumes* cases.[54] But whilst it may be stated simply, its practical application is more complicated and controversial.

---

[54] Above, n. 50.

Community Prohibitions

10.27 As regards prohibitions, the Court of Justice held in the *Wilhelm* case that an agreement could be the subject of prohibitions under both Community and national law.[55] The applicability of the prohibition in Article 85(1) does not mean that the agreement escapes a national prohibition.[56] Moreover a national authority is not prevented from proceeding against an agreement and may even apply a sanction (*e.g.* a fine or penalty).[57] The Court said: "the possibility of concurrent sanctions need not mean that the possibility of two parallel proceedings pursuing different ends is unacceptable."[58] Nonetheless, the application of the national law is still subject to the proviso that it must not prejudice the uniform application of the Community rules. A Community prohibition will prevail over any authorisation or exemption granted by national law.[59] The prohibitions in Articles 85(1) and 86 are directly applicable and under the general principle of the supremacy of Community law will overrule any national provision at variance with it. Any authorisation by national law of an agreement, practice or conduct which is forbidden by Article 85 or 86 will therefore be ineffectual. Parties could not, for example, enforce their agreement in a national court. As the Court of Justice held in the *Simmenthal* case:[60]

> "A national court which is called upon, within the limits of its jurisdiction, to apply provisions of Community law is under a duty to give full effect to those provisions, if necessary refusing on its own motion to apply any provision of national legislation, even if adopted subsequently, and it is not necessary for the court to request or await the prior setting aside of such provisions by legislative or other constitutional means."

National legislative or judicial practices, even on the supposition that they were common to all its Member States, cannot prevail in the application of the Community competition rules.[61]

Negative clearance

10.28 Where the agreement falls outside the scope of Article 85 then there can be no objection to the application of national law. Such application could not be said to prejudice "the full and uniform application of Community law or the effects of measures taken or to be taken to implement it." If the criteria for the applicability of Article 85 or 86 are not satisfied, there cannot by definition be any conflict between national

---

[55] Above, n. 29, at para. 11.

[56] See, *e.g.* s. 5(1) of the Restrictive Trade Practices Act 1976.

[57] See, *e.g. Cast Iron and Steel Rolls*: [1983] O.J. L317/1, [1984] 1 C.M.L.R. 694, where the Commission's procedure followed that of the Cartel Office in Germany.

[58] See n. 55, above.

[59] See *Fire Insurance (D)*: [1985] O.J. L35/20, [1985] 3 C.M.L.R. 246, upheld by the Court in Case 45/85, *Verband der Sachversicherer* v. *Commission*: [1987] E.C.R. 405, [1988] 4 C.M.L.R. 264, in particular paras. 17–24.

[60] Case 106/77: [1978] E.C.R. 629, 645, [1978] 3 C.M.L.R. 263, 284.

[61] See the *Dutch Books* case, above, n. 47.

and Community law. The Court of Justice made this clear in the *Perfumes* cases. It drew attention to the fact that the Commission had expressed the view that the agreements in question did not fall within Article 85(1) because they did not affect trade between Member States. Accordingly, the Court said that there was no obstacle to their being considered by national authorities as regards the anti-competitive effects they might produce in the national context.[62]

Community exemption

10.29   The critical case is that where Community law grants an exemption but national law purports to prohibit the agreement. Advocates of the so-called double barrier theory (*Zweischrankentheorie*) argue that an agreement is only lawful if it passes the tests laid down by both national law and Community law. It is based on a complete philosophy of competition, of which prohibition is considered the material instrument, and exemptions are tolerated but are by no means indispensable.[63] The Commission has said that the Court of Justice rejected this theory in the *Wilhelm* case.[64] It did not, of course, in so many words but, as will be shown below, there must be serious doubt about the validity of the theory in Community law, at least in its purest form.

   It has been suggested that the Court's reference to "certain positive, though indirect, action" of Community institutions means or includes exemption whether by Commission decision or by regulation as in the case of block exemptions.[65] Given the context in which the phrase appears the argument is compelling. There is, however, an alternative interpretation.[66] The positive action referred to means other measures under the Treaty such as directives under Article 102 to Member States to harmonise national laws. Even so, it might still be argued that a national prohibition cannot override the effect of a Community exemption because, as the Court said, the application of national laws must not interfere with "the uniform application throughout the Common Market of the Community rules on cartels and of the full effect of the measures adopted in implementation of those rules." (Indeed it is a consistent theme of the Court's case law that the Treaty imposes a duty on Member States not to adopt or maintain in force any measure which could deprive Articles 85 and 86 of their effectiveness.[67]) Again the meaning of "measures in implementation" may be at issue, but it is also said that the uniform application of Community law would be impeded if an exempted agreement were to be prohibited in some Member States by the operation of "stricter" national law but not in others where there was no such law. The requirement that the uniform application of Community law should not be jeopardised is necessary so that the "ultimate general aim of the Treaty" can be respected and, as the Court added,

---

[62] Above, n. 54, at para. 18. And see Case 31/80, *NV L'Oréal (Brussels), L'Oréal SA (Paris)* v. *De Nieuwe AMCK*: [1980] E.C.R. 3775, [1981] 2 C.M.L.R. 235.
[63] Goldman, *op. cit.*, p. 429.
[64] Fourth Report on Competition Policy, point 45.
[65] See, *e.g.* Ritter, Braun and Rawlinson, *EEC Competition Law: A Practitioner's Guide* (1991), at p. 39. But even they consider the point is not yet settled.
[66] Markert, *op. cit.*, at p. 95.
[67] See Case 13/77, *GB-INNO-BM* v. *ATAB*: [1977] E.C.R. 2115, [1978] 1 C.M.L.R. 283; Case 229/83, *Leclerq* v. *Au Blé Vert*: [1985] 2 C.M.L.R. 286; Case 231/83, *M. Cullet* v. *Leclerq*: [1985] 2 C.M.L.R. 524; Air Tariffs (Cases 209–213/84: [1986] E.C.R. 1425, [1986] 3 C.M.L.R. 173) Case 267/86, *Pascal Van Eycke* v. *Aspa NV*: [1988] E.C.R. 4769, [1990] 4 C.M.L.R. 330 and the Court's recent judgments in Case C–2/91, *Meng*, C–185/91, *Reiff* and C–245/91, *Ohra*: November 17, 1993, not yet reported. The duty mentioned is that in Art. 5(2) E.C.

"any other solution would be incompatible with the objectives of the Treaty and the character of its rules on competition." But, as Advocate General Roemer commented:[68]

> "If national authorities thwart the Community exemption through the application of a national rule of prohibition, they no more threaten the objectives of the Treaty than do the parties to an agreement when they refrain from applying it, which can occur at any time. This conclusion applies as a general rule because in principle cartels cannot be considered as instruments of the organisation of the Common Market."

Indeed, in the absence of a Community provision which requires the performance of an exempted agreement, it is surprising that a Member State could be considered to be under an obligation to relax its national law to permit such performance.

10.30   The *Wilhelm* case was not concerned with a Community exemption but with the application of parallel prohibitions. The Court of Justice therefore did not have to examine the legal nature of such an exemption in this context. An exemption under Article 85(3) is, it is submitted, essentially permissive in character.[69] It operates to negate the prohibition in Article 85(1) leaving the parties free to give effect to their agreement without fear of any sanction under Community law. It is no more and no less. The agreement may be impeached in a national court for a variety of other reasons under the law applicable to the contract. It has never been suggested that an exemption under Article 85 "heals" any lack of capacity, fraud or other provision of national law (commercial, fiscal, criminal, etc.) which may be relevant. Competition law is only another instance where a state's social and economic policies[70] may impinge upon business and contractual relationships.

Even if national competition law must respect Community exemptions, it is by no means clear that all such exemptions must be respected. At one time, the Commission itself acknowledged uncertainty here:[71]

> "The Court's judgment ... leaves open the question whether the primacy of Community exemptions constitutes a strict rule, or whether it should be regarded rather as a flexible principle in the application of which it is permissible

---

[68] Case 14/68: [1969] E.C.R. 1, [1969] C.M.L.R. 100, at p. 23. Goyder considers this statement to be misleading: *EEC Competition Law* (2nd ed., 1993) at p. 435. He argues that even if not applied by the parties the Commission's decision still has value as a precedent and other parties may take account of it accordingly in future cases. This is not, it is submitted, convincing. Leaving aside the value that may be placed on any particular decision as a precedent (some may be heavily fact-dependent) the value as a precedent is not undermined by the application of stricter national law.

[69] A.G. Roemer spoke of the application of Art. 85(1) being waived. *Ibid.* But see A.G. Reischl in the *L'Oréal* case, above, n. 62.

[70] Both Court and Commission have recognised the position of national economic policies. See the *German Fire Insurance* case, above, n. 59.

[71] Fourth Report on Competition Policy, point 45.

to take account of the respective interests of the Community and of Member States."

It has been suggested, for example, that only exemptions granted for reasons of public policy ("political" exemptions) need be respected.[72] But the Commission does not appear to have been attracted by this and indeed has been quite robust about the effect of exemptions, describing block exemption regulations and formal exemption decisions as "the only Commission measures which prevent the application of domestic competition law where this would have the effect of prohibiting or annulling an agreement exempted under Article 85(3)."[73]

It has also looked as though the Court of Justice might take a similar approach. In *Metro II*,[74] Advocate General VerLoren van Themaat remarked that the importance of the case was emphasised by the fact that it followed [from the *Wilhelm* case] that, if the policy contained in the Commission's decision[75] exempting the SABA selective distribution system were accepted "the competition authorities of three Member States (France, the Netherlands and the United Kingdom) will be unable to pursue unaltered their different policy as regards the boycotting of certain forms of distribution."

The relationship between Community law and national law in this context may prove to be more subtle. It is to be noted that the recitals to certain bloc exemptions expressly contemplate the application of stricter national competition laws.[76] The Commission also appears to have returned to a more flexible approach to the question, at least as regards block exemptions. In relation to the application in the United Kingdom of a more strict regime to the sale of beer in tied houses than that contemplated in Regulation 1984/83, the Commission has said:[77]

> "In general, the Commission has always considered that national regulations which are more stringent than bloc exemption regulations drawn up by the Commission are compatible with them, provided they do not affect the essential conditions of such exemptions."

In conclusion, it would appear that the position as regards the status and effects of Community exemptions is uncertain. It is undecided whether all, some or none need necessarily be respected by national law and, if so, to what extent. It is significant that in the *Perfumes* cases the Court of Justice appeared deliberately to leave open the

---

[72] Markert, *op. cit.*, at p. 99. Goyder, *op. cit.*, at p. 434 has criticised this as putting forward a distinction which may be difficult to apply in practice having regard to the application of public policy elements in any case under Art. 85(3).

[73] See the reply to Written Question No. 1508/81: [1981] O.J. C85/6. But note the recognition of national laws and measures in recital 19 to Reg. 1984/83 (the block exemption for exclusive purchasing agreements).

[74] Case 75/84, *Metro-SB-Grossmarkte GmbH & Co. KG* v. *Commission*: [1986] E.C.R. 3021, [1987] 1 C.M.L.R. 118.

[75] See *SABA's EEC Distribution System*: [1983] O.J. L376/41, [1984] 1 C.M.L.R. 676.

[76] See recital 19 to Reg. 1984/83 and recital 29 to Reg. 123/85.

[77] See EP Debates No. 3–416/192. Question No. H–1170/91, reported in [1993] 4 C.M.L.R. 26. The background can be seen in Elland, "Brewing: Recipe for a European Hangover" *Law Society's Gazette* April 26, 1989, p. 19. Questions have also been raised in relation to the implementation of the U.K. Monopolies and Mergers Commission report on automobiles and the application of the new Irish Competition Act. See Holley, "EEC Competition Practice: A Thirty Year Retrospective" 16 Fordham Int. L.J. 342, at pp. 363–364.

question of how the general statements made in the Wilhelm case should be applied in the context of an exemption under Article 85(3).[78] The Court shows wisdom in moving one step at a time in issues such as this. Some clarification may however soon be forthcoming. The Court of Justice has before it the question of the relationship of the bloc exemption for vehicle distribution (Regulation 123/85) and the application of stricter national law.[79]

Practical co-operation between Community and national authorities

10.31   The Court of Justice in the *Wilhelm* case gave some practical guidance as to how to avoid conflicts. In short, where in the course of the national proceedings it appears that there may be a conflict, it is for the national authority to take "appropriate measures."[80] The Commission has put forward two possible solutions; (a) the suppression of the national proceedings until the Commission has given its decision, and (b) consultation with the Commission before adopting the national decision.[81] It is noteworthy that certain provisions of United Kingdom competition law are compatible with the first proposal. Under sections 5 and 21 of the Restrictive Trade Practices Act 1976 the Restrictive Practices Court and the Director General of Fair Trading are given a discretion not to proceed. Other Member States' competition laws may also allow proceedings to be suspended.[82]

On a more general level, if conflicts are to be eliminated, consultation between national authorities and the Commission should be the norm. Where a national authority commences proceedings in respect of a set of circumstances which might also be subject to Community law, the Commission should be informed as early as possible and in any event not later than the time when formal proceedings are begun. (There is at least one Member State, Germany, which has a notification procedure.[83]) It has also been suggested that such notification might be accompanied by similar obligations in respect of information and consultation as are incumbent on the Commission *vis-à-vis* national authorities under Article 10 of Regulation 17. No formal or detailed rules have been settled, and the Member States have indicated their preference for increased exchange of information and consultation as a means of avoiding conflicts, rather than a regulation under Article 87(2)(e) of the Treaty.[84]

---

[78] Above, n. 50, at para. 17.
[79] See Case C–70/93, *BMW* v. *ALD Auto-Leasing*: and Case C–266/93, *Bundeskartellamt* v. *Volkswagen AG*: references from German courts under Article 177.
[80] Above, n. 68, at para. 8.
[81] Fourth Report on Competition Policy, point 46.
[82] Note the actions of the French competition authorities in *Quantel International–Continuum/Quantel SA*: [1992] O.J. L235/9.
[83] Markert, *op. cit.*, at p. 100.
[84] Fourth Report on Competition Policy, point 114. Another explanation for the absence of Community Regulation on the subject may be that there has not in practice been any major conflicts. Ritter, Braun, Rawlinson, *op. cit.*, at p. 41.

Appendix A

COUNCIL REGULATION 17[1]

First Regulation implementing Articles 85 and 86 of the Treaty.

THE COUNCIL OF THE EUROPEAN ECONOMIC COMMUNITY

Having regard to the Treaty establishing the European Economic Community, and in particular Article 87 thereof;

Having regard to the proposal from the Commission;

Having regard to the Opinion of the Economic and Social Committee;

Having regard to the Opinion of the European Parliament;

Whereas, in order to establish a system ensuring that competition shall not be distorted in the common market, it is necessary to provide for balanced application of Articles 85 and 86 in a uniform manner in the Member States;

Whereas in establishing the rules for applying Article 85(3) account must be taken of the need to ensure effective supervision and to simplify administration to the greatest possible extent;

Whereas it is accordingly necessary to make it obligatory, as a general principle, for undertakings which seek application of Article 85(3) to notify to the Commission their agreements, decisions and concerted practices;

Whereas, on the one hand, such agreements, decisions and concerted practices are probably very numerous and cannot therefore all be examined at the same time and, on the other hand, some of them have special features which may make them less prejudicial to the development of the common market.;

Whereas there is consequently a need to make more flexible arrangements for the time being in respect of certain categories of agreement, decision and concerted practice without prejudging their validity under Article 85;

Whereas it may be in the interest of undertakings to know whether any agreements, decisions or practices to which they are party, or propose to become party, may lead to action on the part of the Commission pursuant to Article 85(1) or Article 86;

Whereas, in order to secure uniform application of Articles 85 and 86 in the common market, rules must be made under which the Commission, acting in close and constant liaison with the competent authorities of the Member States, may take the requisite measures for applying those Articles;

Whereas for this purpose the Commission must have the co-operation of the competent authorities of the Member States and be empowered, throughout the common market, to require such information to be supplied and to undertake such investigations as are necessary to bring to

[1] J.O. 204/62, [1959–62] O.J. Spec.Ed. 57; came into force 13 March 1962.

light any agreement, decision or concerted practice prohibited by Article 85(1) or any abuse of a dominant position prohibited by Article 86;

Whereas, in order to carry out its duty of ensuring that the provisions of the Treaty are applied, the Commission must be empowered to address to undertakings or associations of undertakings recommendations and decisions for the purpose of bringing to an end infringements of Articles 85 and 86;

Whereas compliance with Articles 85 and 86 and the fulfilment of obligations imposed on undertakings and associations of undertakings under this Regulation must be enforceable by means of fines and periodic penalty payments;

Whereas undertakings concerned must be accorded the right to be heard by the Commission, third parties whose interests may be affected by a decision must be given the opportunity of submitting their comments beforehand, and it must be ensured that wide publicity is given to decisions taken;

Whereas all decisions taken by the Commission under this Regulation are subject to review by the Court of Justice under the conditions specified in the Treaty; whereas it is moreover desirable to confer upon the Court of Justice, pursuant to Article 172, unlimited jurisdiction in respect of decisions under which the Commission imposes fines or periodic penalty payments;

Whereas this Regulation may enter into force without prejudice to any other provisions that may hereafter be adopted pursuant to Article 87;

HAS ADOPTED THIS REGULATION:

Article 1—Basic provision

Without prejudice to Articles 6, 7 and 23 of this Regulation, agreements, decisions and concerted practices of the kind described in Article 85(1) of the Treaty and the abuse of a dominant position in the market, within the meaning of Article 86 of the Treaty, shall be prohibited, no prior decision to that effect being required.

Article 2—Negative clearance

Upon application by the undertakings or associations of undertakings concerned, the Commission may certify that, on the basis of the facts in its possession, there are no grounds under Article 85(1) or Article 86 of the Treaty for action on its part in respect of an agreement, decision or practice.

Article 3—Termination of Infringements

1. Where the Commission, upon application or upon its own initiative, finds that there is infringement of Article 85 or Article 86 of the Treaty, it may by decision require the undertakings or associations of undertakings concerned to bring such infringement to an end.

2. Those entitled to make application are:
(a) Member States;
(b) natural or legal persons who claim a legitimate interest.

3. Without prejudice to the other provisions of this Regulation, the Commission may, before taking a decision under paragraph 1, address to the undertakings or associations of undertakings concerned recommendations for termination of the infringement.

Article 4— Notification of new agreements, decisions and practices

1. Agreements, decisions and concerted practices of the kind described in Article 85(1) of the Treaty which come into existence after the entry into force of this Regulation and in respect of which the parties seek application of Article 85(3) must be notified to the Commission. Until they have been notified, no decision in application of Article 85(3) may be taken.

2. Paragraph 1 shall not apply to agreements, decisions and concerted practices where:

(1) the only parties thereto are undertakings from one Member State and the agreements, decisions or practices do not relate either to imports or to exports between Member States;

(2) not more than two undertakings are party thereto, and the agreements only:

   (a) restrict the freedom of one party to the contract in determining the prices or conditions of business upon which the goods which he has obtained from the other party to the contract may be resold; or

   (b) impose restrictions on the exercise of the rights of the assignee or user of industrial property rights—in particular patents, utility models, designs or trade marks—or of the person entitled under a contract to the assignment, or grant, of the right to use a method of manufacture or knowledge relating to the use and to the application of industrial processes;

(3) they have as their sole object

   (a) the development or uniform application of standards or types; or

   (b) joint research and development;

   (c) specialisation in the manufacture of products, including agreements necessary for achieving this,

   — where the products which are subject of specialisation do not, in a substantial part of the common market, represent more than 15 per cent. of the volume of business done in identical products or those considered by consumers to be similar by reason of their characteristics, price and use, and

   — where the total annual turnover of the participating undertakings does not exceed 200 million units of account.

These agreements, decisions and practices may be notified to the Commission.[2]

Article 5—Notification of existing agreements, decisions and practices

1. Agreements, decisions and concerted practices of the kind described in Article 85(1) of the Treaty which are in existence at the date of entry into force of this Regulation and in respect of which the parties seek application of Article 85(3) shall be notified to the Commission before 1 November 1962. However, notwithstanding the foregoing provisions, any agreements, decisions and concerted practices to which not more than two undertakings are party shall be notified before 1 February 1963.[3]

2. Paragraph 1 shall not apply to agreements, decisions or concerted practices falling within Article 4(2); these may be notified to the Commission.

Article 6—Decisions pursuant to Article 85(3)

1. Whenever the Commission takes a decision pursuant to Article 85(3) of the Treaty, it shall specify therein the date from which the decision shall take effect. Such date shall not be earlier than the date of notification.

2. The second sentence of paragraph 1 shall not apply to agreements, decisions or concerted practices falling within Article 4(2) and Article 5(2), nor to those falling within Article 5(1) which have been notified within the time limit specified in Article 5(1).

---

[2] Amended by Reg. 2822/71.
[3] Amended by Reg. 59/62. And see Art. 25, *post.*

Article 7—Special provisions for existing agreements, decisions and practices

1. Where agreements, decisions and concerted practices in existence at the date of entry into force of this Regulation and notified within the time limit specified in Article 5(1)[4] do not satisfy the requirements of Article 85(3) of the Treaty and the undertakings or associations of undertakings concerned cease to give effect to them or modify them in such manner that they no longer fall within the prohibition contained in Article 85(1) or that they satisfy the requirements of Article 85(3), the prohibition contained in Article 85(1) shall apply only for a period fixed by the Commission. A decision by the Commission pursuant to the foregoing sentence shall not apply as against undertakings and associations of undertakings which did not expressly consent to the notification.

2. Paragraph 1 shall apply to agreements, decisions and concerted practices falling within Article 4(2) which are in existence at the date of entry into force of this Regulation if they are notified before 1 January 1967.[5]

Article 8—Duration and revocation of decisions under Article 85(3)

1. A decision in application of Article 85(3) of the Treaty shall be issued for a specified period and conditions and obligations may be attached thereto.

2. A decision may on application be renewed if the requirements of Article 85(3) of the Treaty continue to be satisfied.

3. The Commission may revoke or amend its decision or prohibit specified acts by the parties:
    (a) where there has been a change in any of the facts which were basic to the making of the decision;
    (b) where the parties commit a breach of any obligation attached to the decision;
    (c) where the decision is based on incorrect information or was induced by deceit;
    (d) where the parties abuse the exemption from the provisions of Article 85(1) of the Treaty granted to them by the decision.
In cases to which subparagraphs (b), (c) or (d) apply, the decision may be revoked with retroactive effect.

Article 9—Powers

1. Subject to review of its decisions by the Court of Justice, the Commission shall have sole power to declare Article 85(1) inapplicable pursuant to Article 85(3) of the Treaty.

2. The Commission shall have power to apply Article 85(1) and Article 86 of the Treaty; this power may be exercised notwithstanding that the time limits specified in Article 5(1) and in Article 7(2) relating to notification have not expired.

3. As long as the Commission has not initiated any procedure under Articles 2, 3 or 6, the authorities of the Member States shall remain competent to apply Article 85(1) and Article 86 in accordance with Article 88 of the Treaty; they shall remain competent in this respect notwithstanding that the time limits specified in Article 5(1) and in Article 7(2) relating to notification have not expired.

---

[4] Amended by Reg. 59/62. And see Art. 25, *post*.
[5] Amended by Reg. 118/63. And see Art. 25, *post*.

Article 10—Liaison with the authorities of the Member States

1. The Commission shall forthwith transmit to the competent authorities of the Member States a copy of the applications and notifications together with copies of the most important documents lodged with the Commission for the purpose of establishing the existence of infringements of Article 85 or 86 of the Treaty or of obtaining negative clearance or a decision in application of Article 85(3).

2. The Commission shall carry out the procedure set out in paragraph 1 in close and constant liaison with the competent authorities of the Member States; such authorities shall have the right to express their views upon that procedure.

3. An Advisory Committee on Restrictive Practices and Monopolies shall be consulted prior to the taking of any decision following upon a procedure under paragraph 1, and of any decision concerning the renewal, amendment or revocation of a decision pursuant to Article 85(3) of the Treaty.

4. The Advisory Committee shall be composed of officials competent in the matter of restrictive practices and monopolies. Each Member State shall appoint an official to represent it who, if prevented from attending, may be replaced by another official.

5. The consultation shall take place at a joint meeting convened by the Commission; such meeting shall be held not earlier than fourteen days after dispatch of the notice convening it. The notice shall, in respect of each case to be examined, be accompanied by a summary of the case together with an indication of the most important documents, and a preliminary draft decision.

6. The Advisory Committee may deliver an opinion notwithstanding that some of its members or their alternates are not present. A report of the outcome of the consultative proceedings shall be annexed to the draft decision. It shall not be made public.

Article 11—Requests for information

1. In carrying out the duties assigned to it by Article 89 and by provisions adopted under Article 87 of the Treaty, the Commission may obtain all necessary information from the Governments and competent authorities of the Member States and from undertakings and associations of undertakings.

2. When sending a request for information to an undertaking or association of undertakings, the Commission shall at the same time forward a copy of the request to the competent authority of the Member State in whose territory the seat of the undertaking or association of undertakings is situated.

3. In its request the Commission shall state the legal basis and the purpose of the request and also the penalties provided for in Article 15(1)(b) for supplying incorrect information.

4. The owners of the undertakings or their representatives and, in the case of legal persons, companies or firms, or of associations having no legal personality, the persons authorised to represent them by law or by their constitution shall supply the information requested.

5. Where an undertaking or association of undertakings does not supply the information requested within the time limit fixed by the Commission, or supplies incomplete information, the Commission shall by decision require the information to be supplied. The decision shall specify what information is required, fix an appropriate time limit within which it is to be supplied and indicate the penalties provided for in Article 15(1)(b) and Article 16(1)(c) and the right to have the decision reviewed by the Court of Justice.

6. The Commission shall at the same time forward a copy of its decision to the competent authority of the Member State in whose territory the seat of the undertaking or association of undertakings is situated.

Article 12—Inquiry into sectors of the economy

1. If in any sector of the economy the trend of trade between Member States, price movements, inflexibility of prices or other circumstances suggest that in the economic sector concerned competition is being restricted or distorted within the common market, the Commission may decide to conduct a general inquiry into that economic sector and in the course thereof may request undertakings in the sector concerned to supply the information necessary for giving effect to the principles formulated in Article 85 and 86 of the Treaty and for carrying out the duties entrusted to the Commission.

2. The Commission may in particular request every undertaking or association of undertakings in the economic sector concerned to communicate to it all agreements, decisions and concerted practices which are exempt from notification by virtue of Article 4(2) and Article 5(2).

3. When making inquiries pursuant to paragraph 2, the Commission shall also request undertakings or groups of undertakings whose size suggests that they occupy a dominant position within the common market or a substantial part thereof to supply to the Commission such particulars of the structure of the undertakings and of their behaviour as are requisite to an appraisal of their position in the light of Article 86 of the Treaty.

4. Article 10(3) to (6) and Articles 11, 13 and 14 shall apply correspondingly.

Article 13—Investigation by the authorities of the Member States

1. At the request of the Commission, the competent authorities of the Member States shall undertake the investigations which the Commission considers to be necessary under Article 14(1), or which it has ordered by decision pursuant to Article 14(3). The officials of the competent authorities of the Member States responsible for conducting these investigations shall exercise their powers upon production of an authorisation in writing issued by the competent authority of the Member State in whose territory the investigation is to be made. Such authorisation shall specify the subject-matter and purpose of the investigation.

2. If so requested by the Commission or by the competent authority of the Member States in whose territory the investigation is to be made, the officials of the Commission may assist the officials of such authorities in carrying out their duties.

Article 14—Investigating powers of the Commission

1. In carrying out the duties assigned to it by Article 89 and by provisions adopted under Article 87 of the Treaty, the Commission may undertake all necessary investigations into undertakings and associations of undertakings. To this end the officials authorised by the Commission are empowered:
   (a) to examine the books and other business records;
   (b) to take copies of or extracts from the books and business records;
   (c) to ask for oral explanations on the spot;
   (d) to enter any premises, land and means of transport of undertakings.

2. The officials of the Commission authorised for the purpose of these investigations shall exercise their powers upon production of an authorisation in writing specifying the subject matter and purpose of the investigation and the penalties provided for in Article 15(1)(c) in cases where production of the required books or other business records is incomplete. In good time before the investigation, the Commission shall inform the competent authority of the Member States in whose territory the same is to be made of the investigation and of the identity of the authorised officials.

3. Undertakings and associations of undertakings shall submit to investigations ordered by decision of the Commission. The decision shall specify the subject-matter and purpose of the investigation, appoint the date on which it is to begin and indicate the penalties provided for in

Article 15(1)(c) and Article 16(1)(d) and the right to have the decision reviewed by the Court of Justice.

4. The Commission shall take decisions referred to in paragraph 3 after consultation with the competent authority of the Member State in whose territory the investigation is to be made.

5. Officials of the competent authority of the Member States in whose territory the investigation is to be made may, at the request of such authority or of the Commission, assist the officials of the Commission in carrying out their duties.

6. Where an undertaking opposes an investigation ordered pursuant to this Article, the Member State concerned shall afford the necessary assistance to the officials authorised by the Commission to enable them to make their investigation. Member States shall, after consultation with the Commission, take the necessary measures to this end before 1 October 1962.[6]

Article 15—Fines

1. The Commission may by decision impose on undertakings or associations of undertakings fines of from 100 to 5000 units of account where, intentionally or negligently:
   (a) they supply incorrect or misleading information in an application pursuant to Article 2 or in a notification pursuant to Article 4 or 5; or
   (b) they supply incorrect information in response to a request made pursuant to Article 11(3) or (5) or to Article 12, or do not supply information within the time limit fixed by a decision taken under Article 11(5); or
   (c) they produce the required books or other business records in incomplete form during investigations under Article 13 or 14, or refuse to submit to an investigation ordered by decision issued in implementation of Article 14(3).

2. The Commission may by decision impose on undertakings or associations of undertakings fines of from 1 000 to 1 000 000 units of account, or a sum in excess thereof but not exceeding 10% of the turnover in the preceding business year of each of the undertakings participating in the infringement where, either intentionally or negligently:
   (a) they infringe Article 85(1) or Article 86 of the Treaty; or
   (b) they commit a breach of any obligation imposed pursuant to Article 8(1).
In fixing the amount of the fine, regard shall be had both to the gravity and the duration of the infringement.

3. Article 10(3) to (6) shall apply.

4. Decisions taken pursuant to paragraphs 1 and 2 shall not be of a criminal law nature.

5. The fines provided for in paragraph 2(a) shall not be imposed in respect of acts taking place:
   (a) after notification to the Commission and before its decision in application of Article 85(3) of the Treaty, provided they fall within the limits of the activity described in the notification;
   (b) before notification and in the course of agreements, decisions or concerted practices in existence at the date of entry into force of this Regulation, provided that notification was effected within the time limits specified in Article 5(1) and Article 7(2).

6. Paragraph 5 shall not have effect where the Commission has informed the undertakings concerned that after preliminary examination it is of opinion that Article 85(1) of the Treaty applies and that application of Article 85(3) is not justified.

Article 16—Periodic penalty payments

1. The Commission may by decision impose on undertakings or associations of undertakings periodic penalty payments of from 50 to 1000 units of account per day, calculated from the date appointed by the decision, in order to compel them:

---

[6] But see Art. 25, *post.*

(a) to put an end to an infringement of Article 85 or 86 of the Treaty, in accordance with a decision taken pursuant to Article 3 of this Regulation;
(b) to refrain from any act prohibited under Article 8(3);
(c) to supply complete and correct information which it has requested by decision taken pursuant Article 11(5);
(d) to submit to an investigation which it has ordered by decision taken pursuant to Article 14(3).

2. Where the undertakings or associations of undertakings have satisfied the obligation which it was the purpose of the periodic penalty payment to enforce, the Commission may fix the total amount of the periodic penalty payment at a lower figure than that which would arise under the original decision.

3. Article 10(3) to (6) shall apply.

Article 17—Review by the Court of Justice

The Court of Justice shall have unlimited jurisdiction within the meaning of Article 172 of the Treaty to review decisions whereby the Commission has fixed a fine or a periodic penalty payment; it may cancel, reduce or increase the fine or periodic penalty payment imposed.

Article 18—Unit of account

For the purpose of applying Articles 15 to 17 the unit of account shall be that adopted in drawing up the budget of the Community in accordance with Articles 207 and 209 of the Treaty.

Article 19—Hearing of the parties and of third persons

1. Before taking decisions as provided for in Articles 2, 3, 6, 7, 8, 15 and 16, the Commission shall give the undertakings or associations of undertakings concerned the opportunity of being heard on the matters to which the Commission has taken objection.

2. If the Commission or the competent authorities of the Member States consider it necessary, they may also hear other natural or legal persons. Applications to be heard on the part of such persons shall, where they show a sufficient interest, be granted.

3. Where the Commission intends to give negative clearance pursuant to Article 2 or take a decision in application of Article 85(3) of the Treaty, it shall publish a summary of the relevant application or notification and invite all interested third parties to submit their observations within a time limit which it shall fix being not less than one month. Publication shall have regard to the legitimate interest of undertakings in the protection of their business secrets.

Article 20—Professional secrecy

1. Information acquired as a result of the application of Articles 11, 12, 13 and 14 shall be used only for the purpose of the relevant request or investigation.

2. Without prejudice to the provisions of Articles 19 and 21, the Commission and the competent authorities of the Member States, their officials and other servants shall not disclose information acquired by them as result of the application of this Regulation and of the kind covered by the obligation of professional secrecy.

3. The provisions of paragraphs 1 and 2 shall not prevent publication of general information or surveys which do not contain information relating to particular undertakings or associations of undertakings.

Article 21—Publication of decision

1. The Commission shall publish the decisions which it takes pursuant to Articles 2, 3, 6, 7 and 8.

2. The publication shall state the names of the parties and the main content of the decision; it shall have regard to the legitimate interest of undertakings in the protection of their business secrets.

Article 22—Special provisions

1. The Commission shall submit to the Council proposals for making certain categories of agreement, decision and concerted practice falling within Article 4(2) or Article 5(2) compulsorily notifiable under Article 4 or 5.

2. Within one year from the date of entry into force of this Regulation, the Council shall examine, on a proposal from the Commission, what special provisions might be made for exempting from the provisions of this Regulation agreements, decisions and concerted practices falling within Article 4(2) or Article 5(2).

Article 23—Transitional provisions applicable to decisions of authorities of the Member States

1. Agreements, decisions and concerted practices of the kind described in Article 85(1) of the Treaty to which, before the entry into force of this Regulation, the competent authority of a Member State has declared Article 85(1) to be inapplicable pursuant to Article 85(3) shall not be subject to compulsory notification under Article 5. The decision of the competent authority of the Member State shall be deemed to be a decision within the meaning of Article 6; it shall cease to be valid upon expiration of the period fixed by such authority but in any event not more than three years after the entry into force of this Regulation. Article 8(3) shall apply.

2. Applications for renewal of decisions of the kind described in paragraph 1 shall be decided upon by the Commission in accordance with Article 8(2).

Article 24—Implementing provisions

The Commission shall have power to adopt implementing provisions concerning the form, content and other details of applications pursuant to Articles 2 and 3 and of notifications pursuant to Article 4 and 5, and concerning hearings pursuant to Article 19(1) and (2).

Article 25

1. As regards agreements, decisions and concerted practices to which Article 85 of the Treaty applies by virtue of accession, the date of accession shall be substituted for the date of entry into force of this Regulation in every place where reference is made in this Regulation to this latter date.

2. Agreements, decisions and concerted practices existing at the date of accession to which Article 85 of the Treaty applies by virtue of accession shall be notified pursuant to Article 5(1) or Article 7(1) and (2) within six months from the date of accession.

3. Fines under Article 15(2)(a) shall not be imposed in respect of any act prior to notification of the agreements, decisions and practices to which paragraph 2 applies and which have been notified within the period therein specified.

4. New Member States shall take the measures referred to in Article 14(6) within six months from the date of accession after consulting the Commission.[7]

---

[7] Added by the Act of Accession signed at Brussels 22 January 1972, Annex I.

5. The provisions of paragraphs 1 to 4 above still apply in the same way in the case of the accession of the Hellenic Republic, the Kingdom of Spain and of the Portuguese Republic.[8]

This Regulation shall be binding in its entirety and directly applicable in all Member States.
Done at Brussels, 6 February 1962.

[8] Replaced by the Act of Accession signed at Madrid, 2 July 1985, Annex I.

Appendix B

COMMISSION REGULATION 27[1]

First Regulation implementing Council Regulation 17 of 6 February 1962.

(Form, content and other details concerning applications and notifications)

THE COMMISSION OF THE EUROPEAN ECONOMIC COMMUNITY,

Having regard to the provisions of the Treaty establishing the European Economic Community, and in particular Articles 87 and 155 thereof;

Having regard to Article 24 of Council Regulations No. 17 of 6 February 1962 (First Regulation implementing Arts. 85 and 86 of the Treaty);

Whereas under Article 24 of Council Regulation No. 17 the Commission is authorised to adopt implementing provisions concerning the form, content and other details of applications under Articles 2 and 3 and of notifications under Articles 4 and 5 of that Regulation;

Whereas the submission of such applications and notifications may have important legal consequences for each of the undertakings which is party to an agreement, decision or concerted practice; whereas every undertaking should accordingly have the right to submit an application or a notification to the Commission; whereas, furthermore, an undertaking exercising this right must inform the other undertakings which are parties to the agreement, decision or concerted practice in order to enable them to protect their interests;

Whereas it is for the undertakings and associations of undertakings to transmit to the Commission information as to facts and circumstances in support of applications under Article 2 and of notifications under Articles 4 and 5;

Whereas it is desirable to prescribe forms for use in applications for negative clearance relating to implementation of Article 85(1) and for notifications relating to implementation of Article 85(3) of the Treaty, in order to simplify and accelerate consideration by the competent departments, in the interests of all concerned;

HAS ADOPTED THIS REGULATION:

Article 1—Persons entitled to submit application and notification

1. Any undertaking which is party to agreements, decisions or practices of the kind described in Articles 85 and 86 of the Treaty may submit an application under Article 2 or a notification

---

[1] J.O. 1118/62, [1959–62] O.J. Spec.Ed. 132.

under Articles 4 and 5 of Regulation No. 17. Where the application or notification is submitted by some, but not all, of the undertakings concerned, they shall give notice to the others.

2. Where applications and notifications under Articles 2, 3(1), 3(2)(b), 4 and 5 of Regulation No. 17 are signed by representatives of undertakings, associations of undertakings, or natural or legal persons, such representatives shall produce written proof that they are authorised to act.

3. Where a joint application or notification is submitted, a joint representative should be appointed.

Article 2—Submission of applications and notifications

[1. Fifteen copies of each application and notification shall be submitted to the Commission.]²

2. The supporting documents shall be either originals or copies. Copies must be certified as true copies of the originals.

3. Applications and notifications shall be in one of the official languages of the Community. Supporting documents shall be submitted in their original language. Where the original language is not one of the official languages, a translation in one of the official languages shall be attached.

[4. Where applications and notifications are made pursuant to Articles 53 and 54 of the Agreement on the European Economic Area, they may also be in one of the official languages of the EFTA States or the working language of the EFTA Surveillance Authority.]³

Article 3—Effective date of submission of applications and registrations

The date of submission of an application or notification shall be the date on which it is received by the Commission. Where, however, the application or notification is sent by registered post, it shall be deemed to have been received on the date shown on the postmark of the place of posting.

Article 4⁴—Content of applications and notifications

1. Applications under Article 2 of Regulation 17 relating to the applicability of Article 85(1) of the Treaty and notifications under Article 4 or Article 5(2) of Regulation 17 shall be submitted on Form A/B, in the manner prescribed on the Form and in the Complementary Note thereto, as shown in the Annex to this Regulation.

2. Applications and notifications shall contain the information asked for in Form A/B and the Complementary Note.

3. Several participating undertakings may submit an application or notification on a single form.

4. Applications under Article 2 of Regulation 17 relating to the applicability of Article 86 of the Treaty shall contain a full statement of the facts, specifying, in particular, the practice concerned and the position of the undertaking or undertakings within the Common Market or a substantial part thereof in regard to products or services to which the product relates. Form A/B may be used.

Article 5—Transitional provisions

1. Applications and notifications submitted prior to the date of entry into force of the Regulation otherwise than on the prescribed forms shall be deemed to comply with Article 4 of this Regulation.

² Amended by Reg. 3666/93.
³ Amended by Reg. 3666/93.
⁴ Replaced by Reg. 2526/85.

2. The Commission may require a duly completed form to be submitted to it within such time as it shall appoint. In that event, applications and notifications shall be treated as properly made only if the forms are submitted within the prescribed period and in accordance with the provisions of this Regulation.

Article 6

This Regulation shall enter into force on the day following its publication in the *Official Journal of the European Communities*.
This Regulation shall be binding in its entirety and directly applicable in all Member States.
Done at Brussels, 3 May 1962.

N.B. Form A/B and the Complementary Note are reproduced in Appendix F.

Appendix C

COMMISSION REGULATION 99/63[1]

On the hearings provided for in Article 19(1) and (2) of Council Regulation 17.

THE COMMISSION OF THE EUROPEAN ECONOMIC COMMUNITY,

Having regard to the Treaty establishing the European Economic Community, and in particular Articles 87 and 155 thereof;

Having regard to Article 24 of Council Regulation No. 17 of 6 February 1962 (First Regulation implementing Articles 85 and 86 of the Treaty);

Whereas the Commission has power under Article 24 of Council Regulation No. 17 to lay down implementing provisions concerning the hearings provided for in Article 19(1) and (2) of that Regulation;

Whereas in most cases the Commission will in the course of its inquiries already be in close touch with the undertakings or associations of undertakings which are the subject thereof and they will accordingly have the opportunity of making known their views regarding the objections raised against them;

Whereas, however, in accordance with Article 19(1) of Regulation No. 17, and with the rights of defence, the undertakings and associations of undertakings concerned must have the right on conclusion of the inquiry to submit their comments on the whole of the objections raised against them which the Commission proposes to deal with in its decisions;

Whereas persons other than the undertakings or associations or undertakings which are the subject of the inquiry may have an interest in being heard; whereas, by the second sentence of Article 19(2) of Regulation No. 17, such persons must have the opportunity of being heard if they apply and show that they have a sufficient interest;

Whereas it is desirable to enable persons who, pursuant to Article 3(2) of Regulation No. 17, have applied for an infringement to be terminated to submit their comments where the Commission considers that on the basis of the information in its possession there are insufficient grounds for granting the application;

Whereas the various persons entitled to submit comments must do so in writing, both in their own interest and in the interest of good administration, without prejudice to oral procedure where appropriate to supplement the written evidence;

Whereas it is necessary to define the rights of persons who are to be heard, and in particular the conditions upon which they may be represented or assisted and the setting and calculation of time limits;

---

[1] J.O. 2268/63, [1963–64] O.J. Spec.Ed. 47.

Whereas the Advisory Committee on Restrictive Practices and Monopolies delivers its Opinion on the basis of a preliminary draft decision; whereas it must therefore be consulted concerning a case after the inquiry in respect thereof has been completed; whereas such consultation does not prevent the Commission from re-opening an inquiry if need be;

HAS ADOPTED THIS REGULATION:

Article 1

Before consulting the Advisory Committee on Restrictive Practices and Monopolies, the Commission shall hold a hearing pursuant to Article 19(1) of Regulation No. 17.

Article 2

1. The Commission shall inform undertakings and associations of undertakings in writing of the objections raised against them. The communications shall be addressed to each of them or to a joint agent appointed by them.
2. The Commission may inform the parties by giving notice in the *Official Journal of the European Communities*, if from the circumstances of the case this appears appropriate, in particular where notice is to be given to a number of undertakings but no joint agent has been appointed. The notice shall have regard to the legitimate interest of the undertakings in the protection of their business secrets.
3. A fine or a periodic penalty payment may be imposed on an undertaking or association of undertakings only if the objections were notified in the manner provided for in paragraph 1.
4. The Commission shall when giving notice of objections fix a time limit up to which the undertakings and associations of undertakings may inform the Commission of their views.

Article 3

1. Undertakings and associations of undertakings shall, within the appointed time limit, make known in writing their views concerning the objections raised against them.
2. They may in their written comments set out all matters relevant to their defence.
3. They may attach any relevant documents in proof of the facts set out. They may also propose that the Commission hear persons who may corroborate those facts.

Article 4

The Commission shall in its decisions deal only with those objections raised against undertakings and associations of undertakings in respect of which they have been afforded the opportunity of making known their views.

Article 5

If natural or legal persons showing a sufficient interest apply to be heard pursuant to Article 19(2) of Regulation No. 17, the Commission shall afford them the opportunity of making known their views in writing within such time limit as it shall fix.

Article 6

Where the Commission, having received an application pursuant to Article 3(2) of Regulation No. 17, considers that on the basis of the information in its possession there are insufficient grounds for granting the application, it shall inform the applicants of its reasons and fix a time limit for them to submit any further comments in writing.

Article 7

1. The Commission shall afford to persons who have so requested in their written comments the opportunity to put forward their arguments orally, if those persons show a sufficient interest or if the Commission proposes to impose on them a fine or periodic penalty payment.

2. The Commission may likewise afford to any other person the opportunity of orally expressing his views.

Article 8

1. The Commission shall summon the persons to be heard to attend on such date as it shall appoint.

2. It shall forthwith transmit a copy of the summons to the competent authorities of the Member States, who may appoint an official to take part in the hearing.

Article 9

1. Hearings shall be conducted by the persons appointed by the Commission for that purpose.

2. Persons summoned to attend shall appear either in person or be represented by legal representatives or by representatives authorised by their constitution. Undertakings and associations of undertakings may moreover be represented by a duly authorised agent appointed from among their permanent staff.

Persons heard by the Commission may be assisted by lawyers or university teachers who are entitled to plead before the Court of Justice of the European Communities in accordance with Article 17 of the Protocol on the Statute of the Court, or by other qualified persons.

3. Hearings shall not be public. Persons shall be heard separately or in the presence of other persons summoned to attend. In the latter case, regard shall be had to the legitimate interest of the undertakings in the protection of their business secrets.

4. The essential content of the statements made by each person heard shall be recorded in minutes which shall be read and approved by him.

Article 10

Without prejudice to Article 2(2), information and summonses from the Commission shall be sent to the addresses by registered letter with acknowledgement of receipt, or shall be delivered by hand against receipt.

Article 11

1. In fixing the time limits provided for in Articles 2, 5 and 6, the Commission shall have regard both to the time required for preparation of comments and to the urgency of the case. The time limit shall be not less than two weeks; it may be extended.

2. Time limits shall run from the day following receipt of a communication or delivery thereof by hand.

3. Written comments must reach the Commission or be dispatched by registered letter before expiry of the time limit. Where the time limit would expire on a Sunday or public holiday, it shall be extended up to the end of the next following working day. For the purpose of calculating this extension, public holidays shall, in cases where the relevant date is the date of receipt of written comments, be those set out in the Annex to this Regulation, and in cases where the relevant date is the date of dispatch, those appointed by law in the country of dispatch.

This Regulation shall be binding in its entirety and directly applicable in all Member States.

Done at Brussels, 25 July 1963.

ANNEX

referred to in the third sentence of Article 11(3) (List of public holidays)

New Year	1 Jan.
Good Friday	
Easter Saturday	
Easter Monday	
Labour Day	1 May
Schuman Plan Day	9 May
Ascension Day	
Whit Monday	
Belgian National Day	21 July
Assumption	15 Aug.
All Saints	1 Nov.
All Souls	2 Nov.
Christmas Eve	24 Dec.
Christmas Day	25 Dec.
The day following Christmas Day	26 Dec.
New Year's Eve	31 Dec.

Appendix D

COUNCIL REGULATION 19/65[1]

On application of Article 85(3) of the Treaty to certain categories of agreements and concerted practices.

THE COUNCIL OF THE EUROPEAN COMMUNITY,

Having regard to the Treaty establishing the European Economic Community, and in particular Article 87 thereof;

Having regard to the proposal from the Commission;

Having regard to the Opinion of the European Parliament;

Having regard to the Opinion of the Economic and Social Committee;

Whereas Article 85(1) of the Treaty may in accordance with Article 85(3) be declared inapplicable to certain categories of agreements, decisions and concerted practices which fulfill the conditions contained in Article 85(3);

Whereas the provisions for implementation of Article 85(3) must be adopted by way of regulation pursuant to Article 87;

Whereas in view of the large number of notifications submitted in pursuance of Regulation No. 17 it is desirable that in order to facilitate the task of the Commission it should be enabled to declare by way of regulation that the provisions of Article 85(1) do not apply to certain categories of agreements and concerted practices;

Whereas it should be laid down under what conditions the Commission, in close and constant liaison with the competent authorities of the Member States, may exercise such powers after sufficient experience has been gained in the light of individual decisions and it becomes possible to define categories of agreements and concerted practices in respect of which the conditions of Article 85(3) may be considered as fulfilled;

Whereas the Commission has indicated by the action it has taken, in particular by Regulation No. 153, that there can be no easing of the procedures prescribed by Regulation No. 17 in respect of certain types of agreements and concerted practices that are particularly liable to distort competition in the common market;

Whereas under Article 6 of Regulation No. 17 the Commission may provide that a decision taken pursuant to Article 85(3) of the Treaty shall apply with retroactive effect; whereas it is desirable that the Commission be also empowered to adopt, by regulation, provisions to the like effect;

Whereas under Article 7 of Regulation No. 17 agreements, decisions and concerted practices may, by decision of the Commission, be exempted from prohibition in particular if they are

[1] J.O. 533/65, [1965–66] O.J. Spec.Ed. 35.

modified in such manner that they satisfy the requirements of Article 85(3); whereas it is desirable that the Commission be enabled to grant like exemption by regulation to such agreements and concerted practices if they are modified in such manner as to fall within a category defined in an exempting regulation;

Whereas, since there can be no exemption if the conditions set out in Article 85(3) are not satisfied, the Commission must have power to lay down by decision the conditions that must be satisfied by an agreement or concerted practice which owing to special circumstances has certain effects incompatible with Article 85(3);

HAS ADOPTED THIS REGULATION:

Article 1

1. Without prejudice to the application of Council Regulation No. 17 and in accordance with Article 85(3) of the Treaty the Commission may by regulation declare that Article 85(1) shall not apply to categories of agreements to which only two undertakings are party and:
   (a) —whereby one party agrees with the other to supply only to that other certain goods for resale within a defined area of the common market; or
   —whereby one party agrees with the other to purchase only from that other goods for resale; or
   —whereby the two undertakings have entered into obligations, as in the two preceding subparagraphs, with each other in respect of exclusive supply and purchase for resale;
   (b) which include restrictions imposed in relation to the acquisition or use of industrial property rights—in particular of patents, utility models, designs or trade marks—or to the rights arising out of contracts for assignment of, or the right to use, a method of manufacture or knowledge relating to the use or to the application of industrial processes.

2. The regulation shall define the categories of agreements to which it applies and shall specify in particular:
   (a) the restrictions or clauses which must not be contained in the agreements;
   (b) the clauses which must be contained in the agreements, or the other conditions which must be satisfied.

3. Paragraphs 1 and 2 shall apply by analogy to categories of concerted practices to which only two undertakings are party.

Article 2

1. A regulation pursuant to Article 1 shall be made for a specified period.

2. It may be repealed or amended where circumstances have changed with respect to any factor which was basic to its being made; in such case, a period shall be fixed for modification of the agreements and concerted practices to which the earlier regulation applies.

Article 3

A regulation pursuant to Article 1 may stipulate that it shall apply with retroactive effect to agreements and concerted practices to which, at the date of entry into force of that regulation, a decision issued with retroactive effect in pursuance of Article 6 of Regulation No. 17 would have applied.

Article 4

1. A regulation pursuant to Article 1 may stipulate that the prohibition contained in Article 85(1) of the Treaty shall not apply, for such period as shall be fixed by that regulation, to agreements and concerted practices already in existence on 13 March 1962 which do not satisfy the conditions of Article 85(3), where:

A regulation pursuant to Article 1 may stipulate that the prohibition contained in Article 85(1) of the Treaty shall not apply, for such period as shall be fixed by that regulation, to agreements and concerted practices already in existence at the date of accession to which Article 85 applies by virtue of accession and which do not satisfy the conditions of Article 85(3),[2] where:
— within three months from the entry into force of the Regulation, they are so modified as to satisfy the said conditions in accordance with the provisions of the regulation; and
— the modifications are brought to the notice of the Commission within the time limit fixed by the regulation.
The provision of the preceding subparagraph shall apply in the same way in the case of the accession of the Hellenic Republic, the Kingdom of Spain and of the Portuguese Republic.[3]

2. Paragraph 1 shall apply to agreements and concerted practices which had to be notified before 1 February 1963, in accordance with Article 5 of Regulation No. 17, only where they have been so notified before that date.

Paragraph 1 shall not apply to agreements and concerted practices to which Article 85(1) of the Treaty applies by virtue of accession and which must be notified before 1 July 1973, in accordance with Articles 5 and 25 of Regulation No. 17, unless they have been so notified before that date.[4]

Paragraph 1 shall not apply to agreements and concerted practices to which Article 85(1) of the Treaty applies by virtue of the accession of the Hellenic Republic and which must be notified before 1 July 1981 in accordance with Articles 5 and 25 of Regulation 17, unless they have been so notified before that date.[5]

Paragraph 2 [*sic*] shall not apply to agreements and concerted practices to which Article 85(1) applies by virtue of the accession of the Kingdom of Spain and of the Portuguese Republic and which must be notified before 1 July 1986, in accordance with Articles 5 and 25 of Regulation No. 17, unless they have been so notified before that date.[6]

3. The benefit of the provisions laid down pursuant to paragraph 1 may not be claimed in actions pending at the date of entry into force of a regulation adopted pursuant to Article 1; neither may it be relied on as grounds for claims for damages against third parties.

Article 5

Before adopting a regulation, the Commission shall publish a draft thereof and invite all persons concerned to submit their comments within such time limit, being not less than one month, as the Commission shall fix.

Article 6

1. The Commission shall consult the Advisory Committee on Restrictive Practices and Monopolies:
(a) before publishing a draft regulation;
(b) before adopting a regulation.
2. Article 10(5) and (6) of Regulation No. 17, relating to consultation with the Advisory Committee, shall apply by analogy, it being understood that joint meetings with the Commission shall take place not earlier than one month after dispatch of the notice convening them.

---

[2] Added by Act of Accession signed at Brussels 22 January 1972, Annex I.
[3] Replaced by Act of Accession, Annex I.
[4] See n. 2.
[5] Added by Act of Accession signed at Athens, 28 May 1979, Annex I.
[6] Added by Act of Accession signed at Madrid, 12 July 1985.

Article 7

Where the Commission either on its own initiative or at the request of a Member State or of natural or legal persons claiming a legitimate interest, finds that in any particular case agreements or concerted practices to which a regulation adopted pursuant to Article 1 of this Regulation applies have nevertheless certain effects which are incompatible with the conditions laid down in Article 85(3) of the Treaty, it may withdraw the benefit of application of that regulation and issue a decision in accordance with Articles 6 and 8 of Regulation No. 17 without any notification under Article 4(1) of Regulation No. 17 being required.

Article 8

The Commission shall, before 1 January 1970, submit to the Council a proposal for a Regulation for such amendment of this Regulation as may prove necessary in the light of experience.

This Regulation shall be binding in its entirety and directly applicable in all Member States. Done at Brussels, 2 March 1965.

Appendix E

COUNCIL REGULATION 2988/74[1]

Concerning limitation periods in proceedings and the enforcement of sanctions under the rules of the European Economic Community relating to transport and competition.

THE COUNCIL OF THE EUROPEAN COMMUNITIES,

Having regard to the Treaty establishing the European Economic Community, and in particular Articles 75, 79 and 87 thereof;

Having regard to the proposal from the Commission;

Having regard to the Opinion of the European Parliament;

Having regard to the Opinion of the Economic and Social Committee;

Whereas under the rules of the European Economic Community relating to transport and competition the Commission has the power to impose fines, penalties and periodic penalty payments on undertakings or associations of undertakings which infringe Community law relating to information or investigation, or to the prohibition on discrimination, restrictive practices and abuse of dominant position; whereas those rules make no provision for any limitation period;

Whereas it is necessary in the interests of legal certainty that the principle of limitation be introduced and that implementing rules be laid down; whereas, for the matter to be covered fully, it is necessary that provision for limitation be made not only as regards the power to impose fines or penalties, but also as regards the power to enforce decisions, imposing fines, penalties or periodic penalty payments; whereas such provision should specify the length of limitation periods, the date on which time starts to run and the events which have the effect of interrupting or suspending the limitation period; whereas in this respect the interests of undertakings and associations of undertakings on the one hand, and the requirements imposed by administrative practice, on the other hand, should be taken into account;

Whereas this Regulation must apply to the relevant provisions of Regulation No. 11 concerning the abolition of discrimination in transport rates and conditions, in implementation of Article 79(3) of the Treaty establishing the European Economic Community, of Regulation No. 17: first Regulation implementing Articles 85 and 86 of the Treaty, and of Council Regulation (EEC) No. 1017/68 of 19 July 1968 applying rules of competition to transport by rail, road and inland waterway; whereas it must also apply to the relevant provisions of future regulations in the fields of European Economic Community law relating to transport and competition.

[1] [1974] O.J. L319/1.

HAS ADOPTED THIS REGULATION:

Article 1—Limitation periods in proceedings

1. The power of the Commission to impose fines or penalties for infringements of the rules of the European Economic Community relating to transport or competition shall be subject to the following limitation periods:
   (a) three years in the case of infringements of provisions concerning applications or notifications of undertakings or associations of undertakings, requests for information, or the carrying out of investigations;
   (b) five years in the case of all other infringements.
2. Time shall begin to run upon the day on which the infringement is committed. However, in the case of continuing or repeated infringements, time shall begin to run on the day on which the infringement ceases.

Article 2—Interruption of the limitation period in proceedings

1. Any action taken by the Commission, or by any Member State, acting at the request of the Commission, for the purpose of the preliminary investigation or proceedings in respect of an infringement shall interrupt the limitation period in proceedings. The limitation period shall be interrupted with effect from the date on which the action is notified to at least one undertaking or association of undertakings which have participated in the infringement.
   Actions which interrupt the running of the period shall include in particular the following:
   (a) written requests for information by the Commission, or by the competent authority of a Member State acting at the request of the Commission; or a Commission decision requiring the requested information;
   (b) written authorization to carry out investigations issued to their officials by the Commission or by the competent authority of any Member State at the request of the Commission; or a Commission decision ordering an investigation;
   (c) the commencement of proceedings by the Commission;
   (d) notification of the Commission's statement of objections.
2. The interruption of the limitation period shall apply for all the undertakings or associations of undertakings which have participated in the infringement.
3. Each interruption shall start time running afresh. However, the limitation period shall expire at the latest on the day on which a period equal to twice the limitation period has elapsed without the Commission having imposed a fine or a penalty; that period shall be extended by the time during which limitation is suspended pursuant to Article 3.

Article 3—Suspension of the limitation period in proceedings

The limitation period in proceedings shall be suspended for as long as the decision of the Commission is the subject of proceedings pending before the Court of Justice of the European Communities.

Article 4—Limitation period for the enforcement of sanctions

1. The power of the Commission to enforce decisions imposing fines, penalties or periodic payments for infringements of the rules of the European Economic Community relating to transport or competition shall be subject to a limitation period of five years.
2. Time shall begin to run on the day on which the decision becomes final.

Article 5—Interruption of the limitation period for the enforcement of sanctions

1. The limitation period for the enforcement of sanctions shall be interrupted:
   (a) by notification of a decision varying the original amount of the fine, penalty or periodic penalty payments or refusing an application for variation;
   (b) by any action of the Commission, or of a Member State at the request of the Commission, for the purpose of enforcing payments of a fine, penalty or periodic penalty payment.
2. Each interruption shall start time running afresh.

Article 6—Suspension of the limitation period for the enforcement of sanctions

The limitation period for the enforcement of sanctions shall be suspended for so long as:
(a) time to pay is allowed; or
(b) enforcement of payment is suspended pursuant to a decision of the Court of Justice of the European Communities.

Article 7—Application to transitional cases

This Regulation shall also apply in respect of infringements committed before it enters into force.

Article 8—Entry into force

This Regulation shall enter into force on 1 January 1975.
This Regulation shall be binding in its entirety and directly applicable in all Member States.
Done at Brussels, 26 November 1974

Appendix F

FORM A/B

This form must be accompanied by an Annex containing the information specified in the attached Complementary note.

The form and the Annex must be supplied in 15 copies (two for the Commission, one for each Member State and one for the EFTA Surveillance Authority). Supply three copies of any relevant agreement and one copy of other supporting documents.

Please do not forget to complete the 'Acknowledgement of receipt' annexed.

If space is insufficient, please use extra pages, specifying to which item on the form they relate.

To the Commission of the European Communities
Directorate-General for Competition,
200 rue de la Loi,
B-1049 Brussels.

A.1. Application for negative clearance pursuant to Article 2 of Council Regulation 17, as well as Article 53(1) or of Article 54 of the Agreement on the European Economic Area[1].

B.1. Notification of an agreement, decision or concerted practice pursuant to Article 4 (or 5) of Council Regulation 17 with a view to obtaining exemption pursuant to Article 85(3) of the Treaty establishing the European Community, including notifications claiming benefit of an opposition procedure; as well as Article 53(3) of the EEA Agreement.

Identity of the parties

1. Identity of applicant/notifier

Full name and address, telephone, telex and facsimile numbers, and brief description[2] of the undertaking(s) or association(s) of undertakings submitting the application or notification.

For partnerships, sole traders or any other unincorporated body trading under a business name, give, also, the name, forename(s) and address of the proprietor(s) or partner(s).

Where an application or notification is submitted on behalf of some other person (or is submitted by more than one person) the name, address and position of the representative (or joint representative) must be given, together with proof of his authority to act. Where an application

---

[1] Hereinafter referred to as 'the EEA Agreement'.

[2] For example: 'motor vehicle manufacturer', 'computer service bureau', 'conglomerate'.

or notification is submitted by or on behalf of more than one person they should appoint a joint representative (Article 1 (2) and (3) of Commission Regulation 27).

2. Identity of any other parties

Full name and address and brief description of any other parties to the agreement, decision or concerted practice (hereinafter referred to as 'the arrangements').

State what steps have been taken to inform these other parties of this application or notification.

(This information is not necessary in respect of standard contracts which an undertaking submitting the application or notification has concluded or intends to conclude with a number of parties (e.g. a contract appointing dealers)).

Purpose of this application/notification

(see Complementary note)

(Please answer yes or no to the questions.)

Are you asking for negative clearance alone? (See Complementary note—Section V, end of first paragraph—for the consequence of such a request.)

Are you applying for negative clearance, and also notifying the arrangements to obtain an exemption in case the Commission does not grant negative clearance?

Are you only notifying the arrangements in order to obtain an exemption?

Do you claim that this application may benefit from an opposition procedure? (See Complementary note—Sections IV, V, VII and VIII and Annex II.) If you answer 'yes', please specify the Regulation and Article number on which you are relying.

Would you be satisfied with a comfort letter? (See the end of Section VIII of the Complementary note.)

The undersigned declare that the information given above and in the pages annexed hereto is correct to the best of their knowledge and belief, that all estimates are identified as such and are their best estimates of the underlying facts and that all the opinions expressed are sincere.

They are aware of the provisions of Article 15(1)(a) of Regulation 17 (see attached Complementary note).

Place and date: ....

Signatures:

Appendix F

COMMISSION OF THE EUROPEAN
COMMUNITIES

Directorate-General for Competition

Brussels,.....................................

To. ....

ACKNOWLEDGEMENT OF RECEIPT

(This form will be returned to the address inserted above if the top half is completed in a single
copy by the person lodging it.)

Your application for negative clearance dated:..

Your notification dated: ....

Concerning:...

Your reference:..

Parties:

1..

2. ....and others

(There is no need to name the other undertakings party to the arrangement.)

(The be completed by the Commission.)

was received on:..

and registered under No: IV/...

Please quote the above number in all correspondence.

Provisional address:	Telephone:	Fax No:29
200, rue de la Loi	Direct line:29	
B-1049 Brussels.	Telephone exchange: 299 11 11.	

Appendix F

COMPLEMENTARY NOTE

Contents

Additions or alterations to the information given in the Annexes will be published by the Commission from time to time.

NB: Any undertaking uncertain about how to complete a notification or wishing further explanation may contact the Directorate-General for Competition (DG IV) or the Competition Directorate of the EFTA Surveillance Authority in Brussels. Alternatively, any Commission Information Office (those in the Community and in the EFTA States are listed in Annex III) will be able to obtain guidance or indicate an official in Brussels who speaks the preferred official Community language or official language of one of the EFTA States[3]

1. PURPOSE OF THE EC AND EEA COMPETITION RULES

1. Purpose of the Community competition rules

The purpose of these rules is to prevent the distortion of competition in the common market by restrictive practices or the abuse of dominant position; they apply to any enterprise trading directly or indirectly in the common market, wherever established.

Article 85(1) of the Treaty establishing the European Community (the text of Articles 85 and 86 is reproduced in Annex I to this note) prohibits restrictive agreements, decisions or concerted practices which may affect trade between Member States, and Article 85(2) declares agreements and decisions containing such restrictions void (although the European Court of Justice has held that if restrictive terms of agreements are severable, only those terms are void); Article 85(3), however, provides for exemption of practices with beneficial effects if its conditions are met. Article 86 prohibits the abuse of a dominant position which may affect trade between Member States. The original procedures for implementing these Articles, which provide for

[3] For the purposes of this note, any reference to EFTA States shall be understood to mean those EFTA States which are Contracting Parties to the Agreement on the European Economic Area. See the relevant text of the Protocol adjusting the Agreement on the European Economic Area in Annex II to this note, as well as the list in Annex III.

'negative clearance' and exemption pursuant to Article 85(3), were laid down in Regulation 17 (the references to this and all other acts mentioned in this note or relevant to notifications and applications made on Form A/B are listed in Annex II to this note).

2. Purpose of the EEA competition rules

The competition rules of the Agreement on the EEA (concluded between the Community, the Member States and the EFTA States[4]) are based on the same principles as those contained in the Community competition rules and have the same purpose, i.e. to prevent the distortion of competition in the EEA territory by restrictive practices or the abuse of dominant position. They apply to any enterprise trading directly or indirectly in the EEA territory, wherever established.

Article 53(1) of the EEA Agreement (the text of Articles 53, 54 and 56 of the EEA Agreement is reproduced in Annex I to this note) prohibits restrictive agreements, decisions or concerted practices which may affect trade between the Community and one or more EFTA States (or between EFTA States), and Article 53(2) declares agreements or decisions containing such restrictions void (although the European Court of Justice has held that if restrictive terms of agreements are severable, only those terms are void); Article 53(3), however, provides for exemption of practices with beneficial effects, if its conditions are met. Article 54 prohibits the abuse of a dominant position which may affect trade between the Community and one or more EFTA States (or between EFTA States). The procedures for implementing these Articles, which provide for 'negative clearance' and exemption pursuant to Article 53(3), are laid down in Regulation 17, supplemented for EEA purposes, by Protocols 21, 22 and 23 to the EEA Agreement.

II. COMPETENCE OF THE COMMISSION AND OF THE EFTA SURVEILLANCE AUTHORITY TO APPLY THE EEA COMPETITION RULES

The competence of the Commission and of the EFTA Surveillance Authority to apply the EEA competition rules follows from Article 56 of the EEA Agreement. Notifications and applications relating to restrictive agreements, decisions or concerted practices liable to affect trade between Member States, should be addressed to the Commission unless their effects on trade between Member States or on competition within the Community are not appreciable in the sense of the Commission notice of 1986 on agreements of minor importance[5] Furthermore, all restrictive agreements, decisions or concerted practices affecting trade between one Member State and one or more EFTA States should be notified to the Commission, provided the undertakings concerned achieve more than 67% of their combined EEA-wide turnover within the Community[6]. However, if the effects of such agreements, decisions or concerted practices on trade between Member states or on competition within the Community are not appreciable, the notification should be addressed to the EFTA Surveillance Authority. All other agreements, decisions and concerted practices falling under Article 53 of the EEA Agreement should be notified to the EFTA Surveillance Authority (the address of which is given in Annex III).

Applications for negative clearance regarding Article 54 of the EEA Agreement should be lodged with the Commission if dominance exists only in the Community, or with the EFTA Surveillance Authority, if dominance exists only in the territory of the EFTA States, or a substantial part of it. Only where dominance exists within both territories should the rules outlined above with respect to Article 53 be applied.

---

[4] See list of Member States and EFTA States in Annex III.
[5] [1986] O.J. C231/2.
[6] For a definition of 'turnover' in this context, see Articles 2, 3 and 4 of Protocol 22 to the EEA Agreement reproduced in Annex I.

The Commission will apply, as a basis for appraisal, the competition rules of the Treaty. Where the case falls under the EEA Agreement and is attributed to the Commission pursuant to Article 56 of that Agreement, it will simultaneously apply the EEA rules.

III. NEGATIVE CLEARANCE

The purpose of the negative clearance procedure is to allow businesses ('undertakings') to ascertain whether or not the Commission considers that any of their arrangements or behaviour are prohibited pursuant to Article 85(1) or 86 of the Treaty and/or Article 53(1) or 54 of the EEA Agreement. (It is governed by Article 2 of Regulation 17.) Clearance takes the form of a decision by the Community certifying that, on the basis of the facts in its possession, there are no grounds pursuant to Article 85(1) or 86 of the Treaty and/or Article 53(1) or 54 of the EEA Agreement for action on its part in respect of the arrangements or behaviour.

Any party may apply for negative clearance, even without the consent (but not without the knowledge) of other parties to arrangements. There would be little point in applying, however, where arrangements or behaviour clearly do not fall within the scope of Article 85(1) or 86 of the Treaty, and/or Article 53(1) or 54 of the EEA Agreement, where applicable. (In this connection, your attention is drawn to the last paragraph of V below and to Annex II.) Nor is the Commission obliged to give negative clearance—Article 2 of Regulation 17 states that '... the Commission may certify ...'. The Commission does not usually issue negative clearance decision in cases which, in its opinion, so clearly do not fall within the scope of the prohibition of Article 85(1) of the Treaty and/or Article 53(1) of the EEA Agreement that there is no reasonable doubt for it to resolve by such a decision.

IV. EXEMPTION

The purpose of the procedure for exemption pursuant to Article 85(3) of the Treaty and/or Article 53(3) of the EEA Agreement is to allow undertakings to enter into arrangements which, in fact, offer economic advantages but which, without an exemption, would be prohibited pursuant to Article 85(1) of the Treaty and/or Article 53(1) of the EEA Agreement. (It is governed by Articles 4, 6 and 8 of Regulation 17 and, for new Member States, by Articles 5, 7 and 25; with respect to existing agreements falling under Article 53(1) of the EEA Agreement by virtue of its entry into force, it is governed by Articles 5 to 13 of Protocol 21 to the EEA Agreement.) It takes the form of a decision by the Commission declaring Article 85(1) of the Treaty and/or Article 53(1) of the EEA Agreement to be inapplicable to the arrangements described in the decision. Article 8 of Regulation 17 requires the Commission to specify the period of validity of any such decision, allows the Commission to attach conditions and obligations and provides for decisions to be amended or revoked or specified acts by the parties to be prohibited in certain circumstances, notably if the decisions were based on incorrect information or if there is any material change in the facts.

Any party may notify arrangements, even without the consent (but not without the knowledge) of other parties.

The Commission has adopted a number of regulations granting exemption to categories of agreements. These group exemptions also apply with respect to the EEA in the form as contained in Annex XIV to the EEA Agreement. Some of these regulations (see Annex II for the latest list) provide that some agreements may benefit by such an exemption only if they are notified to the Commission pursuant to Article 4 (or 5) of Regulation 17 with a view to obtaining exemption pursuant to Article 85(3) of the Treaty and/or Article 53(3) of the EEA Agreement and if the benefit of an opposition procedure is claimed in the notification.

A decision granting exemption pursuant to Article 85(3) of the Treaty and/or Article 53(3) of the EEA Agreement may have retroactive effect but, with certain exceptions, cannot be made effective earlier than the date of notification (Article 6 of Regulation 17; see also Article 6 of Protocol 21 to the EEA Agreement). Should the Commission find that notified arrangements are indeed prohibited by Article 85(1) of the Treaty and/or Article 53(1) of the EEA Agreement, and cannot be exempted pursuant to Article 85(3) of the Treaty and/or Article 53(3) of the EEa Agreement and, therefore, take a decision condemning them, the parties are nevertheless protected, from the date of notification, against fines for any infringement described in the notification (Article 3 and Article 15(5) and (6) of Regulation 17).

V. PURPOSE OF THE FORM

The purpose of Form A/B is to allow undertakings, or associations of undertakings, wherever situated, to apply to the Commission for negative clearance for arrangements or behaviour, or to notify such arrangements and apply to have them exempted from the prohibition of Article 85(1) of the Treaty by virtue of Article 85(3) and/or of Article 53(1) of the EEA Agreement by virtue of its Article 53(3). The form allows undertakings applying for negative clearance to notify, at the same time, in order to obtain an exemption. It should be noted that only a notification in order to obtain exemption affords immunity from fines (Article 15(5)).

To be valid, applications for negative clearance in respect of Article 85 of the Treaty and/or Article 53(1) of the EEA Agreement, notifications to obtain an exemption and notifications claiming the benefit of an opposition procedure must be made on Form A/B (by virtue of Article 4 of Regulation 27). (Undertakings applying for negative clearance for their behaviour in relation to a possible dominant position—Article 86 of the Treaty and/or Article 54 of the EEA Agreement—need not use Form A/B (see Article 4(4) of Regulation 27), but they are strongly recommended to give all the information requested at X below in order to ensure that their application gives a full statement of the facts.) The applications or notifications made on the Form A/B issued by the EFTA side are equally valid. However, if the arrangements or behaviour concerned solely fall under Articles 85 or 86 of the Treaty, i.e. have no EEA relevance whatsoever, it is advisable to use the present form established by the Commission.

Before completing a form, your attention is particularly drawn to the regulations granting block exemption and the notices listed in Annex II—these were published to allow undertakings to judge for themselves, in many cases, whether there was any doubt about their arrangements. This would allow them to avoid the considerable bother and expense, both for themselves and for the Commission, of submitting and examining an application or notification where there is clearly no doubt.

VI. NATURE OF THE FORM

The form consists of a single sheet calling for the identity of the applicant(s) or notifier(s) and of any other parties. This must be supplemented by further information given under the headings and references detailed below (see X). For preference the paper used should be A4 ($21 \times 29,7$ cm—the same size as the form) but must not be bigger. Leave a margin of at least 25 mm or one inch on the left-hand side of the page and, if you use both sides, on the right-hand side of the reverse.

VII. THE NEED FOR COMPLETE AND ACCURATE INFORMATION

It is important that applicants give all the relevant facts. Although the Commission has the right to seek further information from applicants or third parties, and is obliged to publish a summary of the application before granting negative clearance or exemption pursuant to Article 85(3) of the Treaty and/or Article 53(3) of the EEA Agreement, it will usually base its decision on the information provided by the applicant. Any decision taken on the basis of incomplete information could be without effect in the case of a negative clearance, or voidable in that of an exemption. For the same reason, it is also important to inform the Commission of any material changes to your arrangements made after your application or notification.

Complete information is of particular importance if you are claiming the benefit of a block exemption through an opposition procedure. Such exemption is dependent on the information supplied being complete and in accordance with the facts. If the Commission does not oppose a claim to benefit under this procedure on the basis of the facts in a notification and, subsequently, additional or different facts come to light that could and should have been in the notification, then the benefit of the exemption will be lost, and with retroactive effect. Similarly, there would be little point in claiming the benefit of an opposition procedure with clearly incomplete information; the Commission would be bound either to reject such a notification or oppose exemption in order to allow time for further information to be provided.

Moreover, you should be aware of the provisions of Article 15(1)(a) of Regulation 17 which reads as follows:

> 'The Commission may by decision impose on undertakings or associations of undertakings fines from 100 to 5,000 units of account[7] where, intentionally or negligently, they supply incorrect or misleading information in an application pursuant to Article 2 or in a notification pursuant to Article 4 or 5.'

The key words here are 'incorrect or misleading information'. However, it often remains a matter of judgement how much detail is relevant; the Commission accepts estimates where accurate information is not readily available in order to facilitate notifications; and the Commission calls for opinions as well as facts.

You should therefore note that the Commission will use these powers only where applicants or notifiers have, intentionally or negligently, provided false information or grossly inaccurate estimates or suppressed readily available information or estimates, or have deliberately expressed false opinions in order to obtain negative clearance or exemption.

VIII. SUBSEQUENT PROCEDURE

The application or notification is registered in the Registry of the Directorate-General for Competition (DG IV). The date of receipt by the Commission (or the date of posting if sent by registered post) is the effective date of the submission. The application or notification might be considered invalid if obviously incomplete or not on the obligatory form.

Further information might be sought from the applicants or from third parties (Article 11 or 14 of Regulation 17) and suggestions might be made as to amendments to the arrangements that might make them acceptable.

A notification claiming the benefit of an opposition procedure may be opposed by the Commission either because the Commission does not agree that the arrangements should benefit from a block exemption or to allow for more information to be sought. If the Commission opposes a claim, and unless the Commission subsequently withdraws its opposition, that notification will then be treated as an application for an individual exemption decision.

If, after examination, the Commission intends to grant the application, it is obliged (by Article 19(3) of Regulation 17) to publish a summary and invite comments from third parties. Subsequently, a preliminary draft decision has to be submitted to and discussed with the Advisory Committee on Restrictive Practices and Dominant Positions composed of officials of the Member States competent in the matter of restrictive practices and monopolies (Article 10 of Regulation 17) and attended, where the case falls under the EEA Agreement, by representatives of the EFTA Surveillance Authority and EFTA States who will already have received a copy of the application or notification. Only then, and providing nothing has happened to change the Commission's intention, can it adopt a decision.

Sometimes files are closed without any formal decision being taken, for example, because it is found that the arrangements are already covered by a block exemption, or because the applicants are satisfied by a less formal letter from the Commission's departments (sometimes called a 'comfort letter') indicating that the arrangements do not call for any action by the Commission, at least in present circumstances. Although not a Commission decision, a comfort letter indicates how the Commission's departments view the case on the facts currently in their

---

[7] The value of the European currency unit (ECU) which has replaced the unit of account, is published daily in the 'C' series of the *Official Journal of the European Communities*.

possession which means that the Commission could if necessary—if, for example, it were to be asserted that a contract was void pursuant to Article 85(2) of the Treaty and/or Article 53(2) of the EEA Agreement—take an appropriate decision.

IX. SECRECY

Article 214 of the Treaty, Articles 20 and 21 of Regulation 17, Article 9 of Protocol 23 to the EEA Agreement, Article 122 of the EEA Agreement as well as Articles 20 and 21 of Chapter II of Protocol 4 to the Agreement between the EFTA States on the establishment of a Surveillance Authority and of a Court of Justice, require the Commission, Member States, the EFTA Surveillance Authority, and EFTA States not to disclose information of the kind covered by the obligation of professional secrecy. On the other hand, Article 19(3) of Regulation 17 requires the Commission to publish a summary of your application, should it intend to grant it, before taking the relevant decision. In this publication, the Commission shall have regard to the legitimate interest of undertakings in the protection of their business secrets. In this connection, if you believe that your interests would be harmed if any of the information you are asked to supply were to be published or otherwise divulged to other parties, please put all such information in a second Annex with each page clearly marked 'Business Secrets'; in the principal Annex, under any affected heading state 'see second Annex' or 'see also second Annex'; in the second Annex repeat the affected heading(s) and reference(s) and give the information you do not wish to have published, together with your reasons for this. Do not overlook the fact that the Commission may have to publish a summary of your application.

Before publishing an Article 19(3) notice, the Commission will show the undertakings concerned a copy of the proposed text.

X. FURTHER INFORMATION AND HEADINGS TO BE USED IN THE ANNEX TO FORM A/B

The further information is to be given under the following headings and reference numbers. Wherever possible, give exact information. If this is not readily available, give your best estimate, and identify what you give as an estimate. If you believe any detail asked for to be unavailable or irrelevant, please explain why. This may, in particular, be the case if one party is notifying arrangements alone without the cooperation of other parties. Do not overlook the fact that Commission officials are ready to discuss what detail is relevant (see the *nota bene* at the beginning of this Complementary note). An example that might help you is available on request.

1. Brief description

Give a brief description of the arrangements or behaviour (nature, purpose, date(s) and duration)—(full details are requested below).

2. Market

The nature of the goods or services affected by the arrangements or behaviour (include the heading number according to the Harmonized Commodity Description and Coding System). A brief description of the structure of the market (or markets) for these goods or services—e.g. who sells in it, who buys in it, its geographical extent, the turnover in it, how competitive it is, whether it is easy for new suppliers to enter the market, whether there are substitute products. If you are notifying a standard contract (e.g. a contract appointing dealers), say how many you expect to conclude. If you know of any studies of the market, it would be helpful to refer to them.

3. Fuller details of the party or parties.

3.1. Do any of the parties form part of a group of companies? A group relationship is deemed to exist where a firm:
— owns a more than half the capital or business assets, or
— has the power to exercise more than half the voting rights, or
— has the power to appoint more than half the members of the supervisory board, the board of directors or bodies legally representing the undertaking, or
— has the right to manage the affairs of another.
If the answer is yes, give:
— the name and address of the ultimate parent company,
— a brief description of the business of the group[8] (and, if possible, one copy of the last set of group accounts),
— the name and address of any other company in the group competing in a market affected by the arrangements or in any related market, that is to say any other company competing directly or indirectly with the parties ('relevant associated company').

3.2. The most recently available total, and total EEA-wide turnover of each of the parties and, as the case may be, of the group of which it forms part (it could be helpful also if you could provide one copy of the last set of accounts). The figures and percentage of the EEA-wide total turnover achieved within the Community and within the territory of the EFTA States.

3.3 The sales or turnover of each party in the goods or services affected by the arrangements in the Community, in the territory of the EFTA States, in the EEA territory and worldwide. If the turnover in the Community or in the territory of the EFTA States or in the EEA territory is material (say more than a 5 % market share), please also give figures for each Member State and for each EFTA State[9], and for previous years (in order to show any significant trends), and give each party's sales targets for the future. Provide the same figures for any relevant associated company. (Under this heading, in particular, your best estimate might be all that you can readily supply.)
For the calculation of turnover in the banking and insurance sector see Article 3 of Protocol 22 to the EEA Agreement.

3.4. In relation to the market (or markets) for the goods or services described at 2, give, for each of the sales or turnover figures in 3.3, your estimate of the market share it represents, within the Community, within the territory of the EFTA States, and within the EEA territory as a whole.

3.5. If you have a substantial interest falling short of control (more than 25% but less than 50%) in some other company competing in a market affected by the arrangements, or if some other such company has a substantial interest in yours, give its name and address and brief details.

4. Full details of the arrangements

4.1. If the contents are reduced to writing give a brief description of the purpose of the arrangements and attach three copies of the text (except that the technical descriptions often contained in know-how agreements may be omitted; in such cases, however, indicate parts omitted).
If the contents are not, or are only partially, reduced to writing, give a full description.

4.2. Detail any provisions contained in the arrangements which may restrict the parties in their freedom to take independent commercial decisions, for example regarding:

---

[8] For example: 'motor vehicle manufacturer', 'computer service bureau', 'conglomerate'.
[9] See list in Annex III.

— buying or selling prices, discounts or other trading conditions,
— the quantities of goods to be manufactured or distributed or services to be offered,
— technical development or investment,
— the choice of markets or sources of supply,
— purchases from or sales to third parties,
— whether to apply similar terms for the supply of equivalent goods or services,
— whether to offer different goods or services separately or together.

(If you are claiming the benefit of an opposition procedure, identify particularly in this list the restrictions that exceed those automatically exempted by the relevant regulation.)

4.3. State between which Member States and/or EFTA States[9] trade may be affected by the arrangements, and whether trade between the Community or the EEA territory, and any third countries is affected.

5. Reasons for negative clearance

If you are applying for negative clearance state, under the reference:

5.1. Why, i.e. state which provision or effects of the arrangements or behaviour might, in your view, raise questions of compatibility with the Community's and/or the EEA rules of competition. The object of this subheading is to give the Commission the clearest possible idea of the doubts you have about your arrangements or behaviour that you wish to have resolved by a negative clearance decision.

Then, under the following two references, give a statement of the relevant facts and reasons as to why you consider Article 85 (1) or 86 of the Treaty and/or Article 53 (1) or 54 of the EEA Agreement to be inapplicable, i.e.:

5.2. why the arrangements or behaviour do not have the object or effect of preventing, restricting or distorting competition within the common market or within the territory of the EFTA States to any appreciable extent , or why your undertaking does not have or its behaviour does not abuse a dominant position; and/or

5.3. why the arrangements or behaviour do not have the object or effect of preventing, restricting or distorting competition within the EEA territory to any appreciable extent, or why your undertaking does not have or its behaviour does not abuse a dominant position; and/or

5.4. why the arrangements or behaviour are not such as may affect trade between Member States or between the Community and one or more EFTA States, or between EFTA States to any appreciable extent.

6. Reasons for exemption

If you are notifying the arrangements, even if only as a precaution, in order to obtain an exemption pursuant to Article 85 (3) of the Treaty and/or Article 53 (3) of the EEA Agreement, explain how:

6.1. the arrangements contribute to improving production or distribution, and/or promoting technical or economic progress;

6.2. a proper share of the benefits arising from such improvement or progress accrues to consumers;

6.3. all restrictive provisions of the arrangements are indispensable to the attainment of the aims set out under 6.1 (if you are claiming the benefit of an opposition procedure, it is particularly important that you should identify and justify restrictions that exceed those automatically exempted by the relevant regulation); and

6.4. the arrangements do not eliminate competition in respect of a substantial part of the goods or services concerned.

7. Other information

7.1. Mention any earlier proceedings or informal contacts, of which you are aware, with the Commission and/or the EFTA Surveillance Authority and any earlier proceedings with any national EC or EFTA authorities or courts concerning these or any related arrangements.

7.2. Give any other information presently available that you think might be helpful in allowing the Commission to appreciate whether there are any restrictions contained in the agreement, or any benefits that might justify them.

7.3. State whether you intend to produce further supporting facts or arguments not yet available and, if so, on which points.

7.4. State, with reasons, the urgency of your application or notification.

XI. LANGUAGES

You are entitled to notify your agreements in any of the official languages of the European Community or of an EFTA State. In order to ensure rapid proceedings, you are, however, invited to use, if possible, in case of notification to the EFTA Surveillance Authority one of the official languages of an EFTA State or the working language of the EFTA Surveillance Authority, which is English, or, in case of notification to the Commission, one of the official languages of the European Community or the working language of the EFTA Surveillance Authority.

ANNEX I

TEXT OF ARTICLES 85 AND 86 OF THE EC TREATY, ARTICLES 53, 54 AND 56 OF THE EEA AGREEMENT, ARTICLES 2, 3 AND 4 OF PROTOCOL 22 TO THAT AGREEMENT AND OF ARTICLES 1 AND 2 OF THE PROTOCOL ADJUSTING THE AGREEMENT ON THE EUROPEAN ECONOMIC AREA

ARTICLE 85 OF THE EC TREATY

1. The following shall be prohibited as incompatible with the common market: all agreements between undertakings, decisions by associations of undertakings and concerted practices which may affect trade between Member States and which have as their object or effect the prevention, restriction or distortion of competition within the common market, and in particular those which:
   (a) directly or indirectly fix purchase or selling prices or any other trading conditions;
   (b) limit or control production, markets, technical development, or investment;
   (c) share markets or sources of supply;
   (d) apply dissimilar conditions to equivalent transactions with other trading parties, thereby placing them at a competitive disadvantage;
   (e) make the conclusion of contracts subject to acceptance by the other parties of supplementary obligations which, by their nature or according to commercial usage, have no connection with the subject of such contracts.

2. Any agreements or decisions prohibited pursuant to this Article shall be automatically void.
3. The provisions of paragraph 1 may, however, be declared inapplicable in the case of:
— any agreement or category of agreements between undertakings,
— any decision or category of decisions by associations or undertakings,
— any concerted practice or category of concerted practices,
which contributes to improving the production or distribution of goods or to promoting technical or economic progress, while allowing consumers a fair share of the resulting benefit, and which does not:

   (a) impose on the undertakings concerned restrictions which are not indispensable to the attainment of these objectives;
   (b) afford such undertakings the possibility of eliminating competition in respect of a substantial part of the products in question,

ARTICLE 86 OF THE EC TREATY

Any abuse by one or more undertakings of a dominant position within the common market or in a substantial part of it shall be prohibited as incompatible with the common market in so far as it may affect trade between Member States.
Such abuse may, in particular, consist in:
   (a) directly or indirectly imposing unfair purchase or selling prices or other unfair trading conditions;
   (b) limiting production, markets or technical development to the prejudice of consumers;
   (c) applying dissimilar conditions to equivalent transactions with other trading parties, thereby placing them at a competitive disadvantage;

(d) making the conclusion of contracts subject to acceptance by the other parties of supplementary obligations which, by their nature or according to commercial usage, have no connection with the subject of such contracts.

ARTICLE 53 OF THE EEA AGREEMENT

·1. The following shall be prohibited as incompatible with the functioning of this Agreement: all agreements between undertakings, decisions by associations of undertakings and concerted practices which may affect trade between Contracting Parties and which have as their object or effect the prevention, restriction or distortion of competition within the territory covered by this Agreement, and in particular those which:
  (a) directly or indirectly fix purchase or selling prices or any other trading conditions;
  (b) limit or control production, markets, technical development, or investment;
  (c) share markets or sources of supply;
  (d) apply dissimilar conditions to equivalent transactions with other trading parties, thereby placing them at a competitive disadvantage;
  (e) make the conclusion of contracts subject to acceptance by the other parties of supplementary obligations which, by their nature or according to commercial usage, have no connection with the subject of such contracts.

2. Any agreements or decisions prohibited pursuant to this Article shall be automatically void.
3. The provisions of paragraph 1 may, however, be declared inapplicable in the case of:
— any agreement or category of agreements between undertakings,
— any decision or category of decisions by associations of undertakings,
— any concerted practice or category of concerted practices,
which contributes to improving the production or distribution of goods or to promoting technical or economic progress, while allowing consumers a fair share of the resulting benefit, and which does not:

  (a) impose on the undertakings concerned restrictions which are not indispensable to the attainment of these objectives;
  (b) afford such undertakings the possibility of eliminating competition in respect of a substantial part of the products in question.

ARTICLE 54 OF THE EEA AGREEMENT

Any abuse by one or more undertakings of a dominant position within the territory covered by this Agreement or in a substantial part of it shall be prohibited as incompatible with the functioning of this Agreement in so far as it may affect trade between Contracting Parties.
Such abuse may, in particular, consist in:
  (a) directly or indirectly imposing unfair purchase or selling prices or other unfair trading conditions;
  (b) limiting production, markets or technical development to the prejudice of consumers;
  (c) applying dissimilar conditions to equivalent transactions with other trading parties, thereby placing them at a competitive disadvantage;
  (d) making the conclusion of contracts subject to acceptance by the other parties of supplementary obligations which, by their nature or according to commercial usage, have no connection with the subject of such contracts.

426

Appendix F

ARTICLE 56 OF THE EEA AGREEMENT

1. Individual cases falling under Article 53 shall be decided upon by the surveillance authorities in accordance with the following provisions:
   (a) individual cases where only trade between EFTA States is affected shall be decided upon by the EFTA Surveillance Authority;
   (b) without prejudice to subparagraph (c), the EFTA Surveillance Authority decides, as provided for in the provisions set out in Article 58, Protocol 21 and the rules adopted for its implementation, Protocol 23 and Annex XIV, on cases where the turnover of the undertakings concerned in the territory of the EFTA States equals 33% or more of their turnover in the territory covered by this Agreement;
   (c) the EC Commission decides on the other cases as well as on cases under (b) where trade between EC Member States is affected, taking into account the provisions set out in Article 58, Protocol 21, Protocol 23 and Annex XIV.

2. Individual cases falling under Article 54 shall be decided upon by the surveillance authority in the territory of which a dominant position is found to exist. The rules set out in paragraph 1 (b) and (c) shall apply only if dominance exists within the territories of both surveillance authorities.
3. Individual cases falling under paragraph 1 (c), whose effects on trade between EC Member States or on competition within the Community are not appreciable, shall be decided upon by the EFTA Surveillance Authority.
4. The terms 'undertaking' and 'turnover' are, for the purpose of this Article, defined in Protocol 22.

ARTICLES 2, 3 AND 4 OF PROTOCOL 22 TO THE EEA AGREEMENT

Article 2

'Turnover' within the meaning of Article 56 of the Agreement shall comprise the amounts derived by the undertaking concerned, in the territory covered by this Agreement, in the preceding financial year from the sale of products and the provision of services falling within the undertaking's ordinary scope of activities after deduction of sales rebates and of value-added tax and other taxes directly related to turnover.

Article 3

In place of turnover the following shall be used:
   (a) for credit institutions and other financial institutions, their total assets multiplied by the ratio between loans and advances to credit institutions and customers in transactions with residents in the territory covered by this Agreement and the total sum of those loans and advances;
   (b) for insurance undertakings, the value of gross premiums received from residents in the territory covered by this Agreement, which shall comprise all amounts received and receivable in respect of insurance contracts issued by or on behalf of the insurance undertakings, including also outgoing reinsurance premiums, and after deduction of taxes and parafiscal contributions or levies charged by reference to the amounts of individual premiums or the total value of premiums.

Article 4

1. In derogation of the definition of the turnover relevant for the application of Article 56 of the Agreement, as contained in Article 2 of this Protocol, the relevant turnover shall be constituted:

(a) as regards agreements, decisions of associations of undertakings and concerted practices related to distribution and supply arrangements between non-competing undertakings, of the amounts derived from the sale of goods or the provision of services which are the subject matter of the agreements, decisions or concerted practices, and from the other goods or services which are considered by users to be equivalent in view of their characteristics, price and intended use;

(b) as regards agreements, decisions of associations of undertakings and concerted practices related to arrangements on transfer of technology between non-competing undertakings, of the amounts derived from the sale of goods or the provision of services which result from the technology which is the subject matter of the agreements, decisions or concerted practices, and of the amounts derived from the sale of those goods or the provision of those services which that technology is designed to improve or replace.

2. However, where at the time of the coming to existence of arrangements as described in paragraph 1 (a) and (b) turnover as regards the sale of products or the provision of services is not in evidence, the general provision as contained in Article 2 shall apply.

ARTICLES 1 AND 2 OF THE PROTOCOL ADJUSTING THE AGREEMENT ON THE EUROPEAN ECONOMIC AREA

Article 1

1. The EEA Agreement, as adjusted by this Protocol, shall enter into force, on the date of entry into force of this Protocol, between the European Economic Community, the European Coal and Steel Community, their Member States and the Republic of Austria, the Republic of Finland, the Republic of Iceland, the Kingdom of Norway and the Kingdom of Sweden.

2. As regards the Principality of Liechtenstein, the EEA Agreement, as adjusted by this Protocol, shall enter into force on a date to be determined by the EEA Council and provided that the EEA Council:

— has decided that the condition of Article 121 (b) of the EEA Agreement, namely that the good functioning of the EEA Agreement is not impaired, is fulfilled, and

— has taken the appropriate decisions, in particular as to the application to Liechtenstein of the measures already adopted by the EEA Council and the EEA Joint Committee.

3. Liechtenstein shall be allowed to participate in those decisions of the EEA Council referred to in paragraph 2.

Article 2

1. Since the Swiss Confederation, following its non-ratification of the EEA Agreement, is not a Contracting Party thereto, the reference in the preamble to the EEA Agreement to 'THE SWISS CONFEDERATION' as one of the Contracting Parties shall be deleted.

2. Article 2 (b) of the EEA Agreement shall be replaced by the following:

'the term "EFTA States" means the Republic of Austria, the Republic of Finland, the Republic of Iceland, the Kingdom of Norway, the Kingdom of Sweden and, pursuant to the conditions laid down by Article 1 (2) of the Protocol adjusting the Agreement on the European Economic Area, the Principality of Liechtenstein.'

3. The EEA Agreement shall be adjusted further in accordance with Articles 3 to 20 of this Protocol.

Appendix F

ANNEX II

LIST OF RELEVANT ACTS

(as of 1 January 1993)

(If you think it possible that your arrangements do not need to be notified by virtue of any of these regulations or notices it may be worth your while to obtain a copy.)

IMPLEMENTING REGULATIONS[10]

Council Regulation No 17 of 6 February 1992: First Regulation implementing Articles 85 and 86 of the Treaty (OJ No 13, 21. 2. 1962, p. 204/62, English Special Edition 1959–1962, November 1972, p. 87) as amended (OJ No 58, 10. 7. 1962, p. 1655/62; OJ No 162, 7. 11. 1963, p. 2696/63; OJ No L 285, 29. 12. 1971, p. 49; OJ No L 73, 27. 3. 1972, p. 92; OJ No L 291, 19. 11. 1979, p. 94 and OJ No L 302, 15. 11. 1985, p. 165).

Commission Regulation No 27 of 3 May 1962 implementing Council Regulation No 17 (OJ No 35, 10. 5. 1962, p. 1118/62, English Special Edition 1959–1962, November 1972, p. 87) as amended (OJ No L 189, 1. 8. 1968, p. 1; OJ No L 172, 3. 7. 1975, p. 11; OJ No L 291, 19. 11. 1979, p. 94; OJ No L 240, 7. 9. 1985, p. 11 and OJ No L 302, 15. 11. 1985, p. 166).

REGULATIONS GRANTING BLOCK EXEMPTION IN RESPECT OF A WIDE RANGE OF AGREEMENTS

Commission Regulation (EEC) No 1983/83 of 22 June 1983 on the application of Article 85 (3) of the Treaty to categories of exclusive distribution agreements (OJ No L 173, 30. 6. 1983, p. 1, as corrected in OJ No L 281, 13. 10. 1983, p. 24), as well as this Regulation as adapted for EEA purposes (see point 2 of Annex XIV to the EEA Agreement).

Commission Regulation (EEC) No 1984/83 of 22 June 1983 on the application of Article 85 (3) of the Treaty to categories of exclusive purchasing agreements (OJ No L 173, 30. 6. 1983, p. 5, as corrected in OJ No L 281, 13. 10. 1983, p. 24), as well as this Regulation as adapted for EEA purposes (see point 3 of Annex XIV to the EEA Agreement).

See also the Commission notices concerning Regulations (EEC) No 1983/93 and (EEC) No 1984/83 (OJ No C 101, 13. 4. 1984, p. 2 and OJ No C 121, 13. 5. 1992, p. 2).

Commission Regulation (EEC) No 2349/84 of 23 July 1984 on the application of Article 85 (3) of the Treaty to certain categories of patent licensing agreements (OJ No L 219, 16. 8. 1984, p. 15, as corrected in OJ No L 113, 26. 4. 1985, p. 34), as amended (OJ No L 21, 29. 1. 1993, p. 8), as well as this Regulation as adapted for EEA purposes (see point 5 of Annex XIV to the EEA Agreement). Article 4 of this Regulation provides for an opposition procedure.

Commission Regulation (EEC) No 123/85 of 12 December 1984 on the application of Article 85 (3) of the Treaty to certain categories of motor vehicle distributing and servicing agreements (OJ No L 15, 18. 1. 1985, p. 16); as well as this Regulation as adapted for EEA purposes (see point 4 of Annex XIV to the EEA Agreement). See also the Commission notices concerning this Regulation (OJ No C 17, 18. 1. 1985, p. 4 and OJ No C 329, 18. 12. 1991, p. 20).

Commission Regulation (EEC) No 417/85 of 19 December 1984 on the application of Article 85 (3) of the Treaty to categories of specialization agreements (OJ No L 53, 22. 2. 1985, p. 1), as

---

[10] As regards procedural rules applied by the EFTA Surveillance Authority, see Article 3 of Protocol 21 to the EEA Agreement and the relevant provisions in Protocol 4 to the Agreement between the EFTA States on the establishment of a Surveillance Authority and a Court of Justice.

amended (OJ No L 21, 29. 1. 1993, p. 8), as well as this Regulation as adapted for EEA purposes (see point 6 of Annex XIV to the EEA Agreement). Article 4 of this Regulation provides for an opposition procedure.

Commission Regulation (EEC) No 418/85 of 19 December 1984 on the application of Article 85 (3) of the Treaty to categories of research and development cooperation agreements (OJ No L 53, 22. 2. 1985, p. 5), as amended (OJ No L 21, 29. 1. 1993, p. 8), as well as this Regulation as adapted for EEA purposes (see point 7 of Annex XIV to the EEA Agreement). Article 7 of this Regulation provides for an opposition procedure.

Commission Regulation (EEC) No 4087/88 of 30 November 1988 on the application of Article 85 (3) of the Treaty to categories of franchise agreements (OJ No L 359, 28. 12. 1988, p. 46), as well as this Regulation as adapted for EEA purposes (see point 8 of Annex XIV to the EEA Agreement). Article 6 of this Regulation provides for an opposition procedure.

Commission Regulation (EEC) No 556/89 of 30 November 1988 on the application of Article 85 (3) of the Treaty to certain categories of know-how licensing agreements (OJ No L 61, 4. 3. 1989, p. 1), as amended (OJ No L 21, 29. 1. 1993, p. 8), as well as this Regulation as adapted for EEA purposes (see point 9 of Annex XIV to the EEA Agreement). Article 4 of this Regulation provides for an opposition procedure.

Commission Regulation (EEC) No 3932/92 of 21 December 1992 on the application of Article 85 (3) of the Treaty to certain categories of agreements, decisions and concerted practices in the insurance sector (OJ No L 398, 31. 12. 1992, p. 7). This Regulation will be adapted for EAA purposes.

NOTICES OF A GENERAL NATURE[11]

Commission notice on exclusive dealing contracts with commercial agents (OJ No 139, 24. 12. 1962, p. 2921/62). This states that the Commission does not consider most such agreements to fall under the prohibition of Article 85 (1).

Commission notice concerning agreements, decisions and concerted practices in the field of co-operation between enterprises (OJ No C 75, 29. 7. 1968, p. 3, as corrected in OJ No C 84, 28. 8. 1968, p. 14). This defines the sorts of cooperation on market studies, accounting, R&D, joint use of production, storage or transport, *ad hoc* consortia, selling or after-sales service, advertising or quality labelling that the Commission considers not to fall under the prohibition of Article 85 (1).

Commission notice concerning its assessment of certain subcontracting agreements in relation to Article 85 (1) of the Treaty (OJ No C 1, 3. 1. 1979, p. 2).

Commission notice on agreements, decisions and concerted practices of minor importance which do not fall under Article 85 (1) of the Treaty (OJ No C 231, 12. 9. 1986, p. 2)—in the main, those where the parties have less than 5% of the market between them, and a combined annual turnover of less than ECU 200 million.

Commission guidelines on the application of EEC competition rules in the telecommunications sector (OJ No C 233, 6. 9. 1991, p. 2). These guidelines aim at clarifying the application of Community competition rules to the market participants in the telecommunications sector.

Commission notice on cooperation between national courts and the Commission in applying Articles 85 and 86 (OJ No C 39, 13. 2. 1993, p. 6). This notice sets out the principles on the basis of which such cooperation takes place.

---

[11] See also the corresponding notices published by the EFTA Surveillance Authority.

Commission notice concerning the assessment of cooperative joint ventures pursuant to Article 85 of the EC Treaty (OJ No C 43, 16. 2. 1993, p. 2). This notice sets out the principles on the assessment of joint ventures.

A collection of these texts (as at 31 December 1989) was published by the Office for Official Publications of the European Communities (references Vol I: ISBN 92-826-1307-0, catalogue No: CV-42-90-001-EN-C). An updated collection is in preparation.

Pursuant to the Agreement, these texts will also cover the European Economic Area.

Appendix F

LIST OF MEMBER STATES AND EFTA STATES, ADDRESS OF THE COMMISSION AND OF THE EFTA SURVEILLANCE AUTHORITY, LIST OF COMMISSION INFORMATION OFFICES WITHIN THE COMMUNITY AND IN EFTA STATES AND ADDRESSES OF COMPETENT AUTHORITIES IN EFTA STATES

The Member States as at the date of this Annex are: Belgium, Denmark, France, Germany, Greece, Ireland, Italy, Luxembourg, the Netherlands, Portugal, Spain and the United Kingdom.

The EFTA States which will be Contracting Parties to the EEA Agreement, as at the date of this Annex, are: Austria, Finland, Iceland, Liechtenstein, Norway and Sweden.

The address of the Commission's Directorate-General for Competition is:

Commission of the European Communities
Directorate-General for Competition
200 rue de la Loi
B-1049 Brussels
Tel. (322) 299 11 11

The address of the EFTA Surveillance Authority's Competition Directorate is:

EFTA Surveillance Authority
Competition Directorate
1–3 rue Marie-Thèrése
B-1040 Brussels
Tel. (322) 286 17 11

The addresses of the Commission's Information Offices in the Community are:

BELGIUM
73 rue Archiméde
B-1040 Bruxelles
Tel. (322) 299 11 11

DENMARK
Højbrohus
Østergade 61
Postboks 144
DK-1004 København K
Tel. (4533) 14 41 40

FRANCE
288, boulevard Saint-Germain
F-75007 Paris
Tel. (331) 40 63 38 00

CMCI
2 rue Henri Barbusse
F-13241 Marseille, Cedex 01
Tel. (3391) 91 46 00

FEDERAL REPUBLIC OF GERMANY
Zitelmannstraße 22
D-53113 Bonn
Tel. (49228) 53 00 90

ITALY
Via Poli 29
I-00187 Roma
Tel. (396) 699 11 60

Corso Magenta 61
I-20123 Milano
Tel. (392) 480 15 05

LUXEMBOURG
Bâtiment Jean Monnet
rue Alcide de Gasperi
L-2920 Luxembourg
Tel. (352) 430 11

NETHERLANDS
Postbus 30465
NL-2500 GL Den Haag
Tel. (3170) 346 93 26

PORTUGAL
Centro Europeu Jean Monnet
Largo Jean Monnet, 1–10°.
P-1200 Lisboa
Tel. (3511) 54 11 44

Kurfürstendamm 102
D-10711 Berlin 31
Tel. (4930) 896 09 30

Erhardtstraße 27
D-80331 München
Tel. (4989) 202 10 11

GREECE
2 Vassilissis Sofias
Case Postale 11002
GR-Athina 10674
Tel. (301) 724 39 82/83/84

IRELAND
39 Molesworth Street
IRL-Dublin 2
Tel. (3531) 71 22 44

SPAIN
Calle de Serrano 41
5a Planta
E-28001 Madrid
Tel. (341) 435 17 00

Av. Diagonal, 407 bis
18 Planta
E-08008 Barcelona
Tel. (343) 415 81 77

UNITED KINGDOM
8 Storey's Gate
UK-London SW1P 3AT
Tel. (4471) 973 19 92

Windsor House
9/15 Bedford Street
UK-Belfast BT2 7EG
Tel. (44232) 24 07 08

4 Cathedral Road
UK-Cardiff CF1 9SG
Tel. (44222) 37 16 31

9 Alva Street
UK-Edinburgh EH2 4PH
Tel. (4431) 225 20 58

The addresses of the Commission's Information Offices in the EFTA States are:

AUSTRIA
Hoyosgasse 5
A-1040 Wien
Tel. (431) 505 33 79

FINLAND
31 Pohjoisesplanadi
00100 Helsinki
Tel. (3580) 65 64 20

NORWAY
Postboks 1643 Vika 0119 Oslo 1
Haakon's VII Gate No 6
0161 Oslo 1
Tel. (472) 83 35 83

SWEDEN
PO Box 16396
Hamngatan 6
11147 Stockholm
Tel. (468) 611 11 72

Forms for notifications and applications, as well as more detailed information on the EEA competition rules, can also be obtained from the following offices:

AUSTRIA
Federal Ministry for Economic Affairs
Tel. (431) 711 00

FINLAND
Office of Free Competition
Tel. (3580) 731 41

ICELAND
Directorate of Competition and Fair Trade
Tel. (3541) 27 422

LIECHTENSTEIN
Office of National Economy
Division of Economy and Statistics
Tel. (4175) 61 11

NORWAY
Price Directorate
Tel. (4722) 40 09 00

SWEDEN
Competition Authority
Tel. (468) 700 16 00

Appendix G

This form[1] and the supporting documents should be forwarded in 15 copies together with proof in duplicate of the representative's authority to act.

If the space opposite each question is insufficient, please use extra pages, specifying to which item on the form they relate.

FORM C

TO THE COMMISSION OF THE EUROPEAN COMMUNITIES

Directorate-General for Competition
200 rue de la Loi
B-1049 Brussels

Application for initiation of procedure to establish the existence of an infringement of Articles 85 or 86 of the Treaty, and/or Article 53 or 54 of the Agreement on the European Economic Area[2], submitted by natural or legal persons pursuant to Article 3 of Council Regulation 17.

I. Information regarding parties concerned:

1. Name, forenames and address of person submitting the application. If such person is acting as a representative, state also the name and address of his principal; for an undertaking, or association of undertakings or persons, state the name, forenames and address of the proprietors or members; for legal persons, state the name, forenames and address of their legal representatives.

---

[1] Applications made by using Form C issued by the Commission and Form C issued by the EFTA side are equally valid.
[2] Hereinafter referred to as 'the EEA Agreement'. Any reference to EFTA States shall be understood to mean those EFTA States which are Contracting Parties to the EEA Agreement.

Proof of representative's authority to act must be supplied;

If the application is submitted by a number of persons or on behalf of a number of persons, the information must be given in respect of each applicant or principal.

2. Name and address of persons to whom the application relates.

II. Details of the alleged infringement:

Set out in detail, in an Annex, the facts from which, in your opinion, it appears that there is infringement of Articles 85 or 86 the Treaty and/or Article 53 or 54 of the EEA Agreement.

Indicate in particular:

1. The practices of the undertakings or associations of undertakings to which this application relates which have as their object or effect the prevention, restriction or distortion of competition or constitute an abuse of a dominant position within the common market, within the territory of the EFTA States or within the EEA territory

2. To what extent trade between Member States may be affected.

III. Existence of legitimate interest:

Set out—if necessary in an Annex—the grounds on which you claim a legitimate interest in the initiation by the Commission of the procedure provided for in Article 3 of Regulation 17.

IV. Evidence:

1. State the names and addresses of persons able to testify to the facts set out, and in particular of persons affected by the alleged infringement.

2. Submit all documentation relating to or directly connected with the facts set out (for example, texts of agreements, minutes of negotiations or

meetings, terms of transactions, business documents, circulars).

3. Submit statistics or other data relating to the facts set out (and relating, for example, to price trends, formation of prices, terms of transactions, terms of supply or sale, boycotting, discrimination).

4. Where appropriate, give any necessary technical details relating to production, sales, etc., or name experts able to do so.

5. Indicate any other evidence of the existence of the alleged infringement.

V. Indicate all approaches made, and all steps taken, prior to this application, by you or any other person affected by the practice described above, with a view to terminating the alleged infringement (proceedings commenced before national judicial or administrative bodies, stating in particular the reference numbers of the cases and the results thereof).

We, the undersigned, declare that the information given in this form and in the Annexes thereto is given entirely in good faith.

At..

Signed:

....

....

....

....

....

....

....

....

Appendix G

COMMISSION OF THE EUROPEAN
COMMUNITIES

Brussels.............................

Directorate-General for Competition

```
┌──────────────────────────────────────────────────────────────┐
│  To                                                          │
│                                                              │
│                                                              │
│                                                              │
│                                                              │
│                                                              │
│                                                              │
└──────────────────────────────────────────────────────────────┘
```

ACKNOWLEDGEMENT OF RECEIPT

(This form will be returned to the address inserted above if the top half is completed in a single copy by the applicant)

Your application for a finding of infringement of Article 85 or 86 of the Treaty and/or Article 53 or 54 of the EEA Agreement, dated ....

(a) Applicant:

....

....

(b) Infringing parties:

....

....

was received on...

and registered under No. IV..

Please quote the above number in all correspondence.

437

Appendix H

I

Forms commonly used by the Commission in connection with investigations under Article 14 of Regulation 17:

(a) Authorisation to investigate,

(b) Minute of notification of Commission decision,

(c) Minute recordings failure to produce books and business records.[1]

II

(d) Explanatory note to authorisation to investigate under Article 14(2) of Regulation No. 17.

(e) Explanatory note to authorisation to investigate in execution of a Commission decision under Article 14(3) of Regulation No. 17.

---

[1] This may be adapted to deal with other matters arising during the investigation: for example, failure to supply an oral explanation on the spot or any point of difference or disagreement which might usefully be recorded formally.

Appendix H

COMMISSION
OF THE
EUROPEAN COMMUNITIES
———

Directorate-General for Competition

Brussels,....................................

AUTHORISATION TO INVESTIGATE

Mr. ....

holder of internal service pass No. ....

is hereby authorized to carry out an investigation at...

....

for the purpose of...

....

....

....

To this end, he has been invested with the powers set out in Article 14 Paragraph 1 of Council Regulation No. 17/62, of 6 February 1962 (Official Journal of the European Communities No. 13 of 21 February 1962).
The Commission, with reference to Article 14 Paragraph 2 of Council Regulation No. 17/62, hereby draws attention to the provisions of Article 15 Paragraph 1(c) of that Regulation.[2]

For the Commission,

---

[2] The Commission may, by decision, impose fines of from 100 to 5,000 units of account on undertakings or associations of undertakings which, while submitting to an investigation, intentionally or negligently produce the required books or other business records in incomplete form (Article 15 Paragraph 1 of Regulation No. 17/62 of the Council of the EEC).

MINUTE OF NOTIFICATION OF COMMISSION DECISION

On   at   o'clock, the undersigned:

officials of the Commission of the Directorate-General for Competition of the Commission of the European Communities, and holders of service cards nos. and presented themselves at the premises of the following undertaking:

in the presence of Mr.

representing the competent authority of the relevant Member State for the purpose of Article 14(4) of Regulation No. 17.

The officials notified to the above mentioned company the decision adopted on by the Commission of the European Communities in application of Article 14(3) of Regulation No. 17 of the Council of 2nd February 1962 (Official Journal of the European Communities, No. 13 of 21st February 1962) and handed a certified copy of the original to Mr.

in his capacity as

Mr.   signed the present minute as an acknowledgement of notification of the said decision.

Done at

Commission officials

COMMISSION
OF THE
EUROPEAN COMMUNITIES
————

Brussels,....................................

Directorate-General for Competition

Enquiry ....

File No. ....

Investigation at ....

On...........................at............................am/pm, Messrs...........................
Staff Numbers presented warrants under the procedure set out in Article 14(2) of Council Regulation No. 17/62 to Mr. ....
in his capacity as...
and in the presence of..
and requested him to make available the following material ....
....
....
....
....
....

Mr. .... was made aware of the provisions of Article 14(1) and 15(1) of Regulation No.
17/62.
Mr. .... stated that:
....
....
....
....
....
....
....
....

Attested
....

Explanatory note to authorisation to investigate under Article 14(2) of Regulation No. 17/62

This note is for information only and is without prejudice to any formal interpretation of the Commission's powers of enquiry.

1. The officials of the Commission authorized for the purpose of carrying out an investigation under Article 14(2) of Regulation No. 17 exercise their powers upon production of an authorization in writing. They prove their identity by means of their staff card.

2. Before starting the investigation the Commission officials shall, at the undertaking's request, provide explanations on the subject matter and purpose of the proposed investigation and also on procedural matters, particularly confidentiality. These explanations cannot modify the authorization and may not compromise the purpose of, nor unduly delay, the investigation.

3. The authorization, not being in execution of a Commission decision under Article 14(3), does not oblige the undertaking to submit to the investigation. The undertaking may accordingly refuse the investigation. The Commission officials shall minute this refusal, no particular form being required. The undertaking shall receive a copy of the minute if it so wishes.

4. Where the undertaking is prepared to submit to the investigation, the Commission officials are empowered, pursuant to Article 14(1) of Regulation No. 17:
   (a) to examine the books and other business records;
   (b) to take copies of or extracts from the books and business records;
   (c) to ask for oral explanations on the spot;
   (d) to enter any premises, land and means of transport of undertakings.

5. Officials of the competent authority of the Member State in whose territory the investigation is made are entitled to be present at the investigation to assist the officials of the Commission in carrying out their duties. They shall prove their identity in accordance with the relevant national rules.

6. The undertaking may consult a legal adviser during the investigation. However, the presence of a lawyer is not a legal condition for the validity of the investigation, nor must it unduly delay or impede it. Any delay pending a lawyer's arrival must be kept to the strict minimum, and shall be allowed only where the management of the undertaking simultaneously undertakes to ensure that the business records will remain in the place and state they were in when the Commission officials arrived. The officials' acceptance of delay is also conditional upon their not being hindered from entering into and remaining in occupation of offices of their choice. If the undertaking has an inhouse legal service, Commission officials are instructed not to delay the investigation by awaiting the arrival of an external legal adviser.

7. Where the undertaking gives oral explanations on the spot on the subject matter of the investigation at the request of the Commission officials, the explanations may be minuted at the request of the undertaking or of the Commission officials. The undertaking shall receive a copy of the minute if it so wishes.

8. The Commission officials are entitled to take copies of or extracts from books and business records. The undertaking may request a signed inventory of the copies and extracts taken by the Commission officials during the investigation.

   Where the undertaking makes available photocopies of documents at the request of the Commission officials, the Commission shall, at the request of the undertaking, reimburse the cost of the photocopies.

9. In addition to the documents requested by the Commission officials, the undertaking is entitled to draw attention to other documents or information where it considers this necessary for the purpose of protecting its legitimate interest in a complete and objective clarification of the matters raised provided that the investigation is not thereby unduly delayed.

Explanatory note to authorisation to investigate in execution of a Commission decision under Article 14(3) of Regulation No. 17/62

This note is for information only and is without prejudice to any formal interpretation of the Commission's powers of enquiry.

1. Enterprises are legally obliged to submit to an investigation ordered by decision of the Commission under Article 14(3) of Regulation No. 17. Written authorizations serve to name the officials charged with the execution of the decision. They prove their identity by means of their staff card.

2. Officials cannot be required to enlarge upon the subject matter as set out in the decision or to justify in any way the taking of the decision. They may however explain procedural matters, particularly confidentiality, and the possible consequences of a refusal to submit.

3. A certified copy of the decision is to be handed to the undertaking. The minute of notification of service serves only to certify delivery and its signature by the recipient does not imply submission.

4. The Commission officials are empowered, pursuant to Article 14(1) of Regulation No. 17:
    (a) to examine the books and other business records;
    (b) to take copies of or extracts from the books and business records;
    (c) to ask for oral explanations on the spot;
    (d) to enter any premises, land and means of transport of undertakings.

5. Officials of the competent authority of the Member State in whose territory the investigation is made are entitled to be present at the investigation to assist the officials of the Commission in carrying out their duties. They shall prove their identity in accordance with the relevant national rules.

6. The undertaking may consult a legal adviser during the investigation. However, the presence of a lawyer is not a legal condition for the validity of the investigation, nor must it unduly delay or impede it. Any delay pending a lawyer's arrival must be kept to the strict minimum, and shall be allowed only where the management of the undertaking simultaneously undertakes to ensure that the business records will remain in the place and state they were in when the Commission officials arrived. The officials' acceptance of delay is also conditional upon their not being hindered from entering into and remaining in occupation of offices of their choice. If the undertaking has an inhouse legal service, Commission officials are instructed not to delay the investigation by awaiting the arrival of an external legal adviser.

7. Where the undertaking gives oral explanations on the spot on the subject matter of the investigation at the request of the Commission officials, the explanations may be minuted at the request of the undertaking or of the Commission officials. The undertaking shall receive a copy of the minute if it so wishes.

8. The Commission officials are entitled to take copies of or extracts from books and business records. The undertaking may request a signed inventory of the copies and extracts taken by the Commission officials during the investigation.

    Where the undertaking makes available photocopies of documents at the request of the Commission officials, the Commission shall, at the request of the undertaking, reimburse the cost of the photocopies.

9. In addition to the documents requested by the Commission officials, the undertaking is entitled to draw attention to other documents or information where it considers this necessary for the purpose of protecting its legitimate interest in a complete and objective clarification of the matters raised provided that the investigation is not thereby unduly delayed.

Appendix I

Interim Measures—statement by the Commission given to Camera Care and Hasselblad before the hearing on 20 February 1980 in Case No. IV/29.895.

Introduction to Hearing on Interim Measures

The European Court of Justice has decided that the Commission has the power, under Article 3 of Regulation 17/62, to order by formal decision interim measures pending a final decision. The Court has also given some guidance on how this power should be exercised.

Since this is the first case in which the Commission has to decide whether the power is to be exercised, it may be helpful if the Commission sets out certain principles which it will apply in deciding upon interim measures.

While not relevant to the present case, in general parties should consider whether a similar remedy may not be available from a national court before applying to the Commission—particularly if the national procedures are cheaper or the order more easily policed.

In any event, the Commission will not accept an application for interim measures which is not accompanied or preceded by a formal complaint under Article 3 of Regulation 17/62, unless the Commission has already opened formal proceedings.

The Commission will act strictly in accordance with the principles stated by the Court in its Order in Case 792/79 as far as they apply to cases which arise. The Commission will not normally order interim measures in circumstances in which they are not required by the principles stated by the Court. In cases not governed directly by those principles, the Commission will exercise its discretion in the light of the principles on which the Court itself acts in granting interim measures.

The Commission will take into account all the circumstances as they appear at the time when it adopts its decision on interim measures, and will as far as possible balance all the interests involved. The Commission will also in due course be guided, but not bound, by its own decisions in similar cases.

It must appear that there is a reasonably strong prima facie case that there has been a violation of the rules of competition set out in the Treaty, if interim measures are to be ordered.

The Commission will normally act primarily on the evidence put before it by the parties and will not consider itself bound to investigate the facts fully using its own powers before deciding on interim measures.

Unreasonable delay by a complainant seeking interim measures may be grounds for rejecting the application if this is otherwise appropriate.

It appears from Regulation 17/62 and from the Order of the Court in Case 792/79 that the Commission may upon its own initiative commence a procedure eventually involving interim measures if the practice of any undertaking appears to it to have the effect of injuring the interests of some Member States, causing damage to other undertakings or of unacceptably jeopardising the Community's competition policy.

In deciding upon the duration of any interim measures, the Commission may set a particular time limit by which the matter must be reviewed again, or may order interim measures to remain in force until final decision of the Commission. In either event, the Commission would always consider an application, from either of the parties involved, for review of the interim measures if circumstances have changed. The Commission would also be free to do so on its own initiative.

The Commission will in all cases carefully consider what interim measures are appropriate. Applicants for interim measures will be expected to indicate as precisely as possible the nature of the measures they request the Commission to order. Even so, the Commission is free to order such measures as it feels appropriate. The Commission's decision to grant or refuse interim measures does not affect in any way the Commission's later definitive decision as to whether a violation of the Treaty has occurred. Measures which prejudge the outcome of the Commission's procedure, such as those which irrevocably alter the position of the enterprise suspected of having violated the Treaty, will not be adopted.

The Commission would in appropriate cases order the party requesting interim measures to give a suitable bond or guarantee to indemnify the party against which interim measures are ordered against any loss resulting from the interim measures if the latter party is finally found not to have infringed the Treaty. In an order for interim measures, the Commission may also impose on either or both parties obligations designed to expedite the final decision in the case and so bring about an early termination of the measures.

In the present case, the Commission set out in a telex to the parties indicating the relief claimed some points on which the Commission would like to hear further argument, and various suggestions for the smoother running of the Commission's hearing on interim measures. The parties were invited, if they wished, to make written submissions before the hearing. The time for replying in proceedings for interim measures must necessarily be relatively short and so the oral hearing on interim measures is likely to be more important than in the cases of the normal Commission procedure.

The Commission invited the parties to produce as far as possible an agreed statement of facts and to submit any evidence by means of statements signed by the witnesses offered. These procedures are useful for the expeditious handling of the matter and will be followed for other cases.

Any decision of the Commission in this case will be taken by the Commission according to its normal internal rules. It will be communicated to the parties as soon as it is made and it will be published in the Official Journal in due course. Time under Article 173 EEC Treaty will run, as usual, from the date of communication of the decision to the party concerned.

Appendix J

Article 4[2]

1. The exemption provided for in Articles 1 and 2 shall also apply to agreements containing obligations restrictive of competition which are not covered by those Articles and do not fall within the scope of Article 3, on condition that the agreements in question are notified to the Commission in accordance with the provisions of Commission Regulation No. 27, as last amended by Regulation (EEC) No. 1699/75, and that the Commission does not oppose such exemption within a period of six months.

2. The period of six months shall run from the date on which the notification is received by the Commission. Where, however, the notification is made by registered post, the period shall run from the date shown on the postmark of the place of posting.

3. Paragraph 1 shall apply only if:
   (a) express reference is made to this Article in the notification or in a communication accompanying it; and
   (b) the information furnished with the notification is complete and in accordance with the facts.

4. The benefit of paragraph 1 may be claimed for agreements notified before the entry into force of this Regulation by submitting a communication to the Commission referring expressly to this Article and to the notification. Paragraphs 2 and 3(b) shall apply *mutatis mutandis.*

5. The Commission may oppose the exemption. It shall oppose exemption if it receives a request to do so from a Member State within three months of the transmission to the Member State of the notification referred to in paragraph 1 or of the communication referred to in paragraph 4. This request must be justified on the basis of considerations relating to the competition rules of the Treaty.

6. The Commission may withdraw the opposition to the exemption at any time. However, where the opposition was raised at the request of a Member State and this request is maintained, it may be withdrawn only after consultation of the Advisory Committee on Restrictive Practices and Dominant Positions.

7. If the opposition is withdrawn because the undertakings concerned have shown that the conditions of Article 85(3) are fulfilled, the exemption shall apply from the date of notification.

---

[1] Taken from Reg. 2349/84, the patent licensing agreements block exemption. There are similar provisions in Reg. 417/85, the specialisation agreements block exemption, Reg. 418/85, the research and development block exemption, Reg. 4087/88 the franchising agreements block exemption and Reg. 556/89, the know-how licencing block exemption.
[2] See Art. 4 of Reg. 417/85, and Art. 7 of Reg. 418/85.

8. If the opposition is withdrawn because the undertakings concerned have amended the agreement so that the conditions of Article 85(3) are fulfilled, the exemption shall apply from the date on which the amendments take effect.

9. If the Commission opposes exemption and the opposition is not withdrawn, the effects of the notification shall be governed by the provisions of Regulation No. 17.

Article 13[3]

1. Information acquired pursuant to Article 4 shall be used only for the purposes of this Regulation.

2. The Commission and the authorities of the Member States, their officials and other servants shall not disclose information acquired by them pursuant to this Regulation of the kind covered by the obligation of professional secrecy.

3. The provisions of paragraphs 1 and 2 shall not prevent publication of general information or surveys which do not contain information relating to particular undertakings or associations of undertakings.

---

[3] See Art. 5 of Reg. 417/85, and Art. 8 of Reg. 418/85.

Appendix K

COMPETITION LAWS CO-OPERATION AGREEMENT 1991 (EEC-USA)

ADOPTED BY THE COMMISSION OF THE EUROPEAN COMMUNITIES AND THE
GOVERNMENT OF THE UNITED STATES OF AMERICA

September 23, 1991

Recognising—
that the world's economies are becoming increasingly interrelated, and in particular that this is
true of the economies of the European Communities and the United States of America;

Noting that—
the Commission of the European Communities and the Government of the United States of
America share the view that the sound and effective enforcement of competition law is a matter
of importance to the efficient operation of their respective markets and to trade between them;
the sound and effective enforcement of the Parties' competition laws would be enhanced by co-
operation and, in appropriate cases, co-ordination between them in the application of those
laws;
from time to time differences may arise between the Parties concerning the application of their
competition laws to conduct or transactions that implicate significant interests of both Parties;

Having regard—
to the Recommendation of the Council of the Organisation for Economic Co-Operation and Development Concerning Co-operation Between Member Countries on Restrictive Business
Practices Affecting International Trade, adopted on June 5, 1986; and to the Declaration on
US-EC Relations adopted on November 23, 1990;

THE E.C. COMMISSION AND THE GOVERNMENT OF THE UNITED STATES OF
AMERICA

HAVE AGREED AS FOLLOWS:

Article I

Purpose and definitions

1. The purpose of this Agreement is to promote co-operation and co-ordination and lessen the
possibility or impact of differences between the Parties in the application of their competition
laws.

449

2. For the purposes of this Agreement, the following terms shall have the following definition:

(a) "Competition law(s)" shall mean

    (i) for the European Communities, Articles 85, 86, 89 and 90 EEC, Regulation 4064/89 on the control of concentrations between undertakings, Articles 65 and 66 ECSC and their Implementing Regulations including High Authority Decision 24–54, and

    (ii) for the United States of America, the Sherman Act (15 U.S.C. §§ 1–7), the Clayton Act (15 U.S.C. §§ 12–27), the Wilson Tariff Act (15 U.S.C. §§ 8–11), and the Federal Trade Commission Act (15 U.S.C. §§ 41–68, except as these sections relate to consumer protection functions), as well as such other laws or regulations as the Parties shall jointly agree in writing to be a "competition law" for purposes of this Agreement;

(b) "Competition authorities" shall mean

    (i) for the European Communities the Commission of the European Communities, as to its responsibilities pursuant to the competition laws of the European Communities, and

    (ii) for the United States, the Antitrust Division of the United States Department of Justice and the Federal Trade Commission;

(c) "Enforcement activities" shall mean any application of competition law by way of investigation or proceeding conducted by the competition authorities of a Party; and

(d) "Anticompetitive activities" shall mean any conduct or transaction that is impermissible under the competition laws of a Party.

Article II

Notification

1. Each Party shall notify the other whenever its competition authorities become aware that their enforcement activities may affect important interests of the other Party.

2. Enforcement activities as to which notification ordinarily will be appropriate include those that:

(a) Are relevant to enforcement activities of the other Party;

(b) Involve anticompetitive activities (other than a merger or acquisition) carried out in significant part in the other Party's territory;

(c) Involve a merger or acquisition in which one or more of the parties to the transaction, or a company controlling one or more of the parties to the transaction, is a company incorporated or organised under the laws of the other Party or one of its States or Member States;

(d) Involve conduct believed to have been required, encouraged or approved by the other Party; or

(e) Involve remedies that would, in significant respects, require or prohibit conduct in the other Party's territory.

3. With respect to mergers or acquisitions required by law to be reported to the competition authorities, notification under this Article shall be made:

(a) In the case of the Government of the United States of America,

    (i) not later than the time its competition authorities request, pursuant to 15 U.S.C. § 18a (e), additional information or documentary material concerning the proposed transaction,

    (ii) when its competition authorities decide to file a complaint challenging the transaction, and

    (iii) where this is possible, far enough in advance of the entry of a consent decree to enable the other Party's views to be taken into account; and

(b) In the case of the Commission of the European Communities,

(i)   when notice of the transaction is published in the Official Journal, pursuant to Article 4(3) of Council Regulation 4064/89, or when notice of the transaction is received under Article 66 ECSC and a prior authorisation from the Commission is required under that provision,

(ii) when its competition authorities decide to initiate proceedings with respect to the proposed transaction, pursuant to Article 6(1)(c) of Council Regulation 4064/89, and

(iii) far enough in advance of the adoption of a decision in the case to enable the other Party's views to be taken into account.

4. With respect to other matters, notification shall ordinarily be provided at the stage in an investigation when it becomes evident that notifiable circumstances are present, and in any event far enough in advance of

(a)   the issuance of a statement of objections in the case of the Commission of the European Communities, or a complaint or indictment in the case of the Government of the United States of America, and

(b)   the adoption of a decision or settlement in the case of the Commission of the European Communities, or the entry of a consent decree in the case of the Government of the United States of America,

to enable the other Party's views to be taken into account.

5. Each party shall also notify the other whenever its competition authorities intervene or otherwise participate in a regulatory or judicial proceeding that does not arise from its enforcement activities, if the issues addressed in the intervention or participation may effect the other party's important interests. Notification under this paragraph shall apply only to

(a)   a regulatory or judicial proceedings that are public,

(b)   intervention or participation that is public and pursuant to formal procedures, and

(c)   in the case of regulatory proceedings in the United States, only proceedings before federal agencies.

Notification shall be made at the time of intervention or participation or as soon thereafter as possible.

6. Notification under this Article shall include sufficient information to permit an initial evaluation by the recipient Party of any effects on its interests.

Article III

Exchange of information

1. The parties agree that it is in their common interest to share information that will (a) facilitate effective application of their respective competition laws, or (b) promote better understanding by them of economic conditions and theories relevant to their competition authorities' enforcement activities and interventions or participation of the kind described in Article II(5).

2. In furtherance of this common interest, appropriate officials from the competition authorities of each Party shall meet at least twice each year, unless otherwise agreed, to (a) exchange information on their current enforcement activities and priorities, (b) exchange information on economic sectors of common interest, (c) discuss policy changes which they are considering, and (d) discuss other matters of mutual interest relating to the application of competition laws.

3. Each party will provide the other Party with any significant information that comes to the attention of its competition authorities about anti-competitive activities that its competition authorities believe is relevant to, or may warrant, enforcement activity by the other Party's competition authorities.

4. Upon receiving a request from the other party, and within the limits of Articles VIII and IX, a Party will provide to the requesting Party such information within its possession as the requesting Party may describe that is relevant to an enforcement activity being considered or conducted by the requesting Party's competition authorities.

Article IV

Co-operation and co-ordination in enforcement activities

1. The competition authorities of each Party will render assistance to the competition authorities of the other Party in their enforcement activities, to the extent compatible with the assisting Party's laws and important interests, and within its reasonably available resources.

2. In cases where both Parties have an interest in pursuing enforcement activities with regard to related situations, they may agree that it is in their mutual interest to co-ordinate their enforcement activities. In considering whether particular enforcement activities should be co-ordinated, the parties shall take account of the following factors, among others:

    (a) the opportunity to make more efficient use of their resources devoted to the enforcement activities;

    (b) the relative abilities of the Parties' competition authorities to obtain information necessary to conduct the enforcement activities;

    (c) the effect of such co-ordination on the ability of both Parties to achieve the objective of their enforcement activities; and

    (d) the possibility of reducing costs incurred by persons subject to the enforcement activities.

3. In any co-ordination arrangement, each Party shall conduct its enforcement activities expeditiously and, in so far as possible, consistently with the enforcement objectives of the other Party.

4. Subject to appropriate notice to the other Party, the competition authorities of either Party may limit or terminate their participation in a co-ordination arrangement and pursue their enforcement activities independently.

Article V

Co-operation regarding anti-competitive activities in the territory of one party that adversely affect the interests of the other party

1. The Parties note that anti-competitive activities may occur within the territory of one Party that, in addition to violating that Party's competition laws, adversely affect important interests of the other Party. The Parties agree that it is in both their interests to address anti-competitive activities of this nature.

2. If a Party believes that anti-competitive activities carried out on the territory of the other Party are adversely affecting its important interests, the first Party may notify the other Party and may request that the other Party's competition authorities initiate appropriate enforcement activities. The notification shall be as specific as possible about the nature of the anti-competitive activities and their effects on the interests of the notifying Party, and shall include an offer of such further information and other co-operation as the notifying Party is able to provide.

3. Upon receipt of a notification under paragraph 2, and after such other discussion between the parties as may be appropriate and useful in the circumstances, the competition authorities of the notified Party will consider whether or not to initiate enforcement activities, or to expand ongoing enforcement activities, with respect to the anti-competitive activities identified in the notification. The notified Party will advise the notifying Party of its decision. If enforcement activities are initiated, the notified Party will advise the notifying Party of their outcome and, to the extent possible, of significant interim developments.

4. Nothing in this Article limits the discretion of the notified Party under its competition laws and enforcement policies as to whether or not to undertake enforcement activities with respect to the notified anti-competitive activities, or precludes the notifying Party from undertaking enforcement activities with respect to such anti-competitive activities.

Article VI

Avoidance of conflicts over enforcement activities

Within the framework of its own laws and to the extent compatible with its important interests, each Party will seek, at all stages in its enforcement activities, to take into account the important interests of the other Party. Each Party shall consider important interests of the other Party in decisions as to whether or not to initiate an investigation or proceeding, the scope of an investigation or proceeding, the nature of the remedies or penalties sought, and in other ways, as appropriate. in considering one another's important interests in the course of their enforcement activities, the Parties will take account of, but will not be limited to, the following principles:

1. While an important interest of a Party may exist in the absence of official involvement by the Party with the activity in question, it is recognised that such interests would normally be reflected in antecedents laws, decisions or statements, of policy by its competent authorities.

2. A Party's important interests may be affected at any stage of enforcement activity by the other Party. The Parties recognise, however, that as a general matter the potential for adverse impact on one Party's important interests arising from enforcement activity by the other Party is less at the investigative stage and greater at the stage at which conduct is prohibited or penalised, or at which forms of remedial orders are imposed.

3. Where it appears that one Party's enforcement activities may adversely affect important interests of the other Party, the Parties will consider the following factors. In addition to any other factors that appear relevant in the circumstances, in seeking an appropriate accommodation of the competing interests:

(a) the relative significance to the anti-competitive activities involved of conduct within the enforcing Party's territory as compared to conduct within the other Party's territory;

(b) the presence or absence of a purpose on the part of those engaged in the anti-competitive activities to affect consumers, suppliers, or competitors within the enforcing Party's territory;

(c) the relative significance of the effects of the anti-competitive activities on the enforcing Party's interests as compared to the effects on the other Party's interests;

(d) the existence or absence of reasonable expectations that would be furthered or defeated by the enforcement activities;

(e) the degree of conflict or consistency between the enforcement activities and the other Party's laws or articulated economic policies; and

(f) the extent to which enforcement activities of the other Party with respect to the same persons, including judgments or undertakings resulting from such activities, may be affected.

Article VII

Consultation

1. Each Party agrees to consult promptly with the other Party in response to a request by the other Party for consultation regarding any matter related to this agreement and to attempt to conclude consultations expeditiously with a view to reaching mutually satisfactory conclusions. Any request for consultations shall include the reasons therefor and shall state whether procedural time limits or other considerations require the consultations to be expedited.

These consultations shall take place at the appropriate level, which may include consultations between the heads of the competition authorities concerned.

2. In each consultation under paragraph 1, each Party shall take into account the principles of co-operation set forth in this Agreement and shall be prepared to explain to the other Party the specific results of its application of those principles to the issue that is the subject of consultation.

Article VIII

Confidentiality of information

1. Notwithstanding any other provision of this Agreement, neither Party is required to provide information to the other Party if disclosure of that information to the requesting Party (a) is prohibited by the law of the party possessing the information, or (b) would be incompatible with important interests of the Party possessing the information.

2. Each party agrees to maintain, to the fullest extent possible, the confidentiality of any information provided to it in confidence by the other Party under this Agreement and to oppose, to the fullest extent possible, any application for disclosure of such information by a third party that is not authorised by the Party that supplied the information.

Article IX

Existing law

Nothing in this Agreement shall be interpreted in a manner inconsistent with the existing laws, or as requiring any changes in the laws, of the United States of America or the European Communities or of their respective States or Member States.

Article X

Communications under this Agreement

Communications under this Agreement, including notifications under Article II and V, may be carried out by direct oral, telephonic, written or facsimile communication from one Party's competition authority to the other party's authority. Notifications under Articles II, V and XI, and requests under Article VII, shall be confirmed promptly in writing through diplomatic channels.

Article XI

Entry into force, termination and review

1. This Agreement shall enter into force upon signature.

2. This Agreement shall remain in force 60 days after the date on which either Party notifies the other Party in writing that it wishes to terminate the Agreement.

3. The parties shall review the operation of this Agreement not more than 24 months from the date of its entry into force, with a view to assessing their co-operative activities, identifying additional areas in which they could usefully co-operate and identifying any other ways in which the Agreement could be improved.

The Parties agree that this review will include, among other things, an analysis of actual or potential cases to determine whether their interests could be better served through closer co-operation.

Appendix L

COMMISSION DECISION OF 23 NOVEMBER 1993

On the implementation of hearings in connection with procedures for the application of Articles 85 and 86 of the EEC Treaty and Articles 65 ad 66 of the ECSC Treaty.

Article 1

1. The hearings foreseen in the provisions implementing Articles 85 and 86 EEC Treaty and Articles 65 and 66 ECSC Treaty are decided on by the Member of the Commission responsible for competition and conducted by the Hearing Officer.

2. Implementing provisions in the sense of paragraph 1 are:
   (a) Regulation (EEC) No. 99/63 of the Commission of 25 July 1963 on the hearings provided for in Article 19(1) and (2) of Council Regulation No. 17;[1]
   (b) Regulation (EEC) No. 1630/69 of the Commission of 8 August 1969 on the hearings provided for in Article 26(1) and (2) of Council Regulation (EEC) No. 1017/68 of 19 July 1968;[2]
   (c) Commission Regulation (EEC) No. 4260/88 of 16 December 1988 on the communications, complaints and applications and the hearings provided for in Council Regulation (EEC) No. 4056/86 laying down detailed rules for the application of Articles 85 and 86 of the Treaty to maritime transport;[3]
   (d) Commission Regulation (EEC) No. 4261/88 of 16 December 1988 on the complaints, applications and hearings provided for in Council Regulation (EEC) No. 3975/87 laying down the procedure for the application of the rules on competition to undertakings in the air transport sector;[4]
   (e) Article 36(1) ECSC Treaty;

3. Administratively the Hearing Officer shall belong to the Directorate-General for Competition. To ensure his independence in the performance of his duties, he shall have the right of direct access, as defined in Article 6 below, to the Member of the Commission with special responsibility for competition.

4. Where the Hearing Officer is unable to act, the Director-General, in concert with the Hearing Officer, shall designate another official, who is in the same grade and is not involved in the case in question, to carry out the duties described herein.

[1] O.J. L27 of 20.8.1963, p. 2268/63.
[2] O.J. L209 of 21.8.1969, p. 11.
[3] O.J. L376 of 31.12.1988, p. 1.
[4] O.J. L376 of 31.12.1988, p. 10.

Article 2

1. The Hearing Officer shall ensure that the hearing is properly conducted and thus contribute to the objectivity of the hearing itself and of any decision taken subsequently. He shall seek to ensure in particular that in the preparation of draft Commission decisions in competition cases due account is taken of all the relevant facts, whether favourable or unfavourable to the parties concerned.

2. In performing his duties he shall see to it that the rights of the defence are respected, while taking account of the need for effective application of the competition rules in accordance with the regulations in force and the principles laid down by the Court of Justice.

Article 3

1. Where appropriate in view of the need to ensure that the hearing is properly prepared, and particularly that questions of fact are clarified as far as possible, the Hearing Officer may, after consulting the appropriate Director, supply in advance to the firms concerned a list of the questions on which he wishes them to explain their point of view.

2. For this purpose, after consulting the Director responsible for investigating the case which is the subject of the hearing, he may hold a meeting with the parties concerned and, where appropriate, the Commission staff, in order to prepare for the hearing itself.

3. For the same purpose he may ask for prior written notification of the essential contents of the intended statement of persons whom the undertakings concerned have proposed for hearing.

Article 4

1. After consulting the Director responsible, the Hearing Officer shall determine the date, the duration and the place of the hearing, and, where a postponement is requested, he shall decide whether or not to allow it.

2. He shall be fully responsible for the conduct of the hearing.

3. In this regard, he shall decide whether fresh documents should be admitted during the hearing, whether persons should be heard and whether the persons concerned should be heard separately or in the presence of other persons summoned to attend.

4. He shall ensure that the essential content of the statement made by each person heard shall be recorded in minutes which shall be read and approved by that person.

Article 5

The Hearing Officer shall report to the Director-General for Competition on the hearing and the conclusions he draws from it. He may make observations on the further progress of the proceedings. Such observations may relate among other things to the need for further information, the withdrawal of certain objections, or the formulation of further objections.

Article 6

In performing the duties defined in Article 2 above, the Hearing Officer may, if he deems it appropriate, refer his observations direct to the Member of the Commission with special respnsibility for competition, at the time when the preliminary draft decision is submitted to the latter for reference to the Advisory Committee on Restrictive Practices and Dominant Position.

Article 7

Where appropriate, the Member of the Commission with special responsibility for competition may decide, at the Hearing Officer's request, to attach the Hearing Officer's final report to the draft decision submitted to the Commission, in order to ensure that when it reaches a decision on an individual case it is fully apprised of all relevant information.

Index